Interpreting the
ASIAN PAST

QIU JIN HAILSTORK
WITH CONTRIBUTIONS BY:
ROSEANNE S. DELPARTO
MICHAEL A. NEULANDER

Kendall Hunt
publishing company

Cover images © 2012, Shutterstock, Inc.

Kendall Hunt
publishing company

www.kendallhunt.com
Send all inquiries to:
4050 Westmark Drive
Dubuque, IA 52004-1840

Copyright © 2012 by Qiu Jin Hailstork

ISBN 978-0-7575-9012-2

Printed in the United States of America
10 9 8 7 6 5 4 3 2

Contents

Chapter 1: Introduction

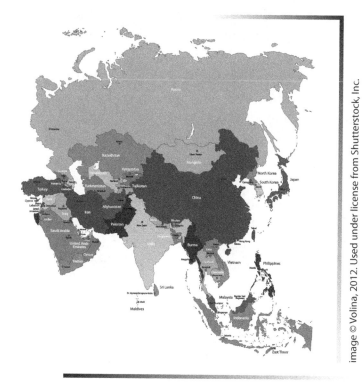

Present-day nations in Asia.

Regions of Asia

INTRODUCTION TO THE REGION

Many argue that while the twentieth century belonged to America and the nineteenth century to Europe, the twenty-first century is an Asian century. The remarkable economic growth in Asia over the past several decades has perpetuated this notion. Japan and the "Four Asian Tigers" (South Korea, Singapore, Taiwan and Hong Kong) took the economic lead in the 1970s and 1980s, followed by the rapid rise of China, India, and other Asian countries since the late 1980s. In 2010, China had a growth rate of 10.3 percent. India, the Philippines, Malaysia, and Thailand, which are known as "newly industrialized countries," also had impressive growth rates.[1] Although the validity of the claim of "an Asian Century" may still be in question, the debate nonetheless highlights the political, economic, and military importance of Asian countries in today's world, and hence rationalizes a more thorough understanding of the continent.

Asia, however, deserves more study by its own merit, even without such a debate. As the largest continent in the world, it comprises one-fifth of the world's total land area, ranging more than 5,000 miles north to south and 6,000 miles east to west, with a total of 17 million square miles. Asia is the home of about 60 percent of the world population and served as the cradle for three out of four of the world's oldest civilizations. As the birthplace of all of the major world religions, Asia is comprised of widespread cultural diversity, as well as a controversial status in terms of its geographical boundaries and political identity.

Geographically speaking, Asia has been defined in different ways. The Ancient Greeks considered the boundaries between Asia and Europe to be the Aegean Sea, the Dardanelles, the Sea of Marmara, the Bosporus, the Black Sea, the Kerch Strait, and the Sea of Azov with the boundary between Asia and Africa being the Nile. After the eighteenth century, the boundaries between Asia and Europe were pushed further east, with the Ural mountains and the Ural river in Russia as the division between Asia and Europe, and by convention, the boundary between Asia and Africa was changed to the Red Sea, and the Isthmus of Suez.[2] These geographical boundaries are now commonly accepted, but not without contention. Some, for example, suggest a unified Asia and Europe because the principle lines of the Urals are relatively arbitrary without representing dramatic change either geographically or culturally,[3] whereas others contest the historical connotation of the term "Asia," believing that the word is more of "an idea than a tangible reality."[4] Many also prefer to define Asia in its narrower sense, based more on its cultural diversity instead of its geography. This narrow definition excludes Turkey, the Middle Eastern countries, and Central Asia, which includes Mongolia and countries recently independent from the former Soviet Union, from Asia. For simplicity's sake, this narrowly-defined Asia, which only focuses on East Asia, the Indian subcontinent, and the Southeastern Asian countries, will be the focus of this book.

Asia, as a whole, has more diversity than commonality in almost every aspect from the physical features and weather patterns to the political and economic systems. Culturally speaking, however, certain regional characteristics can be identified across the sub-regions. East Asia stretches from China in the west to Japan in the east, with adjacent countries in between, such as South Korea, North Korea, Taiwan, and sometimes Mongolia or Vietnam, depending on how the region is defined. The physical features of East Asia range from mountains, plateaus, deserts, and steppe lands in China and Mongolia in the north and northwest, to the mid-latitude hills and coastal lands of the Korean Peninsula and the island countries of Japan and Taiwan. Because of the diversity of the terrain, the weather patterns are also noticeably different in the sub-regions in East Asia. It is dry and cold in the north and northwest of the region, where the dominant lifestyle is nomadic and the population density is low. In contrast, the south and southeast are warm and humid with abundant rainfall, and a rice trade sustains the large population. Culturally speaking, however, the region shares certain common characteristics because of the cultural heritage originating in the Yellow River region of China. In terms of religion, Confucianism and Buddhism are strong in most East Asian countries, but Christianity, Islam, and local religions, such as Shintoism (Shinto), Daoism, and Shamanism, are also practiced in the region.

The center of South Asia is in India. To its east and west are Bangladesh and Pakistan. Other countries in the area include Afghanistan, Nepal, Bhutan, Sri Lanka, and the Maldives. South Asia is physically isolated from the rest of Asia by high mountains; the Himalayan Mountains to the north and the Hindu Kush Mountains to the northwest. Being one of the most formidable barriers in the world, the Himalayan Mountains separated the two earliest civilizations of China and India for centuries, although the two share a long border. As a result, India historically had more cultural exchanges with the Middle Eastern (West Asian) countries than with the East Asian counties. The hills and dense forests along the border of India and Myanmar formed an effective land barrier between South and Southeast Asia. As a result, most Indian cultural influence was spread to Southeast Asia by way of the sea.

The Indus and Ganges rivers nourished the early civilizations on the Indian subcontinent, which provided for a certain common cultural heritage across the entire region. The climate in South Asia is characterized by a monsoon, which means "seasonal wind." Each year, the monsoon draws moisture from the surrounding oceans and turns it into rain upon reaching the land in the summer. Due to changes in atmospheric circulation, in the winter, the now dry winds reverse their course back toward the Indian Ocean. The seasonal changes associated with the monsoon can greatly affect the agriculture in the area. In India, for example, the monsoon accounts for as much as 80 percent of the annual rainfall. Delay of the monsoon will cause droughts across the region.

Southeast Asian countries are generally divided into two groups: continental countries and insular countries. The continental countries include Vietnam, Cambodia, Laos, Myanmar, and Thailand, whereas Indonesia, the Philippines, Malaysia, Singapore, Brunei, and Timor-Leste (commonly known as East Timor) belong to insular Southeast Asia. Similar to South Asia, Southeast Asia is also characterized by a monsoon climate, which first appears as a rainy season and ends with a dry season. Almost all of the Southeast Asian countries are located in the tropical zone with only two different seasons: a dry season in the winter and a wet (rainy) season in the summer. The temperature can climb above 35°C to 40°C in the summer and generally stays around 25°C in the winter. There are, however, significant regional variations. The upland of Myanmar, Thailand, and Laos, for example, can be cold and windy in the winter, and snow falls every year on some of the highest mountains in Indonesia, Vietnam, and Myanmar. The long coastlines of the Southeast Asian countries emphasize a maritime orientation in Southeast Asia's economy; maritime trade developed in Southeast Asia long before the Europeans reached the area. Southeast Asia prospered because of the maritime trade.

Several ancient Southeast Asian cities, such as Oc Eo of the Funan Kingdom, ranked among the richest of the time.

Known for its greater diversity in ethnicity, culture and religion, Southeast Asia has experienced less unity than other Asian regions. Its early culture is generally considered to be a fusion of Indian and Chinese cultures and was later influenced by the cultures of its colonizers. This notion, however, was recently challenged by scholars specializing in Southeast Asian Studies.[5] Southeast Asia is also religiously diverse, and all of the major world religions are practiced there. While Buddhism and Confucianism are the dominant religions in continental Southeast Asia, Christianity, Islam, and Hinduism are also practiced in some southeast countries.

Despite the diversity among the regions, Asia, as a whole, still exhibits considerable commonalities. Three out of four of the oldest civilizations of the world, namely the Mesopotamian civilization, the Indus River civilization and the Yellow River civilization, originated in Asia. Each of these civilizations developed in fertile river valleys, and two of them, the Indus River and Yellow River civilizations, continue to thrive today. Cities, states, and empires that developed in these areas provided models and inspiration for the political, economic and architectural developments of their time. Technological innovations, such as writing, mathematics, the wheel, paper, cloth, silk and gunpowder, etc., were important contributions from these societies.

Most Asian countries, except a few in East Asia, are still highly agrarian, with more than half of the population living and working in rural areas. Agricultural activities in Asia can be traced back to Neolithic times. Between 8,000 and 7,000 BCE, farming communities were formed in Southeast Asia and China. Among the domesticated crops were millets, cabbage, and rice. There is evidence that wheat, peas, sesame seeds, barley, dates, and oranges were cultivated in the Indus valley around the same time, and by 3500 BCE, cotton growing and cotton textiles were quite advanced in the valley. Domestication of animals, such as cattle, pigs, sheep, and goats, was also evident in Asia in the Neolithic age. Many farming tools, such as the plow and spade, were first employed in Asia. Until recently, most crops produced in Asia were labor-intensive crops, such as rice, corn, and beans. Rice is the preferred food wherever there is enough rainfall for its cultivation. Corn and beans are favorable in the areas where precipitation is limited.

Asia has the largest population of any continent in the world, accounting for 60 percent of the world population. Among the twelve countries that have a population of over 100 million, seven are Asian countries, namely China, India, Indonesia, Pakistan, Bangladesh, Japan, and the Philippines. According to the CIA World Factbook, eight out of fifteen of the world's most populous countries are in Asia.[6] China and India combined have about 37 percent of the world's population, which almost equals that of Europe, America, and Africa combined. Population growth in Asia is expected to continue in the twenty-first century at a rate greater than any other region.

Rank	Country	Population
TABLE 1.01 15 MOST POPULOUS COUNTRIES IN THE WORLD (ASIAN COUNTRIES ARE IN BOLD)		
1	**China**	1,343,239,923
2	**India**	1,205,073,612
3	The United States	313,847,465
4	**Indonesia**	248,216,193
5	Brazil	205,716,890
6	**Pakistan**	190,291,129
7	Nigeria	170,123,740
8	**Bangladesh**	161,083,804
9	Russia*	138,082,178
10	**Japan**	127,368,088
11	Mexico	114,975,406
12	**Philippines**	103,775,002
13	Ethiopia	93,815,992
14	**Vietnam**	91,519,289
15	Egypt	83,688,164

The population data in this chart comes from the CIA World Factbook website[7]
*Part of Russia is in Asia.

Many studies have suggested a direct correlation between overpopulation and poverty. As a result, the rapid population increase poses challenges to the governments of many Asian countries. India, for example, may reach 1.5 billion by 2050, becoming the most populous country in the world, followed by China with 1.4 billion. Pakistan and Indonesia, both populations having a chance of exceeding 300 million, will rank fourth and fifth. Continuous population growth may present itself as a threat to prosperity and collective success in many Asian countries. Because of the large population and the increasing level of urbanization, many Asian cities also face the trouble of overpopulation. People living in the countryside continuously migrate into cities because of job opportunities and a higher average standard of living. In the countryside of many Asian countries, residents still have to manage their lives without electricity or running water. Among the ten currently most populated cities, six are located in Asia, or more specifically in southern and eastern Asia, namely, Beijing, Mumbai (Bombay), Calcutta, Seoul, Shanghai, and Tokyo.

Asian countries have played an increasingly important role in the world since World War II and their influence will continue well into the new century. In this age of globalization, we cannot afford to be ignorant of Asia's past and its potential for our future. Therefore, knowledge about Asia may be important or even crucial for a student's future success.

For more information about the topics discussed in this chapter, please visit the website for this textbook. This website can be accessed from http://www.grtep.com/.

1 Paweł Bożyk, "Newly Industrialized Countries" in *Globalization and the Transformation of Foreign Economic Policy* (London: Ashgate Publishing, 2006), 164–165.
2 Martin W. Lewis and Karen Wigen, *The Myth of Continents: A Critique of Metageography* (Berkeley and Los Angeles: University of California Press, 1997), 27–28.
3 Rhoads Murphey, *A History of Asia*, sixth ed. (New York: Prentice Hall, 2008), 1.
4 "The Geography of East and Southeast Asia," accessed July 4, 2011, http://people.hofstra.edu/Jean-paul_Rodrigue/GESA/topic1/topic1_A.html.
5 Milton Osborne, *Southeast Asia: An Introductory History* (Crows Nest Australia: Allen & Unwin), 6.
6 Central Intelligence Agency, The World Factbook, accessed July 15, 2011, https://www.cia.gov/library/publications/the-world-factbook/rankorder/2119rank.html
7 Central Intelligence Agency, the World Factbook, accessed July 09, 2012, https://www.cia.gov/library/publications/the-world-factbook/rankorder/2119rank.html

Chapter 2: Religion

INTRODUCTION[1]

Like no other continent on the planet, Asia has been the birthplace to a plethora of religious and ethical beliefs for a majority of the world's population throughout history. Thus, to understand the history of the Asian people, one must study the rich religious and philosophical heritage that serves as the "gateway" to their diverse cultures. This chapter will explore the Hindu, Jain, Buddhist, and Sikh religions. All of these religions are indigenous to India; however, Buddhism quickly migrated throughout most of Asia. In addition, this chapter will examine Confucianism, which is not a religion, but a philosophy grounded in "virtue ethics." Ironically, Confucianism was born out of the tumultuous Warring States Era of Chinese history and the Daoist religion, which, in many ways, is an antithesis to the teachings of Confucianism. The animistic religion of Shintoism, also indigenous to Japan and very important to the understanding of its socio-political history, will be introduced. Finally, this chapter will look at Islam, a religion that did not have its roots in Asia, but quickly spread throughout much of Asia after its inception. From the hot sands of the Middle East, Islam has played a vital role in shaping Asian culture. I hope that when you have finished studying this chapter, you will have a better appreciation for the precepts of the various religions and philosophies that continue to contribute to the Asian fabric of society and its diverse history.

HINDU RELIGION

One cannot learn the history of India without studying about Hinduism, the oldest of all the major world religions. With over 800 million adherents today, Hinduism has been and still is the spiritual lifeblood of its people.

Hinduism is not just a set of theological beliefs but a societal way of life in India. For example, a major difference between Hinduism and other major present day religions of the world is that Hinduism has been and still is a "cultural" not a "creedal" religion. Like ancient Judaism, one is born a Hindu into the caste system, similar to how in biblical era Judaism, Jews were born into one of the twelve tribes of Israel. Although one cannot really "become" or convert to Hinduism since they are

---

1 All demographic information for this chapter was obtained from the Central Intelligence Agency, *The World Factbook* (Washington, D.C.: Government Printing Office, 2009), https://www.cia.gov/library/publications/the-world-factbook/index.html. (accessed December 28, 2011).

not born into its caste structure, there have been people who have chosen to follow the teachings and rituals of Hinduism.

Hinduism, unlike the other major religions of the world, cannot point to a founder or single canonical text. In addition, most of its religious texts have no named author. However, through the work of archaeologists and linguistic scholars, it has been deduced that two major historical events serve as the foundation for much of Hinduism's rituals and theological beliefs. First, some elements of Hinduism can be traced back to India's first civilization, the Harappan (3000-1800 BCE). For example, archaeological findings show that in Harappan cities, neighborhoods were delineated according to the dweller's occupation, much like Hinduism's caste system. Therefore, many academics see this early use of a caste system as evidence of a socio-political control device, which helps to explain why the caste system became such a vital part of Hinduism from its inception.

The second major historical event that left its indelible mark on Hinduism was the Aryan invasion of India from the mountain ranges of present day Iran around 1600 BCE. This invasion brought with it an ancient form of the Sanskrit language, which is the language of Hinduism's religious scriptures such as the *Vedas*, *Upanishads*, and the *Bhagavad Gita*.

HINDU LITERATURE

Hinduism's *Rig Veda*, the world's oldest religious scripture, is still in use. Not only is its author unknown, its date of origin is debatable as well. Based on the historical references in the work, most historians and linguists place its date of origin about 1500 BCE. However, its origin is difficult to pin down since it was first communicated orally for over a millennium and was only written down between the fourth and sixth centuries CE. The *Rig Veda* contains over 1,028 aphorisms, which are compiled into ten books, and is an essential window into both India's Vedic civilization as well as Hinduism's early beginnings. The *Rig Veda* is Hinduism's first verses of wisdom, describing in poetic aphoristic style many of Hinduism's deities and their functions. For example, the *Rig Veda's* most prominent deity, Indra, is described as Lord of the Universe and Lord of the Thunderbolt, and regarded as the lord protector over people giving them strength to defeat their enemies. Thus, Hindus believe that when they ritually chant the *Rig Vedas* at celebrations and festivals, they are connected to the forces of creation—which in turn renews them spiritually.

Another important Hindu text is the *Upanishads*, which translates to "connection." This text consists of over 200 verses, the earliest of which were composed around the fifth century BCE, and are commonly referred to as the concluding verses of the *Rig Veda*. Replete with mystical and esoteric verses, the *Upanishads* are concerned with the search for immortality and the connections between this world and the cosmos. Similar to the *Rig Veda*, the *Upanishads* depict the Vedic deities as the forces of existence. Most importantly, the *Upanishads* address personal morality and conduct as well as societal mores. In essence, they are a guide for Hindus to discover their self-realization through eternal wisdom. Thus, the *Upanishads* are the segue to Hinduism's most important ethical text—the *Bhagavad Gita*, which means Song of the Lord.

Like other Hindu literature, the author and date of composition is unknown, however, most scholars place it around the third century BCE. Hindus consider the *Gita* a compelling and beautiful poem with a powerful message that encourages individuals to perform their duties in life no matter how unpalatable they may seem. The theme of the poem is a tale of dilemma for Prince Arjuna, who is faced with the necessity of going to war against his relatives and friends whom he loves, even though they are wrongly disputing his rightful claim to the throne. Although, his cause is just, he is stymied into utter inaction by the terrible thought of having to fight and kill people he deeply loves, since he believes doing so would be an evil act. The poem depicts Arjuna in his chariot awaiting the battle to commence; paralyzed by his conflicting emotions, he cannot proceed. Krishna, the deity of love and joy, appears as Arjuna's chariot driver and starts to explain why Arjuna must fulfill his duty even if it means killing those he loves. The logical argument Krishna uses is that since Arjuna is a soldier and his claim to the throne is just, it is imperative that he perform his rightful duty in life, which is also in accordance with maintaining a just society. Thus, Arjuna must go to war against his relatives and friends since it is their evil actions that are really tearing at the fabric of society by fighting against what is truly just. Therefore, the moral concept in the *Gita* that rules the action of Hindus is that the healthy maintenance of the individual and society can only be maintained by everyone performing their duty, which in Sanskrit is *dharma*.

THE FOUR BASIC AIMS OF HINDU LIFE

Hindu teachings recognize that all humans have four basic aims in life, known as *purusartha*; all four aims are seen as important aspects of an individual's well being. Of course, all people seek *kama*, meaning "pleasure, physical or emotional." *Kama* is most often connected with sexual pleasure, and how to obtain sexual pleasure is written about around the second century CE in the book, the *Kamasutra*. Next, everyone desires *artha*, meaning "power, fame, money, and possessions." This aim is also written about in an important Hindu text known as the *Arthashastra*. This book's purpose is to teach a king how to obtain and hold onto power. It was written by Kautilya, an adviser to the Indian king Chandragupta Maurya, who reigned in India from 324-301 BCE. The *Arthashastra* is similar in its goal and scope to Machiavelli's famous political treatise *The Prince*, even though it was written eighteen hundred years earlier. The next aim is *dharma*, meaning "duty, that which upholds or supports." It is an important aim as it helps to control all the other aims through one performing their proper moral duty. *Dharma* is written about in the *Bhagavad Gita*, which was described earlier in this chapter.

These first three aims are interrelated and throughout a person's life produce what is referred to as *karma* meaning "deed." One's *karma* at the end of life determines in what earthly form the soul will be reincarnated for the next life. Hindus believe that a soul cannot only be reincarnated into a human form, but also an animal like a cow or even an insect, a major reason why most Hindus are vegetarians. The last aim, and the one that all Hindu's fervently strive for, is *moksha* meaning "liberation" specifically from *samsara*, "reincarnation." People who obtain this most desirable aim break out of the "curse" of the reincarnation cycle of life, death, and rebirth. Only through the perfection of spiritual self-realization can a Hindu soul reach *moksha* to dwell with the creative force of the cosmos. This could take a soul literally thousands of lifetimes on earth before reaching this ultimate level of enlightened existence. Finally, *samsara* plays a significant role in Hinduism's caste system because the caste one is born in is based upon the *karma* from their previous incarnation.

HINDU CASTE SYSTEM

Varna, meaning color, is a Hindu social class system that has been deeply rooted in Indian culture, most likely since the Harappan civilization. First mentioned in the *Rig Veda*, the *Varna* is considered not a human invention but a divinely created one. During the Vedic civilization, Hindu society was divided into four major caste classifications, which were based on a person's occupation. Since the creation of the *Varna*, a Hindu's class is inherited at birth from the father's line. The *Varna* is clearly a social system that has been used over several millennia to control India's socio-economic and political structure. However, like any class structure based on one's consequence of birth instead of one's abilities, the *Varna* is inherently discriminatory and has caused life-long suffering to hundreds of millions of Indians throughout history.

Members of the highest class are the *Brahmins*, who serve as priests, scholars, and teachers. The second class is the *Kshatriyas*, warriors, administrators, and kings. Interestingly, this is the only class of Hindus who are not vegetarians by rule. The third class is the *Vaishyas*, who are merchants and farmers. The fourth class is the *Shudras*, who are workers, artisans, and service providers. Within the third and fourth classes, there are literally over 2000 subclasses that have developed over time. In addition, there is one group of people who are not even counted within the four classes. Known as the *dalits*, meaning "suppressed," they were commonly referred to as untouchables. People in this category labored in jobs that Hindus considered unclean, such as handling the dead, collecting the trash, butchering animals and tanning their hides. Untouchables were prohibited from entering Hindu temples or from touching members of the higher classes. A higher class Hindu who touched a *dalit* was considered ritually unclean and was required to take a ritual bath to become purified again.

With these prohibitions on the *dalits*, it is easy to understand how they suffered immense discrimination in Indian society. It is important to note that Mahatma Gandhi himself witnessed the pernicious bigotry under which the *dalits* suffered. He worked hard to find a place in Indian society for them, and renamed them *Harijans* meaning "children of God." When India gained its independence in 1948 nearly 25 percent of its population were *dalit*. Fortunately, they gained full rights under Indian law at that time. However, because of the social stigma that many upper class Indians still harbor, many *dalits* have recently converted to Buddhism, which rejects the caste system altogether.

image © forbis, 2012. Used under license from Shutterstock, Inc.

Statue of Lord Shiva

GODS AND GODDESSES

The Sanskrit word for God is *Deva*, meaning "celestial." When one first encounters the pantheon of Hindu deities, one is overwhelmed by how numerous they are. Hindus often mention that there are 330 million gods, but this phrase is more a rhetorical device to explain that all life is really a part of the one Supreme Being or universal Spirit known as *Brahman* who lives in everyone's heart. In fact, the numerous gods and goddesses are nothing more than different functional incarnations known as avatars of *Brahman*. It is these numerous avatars that Hindus are fond of worshipping.

Hindus teach that the cosmic force has three functions: creation, preservation, and destruction. Out of this belief, Hindus have a trinity of avatars that represent these functions and are worshipped quite often. One of the most worshipped avatars is *Shiva*, who is known as lord of destruction and recreation, lord of the fertility, and lord of the dance, which is often how *Shiva* is depicted in both sculptures and paintings. Another avatar is *Brahmā* who exemplifies the creative force of the cosmos. Finally, *Vishnu* is lord of preservation. Since *Brahman* embodies all existence, it contains both male and female characteristics; all gods have male and female avatars. Thus, it is easy to understand why, when Europeans first encountered Hinduism, they classified it as a polytheistic religion because of the panoply of gods. However, as scholars studied Hinduism, they realized that it was essentially monotheistic because Hindus emphasize in their teachings the notion that there is only one Supreme Being, *Brahman*, and that Hindus believe in the immortality of the soul. However, this question still confounds many adherents from the religious traditions of Judaism, Christianity, and Islam.

Other interesting facts about Hinduism seem noteworthy enough to mention. Hindus acknowledge that there is good and evil in the world. However, they teach that these forces are part of everyone's character and it is up to the individual to control their evil inclinations, thus, improving their *karma*. Hinduism does not have a weekly Sabbath day nor does it have a set ceremonial prayer service performed on a certain day. However, Hindus do celebrate several festivals where they gather together. They are the spring festival of *Holi* and the autumn festival of *Diwali*. Observant Hindus chant daily prayers at a home alter and do not need *Brahmins* to intercede on their behalf. However, *Brahmins* are necessary to officiate at significant Hindu life events, such as marriage and death ceremonies. On occasion, Hindus will travel on pilgrimages to leave offerings of food and flowers at Hindu temples.

JAIN RELIGION

The next religion indigenous to India is Jainism, an outgrowth of Hinduism that shares many of its core beliefs and teachings, such as the *samsara* cycle, *dharma*, and *karma*. Jains do, although, reject the Hindu caste system, as well as the *Rig Veda* and *Upanishads* for their violent rhetoric. In addition, Jains reject the *Bhagavad Gita's* authority but not its concept that teaches the necessity for a person to fulfill his/her *dharma*. Finally, Jainism is a religion that is best defined for its strict adherence to *ahimsa*, "pacifism, non-violence," towards all living creatures. *Ahimsa* includes not only a prohibition against killing another living creature because it has a soul, but also not harming another soul physically, mentally, or emotionally. India's violent history during the time of Jainism's founding proves why it became a new religious outgrowth of Hinduism.

THE FOUNDING OF JAINISM

Jains believe that the universe always existed and always will. Therefore, there is no creation story in Jain teachings nor is there a belief in God. To Jains, their religion has always been present. However, historians point to one man as the founder: Mahavira, meaning "great hero," who lived in the sixth century BCE. His true biography is sketchy and there have been all kinds of claims made about his life; these claims are used to enhance Jain religious principals. However, what is known to be true is that around the age of thirty, Mahavira left his birthplace in modern Patna and wandered throughout India naked, for twelve years living the simple life of an ascetic. Soon after, he attained enlightenment, and was revered as the twenty-fourth and last *Tirthankara*, meaning "one who guides others along the path of enlightenment." For over the next thirty years, Mahavira amassed a large following of monks, nuns, and laypeople teaching them to follow his enlightened example. Indabhuti, one of his devoted disciples, gathered his teachings and wrote the *Agnas*, which is the twelve volume foundational scripture for Jains. There are over forty canonical volumes that were written within the millennia after Mahavira's death. While in his seventies, Mahavira died from starvation and obtained *moksha*. The magnificent Jalmandir Temple was erected in his remembrance; it is customary for Jains to make a pilgrimage to it on the anniversary of Mahavira's death.

JAIN THEOLOGY

For Jains, to obtain *moksha* is to live a life of compassionate restraint. Only by improving the *karma* of the present life can a Jain hope to better their birth in a future life, by doing so through the *samsara* cycle, the Jain eventually attains *moksha* in order to end the suffering of life on earth altogether. In order to free themselves of what Jains call the "bondage" of bad karma, they teach that people must restrain from giving into evil inclinations caused by human passions. This is why the word Jain means spiritual victor. To regulate their conduct, Jains have developed a moral code of five principles they vow to follow. Within the five principals, the monastic order of Jains will adhere to a much stricter code of conduct than the laypeople are required to follow.

The first principle is *ahimsa*, non-violence. The strict adherence to this principal sets the religion apart from all others. Jains are strict vegetarians, will not fight in wars, or work as farmers out of fear they will harm organisms living in the dirt. Most Jains work in the business world and are very successful because of their strict adherence to their religious principals. The monastic Jains take extraordinary measures to ensure they do not harm any living creature. These actions include wearing a mask over their mouths so as not to inadvertently swallow an insect, and sweeping the paths in front of them so as not to step on any living creature. The second principle is *satya*, meaning truthfulness. Besides being truthful, Jains vow to speak in a non-harmful manner; thus, connecting this principle to *ahimsa* as a way to refrain from causing emotional harm to anyone. *Satya* also requires being honest in all business dealings. The third principle is *asteya* meaning non-stealing. This principle includes not cheating on taxes, altering weights and scales, or conducting business on the black market. Once again, this principle is connected to *ahimsa* because the prohibited actions are harmful to others. The fourth principle is *brahmacarya*, meaning sexual conduct. Jain laypeople must refrain from adulterous behavior; for the monastic order it means celibacy. Not only is the principle connected to *ahimsa*, but it also regulates one of humanity's strongest passions, that if not repressed, will lead to a bad *karma* and ultimate bondage within the *samsara* cycle. The fifth principle is *aparigraha*, meaning non-materialism. Laypeople are to rid themselves of all thoughts and desires that drive them to obtain material wealth. Although allowed to own property, they should not allow the desire for material wealth to take over their life. For the monastic order, they must give up all earthly possessions. Strict adherence to these five principles is how Jains can improve their soul in their ultimate desire to obtain *moksha*.

Finally, it is important to note that the principle of *ahimsa* played a central role in India's struggle for independence. Mahatma Gandhi grew up in the Porbandar region of India, which had a large Jain community. Although a devout Hindu, he was greatly influenced by the principle of *ahimsa* at an early age and made it a central theme of his non-violent struggle for Indian independence from British rule.

Two Denominations

There was a rift in monastic doctrine soon after Mahavira's death; the residual effects of that rift still exist today. The rift mainly has to do with the conduct of the monks of the *Digambar* sect and the *Svetambar* sect. The *Digambar*, meaning "sky clad," require their monks to go through life in the nude because they believe that attachment to even the simplest of clothing increases the passion of materialism. The *Svetambar*, or "white clad" monks, wear a white seamless cloth wrap for practical reasons and they argue that simple clothing does not inflame materialistic desires in people. This is the major doctrinal split between the two denominations who otherwise agree on almost all other issues. There are over five million Jains today; most of whom reside in India.

BUDDHIST RELIGION

Once again, India is the birthplace to one of the world's largest religions, Buddhism. Around 560 BCE. a Nepalese prince by the name of Siddhartha Gautama was born. As a young man, he embarked on a lifelong quest to find the true path that people could follow to live a life free of suffering. This quest enlightened and transformed Siddhartha into the Buddha, meaning "the Enlightened One," and his teachings ultimately changed the lives of billions of Asians throughout history. Within two centuries, Buddhism gained a most important protégé, Emperor Ashoka of the Mauryan Dynasty in India, who encouraged Buddhist monks to spread their message to the four corners of the earth. What is historically interesting to note is that by the ninth century CE, Buddhism became a major religious and cultural institution throughout most of Asia, while it declined to near extinction in India, the country of its birth. This decline was due to the regenerative growth of Hinduism and the

Muslim invasions into northwest India. To study Buddhism, one must first learn about the extraordinary biography of its founder.

FOUNDER OF BUDDHISM

Much of Siddhartha Gautama's early biography is more legend than historical fact. However, what is known is that he was born to rule the small kingdom of Sakya. Legend has it that when Siddhartha was born, a wise sage told his father, King Suddhodana, that in early manhood Siddhartha would discover the *dukkha*, meaning "suffering," people endured in life, which would cause him to reject the throne and spend the rest of his days searching for and ultimately attaining enlightenment. This prophecy frightened his father, so he ensured that Siddhartha lived a cloistered life of royal privilege free from suffering and hardship. Siddhartha even married and had a son. Despite his father's wishes, an event takes place when Siddhartha is twenty-nine that causes in him a spiritual awakening to the suffering that exists in the world; this event is referred to in Buddhist teachings as the "Four Signs."

The Four Signs of suffering appear to Siddhartha when he ventures beyond the palace walls for the first time in his life. On his first journey, he witnesses the suffering of an old man wracked with injury from age and hard work. On subsequent trips, he comes upon a severely sick man, a corpse being prepared for cremation, and finally a wandering ascetic who by all appearances had the look of peaceful bliss about him. Mortified by the realization that people are doomed to a life of suffering, such as mortality and the false trappings of pleasurable pursuits, Siddhartha is drawn to the ascetic life. He quickly renounced his possessions, left his wife and child behind, and with nothing but a begging bowl and a loin cloth, lived the austere life of an ascetic on a quest for the truth to enlightened human existence.

After many years of material deprivation, while at the same time perfecting the practice of yoga, meaning to control, from the best Hindu and Jain practitioners at that time, Siddhartha still did not believe he had reached his goal of extinguishing the passions that drove him towards suffering; what the Buddhists refer to as *nirvana*, a Sanskrit word meaning "to extinguish." It is this reality that caused Siddhartha, who by this time had become emaciated from years of asceticism, to realize that his suffering did not lead to the path of true enlightenment.

He learned two important lessons from this realization. First, the soul will not be improved by punishing its vessel, the body. Second, happiness is not necessarily the antithesis to enlightenment. If one could embrace happiness freed from the yearnings of destructive passions of lust and greed for example, then happiness could be a path to enlightenment. These revelations became the great foundational truths that Buddhism was built upon, known as the "Middle Way," which is the ability to avoid the extremes of self-gratification and self-mortification.

With this new knowledge, Siddhartha, at age thirty-five, sat under a bodhi tree promising that he would not move from under it until he discovered all of life's truths. He began a state of deep meditation that lasted for forty-nine days. During this period, Mara, the demonic embodiment of death and evil, threatened Siddhartha with death, the ultimate fear of all humans. Siddhartha showed no fear of dying, Mara tries to entice him with worldly pleasures. Although, Siddhartha was severely tested, he ultimately conquered the great fear of death and the temptations of pleasure. Armed with this newfound knowledge, he emerged from his meditative state to be forever after recognized as the Buddha, "Enlightened One." The Buddha's newfound knowledge is his recognition of what causes human suffering, known as the "Four Noble Truths," and the steps necessary to avoid suffering which is known as the "Eightfold Path." The Buddha spent the rest of his life wandering throughout India preaching about his newfound enlightenment until he eventually died at the age of eighty.

THE BASIS OF BUDDHIST DOCTRINE

The Four Noble Truths are at the heart of Buddhist doctrine. They are: (1) life is full of *dukkha*, "suffering," (2) suffering is caused by urges to fulfill desires, (3) suffering can only end when people ignore their desires, and (4) liberation from suffering can only be obtained by following the "Eightfold Path." Understanding the conditions of suffering is not enough to break out of the reincarnation cycle. Only by living the Eightfold Path can a Buddhist soul enter into a state of *nirvana*. The Eightfold Path is often depicted in Buddhism as a wheel with eight spokes known as a *dharma* wheel; each path is an action to perform and it takes the unity of all eight actions to reach *nirvana*.

In addition, the eight actions are divided into three maxims that define the Buddha's "Middle Way." The first maxim is wisdom, and the first two paths are (1) right understanding and (2) right intention. The second maxim is moral conduct, and the next three paths are (3) right speech, (4) right action, and (5) right livelihood. The third maxim is contemplation, and the last three paths are (6) right effort, (7) right mindfulness, and (8) right concentration. The word right connotes more than just "truth." It also implies those actions that advance an end to suffering. It is important to understand that the maxims of the Middle Way are interconnected; an advancement in any one maxim is dependent upon advancement in the other two.

Finally, unlike Christianity, the Buddha's teaching of liberation from suffering in the Four Noble Truths is not about receiving divine grace or a heavenly gift bestowed by God. Buddha taught that individuals are the cause of their own suffering, and only through a life full of discipline and effort in exhibiting proper conduct as listed in the Eightfold Path can they free themselves from suffering.

TWO MAJOR DENOMINATIONS

Within a century of Buddha's death there was a major rift within the Buddhist community that formed two doctrinal paths. The oldest and closest to early Buddhism is the Theravada, meaning "the way of the elders." It adheres to the original Pali canon, which contains the earliest lessons of the Buddha. In addition, it emphasizes the notion that acts of good deeds, such as charitable donations, could erase past transgressions and improve a person's *karma*. Theravada Buddhism is predominantly found in Sri Lanka, Myanmar, Thailand, Cambodia, and Laos, and has a majority of Buddhist adherents in the world. In addition, this is the school of Buddhism that is prevalent in most countries outside of Asia. Mahayana Buddhism, meaning "great vehicle," developed around the first century CE during India's Kushan Empire. Mahayana Buddhists adopted many later scriptures to help guide their adherents to *nirvana*. The most significant are the Lotus Sutra and the Diamond Sutra. In addition to new scripture, the Mahayana school also introduced a new set of theological beliefs. The Mahayana denomination tends to ascribe Buddha with the characteristics God. In addition, they developed the notion of *bodhisattvas*, meaning "enlightened beings", who out of kindness have forestalled their entrance into *nirvana* so that they can help guide adherents to *nirvana*. This new theology caused a new form of worship including the institution of elaborate rituals and the worship of a new group of images.

It is important to note that besides these few differences between the two denominations, there is much more upon which they agree. For example, all Buddhists adhere to the importance placed on following the Middle Way, Four Noble Truths, and The Eightfold Path. In addition, all Buddhists accept the Buddha as their guide. Mahayana Buddhism is most prevalent in China, Tibet, Singapore, Korea, Japan, and most of Vietnam. There are over 350 million Buddhists in the world.

SIKH RELIGION

The last indigenous religion that arose in India is the Sikh religion. Sikhism is seen in many ways as a melding of some of the core beliefs of both Hinduism and Islam. For example, although Sikhs adopted Hinduism's reincarnation cycle, they rejected the Hindu caste system. Sikhs have adopted Islam's belief in only one God who is formless and eternal, making Sikhism a monotheistic religion. The confluence of beliefs of these two religions into Sikhism is definitely born out India's violent history of at the time of Sikhism's founding in the fifteenth century CE.

FOUNDER OF SIKHISM

The founder of Sikhism, Nanak Dev, was born a Hindu in 1469 CE. in present day Lahore Pakistan. His family was of the *kshatriyas* caste, and his father was a tax collector for the Muslim governor of the area. He was well educated and by the time he was a teenager had already rejected Hinduism. Having been raised in a predominantly Muslim neighborhood, he studied the tenets of the Islamic faith but became equally dissatisfied in Islam as a substitute for Hinduism. Legend has it that at the age of thirty, Nanak went missing for three days in a river and was given up for dead. When he miraculously reappeared, he related a story that he was brought to God's heavenly court, was invested with the truth of God's eternal and ever present existence in the world, and was instructed by God that it was his calling to teach others to rejoice in the knowledge of God's existence in the heart of every person. Thus, Sikhism was founded and Nanak's new found enlightenment earned him the title of Guru, meaning "disciple and teacher." Finally, Guru Nanak spent the rest of his days preaching that the path to God's salvation was not through following the tenets of Hinduism or Islam. For Sikhs the only way to break the reincarnation cycle and reach union with God's love is to recognize that God lives in the hearts of all people, and that one gains salvation by relinquishing the "Five Evils": ego, anger, greed, attachment, and lust. Guru Nanak and his followers formed the first Sikh community. Sikh teachings and its rituals have changed over time through the enlightened words of an unbroken chain of nine other subsequent Gurus, the last being Guru Gobind Singh in 1708 CE. From this time forward, all rituals and scriptures were finalized and formed the basis of beliefs upon which Sikhs live their lives.

SIKH OBSERVANCES

The collected wisdom of all ten gurus is contained in the scripture known as the Guru Granth Sahib. It has more than 5,000 hymns that are used in Sikh rituals and daily prayers recited after rising and bathing each morning. The Sikh place of worship similar to a temple is known as a *gurwara*. It will not have any images of God, and in the main hall, passages from the Guru Granth Sahib are read. There are no priests in the Sikh religion; however, members of the Sikh community serve as custodians of the *Guru Granth Sahib* in the *gurwara*. All attendees share in an afternoon meal that is open to anyone who is hungry regardless of religious affiliation. Sikhs partake in life cycle ceremonies to include birth, marriage, and death ceremonies. The Sikh baby naming ceremony is quite fascinating. Upon the birth of a child, the Guru Granth Sahib is randomly opened to any page and the first letter in the upper left corner of the left page is used as the first letter of the child's name.

The Sikhs also have a baptism ceremony that is a direct result of the perilous attacks on their community from the Mughal Emperor Aurangzeb in 1699 CE. In fact, because of Aurangzeb's intolerance of all religions except Islam, Sikhs developed one of their distinctive characteristics, which is a reputation for being excellent warriors. The last guru, Gobind Singh, emphasized that their community was in danger of extinction by Aurangzeb's army, and that in order to survive, Sikhs would have to unite and fight in the common cause to save the community. The Guru instituted a baptism ceremony known as the *Khalsa*, meaning "free or pure." The initiates were given a code of conduct to live by that subsequently has been adopted by all Sikhs and prohibits tobacco products, eating meat that was slaughtered according to Muslim custom, and sexual relations with Muslims. In addition, the baptized were required to study the martial arts in order to hone their skills as warriors. The Guru Gobind also required the men to wear five articles as a sign of their baptism. Known as the Five Ks, they are: (1) wrapping uncut hair in a turban, *kes*, (2) wearing a wooden comb in the hair, *kangha*, (3) wearing an iron wrist bracelet, *kara*, (4) wearing short underpants, *kach*, (5) wearing a curved sword or dagger, *kirpan*. In addition, all male initiates by Guru Gobind Singh took for their surname Singh meaning "lion," and the female initiates took the surname of Kaur meaning "princess."

The Sikh community survived the attacks by the Emperor Aurangzeb and has flourished into a vibrant part of India's culture and society. There are over 26 million Sikhs today with over 75 percent of the community living in the Punjab region of India. Starting in the nineteenth century there has been a large migration of Sikhs throughout the world including to North America.

CONFUCIAN PHILOSOPHY

Confucianism has had a greater effect on the moral conduct of the planet's population throughout the last 2,000 years of history than any of the world's religions. Yet Confucianism is not a religion; it is a philosophy very similar to the virtue ethics teachings of the famous Greek philosopher, Aristotle. Most interestingly, Confucianism has existed in syncretistic harmony with the religions of billions of East Asians over the last two millennia. Confucianism is best understood as an ethical code adopted by East Asians to improve the character of its citizenry and produce a doctrine of behavior for the members of its political ruling class.

The story of the founder of Confucianism and his plan to find an ethical way of life for China's people and their political leaders during the tumultuous period of the Zhou Dynasty, reveals why this philosophy has become so popular in East Asia.

FOUNDER OF CONFUCIANISM

Kong Fuzi (551-479 BCE) is known throughout the world by his Latinized name Confucius. During his lifetime, Confucius traveled to many of the seventy states of the Zhou Dynasty trying to convince kings to hire him as their minister of state so that he could institute his new philosophy for improving society in

image © Philip Lange, 2012. Used under license from Shutterstock, Inc.

their kingdoms. Unfortunately, he was unable to convince any ruler to provide him anything but a minor office, which caused him to spend most of his life as a wandering philosopher. At the time of his death, he considered himself an abject failure because he could not convince a ruler to adopt his ethical philosophy. However, his ethical teachings did attract a substantial following of young intellectuals who were responsible for sowing the seeds of Confucianism throughout China. Soon after the start of the Han Dynasty in 206 BCE, Emperor Wu adopted Confucianism as the ruling philosophy for the state and society, and from that time until the Communist takeover of China in 1949, Confucianism was the ruling philosophy of China. Interestingly, Confucius's family, the Kongs, has a great genealogical legacy in human history. Confucius has the longest recorded father-to-son lineal descent in the world today; it is in its eighty-third generation.

CONFUCIUS' DOCTRINE

At the center of Confucius' doctrine are two beliefs for improving society. First, is his belief that people by nature are good and that it is possible to teach all people to improve and act upon their good inclinations—what Confucius called the Doctrine of the Mean. His Doctrine of the Mean is the notion that all virtues have two extremes. On one end is excess while on the other is deficiency. The goal of society should be to cultivate the character of individuals so they may successfully find the "golden way" which leads them to the proper performance of a virtuous act. In addition, Confucius recognized that there are three "universal virtues" that have to be cultivated in society: wisdom, benevolence, and fortitude. Second, is his notion that in order to improve upon the harmony between the citizens and the state, the state must be led by wise leaders. Thus, Confucianism's faith in the inherent goodness and perfectibility of people has had immense implications for the development of the Chinese political structure throughout history. Within the Confucian model of the political state, the sovereign's main purpose is to educate and improve the ethical character of the people. This was ideally accomplished not by coercive power, but by the sovereign setting the ethical example for all of their subjects to follow. Another philosophical precept in Confucianism teaches that as long as the sovereigns rule by virtuous example then they will have and maintain "The Mandate of Heaven." However, heaven would be disappointed with a despotic sovereign and would remove its mandate, leading to a more worthy person supplanting the toppled ruler. Thus, The Mandate of Heaven would then pass onto a new sovereign who would rule virtuously.

Similar to the concepts of Aristotelian ethics, Confucianism espouses the notion that through education and the constant practice of good ethical decision making, individuals will act ethically in society; this makes it unnecessary to rule people with an overabundance of restrictive laws and harsh punishments to regulate society. Confucius also taught that in order to properly regulate society, it was necessary to properly regulate the foundation upon which all societies are built upon—the family unit. Thus, Confucius observed that there were five relationships within the family and society that were of vital importance to the well being of all society. They are: (1) sovereign-subject, (2) husband-wife, (3) parent-child, (4) elder brother-younger brother, (5) friend-friend. Confucius realized that everyone was born into particular relationships that come with certain duties to perform. For example, one has a duty to be loyal to the sovereign, a filial duty to parents, a duty to aid friends, and a duty of common benevolence towards the rest of society. However, these duties are not of equal importance. An individual's duty to his sovereign and parents takes precedent over his/her duty to his/her friends and fellow citizens. It was Confucius' core argument that if everyone in society lived up to their duties according to their station in life, then political order and harmony within society would prevail. Therefore, it is not an over exaggeration to state that the five relationships are the foundation upon which not only Chinese but all of East Asian society has been regulated and maintained for over 2,000 years.

CONFUCIAN LITERATURE

Although Confucius did not write down any of his philosophy, we know his philosophy through the writings of his disciples, which were written about thirty years after his death, and the plethora of commentaries on his teachings that are still published to this day. The literature that is at the heart of Confucius philosophy is known as *The Four Books of Confucianism*. First is "The Great Learning," which has a short text devoted to Confucius' ideas on political philosophy and nine chapters of commentary by one of his disciples. The second is "The Doctrine of the Mean," written by Confucius' grandson Zisi, which consists of thirty-three chapters espousing the significance of following the "golden way" to obtain virtue. The third is "The Analects of Confucius," which is a compendium of lectures and discussions Confucius had with his disciples. It contains all of Confucian philosophy. The fourth is "Mencius," written and named after a pupil of Confucius' grandson. Mencius is recognized as the greatest Confucian scholar in history. His work is an anthology of long dialogues he had with several kings about the proper way to rule.[2]

Historians recognize that *The Four Books of Confucianism* along with many others, served a very important function in Chinese society. Since Confucianism taught that the state was the ethical guardian of society, for over two millennia any man wanting to serve in China's bureaucracy had to pass a written civil service exam proving his knowledge of the classical Confucian literature. Known as the Imperial Examinations, these tests were given every year to men who spent years studying Confucianism in hopes of obtaining an Imperial appointment to work for the government. The intended result of Imperial Examinations was to ensure that the most virtuous men in China's society would work for the Emperor and help run all of the government agencies based on a political system built on a meritocracy and not political patronage. Another important byproduct of the Imperial Examinations was that since these men were Confucian scholars and thus paragons of virtue, they would be less likely to take bribes or embezzle from the government coffers in the performance of their duty to the state.

LEGACY OF CONFUCIANISM

Many scholars have credited Confucianism for the post World War II economic development of East Asian countries like Japan, Korea, and Taiwan. These countries shared Confucian beliefs that taught individuals to collectively work together for the common good of the whole society in strengthening the nation over the desires of the individual. This is just one indication of how strong a grip Confucianism has on East Asian society.

A more recent indication of Confucianism's legacy is easily discernable in the history of the People's Republic of China (PRC). When Mao Zedong became the Communist leader of mainland China in 1949, one of his first acts in transforming Chinese society was to replace Confucianism with Communist doctrine as the ruling philosophy for China's citizens. Mao argued that Confucianism supported the decrepit feudal society, which forced peasants to accept their subservience under the bourgeois elites of society. Until Mao's death in 1976, this was an ongoing fervent project. However,

---

2 There are other early significant Confucian works that are just too numerous to mention here.

soon after his death it became apparent that his attempt had failed, and at best, Mao's project only succeeded in driving Confucianism underground and not out of the hearts and minds of the people. The new ruling elite of the Communist Party realized that over 2,000 years of Chinese education and tradition is not easily eradicated from society. Thus, the new leaders found ways to meld Confucius philosophy with Communist doctrine in a way to ensure that the people worked for the collective good of the government while maintaining a harmonious society. This synthesis of philosophies has had a profound impact on China's recent rapid economic growth.

DAOIST RELIGION

Daoist teachings claim that the religion was founded in China around the fourth century BCE by Laozi, meaning The Old One. He is also credited with writing its central text, the *Daodejing*, meaning "Classic of the Way." However, historians are in agreement that most of Daoism's rituals and its foundational text were set during the Han Dynasty. Daoism is a fusion of a philosophy teaching people to live in harmony with nature, and a religion that contains rituals, gods, and priests. The Dao or "the Way," rapidly spread throughout much of East Asia much like Confucianism. Daoist philosophy and religion is explained in its principal document the *Daodejing*. Most historians argue it could not have been written by Laozi, or probably any one person for that matter, since much of what it contains refers to historical events that spanned three centuries and its theme varies throughout the text. The *Daodejing* is written in a paradoxical nature making it very hard to understand by the casual reader. Also central to Daoism are additional texts containing important commentaries on the *Daodejing*, as well as books on astrology, magic, and alchemy. Interestingly, Daoism's philosophical side is a counter argument to many Confucian philosophical precepts.

DAOIST PHILOSOPHY

Daoist philosophy uses the symbol of the *yin* and the *yang* to espouse its central teaching that all of nature is composed of complementary opposite but equal forces that exist in harmony. According to Daoism, everything in nature can be arranged within the yin and yang model. For example, *yin* is night, *yang* is day; *yin* is winter, *yang* is summer. In addition, Daoism uses an example from nature to show how opposite forces exist in harmony with each other in a parable that teaches that the hardest substance in the world is a rock and the softest substance is water, yet they both exist in harmony. When water is flowing in a stream and a rock is placed in its path, water easily finds its way around the rock to continue flowing down the stream. In fact, after eons of time, the soft water will smooth out the rough, hard edges of the rock. Thus, Daoism's central philosophical doctrine is that humans must accept this structure of nature and learn to live within the state of nature in a harmonious fashion without trying to alter it.

Daoist philosophy argues that humans are meant to live in a state of nature, and not in contrived social structures like villages and towns; that humans should be farming the land and be free of government constraints. Daoism preaches that all of Confucianism's stress on reshaping human behavior so that people can live in "polite" society actually goes against the grain of human nature. Thus, Daoist doctrine rejects Confucianism's philosophy that people should be educated to live a virtuous life in a large social structure submitting to the will of a sovereign as their master. Interestingly, for all of Daoism's rejection of Confucianism's stress on living a virtuous life, Daoism does have an ethical component that it stresses in order to regulate people's behavior as well, which is *sanbao*, meaning "The Three Jewels." These jewels are compassion, moderation, and humility.

DAOIST RELIGIOUS PRACTICE

Daoism's pantheon of gods, known as "The Three Pure Ones," and "The Eight Immortals" makes it a polytheistic religion. In addition, most of the gods referred to in Daoism actually date from ancient Chinese animistic folklore. Among the Three Pure Ones, is Yuqing, meaning "The Jade Purity," who is the god of creation. Shangqing, meaning "The Supreme Pure One," is connected with the yin and yang. Taiqing, meaning the "Grand Pure One," is also known by Daoist as "The Universally Honored One of Dao and Virtues" and throughout history has manifested itself into many incarnations on earth, most notably as Laozi, Daoism's founder. The Eight Immortals are a group of mortals from mostly Tang and Song Dynasty China who, through an extraordinary event in their lives, have transcended the earthly world and have become saints. These immortals are the personification of forces that can improve life or obliterate evil. For example, He Xian Gu is the only female god among The Eight Immortals, and she is the personification of health. In fact, Daoist adherents have rituals to invoke the help of all of these gods in times of need. In addition, Daoism is one of the few religions that practices equality between the sexes. For example, there are male and female deities and Daoism allows both sexes to join the priestly order of the religion.

Daoism has many festival days and life cycle rituals whereby adherents conduct animal sacrifices and make offerings of prepared food and tea to different deities or to their ancestors. For example, The Qingming Festival, occurring on the fifteenth day after the Spring Equinox, is set aside for Daoists to clean the graves of their ancestors and leave food and tea in their honor. Certain festival days, such as the Chinese New Year, are very raucous affairs for Daoists. They set off firecrackers, have flower-covered floats, and perform the Dragon Dance. This is a famous ritual whereby upwards of fifty people perform an undulating dance within an elaborately decorated dragon on poles. Daoists believe that the people are not merely performers, but are actually possessed by the deities. In addition, astrology and fortune telling have been important ritual aspects of Daoism.

DAOISM'S LEGACY

Daoism has left an indelible mark, especially on the culture of China as well as many other East Asian countries, in two very opposite human pursuits—warfare and the arts. For example, during the Warring States Era in China 475- 221 BCE, Daoism became an instrumental influence on Chinese war fighting. Soon after Daoism was founded, one of the most influential treatises in history on the conduct of warfare was written, *The Art of War* by Sun Tzu. Sun Tzu, a great military sage, envisioned that a successful military commander had to become adept at mastering the Daoist principals of using the opposite forces of the yin and yang in order to successfully plan and fight military campaigns. This text revolutionized warfare for over two millennia in East Asia. The Daoist stratagems of effectively using the elements of surprise and guerilla warfare served as the guiding principal by which Mao Zedong in China, and Ho Chi Minh in Viet Nam fought victoriously against superior forces.

In the arts, Daoism has had an enormous impact, first on Chinese and later on East Asian poetry and landscape painting. The Daoist concept of the yin and yang dualism, which teaches about the need for humans to live harmoniously in nature, is the bedrock upon which Chinese poetry is based. The golden age of Chinese poetry occurred during the Tang Dynasty and was best represented by the work of the poet Li Bo (701-762 CE), who constantly used themes of humans seeking spiritual communion with nature. Li Bo's theme was also at the center of Chinese landscape paintings of the Song Dynasty (960-1279 CE). The legendary Chinese landscape painter Ma Yuan (1190-1225 CE) used themes depicting monumental landscapes with great mountains towering above the smaller mountains with men depicted as the smallest subject in the paintings, as a Daoist metaphor of a natural ruler (mountains) lording over its subjects (humans).

Daoism continues to influence the lives of at least 20 million adherents today.

SHINTO RELIGION

When historians look at the socio-political, and cultural development of Japan's history, it is abundantly clear that most of its development reflects a distinctive Chinese influence. Historians have been able to trace the origins of early Shintoism, meaning the way of the gods, back to the ancient tribal migration from the Korean peninsula to Japan some 35,000 years ago. Since the tribal migration to Japan took place over a long period of time, different tribal *uji*, meaning "clans," tended to form separate social units with varying Shinto practices. However, all of the tribes believed in one similar idea concerning supernatural forces working in the world.

Shinto belief holds that everything has a *kami* or spiritual essence. *Kami* is not easily defined since it seemingly stands for so many different entities. Essentially, the *kami* are the gods responsible for creation, not only on earth, but in the cosmos. In addition, since Shintoism espouses the notion that *kami* is present in everything including the spirits of ancestors, the early Japanese felt the constant presence of all of the supernatural forces around them, especially the presence of their ancestor's spirits. There is no doubt that the significance Shintoism places on the belief in the supernatural powers of ancestors plays an important cultural role in the reverence the Japanese people have had for ancestral worship throughout their history.

Another aspect of ancient Shinto practice reveals that each individual clan worshipped and regarded an individual *kami* as its ancestral founder. As a clan migrated within Japan, it brought its founding *kami* with it. Throughout early Japanese history, as larger clans defeated smaller clans in battle, they would incorporate the captives into their clan structure forcing them to adopt the *kami* of the victorious clan.

SHINTO LITERATURE

Historians cannot point to a founder of Shintoism nor is there a religious scripture associated with it. However, there is plenty of archeological evidence dating back to the Yayoi Period (200 BCE–200 CE) to show that some aspects of Shinto practice did exist hundreds of years before the publication of the first Shinto texts. Around the eighth century CE, the first written Shinto chronicles that tell the story of creation and the early history of Japan were actually authored due to an Imperial decree. The oldest of the six chronicles is the *Nihon Shoki, The Chronicles of Japan*, which is the basis of Shinto creation mythology of Japan and includes instructions for ritual purification. These six chronicles were written some 200 years after the adoption of Buddhism as Japan's official religion, and scholars have noted that the texts have been "colored" by Buddhist and Confucian thought.

SHINTO RELIGIOUS PRACTICE

Shintoism does not have many of the usual trappings of a religious organization, such as a religious dogma or an ethical code it expects adherents to follow. Shintoism is a polytheistic religion because it is founded on an animistic belief that everything on earth and in the cosmos has a *kami*. Japan is dotted with over 3,000 Shinto shrines. The most significant is the Izumo-taisha shrine, which Shinto legend claims is the place that the Sun Goddess, Amaterasu, gave as a gift to Okuninushi, the god who is considered the creator of Japan. Although it is chronicled to be one of the oldest Shinto shrines, the present shrine only dates back to about 950 CE. All Shinto shrines are placed in significant geographical locales, such as near waterfalls or picturesque mountain settings. In addition, these shrines are considered to contain extra supernatural energy and are, therefore, places where people can come in closer proximity to and commune with the *kami* forces in nature. Typically, Shinto shrines have a water trough where visitors can wash their hands and face for ritual cleansing; this practice is of paramount importance to Shinto ritual before entering into a one-room shrine. When a person "attends" a shrine, they offer a *Norito*, meaning "prayer," which Shintoism teaches has supernatural powers that deliver a favorable outcome for the visitor when delivered correctly. In addition, visitors leave offerings of food and money. In many instances, visitors write down a wish they want fulfilled on a small piece of wood and leave it in the shrine. A visitor can also purchase an *omamori*, meaning "amulet," at a shrine for the purposes of providing protection or good health when worn.

Shintoism also has a priesthood whose main functions include attending to the shrines and conducting purifying rituals at certain life cycle events like birth, illness, and death.

SHINTOISM'S LEGACY

Buddhism was adopted by Japan's emperor after it was presented as a gift from the king of Paekche in Korea in 552 CE, and quickly permeated Japan's society. Yet Buddhism, with its political and societal power, did not supplant Shintoism. Buddhism helped transform Shinto practice and kept it from becoming a competing religion. Thus, Japanese society was able to carve out a place for both beliefs to exist in harmony. Shintoism became significant to the power structure and society of Japan when the political power of the emperor was restored in 1868 CE in the period known as the Meiji Restoration. In order to help wrest political power from the *Shogun*, or "generalissimo," and to reinvest the emperor with full power to lead the nation, Shintoism became more significant in Japanese society because of its ancient teaching that the emperor was God's representative on earth and had to be revered as such by all of his subjects. The Japanese people accepted this notion wholeheartedly, and thus provided the emperor and his political advisors with a very effective means by which they could control all of the facets of Japan's socio-economic and political structure. This Shinto belief in the emperor's divinity was at the center of Japan's political structure until their defeat by the military forces of the United States in 1945. After World War II, Shinto practice was discouraged by the American occupation power and visits to the shrines declined. Starting in the 1970s, Shintoism experienced a steady increase in participation. It is important to note that Shintoism never required its adherents to exclude themselves from practicing Buddhism and/or Confucianism. All three of these institutions exist in syncretism with each other.

There are over 110 million Japanese who practice some form of Shintoism today. Thus, Shintoism, which started as a tribal religious practice, is still recognized as a Japanese cultural icon to this day.

ISLAMIC RELIGION

Although the Islamic religion is not indigenous to the Asian continent, it became the second largest religion on the Indian subcontinent starting in the eleventh century CE. Before exploring the founding and tenets of Islam, it is important to understand the historical background of how the last of the three great Western religions advanced into Asia. Islam quickly swept through Asia—mainly along the Silk Road. The Mongol Empire, starting in the thirteenth century CE, conquered most of Eurasia and provided the real impetus for Islam and its adherents to flourish throughout Asia. From this date forward, Islam began to make a significant contribution to the socio-economic, political, and cultural landscape of Asia lasting to this day.

Islam entered India through several bloody invasions of Turkish Muslims led by Mahmud of Ghazni, known as The Sword of Islam. His aim was plundering and destroying Hindu temples, as well as enslaving Hindus as a means to eradicate Hindu resistance and to pay for his vast army and his philanthropic donations to Islamic mosques and libraries. This is the description in India's history books of Mahmud's activities. Meanwhile, he is described in Islamic history as a religiously pious man and a heroic figure for bringing the Islamic religion to a heathen territory and for his philanthropy to Islamic religious and cultural institutions. Mahmud's forays into India eventually paved the way for the permanent invasion, conquest, and settling by Muslims throughout most of the Indian subcontinent in the early sixteenth century by Babur, the founder of the Mughal Empire, which lasted some 250 years. The 500-year time span between Mahmud and Emperor Aurangzeb, last of the great Mughal rulers, marks a period when India's Hindus suffered millions of deaths and went through a cultural transformation that still affects the societies of India and Pakistan today.

FOUNDER OF ISLAM

Islam was founded by Muhammad (570–632 CE), who belonged to a mercantile family in the merchant town of Mecca in Arabia. Muhammad was recognized as a prophet when, at the age of 40, he received enlightened wisdom when the Archangel Gabriel invested him with the word of God. In Islamic teachings the Muhammad is not considered so much as the founder of the faith but rather the last and greatest prophet, in line with Adam, Abraham, Moses, and Jesus preceding him. Muhammad is also the prophet that Allah, meaning "one God," invested with the *Koran* meaning recitation text, which is the central religious scripture of Islam. After 610 CE, Muhammad traveled throughout Arabia giving public sermons with his central theme being a monotheistic message. First, he espoused that there is only one God who is formless, absolute, and eternal. Second, he sternly condemned the polytheism that was prevalent in Arabia at the time. Third, he argued for an improvement in the moral behavior of mankind. His new monotheistic message drew a large following; however, he encountered strong opposition from businessmen in Mecca who financially gained from pagan visitors to the Kaaba shrine. Thus, in 622 CE the Prophet and his retinue moved to the town of Medina where he continued to preach a message of resistance against the polytheistic practices in Mecca. Muslims recognize this move to Medina as the *hijrah* or emigration. This event marks Muhammad's new political and religious master plan and is the starting point of the Islamic calendar. Within a few years, Muhammad and his followers fought several battles to cut off the trade routes to Mecca, and by 629 CE they conquered the city and finally united most of the people of Arabia under the banner of Islam.

TENETS OF ISLAM

There are six articles of faith that practicing Muslims believe are essential truths. First, Muslims have a strict belief in a monotheistic god, with no intermediaries such as priests or saints standing between God and the individual. Second, they believe that angels exist and perform several functions including communicating God's message, at times protecting people on earth, and carrying the soul upon the death of the individual. Third, Muslims believe in the revelations of God in the form of the Old and New Testaments, and in his last and perfected revelation, the *Koran*, which was communicated to Muhammad by the Archangel Gabriel. The *Koran* has 114 chapters containing over 6,000 verses and is Islam's primary written source dealing with spiritual and moral topics to guide the Muslim community. Fourth, Muslims believe that there were several biblical figures who had a prophecy to deliver to humankind. However, God chose Muhammad to be the last prophet of God's revealed truth. Fifth, the *Koran* has extensive descriptions concerning the Day of Judgment wherein one's sins are recounted and can cause the soul to be sent to hell or heaven. Sixth, Muslims believe in predestination whereby God has decreed all of the occurrences on earth. However, Koranic theology also teaches that people have free will to choose between good and evil and are, therefore, responsible for the path they choose.

Besides the articles of faith, Muslims also adhere to a set of obligations they must perform throughout their lives, known as the Five Pillars of Islam. First, Muslims and all who convert to Islam must testify to the *Shahada*, meaning "to witness." This testimony is the basic credo of Islam testifying that there is only one god worthy to worship, and that Muhammad is his messenger. Second, Muslims are required to pray five times a day using verses from the *Koran* to bring one in close communication to God. These prayers are usually performed in a mosque, which also serves as a center for learning. Third, all Muslims are obliged to refrain from eating, drinking or partaking in other restricted activities from dusk to dawn during a period known as the fast of Ramadan. Fourth, Alms-giving by Muslims is a requirement to assist the less fortunate and to support institutions that spread the word of Islam. Fifth, if financially able, all Muslims are obliged to make a *Hajj*, meaning "pilgrimage" at least once in their life to the Kaaba in Mecca.

ISLAMIC SCHISM

After Muhammad's death in 632 CE, the Muslim community was leaderless because Muhammad had not appointed a successor, and none of his male heirs survived into adulthood. Some of Muhammad's most trusted followers proposed his father-in-law, Abu Bakr, become the *Caliph* or Muslim head of state. Muslims who believe Abu Bakr to be Muhammad's true successor are members of the Sunni sect. However, other followers threw their support behind Ali, Muhammad's cousin and son-in-law, designating him as *Imam* meaning leader of the Muslim state. Followers of Ali are members of the Shia sect. The extreme hatred between these two sects, which lasts to this day, stems from the murder of Ali and his heirs by Sunnis who did not recognize his claim to Muslim leadership.

Finally, Shia or Sunni have a choice to follow a different path known as Sufism. Sufism, the mystical and ascetic path in Islam, started in Baghdad during the eighth century CE. Sufis believe that Muslims do not have to wait for death to get closer to God. Sufism teaches that through intense prayer, similar to meditation and ascetic practices, one can come closer to God. Some of Islam's most beautiful literature, poetry, and music were composed by Sufi mystics such as Jalāl ad-Dīn Muhammad Rūmī

ISLAMIC DEMOGRAPHICS

Islam's legacy in Asia's history is undoubtable and will be told in the succeeding chapters. A few statistical facts will show how important Islam is to Asia's population. Presently there are over 1.5 billion Muslims in the world today, making it the second largest religion after Christianity. Over 60 percent of the world's Muslims live in Asia. Over 228 million Muslims live in Indonesia, which has the largest Muslim population in the world. Pakistan is the country with the second largest Muslim population with over 172 million. Interestingly, India, which borders on Pakistan and is the home-land to over 800 million Hindus, is the home to the world's third largest Muslim population at over 160 million. Unfortunately, India's and Pakistan's shared history, fraught with religious strife between Muslims and Hindus, makes it one of the most violent regions on the planet. Even in China, far from the Arabian Peninsula, Islam arrived with the caravans of merchants plying their trades along Silk Road less than 100 years after Muhammad's death. These Islamic merchants took up residence in places like Xi'an China, home to the oldest Islamic mosque in the country, which was erected in 742 CE. Although religious demographics are sketchy in Communist China, the CIA's World Factbook estimates that there are over 20 million Muslims residing in China today.

Conclusion

Since Asia is the world's largest continent both geographically (over 16 million square miles), and demographically (over 3.8 billion inhabitants), it should not be surprising that it would also be the most culturally diverse area on the planet. In addition, Asia's culture was further enriched by the numerous invasions, mercantile activity, and migrations that occurred throughout its history. Little wonder that Asia would embrace a plethora of religious and philosophical institutions dedicated to providing a moral structure by which people could learn to live harmoniously in society. Interest-ingly, there are two important theological differences between Asia's indigenous religions and moral philosophies and the Western religions of Judaism, Christianity and Islam. These differences have to do with their notions of good and evil's place in the world and beliefs regarding sin.

The first difference between Asian and Western theology and moral philosophy has to do with humankind's place in the natural world. Asia's religious and philosophical traditions teach that na-ture, created by the gods, is a force that cannot be tamed by mankind, including the forces of evil, and only through an individual's acceptance of their insignificant stature in nature's realm can he/she learn to live in harmony with nature first, and then in society. This is unlike the Western religious tradition that teaches that nature is seen as a receptacle full of evil temptation and is, therefore, an enemy of mankind who is doomed to constantly struggle with nature. In addition, the Western reli-gious tradition views humankind's place in the cosmos as being far more significant to God than the natural world. Second, both Asian theology and philosophy profess that although people may com-mit evil acts at times, they are primarily good by nature, and a society based on a solid moral code can educate people to remain good. This is unlike Christianity's belief that people are predisposed to give into their natural evil inclinations causing them to be more likely to commit sinful acts instead of good acts.

Another aspect of paramount importance to the understanding of Asian history comes from studying the effects its various religions and philosophies had in helping to color the tapestry of Asia's culture. For example, in the field of the arts, Asian religions have left a breathtaking visual record. Architecturally, the Islamic religion was responsible for the building of the Taj Mahal, one of the most magnificent buildings listed among the Seven Man Made Wonders of the Modern World. A confluence of Hindu and Buddhist religious beliefs is responsible for the stupendous temple site, Ankgor Wat, in the jungles of Cambodia. Just these two sublime examples of Asian architecture stand as testaments to Asian leaders and artists who were inspired by Asia's rich religious influences to build superlative places of worship that rival, if not surpass, all of Europe's cathedrals. Finally, armed with this knowledge of the religions and philosophies of Asia, you should now be able to better understand the historical development of Asia's social institutions.

References

Bowring, Richard. 2008. *The Religious Traditions of Japan: 500-1600*. Cambridge: Cambridge University Press.

Cragg, K., and Speight, R. M. 2002. *The House of Islam*. 3rd ed. Belmont, CA: Wadsworth.

Coogan, Michael D., general ed. 2005. *Eastern Religions: Hinduism, Buddhism, Taoism, Confucianism, Shinto*. Oxford: Oxford University Press.

Doniger O'Flaferty, Wendy. 2004. *Hindu Myths: A Sourcebook Translated from the Sanskrit*. London: Penguin Classics.

Dundas, Paul. 2002. *The Jains*. 2nd ed. London: Routledge.

Koller, John M., 2006. *The Indian Way: An Introduction to the Philosophies and Religions of India*. 2nd ed. Upper Saddle River, NJ: Pearson Prentice Hall.

Lopez, Donald S., Jr. 2002. *The Story of Buddhism: A Concise Guide to Its History and Teachings*. New York: Harper Collins.

McLeod, W.H. 1990. *Textual Sources for the Study of Sikhism*. Chicago: University of Chicago Press.

Oxtoby, Willard G.., and Amore, Roy C., ed. 2010. *World Religions: Eastern Traditions*. 3rd ed. Oxford: Oxford University Press.

Roth, Harold D. 1999. *Original Tao: Inward Training and the Foundations of Taoist Mysticism*. New York: Columbia University Press.

Yoa Xinzhong. 2000. *An Introduction to Confucianism*. Cambridge: Cambridge University Press.

Chapter 3: Ancient India

THE CIVILIZATION OF ANCIENT INDIA

Historians have long pondered what accounts for the historical characteristics of a particular civilization. One can find numerous answers to this question; few historians, however, can overlook the impact of geographical location on the evolution of a mature civilization. Therefore, we start this chapter with a discussion of geographical features of the Indian subcontinent.

SOUTH ASIA: DIVERSITY AND COMMONALITY

The Indian subcontinent stretches from the mountains in Afghanistan in the west to the Bay of Bengal in the east and from the Himalayan Mountains in the north to the southern tip of the peninsula at Kanyakumari (Cape Comorin). It is about the size of Europe, but may have more diversity in terms of its culture, physical features, and languages. The region has a greater variety of geographical features than most other regions, ranging from mountains covered by glaciers and plateaus, to river valleys, plains, deserts, and grasslands. The wide range of physical geography, in collaboration with other factors, such as latitude, differences in the proximity to the mountain range or the sea, and the impact of the monsoon, brings a variety of weather patterns to the area.

The Himalayan Mountains in the north are the highest mountain range in the world and the home of the highest peak on earth, Mount Everest at 8,848 meters (29,029 ft.) above sea level. The highest parts of the Himalayas are snowbound throughout the year and host the largest glaciers outside of the polar regions. These glaciers store about 12,000 km^2 of freshwater and are the source of the ten largest river systems in Asia, including the Indus and the Ganges on the Indian side. The Himalayas have a profound impact on the climate, agriculture, life, and culture on the Indian subcontinent. For example, they prevent the monsoon winds from the Indian Ocean from blowing further north and cold western winter winds from traveling east into northern India. As a result, it snows during the winter in Kashmir, but only rains in Punjab, India. The Himalayas, however, have a profound impact on the Indian subcontinent in more ways than just weather. They have also shaped the cultures of South Asia. The mysterious nature of the Himalayas, for example, has stimulated people's imaginations, and some spots in the mountains, such as Amarnath Cave, Kedarnath temple, and Hemkunt Sahib, are sacred places in Hinduism, Buddhism, and Sikhism.

North of the Himalaya Range lies a large plain. This vast plain, known as the Indo-Gangetic Plain, stretches from Jammu and Kashmir in the west to Assam in the east and is dominated by three rivers, the Indus, the Ganges, and the Brahmaputra, along with their tributaries. These river systems originate from the Himalayas and the areas near these river systems are today home to more than two billion people; nearly half of the Indian population lives in this region. The rich soil formed by the depositing of the silt from the rivers, the abundant rainfall, underground water, and the warm and humid weather make the plain an ideal location for agricultural production. Home of the earliest Indian civilizations and capitals of the major Indian dynasties and empires, the Indo-Gangetic Plain is traditionally regarded as the "geographical core and cultural heartland of the subcontinent."[1]

To the west of the Indo-Gangetic Plain is the Thar Desert, which ranks as one of the top ten largest deserts in the world. Most of the Thar Desert is in Rajasthan, currently the largest state in the Republic of India and formerly home to the early Indus River Civilization, but it also extends into neighboring Pakistan. Similar to the atmosphere of other deserts, the weather here is dry and cold in the winter and baking hot in the summer. Covered by sand dunes and rocky surfaces with scarce rainfall, the region lacks favorable conditions for agriculture. The natural vegetation and wildlife, on the other hand, are relatively rich in comparison to other deserts. This is most likely due to the diversified landforms in the desert region: the sandy soil, the rocky plains, and the semi-arid area surrounding the mountain range of Aravalli in western India and eastern Pakistan.

Further south of the Indo-Gangetic Plain are the Central Highlands, which are comprised of three plateaus: the Malwa Plateau in the west, the Deccan Plateau in the south and the Chota Nagpur Plateau in the east. These plateaus cover most of the rest of the Indian subcontinent, tilting gently from the west to the east down all the way towards the southern tip. Much of the plateaus are covered by forests, ranging from thorn scrub forests to tropical and subtropical dry broadleaf forests. Although the physical features of these plateaus have never interrupted the passage of people and the exchange of products, they largely account for the greater historical and political isolation of the south. The Deccan Plateau is the largest of the three plateaus, containing most of the mineral wealth of India: copper, iron, gold, manganese, and coal.[2]

On each side of the Central Highlands run the coastal plains. The Eastern Coastal Plain is a wide stretch of land running southward along the Bay of Bengal, and the Western Coastal Plain runs through a narrow strip of land sandwiched between the Western Ghats and the Arabian Sea. Historically, these offshore areas served as major windows for cultural exchanges between the subcontinent and other areas. While trade, early migrations, and religions, such as Buddhism and Islam, reached Southeast Asia from India's eastern shores, the early European influence during the colonial era reached India through its western shores.

These diversified physical features and weather patterns have helped shape major characteristics of the Indian subcontinent and have had a direct impact on the historical and cultural development of India, as observed by Burton Stein and David Arnold.[3] India is often referred to as one of the oldest living civilizations. Throughout its long history, however, the Indian subcontinent was only occasionally unified under a single power. A lack of political unity and a strong totalitarian tradition have slowed down the process of cultural and ethnical assimilations in the region. There are currently more than 2,000 ethnic groups in South Asian countries. The culture of the subcontinent is comprised of many different subcultures with distinctive characteristics. Strong local variations are most obvious in the south, where the dominant Dravidian culture is quite different from the northern cultures derived from the Indo-Aryan, Iranian, or Muslim traditions. The culture of India is an amalgamation of diverse subcultures with genuine local flavor.

Linguistic diversity is equally obvious in the Indian subcontinent. The official language of the Republic of India is Hindi with English as an additional language for official work. Through legislation, however, each state can choose additional languages as its own official languages. By some account, there are currently about two hundred languages in use in India, among which, twenty-one languages, in addition to Hindi, have entered the list of "The Eighth Schedule to the Indian Constitution" as "scheduled languages," which means that these languages are officially recognized as the bases that "would be drawn upon to enrich Hindi , the official language of the Union."[4] According to the 2001 Indian census, the official language of Hindi claimed only 422 million people, a little above 41 percent of the population in India, as its native speakers. There are twenty-nine other languages in India of which one million people claim as their mother tongue.[5] The Republic of India has various complicated rules about the use of official or non-official languages. Other than the Constitution, there are other detailed legislative acts, such as the Official Language Act (1963), Official Languages Rules (1976), and various other rules and regulations made by the central government and the states.[6] Because of the language differences, even the denomination and the word rupee on Indian Currency are printed in several different languages.[7]

Being the birthplace of several major world religions, such as Hinduism, Buddhism, Jainism, and Sikhism, South Asia is also one of the most religiously diverse regions in the world. Nearly all of the major world religions are practiced here. While eighty percent of the population in India and Nepal practice Hinduism, Islam is the dominate religion in Afghanistan, Bangladesh, Pakistan, and the Maldives. Buddhism, on the other hand, is at the center of the life of the people of Sri Lanka and Bhutan, whereas Christianity, Sikhism, Jainism, and Zoroastrianism also attract large populations in several South Asian countries.

THE INDUS VALLEY CIVILIZATION (CA. 3000 BCE—1500 BCE)

Despite the diversity discussed above, one can still discern certain cultural commonalities across the Indian subcontinent, commonalities that stemmed from a similar historical and cultural heritage. The Indian subcontinent was the home to one of the earliest civilizations in the world. There exists evidence of agricultural activities in the Indian subcontinent as early as 7000 BCE. Around 3000 BCE, extensive settlements spotted the Indus River valley and its tributaries, extending from northwest India to Pakistan and Afghanistan. These settlements are referred to as the Indus Valley Civilization, or the Harappan Civilization, after its first excavation site.[8] According to Gregory L. Possehl, "the roots of sedentism and the village farming community have now been documented in the seventh millennium BC, at the site of Mehrgarh on the Kachi Plain of the central Indus Valley."[9] The Mature Harappan civilization likely existed between 2500 and 1900 BCE.[10] At least 96 Mature Harappan

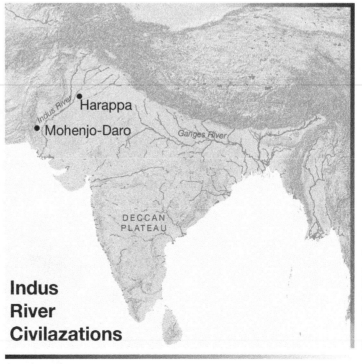

Some Early Indus Valley Settlements

settlements have been excavated. They are scattered over an area of some 1,260,000 km² from the Indus River Valley east to the upper Ganges, south to the west coast of India, and west to Afghanistan.[11] The Indus River civilization, thus, covered the largest area of any known ancient culture. It is believed that at the peak of this civilization there may have been between two and five million people in these settlements.[12]

In comparison to other early civilizations, the most remarkable feature of the Indus Valley Civilization is its city design. When Harappa and Mohenjo-Daro were excavated in the 1920s, the sophisticated city design of these settlements astonished archeologists.[13] The ancient city of Harappa was located in Punjab in today's Pakistan; the name is taken after a modern nearby village. The excavations at Harappa and Mohenjo-Daro revealed complicated city layouts in both cities, including "differentiated living quarters," "fortified administrative or religious centers" and even public bathrooms.[14] A reconstructed map of a citadel of Mohenjo-Daro, which was built around 2600 BCE and abandoned around 1800 BCE, includes a central market place, assembly halls, a granary, a college, a public bath, guarding towers and fortifications, and a large residential area that could house 5,000 people. The brick houses, which lined the city streets, were equipped with wells, bathrooms, water pipes, and a drainage system. Some of them, which may have belonged to wealthier people, were two stories with separate rooms for bathing. One of them even had an underground furnace for heating the water. The amazing achievements in plumbing by this 4,000-year-old city were comparable to nineteenth century cities in western Europe and North America.

The abundant river systems nearby provided the water for extensive usage. This attachment to the personal use of water in the life and culture of Hindus has continued on the Indian subcontinent, accounting for a distinctive emphasis on bathing and ritual purity. Other excavations reveal even more sophisticated cultural systems related to this civilization, including a writing system, a diversified social and economic system, and religious orientations. The weights and measurements were highly standardized, and several metals, including copper and bronze, were used. Cotton was woven for clothes and dyed for decoration; dietary needs were met by a variety of grains, vegetables, and fruits. City administrative buildings and other differentiated property often were marked by a variety of seals, which carried distinctive Indus symbols of religious life as well as evidence of a script that has yet to be deciphered. Trade and commerce activities were also evident in these cities.

© CORBIS

Two oxen pulling a woman in a cart, found at Mohenjo-Daro

Statue of a dancing girl, found at
Mohenjo-Daro

Sculpture of "Priest-King", found at
Mohenjo-Daro

Lothal, for example, claimed the world's earliest known dock, which was located on the trade routes to Harappan cities which probably went all the way to Mesopotamia. Among excavated artifacts are wheel-made pottery, toy models, and bronze and clay statues. The artifacts excavated from Mohenjo-Daro reveal many cultural and technological clues about the civilization. A terra-cotta toy cow with a moving head suggested a tradition of worshipping the cow; the figure of two oxen pulling a woman in a cart showed the domestication of the ox and the usage of the cart as a means of transportation; the copper statue of "the dancing girl" indicated certain dancing styles that are still common on the subcontinent; a statue of the god Shiva represented a connection between the early religion of the Indus Valley and the later development of Hinduism; and "the priest-king" has become symbolic of the lifestyle of the dominant class.

As rich and sophisticated as the historical and cultural traditions of the Indus Valley Civilization were, we know very little about that civilization other than its geographical location and what the excavation sites tell us. For example, we know little about the people who built this great civilization. Both the names of Mohenjo-Daro and Lothal mean "the mount of the dead" in local languages. Neither do we know for sure the reasons for the decline of this great civilization. Around 1800 BCE, signs of a gradual decline began to emerge, and between 1800 and 1700 BCE, many of the cities were abandoned in a rather abrupt way.[15] Some early scholars have suggested that the Indus Valley Civilization ended due to an invasion by the Aryans.[16] The discovery of 37 bodies at Mohenjo-Daro was cited by one such scholar, Sir Mortimer Wheeler, as evidence that Mohenjo-Daro had ended due to a massacre. Most scholars, however, later came to reject the Aryan invasion as the cause of the decline of the Indus River Civilization. George Dales has noted that there is a lack of strong evidence in support of the Aryan invasion theory. Kenneth Kennedy studied 34 of the 37 bodies and found that all the marks on 32 of those skulls were caused by erosion. Of the remaining two skulls studied by Kennedy only one had a mark which may indicate a violent death. The other had a mark from a wound which had healed and was not fatal.[17] Although the discovery of bodies at Mohenjo-Daro promoted some early theories, which attributed its decline to an outside invasion coinciding with the advance of the Aryans to the region, the absence of evidence of violence in excavation sites and the fact that few weapons have been found in the region led many to question this theory. Other scholars suggest instead that climatic change or changes in the course of the river might have damaged agricultural production and deprived the cities of their water sources. Still others identify additional causes that may have attributed to the ruins of this civilization, including decline of trade with other regions, deforestation, floods, droughts, and new groups of immigrants.[18]

For whatever reasons, the Indus Valley Civilization was in obvious decline between 1500 and 1000 BCE. The process of the deterioration of the entire civilization was probably gradual, with clear evidence of the progressive shrinking of the area under cultivation and irrigation; thus the grain surplus that had supported the cities started to disappear. Bit by bit, this great civilization eventually sank into oblivion, although the traits of this ancient culture can still be found in many later Indian subcultures, especially in the east and south of the subcontinent. When waves of nomadic Aryans moved into the Indus Valley through the mountain passes of Afghanistan between 1500 and 1200 BCE, the Indus Valley Civilization had probably long passed its peak, making it easier for the new settlers to establish themselves in the region.

ARYAN AND VEDIC CULTURE (1700 BCE—600 BCE)

The word Aryan, in its strictest sense, is a linguistic term, referring to the Indo-Iranian or Indo-Aryan languages. It also often refers to the people who speak these languages. In terms of Indian history, the term describes the people who spoke the language of Sanskrit, a historical Indo-Aryan language, and who moved in waves to India after 1700 BCE. These Aryan speaking people dominated northern India from the late Harappan period to the rise of the Mauryan Empire around 322 BCE and influenced Indian history both politically and culturally.

The use of the term Aryan, however, is still under much debate among scholars of Indian History. Derived from *arya*, a Sanskrit term which means "noble" or "pure," the word Aryan is loaded with the notion of superiority over the indigenous non-Aryan people. Originally, these new immigrants used the term in their sacred hymns, which mentioned victorious *arya* who successfully subjugated their enemies.[19] This established the first association between these people and the term, and hence, it has been accepted in Western literature to use the term Aryan when referring to the Aryan-speaking groups during this time of Indian history. The more cautious historians, especially those in India, suggest some modified terms for these people, such as Indo-Aryan or Vedic-Aryan. The latter derives from the word *Veda*, which refers to the sacred books of Indo-Aryan people.

Similarly, the origin of the Indo-Aryans is also in much debate among scholars of Indian history, and so are the actual dates of their immigration to India. Some suggest the Aryans who had migrated from Central Asia may have had direct contact with the local Indus people and may even have conquered the Harappan cities and settlements in northern India, whereas others insist on a native Hindu identity of these Aryans—the newly immigrated groups were assimilated into the more refined Indus tradition.[20] The latter view is especially popular among the historians in India.[21] In this sense, the Aryans continued the Hindu tradition that had developed during the early Indus River Civilization.

In either case, whether by migration or infusion, the political and cultural dominance of the Indo-Aryans and their culture became obvious around 1000 BCE. The Aryan-speaking groups became politically privileged elites. Their culture, represented by a vast body of their sacred texts known collectively as the *Vedas*, prevailed in northern India. The texts of the *Vedas* are an invaluable source for our understanding of the era, and the word Vedic, an adjective form of *Veda*, is used to refer to both the people and the era. Although it is in dispute whether the introduction of horses, spiked wheels, chariots, and metal-tipped weapons were exclusive to the *Vedic* period, few would argue against the importance of Sanskrit, an Indo-Aryan language, and its representative literature, the *Vedas*, to the political and cultural development of India.

Unlike the study of the Indus Valley Civilization, which relied heavily on the excavation of the remains of ancient sites, our understanding of the Vedic period essentially relies on the interpretation of the sacred texts of the *Vedas*. Different interpretations gave rise to different theories. For example, some believe that these *Vedas* actually tell the story of Aryan victories over their enemies, whose cities they conquered and destroyed. The Aryan gods, riding in a chariot drawn by two or three horses, led the Aryan heroes through the enemy lands, breaking their forts and nullifying their resistance. In many cases, the *Vedas* also recorded the fighting among the Vedic people themselves. As a result, there was a disproportionate emphasis and a glorification of war in Vedic culture, in comparison to more peaceful and refined cultures during the Harappan era.[22] Other contending theories, however, also use the *Vedas* as a source of their interpretations.[23]

The *Vedas* also provide detailed information about the religion and society at the time. The early Aryan religion centered on their gods, who were mighty and omnipotent, not much different from those deities in ancient Greece or Rome. One way to keep their great gods, such as Indra, the chief deity and the god of war, and Agni, god of fire, happy was through sacrifice. In order to appease these gods, it was crucial to prepare and perform the sacrifice appropriately, precisely following the sacrificial rituals. No one could be excluded from following the meticulous rituals during these procedures, be it a powerful king or an ordinary subject. The complicated ceremony of the sacrifice called for the service of Brahman priests, who supposedly possessed the exclusive knowledge concerning these rituals. As a result, the priests occupied the highest position in Indo-Aryan social stratification.

Important religious practices produced a rich body of Vedic literature, and the most important are known as *Veda*, which means knowledge. The chanting hymns in praise of a pantheon of Aryan gods were collected in *Rig-Veda*, the oldest and the principal *Veda* in Indo-Aryan culture. *Rig-Veda* is known today as the oldest written text in India still in use, and the first major composition in any Indo-European language. It is commonly believed that various sage families produced the hymns collected in the book over a period of 300 to 500 years. Although the dating of the book has yet to be definitively identified, all the hymns had most probably been produced by 900 BCE.[24] The content of the book has been memorized syllable by syllable and passed orally up to the present day, even in spite of the availability of various written versions since 1000-900 BCE. To many, *Rig-Veda* is the best source of knowledge of early Aryan life; it depicts the socioeconomic transformation of the Vedic culture from the era of early Aryan migration to the late Vedic age when the Indo-Aryan culture laid the foundation for Hinduism.

Other than the *Rig-Veda*, there are three other *Vedas*. The *Yajur-Veda* (the textbook for sacrifice) and the *Sama-Veda* (the hymnal) are considered supplemental to the *Rig-Veda*. The *Yajur-Veda* is the manual of the priests, and the *Sama-Veda* consists of a rearranged version of some of the hymns of the *Rig-Veda*, setting them to music. The *Sama-Veda* serves as a songbook for the priests who "sing" through their chanting, an important custom for Hindu rituals. Unlike the other three *Vedas*, the *Atharva-Veda* has less to do with sacrifice. It is a collection of magic spells, which are used to dispel demons and cure diseases. Some consider it the first Indian text on medicine since it includes many references to plants and herbs as well as their functions.[25] All the *Vedas* are considered sacred writings, and the "revealed" knowledge contained in them carried the ultimate canonical authority to Indo-Aryans and later to all Hindus, as the *Vedas* maintained their sacred nature in Hinduism. From a more secular point of view, however, some have described the *Vedas* as "a vast and complex instruction manual for sacrifice."[26] The *Atharva-Veda* also contains what R.C Zaehner called "cosmological hymns," which represent a type of philosophical thinking that is further explored in the *Upanishads*.[27]

Other categories of Vedic texts include *Brahmana* (commentaries on sacrificial rituals) and *Upanishad* (esoteric philosophical treatises). These are prose texts that interpret the sacrificial rituals, explaining their themes and meanings. The *Brahmanas* may either stand alone or be an attachment to the *Vedas*. Some *Brahmanas* provide information on astronomy (determining the auspicious time for the sacrifice) and geometry (used in designing fire altars), while others are concerned with mysticism. The *Upanishads* are the most philosophical works among the Vedic texts. They pose deep questions concerning the soul and its personal position in the cosmos, and contain spiritual interpretations of the *Vedas*. Some scholars maintain that the *Upanishads* presents a "gradual transition from the mythical world-view of the Early Vedic age and the magical thought recorded in the *Brahmana* texts to the mystical philosophy of individual salvation".[28] They find in the *Brihadaranyaka Upanishad*, one of the older primary *Upanishads*, examples of the reinterpretation of the meaning of the sacrifice as "a comic symbolism" which serves as "a point of departure for meditation."[29] Many abstract concepts explored in the *Upanishads*, such as the universal soul (*Brahman*), the individual soul or self (*Atman*), and union with the ultimate soul through meditation, paved the way for later developments in Hinduism, Buddhism and Jainism.

SOCIAL DIFFERENTIATION AND THE EMERGENCE OF THE CASTE SYSTEM

Interpretations of the Vedic texts justify a differentiated society in the Vedic world; from this differentiated society, a rigid caste system was born on the Indian subcontinent. It is still under debate whether or not the caste system was an essential part of the Vedic religion as well as Hinduism. There are some indications in the Vedic texts of social classification by *varna* (color): one hymn in the *Rig-Veda* specifies four ranked groups, *brahmans* (priests), *kshatriyas* (warriors), *vaishyas* (farmers, merchants), and *shudras* (craftsmen, servants), from top to the bottom.[30] As a result, the Vedic texts are believed to have provided a justification and laid a foundation for the development of the more complicated and rigid caste system that has had an enduring impact on the Indian subcontinent. The *varna* system described in the scriptures is commonly interpreted as a distinctive Aryan/non Aryan division in Vedic society; the word *varna* itself gave rise to many further assumptions because the Aryans were white or lighter in skin color.[31]

Others, however, point out that social differentiations in the Vedic society were not the same as the social stratification of the caste system practiced later. There was much more flexibility and mobility within the original *varna* system, and the four castes were not exclusive. The first two castes, priests and warriors, for example, were not necessarily preserved for the triumphant Aryans. The main reason argued by Avari for the non-Aryans in the other two categories may have had more to do with the reality that Indus Valley populations were the people who possessed skills as farmers, merchants or craftsmen, while most Aryans were still nomadic in nature.[32] As a result, the original fourfold division was more based on function than social discrimination. These arguments modified the general belief that the origin of the caste system was derived from the insecurity of the Aryans who wanted to distinguish themselves from the rest of the indigenous people who outnumbered them.[33]

Whatever the origins and intended design of the caste system in the Vedic era, the caste system later developed into a full-fledged social stratification system, known in the modern era for many ill practices such as discouraging intermarriages and restricting the ability of different castes to associate, or even eat at the same table. Those who violated the rules would be thrown out of their castes and hence become outcasts, or untouchables. The caste system and its practice in India, however, may have been much more complicated than what meets the eye. Some argue that modern evaluations may not necessarily be a faithful reflection of its historical evolution as well as its complexity. In addition to an entity with political and religious beliefs, the caste system evolved into a socioeconomic system accepted by many Indians. It is a system of *jati*, a term that refers to the community or individual caste, based more on the occupations than the original hierarchy of the *varna* system. In time, hundreds of subgroups were added to the system. A 1901 census conducted under British rule reported 2,378 separate tribes and castes, some with millions in number, but others only having a few hundred.[34] It was a very confusing process to match a particular *jati* with the original *varna* (used by the British as a division of social classes), and in some cases even lawsuits were used in order to properly categorize certain *jati*.

The caste system, viewed as a hereditary system based on occupation, played an essential role in economic activities in India. The function of the caste system, some argue, was similar to that of guilds in medieval Europe. As such, some believe that the caste system in India may have contributed to social stability, as many seem to have accepted and felt comfortable with the stratified groups. A caste association, as observed by Avari, can provide "a secure psychological umbrella" for someone who would be otherwise lost.[35] Although social mobility may have been limited, there were opportunities for some mobility within the caste.[36] In his study of south India, M. N. Srinivas, an Indian sociologist, questioned the general assumption of rigidity in caste.[37]

Even in today's India, there is still ambiguity concerning the status of the caste. Although the 1950 Constitution of India put restrictions on the practice of the caste system, especially on discriminative treatment of the untouchables, there are still many ongoing debates in India over the politics of the caste system. For example, the Indian government's decision to carry out a caste census as part of the 2011 census led to much public debate.[38]

INTELLECTUAL CHALLENGES TO VEDIC CLASSICS: THE RISE OF BUDDHISM AND JAINISM

In the years after the peak of the Vedic period, between 600 to 200 BCE, the history of the Indian subcontinent was dominated intellectually and politically by two major trends. One was the emergence of Buddhism and Jainism, partially as an intellectual movement against the dominant Vedic culture, and the other was the rise of the Mauryan Empire, which put an end to Aryan dominance in northern India. Both had an enduring impact on the history of India, and Buddhism later spread from India, finding many compassionate believers around the world. This discussion of Buddhism focuses on its historical significance, since Buddhism as a religion was discussed in detail in Chapter 2.

The sixth century BCE was a period that saw the spread of great ideas around the world and the emergence of several great intellectual schools of thought such as Greek philosophy represented by Plato and Socrates in the West; Buddhism and Jainism in India; and Confucianism and Daoism in China. As Avari noted, by the sixth century, India entered a stage of religious fervor and social disturbance. Vedic society had become highly stratified, with the lower caste, *shudras*, at the bottom. The monopoly of the priesthood, the political domination of the kings and warriors, and the increasing wealth of the merchants aroused a sense of injustice among the less privileged at the bottom of the social stratification. The more affluent people, on the other hand, were increasingly bewildered over the meaning of the sacrifice as well as the extravagance of the related rituals. Even among the priests themselves, as discussed before, some started to explore deeper philosophical questions over the relation between the universe and the individual, represented by the intellectual inquiries in the later *Upanishads*.[39] All this led to the emergence of other religious forms, specifically Jainism and Buddhism, both of which began as a revolt against the dominant Vedic culture.

Both Jainism and Buddhism, however, shared some key concepts from Vedic Brahmanism, the essential part of Hinduism. For example, the dual concept of universal *Brahman* and individual *Atman* that was first explored in the *Upanishads* became the core of Buddhist beliefs. Some other Vedic or maybe pre-Aryan concepts, such as *samsara*, the cycle of birth, life, death, rebirth or reincarnation; *karma*, actions or deeds, or *moksha*, release from *samsara*, also found their way into Buddhism. In this sense, both Buddhism and Jainism appeared as a reform to the orthodox Vedic religion instead of a total rejection.

Among the new additions to the Vedic tradition, in both religions, is the significance of nonviolence, and most importantly, compassion to grant everyone an equal opportunity for salvation, no matter whether a person is a king or a slave. In a society that had become complacent due to the caste system, this last point may well have served as a needed remedy to many who would be more than eager to find salvation from the burden of human suffering. It may also account for the immediate popularity of Buddhism, even during the lifetime of the Buddha. Buddha's messages were more accessible; those messages were simple and more ethical than mythical and hence had more appeal to the general audience.[40] In addition, instead of using Sanskrit, which was the classical language of the *Vedas*, Buddhist disciples chose to use *Pali*, a vernacular of the common people in north India, for the Buddhist scriptures. This gave more people access to Buddha's teaching at the time.[41]

THE RISE OF THE MAURYAN EMPIRE

The rise of Buddhism was only part of a newly merged Gangetic civilization, which was characterized by the extensive emergence and urbanization of Gangetic kingdoms. Buddhism served as a "spiritual expression" of this historical change.[42] In the centuries after the Vedic Aryans dominated northern India, they continued advancing eastward towards the Ganges Valley. Accompanying with this eastward movement was the emergence of numerous small polities on the eastern and southern Gangetic plain. It is, however, still difficult to obtain the details of this eastward expansion. As in the study of the early Vedic era, many available accounts of the expansion are based on literary sources, such as the epics of *Mahabharata* and *Ramayana*, which, many believe, are based on true stories and hence contain clues to the social and political life of Indian society from 1000 BCE onward.[43] As useful as these literary sources are, caution needs to be exercised, as literary descriptions should not be taken at face value.

What we do know is that more powerful kingdoms gradually replaced the early states. The rise of these kingdoms might be the result of the new economic prosperity that emerged in the late Vedic era. This prosperity was largely promoted by the extension of agricultural activities into the Ganges, a potentially more productive area, as well as the introduction of iron tools and new farming technology. This gave rise to the "second urbanization" after the fall of the Harappan cities.[44] Agricultural surplus supported a growing urban population and increasingly larger urban centers, which in turn hosted the institutions of the monarchy.[45] This change was most obvious in the Ganges valley. Sixteen major states and regions, known collectively as *Mahājanapadas* (Great Countries in Sanskrit) were established in the sixth century BCE, and more than half of them were located in Gangetic Plain. Magadha, the most powerful among them, controlled the south of the Ganges valley from the middle of the sixth century to 321 BCE. Its power and prosperity, however, only precipitated the rise of the Mauryas, who built the first great empire in Indian history.

From the very beginning, these newly formed kingdoms faced the challenge of foreign intrusions, the best known of which was the expedition of Alexander the Great who led a campaign into northern India between 327 and 324 BCE. Encouraged by his dream to conquer the world, this mighty Macedonian king led 35,000 soldiers into India, fighting along the way against the armies of the Indian *raja* (Indian word for monarch) that were equipped with war elephants. Alexander ventured as far east as the rich river valleys of India, but then his troops, who were exhausted after a two-year exploration and from fighting against wave after wave of Indian resistance, refused to go any farther. Yielding to the wishes of his generals and troops, Alexander promised to take them home. In the following year, Alexander died of illness in Babylon at the age of 32. Although Alexander's campaign in India did not leave a lasting political or historical impact on the region, it opened the door of India to the West, and vice versa. The Hellenistic kingdoms in northwest India exerted an enduring influence on Indian arts and architecture, whereas Indian philosophy, mathematics, and medicine found their ways into classical Greek culture.[46]

Another indirect legacy of Alexander's campaign may have been the inspiration that he incidentally offered to a young ruler, Chandragupta Maurya (r. 322–296 BCE), the founder of the Mauryan Empire. According to Greek sources, Alexander had met with a number of Indian princes, including Chandragupta.[47] Others, however, question the historical likelihood that the two had ever met. The Mauryan conquest of India did not begin until two years after Alexander's venture into India.

The rise and fall of the Mauryan Empire (321–185 BCE) is one of the most significant events in Indian history. It was the first time in Indian history that a single dynasty exerted its rule over most of the Indian subcontinent. Even though our knowledge about the early life and rule of India's first unifier is still limited, evidence can be found about the Mauryas and their empire from sources outside of India, such as Greek annals and the diaries of the first Greek ambassador to the Mauryan court. One legend put the early life of Chandragupta Maurya at the Nanda court, a powerful state of Magadha, with his mother being a concubine to the king. He eventually seized power with the help of his mentor and minister, a Machiavellian Brahman named Kautilya, who gained popularity mostly because of the *Arthashastra*, a book presumably written by him. The book was the most famous Indian treatise on the art of government, although the assumption of his authorship was later proven to be false.[48]

After he gained power in 321 BCE, Chandragupta Maurya assumed control of all of northern India, using means of war, threat of war, and political negotiation. He brought unity for the first time to the subcontinent, not only in the form of a unified political institution, but also through regulations in trade, agriculture, and other aspects of life in India. By the time his reign ended, his empire stretched some 2,000 miles across northern India, from the Bay of Bengal in the east to the Hindu Kush in the west. One of his greatest victories was his negotiation with Seleucus Nicator, the Greek Viceroy of Alexander, in which he secured the northwest border of his empire. Seleucus agreed to cede eastern Afghanistan, Baluchistan, and the area west of the Indus in exchange for 500 war elephants. This also led to the four-year presence of Megasthenes, the first Greek ambassador at the Mauryan court, whose diaries were among the best-known sources for knowledge of life and politics in the Mauryan Empire.[49]

THE EMPIRE OF ASHOKA

Chandragupta died about 297 BCE, leaving his vast empire to his son, Bindusara (r. ca. 297–272 BCE.). Even less is known about the life and twenty-five-year reign of Bindusara than of his father. He conquered Deccan, the great plateau that covers central India, and maintained the Greek connection established by his father, having asked for gifts from a Seleucid King of Syria. Bindusara's death in 272 BCE opened the door for his son, Ashoka (r. 273–232 BCE), the greatest Indian ruler ever. There may have been a succession struggle among his sons, but eventually Ashoka secured the throne and initially ruled the Mauryan state the same way that any other Indian monarch would have done, consolidating and expanding the territory under his control.[50] Ashoka extended Mauryan rule to the whole subcontinent except for a few states in the far south, and thus built one of the largest empires in Indian history, which was only matched by the Mughal Empire that evolved nearly two thousand years later.

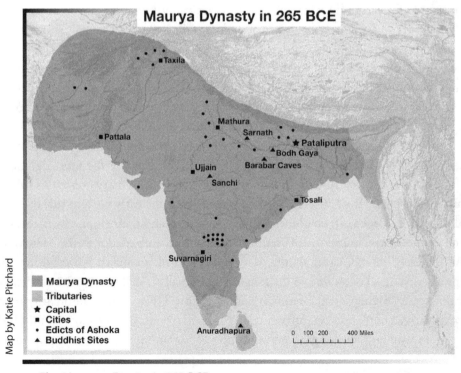

The Mauryan Empire in 265 BCE

A war which Ashoka waged against the kingdom of Kalinga became the turning point in both his life and his reign. His response to the war was later recorded in his 13th rock edict, according to which "One hundred and fifty thousand were deported, one hundred thousand were killed and many more died (from other causes). After the Kalingas had been conquered, [Ashoka] came to feel a strong inclination towards the Dhamma, a love for the Dhamma and for instruction in Dhamma. Now [Ashoka] feels deep remorse for having conquered the Kalingas."[51] Although he did not entirely disengage from warfare, he devoted the rest of his life to following the Buddhist teaching of *Dhamma* (a word in Pali, *Dharma* in Sanskrit), meaning law or natural law, or moral virtues, and replaced the concept of "conquest by force" with the concept of "conquest by righteousness."[52]

Accordingly, Ashoka implemented new imperial policies based on moral virtues. He restricted his people from hunting and eating meat and championed the concept of non-violence. In order to get his new message across the nation, he issued numerous edicts specifying the principles of *dhamma* and had them inscribed on the faces of hillocks or on 32-foot tall, highly polished sandstone columns. These edicts, preserved by means of the rocks and pillars, provide knowledge about the life and rule of the Ashoka Empire. They are Ashoka's proclamation of his devotion to *dhamma* and other Buddhist teachings. In some of his edicts, he referred to his subjects as his "children" and took it as his responsibility to provide for them. In order to raise standards of morality in his realm, he appointed "*dhamma* officials," whose responsibility included investigation of public welfare problems and supervision of agricultural improvements in the countryside. He often toured around his empire to monitor their work. He instituted beneficial public works and brought just governance to the local level. One of the major rock edicts even mentions his efforts at securing medical help for the sick and building houses for travelers to rest in.[53]

Ashoka's religious devotion to Buddhism was beyond any doubt. He took Buddhism extremely seriously after his conversion and was even more pious as he grew older. In his time, he was the most important patron to Buddhism, having funded many Buddhist temples throughout his empire. In 250 BCE, he endorsed and funded the Third Buddhist Council at Pataliputra, his capital, and also sponsored Buddhist missions to Hellenistic kingdoms, Tibet, Nepal, the deep south of India, and Ceylon (today's Sri Lanka). Later, Buddhist missionaries reached as far as Burma and Java in Southeast Asia, and Egypt in Middle East.[54]

His support of Buddhism, however, was never exclusive. His Buddhist faith

A statue of regal lions watching in four different directions never prevented him from stressing tolerance of all traditions and religious beliefs. According to Avari, Ashoka desired a harmony among all religious sects, for all had the same goal of seeking "self-control and purity of mind."[55] He urged his subjects to honor other sects and to be tolerant of different viewpoints. This "profound sensitivity towards issues that arise from a multi-faith society" is probably the most important legacy of Ashoka's reign.[56] He evidently understood some of the most urgent needs of his new empire. Other than addressing the material needs of the millions of people under his reign, exercising tolerance of cultural, linguistic, and religious issues was probably the best way to achieve his *dhamma* of "conquest by virtue."

Unfortunately, Ashoka's model of rule was largely based on his personal beliefs and virtues, and did not have enough time to be institutionalized. Buddhist doctrine and his religious tolerance alone could not keep this vast empire together for long. Fifty years after Ashoka's death, the Mauryan Empire fell apart. Local dynasties soon took advantage of his weak successors to break away from the empire and would remain as local powers for many years to come. What Ashoka did was soon forgotten, and even his name fell into oblivion until it was rediscovered in the British era. The name of Emperor Ashoka lives on today as a symbol of enlightened rule in India as well as in the world. The Republic of India has adopted as its official emblem the regal lions that watched the four different directions from the top of one Ashokan pillar.[57]

For more information about the topics discussed in this chapter, please visit the website for this textbook. This website can be accessed from http://www.grtep.com/.

1 Burton Stein and David Arnold, *A History of India, 2nd ed.* (Malden, MA: John Wiley and Sons, 2010), xv.
2 "South Asia, Physical Geography," accessed June 23, 2011, at http://www.harpercollege.edu/mhealy/g101ilec/sasia/ssd/ssphys/ssphysfr.htm.
3 Stein and Arnold, *History of India*, 9
4 *The Constitution of India*. accessed May 9, 2012, at http://india.gov.in/govt/documents/english/coi-eng-schedules_1-12.pdf.
5 "Census of India, 2001," Ministry of Home Affairs, Indian Government, accessed June 25, 2011, at http://censusindia.gov.in/Census_Data_2001/Census_Data_Online/Language/Statement4.htm.
6 India.gov.in. "Official Language," accessed on May 7. 2012, at http://india.gov.in/knowindia/profile.php?id=33.
7 "India seeks global symbol for rupee," Hindustan Times 2009-03-06, accessed June 28, 2011, at http://www.hindustantimes.com/StoryPage/StoryPage.aspx?sectionName=HomePage&id=c8097698-a806-4cc2-8c67-668d594057dc&Headline=India+seeks+global+symbol+for+rupee.
8 Gregory L. Posshel, *The Indus Civilization: A Contemporary Perspective* (Walnut Creek, CA: Altamira Press, 2002), 1.
9 Gregory L. Possehl, "Revolution in the Urban Revolution: The Emergence of Indus Urbanization," *Annual Review of Anthropology* 19 (1990):261.
10 Posshel, *Indus Civilization*, 1.
11 Posshel, *Indus Civilization*, 20.
12 PBS. The Story of India. "Indus Valley" and "Climate Change," accessed on May 10, 2012, at http://www.pbs.org/thestoryofindia/gallery/photos/3.html.
13 Posshel, *Indus Civilization*, 10.
14 Library of Congress, Country Studies1995, "Harappan Culture," accessed June 23, 2011, at http://lcweb2.loc.gov/cgi-bin/query/r?frd/cstdy:@field (DOCID+in0013.
15 Hermann Kulke and Dietmar Rothermund, *A History of India, 5th ed.* (New York: Routledge, 2010), 10.
16 Edwin Bryant, *The Quest for the Origins of Vedic Culture: The Indo-Aryan Migration Debate* (New York: Oxford University Press, 2001), 159–160.
17 Bryant, *Quest*, 159–160.
18 Posshel, *Indus Civilization*, 238, 240; and Bryant, 332.
19 Kulke and Rothermund, *History of India*, 11.
20 Kulke and Rothermund, *History of India*, 13–14.
21 See, for example, an internet article, "The Myths of Aryan Invasion of India," accessed May 25, 2011, at http://www.tri-mu3rti.com/ancientindia/aryan2.html#a12; and Burjor Avari, *India: the Ancient Past: A History of the Indian Sub-Continent from c. 7000 BC to AD 1200*, new ed. (New York: Routledge, 2007), 60–66.
22 Rhoads Murphey, *A History of Asia*, 6th ed. (Upper Saddle River, NJ: Prentice Hall, 2008), 71; and Kulke and Rothermund, *History of India*, 15–18.
23 For other contending theories, see Avari, *India*, 64–66.
24 Avari, *India*, 77; and Kulke and Rothermund, *History of India*, 14–15.

25 Avari, *India*, 78–79.

26 Avari, *India*, 78.

27 R. C. Zaehner, *Hindu Scriptures* (London: Everyman's Library, 1966), vii.

28 Kulke and Rothermund, *History of India*, 25.

29 Kulke and Rothermund, *History of India*, 25.

30 Michael Edward, "Hindu India under the Aryans" in *India*, ed. by Jann Einfeld (San Diego: Greenhaven Press, 2003), 49.

31 Edward, "Hindu India," 49.

32 Avari, *India*, 74.

33 Edward, "Hindu India," 49, 52; and Avari, *India*, 74. For the argument on the insecure Aryans, see Kulke and Rothermund, *History of India*, 17; Murphey, *History*, 45–46; and N. Prinja, ed. *Explaining Hindu Dharma: A Guide for Teachers* (Norwich, England: Religious and Moral Education Press, 1996).

34 Edward, "Hindu India," 52.

35 Avari, *India*, 74; and Prinja, *Dharma*, 69–72. According to Avari, Prinja's interpretation provides a more balanced view on the Caste system. Avari, *India*, 74 and note 61.

36 Murphey, *History*, 45–46.

37 M.N. Srinivas, *Religion and Society among the Coorgs of South India* (Oxford: Oxford University Press, 1952), 32; and *Caste in Modern India; and Other Essays*, 11th reprint, (Bombay: Media Promoters & Publishers, 1994), 48.

38 Vikhar Ahmed Sayeed, "The Caste Factor," accessed May 23, 2011, at http://www.frontlineonnet.com/fl2718/stories/20100910271810500.htm.

39 Avari, *India*, 96–97.

40 Edward, "Hindu India," 56–57.

41 Avari, *India*, 110.

42 Kulke and Rothermund, *History of India*, 28–29.

43 Stanley Wolpert, *A New History of India*, 4th ed. (New York: Oxford University press, 1993), 37–42.

44 Avari, *India*, 93–94.

45 Kulke and Rothermund, *History of India*, 28–29.

46 Murphey, *History*, 72–73; Avari, *India*, 86; and Kulke and Rothermund, *History of India*, 33–34.

47 Murphey, *History*, 73; Wolpert, *New History*, 56; and B.G. Gokhale, "The Great Ancient Empires: The Mauryan Dynasty and the Glorious Gupta Age," in *India*, ed. by Jann Einfeld (Farmington Hills, MI: Greenhaven Press, 2003), 58.

48 Murphey, *History*, 73–74; Wolper, *New History*, 57; and Avari, *History*, 107–108.

49 Avari, *History*, 108–110; and Murphey, *History*, 74.

50 Gokhale, "Great Ancient Empires," 60.

51 Dhamikka, Ven. S. trans. *The Edicts of King Ashoka* (Kandy, Sri Lanka: Buddhist Publication Society, 1993). DharmaNet edition, 1994, accessed on May 10, 2012, at http://www.cs.colostate.edu/~malaiya/ashoka.html#KALINGA.

52 New World Encyclopedia, "Ashoka,", accessed June 16, 2012, at http://www.newworldencyclopedia.org/entry/Ashoka.

53 Avari, *History*, 112;

54 Avari, *History*, 114; and Murphey, *History*, 76.

55 Avari, *History*, 114.

56 Avari, *History*, 114

57 Avari, *History*, 111.

Chapter 4: Ancient China

THE CIVILIZATION OF ANCIENT CHINA

Similar to the formation of Indian civilization, the Chinese civilization was also significantly influenced by geographical features. Until the modern era, formidable geographic barriers separated China from other centers of civilization. As mentioned earlier, the Himalayas separated China from its southwest neighbor, India, although the two appear adjacent to each other on maps. Northwest of the Himalayas and the Tibetan Plateau is the cold Taklimakan desert, which covers 130,116 square miles.[1] In northern China, there is the Mongolian steppe (or prairie), which is covered by grasslands that are only suitable for a nomadic lifestyle. Beyond the steppe are the freezing and bleak terrains of Siberia. On the east and southeast China is bordered by the vast Pacific Ocean and on the south and southwest by the almost impenetrable jungles that divide China from its neighbors, Vietnam, Laos, and Myanmar.[2] China and the United States are similar in size and latitude, but China stretches more from the north to the south. Accordingly, the weather patterns vary tremendously from subarctic cold in Manchuria to tropical hot and humid on Hainan Island. In geographical terms, China is even less unified than the Indian subcontinent.

These formidable geographical barriers prevented the early Chinese civilization in the Yellow River Valley from making direct contact with other early civilizations such as the Mesopotamian, Egyptian, and Indus Valley civilizations.[3] Scholars still debate to what extent the early civilizations influenced each other, since a variety of evidence seems to point in different directions.[4] While some evidence shows that the Chinese may have adopted rice production and the use of light chariots from India or Southeast Asia, China definitely developed its language, potteries, and bronze vessels independently.[5] Despite this debate, many agree that China's isolation from other civilizations served as a unifying factor for the Chinese civilization and contributed to the continuity of its distinctive culture.[6]

Within the boundaries of Chinese territories, there are regional boundaries, two of which most notably stand out. The first is the difference between what is known as "China proper," which covers the area south of the Great Wall, and the peripheral territories that had traditionally been inhabited by Non-Han Chinese such as the Tibetans, the Mongolians, and the Turkish people.[7] The contrast between these two regions, in the words of John King Fairbank, "is a striking one in nearly every respect."[8] While the peripheral areas have been of strategic importance to the Chinese, most cradles

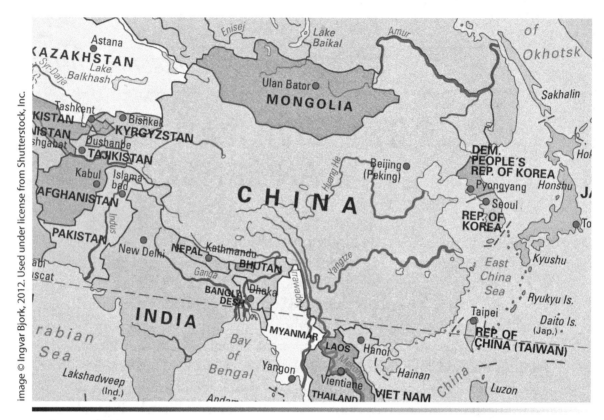

A map of China

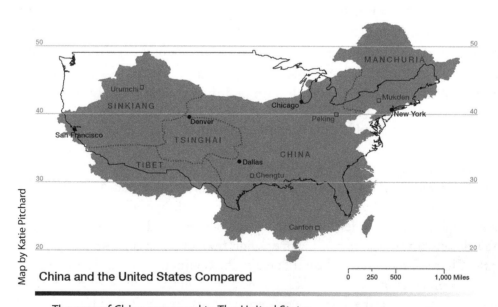

China and the United States Compared

The area of China compared to The United States

of early Chinese civilizations were located in China proper, and until the powerful Qing Dynasty (1644–1911), most Chinese dynasties were established within the boundary of China proper. Consequently, China proper is the center of early Chinese culture. While the population in the peripheral areas is thinly scattered, China proper accounts for one of the world's highest population densities, with nearly 84 percent of today's Chinese population crowded into the area.[9]

Agriculture is always a precarious business in China, because China has to feed 23 percent of the world's population with its limited amount of cultivated land, which accounts for only 7 percent of the world's total.[10] This means that the total cultivated area of China, which is only roughly half the size of the cultivated land in the United States, supports four times as many people.[11] In China proper, therefore, agricultural activities are heavily concentrated, and people cannot afford to use their valuable land to raise cattle for meat or milk. In fact, 90 percent of the land that can be used for agriculture in China is cultivated for crops; in comparison, only 40 percent of the arable land in the United States is used for crops.[12]

The second distinction within the Chinese boundary is the north-south division. The mountain range of Qinling in the West and the Huai River in the East roughly separate China into two halves: the Yellow River zone of the north, and the Yangtze River zone of the south.[13] There is a wide range of difference between the "dry wheat-millet area of North China and the moist rice-growing areas of the south," from the terrain and weather to crop cultivation and living habits.[14] The weather of the south is usually hot and humid with abundant rainfall; whereas the weather of the north is dry and cold with limited and uncertain rainfall. The growing season, accordingly, is eight to twelve months long in the south, but only four to six months long in the north. Due at least in part to these different geographical and weather patterns, there is a significant difference between the people in the north and the people in the south in terms of living habits and socioeconomic patterns.[15]

Ethnicity and language further demonstrate diversity within China. Today, the Chinese government officially recognizes fifty-six ethnic groups, including Han Chinese which constitute about 92 percent of the nation's population.[16] Most minority groups live in the outlying areas, such as the Tibetans in Tibet, the Mongolians in Inner Mongolia, and the Uighurs in Xingjiang. Many minority groups inhabit China's south and southwest borders, the Zhuang in Guangxi, and the Miao and the Yao in Guizhou and Yunnan. Most minority groups distinguish themselves from the Han by their languages, customs, and clothes. The languages used in China include languages from all major linguistic families, including Sino-Tibetan, Altaic (e.g. Korean, Mongolian, Uyghur, etc.), Austro-Asiatic (e.g. Mon-Khmer,) and Indo-European (e.g. Tajik).

There are also considerable variations within the Chinese language itself. Chinese officials often describe these linguistic variations as differences in dialects, but many of these dialects in fact are different from one another in a wider range of linguistic features than those between different European languages. For example, Cantonese, a dialect used in Guangdong and Hong Kong, has eight tones in its pronunciation instead of the four tones that are associated with standard Chinese, sometimes known as Mandarin, which is based on a dialect of Beijing. Other than standard Chinese, there are at least five other major dialectic groups: namely Wu dialects, Cantonese dialects, Hunan and Guangxi dialects, South Min (Fujian) dialects, and Haka dialects. Although they share certain grammatical structures and vocabulary, these dialectic groups are not mutually intelligible in oral communication. Regional linguistic variations partially explain why feelings of local affinity usually run deep in China.

image © Ingvar Bjork, 2012. Used under license from Shutterstock, Inc.

Oracle Bone Script

Then, how do the Chinese communicate with each other? The answer lies in the written language. All Chinese people use the same written system, no matter which dialect they speak. Hence, they can always communicate with other people in writing. The Chinese language is one of the oldest languages that are still in active use. Evidence of the earliest known form of Chinese was discovered around the turn of the twentieth century. One scholar of the Qing Dynasty found, among the elements of his Chinese herb medicine, pieces of "dragon bones," on which some strange scripts were carved. Subsequently, Chinese scholars identified these strange scripts as an ancient form of language related to modern Chinese. More than 20,000 pieces of similar bones, known later as the Oracle Bones, were excavated from today's city of Anyang in the Henan province, which was later identified as the capital of a legendary dynasty in Chinese history, the Shang dynasty (ca. 1766–1122 BCE). Although Chinese scholars have not been able to decipher all of the scripts on these animal bones, which are usually shoulder bones of ox or turtle shells, they have established definitive connections between the Oracle Bone Script and the modern Chinese language.[17]

RIVER SYSTEMS AND CHINESE CIVILIZATION

The Chinese civilization is one of the world's oldest civilizations and, along with India, one of the two oldest continuous civilizations. In comparison to India, the Chinese civilization reveals more consistencies between earlier and more modern times. One such example can be found in the Chinese language system discussed above, and another is reviewed in the earlier discussion of Confucianism in Chapter 2. Thus, cultural continuity is one of the most distinct features of this civilization. Even today's autocratic Chinese government contains traces that "came down directly from prehistoric times."[18]

Similar to the case of the Indus River Valley and other early civilizations, early centers of Chinese civilization were born along river systems. There are two major river systems in China: the Yellow River (Huanghe) in the north and the Yangtze River (Changjiang) in the south. Both of the rivers originate from the Himalayan Mountains and run from west to east to enter the Pacific Ocean. The Yangtze River is the third longest river in the world, only after the Amazon and the Nile. It pours down from the Tibetan Plateau into the Sichuan basin and gushes into the central plain of the Hubei province and then through the Jiangsu province into the East China Sea from Shanghai. The river has been a blessing to the Chinese, bringing abundant water into the rice fields along the river. Its delta in the lower reaches of the river, known as the Yangtze delta, is one of the most productive areas in China.[19] The Yangtze River is deep, wide, and navigable almost all the way from the upper reaches to the Pacific, and has been a major means of transportation for the Chinese since ancient times. Moreover, the river seldom floods except in cases of excessive rainfall.[20]

In contrast, the Yellow River is known for its malevolence. It runs through the treeless high plateaus in the northwest and tumbles down through the Loess Plateau of the Gansu, Ningxia, and Shanxi provinces, absorbing a heavy deposit of yellow soil into its water, making it very muddy. According to one source, the Yellow River's "average silt concentration per cubic meter is 34 kilograms (kg) as compared with 10 kg in the Colorado, 4 kg in the Amu Darya, and 1 kg in the Nile."[21] This sediment-laden river gained its name, Yellow, from the color of its water. The heavy soil content gradually sinks to the bottom of the river, adding layers of dirt to its riverbed. As the soil accumulates on the riverbed and raises the water level, the river often breaks its natural dikes, and sometimes even dramatically changes its courses in its lower reaches. It is said that in the past 3,000 years, the river breached its dikes, or more specifically, the levee embankments, more than 1,500 times and changed its courses twenty-six times.[22] Hundreds of thousands of Chinese have died as a consequence of flooding and subsequent famines and plagues. The Yellow River is thus known as "China's sorrow."[23]

From the early beginning of their civilization, the Chinese have worked collectively to construct levees, especially along the lower reaches of the Yellow River, in order to contain the water in its channel. As the riverbed became higher, so did the constructed levees. Because of thousands of years of levee construction, the Yellow River now flows high above the surrounding land in the middle and lower reaches. Near the city of Kaifeng in the Henan province, for example, the levees stand as high as thirty feet above the city level. These levees were first linked into a complete system in about 200 CE. This system has protected the cities and farmlands from being flooded for centuries. Today, it is still viewed as a "marvel in civil engineering, comparable in grandeur to the building of the Great Wall."[24]

The Yellow River, however, has been both a curse and a blessing for the Chinese.[25] Other than being negatively known as China's sorrow, it is also called "the cradle of Chinese civilization" and "the Mother River." Similar to the Nile, the frequent flooding of the Yellow River also brought rich soil to its surrounding areas, making them suitable for agricultural activities. It is in the Yellow River valley that evidence of the earliest Chinese civilization has been discovered, which dates back to 3,000 BCE, if not earlier. Although accounts of the origins of the Chinese civilization are mythical and subject to much debate, early Chinese civilization is usually called the Yellow River Civilization.

ORIGINS OF CHINESE CIVILIZATION: MYTHS AND DISCOVERIES OF ARCHEOLOGY

There are two important sources for studying early Chinese civilization: Chinese mythology and archaeological evidence. Similar to other early cultures, early Chinese civilization is shrouded by creational myths, which were recorded in various written sources years later. Chinese mythology is rich in its content; it is different from the mythology of many other cultures because most of its characters are not godlike figures, but cultural heroes. Other than Pangu, a powerful creature who is said to have chopped a colossal stone into heaven and earth, all of the other major mythological figures are admired as cultural and political champions.[26] For example, some versions of Chinese mythology mention the following as being the Three Sovereigns: Fuxi, (Ox Tamer) who is credited with domestication of animals; Shennong, (Divine Farmer), who invented farming tools and taught people techniques of agriculture; and Huang Di (Yellow Emperor).[27] The last one, Huang Di, is considered the ancestor of all Han (or Huaxia) Chinese, and supposedly reigned from about 2697 to about 2597 BCE.[28] The reign of Huang Di saw many achievements, including the introduction of the Chinese language (Oracle Bone Script), the Chinese calendar, Chinese music principles, Chinese medicine, wooden houses, boats, bow and arrows, and ceramics. His wife taught people how to dye clothes and how to weave silk from the thread of silkworms.[29]

ANCIENT XIA AND SHANG DYNASTIES

According to ancient historical chronicles, other legendary rulers, such as Yao (r. 2357–2256 BCE), Shun (r. 2255–2205 BCE), and Yu (r. 2205–2198 BCE), were all revered leaders whose work eventually led to the creation of the first Chinese legendary dynasty, Xia (ca. 2200–1766 BCE), in the areas along the Yellow River, including today's Luoyang, Henan Province.[30] Yu the Great, the first ruler of the Xia, was especially known for his altruistic personal sacrifices for the sake of his people. One of his biggest challenges at the time was a great flood. Yu successfully organized his people to dredge channels in order to guide the floodwaters out to the sea. He worked so hard that he did not have time to visit his family even though he passed his house three times and heard his wife and children crying.[31] This legend showed a model king for the later rulers to emulate. Yu's people loved him so much that they decided to ignore the early practice, as well as Yu's own wish, to choose from the Chinese the most capable person to rule the country. Instead, Yu's son became the next king and hence started the Chinese hereditary imperial tradition.

The Xia dynasty was replaced by another ancient dynasty, the Shang Dynasty (1766–1122 BCE), although the two might have overlapped for a certain time.[32] The literature of the Shang is particularly rich. J.A.G. Robert sums up three themes of the Shang: the organization of the Shang state, the significance of the Oracle Bones Script, and magnificent Shang bronze.[33] Many of the features that would influence the Chinese political system and cultural tradition for thousands of years started to take shape during the Shang dynasty. Around 1122 BCE, the Shang dynasty was replaced by the Zhou dynasty, which lasted until 256 BCE.[34] The Zhou dynasty, together with the Xia and the Shang, are known as the three legendary dynasties of ancient China.[35]

Not everything we know about these dynasties is established by legends. Although studying prehistory through archaeology is a modern phenomenon in Chinese history, many archaeological achievements have provided impressive evidence that support the legendary assertions of early records.[36] Excavations in central China have found evidence of several Neolithic cultural centers. The Yangshao Culture, a Neolithic culture that existed from 5150 to 2960 BCE, stretched across a vast region along the Yellow River in the Gansu, Shaanxi, and Henan provinces.[37] The Yangshao people clustered into villages and cultivated millet, rice, turnips, cabbage, and yams. Their diet was also supplemented with meat and fish obtained through hunting or fishing. The villagers also domesticated chickens, ducks, pigs, dogs, and cattle, and made colored pottery, a common artifact of this culture.[38] Another nearly contemporary Neolithic culture, the Longshan Culture (ca. 3000–2000 BCE), was discovered in the Shandong and Shaanxi provinces. Because of its distinctive patterned black pottery that has been unearthed across the excavation sites, the Longshan Culture has been given the name "Black Pottery." The Longshan people had permanent walled communities larger than villages, as well as bronze weapons and tools.[39] Evidence also showed their religious orientation as well as their use of oracle bones for divine purposes, a practice that became popular in the Shang dynasty.[40] The excavations at Erlitou of the Henan province uncovered another set of large palaces and tombs dated 2100 to 1800 BCE; these appeared to be evidence of the Longshan Culture and may have been a capital of the Xia dynasty.[41] Among the artifacts found at this site were the earliest known bronze vessels in the world.[42]

Excavations at these Neolithic sites provide evidence that connect these Neolithic cultures with the legendary Xia and Shang dynasties. Although some scholars still question the real existence of the Xia dynasty, most scholars accepted these ancient dynasties as genuine dynasties of early Chinese civilization.[43] The archaeological evidence for the Shang dynasty is particularly overwhelming. Through excavation sites in today's Anyang, archeologists have identified a city called Yin in ancient times as one of the capitals of the Shang. At its peak, the city may have covered as much as ten square miles with impressive monumental buildings, streets, and tombs.[44] As mentioned before, the excavation of the large pits that contained thousands of pieces of Oracle Bones in Anyang have brought to light the Shang archives.[45] The Oracle Bone Script gives us detailed knowledge of the Shang political system. The Shang kings were powerful and monarchical, passing the throne to the members of their own family. They declared wars against their enemies and demonstrated their power through massive public works. They also controlled the production of bronze vessels, which were crafted more for ceremonial than utilitarian purposes.[46] Shang bronze perhaps represented the highest achievement of technology in the era. Many of bronze vessels bear complicated decorations, and some larger types, such as the Ding, weighed as much as 1,500 pounds.[47] The high craftsmanship represented in bronze metallurgy during the Shang and later Zhou dynasties have never been surpassed and "are still one of humankind's great artistic achievements."[48]

Perhaps the greatest purpose of these archaeological excavations is to provide evidence of the "successive phases of a single cultural development" from the Yangshao villages to the Longshan communities, and then to the capital cities of the three ancient dynasties. Differing from the early history of the Indian subcontinent, there is no evidence of outsider invasions in the formative stages of the Chinese civilization between 3000 BCE and the beginning of the Christian era. It is not difficult for one to discern a high degree of cultural consistency and continuity among these cultural centers and previous or overlapping dynasties.[49]

THE ZHOU DYNASTY

The Zhou dynasty is traditionally dated from 1122 to 256 BCE.[50] Historians further divide the dynasty into the Western Zhou (ca. 1122–771 BCE) and the Eastern Zhou (770–256 BCE), using the move of their principal capital from Xi'an to Loyang in 771 BCE as the demarcation.[51] We know more about the Zhou dynasty than the earlier Xia and Shang dynasties. Much of our knowledge is based on what the Zhou people recorded about their own activities, and in fact, much of the written information of early Chinese history, including the Three Sovereigns, the Five Emperors, as well as the Xia and Shang dynasties, were recorded in the Zhou era.[52] In addition, Confucian classics included the great deeds of the early Zhou rulers whom Confucius himself greatly admired and wanted later rulers to emulate.[53]

The origin of the Zhou people is not clear. According to some literary traditions, they might have been a mixed group of Turkish and Chinese blood, who settled down in the Wei River valley. Linguistically there was no evidence that they travelled from afar. They later justified their rebellion against the Shang in the same language that the Shang people had used. Most likely, they were Chinese-speaking descendants of the Longshan Neolithic people.[54] The Zhou people adopted the Shang style of agriculture and became a powerful state at the west periphery of Shang territory. Under the reign of King Wen (Cultured King), the Zhou people started to maneuver against the Shang ruler, and King Wen's son, King Wu (Marshal King) eventually sacked Anyang, the last capital of the Shang in 1122 BCE, and thus ended the Shang dynasty.

King Wu returned to the Zhou's original capital, Xi'an, which was called Hao at the time, leaving a couple of his brothers to keep the Shang capital under control.[55] It was his brother, known as the Duke of Zhou, who finally gained full control over the vast Shang domain and laid the political foundation of the Zhou dynasty. The Duke of Zhou relentlessly suppressed rebellions by the remnants of the Shang as well as by his other brothers, and built a new capital in Louyang in order to control the Zhou dynasty's new conquests in the east. Many elite families of the Shang were relocated from Anyang, which was leveled, to the new city. Although the Duke of Zhou enjoyed enormous power, he never took the throne himself. He only served as a regent for his nephew, the young King Cheng, whom he diligently coached about the responsibilities of a king.[56]

The Zhou state was not totally unified. Some scholars suggest that the political system of the Zhou was similar to the feudal system in medieval Europe, whereas others try to avoid the loaded word of "feudal" to describe the Zhou's political realm.[57] In either case, Zhou rulers never exerted an absolute control over their domain. Instead, they delegated power over local states to members of the royal family, generals, and formal commanders of the regional city-state, giving them ranked titles similar to the English titles of duke, marquis, earl, viscount, and baron.[58] When Zhou rulers became weak after three centuries of reign, the most powerful of these lords, known collectively as *zhuhou* (the various marquises), brought power into their own hands. In the meantime, the non-Han Chinese from the west and the north constantly harassed the Zhou's capital in Xi'an, and one group from the north even sacked the city in 771 BCE, killing the Zhou king. As mentioned earlier, Zhou's decision to move the main capital from Xi'an to Luoyang marked the beginning of the Eastern Zhou.[59]

The Eastern Zhou is oftentimes further divided into two time eras. One is known as the Spring and Autumn period (771–481 BCE) after famous annals that describe the events of those years in the small state of Lu, Confucius' hometown. The other period, the Warring States period, began in 481 BCE with the partitioning of the territory of the powerful lord of Jin and ended in 256 BCE when the rest of Zhou territory was annexed by the Qin state.[60]

Actually, Warring States is an apt description of the Eastern Zhou period in general, since the dominant theme of the period was a competition for power among the most powerful *zhuhou guo* (marquis states). With the decline of royal authority, war became epidemic among *zhuhou*, who had become kings of their own domain instead of servants to the Zhou king. In the earlier Spring and Autumn period, there were about 170 local states, among which fifteen or so had significant size, riches, and power.[61] These states fought with each other for control of more land and resources, but sometimes they formed alliances against one another. One calculation speculates that only thirty-eight years of this time were peaceful.[62] By the late Spring and Autumn era, only thirteen of the

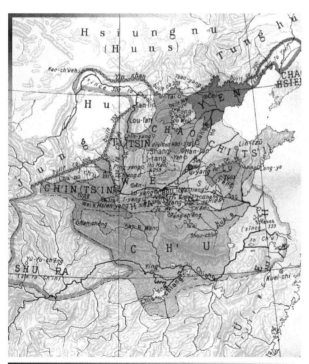

China during the Warring States Period

most powerful had survived, and that number was further reduced to seven by the beginning of the Warring States.

The rulers of these states not only competed with each other for more land and resources, but they also tried to outdo each other in terms of securing talented people. Constant war brought such rapid social and political changes that the rulers needed talented people to advise them. This gave rise to a new elite group, intellectuals known as *shi*, who were especially active in exploring social, political, and philosophical ideas for answers to political or philosophical problems.[63]

The Eastern Zhou is thus known as the era of the Hundred Schools of philosophy. The most important schools among them were Confucianism, Taoism, and Legalism. Confucius, (Kong Qiu or Kong Fuzi in Chinese), the founder of Confucianism, lived in the Spring and Autumn period of the Eastern Zhou dynasty. In his teachings, which were discussed in detail in Chapter 2, Confucius emphasized a social/ethical code that should guide "the individual's conduct along lines of proper ceremonial behavior."[64] Confucius presented his most important principle in his own words: "Let the ruler rule as he should and the minister as a minister should. Let the father act as a father should and the son as a son should" (*junjun chenchen fufu zizi*).[65] Although Confucius could not successfully promote his ideas to various state rulers in his time, his philosophy has been a major cultural influence in China since the Han dynasty. In contrast to Confucianism's worldly view of human relations in a society, Taoism emphasizes human relations within a larger cosmic sphere, not far off from the guiding principles of Buddhism. Confucianism and Daoism, however, are not mutually exclusive. Instead, "the Chinese scholar was a Confucian when in office and a Daoist when out of office."[66] Similar to Confucianism, its counterpart, Daoism, also exerted considerable influence over the life of the peoples around the world. Legalism, which focused on governance, had a particularly strong influence over the emperor of the Qin dynasty (221–206 BCE), the first of the undisputed dynasties in China.

Other intellectual achievements of the Zhou dynasty include several important Chinese classics. *Zhouli* (Zhou Ritual), which was traditionally ascribed to the Duke of Zhou, and *Liji* (Book of Rites), which may have been written by Confucius himself, are important records of the rituals of the Zhou dynasty. In addition to describing etiquette and proper rituals, *Zhouli* also contains information about governmental organizations and the obligations of officers.[67] Another important classic, *Yi jing* (*I Ching*, or *Zhouyi*, Book of Change) was also composed during the Zhou era. *Yi jing*, a handbook for diviners, "is used on the simplest folk-culture level for fortune-telling and on the highest intellectual level for gaining somewhat mystical insights into the nature and workings of the cosmos."[68]

Another important genre of Zhou literature focused on military strategy. As agricultural production and the population continued to increase in these states, the warfare expanded to a larger scale and became more ruthless in the period of the Warring States.[69] Some records provide information describing an army of as many as 600,000 men.[70] Military specialists were in high demand among the competing rulers. Sun Wu, also known as Sun Zi (Sun Tzu), for example, emerged as one of the best military strategists. He designed various strategies to build up the morale of his soldiers and to lure and deceive his enemies. *The Art of War*, which may have been written by Sun Zi, is among the best work in the genre of military strategy and philosophy of war. Its contents cover a wide range of military strategies, from how to organize a battle, to how to evaluate a terrain, to whether or not to choose an offensive or defensive strategy, to how to guarantee logistic supply, to how to discover and take advantage of an enemy's weakness using strategies such as deception and diplomacy.[71] As such, *The Art of War* has served as a reference for many military leaders in and outside of China. Many military academies around the world still choose the book as part of their curricula.

UNIFICATION OF CHINA UNDER THE QIN

As mentioned before, by the third century BCE, only seven states had survived the early rivalry: Qi in the east in today's Shandong; Chu in the south in today's Hubei in the middle reaches of the Yangtze river; Qin in the west in today's Shaanxi, Shanxi, and Sichuan; Yan in the northeast near today's Beijing; and Wei, Zhao, and Han, three offspring states which arose from the partition of the early, powerful Jin state, in the center. Even Confucius' hometown, the state of Lu, had been eliminated by this time. Although there were certain commonalities among these states, considerable cultural, linguistic, and even ethnical differences divided these states.[72]

In 221 BCE, the state of Qin managed to eliminate the last of its six opponents and unified China for the first time in its history. Qin had started as one of the smallest states with the poorest resources because of its peripheral location.[73] Among the many reasons why Qin emerged victoriously over other competitors, one stands out: the outstanding work of Qin ministers and kings. The open-mindedness of Qin kings was essential in attracting the most talented people from the other competing states. Shang Yang (390–338 BCE), from the state of Wei, became a chief advisor to the Qin king. He introduced political reform in Qin, including a law code, land reform, regulated pay for soldiers in terms of land and according to their military contribution, and severe punishment for those who broke the king's law.[74] Although he was later executed after his patron died, his reforms were picked up by other Qin statesmen, such as Li Si (280–208 BCE), who was originally from the state of Chu. Li Si had studied legalism directly under Xun Zi, the father of the school, together with Han Feizi (ca. 280–234 BCE), who became one of the foremost theorists of Legalism.[75] Li Si later became prime minister to Ying Zheng, the last king of the Qin state or the first emperor of China, who adopted Li's legalistic policies in his process of the unification and reign of China.[76]

The unification of China under the Qin dynasty was a major watershed in Chinese history. The Qin dynasty (221–206 BCE) is the first in a series of Chinese dynasties that flourished in China until 1911. Although it is the shortest dynasty in Chinese history, its reign of China began a political and administrative tradition that was followed by later dynasties. The imperial unity of China, for example, has been the highest goal of a political leader in China ever since the time of the Qin dynasty. Ying Zheng, who called himself *Qin Shi Huangdi* (the First Emperor of Qin) was the first emperor of the Qin dynasty. The new title of emperor, *Huangdi, Huang* or *Di*, was subsequently used by later Chinese imperial rulers. The First Emperor continued his conquest by attacking areas south of China and even expanded Chinese control over Northern Vietnam.[77] The emperor, however, was not simply satisfied with putting the land under his control. Together with his advisors, he started to create a centralized legalist state aimed at a high level of political, social, and cultural unification of all of China, which had been a goal for many other rulers since the East Zhou, but one that none of them had achieved.[78]

One of the major goals of the emperor's empire building was to create a centralized bureaucratic administration.[79] For that purpose, the first emperor and his prime minister, Li Si, created a series of political and economic reforms. The emperor divided the country into thirty-six commanderies (*jun*), which were subdivided into a number of counties (*xian*). The governors of the *jun* and the magistrates of the *xian* were centrally appointed and under the close supervision of the central government. These *jun* and *xian* were administrative divisions under a united government, and in this sense, differed greatly from the semi-independent states which had existed during much of the early Zhou period.[80] Moreover, court appointments were nonhereditary and service-based, and the emperor constantly evaluated the performance of each bureaucrat who received such an appointment.[81]

Centralization was accompanied by standardization, which further uprooted the remnants of the localism that had occurred as a result of separate Zhou states.[82] The First Emperor imposed strict controls on his people, setting up unified standards in several important areas, including law codes, writing, currency, weights, measuring units, and even the axle length of the carts so that they would not tilt over the tracks on a muddy road that had been made by a previous cart.[83] The frenzy of standardization also extended to the intellectual realm. The emperor's legalistic advisors strongly opposed the Confucian ideas of educating people to be gentlemen and believed instead that punishment was the best way to install obedience among the populace. As a result, the emperor ordered the notorious "burning of books," followed by the execution of as many as 460 Confucian scholars as a warning to anyone who dared to criticize his rule, although the exact number of the victims of this event is still in dispute.[84] His anti-intellectual atrocities elicited especially harsh criticisms of him in Chinese dynastic histories, most of which were composed by Confucian scholars.

The emperor's ambition also led him to undertake massive construction projects, including constructing a magnificent palace for himself and building as many as 4,000 miles of roads to connect his capital with other cities in order to facilitate his tours around his new domain.[85] Construction of two of China's most symbolic monuments occurred during his reign: the Great Wall of China and his mausoleum near Xi'an, which was guarded by thousands of life-size terracotta soldiers, generals, and horse-drawn chariots. These massive construction projects caused the emperor to ruthlessly tap the human and financial resources of the nation.[86] Over a million people may have died in building the Great Wall alone.[87] Soon after the sudden death of the First Emperor of Qin at the age of 49 in 210 BCE, his dynasty started to shatter and was overwhelmed by massive rebellions throughout the country. The Qin dynasty soon gave way to a new dynasty.

The Great Wall of China

Terracotta Soldiers

CHINESE EMPIRE UNDER THE HAN DYNASTY

Out of the chaos of the late Qin dynasty emerged a rebel leader, Liu Bang, who eventually founded a new dynasty, the Han dynasty (202 BCE–220 CE), which was one of the longest reigning dynasties, if not the longest reigning dynasty, in Chinese history. Han rulers consolidated the political and cultural traditions that they had inherited from the Qin and other early Chinese dynasties. Many long lasting Chinese characteristics took shape during this time, and the cultural achievements of the Han dynasty, including the establishment of Confucianism as the official ideology of China, still influence Chinese society today. As mentioned before, about 92 percent of residents in China still identify themselves as Han Chinese who are distinctively different from non-Han minorities in China.[88] During its time, the Han empire, together with the Roman and Indian Mauryan empires, was one of the three most powerful empires in the world; among these three, the Han empire was the largest, if not the most populous, with a population of approximately 60 million, as well as the richest.[89]

Unlike most founding fathers of Chinese dynasties, Liu Pang, also known by his posthumous title Han Gaozu (high ancestor), was one of the few Chinese emperors who emerged from a peasant family.[90] He became a minor official in the Qin government and was put in charge of building the tomb of the first emperor, but abandoned that post for fear of his life. After the death of the First Emperor, Liu led a rebellion against the Qin government and initially joined hands with another rebel leader, Xiang Yu (232–202 BCE), who later became Liu's major competitor for central power. Xiang was militarily stronger, but Liu managed to rally more support and eventually defeated Xiang and established a new dynasty.[91] Liu chose Han as the name of his dynasty, based on his earlier title: King of Han.[92]

Having known poverty and having suffered himself under the oppressive Qin, Gaozu immediately softened Qin's legalistic approach to give people a chance to recover from their earlier suffering.[93] He reduced the taxes of the peasants and the merchants and encouraged education, which had been destroyed by the Qin dynasty. The longevity of the Han dynasty may have been the result of the shrewd policies of Gaozu and his successors. In order to avoid repeating the tyranny of the First Emperor of Qin, Gaozu gave credit to his courtiers who rendered him advice or even criticism, and accepted more humane, Confucian approaches of governance, an approach which emphasized that the government should take consideration of the need of the people.[94] He was credited with the practice of selecting talented young men who were well educated in Confucian precepts to be government officials.[95]

Nonetheless, Gaozu did not dismantle Qin's administrative structure, nor did he abandon Qin's superimposition of state hegemony on most aspects of

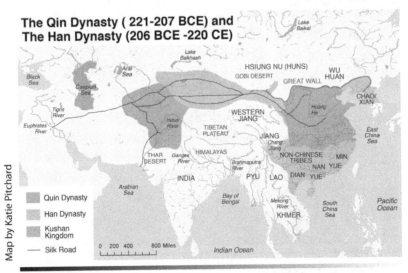

The Han dynasty and the earlier Qin dynasty. The Silk Road is also shown.

the people's lives. He not only generally perpetuated the Qin political system, but also improved on it with the creation of a systematic bureaucracy consisting of the three most senior officials, who were, in turn, aided by nine ministers.[96] Gaozu exerted direct control over fourteen commanderies in the West, but granted ten hereditary princedoms as rewards to his strongest generals.[97] This was probably the most drastic change that Gaozu made to the Qin system. Gaozu, however, gradually replaced the rulers of these princedoms with his family members and reduced them in size. These princedoms never enjoyed the same degree of power and wealth that the early Zhou kingdoms had.[98] Throughout his reign, Gaozu was conscious of the problems that the Qin dynasty had brought to the empire and cautiously implemented his moderate policies so as not to disturb the peace and prosperity of the country. Gaozu's "laissez-faire style of governing" continued during the first sixty years of the Han dynasty, despite the fact that he reigned for less than a decade.[99]

EXPANSION AND CONSOLIDATION UNDER HAN WUDI

The reign of Emperor Liu Che, also known as Han Wudi (marshal emperor of the Han, r. 141–87 BCE), marked the zenith of the Han Empire. Benefited by the prosperity achieved through the prudent policies of early Han emperors, Wudi started to employ aggressive policies, which brought more changes. His military achievements extended China's territorial control to as far as northern Vietnam in the south, northern Korea in the northeast, and part of central Asia in the west.[100] In order to combat the Xiongnu, who had been settled along China's northern borders since the Qin dynasty, Wudi sent Zhang Qian as an envoy to find the Yuezhi, who had moved westward and eventually entered northern India. The purpose of Zhang Qian's trip was to seek an alliance with the Yuezhi in China's struggle against the Xiongnu, but Zhang was captured by the Xiongnu before he could find the Yuezhi.[101] When Zhang eventually returned to the Han capital after thirteen years, including spending ten years in Xiongnu's captivity, he brought back reliable information about Central Asia, India, and the Roman Empire. Meanwhile, Wudi organized massive campaigns against the Xiongnu, driving them at least temporarily out of today's Inner Mongolia and Xinjiang.[102] One of the Chinese exploratory troops went as far as northern India, and this might have put them in proximity of Roman troops who were campaigning against the Parthian kingdom of Persia. However, the Chinese and the Romans never had direct contact with each other.[103] These military battles, supplemented with other strategies, such as an "intermarriage system" of diplomacy, where Han princesses married the leader of the Xiongnu, and a "tributary system," helped Wudi and his successors keep the Xiongnu under control.[104]

Wudi's reign was also marked by noticeable changes in other areas. He further centralized and extended imperial control in domestic affairs. He introduced new taxes on commerce and established governmental monopolies of some essential trade items, such as iron, salt, and liquor. Chinese cities traded with India, the Mediterranean, and Rome. Merchants travelled along the Silk Road, carrying Chinese goods such as silk, lacquered ware, and an early form of porcelain, from Chang'an, the Han capital. They traded these goods in return for gold, spices, and other commodities, which they brought back to China.[105]

The most important reform, however, was in the area of national ideology, which had a lasting influence on Chinese government and society. Upon the suggestion of Dong Zhongsu, a court official, Wudi agreed to adopt Confucianism as the exclusive governmental ideology. He ridded his court of non-Confucian officials and in 124 BCE established a university to train officials in Confucian orthodoxy.[106] Civil service examinations began to be used in the hiring of government officials. Wudi asked senior officials to recommend talented young men to study at the university to prepare for the exams. If they passed, they would be eligible for an official appointment regardless of their birth. The new hires remained a source of strength for Wudi, helping him neutralize the power of the hereditary princedoms and eliminate many of them during his reign.[107]

HAN CULTURE

The stability and prosperity of the first two centuries of the Han Empire provided a benevolent environment for cultural developments in all fields, but particularly in the areas of political philosophy, the writing of history, and technical inventions.[108] Confucianism would flourish for the rest of the Han dynasty after Han Wudi propagated it. However, as John King Fairbank points out, the Confucianism that was practiced as a ruling philosophy during and following the Han dynasty was different "both from the original teaching of Confucius, Mencius, et al. and from the secular and personal Confucian philosophy that arose during the Song times."[109] Fairbank called it "Imperial Confucianism," which is actually a "Legalist-Confucian amalgam," the essence of which was that "Legalism was liked by rulers and Confucianism by bureaucrats."[110] A Chinese emperor could enjoy enormous power, rewarding as well as punishing his people as he wished, but the ministers should follow Confucian doctrines to advise and sometimes even put constraints on the emperor, as part of their duty to the nation not as defiance of the ruler.[111] The influence of this kind of special relationship between the Legalist emperor and Confucian ministers on Chinese political thought can still be seen in the Chinese political system today.

Han Confucianism was best manifested by the national university founded by Wudi. Under his patronage, Confucian scholars searched diligently for the remaining texts of Confucian classics that might have survived Qin Shi Huangdi's burning of the books. They then compiled these texts, added their own commentaries to them, and circulated them. These newly compiled texts from the Han era are known in Confucian tradition as the "new texts," in comparison to the "old texts" that had existed before the Han era.[112] The academy chose five classics as the core of its curricula, namely *Yi jing* (Classic of Changes); *Shu jing* (Classic of History); *Shi jing*, (Classic of Songs); *Chun qiu* (Spring and Autumn Annals); and *Li ji* (Classic of Rites).[113] These Five Classics, together with the Four Books—*Daxue* (Great Learning), *Zhong yong* (Doctrine of the Mean), *Lun yu* (Analects of Confucius), and *Meng zi* (Mencius)—have formed the core of Confucianism ever since.

The writing of history has always been an important part of Chinese cultural tradition. The Chinese are always proud of their historical heritage and extremely keen on keeping records with painstaking scrutiny. This literary tradition has produced an extensive chronicle of dynastic history, which consists of 3,213 volumes, covering Chinese history from 3000 BCE to the Ming dynasty (1368–1644). This tradition started with Sima Qian (Ssu-ma Ch'ien, ca. 145–86 BCE), whose monumental work, *Shi ji* (Records of the Grand Historian), continues to be one of the most important sources of early Chinese history. Sima Qian spent more than ten years writing his 130-volume history, which covered early Chinese history from the Five Emperors, Xia, and Shang to his own time.[114] More important was the organization and the style of *the Records of the Grand Historian*, which established a model for later Chinese historians to follow. Sima Qian worked diligently to "approach facts of history with a spirit of respect and objectivity."[115] Although in some places he did not hesitate to fill in the blanks with his own invented speeches and dialogues, the significance of his work to our knowledge of early China as well as to the Chinese historiography is seldom overestimated.[116]

The Han dynasty saw several scientific and technological inventions. Around the second century CE, a court eunuch, Cai Lun, improved on some earlier technology in the standardization of paper-making. This, together with the invention of the compass, gunpowder, and printing, are known as the four great inventions of ancient China. The magnetic compass, first referenced in a Chinese book believed to have been written in the fourth century BCE, was in wide use in China 1000 years before the European sailors employed compasses.[117] Chinese ships, which were guided by compasses and equipped with watertight compartments and sternpost rudders, sailed along what is known as the maritime Silk Road, from southern China through the Malacca Straits to Southeast Asia, Sri Lanka, India, and then to the Persian Gulf and the Red Sea.[118]

Rhoads Murphey summarizes some equally impressive but less known achievements in terms of science and technology during the Han Dynasty:

> Han Dynasty alchemists invented the technique of distillation, not discovered in Europe until the twelfth century AD.... Metallurgy, already well advanced, was given a further boost by the invention of a double-acting piston bellows, something not achieved in the West until the seventeenth century. The wheelbarrow had made its appearance by late Han, better balanced than its later Western copy since the single wheel was placed in the middle instead of at the end, thus enabling a much greater weight to be transported with less effort. The square-pallet chain pumps, for moving or raising water, and the suspension bridge were also Han innovations. The circulation of the blood was also first discovered in Han, despite the traditional Western claim for its discovery by William Harvey in the seventeenth century.[119]

THE DECLINE OF THE HAN DYNASTY

While Han Wudi may have expected to perpetuate Han rule of China through Confucian teaching, ironically, that ideology may have formed a theoretical basis for a temporary interruption of the rule of the Liu family by a powerful prime minister, Wang Mang, who usurped power from the Liu and established his own dynasty of Xin (the new dynasty, 9–23 CE). Dong Zhongshu had anticipated the emergence of a real Confucian state reigned by a philosopher-king, and this prophesy was used by Wang Mang, a devoted Confucian scholar, to justify his takeover of the Han throne.[120] Wang Mang carried out a series of reforms in order to build a new state according to the Early Zhou model, which was greatly admired by Confucius.[121] Due to lack of military connections, however, Wang's dynasty was short-lived. The Liu family soon restored their power and moved the capital from Chang'an to Luoyang in 23 CE. Parallel to the early move of the capital eastward that divided the Eastern Zhou from the Western Zhou, the same move distinguished the Eastern or Later Han (25–220 CE) from the Western or Former Han.[122]

Another comparison to the history of Zhou was that the Later Han similarly lost its early momentum. Although its first few rulers were capable of restoring the prosperity and power of the former Han, they were followed by a series weak emperors who started to lose control of the country.[123] One major achievement of the Later Han was that it finally settled the score with the Xiongnu, who had been a major problem for the Han since the time of Gaozu. Taking advantage of an internal split of the Xiongnu, coalition forces of the Han, the Xiongnu division of southern Xiongnu, and other tribes finally defeated the northern Xiongnu, who subsequently moved further west and may have reemerged years later as the Huns who sacked Rome, although this connection is still under debate.[124] In his pursuit of the Xiongnu, one Han general led his army all the way to the Caspian Sea and may have reached either the Persian Gulf or the Black Sea.[125]

Toward the end of Later Han, the same problems that haunted the Qin returned. A widespread peasant rebellion, known as the Yellow Turban Rebellion, broke out in 184 CE. Instead of fighting against the rebels, some generals took advantage of the chaos to make themselves local masters. In 190 CE, one of these new warlords seized Louyang, removed the emperor, and murdered the empress dowager and a prince. Several years later, another warlord, Cao Cao (155–220 CE), put the emperor under his control. After Cao Cao died in 220 CE, his son forced the last Han emperor to abdicate, and thus, ended nearly 400 years of Han rule.

For more information about the topics discussed in this chapter, please visit the website for this textbook. This website can be accessed from http://www.grtep.com/.

1 Jimin Sun and Tungsten Lou, "The Age of the Taklimakan Desert," *Science*, vol. 312 (June 2006), 1621.
2 David C Wright, *The History of China* (Westport, CT.: Greenwood Press, 2001), 1.
3 Richard Smith, *China's Cultural Heritage: the Qing Dynasty, 1644–1912, 2nd ed.* (Boulder: Westview Press, 1994), 16.
4 Murphey, *History*, 88.
5 Murphey, *History*, 89.
6 Murphey, *History*, 88; Charles Hucker, *China's Imperial Past: an Introduction to Chinese History and Culture* (Stanford: Stanford University Press, 1975), 2; and Smith, *Heritage*, 16.
7 Hucker, *Imperial*, 1–2; and Smith, *Heritage*, 16.
8 John King Fairbank, *China: A New History* (Cambridge, Mass.: The Belknap Press of Harvard University Press, 1992), 23.
9 Wright, *History*, 10–11; and National Bureau of Statistics of China, "The sixth national census data in 2010 (bulletin No. 2)" accessed on June 4, 2012, at http://www.stats.gov.cn/tjgb/rkpcgb/qgrkpcgb/t20110429_402722510.htm.
10 John King Fairbank, Edwin Oldfather Reischauer, and Albert M. Craig, *East Asia: Tradition & Transformation* (New York: Houghton Mifflin, 1989), 11.
11 Fairbank et al., *Tradition*, 5; and Wright, *History*, 10.
12 Fairbank et al., *Tradition*, 15.
13 Smith, *Heritage*, 18; Hucker, *Imperial*, 2; and Fairbank, *New History*, 4–11.
14 Fairbank et al., *Tradition*, 5.
15 Smith, *Heritage*, 23–24; and Fairbank et al., *Tradition*, 4–5.
16 Some minorities have not gained official recognition as a separate minority group, such as the Jewish, Tuvan, and Oirat minorities. For more about how to determine minority groups in China, see Thomas Mullaney, "Seeing for the State: The Role of Social Scientists in China's Ethnic Classification Project," *Asian Ethnicity* 11: 3 (2010): 325–342; and Katherine P. Kaup, "Regionalism versus Ethnicnationalism," *The China Quarterly* 172 (2002): 863–884.
17 Hucker, *Imperial*, 29–30.
18 Fairbank et al., *Tradition*, 19.
19 Hucker, *Imperial*, 3.
20 Wright, *History*, 5.
21 Thomas. R. Tregear, *China, a Geographical Survey* (New York: John Wiley & Sons, 1980), 9.
22 Thomas. R. Tregear, *A Geography of China*, (London: University of London Press, 1965), 218.
23 Wright, *History*, 3.
24 "Yellow River Basin," ZSTPC, accessed August 26, 2011, at http://www.zstpc.org/eWebEditor/file/201004/5887.htm.
25 Wright, *History*, 3.
26 Hucker, *Imperial*, 22.
27 Hucker, *Imperial*, 22.
28 Hucker, *Imperial*, 22–23.
29 Hucker, *Imperial*, 23; and Murphey, *History*, 89.
30 The exact dates of the Xia dynasty are still not clear. The source for the dates listed here is J.A.G. Roberts, *A Concise History of China* (Cambridge, Mass.: Harvard University Press), 2–3.
31 Hucker, *Imperial*, 23; and Wright, *History*, 11–13.
32 Roberts, *Concise*, 3.
33 Roberts, *Concise*, 4–6.
34 Roberts, *Concise*, 7–8.
35 Fairbank et al., *Tradition*, 33.
36 Fairbank et al., *Tradition*, 19.
37 Jacques Gernet, *A History of Chinese Civilization*, Trans. by J. R. Foster and Charles Hartman (Cambridge: Cambridge University Press, 1972), 38.
38 Hucker, *Imperial*, 25; Fairbank et al., *Tradition*, 32; and Gernet, *Civilization*, 38.
39 Murphey, *History*, 88–89; and Hucker, *Imperial*, 25–26.
40 Hucker, *Imperial*, 25.
41 Fairbank et al., *Tradition*, 34–35.
42 Roberts, *Concise*, 3.

43 Murphey, *History*, 89.
44 Murphey, *History*, 90.
45 Hucker, *Imperial*, 27–30.
46 Hucker, *Imperial*, 28–30.
47 Hucker, *Imperial*, 28; and Murphey, *History*, 90–91.
48 Fairbank et al., *Tradition*, 34.
49 Fairbank et al., *Tradition*, 35.
50 Roberts, *Concise*, 7; and Hucker, *Imperial*, 30.
51 Hucker, *Imperial*, 35; and Fairbank et al., *Tradition*, 49.
52 Murphey, *History*, 92.
53 Gernet, *Civilization*, 51.
54 Roberts, *Concise*, 7; Murphey, *History*, 92; and Hucker, *Imperial*, 30–31.
55 Hucker, *Imperial*, 30–31.
56 Hucker, *Imperial*, 32.
57 Hucker, *Imperial*, 33; and Gernet, *Civilization*, 52
58 Hucker, *Imperial*, 33.
59 Hucker, *Imperial*, 34–35; and Murphey, *History*, 93.
60 Roberts, *Concise*, 11.
61 Fairbank et al., *Tradition*, 49; and Roberts, *Concise*, 11.
62 Roberts, *Concise*, 11.
63 Hucker, *Imperial*, 40; and Roberts, *Concise*, 12.
64 Fairbank et al., *Tradition*, 52.
65 Fairbank et al., *Tradition*, 52.
66 Fairbank et al., *Tradition*, 53.
67 Hucker, *Imperial*, 48–49.
68 Hucker, *Imperial*, 72.
69 Murphey, *History*, 93.
70 Roberts, *Concise*, 13.
71 Hucker, *Imperial*, 73.
72 Murphey, *History*, 93; and Fairbank et al., *Tradition*, 54–55.
73 Murphey, *History*, 95.
74 Hucker, *Imperial*, 42; Roberts, *Concise*, 20–21; and Fairbank et al., *Tradition*, 55.
75 For more on Han Feizi and Legalism, see Gernet, *Civilization*, 90–91; Hucker, *Imperial*, 93; and Roberts, *Concise*, 21.
76 Roberts, *Concise*, 21–22; and Murphey, *History*, 98.
77 Murphey, *History*, 96; and Hucker, *Imperial*, 45.
78 Hucker, *Imperial*, 42–44.
79 Hucker, *Imperial*, 43–44.
80 Fairbank et al., *Tradition*, 56.
81 Hucker, *Imperial*, 54.
82 Hucker, *Imperial*, 43.
83 Murphey, *History*, 96; and Hucker, *Imperial*, 43.
84 Fairbank et al., *Tradition*, 56; Hucker, *Imperial*, 43–44; and Gernet, *Civilization*, 109.
85 Fairbank et al., *Tradition*, 56; and Hucker, *Imperial*, 44.
86 Fairbank, *Imperial*, 56.
87 Murphey, *History*, 97.
88 Murphey, *History*, 103.
89 Hucker, *Imperial*, 172; and Murphey, *History*, 103.
90 Murphey, *History*, 100; Hucker, *Imperial*, 122; and Roberts, *Concise*, 26–27.
91 Hucker, *Imperial*, 122; and Roberts, *Concise*, 27.
92 Roberts, *Concise*, 27.
93 Roberts, *Concise*, 27.
94 Hucker, *Imperial*, 123; and Roberts, *Concise*, 28.
95 Murphey, *History*, 100; and Roberts, *Concise*, 28.
96 Roberts, *Concise*, 28; and Hucker, *Imperial*, 149–151.
97 Fairbank et al., *Tradition*, 57.
98 Fairbank et al., *Tradition*, 57; and Roberts, *Concise*, 27
99 Hucker, *Imperial*, 123; and Murphey, *History*, 100.
100 Roberts, *Concise*, 30; and Fairbank et al., *Tradition*, 125–127.
101 Roberts, *Concise*, 30.
102 Hucker, *Imperial*, 128; Murphey, *History*, 102; and Wright, *History*, 54–60.
103 Murphey, *History*, 103.
104 Wright, *History*, 57–59.
105 Hucker, *Imperial*, 124; and Murphey, *History*, 103–104.
106 Hucker, *Imperial*, 194.
107 Roberts, *Concise*, 31; and Murphey, *History*, 104.
108 Murphey, *History*, 104.
109 Fairbank et al., *Tradition*, 62.

110 Fairbank et al., *Tradition*, 62.
111 Fairbank et al., *Tradition*, 62–63.
112 Hucker, *Imperial*, 197.
113 Fairbank et al., *Tradition*, 67.
114 Hucker, *Imperial*, 223.
115 Hucker, *Imperial*, 225.
116 Hucker, *Imperial*, 223–226; Fairbank, *Tradition*, 70–71; and Gernet, *Civilization*, 167.
117 Murphey, *History*, 108.
118 Murphey, *History*, 108.
119 Murphey, *History*, 108. For more on this, also see Wright, *History*, 39–43.
120 Hucker, *Imperial*, 128–130.
121 Roberts, *Concise*, 34–35; and Wright, *History*, 59.
122 Hucker, *Imperial*, 130.
123 Murphey, *History*, 106.
124 Wright, *History*, 59–60.
125 Hucker, *Imperial*, 131.

Chapter 5 Gupta India and the Rise of Islam

After the collapse of the Mauryan Empire in 185 CE, the Indian subcontinent once again slipped back into upheaval. Political diffusion prevailed in northern India, making it particularly vulnerable to foreign invasions. Much of the northwest was occupied by different groups from across the border in Bactria, today's Afghanistan. By 190 CE, a number of new kingdoms had emerged in Bactria, and the Greco-Bactrian invaders took control of all of Punjab.[1] New waves of invaders from Central Asia also ventured into northern India and established their own kingdoms. These new dynasties were neither Indian nor ethnically mixed. They included the dynasties established by Indo-Greeks in the northwest, by Central Asian Kushans in the north, and by Shakas, another Central Asian group, in the west.[2] The political fragmentation of India continued for nearly five centuries before another single dynasty would once again claim central control of the entire northern India region.

KUSHAN KINGDOM

Among all the new settlers, the northern kingdom of Kushan (ca. 135 BCE and 250 CE) emerged as the strongest, and as such, had a lasting impact on the Indian subcontinent. According to some scholars, the Kushans built their kingdom into "one of four major centers of civilization in Eurasia" at the time, along with Rome, China, and the Parthian empire of Iran.[3] As is the case with very early kingdoms in India, information about the people who built the Kushan empire is still hard to come by, even though by the time of the Kushan empire, more information was available from Indian and foreign written sources.

As a result, the origin of the Kushans and the exact length of their reign are still not clear. Chinese sources described the Kushan (*Guishuang*) as one of the five tribes of the Yuezhi, a loose confederation of Indo-European peoples. After they had been driven out of northwestern China between 176–160 BCE, they reached Bactria around 135 BCE, where the Hellenic kingdoms of Greco-Bactria had resettled after the collapse of the Mauryan Empire.[4] After the Kushans subdued the other four Yuezhi tribes, they soon supplanted not only the Greek dynasties, but also the kingdoms of the Northern Shakas, driving the Shakas out of Bactria. For the next two centuries, the Kushans continued their expansion under their early kings. They settled in the northwest Indian region traditionally known as Gandhara (now Pakistan and Afghanistan), and established their capital near Kabul.[5] From there, they extended their political power over northern India as far as the central Ganges valley. By the reign of their third emperor, Kanishka, who reigned from the late first to the early/mid-second century CE, the Kushan kingdom had reached its zenith and controlled a vast area "ranging from the

Aral Sea through areas that include present-day Uzbekistan, Afghanistan, and Pakistan into northern India as far east as Benares and as far south as Sanchi."[6] The Kushans might have had direct contact with the Chinese who had extended their power into Central Asia, and they may have cooperated with the Chinese in their fighting against nomadic groups in the area. However, they later fought against the Chinese because the Chinese refused their request for a Chinese princess. A Chinese general, Pan-chao, defeated the Kushan army at Khotan in the year 90 CE.[7]

THE KUSHANS AND THE SILK ROAD

The Kushans benefited greatly from the international trade between two great empires of the time: the Roman Empire in the west, and the Han Empire in the east. The Silk Road and the sea-faring trade routes connected these two empires and other countries on the Pacific with those of the Mediterranean Sea. The bulk of the goods that were transported by land between the Roman Empire and China were silk, a product originating from China, but highly desirable in Rome. The caravan routes through Central Asia and northern India were therefore known as the Silk Road. There were several different routes, but an important segment of them passed through areas controlled by the Kushans.[8]

The trade between the east and the west had long preceded the rise of the Kushan kingdom and the Roman Empire. The rapid rise of the power and wealth of Rome, however, greatly boosted the volume and the range of the trade after the first century BCE. The expansion of the Chinese into Central Asia during the Han dynasty also greatly facilitated the revived interest in trade. Around the first century BCE, Han Wudi secured the northern routes of the Silk Road by putting an end to the harassment of the merchants by nomadic tribes. These routes travelled northwest from Chang'an, the capital of the Han Empire, following the mountain ranges north and south of the Taklimakan Desert to reach Kashgar on the western edge of the desert. The routes then entered Central Asia and the territories controlled by the Kushans. From there, they went through the Pamir Mountains into the Indus Valley and to the ports on the west coast of the Indian subcontinent. From these ports, the goods were eventually shipped to Rome and other Mediterranean countries.[9] In addition to goods such as gold, silver, wine, and perfumes from Rome, as well as silk and lacquers from China, merchants picked up a variety of other commodities along these routes: dates, saffron powder, and pistachio nuts from Persia; ivory, spices, precious stone, and sandalwood from India; and cloth and glass bottles from Egypt. These goods would then be transported to other parts of the world.[10]

Sitting at the middle of these important trade routes, northern India under Kushan rule thrived from the commerce that passed through their territories. The influence of international trade is evident from the relics that were excavated from the Kushan summer capital of Bagram (north of Kabul). These relics included painted glass from Alexandria, bronzes and alabasters from Rome, carved ivories from India, and lacquers from China. International trade in the Kushan kingdom was so profitable that, according to an observer at the time, "there is no year in which India does not attract at least 50 million sesterces [Roman coins]."[11]

These Roman coins are hard to find among the excavations in northern India today. One answer to this puzzle may be found in the Kushan production of their own gold coins, which depicted their kings. The tradition of making gold coins started with their first king and was continued by each subsequent king. Many Roman coins may have been used to produce these high quality coins, which have remained a reliable source for the identities and lives of the Kushan rulers.[12]

A Roman Coin

THE SIGNIFICANCE OF KUSHAN RULE

The emergence of the Kushan kingdom as a major power was due not only to the military and commercial success of the kingdom, but also to its contribution to the rising popularity of Buddhism.[13] The Kushans were great patrons of Buddhism and Buddhist arts. Their greatest ruler, Kanishka, is ranked as having been one of the greatest patrons of Buddhism, second only to Ashoka Maurya.[14] Buddhist *stupas*, (a type of reliquary with tall bell domes, which was originally designed to contain the relics of Buddhist saints) were erected across his kingdom, and one of them, the great *stupa* near Peshawar, was described by a Chinese source as standing 600 feet high. Modern archaeologists have confirmed that the foundation of this *stupa* is 286 feet in diameter. This giant *stupa* may have been the tallest building in the world at the time.

Under Kanishka and other Kushan kings, an intimate and mutually beneficial relationship was established between Buddhist monasteries and the local merchant community. Many merchants became enthusiastic patrons of Buddhism and "were eager to build stupas and donate money to monasteries in return for social prestige and the implied promise of a better life in this world or the hereafter."[15] Their enthusiasm for Buddhism made them instrumental in bringing the religion to Central Asia and China through the Silk Road. They were amply rewarded as the demand for Buddhist artifacts from India significantly increased.[16]

It is also believed that Kanishka may have convened a Buddhist council in Kashmir, which stimulated the development of Mahayana Buddhism.[17] Mahayana Buddhism travelled along the Silk Road to China, and from there spread to Korea and Japan. It still dominates Buddhist practices in East Asia today, in contrast to Theravada Buddhism, which is more popular in Southeast Asia. Kanishka, however, also demonstrated his tolerance for other Indian religions, which was reminiscent of Ashoka's policy of religious tolerance. Kanishka's coins show an image of gods from different traditions, such as Hindu, Buddhist, Greek, and Persian. There were so many different religious and cultural traditions in his kingdom that only policies with that a policy of religious tolerance would help to consolidate his rule.

Cultural synthesis is also highly visible in Kushan art forms. Kanishka and his successors were great patrons of Gandhara Buddhist arts, a classically blended style also known as Greco-Buddhist arts.

The Gandhara region was home to a multiethnic society. This was a result of constant competition over control of the region. The conquests of Alexander the Great and his successors, including the Hellenistic Greco-Bactrian kingdoms (ca. 250–130 BCE) to the west of Gandhara, had first brought Greek influence to the region. Greek culture was further blended with the regional culture during the time of the Indo-Greek kingdoms (180–10 BCE) in Gandhara. It may have been under Kushan rule that Greek and Roman artistic influence found its best expression in Buddhist art. The royal patronage to Buddhism under the Kushans encouraged the artists to explore the Buddhist theme in Indo-Greco style, a style that had a strong emphasis on realism.

Under the Kushans, the Gandhara Buddhist artists produced a large number of sculptures, including one of King Kanishka, the very first presentations of the Buddha in human form, and the earliest depictions of *bodhisattvas*. During the period when the Kushans dominated the region, the statues of Buddha and *bodhisattvas* were probably produced under the influence of newly developed Mahayana Buddhism. Neither Siddhartha Gautama (the Buddha) himself nor the traditional Buddhist doctrines recognized Buddha as a divine figure. The most important Buddhist ideology, according to Burjor Avari, was traditionally presented by what was called the Three Jewels: lessons from the life of Buddha, the *Dhamma*, and puritanical life in a monastic community.[18] In the early tradition, Buddha had been portrayed with symbols such as the stupa, the bodhi tree, the empty seat, the wheel, or the footprints.[19] The advocates of the Mahayana school, however, argued that it was important to have a Buddha image available for the masses to worship and that this would encourage them to achieve nirvana through their faith and devotion to Buddha. The ideas of the deification of Buddha and salvation by faith marked the division of the Mahayana school from the traditional Theravada.[20] As a manifestation of the new Mahayana beliefs, presentations of Buddha in human form were created for people to worship.

During the Kushan time, the production of Buddhist sculptures mushroomed in the northern part of the Indian subcontinent, and many sculptures could be seen along the Silk Road all the way to Central and East Asia. Equipped with a highly sophisticated Greek sculptural style, the Gandhara Buddhist artists produced the finest quality presentations of Buddha of all time.

© Bettmann/CORBIS

Kushan carving of Buddha

The Gandhara Buddhist carving arts have actually had a more enduring influence than the Kushan kingdom itself. The Gandhara Buddhist tradition continued long after the political reign of the Kushan kingdom. The world's two largest Buddha figures (180 and 120 feet tall, respectively), which were carved into a cliff at the Bamiyan Valley in Afghanistan in the middle of the sixth century CE, were made in the same Gandhara Buddhist style. Unfortunately, in 2001 the Taliban government that ruled Afghanistan at the time ordered the destruction of these valuable "Buddhas of Bamiyan."[21]

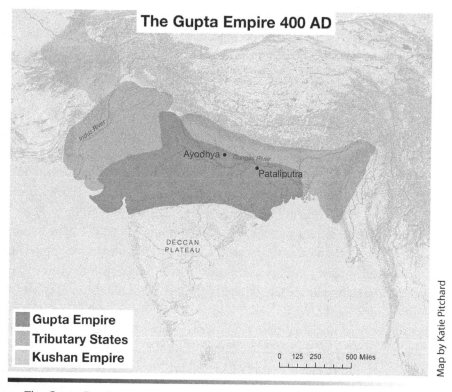

The Gupta Empire

THE GUPTA EMPIRE

The Kushan kingdom ended under uncertain conditions in the third century CE. Its rule in the east may have lasted until the mid-fourth century CE when the emerging Gupta dynasty, which established what was probably the greatest empire on the Indian subcontinent since the Mauryans, subjugated the remnants of the Kushan kingdom. Many Indians consider the Gupta era a high point of their civilization. Not only did the Gupta reunite most of the Indian subcontinent that had been held by the early Mauryan Empire, but it also opened a new classical age of Indian civilization, during which a variety of foreign influences that had come to India were assimilated into Indian culture. Under the Gupta, a classical form of Hindu culture started to influence the Indian subcontinent and gave the region a certain cultural-linguistic unity. In terms of cultural significance, Gupta India is considered an equivalent to Augustinian Rome or Tang China.[22] Some scholars, however, caution against the overrating of the Gupta as the Golden Age of Indian history, believing that it might be an exaggerated notion.[23]

The glory of the Gupta dynasty began with a local *raja* (ruler), whose name was Chandragupta, not to be confused with Chandragupta Maurya, the founder of the Mauryan dynasty. There were no connections between these two Chandraguptas, except that Chandragupta I of Gupta may have had an ambition to model his empire after that of the Mauryans.[24] His coronation as "Overlord of the Great Kings" (*maharaja-adhiraja*) in 320 CE marked the beginning of another grand imperial dynasty in Indian history. Following in the footsteps of the Mauryans, Chandragupta I and his descendents extended their territorial control from Magadha to the entire Ganges Valley, and then pushed the frontier of their empire to Punjab in the west, and Bengal in the east.[25] They even set up their capital at the old Mauryan capital, Pataliputra.[26] Written records have not provided us adequate information about the life and reign of the Guptas, so much of what we know about them comes from inscriptions, coins depicting their kings, reports by Chinese missionaries who visited the subcontinent to obtain Buddhist scriptures, and Hindu literature.[27]

TWO GREAT EMPERORS

The real engineers of the Gupta empire were Chandragupta's son, Samudragupta (r. 335–375 CE), and grandson, Chandragupta II (r. 375–415 CE), who are considered the greatest kings of Indian history, along with Chandragupta Maurya, Ashoka Maurya, and Kanishka of Kushan.[28] It was under Samudragupta that the Gupta Empire extended all the way to the foothills of the Himalayas in the north, over eastern Deccan, and down a long stretch of the eastern coastline to the southern tip of the subcontinent. He had three successful military campaigns, two in the north and one in the south.[29] Samudragupta detailed his glorious victories in his famous undated Allahabad inscription, which was engraved on an old Ashokan pillar. It contains a long list of kingdoms that he defeated, but only half of the kingdoms on the list have been identified today.[30] Based on the list, some scholars have calculated that Samudragupta eliminated "nine kings of north India, humbling eleven more in the south while compelling another five on the outskirts of his empire to pay 'tributes' as his 'feudatories.'"[31] The inscription also indicated that the Gupta sphere of influence was still larger, including some of the remnants of the Kushan and Saka kingdoms of the northwest, the Dravidian states in the south, the eastern coast of India, and possibly Ceylon (Sri Lanka).[32] The pattern of taking vassalage, however, was noticeably different from the political rule of the Mauryans. It seemed that Samudragupta was quite willing to accept a defeated ruler as a vassal prince rather than assert his direct rule over the defeated kingdom, especially in the cases of some remote kingdoms.[33] Since no failure was recorded on the inscription, Samudragupta was credited with continuous victories against as many as twenty-four kings without defeat; hence, he was described as a Napoleon of Ancient India, but without a Waterloo.[34]

Samudragupta was more than a talented military leader. He was also a talented cultural figure, a poet, and a musician. He sponsored a group of scholars and artists and promoted "a high culture" at his court.[35] He himself was a follower of Hinduism and revived some of the Hinduist tradition, such as performing horse sacrifices. Similar to Emperor Ashoka, he was also tolerant of other religions on the subcontinent.[36] Upon the request of the Sri Lankan king, for example, he donated generously to a famous Buddhist monastery at Bodh Gaya, Sri Lanka. He also provided a gold rail around the Bodhi Tree, under which the Buddha had supposedly achieved his enlightenment.[37]

The Gupta Empire reached its zenith under the rule of Samudragupta's son, Chandragupta II, similar once again to the situation of the Mauryans. Under Chandragupta II, India enjoyed a peace and prosperity that few other countries in the world could match at the time. A partial explanation of his success was his "bold and lively personality," which was portrayed in a popular Sanskrit drama that tells of Chandragupta II's courageous deeds of saving the kingdom.[38] The play indicated that the immediate heir of the empire was not Chandragupta II, but his brother Rama, who, however, proved himself weak and treacherous. Rama surrendered to a Shaka ruler and promised to send his wife to that Shaka monarch. Disagreeing with his brother's decision, Chandragupta II bravely entered the enemy's harem, disguising himself as the queen. He returned triumphantly after he murdered the Shaka king. According to the play, Chandragupta II later had his brother murdered and then married his widow. Historians, however, question whether the above play is a reconstruction of historical facts or simply an imaginative drama.[39]

Others attribute his success more to his political shrewdness, with which he craftily combined "the aggressive expansionist policy of his father with the strategy of marital alliance of his grandfather."[40] He further expanded into the territories controlled by the mighty Shaka dynasty of west India. Among his marriage alliances with other kingdoms, which were done to further his political agenda, one of the most important was to marry his daughter to a powerful king in west Deccan. Upon the death of that king, his daughter actually controlled the kingdom, and thus brought west Deccan under the Gupta reign.[41] Meanwhile, he maintained good diplomatic relations with the neighboring kingdoms, such as Assam, Nepal, Kashmir, and Sri Lanka. During the Gupta era, Chandragupta II's political influence was even evident as far away as Southeast Asian countries, such as Indonesia, where an old Sanskrit inscription contained a reference to "kingdoms on the Indian pattern."[42]

GUPTA CULTURE

As mentioned before, the Gupta era saw a boom in classical Hindu culture. The Gupta monarchs had eliminated most of their competitors and had thus provided security, peace, and stability to more than half of the Indian subcontinent for the first time since Ashoka. Under Gupta rule, most of the Indian subcontinent not only saw political unity for over two centuries, but also experienced a certain unity across the region in the form of revived Sanskrit literature and "popular Hinduism."[43] The conscientious patronage of the Gupta monarchs to arts, together with the decline of outside cultural influences, provided a golden opportunity, in the words of Avari, for the Indian "Brahmanic-Buddhist-Jainistic civilization" to revive itself to "a particularly splendid height under the Guptas."[44] The classical Hindu style flourished in artistic and literary productivities of all forms, such as poetry, painting, sculpture, dance, drama, and music.[45] The best examples of this development can be found in the Sanskrit literature of the time, as well the sculptures and wall paintings of the Ajanta caves.

One of the greatest patrons of Sanskrit literature was Chandragupta II, whose court was culturally graced with the presence of a group of nine excellent literary artists, known as the Nine Jewels. Among them was the famous Kalidasa, whose works earned him a reputation as the "Shakespeare of Sanskrit language."[46] Little, however, is known about the life and the dating of Kalidasa, and his identity is still under debate. We only know that his name literarily means "slave of the Goddess Kali," who is a consort of god Shiva in Hindu tradition. This may reveal, according to Wolpert, his background as a south Indian *shudra*, but others sources suggest that he might have been a *brahman* from Mandasor or Ujjain.[47] While most scholars now put him under the patronage of Chandragupta II, there are other suggestions that put his existence in a wide time spectrum from "the reign of Agnimitra, the second Shunga king (c. 170 BC)" to the time of "the Aihole inscription of AD 634 which praises Kalidasa's poetic skills."[48]

In spite of these controversies, few have questioned the quality of Kalidasa's works and his contribution to Sanskrit literature. Among his six surviving works, the best presentation is his play, *Shakuntala*, which tells a story of the love between a forest nymph, Shakuntala, and King Dusyanta, who was so enticed by the beauty of Shakuntala that he married her and had a child with her, but forgot about her after his return to his kingdom.[49] Many verses in the play were so beautifully written that *Shakuntala* caught the imagination of many literary figures around world, including a German poet, Johann Wolfgang von Goethe (1749-1832), whose words of praise best illustrated the charm of this play:

> If you want the bloom of youth and fruit of later years,
> If you want what enchants, fulfills, and nourishes,
> If you want heaven and earth contained in one name -
> I say *Shakuntala* and all is spoken.[50]

The revival of interest in Sanskrit was also represented in Buddhist literature. Although the early literature of Buddha's life and teaching was in Pali, a vernacular language in north India, rather than Sanskrit, which was the language of Hinduism, most of the literature of Mahayana Buddhism developed during the Kushan era was in Sanskrit. Under the Guptas, Buddhism continued to flourish in both forms, and Buddhist artwork has been preserved in the Buddhist caves of Ajanta, which are located in the present-day state of Maharashtra, India. Between the second century BCE and the sixth century CE, nearly thirty caves were carved into the mountains where the Buddhist monks would dwell and pray. The wall paintings and sculptures in these caves, which are devoted to the life of Buddha, his incarnations, and *bodhisattva*, represented the finest craftsmanship with infinite charm. Accomplished over a period of 800 years, these works of art reveal an evolution of the artistic style of Buddhist arts and architecture. Some of the finest caves were built during the Gupta era. They contained paintings reflecting the fashion at the Gupta courts. Some of them, such as the painting of *Avalokitesvara*, a *bodhisattva* of mercy and compassion, rank high among the greatest Buddhist artworks in the world.[51]

image © Aleksandar Todorovic, 2012. Used under license from Shutterstock, Inc.

Buddhist caves of Ajanta

Another category of Sanskrit literature is the *Puranas* (of ancient times), which had performed an essential role in the popular form of Hinduism.[52] Beginning in the sixth century BCE, Vedic Brahmanism had suffered a decline in popularity as the result of the rise of Buddhism and Jainism, especially during the Ashoka era. In the post-Mauryan era, however, Vedic Brahmanism, the oldest religious tradition on the Indian subcontinent, experienced a gradual revival by adopting some Buddhist practices. Two modified forms of Vedic Brahmanism began to emerge: *Vaishnavism* and *Shaivism*.[53] Both of them centered on a supreme deity in the form of either Vishnu, originally a Vedic god of lesser importance, or Shiva, an ancient pedigree in Vedic mythology, but may also be a Harappan deity. As part of a movement later known as *bhakti* (loving devotion), these new sects embraced the notion that salvation was possible by means of intensive love and devotion to the deity, and through the grace of Vishnu or Shiva.[54] Although they did not break away from the main Vedic tradition, the adherents rejected some Brahmanistic practices, especially animal sacrifice, the austere and extravagant rituals associated with such a sacrifice, and the rigidity of the caste system. Hindu temples for Vishnu or Shiva were erected for people to worship. In these new forms, *Vaishnavism* and *Shaivism*, may have emerged as a compromise to a Buddhist challenge as well as to the popular demands of the time. Thanks to the efforts of brilliant Hindu scholars who bridged the different strands, Vedic Hinduism avoided a destructive separation from these new trends.[55] Instead, Hinduism experienced an internal change, gradually departing from its early Vedic focuses on the Aryan gods and on the rituals of sacrifice to new emphases on daily morality (*karma*) and social norms (e.g. Hindu marriage custom) guided by eternal laws (*dhamma*). These new focuses were not much different from the essential beliefs of Buddhism and Jainism.

This gradual shift from Vedic Hinduism to popular Hinduism may have helped revitalize this old tradition. While many of the higher classes still adhered to orthodox doctrines, the new popular forms "swept through India like a whirlwind."[56] Being revived in more popular forms, Hinduism survived the severe challenge of Buddhism and Jainism, and remained a compelling force in Indian societies. In the post-Mauryan societies, Hinduism received royal patronages from kings at the top and popular acceptance from the masses of the lower castes. Accompanying this popular movement was the development of new Hindu scriptures to serve the needs of the new converts; among these new scriptures were the great epics of *Ramayana* and *Mahabharata*, and the *Puranas*.

The epics of *Ramayana* and *Mahabharata* had a dim origin in the Vedic period long before they were incorporated as part of the Hindu canon. The stories probably developed during the sixth century BCE. It was centuries, however, before they were written down in their modern forms in Hinduism, Buddhism, and Jainism, and, after Indian cultural influence spread to Southeast Asia, in different languages in what are now the countries of Indonesia, the Philippines, Thailand, Laos, Myanmar, and Malaysia. The epics conveyed important messages of Vedic values, especially those of *dhamma* through the actions of the major characters. *Ramayana*, for example, told a story of a perfect prince, Rama. As an ideal son, he obeyed the order of his father to be banished into the forest even though he knew that it was due to an evil act by his stepmother. His wife, Sita, voluntarily went with him in order to perform her duty as an ideal wife. Rama's half brother, as an ideal brother, came to the forest, begging Rama to return. Rama, however, needed to stay in the forest not only to stick to his principles of a good son, but also to rescue his wife from the king of Lanka Island (Ceylon), who had abducted her. Hanuman, a monkey king, was an ideal servant who rallied an army of monkeys to aid Rama's efforts. When Rama eventually returned to the kingdom of Ayodhya with his wife, he was crowned king and ruled the country as an ideal king ever after. These epics thus served as important tools to educate many Hindus who still did not have direct access to the sacred *Vedas*.

The *Puranas* arrived at their popularity in a similar way. There are two categories of Hindu scriptures: *Smriti* (remembered) and *Sruti* (revealed).[57] The *Puranas*, which belong to the first category, may have existed as early oral traditions, but the earliest written versions date from the time of the Gupta Empire.[58] These *Puranas* contain stories about the history of the universe, genealogies of important people, such as kings, heroes, sages, and demigods, as well as other information. There are eighteen Great *Puranas*, which are supplemented by Less *Puranas*.[59] Some *Puranas* focus on a particular Hindu deity or a particular Hindu holy place, and thus the written *Puranas* were closely associated with the new sects of Hinduism that emerged during the Gupta era, which centered upon a particular deity. The *Vishnu Purana*, for example, is one of the most important scriptures to the Vaishnavas. Since all the texts of the *Puranas* were written in Sanskrit, the popularity of the *Puranas* made a great contribution to the resurgence of Sanskrit. The blossoming of Sanskrit literature had not only a great impact on the Sanskrit language itself, which completed its transition from Vedic Sanskrit to Classical Sanskrit, but also had a lasting influence on regional languages used on the Indian subcontinent.[60] Regional languages thrived alongside Sanskrit, since many Sanskrit texts had to be translated into regional languages in order to reach a greater range of audiences.[61]

Because of the splendid cultural achievements during the Gupta era, many view the Guptas as having overseen a golden age of classic Hindu traditions. Although the Gupta monarchs were great patrons to all of the traditional religions of the region, they were essentially followers of Hinduism. It was under Gupta patronage that Hinduism "secured the opportunity to establish itself more firmly in the religious life of the people."[62] Under the Guptas, Hinduism became a more coherent and codified religion that still influences millions of people on the Indian subcontinent and around the world.

ADVANCE OF ISLAM TO INDIA

The birth of Islam in the year 622 CE changed the course of history in many areas. After Muhammad established the Islamic faith and practice, thousands of his enthusiastic followers spread this faith "by tongue" or "by force" into the neighboring areas. Islamic political power soon spread far beyond the Arabian Peninsula into other areas of the Middle East, North Africa, the Indian subcontinent, Central Asia, and the Iberian Peninsula. Concerning the Indian subcontinent, Islam brought more fundamental changes to the region than any previous cultural influences since the Aryans established their influence on the Indian subcontinent more than 2,000 years earlier. Its impact is still felt in the region where tens of millions of Muslims live in Afghanistan, Pakistan, Bangladesh, and India.

The Islamic advance into India was preceded by political fragmentation that, after the decline of the Gupta Empire, once again prevailed in northern India. Similar to their predecessors, the Guptas could not hold their empire together after their first few great kings were gone. In the late fifth century CE, the Guptas seemed to be able to withstand the first challenge from the Huns, who came down from Central Asia; but, when the Huns returned in the next century, the good fortune of the Guptas came to an end, although it may have returned for a while during the reign of Harsha (606–648 CE).[63] Culturally, the Indian artistic tradition consolidated during the Gupta era continued well into the Muslim era; politically, the Indian subcontinent returned to its usual pattern of regionalism.[64] Between the mid eighth century and the end of the tenth century, there were a number of regional kingdoms in the north and several in the Deccan and southern areas. None of them, however, could bring unity back to the Indian subcontinent. Due to this vacancy, Muslim powers started to enter northern India.

The earliest Muslim exploration into northern India can be traced back to as early as 644 CE when an Arab commander reported from Sind that "water is scarce, the fruits are poor, and the robbers are bold; if a few troops are sent they will be slain, if many, they will starve."[65] Reports such as this discouraged further Arab advances into India until a Muslim army plunged into Sind in 711 CE to retaliate against Indian pirates who had intercepted an Arab merchant ship. In an effort to convert the "infidels" in the area, they set up Muslim communities in Sind.[66] These communities, however, confined their activities to a particular area and had little interest in further expansion. It took nearly three centuries before a major Muslim initiative was launched against northern India through a mountain pass in today's Afghanistan.[67]

MAHMUD OF GHAZNI AND MUHAMMAD OF GHUR

In 997, Mahmud of Ghazni (971–1030) began his raids in India. He was the grandson of the king of Ghazni, the first independent Turkish Islamic kingdom located in the south of Kabul. He was the first ruler to carry the title sultan (authority), a secular royal title in contrast to caliph (deputy of God), the Prophet's temporal successor.[68] At its height, Mahmud's kingdom included today's Iran, Afghanistan, Pakistan, and northwest India. His invasions into India were especially harsh. As the "Sword of Islam," Mahmud of Ghazni led as many as seventeen assaults into India each year.[69] In 1018, he invaded northern India in two major campaigns, during which he destroyed Hindu temples, looted India's cities of their treasure, and left thousands of dead bodies behind him. Having witnessed the atrocities of the Turkish-Muslim army, some proud local *Rajput* (a member of a ruling clan in northern India) warriors practiced *jauhar*—an ancient Indian tradition that required warriors to kill their families before they engaged in fighting against the odds.[70] By the time of his death, Mahmud had annexed the Punjab and made other Hindu kingdoms into his vassal states.[71]

A little over a century after the death of Mahmud of Ghazni, a Turkish leader known as Muhammad of Ghur (1150-1206), conquered the city of Ghazni in 1173 and uprooted Mahmud's empire. Two years later, he invaded India from Afghanistan. Unlike Mahmud of Ghazni, who spent most of his time in Afghanistan, Muhammad of Ghur was determined to rule northern India instead of just looting it. In 1192, after his troops defeated a group of local *raj* (kingdom), he established a capital at Delhi, a strategic location from which he could control movement between the upper Indus and the Indo-Gangetic plain.[72] Over the next few years, he conquered most of northern India. During the three decades of his rule, Muhammad ran a vast kingdom from Ghur in the west to Bengal in the east. He was constantly in battle against the local insurgence, marching from border to border. In 1206, he was assassinated on his way back to Ghazni after he suppressed a rebellion in Punjab.

DELHI SULTANATE

Before he died, Muhammad had appointed Qutb-ud-din Aibak, one of his generals, as the governor of the Indian part of his empire. Shortly after Muhammad's death, Aibak claimed independence and hence became the first sultan of Delhi. His rule was followed by a line of rulers known as the *Mamluk*, which means slave. As a result, the dynasty was also known as the Slave dynasty, because Aibak and several of the sultans who succeeded him were originally military slaves. Aibak was succeeded by his son-in-law, Iltutmish (r.1210–1235), who is considered to have been one of the most capable rulers of this dynasty. Interestingly, Iltutmish's rule was followed by the rule of his daughter, Razia Sultana (r.1236–1240), who was the first female ruler in the Muslim world.[73] Although she was a capable and fitting ruler, her reign saw the revolt of her nobles who eventually killed her. Mostly

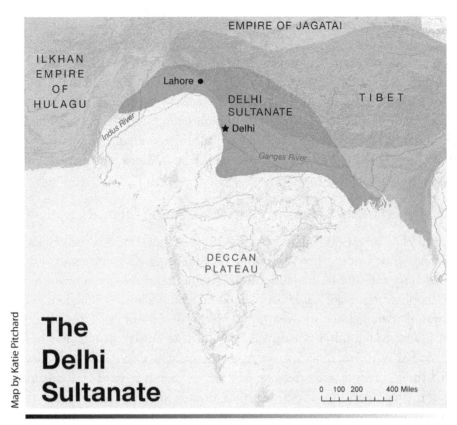

The Delhi Sultanate

weak, the remaining sultans of the Slave dynasty only ruled for short periods, except Mahmud (r.1246–1266), Iltutmish's son, and Balban (r.1266–1287), who was raised by Iltutmish and later became the son-in-law of Mahmud.[74] Balban was notorious for his cruelty. Not only did he crush defiant Hindu Rajputs, but he also murdered his competitors, together with their families, as well as disloyal Turkish rulers.[75] Shortly after the death of Balban, the dynasty fell apart in 1290.

Between 1290 and 1526, four other dynasties rose and fell in northern India. The rule of these four dynasties, together with that of the Slave dynasty, is known collectively as the rule of the Delhi Sultanate (1206–1526). The dynasty that immediately followed the Slave dynasty, the Khalji dynasty (1290–1320), was short-lived, but its achievements were impressive. The second king, Ala al-Din Khalji (r.1296–1316), conducted conquests in India that no other monarch had conducted since Ashoka Maurya. His conquering forces brought central and deep southern India under his control. He also successfully prevented the Mongols from the north from capturing Delhi. His empire, however, collapsed soon after he was killed in battle in 1316.[76]

The Delhi Sultanate's power reached its zenith during the next dynasty, the Tughluq dynasty (1320–1413). Muhammad bin Tughluq (r. 1325 to 1351), the second Tughlug sultan extended his control into central and southern India and controlled even more territory than Ala al-Din. Muhammad Tughluq was an intelligent and well-educated ruler, being knowledgeable in logic, philosophy, mathematics, astronomy, physical sciences, and medicine. However, his "unbridled ambition," according to some scholars, brought the final destruction of the dynasty.[77] His political policies were often disastrous and "eccentric," which caused revolts from Hindu kingdoms in the south, as well as from his own generals and ministers. For example, he moved the capital 700 miles south into the city of Devagiri of the northern Deccan, "without any consultation, without carefully looking into the advantages and disadvantages on every side."[78] It may have been a strategic move for the purpose of being closer to his newly conquered central and southern India, but his decision to transfer the entire population of Delhi proved to be disastrous. This policy was greatly resented by his generals and ministers who hated to lose the comfort of their homes in Delhi. In addition, the water source in the new capital could not meet the needs of the larger population, especially during the dry summer. After wasting much of his treasure and labor to build palaces in Devagiri, Tughluq had to move the capital back to Delhi after only two years, but by that time the city had already been damaged beyond repair.[79] Taking his return to the north as a sign of weakness, the southern Hindu kingdoms revolted against him. Other central and western kingdoms followed suit and also revolted, and his empire began to fall apart. As a result, the word *Tughluqi* has become synonymous with "brilliant if stubborn eccentricity" in Urdu, a language of the Muslims in South Asia.

The Tughlug dynasty continued to decline after the death of Muhammad Bin Tughluq, losing its control of the central area, as well as of the south. The biggest challenge to the dynasty, however, loomed outside the Indian subcontinent. In 1398, a Mongol-Turkish ruler, Timur (1336–1405), mercilessly sacked Delhi after looting the Punjab.[80] The city was destroyed, and most of the people were either killed or dragged away as slaves. It is said that the ferocity in Delhi even shocked Timur, who claimed in his alleged autobiography that only his soldiers, not him, should be blamed for this terrible event.[81] The Delhi sultanate never fully recovered from the destructiveness of Timur. Fifteen years after this event, the Sayyid dynasty (1414–1451) would come to rule from Delhi. The Sayyid dynasty was later replaced by the Lodi dynasty (1451–1526), which continued to rule from Delhi until the emerging Mughals absorbed it in 1526.

The political history of the Delhi Sultanate is thus not a pleasant one, but one full of "bloodshed, tyranny and treachery."[82] Its dynasties were short and weak, and of the thirty-five sultans of the five dynasties, Muslim rebels assassinated nineteen.[83] While its political power was often abused and its resources wasted, its cultural achievements earned a reputation as an "Indian cultural renaissance" for the period.[84] The fusion of Muslim culture with the rich Hindu heritage resulted in a boom of architecture, music, literature, and religion. One important example of this cultural integration is the creation of the Urdu language, which is still used by Muslims in northern India. Urdu is similar to Hindi, a traditional language of Hindus, in grammatical structure, but different in vocabulary and script. While most of the Hindi vocabulary derives from Sanskrit, Urdu contains many Persian, Arabic, and Turkish words. Hindi is written in Devanagri script, from left to right, but Urdu is written in a Persio-Arabic script from right to left. In 1947, disagreement over these languages, Hindi and Urdu, was one of the major issues that eventually contributed to the partition of British India into two separate countries, India and Pakistan.[85] While Urdu is the official language of Pakistan, Hindi is the main official language in India, even though India accepted Urdu as one of the twenty two "scheduled languages."

For more information about the topics discussed in this chapter, please visit the website for this textbook. This website can be accessed from http://www.grtep.com/.

1 Wolpert, *New History*, 70.
2 Avari, *India*, 128–129.
3 Albert Craig, William Graham, Donald Kagan, Steven Ozment, and Frank M. Turner, *The Heritage of World Civilizations, 4th ed.* (Upper Saddle River, NJ: Prentice Hall, 1997), 133.
4 Meredith L. Runion, *The History of Afghanistan* (Westport: Greenwood Press, 2007), 46.
5 Craig et al., *Heritage*, 133–134.
6 "Kushan Empire," The Metropolitan Museum of Art, accessed July 3, 2011, at http://www.metmuseum.org/toah/hd/kush/hd_kush.htm.
7 Kulke and Rothermund, *History of India*, 50; and Rafe de Crespigny, *A Biographical Dictionary of Later Han to the Three Kingdoms, 23–220 AD* (Leiden: Koninklijke Brill, 2007), 5–6.
8 William J. Duiker and Jackson J. Spielvogel, *World History, Vol. I.* (Minneapolis/St. Paul: West Publishing Company, 1994), 338ff.
9 Francis Wood, *The Silk Road: Two Thousand Years in the Heart of Asia* (Berkeley, CA: University of California Press, 2002), 9–23; and Avari, *History*, 135–137.
10 Wood, *Silk Road*, 9–23; and Ulric Killion, *A Modern Chinese Journey to the West: Economic Globalization and Dualism* (New York: Nova Science Publishers: 2006), 66.
11 Kulke and Rothermund, *History of India*, 50.
12 Kulke and Rothermund, *History of India*, 50; and Avari, *India*, 134.
13 Duiker and Spielvogel, *World History*, 339
14 Kulke and Rothermund, *History of India*, 50.
15 Duiker and Spielvogel, *World History*, 339; and Avari, *India*, 135.
16 Avari, *India*, 137.
17 Avari, *India*, 137; and Kulke and Rothermund, *History of India*, 52.
18 Avari, *India*, 139–140.
19 Katsumi Tanabe, *Alexander the Great, East-West Cultural Contacts from Greece to Japan* (Tokyo: NHK Promotions, 2003), 19–23.
20 Duiker and Spielvogel, *World History*, 342–344.
21 For more on this, see Llewelyn Morgan, *The Buddhas of Bamiyan* (Harvard University Press, 2012).
22 Craig et al, *Heritage*, 286; Duiker and Spielvogel, *World History*, 340; and Avari, *India*, 168.
23 Avari, *India*, 155–156, also, note 1; and Craig et al, *Heritage*, 286–86.
24 John McKay, Bennett Hiss, John Buckler, *A History of World Societies*, 4th ed. vol. I (Boston: Houghton Mifflin Company, 1996), 311.
25 Avari, *India*, 157; and Wolpert, *New History*, 88–89.
26 Kulke and Rothermund, *History of India*, 54.
27 Duiker and Spielvogel, *World History*, 340–341; and Gokhale, "Great Ancient Empires," 65–66.
28 Avari, *India*, 157.
29 Avari, *India*, 157; and Kulke and Rothermund, *History of India*, 54–56.
30 Kulke and Rothermund, *History of India*, 54–56.
31 Wolpert, *New History*, 89.
32 Duiker and Spielvogel, *World History*, 340; Wolpert, *New History*, 88–89; Kulke and Rothermund, *History of India*, 56; and McKay et al., *World Societies*, 312.
33 Avari, *India*, 159.
34 The expression probably first appeared in Vincent A. Smith, *The Early History of India: From 600 B.C. to the Muhammadan Conquest* (Oxford: Oxford University Press, 1924), 306; Also see Avari, *India*, 158; Wolpert, *New History*, 88; and Gokhale, "Great Ancient Empires," 66.
35 Avari, *India*, 158.
36 Kulke and Rothermund, *History of India*, 55.
37 Avari, *India*, 158; and Kulke and Rothermund, *History of India*, 56.
38 Wolpert, *New History*, 89.
39 Wolpert, *New History*, 89; and Kulke and Rothermund, *History of India*, 60.
40 Kulke and Rothermund, *History of India*, 58.
41 Avari, *India*, 158.
42 Kulke and Rothermund, *History of India*, 58.
43 Avari, *India*, 166.
44 Avari, *India*, 168.
45 Craig et al, *Heritage*, 286–288.
46 Craig et al, *Heritage*, 286; Wolpert, *New History*, 89; and Avari, *India*, 171.
47 Wolpert, *New History*, 87.
48 Mamta Pandey, *Encyclopedia of Kalidasa Literature*, Volume 2, Kālidāsa (New Delhi, India: Anmol Publications, 2009), vii.
49 William Theodore De Bary and Irene Bloom, *Eastern Canons: Approaches to the Asian Classics*, (New York: Columbia University Press, 1990), 169, and 395; and also see Wolpert, *New History*, 88.
50 De Bary and Bloom, *Canons*, 165.
51 Wolpert, *New History*, 89.
52 Kulke and Rothermund, *History of India*, 60.
53 Avari, *India*, 140–141.

54 Craig et al, *Heritage*, 290–291; and Avari, *India*, 141, and 239.

55 Avari, *India*, 239.

56 Avari, *India*, 239.

57 Gavin Flood, *An Introduction to Hinduism* (Cambridge: Cambridge University Press, 1997), 39; and Thomas B. Coburn, "Scripture in India: Towards a Typology of the Word in Hindu Life," *Journal of the American Academy of Religion*, 52: 3 (September 1984): 439.

58 W. J. Johnson, *A Dictionary of Hinduism*. (Oxford: Oxford University Press, 2009), 247.

59 Kulke and Rothermund, *History of India*, 60.

60 J. F. Staal, "Sanskrit and Sanskritization," *The Journal of Asian Studies* 22:3 (1963): 261–275.

61 Kulke and Rothermund, *History of India*, 105.

62 Kulke and Rothermund, *History of India*, 165.

63 Kulke and Rothermund, *History of India*, 62; and Murphey, *History*, 83.

64 Avari, *India*, 203–222.

65 H.M. Eliot and John Dowson, eds., *The History of India, As Told by Its Own Historians: The Muhammadan Period: Historians of Sind*, I, 2nd ed. (Calcutta: Susil Gupta, 1955), vol. 25, 17. Quoted from Wolpert, *New History*, 106.

66 Wolpert, *New History*, 107.

67 Eliot and Dowson, *History of India*, 17; and Milton Meyer, *Asia: a Concise History* (Oxford: Roman & Litterfield, 1997), 52.

68 Wolpert, *New History*, 107.

69 Wolpert, *New History*, 108; and Kulke and Rothermund, *History of India*, 114–115.

70 For the origins of the Rajput, see Kulke and Rothermund, *History of India*, 77–78; and Meyer, *Asia*, 53.

71 Wolpert, *New History*, 108–109.

72 Meyer, *Asia*, 53; and Kulke and Rothermund, *History of India*, 116–117.

73 Kulke and Rothermund, *History of India*, 118.

74 Peter Jackson, *The Delhi Sultanate: A Political and Military History* (Cambridge: Cambridge University Press, 2003), 44–50.

75 Kulke and Rothermund, *History of India*, 118

76 Kulke and Rothermund, *History of India*, 120–133.

77 Kulke and Rothermund, *History of India*, 123.

78 Kulke and Rothermund, *History of India*, 124.

79 Wolpert, *New History*, 115–116.

80 Richard L. Greaves, Robert Zaller, Philip V. Cannistraro, and Rhoads Murphey, *Civilizations of the World: The Human Adventure* (New York: Harper & Row, 1990), 226.

81 Kulke and Rothermund, *History of India*, 125.

82 *Academic American Encyclopedia*, Vol. 10 (New York: Grolier Incorporated, 1994), 91, accessed on July 20, 2011, at http://gme-ada.grolier.com/article?assetid=0146990-0.

83 D.P. Singhal, *A History of the Indian People* (London: Methuen, 1983), 173. Quoted from Murphey, *History*, 118.

84 Thomas Walter Wallbank, Nels M. Bailkey, and George F. Jewsbury, *Civilization Past & Present*, 6th ed. (New York: HarperCollins College Publishers, 1996), 206.

85 Robert D. King, "The Poisonous Potency of Script: Hindi and Urdu," accessed July 20, 2011, at http://languagelog.ldc.upenn.edu/myl/llog/King2001.pdf.

Chapter 6 :   Golden Age of China

THE ERA OF DIVISION

After the fall of the Han dynasty, China once again entered an era of divisiveness and chaos. Competing warlords dominated China for the next 350 years. Eventually, three of these warlords became dominant, and each one established his own powerful kingdom. These kingdoms were: the Wei kingdom, which was based in Luoyang and controlled central China; the Shu kingdom, which was based in Chengdu and controlled Sichuan and the southwest; and the Wu kingdom, which was based in Nanjing and controlled the area south of the Yangtze River.[1] Their competition ushered in a new era known as the Three Kingdoms period (220–280 CE), which began with the establishment of the Wei kingdom in 220. The ending of the era was somewhat fluid. Some historians consider the destruction of the Wu in 280, presumably by the Wei, to mark the ending of this period. By 280, however, control of the Wei kingdom had already shifted from its original ruling family, the Cao family, to the Sima clan. The Sima clan actually claimed the establishment of the Jin dynasty in 265, two years after the elimination of the Shu. As a result, historians associate different endings to the era, either 265 or 280.

Despite the fact that the era of the Three Kingdoms did not have any remarkable impact on China's political and economic systems, it is one of the most romanticized historical periods in Chinese history. Owing to the popularity of *Sanguo yanyi* (the Romance of the Three Kingdoms),[2] one of the most famous Chinese classics, many historical figures of the Three Kingdoms period have become household names in China, such as three sworn brothers, Liu Bei, Guan Yu, and Zhang Fei, who were not related in blood, but swore to be brothers for the rest of their lives, and Liu Bei's advisor, Zhuge Liang, who has become an icon as a scholar and military strategist.[3] The wars between the kingdoms, such as the Battle of Red Cliffs, have inspired movie producers and video game programmers. The four-hour Chinese movie *Red Cliff* (2009), for example, reconstructs the major events of the battle.

After the Three Kingdoms period, the political situation became even more chaotic. Historians of Chinese history usually do not consider the subsequent Jin dynasty (265–420) to be a major unified dynasty. It soon lost control of northern China, where as many as sixteen different kingdoms were established, and various nomadic groups, known together as *wu hu* (five barbaric tribes), controlled most of them. The Jin dynasty later moved its capital from Loyang, which was destroyed by the nomadic groups, to today's Nanjing in southern China, leaving the north in the hands of these nomadic groups. As a result, southern China and northern China developed separately for over a century during the era of what is known as the East Jin (317–420) period.[4]

One important cultural development in this chaotic era was the spread of Buddhism in China. By way of the Silk Road that connected China with India, Buddhist monks traveled to China to advocate this new faith. Buddhism was first embraced and patronized in China by the rulers of the kingdoms in northern China, where numerous Buddhist cave temples were built in a style similar to those in India.[5] Buddhism was probably known to the Chinese during the Han dynasty, but it had not been able to firmly establish itself until after the political decentralization that had prevailed in China ended.[6] With its basic message of learning to endure suffering, the new faith provided a new level of comfort to the Chinese, whose lives, at the time, were severely disrupted by the wars among competing kingdoms.[7] Moreover, some Buddhist doctrines, such as its emphasis on the "disdain of worldly power" and "the goal of inner contentment," were similar to Chinese Daoist tradition. In fact, some Chinese initially accepted Buddhism as a variant of Daoism, which had gained enormous popularity in Han China.[8]

As a result, the similarity between Buddhism, especially Mahayana Buddhism, and Daoism contributed to Buddhism's success in China at the time. Unlike Theravada Buddhism, the transformation of Buddha to a supreme godlike spirit in Mahayana Buddhism gave the Chinese a comfortable association with Daoist immortals and the mythical place of Penglai, where the immortals inhabited.[9] Early Buddhist monks deliberately explored the similarities between the Buddhism and Daoism in order to attract more Chinese adherents. Hucker notes that these monks deliberately combed the writings of Laozi and Zhuangzi, the two most important writers of Daoist classics, for "analogies that 'they could use to suggest Buddhist concepts that were utterly foreign to the Chinese tradition.'"[10] The similarity between the two led Daoist monks to make a strange argument that Lao Zi (Lao-tzu), the founder of Daoism, and the Buddha may have been the same person, since Lao Zi disappeared in his old age and may have eventually ended up in India to spread his doctrines in the form of Buddhism.[11] Moreover, the Chinese developed a number of Buddhist sects based on a single text or a particular practice. Two of them, *Jingtu* (Pure Land) and *Chan* (Zen), not only became popular in China, but were also influential in Korea and Japan.[12]

EMERGENCE OF THE SUI DYNASTY

Luo Guanzhong, the author of *The Romance of the Three Kingdoms*, wrote at the beginning of his book, "The empire, long divided, must unite; long united, must divide. Thus it has ever been."[13] This statement highlighted a pattern in Chinese imperial history, known as a "dynastic circle," which started with the Qin dynasty. After over 350 years of disunity, China was once again unified under a single dynasty, the Sui dynasty. Although the Sui is one of the shortest dynasties in Chinese history, it made some important achievements.

The Sui dynasty was established by a Chinese general, Yang Jian, who had served at the court of a northern kingdom, the northern Zhou.[14] Yang eventually usurped control of that kingdom, and from there, he started efforts toward the unification of China. In 581, he inaugurated a new dynasty, the Sui (581–618), at Chang'an, the former capital of the Qin and Han dynasties. With the help of other generals, he unified most of China and thus ended the over three centuries of chaos which had followed the end of the Han dynasty.[15] During his reign from 581 to 604, Yang Jian, known posthumously as Sui Wendi, proved to be one of the greatest Chinese emperors. He was open-minded enough to recognize the cultural differences between the north and the south that had developed during the age of separation. He adopted a flexible policy toward religion, endorsing various ideas, including Buddhism, Daoism, and Confucianism. The prudent administration of his court gave the country a few decades of much needed peace, and China started to recover from the previous destruction.[16]

One of the greatest achievements of Sui Wendi was his project to rebuild an old canal to connect his capital, Chang'an, in the north with the agriculturally rich south. Known later as the Grand Canal of China, it is by far the longest man-made canal in the world. Due to the efforts of Wendi and later Chinese emperors, the canal today stretches 1,103 miles; whereas, the Panama Canal is only 48 miles long and the Suez Canal is only 120 miles long.[17] Wendi's successful and profitable work for his dynasty, however, did not last long. His son, Yang Guang, known as Sui Yangdi (r. 604–618), soon undermined his father's achievements after he become the second emperor of the Sui. Inheriting a strong-mindedness from his parents, Yangdi was ambitious but impudent, reportedly ascending the throne through the poisoning of his father.[18] Although he continued most of his father's administrative and foreign policies, his passion for expansion and a lavish lifestyle brought destruction to the dynasty. He built an extravagant palace for himself at his new capital of Luoyang and ordered the reconstruction of the Great Wall before the Sui accomplished the project of the Grand Canal.[19]

Dreaming about military glories, he sent troops to areas as far away as central Vietnam, Taiwan, Central Asia, and Korea. After his army conquered northern Vietnam, he launched three consecutive field and naval campaigns to conquer northern Korea in 612, 613, and 614, but none of them was successful. Then he turned his attention to the Turkish people in Central Asia, but became discouraged after his enemy almost captured him in a battle in 617. After that, Yangdi fled to the south, leaving command of the military to one of his generals, Li Yuan (566–635), the Duke of Tang, who soon took advantage of massive domestic rebellions by engaging in battles against the Sui dynasty.[20] With the help of his sons, who were all excellent military generals, Li Yuan soon captured Chang'an, the old capital of the Sui, and made one of Yangdi's grandsons the new emperor in 617, despite the fact that Yangdi was still in power in the south. In the subsequent chaos, another general murdered Yangdi, and appointed one of Yangdi's other grandsons to the throne. Eventually, Li Yuan emerged as the strongest competitor and defeated all eleven other major power contenders.[21] In 618, he declared himself the emperor of his own dynasty, the Tang dynasty.

THE GLAMOROUS TANG DYNASTY

Li Yuan, canonized as Tang Gaozu (r. 618–626), thus inaugurated a new dynasty, the Tang Dynasty, which was one of the most powerful and successful dynasties in Chinese history. The imperial Li family, according to some scholars, symbolized a changed China. Although the family altered its past lineage in order to be somehow related to a former Han general, Li Yuan's sons could be considered as only half Chinese, due to the

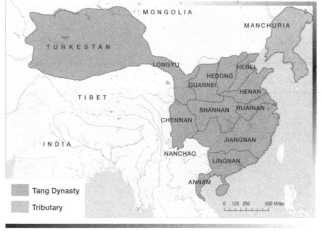

Map by Katie Pitchard

The Tang Empire

Turkish origin of their mother.[22] Although the Tang dynasty built up its power on top of the political, economic, and cultural strength of the Sui and the earlier northern dynasties, many scholars describe the Tang period as a golden era of the development of Chinese culture and an age of greatness comparable to the Han dynasty.[23]

Similar to the situation of the late Han dynasty, the early Tang dynasty was dominated by power struggles among Li Yuan's capable sons. His second son, Li Shimin (600–649), was especially vigorous in these struggles. It was he who actually provoked his father to rebel against Sui Yangdi in 617 and later helped him secure northern China.[24] In 626, Shimin murdered the crown prince and another brother and forced his father to name him as heir apparent. Li Yuan abdicated soon afterwards and passed the throne to Shimin, who was posthumously known as Tang Taizong (r. 626–649). Because of Taizong's great achievements for the Tang, some scholars deem Taizong as "the real founder of the dynasty" and one of "the most heroic rulers of all Chinese history."[25]

As emperor, Taizong continued his military success. Intimidated by his military power, the Turkish groups in Mongolia acknowledged him as their grand *khan* (a title in Mongolian or Turkic languages, equivalent to an emperor). He was the first Chinese ruler to obtain such power. He subjugated the Turkish tribes in the northwest and extended Chinese control to central Asia and into Afghanistan. The Tang dynasty maintained its domination of the Turkish groups for over half a century, and hence secured the Silk Road, along which Chinese and other merchants actively carried out international trade between China and Europe. Following Sui Yangdi's example, Taizong also made expeditions into the Korean peninsula, but had to retreat after encountering severe resistance.

Taizong was equally vigorous in his pursuit of political and economic policies. Chinese historians often described him as a model ruler, who ruled the country with fairness and benevolence, fostering education, economic developments, and religious tolerance. It was during his rule that Xuanzang, a Buddhist monk, made his famous sixteen-year trip to India and brought Buddhist scriptures back to China. *Xiyou ji* (The Journey to the West), a book based on his trip, is one of the most renowned Chinese classics. In addition, Taizong endorsed the request of Nestorian Christian missionaries, to build a church in Tang territory in central Asia.[26] The reign of Taizong laid the foundation for the prosperity of Tang dynasty, which by the early eighth century, was the wealthiest and most powerful empire in the world. Its capital had become "the largest city in the world and surpassed Constantinople in splendor."[27]

706 AD. Artist unknown.

A mural from a Tang era tomb

EMPRESS WU ZETIAN, CHINA'S FIRST AND ONLY WOMAN EMPEROR

Taizong's son, Gaozong (r. 649–683), continued his father's policies, but is probably best remembered for his affair with one of his father's concubines, Lady Wu. After he became the emperor, Gaozong recalled Lady Wu back from the Buddhist monastery where royal women often retreated after an emperor's death, and eventually made her his empress. After Gaozong died in 683, Empress Wu, or Wu Zhao to use her maiden name, became the regent for two of her sons, but in 690, she finally assumed the throne herself as Empress Wu Zetian (r. 690–705), and thus became the first and only woman emperor in Chinese history. She changed the name of the dynasty to Zhou, and ruled until 705, when a palace coup forced her to abdicate.[28] Traditional Chinese historians often portray Empress Wu as a usurper of power and blame her for many problems of the time. Actually, she was quite a capable ruler, especially in terms of foreign policy. As the wife of Gaozong, she had helped the emperor implement a vigorous policy toward Korea, which focused on supporting the state of Silla, one of the three competing powers of the Korean Peninsula, and the one that eventually unified Korea for the first time in its history.[29] Meanwhile, she is also well remembered for her efforts to foster an examination system for civil service appointments, a practice that gained full strength under the Song dynasty and remained a corner stone of Chinese imperial governance until it was abolished in 1905, toward the end of the Qing dynasty.

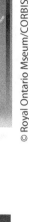

Tang era sculpture of a man and a horse

After Empress Wu's abdication, the Li family returned to power, and the Tang dynasty was restored. Several years later, the power went to Li Longji, known as Tang Xuanzong (r. 712–756), who restored the Tang dynasty to its earlier grandeur, and therefore came to be known as Tang Minghuang (emperor of brightness). Not only was he one of the most capable rulers in Chinese history, but he was also the greatest patron of Chinese art since Han Wudi.[30] Chinese culture flourished in all forms under his reign, especially in music, dance, painting, literature, and poetry.

Tang Minghuang's capital, Chang'an, had become a symbol of the splendor of the Tang and a cosmopolitan city

A Tang era celadon jar

which attracted many people from places outside of China, including Indians, Persians, Syrians, Vietnamese, Koreans, Japanese, Jews, Arabs, and Nestorian Christians.[31] The architecture and the structure of Chang'an later became a model for other East Asian countries, such as Japan, to emulate.[32] In order to attract more talent to his court, Xuanzong established the Hanlin Academy, which started a tradition of imperial sponsorship of talented scholars that influenced the subsequent Song Dynasty. His reign fostered some of the greatest literary geniuses in Chinese history, including the premier poets of Chinese tradition, Li Bai (Li Po, 701–762) and Du Fu (Tu Fu, 712–770).[33]

DECLINE OF THE TANG

Signs of trouble, however, began after a few decades of his reign. Xuanzong, who seemed to be tired of the tedious process of reviewing documents and conducting palace meetings with his chancellors, started to indulge himself in a luxurious lifestyle and surrounded himself with beautiful court women. At the age of 60, he fell in love with Yang Yuhuan, a 22-year-old concubine of one of his sons. Despite protests from his courtiers, Xuanzong made her one of his own royal consorts, giving her the title of Guifei (precious consort). Yang Guifei took advantage of the situation by having some of her relatives promoted to important positions. According to Hucker, she became the most notorious *femme fatale* in Chinese history.[34] Her second cousin, Yang Guozhong, dominated court politics for

Artist unknown.

A painting of an audience being given by Emperor Tang Xuanzong

years when Xuanzong detached himself from the court in order to spend more time with his beloved Guifei. This greatly upset Xuanzong's courtiers and generals, and one of them, An Lushan, rebelled against the Tang in 755. An Lushan's troops captured the capital, Chang'an, and forced Xuanzong to flee the city. On their way to Sichuan, Xuanzong's guards, who blamed Yang Guifei for all the trouble, forced Xuanzong to allow them to strangle her and throw her body into a pit. Extremely ashamed and depressed, Xuanzong abdicated from the throne and, a few years later, died of depression.[35]

An Lushan's rebellion was a turning point in the history of the Tang. The dynasty never fully recovered from the devastation caused by this rebellion and rapidly lost its vigor. None of the subsequent emperors were as strong and capable as the early, brilliant emperors, such as Taizong and Xuanzong. In addition to the social and economical disruption caused by An Lushan's and other rebellions, two important political changes further undermined the power of the Tang. In the domain of foreign policy, the Tang lost control of Central Asia. Except for the era of the Mongol-controlled Yuan dynasty (1271–1368), China did not return to the area until the Qing dynasty (1644–1911). Another political problem that haunted the late Tang dynasty was factionalism; powerful cliques of ministers, generals, and palace eunuchs had risen to prominence during the suppression of the rebellion. These cliques took advantage of the chaotic situation to start building their own dynasties and kingdoms. One aboriginal chieftain established the state of Nanzhao, which prospered in the Yunnan area until the tenth century. After a long political and economic decline, the Tang was once again devastated by a grand rebellion, and the last Tang emperor abdicated in 907.[36]

With the demise of the Tang, China plunged into chaos again for the next half century. Similar to the anarchic situation before the rise of the Sui, competing warlords fought against each other and established their own kingdoms and dynasties. As a result, the era between 907 and 960 is known as the Five dynasties and Ten kingdoms period. In the north, five dynasties rose and fell in quick sequence, whereas ten kingdoms contended against each other in the south, but none of them was strong enough to unify the entire south.

THE AUTOCRATIC SONG DYNASTY

The problem of half-century-long instability was gradually resolved with the establishment of a new state in the north, which eventually unified China again under the reign of the Song dynasty (960–1279). The founder of the Song dynasty was Zhao Kuangyin, a military general who initially served at the court of one of the dynasties in the north, the Late Zhou dynasty. Zhao engineered a coup against the young emperor of the Late Zhou and became the emperor of a new dynasty in 960. The Song dynasty period is divided into the Northern Song period (960–1127), during which the Song capital was at Kaifeng, and the Southern Song period (1127–1179), which began when a Song emperor moved his capital to Hangzhou.

Although the Song emperors often carried the dream of restoring the glory that had existed during the Tang dynasty, they never reached the same level of glamour in terms of Tang's territorial expansion and cosmopolitan style. They gave up controlling central Asia, the northern part of Korea, and the northern part of Vietnam, which had been controlled by the Chinese during the Han dynasty and the Tang dynasty, and redefined China's border along what is known as China proper.[37] The Song dynasty, however, presided over an era when the Chinese stabilized their political institutions and experienced unprecedented economic and commercial growth. The aristocracy that dominated early Chinese history fell apart during the Song dynasty and was replaced by scholarly officials chosen by rigorous civil service examinations.[38] During the Song dynasty, traditional Chinese culture fully developed in many areas, including literature, landscape painting, and porcelain artwork.

SONG TAIZU AND THE NORTHERN SONG

After Zhao Kuangyin, who was posthumously known as Song Taizu, became the emperor of the Song dynasty, he established his capital at Kaifeng and implemented a series of policies to stabilize the political situation. He gave up the aggressive foreign policies of the Tang and retreated militarily from the peripheral areas in the north and northwest in order to focus on campaigning against other Chinese kingdoms in the south.[39] After he finally unified China, Taizu concentrated on ensuring his supremacy and the loyalty of court officials. Learning a lesson from the factionalism of the late Tang dynasty, Taizu persuaded his capable generals to give up their military command in exchange for a generous pension, and he moved to eliminate the power of court eunuchs, who had often taken advantage of emperors' trust to advance their own wealth and interest. He greatly expanded the practice of recruiting court officials through civil service examinations and replaced hereditary aristocratic elites with newly recruited scholar-officials. This system opened the door to many highly talented people who tended to be loyal to the emperor, since their position almost entirely depended on imperial favor.[40] These talented officials greatly improved administrative efficiency.

Portrait of Song Taizu

© Charles & Josette Lenars/CORBIS

As a result, the civil service examinations, also known as the Imperial Examinations, reached their peak during the Song dynasty. The tradition started early in the Sui dynasty and may even be traced back to the era of Han Wudi, who asked for recommendations of talented people to take exams on Confucian classics. Wudi subsequently chose the best among the students to enter his service. The rulers of the Tang dynasty were the first to employ the civil service examinations to recruit court officials, but only on a limited scale.[41] Under the Song, however, the civil service examinations developed into a full-fledged system, which allowed all Chinese males to take the exams. The youngest recorded examinee was six whereas the oldest was sixty.[42]

All students needed to take three exams: one at the county level, one at the provincial level, and one at the capital level. They would earn consecutive titles, *xiucai*, *juren*, and *jinshi* as they passed each exam. The successful candidates would be placed in the administration according to their final scores. The higher the scores they achieved, the higher the positions they obtained. The most successful ones would enter the court, whereas the rest of them would be sent to provinces or counties. None of them, however, could go back to their own hometown, lest they would practice nepotism.[43] Also, these administrators could only stay on a post for three years before they were shifted to another one. Every three years, the examination system would produce about 20,000 capable scholarly bureaucrats who brought the real strength of the Song administration. This political system created by Taizu was much more efficient than the early bureaucracy dominated by aristocrats. It opened the door to men of merit regardless of their backgrounds and thus created a remarkable degree of social mobility that was unheard of "in any premodern society or even in many modern ones."[44] As a result, the Song political institution changed the Chinese political structure from aristocratic to autocratic. In other words, the Song political institution allowed the emperor to enjoy a high concentration of power and loyalty from his bureaucrats, instead of having to share power with competing aristocrats.

Taizu died relatively young at the age of 41 before he could fulfill all of his ambitions. Fortunately, his brother, known as Song Taizong (r. 976–997), continued Taizu's policies. After two failed military expeditions against the Kitan, who had established their Liao dynasty (947–1125) on China's northern borders, Taizong made peace agreements with the Kitans and promised the Liao generous annual gifts in exchange for their peace agreement with China. Thanks to the capable reigns of Taizu and Taizong, China, under the early Song dynasty, experienced much needed political and domestic stability.[45]

Similar to the situation of the early dynasties, however, the subsequent rulers of the Song dynasty didn't have the ambition and vigor of the founding emperors. Most of the Song emperors after Taizong spent a lot of time pursuing personal interests and pleasure, leaving the administration of the court in the hands of their ministers. Fortunately, these ministers, chosen through the vigorous process of the civil service examinations, were tremendously talented. As a result, these ministers could push forward reforms to solve the problems of the dynasty, even without the spirited leadership of the emperor.

Map by Katie Pitchard

The Northern Song Dynasty

Fan Zhongyan (989–1052) was the first of such reformers. Fan's highly moralized statement, "the true scholar should be the first to become anxious about the world's troubles and the last to enjoy his happiness," became the motto for later Confucian scholars.[46] Although Fan's reforms were eventually sabotaged by conservatives, Wang Anshi (1021–1086), one of his protégés and later a chief councilor of Emperor Shenzong, carried out vigorous reforms in many areas, including the economy, fiscal administration, the military, education, and personnel recruitment. Wang's reforms saved the dynasty from a crisis that it was experiencing at the time.[47] Interestingly enough, many conservatives were gifted scholars themselves. For example, both Ouyang Xiu (1007–1072) and Sima Guang (1019–1086), who opposed Wang's reforms, were gifted poets and painters, and another conservative, known as Su Shi or Su Dongpo (1037–1101), was one of the most famous Song literati. These scholars, whether they were reformers or conservatives, were more famous in Chinese history for their literary achievements than their political careers.[48]

The military weakness of the Song eventually cost the dynasty the northern half of its territories. The situation on the northern Chinese border had become increasingly messy. After having kept their promise of peace with China for several decades, the Liao dynasty resumed its military actions and gradually extended its control over large areas of northern China. Meanwhile, the Tangut, who were probably a mixture of Tibetan and Mongolic minorities, established their dynasty, the Xi Xia (West Xia, 1038–1227), in northern China. The third power group, the Jurchens, the ancestors of the Manchus, who would establish China's last dynasty, the Qing dynasty, also entered the competition in northern China. The Jurchens, at first, cooperated with the Song and helped drive the Liao out to Central Asia, but after that, they broke their alliance with the Song and established their own Jin dynasty (1115–1234). In 1125, they marched southward and besieged the Song capital, Kaifeng, but retreated after the Song emperor accepted their terms. The Song, however, failed to follow up with the agreed terms, and the angry Jurchens returned in 1127. This time, they sacked the Song capital and took Emperor Huizong and 3,000 other captives back to their kingdom.[49] The Song reestablished its court in Hangzhou, a city south of Shanghai, and thus started the new era of the Southern Song.[50] In 1142, the new Song emperor agreed to cede to the Jurchens the areas north of the Yangtze River, thus officially acknowledging the Jurchens' incorporation of the area into their dynasty, the Jin.

THE SOUTHERN SONG AND THE DEVELOPMENT OF JIANGNAN.

Similar to the late Northern Song, the Southern Song was characterized by weak emperors, but capable councilors. During the Southern Song, the chief councilors obtained even greater power than those in the same position had had in the Northern Song. They extended their control over the whole officialdom without much interference from the emperor.[51] The problem was that the high officials at the court were divided between those who wanted to maintain peace with the Jurchens of the Jin dynasty and those who desired to recover the northern territory. Factionalism weakened the Southern Song court. Weakened leadership, however, did not seem to have a strong impact on economic and cultural development. Far away from the troubled northern border, the south enjoyed an economic and cultural boom throughout the entire Southern Song period. Many Chinese, including the talented and the wealthy, migrated to the south because of the instability in the north. As a result, the important commercial centers shifted from the region around the Yellow River to the Yangtze River valley, and the south experienced an economic and cultural boom that it had never experienced before.

The thriving economy in the south was partially the result of the cultivation and processing of tea, which had originally been brought to China from India and Southeast Asia. Tea was initially used for medicinal purposes, but during the Tang dynasty, it was generally used as a stimulant and hence became a popular beverage. The climate in southern China was suitable for growing tea

Paper money from the Northern Song dynasty. Paper money had been invented in China by the late eighth or early ninth century. The first Western paper money was issued in 1661 in Sweden.

bushes, and the large population could easily fulfill the needs of the labor-intensive tea industry. The trade volume of tea and other commodities became so large that the traditional means of monetary transactions, copper coins, were no longer practical. Instead, Chinese merchants began to pay for large transactions with paper monetary notes, which were created by block printing, a technology that had been available since the Tang dynasty. The court usually insured these paper money notes.

Booming commerce led to the further development of urbanization. The Song dynasty, in both the era of the Northern Song and the era of the Southern Song, experienced the industrialization of its cities. Similar to the previous Song capital, Kaifeng, the new capital, Hangzhou, quickly developed into a metropolis with millions of residents. Many other cities mushroomed in the south. Suzhou and Fuzhou, for example, had a population that well exceeded one million, and there were at least six other cities located between them. With a population of over 1.5 million, the capital, Hangzhou, was "the biggest, the richest, the most populous, and altogether the most marvelous city,"[52] which was "not matched in the Western world until the nineteenth century."[53]

During the Southern Song period and during the subsequent Yuan dynasty (1271–1368), the volume of China's overseas trade was far larger than that of Europe at its own trading peak in the late nineteenth century. Many cities in the south became important centers of maritime trade, and Chinese entrepreneurs advanced their commercial interests in other Asian areas. Merchant ships from Southeast Asia and India swarmed into the harbors along China's southeast coast. Marco Polo (1254–1324), who travelled from Venice, Italy, estimated that the number of ships that came into the busy seaport of Quan Zhou, in today's Fujian province, on a single day was larger than the number of the ships that anchored at Venice or Genoa in a whole year.[54] Using newly developed technology, Chinese ocean-going ships carried Chinese merchants into the Philippines, Java, Vietnam, Thailand, and Malaya. According to Rhoads Murphey, it was the maritime technology that was perfected during the Song dynasty that prepared China for its famous maritime explorations during the Ming.[55]

Once again, military weakness against an enemy to the north proved to be disastrous for the Song. A new and more dangerous enemy loomed in the north and soon devastated the Southern Song. Inspired by their legendary leader, Chinggis Khan, the aggressive Mongols took control of Hangzhou in 1276 and thus ended the Southern Song dynasty in 1279. The last imperial heir of the Song was drowned off the coast of Canton during the last naval battle of the Song fleet.[56]

PHILOSOPHY, LITERATURE AND ARTS DURING THE TANG AND SONG

The era of the Tang and the Song is widely known as the golden era of the development of Chinese culture. The Tang emperors revitalized Chinese culture in the style of the Han dynasty, even though the early founding emperors were part Chinese and part Turkish.[57] The cultural boom continued during the Song dynasty, and as a result, the era of the Tang and the Song saw the flourishing of Chinese culture, from political culture to the visual arts and music. In terms of Chinese political tradition, one important change during the Song dynasty concerned the function of the emperor, which had changed from the head of an aristocratic state to an absolute ruler. This same autocratic style continued to define the relationship between the emperor and his courtiers until the end of imperial China. If a Tang emperor sat to discuss national affairs with his councilors, these councilors would likely be aristocrats who were not much different from the emperor himself. A Song emperor, on the other hand, who had been transformed into an autocrat, was high above his bureaucracy, which mainly consisted of scholar-officials. Most subsequent imperial rulers, Chinese or non-Chinese, followed the Song model, and by the time of the Ming and the Qing dynasties, councilors and other court officials had to follow rigid protocol, which required them to kneel at the presence of the emperor.[58]

Another political tradition developed in the Tang-Song era exerted great influence over China. Ever since the Song dynasty, the rigorous civil service examinations by which court officials were recruited influenced millions of Chinese. Education had become the most effective way for the talented, politically ambitious, but underprivileged person to pursue his dreams. This practice enticed millions of Chinese families to invest heavily in their children's education for the sake of their or their family's future, a practice that continues even today. The civil service exams also helped perpetuate the official ideology, Confucianism. During the Tang dynasty, Buddhism gained considerable prominence because of royal patronage. Tang emperors patronized Buddhist establishments and clergy, and built many Buddhist monasteries, granting them money and tax-free lands. Although Confucianism never lost its prestige, the Tang dynasty represented a golden era of Buddhist development in China. Some Buddhist monks even served as advisors to the emperor.

The Song emperors, returning to early Han policies, revered Confucianism as the sole national ideology and strengthened their position through the implementation of the civil service examinations. Confucian classics were the most important subjects for the exams, and without knowledge of them, one could not pass the exams. Confucian scholars, as a result, dominated the Song court. New interpretations of Confucian classics, known as Neo-Confucianism, emerged during the Song dynasty. In a sense, Neo-Confucianism was an intellectual response to the earlier booming of Buddhism during the Tang dynasty. Zhu Xi (1130–1200), who was largely responsible for this development, incorporated ideas from both Buddhism and Daoism with the intention of proving that Confucianism was indeed desirable. One of the well-known motifs of Neo-Confucianism was portrayed in a painting where Confucius, Buddha, and Lao Zi are all drinking out of the same jar. This illustrated the Neo-Confucian slogan of "the three teachings are in one!"[59]

In Neo-Confucianism, Zhu Xi advocated a dynamic combination of dual concepts, *li* (abstract principles) and *qi* (matter).[60] *Li* would never change in any way, and the ultimate expression of all *li*, according to Zhu Xi, was *taiji*, (the supreme ultimate), which in a sense is similar to Dao in Daoism and dhamma in Buddhism. All men were equipped with the same *li*, but *qi* was responsible for the differences. The polluted *li*, according to Zhu Xi, could be compared to a pearl that was buried in mud. In this sense, Confucianism would serve as a tool to help purify *li* from polluting *qi* for those who would follow Confucian ethical guidance towards self-cultivation. Through the explanation of how the dual concept of *li* and *qi* would work, Zhu Xi incorporated metaphysical explanations of the world and worldly behavior into Confucianism, explanations which came from the core of both Buddhism and Daoism. Neo-Confucianism developed in the Song dynasty and later influenced philosophical thinking in Japan and Korea.

Chinese literature reached its height during the Tang and Song era. Tang poetry, for example, represents the highest achievement of Chinese poetry, even today.[61] Through the patronage of the emperors, Chinese poetry entered its golden age during the Tang dynasty, and poem writing became a daily activity for the educated. An eighteenth century anthology of Tang poems, *Quan tang shi* (Complete Tang Poetry), contains about 48,900 poems from about 2,300 poets, among whom, Li Bai, Du Fu, and Bai Juyi (772–846) stand out as the best.[62] Li Bai was one of the most famous Chinese poets and probably the most productive as well. Among his 20,000 poems, 1,800 pieces, which cover a wide range of subjects reflecting his flamboyant personality, have survived.[63] He was known as a Daoist wanderer and a wine lover. It is said that some of his best poems were produced in his drunken ecstasy, and that wine was an important theme and metaphor throughout his poetry. Even the legend of his death was related to wine drinking. Although this story may not be historically true, he is said to have drowned while reaching out for the moon after a heavy dose of drink alone on a boat, since he only touched the reflection of the moon and fell off the boat.[64]

In comparison to Li Bai, Du Fu was a much more serious writer. Having experienced social turmoil caused by the loss of many territories in the north and the An Lushan rebellion, Du Fu was deeply concerned with human suffering. Many of his poems deal with heavy subjects such as war, social anxiety, and political disturbance.[65] Similarly, Bai Juyi, who was an official member of the Hanlin Academy and the best-loved poet of the late Tang dynasty, also had a strong sense of social responsibility. The most famous among his 2,800 poems are his two long narrative poems, *Chang hen ge* (The Song of Everlasting Sorrow), which tells the story of Tang Xuanzong and Yang Guifei, and *Pipa xing* (The Song of the Pipa Player).[66] Through the achievements of these great Tang poets, Tang poetry exerted considerable influence over cultures outside of China, and Tang poets were celebrated in countries such as Japan, Korea, and Vietnam.

The Tang style of poetry continued during the subsequent Song dynasty, and many officials at the Song court were working poets. During the Song dynasty, some particular forms of lyric poems, known as *ci* or *Song ci* (Song poetic style), became popular. Most of the Tang poems or *Tang shi* employed equal lengths of sentences, such as five characters or seven characters per sentence, and the Tang poems were also expected to have a fixed length. *Song ci,* on the other hand, allowed variation in sentence lengths, as well as in tempo when they were set to tunes. As mentioned earlier, many Song scholar-officials were actually remembered more as great literary figures than as important statesmen. For example, Ouyang Xiu (1007–1072), a major player of the political reform of 1043–1045, was recognized more as a versatile literary master than a reformer.[67] Not only were his poems in *ci* style instrumental in driving the popularity of this style, but he also revitalized a classical prose style, known as *guwen* (old-style prose), which emphasized clarity and directness instead of fancy rhetoric. The *guwen* style had first been developed by some acclaimed Tang scholars, such as Han Yu (768–842) and Liu Zongyuan (773–819). Ouyang invented new genres of prose based on the early style. The purpose of his promotion of the *guwen* may have been a practical one—to encourage Confucian scholars to write their memorandums to the emperor in a clear style so that the emperor would pay more attention to their opinions.

Another famed scholar of the Song dynasty was Su Shi, who was a government official in charge of a few cities, including Hangzhou, Xuzhou, and Minzhou. Like many other scholar officials, he is also best remembered for his literary achievements. One of the most versatile scholar-officials during the Song dynasty, he was an accomplished writer in poetry, both in the styles of Tang *shi* and Song *ci*, prose, and travel literature. He left behind him a rich cultural heritage of about 2,700 poems and numerous pieces of prose.[68] Su Shi, along with many other eminent Song scholars, was also famous for his calligraphy. Calligraphy played an essential role in the civil service examinations since beautiful handwriting could only increase the chance of getting a positive response from the examination officials.

The Tang and Song era also saw the vigorous development of the writing of history and the development of early Chinese historiography. The Chinese tradition that the government is responsible for compiling an official history started with the Tang dynasty's official historiographic commission, which compiled the history of the previous Sui dynasty.[69] Song scholars followed a similar tradition. Ouyang Xiu, one of the most prominent Song scholars, participated in the composition of the official history of the Tang Dynasty.[70] The Tang and Song historians added a few new genres, such as *Shilu* (True Records) and *Hanlin zhi* (History of Hanlin [academy]), to the Chinese historical tradition. *Shilu* was a particular style of history, which recorded detailed court chronicles for each emperor, and thus has become invaluable resources for later historians who study the Tang history. *Hanlin zhi* was a short history of Tang Hanlin Academy, and thus initiated a tradition of writing histories of particular institutions.

The visual arts were another area in which the artists of the Tang and Song period scored noticeable achievements. Tang visual arts reflected the cosmopolitan nature of the era; it was an artistic style that blended traditional Chinese influences with Buddhist, Indian, Persian, and Central Asian influences. Although early Tang paintings inherited the earlier Chinese styles, which usually focused on figure painting, the subjects, colors, and techniques used in paintings changed dramatically during the Tang and Song dynasties. Because of the influence of Buddhist culture, Tang artists used colors that were both brighter and darker, especially in their religious paintings, than the colors that had normally been used in the traditional Chinese paintings of earlier periods.

By late Tang, landscape painting, a style that influenced not only the painters in the next Song dynasty, but also the artistic values of the neighboring countries, such as Korea and Japan, had become popular. The artists of the Song dynasty refined many of the developments of the Tang dynasty. They brought many techniques developed during the Tang to full maturity in their watercolor landscape paintings. The Song court was filled with talented scholar-officials who greatly contributed to the achievements of Song painting, especially during the time of the Southern Song. Some of the Song emperors were talented painters themselves. Song Huizong, who lost northern China to the Khitan, was a renowned artist, in addition to being a great patron of the arts. He established the Hanlin Imperial Painting Academy, which was responsible for developing a style of realistic watercolor landscape paintings.

In the south, an impressionistic style of monochromatic landscape paintings became popular. This style was probably influenced by the abstract or metaphysical philosophies of Neo-Confucianism developed during the Song dynasty. Many painters who belonged to this school were drawn to Daoist interpretations of nature. To them, expression was more important than representation, and as a result, painting was only a way to realize the eternal Dao, and was merely used as a tool to reveal their feelings. Many Chinese classical paintings were put on scrolls, which were made of a mixture of thick layers of paper and silk, and had wooden cylindrical bars on each end. The length of these scrolls varied, usually from three to ten feet long, and some were even longer.[71] The original of one of the most famous paintings of the Song dynasty, *Qingming shanghe tu*, (Along the River during the Qingming Festival), is over seventeen feet in length and about one foot in width.[72] The paintings of the Song dynasty, as well as those from the subsequent Yuan dynasty, (1271–1368) are considered "the apogee of painting in traditional China,"[73] and landscape painting is considered China's greatest contribution to the history of artistry.[74]

The Tang and Song dynasties also witnessed great technological developments. Many cultural achievements in historiography, religion/philosophy, poetry, prose writing, and painting may not have been possible without the continuing development of technology during the Tang and the Song dynasties. While the invention of paper during the early Han dynasty had greatly facilitated scholarly events, the development of printing in the seventh century further boosted the extent of literary activities.[75] For example, woodblock printing, which gradually moved toward the direction of movable type, made it possible for scholars to share ideas and their works with a larger audience than they ever could before. Moreover, many of the invaluable paintings, poems, historical and lyric writings, and calligraphies may have never reached our modern age without the continued improvement in the quality of paper and ink. Many classical works of Buddhism and Confucianism were printed and reproduced in thousands of copies during the Song dynasty. Although the volume of produced works was still relatively small, the preserved written materials are precious resources for later scholars who want to gain knowledge of the Tang, the Song and even the earlier dynasties.[76]

Improved technologies also enabled the artists of the Tang and the Song dynasties to produce more refined pieces of porcelain. Tang artists were famous for their production of *sancai* (three colors) ceramics, a type of lead-glazed earthenware in the figure of horses, camels, or people. The artists used different materials, such as copper (for green color), iron (for brownish yellow color) and manganese or cobalt (for blue color), to produce a polychrome effect.[77] Today, Tang *sancai* figurines are among the most sought out items for collectors. The artists during the Song dynasty also developed techniques of producing more colors. For example, they produced celadon, which was grayish blue in color.[78] Before the development of the tea trade in the eighteenth century, Chinese porcelain, with different designs and colors, was the most popular Chinese export. Chinese merchants carried porcelain pieces to Europe, Central Asia, the Mediterranean, and Southeast Asia. Examples of the early Chinese porcelain are preserved in museums around the world.

For more information about the topics discussed in this chapter, please visit the website for this textbook. This website can be accessed from http://www.grtep.com/.

1 Hucker, *Imperial*, 133.
2 There are several translations with different English titles. See for example, Lo Kuan-chung, *Romance of the Three Kingdoms*, trans. by Robert Hegel, and Intro. by C.H. Brewitt-Taylor (Boston:Tuttle Publishing, 2002); Luo Guanzhong, *Three Kingdoms*, trans. by Moss Robert, (Beijing: Foreign Languages Press, 1995); and Luo Guanzhong, *Three Kingdoms: a Historical Novel*, trans. by Moss Robert (Los Angeles: University of California Press, 2004).
3 Hucker, *Imperial*, 134.
4 Hucker, *Imperial*, 134–136.
5 Murphey, *History*, 134; and Hucker, *Imperial*, 137.
6 Hucker, *Imperial*, 209–210; and Wright, *History*, 62.
7 Wright, *History*, 62–64.
8 For more on Daoism in Han era, see Hucker, *Imperial*, 201–206.
9 Hucker, *Imperial*, 203.
10 Hucker, *Imperial*, 210.
11 Hucker, *Imperial*, 216–217.
12 Hucker, *Imperial*, 213–215.
13 Luo Guanzhong, *Three Kingdoms*, trans. by Moss Robert, 3.
14 Hucker, *Imperial*, 137–138.
15 Murphey, *History*, 134.
16 Hucker, *Imperial*, 138.
17 Joseph Needham, Science and Civilization in China: Volume 4, *Physics and Physical Technology, Part 3, Civil Engineering and Nautics.* (Taipei: Cambridge University Press, 1971), 307.
18 Hucker, *Imperial*, 138–139.
19 Murphey, *History*, 135; and Hucker, *Imperial*, 138–139.
20 Hucker, *Imperial*, 138–139; and Wright, *History*, 68
21 Hucker, *Imperial*, 140.
22 Hucker, *Imperial*, 140 .
23 Murphey, *History*, 135; and Hucker, *Imperial*, 139–140.
24 Hucker, *Imperial*, 140.
25 Hucker, *Imperial*, 140.
26 Hucker, *Imperial*, 141–142.
27 Wright, *History*, 69.
28 Hucker, *Imperial*, 142.
29 Hucker, *Imperial*, 143; and Wright, *History*, 69.
30 Wright, *History*, 69.
31 Murphey, *History*, 138; and Wright, *History*, 72.
32 Murphey, *History*, 138–39.
33 Hucker, *Imperial*, 143.

34 Hucker, *Imperial*, 143.

35 Hucker, *Imperial*, 144.

36 Hucker, *Imperial*, 146–47.

37 Murphey, *History*, 140.

38 Hucker, *Imperial*, 267.

39 Hucker, *Imperial*, 269–271; and Wright, *History*, 74–75.

40 Hucker, *Imperial*, 270; and Murphey, *History*, 140.

41 Wright, *History*, 70.

42 Hucker, *Imperial*, 315–322.

43 Murphey, *History*, 140–141

44 Murphey, *History*, 141, 315–321.

45 Wright, *History*, 77.

46 Hucker, *Imperial*, 274.

47 Hucker, *Imperial*, 274; and Murphey, *History*, 143–144.

48 Hucker, *Imperial*, 274–275.

49 Hucker, *Imperial*, 275–276.

50 Murphey, *History*, 144–146

51 Hucker, *Imperial*, 307–308.

52 Murphey, *History*, 146.

53 Hucker, *Imperial*, 278.

54 Hucker, *Imperial*, 278; and Murphey, *History*, 146.

55 Rhoads Murphey, *East Asia: A New History*, (Harlow, England: Longman, 1996), 114.

56 Hucker, *Imperial*, 279.

57 Wright, *History*, 69.

58 Hucker, *Imperial*, 303–305; and Wright, *History*, 82

59 John W. Head, *China's Legal Soul: The Modern Chinese Legal Identity in Historical Context* (Durham, NC Carolina Academic Press, 2009), 168.

60 Wright, *History*, 81.

61 Wright, *History*, 71.

62 Hucker, *Imperial*, 236.

63 Hucker, *Imperial*, 246–247; Murphey, *East Asia*, 135; and Duiker and Spielvogel, *World History*, 395.

64 Hucker, *Imperial*, 247; and Duiker and Spielvogel, *World History*, 395.

65 Hucker, *Imperial*, 249–251.

66 Hucker, *Imperial*, 252.

67 Hucker, *Imperial*, 387–388

68 Hucker, *Imperial*, 396; and Duiker and Spielvogel, *World History*, 394.

69 Hucker, *Imperial*, 227.

70 Hucker, *Imperial*, 389.

71 Duiker and Spielvogel, *World History*, 399.

72 Karen Hosack Janes, *Great Paintings: The World's Masterpieces Explored and Explained* (New York: DK Adult., 2011), 10.

73 Duiker and Spielvogel, *World History*, 398.

74 Hucker, *Imperial*, 262.

75 Duiker and Spielvogel, *World History*, 393.

76 Duiker and Spielvogel, *World History*, 393–394.

77 Nigel Wood, *Chinese Glazes:Their Origins, Chemistry, and Recreation* (London: A & C Black Publishing, 1999), 200–202.

78 Duiker and Spielvogel, *World History*, 400.

Chapter 7: Early and Medieval Japan and Korea

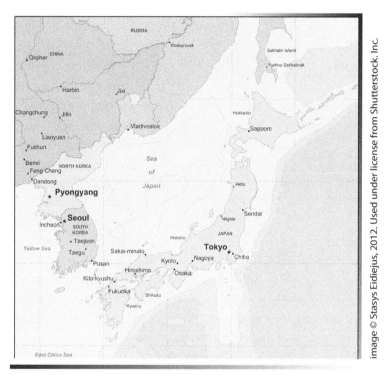

Present-day Japan, South Korea, and North Korea

image © Stasys Eidiejus, 2012. Used under license from Shutterstock. Inc.

Japan and Korea are both situated near one of the earliest centers of civilization, China, and as a result, were influenced by Chinese culture. Both of them, however, have long histories of their own with significantly distinctive features, even if their early history was somewhat overshadowed by their powerful neighbor, China. This chapter will cover the early and medieval eras of these two countries.

JAPAN, THE LAND AND THE PEOPLE

As mentioned earlier, geography often plays a principle role in shaping a civilization. Japan is an island country, which consists of four main islands: Hokkaido, Honshu, Shikoku, and Kyushu, from the north to the south. Hokkaido is just south of Sakhalin island in Russia, while Kyushu is southeast of Korea. Three thousand other islands are scattered along the coasts of the main islands, but only some of these islands are big enough to sustain human societies. There is also an important island chain, the Ryukyu Islands, which stretches from south of Kyushu toward Taiwan. In comparison to the British Isles, Japan is more isolated from the continent. While the Strait of Dover that separate

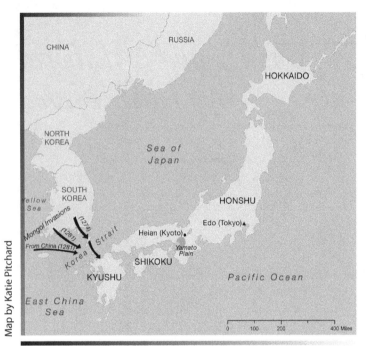

Map by Katie Pitchard

Japan

rate England from France is 21 miles wide, the Tsushima Strait that divides Kyushu from the Korean Peninsula is about 115 miles.[1] The straits not only protected Japan from the Mongol invasions in the thirteenth century, they also gave Japan enough distance from its neighbors for Japan to maintain a large degree of autonomy and control over its own affairs.

The distance of Japan from the continent is thus one of the most important reasons why Japan could develop its own distinctive features without much interruption. It could voluntarily adopt new ideas from its neighbors without the danger of being overwhelmed by a foreign culture. Changes usually came from within instead of being forced upon the Japanese by an outside invasion. This was an advantage that Japan enjoyed during its formative stages; an advantage which Korea and Vietnam did not have during their early histories. Other than the Allied Occupation after World War II, Japan seldom experienced the threat of a foreign invasion. As a result, indigenous cultures were able to survive into the modern era. The Japanese enjoy a traditional game of Sumo wrestling the same way as they enjoy a baseball or soccer game, and a performance of the Noh drama attracts as many enthusiastic audiences as a rock concert.

In comparison to China or the United States, Japan is a small country in terms of land area. Japan is about the same size as the state of Montana or California. However, if it is compared with the nations in Europe, it is not as small as it may seem. It is larger than Great Britain, Germany, and Italy.[2] In today's world, Japan is definitely a big country in terms of population. It traditionally has a larger population than many of the European countries, and in 2010, Japan's population was over 126 million, ranking tenth among the most populous countries in the world. In terms of economy, Japan is definitely a modern giant. Scholars often describe Japan's rapid economic development after World War II as a miracle. Japan's economy became the second largest in the world in 1985, only after the United States, and was only surpassed by China in 2010.[3] Still, it will probably continue to hold the third position for the next several years.

Surrounded by the ocean, Japan's climate is generally mild, but with a variety of weather patterns because of the long stretch of its islands. Hokkaido lies at the same latitude as New England; whereas Kyushu is at the same latitude as the state of Georgia, although Kyushu has more subtropical features than Georgia. In winter, northern Japan can sometimes have as deep as six feet of snow on the ground, but its coasts on the southern Pacific seldom see any snow at all.[4] Its long coastal lines provide beautiful sceneries for tourists and provide for the livelihood of the locals.

Japan is rather mountainous with 73 percent of its territory covered by mountain ranges. Every main island has a mountain range in the middle, and Honshu, the largest island, has at its center an active volcano, Mount Fuji, which is the highest mountain in Japan. The land that is suitable for agriculture is less than 15 percent of the total terrain.[5] Most Japanese peasants settle at the narrow river valleys or plains along the coast. Lack of adequate arable land has made it difficult for Japan to maintain its large population. Agriculture, therefore, has always been a high priority for the Japanese government. Japan is divided into forty-seven administrative units, which include three metropolitans, Tokyo, Osaka, and Kyoto, and forty-three prefectures.[6] These administrative units vary greatly in size and in population.

Ethnically, Japan is traditionally considered to be a more homogenous society than other countries. About 96 percent of Japanese people belong to the same Mongoloid race, known in Japan as the *Yamato* race. Recent research, however, indicates that there is more ethnic variety in Japan than people usually assume. Other than Koreans, who have lived in Japan since the beginning of its civilization, the second largest minority group in Japan is the Ainu, who are noticeably different from other Japanese people, both physically and linguistically.[7] A full blood Ainu has lighter skin and more body hair than other Japanese people do. The origin of the Ainu is still under debate. The proposed theories of their origin include the Caucasoid Theory, the Oceania Race Theory, the Old Asian Race Theory, the Solitary Race Theory, and the double Mongoloid Theory. Most scholars, however, agree that the Ainu are indigenous people who are descendants of the people from the Jomon era (ca.10000 to 250 BCE), the earliest identified era in Japanese history.[8] The Ainu originally inhabited northern Honshu, but later discrimination against them pushed them further north to Hokkaido, where they were the chief inhabitants until the twentieth century. It was not until 2008 that the Japanese Diet passed a bill urging the government to recognize officially that the Ainu are "indigenous to Japan."[9] Today, there are about 25,000 people registered as Ainu in Japan.

There is also cultural diversity in Japan. One such example is the culture of the Okinawans from the Ryukyu Islands. There were ancient kingdoms on the Ryukyu Islands since the twelfth century, and between the fifteenth and nineteenth centuries, the Ryukyu Kingdom controlled Okinawa and most of the Ryukyu Islands. Taking advantage of its strategic position between China, Japan, and Korea, the kingdom prospered from the maritime trade in the region. It also developed its own culture, which is a mixture of Japanese, Korean, and Chinese cultures. In 1609, Japan invaded the islands and brought them under the control of the Satsuma lord. Japanese control, however, was exercised through the Okinawan king. Ironically, under the Tokugawa bakufu, neither the Japanese shogun nor the Okinawans considered the Japanese and the Okinawans to be the same people. The shogun and the Satsuma *daimyo* (big name, a feudal lord in Japan) tried their best to make sure that the Ryukyu Islands remained as foreign soil, forbidding the Okinawans from adopting Japanese names, clothes, customs, and language. Japan continued to rule the area through the Okinawan kings until 1879, when it formally annexed the Ryukyu Islands. At the end of World War II, the United States occupied Okinawa and only returned it to Japan in 1960. As a result, many Okinawans feel that they are culturally different.

Similar to the situation of other cultures, the so-called homogenous Japanese race and culture may have been the result of a long-term assimilation of ethnic differences. Peter Duus, for example, makes the following statement concerning the diversity in Japanese society:

> "To late Tokugawa Japanese, what would have been most noticeable when they
> traveled away from their native places was not similarity or familiarity but immense
> diversity and variety. The most important cultural boundary separated the eastern and
> western parts of the country. Since the thirteenth century, the region west of the bar-
> rier station at Otsu became known as *Kanto* ("east of the barrier") in contrast to the
> *Kansai* region ("west of the barrier"). While this political boundary lost significance
> over time, as a cultural boundary it remained an important dividing line on mental
> maps of the country."[10]

EARLY JAPANESE HISTORY

What historians know about early Japanese history comes from a combination of contemporary Chinese written records, later Japanese accounts of their creational myths, and archaeological evidence. One of the earliest accounts of Japan in Chinese histories mentions a route from Korea to Japan with a detailed description of the people who lived on the islands of Japan as early as the second century CE. At that time China was under the Han dynasty, during which it established colonies in North Korea. According to the accounts of some Chinese travelers who visited Japan from Korea, the inhabitants of Kyushu had been organized into more than one hundred clans. These accounts were compiled no later than 191 CE, and these Han records remain to be the earliest mentioning of Japan.[11]

Other than an occasional mention of the Japanese, the Chinese records do not paint a clear picture of early Japanese history. Early Japanese records, on the other hand, focused on the creational myth of Japan. Two of the earliest Japanese histories, *Kojiki* (Record of Ancient Matters), written in 712 CE; and *Nihon shoki* or *Nihongi* (History of Japan), written in 720 CE, put together creational myths centered around a divine brother and sister, who gave birth to the islands of Japan and a group of deities, among whom the Sun Goddess Amaterasu was especially influential. Amaterasu later sent her grandson, Ninigi, to Kyushu, giving him what was known as "the Three Imperial Regalia," namely a bronze mirror, which is the symbol of the Sun Goddess, an iron sword, and a necklace of "curved jewels."[12] Ninigi's great grandson, known posthumously as Emperor Jimmu, "the Divine Warrior," conquered Honshu and established the first Japanese state of Yamato in 660 BCE. Emperor Jimmu, therefore, is assumed to be the ancestor of all of the subsequent Japanese emperors, or *Tenno* in Japanese. Because of this connection to the Sun Goddess, Amaterasu, through Jimmu, the Japanese emperor was considered divine until 1945.[13]

Archaeologists found evidence that the Japanese archipelago was first inhabited as early as 5,000 BCE. The earliest period in Japanese history is known as the Jomon period, which lasted from approximately 4500 BCE to 250 BCE. The term Jomon means "cordmaking," which describes a dominant pattern of pottery dating back to that period. People in the Jomon era were hunters and gatherers.

Artist unknown.

Jomon Pottery

Around 250 BCE a new culture, known as the Yayoi culture, emerged; it was named after a famous excavation site and lasted from about 250 BCE to 250 CE. The Yayoi people had employed irrigation systems for rice cultivation and made use of technology to produce bronze artifacts and iron tools. The origin of the Yayoi culture, however, is still under debate. Chinese coins and bronze mirrors from the Han dynasty were among the uncovered artifacts from Yayoi; these items indicated the influence of a culture which had newly developed in Han China—the bronze and iron culture.[14] Archaeological evidence also revealed influence from the Korean Peninsula. In fact, the new culture started in northern Kyushu, slowly spread to Honshu and may have eventually merged with the old Jomon culture. Scholars, however, detected distinction between the Yayoi and the old Jomon cultures, and the distinction was clearly indicated by the different styles of pottery and the different ways in which the pottery was produced. Yayoi pottery was decorated differently from Jomon pottery, and the Yayoi made pottery with a pottery wheel, instead of by hand. This evidence illustrated cultural influences from Korea and China, and later gave rise to a theory of invaders from Korea to Japan. Other scholars point out that immigration alone would not provide a full picture of the transformation from the Jomon culture to the Yayoi culture around the third century BCE. There was also a clear indication of the influence of the old Jomon culture on the new Yayoi culture, and these indications suggested a continuity between the two cultures.[15]

Some scholars refer to the era that followed the Yayoi period as the "Tomb Period" (*kofun,* 250–538 CE) because of the discovery of burial mounds near Nara, which date back to between the third and sixth century CE.[16] Unlike the earlier Japanese tradition of building tombs on hills, these large tombs were built on the plain, and the artifacts uncovered from the tombs, including *haniwa* (clay figurines), revealed a cultural influence from Korea. These new tombs were aristocratic in nature. The largest, which is believed to be that of "emperor" Nintoku of the early fifth century (r. 395–427 CE), is about 120 feet high and 2,695 feet long, covering nearly eighty acres in the shape of a keyhole.[17] The origins of this new tomb culture are under heated debate. Some scholars propose a Horse Rider Theory, which credit the new immigrants of horse riders for the changes, but other scholars argue that there is a close link between this culture and the emergence of the Yamato court in the fifth century CE.

Artist unknown.

A haniwa horse figurine

Despite all of the debate about early Japanese history, sources of early Japanese history, Japanese mythology, Chinese records, and archaeological evidence present a much clearer picture of Japanese history from the late fifth century CE onward. Although the origin of the Yamato state is still under debate, all of the sources are consistent with the view that by the fifth century, the Yamato clan had unified or at least exerted their control over a large part of Kyushu and the Kanto region of Honshu. The early Yamato society was formed into *uji,* a Japanese word that is an equivalent to the English word "clan." Each *uji* shared the same lineage and had its own deity, known as *kami* in Japanese. The Yamato clan gradually conquered other *uji* groups and rearranged them into ranks, among which the largest were *Omi,* which was held by the Yamato family, and *Muraji,* which was for unrelated *uji.*[18] Japan's indigenous religion, Shinto, was a dominant force at the early Yamato court. By this time, however, the Sun Goddess, Ametarasu, who was the chief goddess of the Yamato clan, became prominent over other *kami.* As discussed earlier, Ametarasu was deemed the source of authority for all of the Japanese emperors until the end of World War II.

Meanwhile, other cultural forces from neighboring countries found their way into the Yamato court and became tools for the Yamato elites to consolidate their power over Japan. Among them were the reported introduction of Paekche scribes around 400 CE, and later the official introduction of Buddhism to Japan through Korea around 552 CE.[19] The latter was of particular importance. The foreign challenge forced the Japanese to rethink their own indigenous religion. The word of Shinto, "the way of the Kami" was adopted after the introduction of Buddhism, which was known in Japan as "the way of Buddha." Even the practice of building a shrine to house a Shinto deity, such as the building of the Ise Shrine for the Sun Goddess Ametarasu, may have been a foreign import.[20]

In the early seventh century, the Yamato state was greatly strengthened through a series of political reforms. Prince Shotoku Taishi (574–622 CE), who was from the powerful Soga clan and served as the regent to the Yamato throne, initiated reforms. Prince Shotoku was the most notable intellectual at the Yamato court. Being a devote Buddhist, but also well-read in Confucian literature, he decided to remodel the Japanese government according to the Chinese model.[21] Since the early ties with the Korean Pakchea kingdom had been severed by this time, Prince Shotoku initiated relations with China and sent six envoys to the Chinese court to study the Chinese political system. These students brought back many ideas from China, and among them were the Chinese calendar and a Confucian style of government. In 604, Prince Shotoku published a "Seventeen Article Constitution," which was based on Confucian ethics and some Buddhist concepts. Although this "constitution" was by no means a constitution in a modern sense, it aimed to strengthen the power of the Yamato court and to spell out its moral obligations to its subjects or vice versa.[22]

These reforms, however, were temporarily interrupted by the death of Prince Shotoku in 622 CE, and the subsequent bloody power struggle gave rise to a powerful opponent of the Soga clan, the Nakatomi clan. Nakatomi no Kamatari, a member of the Nakatomi clan, was later given a new family name of Fujiwara, and the Fujiwara family dominated the Japanese court for centuries to come. Despite the political power struggle, the new court in 645 announced a larger scale reform, the *Taika* (great change) Reforms, which was more thorough than what Prince Shotoku had started.[23] The resulting political system endorsed absolute authority for the emperor, implemented a centralized bureaucracy headed by three ministers, and divided the country into provinces headed by governors. The government would maintain a standing army and levy the land and labor taxes. The *Taiho Code* (*Taiho-ritsuryo*), implemented in 702 CE, further consolidated the political changes of the *Taika* Reforms. All of these reforms further transformed the Yamato court from a confederation based on *uji* groups to a well-organized state.

THE NARA ERA

Prince Shotoku's reforms and the subsequent *Taika* Reforms exerted a long-lasting influence on Japanese political and cultural systems. One direct result was the building of the first capital in Nara, which was modeled after Chang'an, the capital of Tang China. In 710, the Japanese court moved into Nara on a permanent basis, ending its early tradition of moving its capital after the death of each emperor. Nara soon grew into Japan's first urban center with a population of 200,000, which accounted for 4 percent of the country's total.[24] The Nara era (710–784) saw the continuing influence of Chinese culture at the court. Following the Chinese tradition of documenting official history, for example, the first two historical works, the *Kojiki* (ca. 711) and the *Nihon shoki* (720), were compiled during the Nara era. Both were political in nature, with clear goals for justifying the supremacy of the Japanese emperor, as well as that of the Japanese race, as discussed earlier.[25] Similarly, writing poetry, which was much admired in Tang China, also gained popularity at Nara, Japan. *Manyoshu*, the first large collection of Japanese poetry, was published in 759. *Manyoshu* used Chinese characters to represent sounds in the Japanese language. This style of writing was known as *manyogana*, which was later displaced by *katakana*, a syllabary invented in the Heian era (794–1185).[26]

Meanwhile, Buddhism also gained a firm ground at the Nara court. With the enthusiastic patronage of the emperors and the aristocrats, Buddhist congregations built large Buddhist temple complexes in Nara, as well as in the provinces. An edict in 741 required every province to build a Buddhist temple. The Horyu-ji temple, the oldest surviving temple in Japan, is one of the finest examples of Buddhist architecture and arts of Nara Japan.[27] The Todai-ji (Eastern Great Temple) temple complex, built in 728, has the largest wooden building in the world and one of the world's largest bronze Buddha statues, known as *Daibutsu*. With the support of royal rulers, especially the empresses, Buddhist priests shared power with the aristocracy, such as the Fujiwara family, at court. The power of Buddhist monks culminated when an ex-empress, Koken (r. 749–758), resumed the throne as Empress Shotoku between 764 and her death in 770.[28] Empress Shotoku was especially known for her passionate endorsement of Buddhist culture. It was said that she might even have wanted to see her favorite monk as the emperor. This decision greatly damaged her reputation as a rational and capable ruler. Royal women were later no longer trusted with imperial power following the reign of Empress Shotoku. Since her death, there have only been two empresses out of seventy-six Japanese emperors; in comparison, there were nine empresses out of the first forty-nine Japanese emperors. The court also prohibited Buddhist monks from participating in court politics.[29]

COURT AND CULTURE OF THE HEIAN PERIOD

This episode of negative Buddhist influence on Japanese court politics may have contributed to the decision of Emperor Kammu (r. 781–806) to abandon Nara in 784. After temporarily residing at Nagaoka a few miles north of Nara, in 794 Emperor Kammu moved his court to Heian-kyo (the city of peace), today's Kyoto, where the Japanese imperial court stayed for the next 1,000 years or so until the Meiji Restoration in 1868.[30] The move of the court to Heian ushered in a new era in Japanese history. The word "Heian" means "peace and tranquility" in Japanese, a phrase that highlights the general character of the era, at least until the late Heian era.

The Heian period was the time when the Japanese assimilated what they had borrowed and consolidated their own culture. After over two centuries of extensive borrowing from China and Korea, the era of China-inspired reforms ended. Actually, the strong reaction against Buddhism and Chinese culture even led to a court decision to cut off its relations with China after 838. Imperial politics embarked along a similar path, departing from the imported Chinese model. While the Chinese emperor often forcefully controlled the court, the Japanese emperor, except for a few assertive rulers such as Emperor Kammu, was considered the spiritual head of the country, but had limited temporal power. The real power went to the court aristocracy, who not only controlled court politics, but also had almost complete control of the royal family.[31] The reigning emperors were often pressured into retirement and eventually retreated to Buddhist monasteries when their male heirs were old enough to perform the Shinto ceremony. The boy emperor, who was usually immature and inexperienced, was often subjected to the control of his regent, a position filled by an individual from the most powerful aristocratic family.

During the Heian era, the regent was almost always a member of the Fujiwara family. The power and influence of this one particular family was so strong that some scholars even adopted the phrase, "the Fujiwara period," to describe the Heian culture of the tenth and eleventh centuries.[32] One method that the Fujiwara used to guarantee their dominance was to marry their daughters to the emperors. Fujiwara Michinaga (966–1027), "the apotheosis of Fujiwara power and glory," dominated the Heian court for nearly thirty years through a web of such connections. He was "the brother of two empresses and the father of four, the uncle of two emperors, and grandfather of two more, and the great-grandfather of another."[33] In addition to being a controller of court politics, Michinaga was also a great cultural sponsor, and his time was known as the golden age of Japanese court culture. Books produced during this time reflected the exquisite style of court life during the Heian period. Among them, Murasaki Shikibu's *Tale of Genji* was considered the best.

Not much about the life of Lady Murasaki is known, except that she was born into a minor branch of the Fujiwara family and got married; unfortunately, her husband died three years later. Probably because of her literary talent, she caught the attention of Michinaga, who hired her to serve his daughter, Empress Akiko, the wife of Emperor Ichijo. Lady Murasaki was impressively knowledgeable of history and poetry, and often gave the young empress lessons on these subjects. Her intellect and talent were reflected in her famous work, *The Tale of Genji*, a phenomenal novel focusing on the life of a royal prince, *Genji*. Finished around 1000 CE, this book was, in many senses, the world's first modern novel. It is highly emotional, reflecting the value and the lifestyle of the Heian court.[34] Holding mostly meaningless positions without any functional government responsibility, the court nobles spent most of their time on menial tasks such as flower arranging, poem writing, and custom designing.

Another long lasting impact of Murasaki's works was her contribution to the Japanese script. Most intellectuals of the time were men who were using Chinese characters in their writing, but Murasaki and other noble ladies experimented with writing in Japanese. Works such as *The Tale of Genji* helped establish the *kana* syllabaries, which gradually grew into their maturity after the Heian era.[35]

THE RISE OF A SEMI-FEUDAL SOCIETY

While the court nobles were indulging in their exquisite lifestyle in the capital, Heian-kyo, the countryside was going through some profound changes. Two of them, the formation of the *shoen* system and the rise of the samurai class, would prove to be of fundamental importance in Japan's future development into a semi-feudal society. Although the elites in the provinces had aristocratic values that were similar to those held by the elites in the capital, there were considerable differences between the capital and provinces. The center of life in the provinces was the agricultural estate, *shoen* in Japanese, which thrived in Japan between the eighth and fifteenth centuries. After the *Taika* Reforms in the seventh century, all of the land belonged to the emperor, and the government collected land taxes through provincial governors. In the Nara era, however, the emperor started to grant tax-free land as gifts to the Buddhist monasteries and members of the royal families, and exempted those lands from state tax. The *shoen* system, which started as a reward system, continued to disrupt the results of the land reforms introduced by the *Taika* Reforms.[36] Unlike European manors, which were usually based on villages and common pastoral land, *shoen* in Japan were initially irrigated paddy fields that varied greatly in size. Some were no larger than a small farm, but others could contain paddy fields across several provinces. During the Nara era, the large Buddhist monasteries became the biggest landholding institutions, and their holdings ranged from 1,000 to 10,000 acres apiece.

During the Heian period, the emperors granted more tax-free land to the minor branches of the royal families and their favorites. The Fujiwara family also obtained the right to grant *shoen* estate to their family members and friends, and later, even provincial governors took it upon themselves to grant tax-free land to their beneficiaries. Moreover, the 30 percent decline in the population as a result of an epidemic in the late eighth century freed up a lot of agricultural land. The government encouraged the reclamation of these lands, as well as wastelands; they allowed these reclaimed lands to be held as private estates with reduced taxes. This greatly increased the amount of privately owned land. By design, the owners were supposed to return the reclaimed land to the public domain after one to three generations, but most of them chose to ignore this rule. Giving up on the situation, the government eventually granted permanent ownership to these lands. The government later tried to curb further possession of *shoen*, but these efforts proved to be futile, because the imperial and noble families were the biggest beneficiaries of the system. By the beginning of the tenth century, *shoen* prevailed throughout the country. By the twelfth century, less than 10 percent of the land remained in the public domain. The *shoen* owners later gained another privilege—they could deny the entrance of government officials to their estates and thus, manage their estates without government supervision. As a result, the *shoen* system paved the way for a feudalist or semi-feudalist society in Japan.[37]

The *shoen* was originally managed by the owner and cultivated by his tenants. Later, many *shoen* owners were attracted to the exquisite city lifestyle in Heian-kyo and moved to the city, leaving the affairs of their estates to a hired manager. With their master living far away from the *shoen*, these managers gained considerable authority over the estate. Some of the managerial positions became hereditary, and many managers even had the authority to levy taxes for themselves.[38]

THE RISE OF WARRIOR CLASS

The development of the *shoen* system resulted in a steady decline of centralized control of the provinces. As the position of emperor became increasingly weaker, and the government continued to lose revenue because of the *shoen* system, the central government's military forces also declined drastically. Without protection or help from the central government's military or police forces, the *shoen* owners and their managers took the matter of security into their own hands. This led to the rise of the *samurai* class in Japan. The hard core of the armed soldiers who were hired to protect the estates had kinship ties among themselves as they usually came from the same clan according to the old *uji* system. These warriors gradually formed a feudalistic lord-vassal relationship with their masters, with their loyalty shifting towards their lord instead of to the central government.[39] Their lords adopted measurements to assure their loyalty. Up to the time of the Meiji Restoration in the mid-nineteenth century, Japanese peasants and commoners were not permitted to bear a family name. A family name had been preserved as a special privilege for the aristocracy, and on many occasions, only the emperor had the right to grant a family name, a way to dignify the rewarded.

In the late Heian era, it became commonplace for estate owners in the provinces to allow their warriors to use the place name in identifying themselves. They would also be provided with a piece of their own land and be allowed to collect taxes on their own. By the end of the twelfth century, these warriors had come to be bound by a certain set of common rules of ethical behavior, known later as *Bushido*. They identified themselves as members of a distinctive class known as *samurai*, or *bushi*, who, together with their lords, dominated Japanese history over the next several centuries. The influence of the *samurai* class can still be found in Japanese culture and society today.[40]

THE RIVALRY BETWEEN THE TAIRA AND THE MINAMOTO

The dominance of the *shoen* system and the rise of the *samurai* class greatly redefined politics in the provinces. Powerful families, many of them related directly to the imperial family, emerged in the provinces and managed their estates as semi-independent kingdoms. They competed with each other in order to gain more control of the land and resources. Meanwhile, court politics at Heian became messy as the power of the Fujiwara family declined dramatically after the death of Michinaga. When issues arose at the court, especially those concerning succession, different factions of the court often counted on elite families in the provinces to provide military support. This provided the most powerful families in the provinces with an opportunity to intervene in court politics and thus, to enhance their own control over the imperial court.

Two such families played a particularly important role in this process, namely the Taira (or Heike)[41] family and the Minamoto (or Genji)[42] family, both of whom were related to earlier emperors, but were later given their own family names when their tie to the imperial line was officially severed.[43] The name of Taira was first given to a grandson of the emperor Kammu, who had been responsible for moving the imperial court from Nara to Heian. The Taira family was initially established in the Kanto region, but moved further west to the Ise area. The Taira family gradually gained prominence by trading with China and helping the court repress local rebellions. The Taira family also built close ties with the retired emperors, who sometimes were known as "cloistered emperors." The name of Minamoto was given by the Emperor Saga (r. 809–823) to his sons and brothers, and some of the Minamoto branches were also related to the emperor Seiwa (r. 858–876). The Minamoto family established their power and fame by subduing the rebellions in the Kanto region and by helping the court conquer Northern Honshu during the 10th century.[44] During the process, it gained close sponsorship from Fujiwara Michinaga. The Taira and Minamoto families were in conflict from the eleventh century forward.

In the twelfth century, increasingly chaotic court politics over the issue of succession, as well as continued competition between the Taira and Minamoto families, eventually ushered in a half-century of warfare in Japan. The problem started when the emperor Konoe (r. 1142–1155) died without leaving an heir of his own. The throne went to a brother, the emperor go-Shirakawa (r. 1155–1158). His legitimacy to rule, however, was challenged by a retired emperor, who had interfered in court politics during the reign of the deceased emperor Konoe. A brief civil war, known as the Hogen Rebellion (1155), broke out. All of the important families, the Fujiwara, the Taira, and the Minamoto, were involved in the dispute, but different branches of the three families were on opposite sides of the dispute. For example, Minamoto no Tameyoshi, head of the Minamoto clan, supported the retired emperor, but his eldest son, Minamoto no Yoshitomo sided with some members of the Taira family to aid the reigning emperor.[45] Eventually, the emperor go-Shirakawa, the reigning emperor, gained an upper hand, and the retired emperor was banished to Shikoku.

The emperor go-Shirakawa retired in 1158, giving the throne to his son, the emperor Nijo (r. 1158–1165), but go-Shirakawa still managed the court as the new retired emperor. Meanwhile, the Fujiwara family and the Minamoto family became increasingly uncomfortable with the dominance of Taira no Kiyomori, the head of the Taira family, over court affairs. The two families started to plot together against Taira no Kiyomori, and this led to another brief civil war, known as the Heiji Rebellion (1159–1160). Although both the Hogen Rebellion and the Heiji Rebellion each lasted only a brief time, the Heiji Rebellion was fundamentally different in nature from the Hogen Rebellion. While the opposing sides in the Hogen Rebellion each had both members from the Taira family and members from the Minamoto family, the Heiji Rebellion highlighted the power struggle between the Taira and the Minamoto families.[46] The disturbance began when Kiyomori was away from Kyoto in January, 1160. Minamoto no Yoshitomo and some Fujiwara members made their move and took control of the palace. Upon his return, however, Kiyomori quickly gained an upper hand over the rebels, ensuring a total victory. Members of the Fujiwara family were killed, and so was Yoshitomo, who was killed by his own retainer after he had retreated from Kyoto.

The civil wars, the Hogen Rebellion and the Heiji Rebellion, ended quickly, but the changes that they brought to court politics were significant and, to a certain extent, unexpected. The power of the Fujiwara family declined greatly, and the supremacy that they had enjoyed over the last two centuries was passed onto other strong families, despite the fact that the members of the Fujiwara continued to hold court positions. The power of the royal court shifted to the provincial military cliques. The triumphant Taira family, under the strong leadership of Kiyomori, now controlled the court in the same way that the Fujiwara family had, allowing the emperor, the royal family, and the Fujiwara family to assume only empty titles and powerless positions. Kiyomori even followed the Fujiwara practice of having his daughter marry the emperor, and eventually in 1880, he put his own infant grandson on the throne as the Emperor Antoku.[47]

Meanwhile, the defeat of Yoshitomo only temporarily weakened the Minamoto family. After Kiyomori defeated the Minamoto in 1160, he ordered the execution of all of the members of the family and the seizure of their wealth, but spared the life of the young son, Minamoto no Yoritomo (1147–1199), who was exiled to the island of Izu. This proved to be a fatal mistake on the Taira side. While the Taira struggled to control the court at Heian, Yoritomo assumed the leadership of the Minamoto family and gradually regained strength with the support of loyal retainers. In 1177, a plot against the Taira broke out at court, and a royal prince called the Minamoto family for help. The plot was soon destroyed, but the struggle between the Taira and the Minamoto surfaced again. Yoritomo, now a mature man, gained the support of many other families who were dissatisfied with Taira no Kiyomori's domination of the court and openly challenged Kiyomori in 1180. This started the five-year Genpei War (1180–1185) between the two families. With the support of other powerful families, Yoritomo soon seized the Kanto region, defeating the forces that were sent from Heian. His cousin, Minamoto no Yoshimitsu, began fighting his way toward the capital from a province in the north in 1183. The Taira forces, which were greatly weakened by the death of Kiyomori in 1181, fled the capital to the north coast of Shikoku, taking the infant emperor Antoku with them. Yoritomo sent two of his brothers, Noriyori and Yoshitsune, to pursue the Taira forces. Yoshitsune, who was instrumental in the Minamoto's success, destroyed the Taira base at Shikoku and annihilated the remnants of the Taira forces at a decisive naval battle.[48] The Emperor Antoku drowned in the sea, and the *Kusanagi*, the sword that was one of the Three Imperial Regalias, went down with him, lost to the waves.

KAMAKURA BUKUFU

The victory of the Minamoto over the Taira paved the way for the establishment of the first Bakufu (tent government) in Japanese history. In 1192, Yoritomo was given the title of Shogun from the emperor, which initially was the abbreviated form for *Sei-I-tai-shogun*, (barbarian conquering generalissimo); it was later developed into a full-fledged position to control the nation.[49] Yoritomo established his headquarters in his home city, Kamakura, and thus ushered in a new era in Japanese history—the rule of the military government.

Minamoto no Yoritomo

The Bakufu (or shogunate) dominated Japan until 1868 when the last Tokugawa shogun was overthrown. During these years, the shogun assumed the real power, while the emperor at the Kyoto court was further reduced to merely a nominal ruler and the head of the Shinto religion.[50]

The Kamakura bakufu ruled Japan in the name of the emperor from 1185 to 1333. Some scholars characterized the system set up by Yoritomo as "feudal"—"a hereditary military clique held together by the personal loyalty of the vassals to their lord."[51] Yoritomo himself controlled large amounts of land as his own *shoen*, appointing loyal retainers as managers to run the land for the family. Other strong provincial aristocrats, who had taken advantage of the previous wars to gather large amounts of land, followed suit. While claiming their allegiance to the Kamakura Shogunate, they also rewarded their warriors with pieces of their estates or with managing rights of their *shoen*. Eventually the estate managers throughout Japan proclaimed their loyalty to the Kamakura bakufu. Kamakura Japan, however, might not be the same type of feudalistic society that developed in Europe in the Middle Ages. The Kamakura Shogunate did not seek to replace the imperial court, but only to assume control over the country in the name of the emperor, and in theory, the final authority over the land still rested with the emperor, not with the shogun.[52] The system that was established by Yoritomo, in a sense, was a continuation of what had been established by the Fujiwara family in the late Heian era and was only different because of an institutional separation of a military regime from the royal court.[53]

HOJO REGENCY

As soon as Yoritomo consolidated his power, he started to turn against the members of his own family. He soon found excuses to execute his siblings, including Yoshitusme and Noriyori. He gave more power to his wife, Masako, and her family, the Hojo family, who had hosted the young Yoritomo during his early years of exile after Taira no Kiyomori had spared his life when Kiyomori executed other members of the Minamoto family. As a result, after his death in 1199, the power went to his widow, Masoko Yoritomo, who was also known as "nun-shogun." Although Masoko ruled through her sons in the name of the Minamoto family, she greatly promoted the interest of the Hojo family, appointing her brother to important positions and established her father as a regent to the shogun.[54] In 1221, a disturbance against the Hojo broke out when a retired emperor denounced Masako's brother as an outlaw. The Hojo family, however, quickly subjugated the opposition, and emerged even stronger by confiscating the *shoen* of those who had opposed them and by tightening their control over the imperial court. The Hojo later reorganized the shogunal administration into a thirteen-member council, headed by the senior members of the Hojo family, and in 1232, issued a new code, the *Joei Code*, to define property rights and land tenure, and to discipline the estate managers.[55] Members of the Hojo family maintained their regency to the shogun until 1333.

THE MONGOL INVASION AND THE FALL OF THE KAMAKURA BUKUFU

After the Mongolian ruler, Khubilai Khan (1215–1294), conquered both China and Korea, he directed his troops to invade Japan twice, in 1274 and 1281. The Mongol invasions greatly affected Kamakura Japan. Khubilai Khan sent his envoy to Japan in 1268, demanding that Japan submit to his power. The shogunate, however, proudly rejected this request. Khubilai then dispatched a large fleet, consisting of 900 ships and a mixed force of 25,000 Mongols and Koreans, as well as 67,000 ship workers, on a punitive expedition against Japan.[56] When the Mongol troops approached Hakata Bay in North Kyushu, the shogunate hastily gathered a force to fight against the Mongols, but the enemy proved to be too strong. The Japanese warriors soon abandoned Hakata Bay and retreated to an inland fortress. The Mongols, however, vanished the next day as a powerful typhoon destroyed most of their ships.

The Mongols resumed their efforts to conquer Japan in 1281, since the shogunate repeatedly rejected Khubilai's requests after the first invasion. Two even larger Mongol fleets came from two separate routes, with a total of 4,400 ships and a combined force numbering about 140,000 men, the largest expedition of forces that the world had ever seen.[57] Using a recently constructed stone wall along the shoreline of Hakata Bay, the Japanese warriors held the Mongols at bay in a narrow strip of beachhead for nearly two months. Then, another typhoon struck, which forced the Mongols to retreat for the second time. Although storms were quite frequent in Japan during the typhoon season in late summer, the fact that the typhoon had destroyed the Mongolian fleet twice convinced the Japanese that they were truly blessed by a "divine wind" or in Japanese, *kamikaze*.

The Mongol invasions had a mixed impact on the Kamakura regime. On one hand, the invasions gave the shogunate a chance to extend its control over Kyushu and other areas originally outside of its jurisdiction. In these cases of national crisis, all of the samurai answered the call of the shogun.[58] The increased power of the shogunate, on the other hand, only resulted in the further division of the Hojo family, who had aroused jealousy of the royal family and other aristocrats, and an increasing discontent among the samurai class. One major source of the samurai's dissatisfaction was the lack of rewarding land in the aftermath of the Mongol invasions. The warriors had fought against the Mongols at their own expense, and without proper rewards, many ended up in poverty and subsequently lost their land because they had to sell or pawn it.[59] The shogunate, on the other hand, could not help them because the victory over the Mongols did not result in increased land holdings or financial benefit. On the contrary, even though the Mongols never returned, preparations for that future possibility drained the country financially.

The worst problem for the shogunate, however, was its rivalry at the court. Emperor Go-Daigo (r. 1318–1339), who was an unusually active monarch, took the lead in an anti-bakufu movement. Particularly resentful of the shogunate's involvement in court politics, the emperor was determined to return the court to its original emperor-centered governance. The emperor was soon able to gather a considerable amount of support from discontented warriors, but his initial plan to uproot the shogunate failed, and the emperor was exiled in 1331.[60] The anti-bakufu movement, however, had already achieved momentum, and in two years, the Kamakura regime came to an end.

ASHIKAGA NO TAKAUJI AND THE ASHIKAGA BAKUFU

The person who was instrumental for the overthrow of the Kamakura bakufu in 1333 was Ashikaga no Takauji (1305–58), whose family was remotely related to the Minamoto family; the family name of Ashikaga was derived from the place where their family *shoen* was located. In 1333, when the Emperor Go-Daigo escaped from his exile and was on his way back to Kyoto, the Kamakura shogun dispatched a force under Ashikaga no Takauji from Kamakura to Kyoto on a rescue mission of the Kamakura headquarters in the capital. Tagauji, however, was ready to switch his loyalty, and upon receiving a personal endorsement from the Emperor Go-Daigo, he joined the emperor to fight against the Hojo.[61] After he and others helped the emperor secure the city of Kyoto, Takauji led a force back to Kamakura and toppled the Kamakura forces, thus rendering himself the leader of the warriors in the Kanto region.

Almost immediately after the victory, the coalition fell apart between the emperor, who planned to implement "the Kemmu Restoration" to restore real power to the emperor, and Takauji, who desired to establish his own bakufu to replace the one at Kamakura. As a result, the period between 1333 and 1336 saw a struggle between the Emperor Go-Daigo, and Takauji.[62] After having suffered a few initial defeats, Takauji finally took over the city of Kyoto in 1336 and forced Emperor Go-Daigo to flee to the south. Takauji placed Go-Daigo's cousin on the throne and built his headquarters at Muromachi, a district in the suburb of Kyoto. In 1338, he received the title of shogun from the new emperor and thus started the second shogunate in Japanese history, known as the Ashikaga shogunate, after the family name, or the Muromachi shogunate, after the place of its headquarters.[63]

The establishment of the Ashikaga bakufu did not bring peace back to Japan. Power struggles continued between the shogunate and the imperial courts, as well as within the Ashikaga family. The Emperor Go-Daigo fled to the south and established a rival southern court in Yoshino, and until 1392, Japan had two courts simultaneously, the northern court and the southern court. The southern court benefited from a bitter competition between Takauji and his brother, Tadayoshi, who was a pivotal figure in the Ashikaga's success over the Hojo and Emperor Go-Daigo. Despite Taukaji's being the shogun, Tadayoshi was the real leader of the Ashikaga bakufu in its first decade. In 1351, Tadayoshi rebelled against Taukaji and joined the Southern court. In 1392, Ashikaga Yoshimitsu, the grandson of Takauji and the third Ashikaga shogun, succeeded in reaching an agreement with the emperor at the southern court; the emperor would return to Kyoto on the condition that the throne would alternate between the two family lines, but Yoshimitsu never honored that agreement.[66] Actually, Yoshimitsu's reign marked the summit of Ashikaga power. None of the later shoguns, except for the sixth one, Yoshimasa (r. 1449–1473), were able to exercise their power over all of Japan.

Scholars traditionally evaluate Ashikaga Japan in two contradictory ways. In terms of political rule, the Ashikaga bakufu was the weakest among the three military governments. For a while, it hardly extended its control beyond Kyoto and probably never gained control of the entire nation. Social unrest became epidemic during its tenure. Other scholars, however, suggest that one should not dismiss too easily the significant social and institutional changes during the Ashikaga rule, which lasted over two hundred years.[64] It was under the Ashikaga that the *shugo* (governors), who were originally appointed by the shogun to administrate the provinces during the Kamakura era, were also given the power to claim their own land, build up their own *shoen*, and take care of their own retainers. This led to the further disintegration of central control—neither the court nor the shogunate could effectively control Japan any more. Not only did the imperial court continue to lose its vitality, but the shoguns also relied heavily on the support and loyalty of the *shugo*.[65] As a result, the *shugo*, and later the emerging warlords, *daimyo*, played the most important role, especially in the late Ashikaga period. Yet, in cultural terms, the Ashikaga period was one of Japan's most creative periods of stunning artistic achievements in many cultural fields.

MUROMACHI CULTURE

Despite political disunity and social unrest, a new national culture, sometimes called the Muromachi culture, emerged from the bakufu headquarters in Kyoto and influenced the entire country. This was probably due, in large part, to the proximity of the imperial court to the bakufu. The many interactions between the members of the imperial family, the aristocrats, the samurai, and the priests provided an environment for the growth of the new culture, which embodied the key values of all of the groups. As a result, the dominant value of the time, "a notion of beauty and elegance modified by stern simplicity," was a combination of aristocratic aesthetics with the values of the new samurai class.[67] Above all, two influences, Buddhist and Chinese, helped sustain these enduring cultural changes.

Although after the Heian era, Buddhist monasteries lost their power to intervene in court politics, their ties with the imperial family were never completely severed, especially since the retired emperors usually lived in a monastery. The Buddhist monasteries also remained strong players socioeconomically. Many of them held large amounts of tax-free land; some pieces of land were given as gifts by their royal patrons, but other pieces of land were received as "donations" offered by surrounding landowners, who registered their land with the monasteries in order to evade government taxes or to seek protection in times of social upheaval. At first, the monasteries recruited their own armies for the sake of protecting their property, but later, their forces were also involved in the wars among the warlords.

Since the introduction of Buddhism to Japan in the sixth century, several Buddhist schools had developed into separate forms, such as the *Shingon* (True Word) school, the *Tendai* school (related to Lotus Sutra school), the *Jōdo* (Pure Land) school, and the Zen school. Zen Buddhism, in particular, exerted many direct influences on Japanese culture and arts during the era of military governments. Zen Buddhism was the Japanese equivalent to the "Chan" sect, which originally developed in China around the time of the Tang dynasty. It came to Japan with other Buddhist sects, but was only developed into a distinctive school during the Kamakura era. During the Ashikaga period, Zen Buddhism became the most successful Buddhist sect in Japan. The Zen temples and their monks became instrumental in spreading not only their religious doctrine, but also the artistic values derived from Chinese architecture and landscape painting.

The Zen masters, such as Muso Soseki, developed close ties with powerful political figures, such as those of the Hojo family, Emperor Go-Daigo, and Ashikaga Takauji.[68] With the patronage of Takauji, Yoshimitsu, and other Ashikaga shoguns, Zen temples were erected throughout Japan. All of these Zen temples, at least one major temple in each province, were ranked in a hierarchical order. Because of their knowledge of China and the Chinese language, the highest priests enjoyed enormous advisory power to the shoguns over matters of administrative appointments, promotion, and even foreign trade.[69] These Zen temples were usually decorated with elegant halls and a special style of garden made of sand and stone, designed to illustrate Zen aesthetic principles like "unity with nature."[70] As a result, Zen Buddhism affected architecture and other related art forms in Japan. Muso himself was responsible for the finest temple-gardens, the Tenryū-ji and the Saihō-ji at Kyoto.[71]

Among the finest examples of Zen Buddhist influence on Japanese architecture are two monumental buildings in Kyoto, the Golden Pavilion (*Kinkaku-ji*) and the Silver Pavilion (*Ginkaku-ji*). The former was built by the Shogun Yoshimitsu between 1397 and 1407, and the latter by Yoshimitsu's grandson, the Shogun Yorimasa, after 1482. The Golden Pavilion is the best illustration of the aesthetic principles of the time, "a notion of beauty and elegance modified by stern simplicity,"

Ryoan-ji Garden

The Golden Pavilion

which is a combination of Heian "sensibility" and Kamakura "austerity."[72] Both were designed as villas to the shoguns, but both were also used as Zen temples. The Golden Pavilion, whose roof and top two stories were covered with gold leaf, embodied the power and wealth of the shogun. It was set on a platform overseeing an artificial pond, which enhances the elegance of the building.

Its plain surface of natural wood and its simple structure, however, "preserved the Japanese tradition of simplicity."[73] Echoing the beauty of the Golden Pavilion, the Silver Pavilion is somewhat smaller and less glamorous, reflecting the problems of the age when it was built. This, however, does not affect in any sense the beauty, tranquility, and simplicity embodied through the exquisite arrangement of its halls, the pond, and the garden. Its well-known sand garden, with a mound of carefully arranged sand, supposedly represented Mount Fuji.[74]

The Golden and Silver Pavilions also illustrate the influence of Chinese culture at the time. The Zen Buddhist masters played a particularly important role in encouraging the Japanese authorities to resume relations with China. Upon the advice of Muso Soseki, for example, the Emperor Go-Daigo sent an official envoy to China in 1325, almost 500 years after the relationship was severed.[75] At the time, China was under the rule of the Mongol Yuan dynasty, but the important cultural developments during the previous Song dynasty continued; the Song culture flowed into Japan during the Ashikaga era, influencing Japanese architecture, painting, and landscape. The use of the ponds in both villas, for example, was probably inspired by the famous West Lake in Hangzhou, the capital of the Southern Song. The art of the gardens and the landscaping were also heavily influenced by Chinese themes, styles, and techniques of Chinese brush and ink painting that were particularly popular during the Tang-Song era in China. As in the case of the pre-Heian era, however, Japanese artists were selective in their borrowings, and they never stopped developing Japan's own cultural aesthetics and styles. Conrad Schirokauer describes the art of the Japanese garden in the following:

> In Japan, too, the aesthetics of garden design and landscape painting were closely related. The garden artist also could choose rich, colorful landscapes, using tree and shrub, rivulet and waterfall, pond and bridge, or he could confine himself to stone and carefully raked sand, much like the ink painter who rejected color. Such sand and stone gardens can be viewed as three-dimensional monochrome landscapes, the sand representing water, the rocks functioning as mountains, or they can be enjoyed as abstract sculptures inviting the viewer to exercise his or her imagination. Like Zen, they concentrate on the essentials.[76]

The finest example, according to Schirokauer, can be found in the Ryōan-ji, a Zen temple in Kyoto. There are fifteen stones in the sea of sand, but there is no particular angle, except from above, from which all of them can be seen.[77] It is said that only after a person obtains spiritual enlightenment through deep Zen meditation, can that person detect the last unseen stone with the mind's eye.[78] In addition, many Zen monks were also great masters of landscape painting, landscaping arts, and calligraphy (writing Chinese characters in brush and ink style).

The Tea Ceremony was another art form that was closely associated with the Zen temples, an art that contained Japan's own form and value. Tea was first introduced to Japan through Buddhist monks in the eighth century and had become a drink used at the court and the shogunate. Zen Buddhist monks during the Ashikaga era were probably responsible for popularizing the tea culture of this period. Most Zen temples had a tearoom—a small simple room usually facing the garden. Accordingly, the tea ceremony was first developed at a Zen temple. Tea masters began to ceremoniously prepare powdered tea for their guests; the tea is intended to purify the mind and make it merge with nature in a tranquil and peaceful way. As a result, the ceremony was performed with "a motion as deliberate as those of an actor on the Noh stage."[79] Soon, the ceremony, the particular setting of the tearoom, and the specific tea equipment, such as tea wares, became popular, particularly among the higher social classes, including the samurai class and wealthy merchants. In contrast to the fine porcelain from China, the most popular Japanese tea wares were plain and unevenly shaped, illustrating Japan's elegant simplicity (*wabi* and *sabi*).[80] The central theme of the ceremony, "peace and tranquility," was intended to "assimilate warriors and priests to aristocratic standards of taste," and was probably the main reason for the swift popularity of the tea ceremony, especially among the samurai class. Until the Meiji Restoration, the tea ceremony was practiced exclusively by men; women were only allowed to join after the restoration.[81]

The Noh drama is another authentic Japanese form of visual arts that reflected Japanese values. It first took form at Yoshimitsu's court in the late fourteenth century.[82] The chief actors usually performed on a bare stage, wearing facial masks. The actors were "possessed" by spirits of the dead who made them revisit places that were important to them, a battlefield where they died or a scene that was important for their romantic love. The singing, dancing, and costumes created highly emotional scenes for the audience, and every precise movement and gesture was highly structured to convey very specific messages. Together with tea ceremonies and the core Zen practice of meditation, the Noh drama might have provided a temporary emotional relief for the samurai, who often lived a bloody and ruthless life.[83] Although the Noh drama may be difficult for a foreign audience to understand, they are still popular in Japan today.

THE ONIN WAR AND THE RISE OF DAIMYO

The power of the Ashikaga shogunate was greatly diminished due to the Onin War in 1466–1467. Similar to many of the earlier wars, the Onin War started with a succession problem. Shogun Yoshimasa had promised his brother the title of shogun before his own son was born. Trying to assure that the title of shogun would go to her son, Yoshimasa's wife rallied support from the powerful Yamana family, one of the three families that could provide candidates for the position of *kanrei*, (deputy shogun); the other two families were the Hosokawa and the Hatakeyama. The Hosokawa, however, preferred Yoshimasa's younger brother. A war broke out in May 1466 right in the streets of Kyoto, and by the end of the war, most of the city was burned or destroyed, but there were still no clear winners. Even though Yoshimi, Yoshimasa's son, became the next shogun with the support of his father, the Ashikaga bakufu fell apart. From the position of *kanrei*, the Hodokawa family completely controlled the shogunate, forcing the shogun to flee Kyoto.[84] This also gave powerful families in the provinces the opportunity to intervene in the shogunal politics in Kyoto.

As a result, the Onin war was only the first of many other wars to occur in the following decades, a period later known as the *Sengoku jidai* (warring states period). The period, which lasted from the beginning of the Onin War to 1568, when Oda Nobunaga took control of Kyoto, was completely dominated by the warrior class led by their powerful warlords, now known as *daimyo*. Although some *daimyo* were *shugo*, members of powerful families who had been loyal to the shoguns, and were, therefore, appointed as provincial governors, *daimyo* were different in many ways from the earlier warrior elites. Many of them, known as *sengoku daimyo*, emerged from the position of estate managers to topple their masters, taking advantage of the absence of their lords who lived in the capital. They were self-appointed, ambitious, and ruthless. The only thing that mattered was the military prowess that would ensure their victories. After gaining power, these *daimyo* rewarded their retainers with land that they grabbed from others in order to assure their continued loyalty; they totally ignored the complicated rules of claiming *sheon* in the process. This practice led to the inevitable demise of the *sheon* system, but the Ashikaga shogunate was powerless to stop this process.[85] Japan was quickly divided into many big and small principalities, headed by *daimyo*. The decline of the shogunate's power was compounded by the collapse of the old socio-economic system that had formed the foundation of Ashikaga rule.

THREE GREAT UNIFIERS AND THE ESTABLISHMENT OF TOKUGAWA BAKUFU

The late Warring State era saw the rise of the three greatest warriors in Japanese history, Oda Nobunaga (1534–1582), Toyotomi Hideyoshi (1536–1598), and Tokugawa Ieyasu (1543–1616). The last one, Tokugawa Ieyasu, eventually ended a century of warfare and unified Japan under the Tokugawa bakufu in 1600.

Oda Nobunaga was a *daimyo* from Owari, which is located in a strategic location between Kyoto and Kamakura. The family gained control of the province under the leadership of Nobunaga's father. The family became divided after his father's death, but with much struggle, Nobunaga eliminated all of his opponents and firmly controlled Owari. The quick rise of Nobunaga in the sixteenth century was largely due to his military prowess and political shrewdness. Politically, he was not shy in securing alliances through all means that were available to him, including political marriage, family adoption, and bribery.[86] In terms of military skills, he was a daring tactician who was keen on taking advantage of newly introduced western technology. Nobunaga was among the first in Japan to arm his men with muskets and thus, boldly changed the fighting techniques from those of the traditional mounted warrior to those of the armed foot soldier. The chaotic situation after the Onin War also gave the family great opportunities for extending their power. In 1560, Nobunaga defeated a long-standing opponent of the family, the Imagawa clan, and this victory gained him a national reputation. Having recognized Nobunaga's power, both the emperor and the Ashikaga family started to ask for his assistance. In 1568, Nobunaga entered Kyoto at the request of Ashikaga Yoshiaki and secured the position of the shogun for Yoshiaki. In return, the shogun offered him the position of *kanrei*, but Nobunaga refused; he had his own dream of establishing his hegemony over the entire country.[87] As Yoshiaki became increasingly nervous of Nobunaga's power, he sent out letters in 1573, calling other *daimyo* to engage in military action against Nobunaga, but this only hastened the demise of the Ashikaga shogunate. Nobunaga drove Yoshiaki out of Kyoto and thus officially ended the reign of the Ashikaga bakufu, although some prefer to use the death of Yoshiaki in 1597 as the ending of that historical period.[88]

Nobunaga continued battling against other *daimyo*, as well as monastery forces, Ikko (True Pure Land) forces, and other forces of the Buddhist temples. Nobunaga ruthlessly destroyed the Ikko forces and many Buddhist monasteries outside Kyoto.[89] By 1580, Nobunaga's victories over his major competitors gave him control of over half of the provinces. Two years later, however, he was assassinated by his vassal, Akechi Mitsuhide, who held some personal grudges against Nobunaga. Taking advantage of the fact that most of Nobunaga's forces were battling in the provinces, Mitsuhide trapped Nobunaga by surprise. In desperation, Nobunaga took his own life.

When Mitsuhide murdered Nobunaga, Toyotomi Hideyoshi, Nobunaga's chief vassal, was fighting against the Mori clan in western Japan. As soon as he heard of Nobunaga's death, he made a quick truce with the Mori and returned to Kyoto to avenge the death of Nobunaga. He hunted down Mitsuhide and destroyed his forces. He later claimed himself as the head of Nobunaga's forces after he defeated all of the other competitors, including Nobunaga's son.[90] Hideyoshi soon succeeded in subduing most of the regional forces, either by destroying them or by forcing them to claim allegiance to him. By 1590, he accomplished Nobunaga's dream of unifying all of Japan. His humble origins from a peasant family, however, curbed his ambition to become a shogun. He did not even have a family name. He adopted the name Toyotomi (abundant provider) only after he became the commander of Nobunaga's forces. He could not therefore claim any blood-tie with Minamoto no Yoritomo, the first Japanese shogun. Hideyoshi eventually agreed to be the regent to the emperor in 1558, after he managed to have the Fujiwara family adopt him.

Hideyoshi established his headquarters in Osaka, where he built his famous castle, and from there extended his power over Japan. The period from 1573–1615 is often known as the "Azuchi-Momoyama period," taking the names from the castles of Nobunaga and Hideyoshi, respectively. In addition to his military prowess, Hideyoshi also proved to be one of the greatest politicians of his time. Many of the social policies adopted later by the Tokugawa bakufu actually originated with Hideyoshi. He centralized the taxation system; froze social mobility to prevent the peasants from being warriors or vice versa; staged the famous "sword hunt" to disarm non-samurai in order to secure a new national order; issued orders against the Christian missionaries; and controlled the *daimyo* through reshuffling their locations and keeping the most dangerous with him, away from their families, as hostages.[91]

His boldest moves, however, were his invasions of Korea in 1592 and 1597. This may have been the first step of his grandiose plan to conquer China.[92] The invasion of Korea in 1592 was the first time that Japanese forces had ever reached foreign soil outside of Japan. At the time Korea was a tributary state of China, so Hideyoshi's invasion triggered a Chinese intervention. Neither side could easily subjugate the other, so after a truce was negotiated, Hideyoshi ordered a retreat of his forces with the illusion of being victorious over both Korea and China. Being disappointed at the fact that nothing had happened in the following years, he ordered the troops to return to Korea in 1598. His death a few months later, however, led to an immediate withdrawal of his troops from Korea. This fact may suggest that Japan's invasion of Korea at this time was for no other reason than Hideyoshi's inordinate ambition for "leaving a great name behind me," so he said in a letter to his wife.[93]

The death of Hideyoshi opened the door for the last of the great Unifiers, Tokugawa Ieyasu, who, according to Mikiso Hane, "was the most patient, the shrewdest and the luckiest of the three," and "had a broad vision—a historical perspective and political acumen—that the other two may have lacked."[94] Ieyasu was born into the Matsudaira family in the Mikawa province, which bordered the Owari province where two powerful families, the Oda and the Imagawa, resided. In 1548, when the Oda clan invaded Mikawa, Ieyasu's father agreed to send his six-year-old son to the Imagawa family as a hostage in exchange for support, and thus the young Ieyasu remained a hostage for about 10 years. He was first promised to the Imagawa, but was abducted by the Oda family, and later was even betrayed by his own father when the head of the Oda family threatened to kill Ieyasu if his father continued to side with the Imagawa. Ieyasu's father refused to give in even at the risk of losing his son. A year later, Ieyasu was returned to the Imagawa family and stayed there as a hostage until he was 15. He eventually shifted to the Oda's side after Nobunaga defeated the Imagawa in 1560.[95] In 1567, Ieyasu changed his family name to Tokugawa, claiming that he was a descendent of the Minamoto family, although no hard proof was found for such a claim.[96]

Afterwards, Tokugawa Ieyasu served as vassal under both Nobunaga and Hideyosi. In order to bind Ieyasu to him, Nobunaga married his daughter to Ieyasu's eldest son, but later asked Ieyasu to kill both his wife and his son, because Nobunaga suspected these two were involved in a conspiracy against him. Ieyasu complied, putting his own wife to death and ordered his son to perform *seppuku* (belly cutting, a ritual suicide for samurai); he deeply regretted these actions later. By the time that Hideyoshi succeeded Nobunaga, the Tokugawa forces had become too strong to be easily subjugated. Hideyoshi was compelled to make Ieyasu an ally by adopting Ieyasu's second son and marrying his own sister to Ieyasu. Ieyasu firmly established himself in eastern Japan, becoming the Lord of Edo (today's Tokyo).

Before his death, Hideyoshi appointed his five-year-old son, Hideyori, as his successor, and established a council of five regents, including Tokugawa Ieyasu, to assist him. Ieyasu, however, had no intention of working for young Hideyori. Taking advantage of a split among Hideyoshi's generals between the "administrators," led by Ishida Mitsunari (1560–1600), and the "combat officers," Ieyasu openly challenged Hideyori, who was supported by Mitsunari.[97] In October 1600, the two factions, which were also roughly divided into geographic regions, the western clan headed by Mitsunari, and the eastern clan led by Ieyasu, had a decisive showdown at Sekigahara in central Honshu. With all of the "combat officers" joining the eastern clan because of their dislike for Mitsunari, Ieyasu achieved a total victory at the Battle of Sekigahara. Mitsunari was captured and executed.

The popular saying that Tokugawa Ieyasu ate the pie that Oda Nobunaga baked and Toyotomi Hideyoshi baked sums up the relations between the three great unifiers in the sixteenth century. In 1603, Ieyasu received the title of Shogun and named Edo as his headquarters. As the ultimate unifier of Japan, Ieyasu and the shogunate that bore his family name, the Tokugawa bakufu, controlled all of Japan, and provided relative peace to the country for the next 250 years.

KOREA AND ITS EARLY HISTORY

Korea is a peninsula located between China and Japan. The peninsula is surrounded by water on three sides: the Yellow Sea to the west, the East Sea (or Sea of Japan) to the east, and the South Sea (or Straits of Tsushima) to the south. To the north, it borders Manchuria in China. Although Korea is smaller by land area than both China and Japan, it is larger than Britain and several other European countries. Korea is a country dominated by mountains. In the north, the Changbaek Mountains (known as the Changbai Mountains in China), separate Korea from China and run toward the central part of the peninsula. Another major mountain range, the Taebaek Mountains, stretches over 500 kilometers from the north to the south along the east coast. Two important rivers in South Korea, the Han River and the Nakdong River, originate in the Taebaek Mountains. Korea is a very mountainous country, with only about 16 percent of its land suitable for cultivation.[98] Despite making travel very difficult, the mountains and hills in Korea decorate the country with beautiful scenery. The Koreans call their nation the "Land of Morning Calm" or the "Land of Morning Freshness."[99]

Throughout its history, Korea found itself in a constant struggle with its powerful neighbors, China and Japan, both of which were sources of influence as well as sources of conflict for the Koreans. Although all three countries share a certain cultural heritage with similar characteristics, Korea developed its own distinctive culture, including its own language, food, and customs. One would hardly mistake Korean peppery *kimchi* as Chinese or Japanese food; or the *dang'ui* and *chima* (traditional Korean dress) for the *qipao* (traditional dress for Chinese women) and *kimono* (Japanese traditional garment). Although Chinese characters are used in the Korean language, as they are in Japanese Kanji, the Korean language is uniquely different in its pronunciation and its alphabet, known as *Hangul*, which should not be confused with either Chinese writing or Japanese *kana* syllabary. Although the Korean and the Japanese languages are similar in their grammatical structures, no close vocabulary parallels between the Korean and the Japanese have been established.[100]

Before Buddhism spread to Korea, Shamanism was the major religious practice in Korea. Shamanism purports a strong belief in spirits, both in human beings and in all objects. The major obligation of the shamans was to perform proper rituals to control or appease these spirits. Because of the influence of the Shamanism, *Pung-siu* (or *Feng shui* in Chinese) has been a very important practice in Korea, especially before a house or a monastery is constructed. After Buddhism arrived in Korea in the fourth century CE, many Shamanist practices were quickly assimilated into Buddhism, making Korean Buddhism, in many senses, a unique form of Buddhism.

Similar to the case of early Japanese history, archaeological evidence, mythology, and Chinese historical records are sources of early Korean history. The Koreans probably came down to the peninsula from north central Asia; their language belongs to the Altaic language family, which also includes the Turkish, Mongolic, Tungusic, and Japanese languages. Archaeological evidence indicates that there were residents on the Korean peninsula probably as early as 4,000 BCE, but their identity has not been established. Mythological histories, centered on a bear-woman who gave birth in 2223 BCE to Tangun, the ancestor of the Korean people, only serve the purpose of establishing a separate Korean identity, and contain little guidance for understanding early Korean history. According to a Chinese source, *Shiji* by Sima Qian, there was a Korean state called Choson around 1000 BCE.[101] The Choson state seemed to be organized in a way similar to neighboring Chinese states; communal life, and bronze and iron tools were employed for agricultural work. Iron and copper coins similar to the Chinese style were also discovered at the tombs dated to the fifth century BCE.[102] It is said that the Chinese state of Yen (or Yan, 1122–255 BCE) pushed the Choson people from the Liaodong basin to the northern part of the Korean peninsula, where they established their capital in Pyongyang in the third century BCE.

Between 109 and 108 BCE, the Chinese, under the Han dynasty, invaded Choson and established colonies on the northern Korean peninsula; they supervised the region from their base north of Pyongyang, known as Lo-lang, which became a center of Chinese art, philosophy, and commerce for the next few centuries. Artifacts excavated from tombs of the era indicated a strong connection with the Han culture. The Chinese controlled North Korea until 313 CE, when a Korean state put an end to Lo-lang and the other four Chinese commanderies.[103]

THE ERA OF THREE KINGDOMS

With the Chinese retreating from Korea in the fourth century CE, the Koreans took the opportunity to consolidate their kingdoms on the peninsula. The three strongest ones, Koguryo in the north, Paekche in the Southwest, and Silla in the southeast, gave the name of "Three Kingdoms" (57–668 CE) to the era. When Silla overran Koguryo after it ousted Paekche in 668 CE, the end of the "Three Kingdoms" was marked, and the era of United Silla began.

The Three Kingdoms period

Among the three kingdoms, Koguryo had the longest history and was initially the strongest. It originated in the mountain areas along the border of Manchuria and the Korean peninsula, and gradually spread its power southward, becoming formidable opponents to the Chinese establishment in northern Korea. In the fourth century, Koguryo finally eliminated the Chinese colonies, and in the next century, it firmly established itself on the northern part of the peninsula with its capital in Pyongyang. It maintained close ties with China; both Buddhism and Confucianism had a strong influence over Koguryo society. At the height of its power, it controlled two thirds of Korea, as well as the southern part of Manchuria.

Meanwhile, two other states, Paekche and Silla, established their kingdoms in the south. They shared a similar ancestry with Koguryo, but tried to maintain their political status as free from Koguryo's control. Because of their geographical locations, Paekche and Silla were closer to Japan than to China. There was actually a third tribal group called Kaya in the south, which had an especially close tie with Japan. The Kaya League, however, was never considered an effective competitor for controlling Korea, as the other three states were.[104]

Similar to the case of Koguryo, which was established in 57 CE, the history of Paekche could also be traced back to the same period, around 19 CE. It was originally known as Mahan, one of three Han confederates in the south. One of the chiefdoms of the Manhan confederation gradually grew into the state of Paekche.[105] In the fourth century CE, Paekche actively sought a relationship with China, probably with an expectation of Chinese support in its struggle against other states. It is said that Buddhism was officially introduced to Paekche in 384 CE, and the Chinese style of arts and crafts developed accordingly in Paekche.[106] As mentioned earlier, Paekche actually played an important role in transferring Buddhism and Chinese culture to Japan.

In its warfare with Koguryo, Paekche won the first round, taking advantage of Koguryo's problems with the Chinese in the north. Paekche invaded Koguryo in 371 CE, killing its king and taking control of the best agricultural regions around the Han River. Paekche, however, could not maintain its victory over Koguryo for long. Under their strong warrior King, Gwanggaeto (391–413 CE), Koguryo soon regained its strength as a paramount power and waged wars against not only Paekche, but also the Japanese-supported Kaya League, as well as the Chinese in Manchuria. Between 475 and 538, Koguryo forced Paekche to move its capital twice to cities further south. Paekche relied on its alliances with Silla and the Kaya League in combating the aggressive Korguryo.[107]

Silla, initially the smallest and the weakest state among the three, was originally associated with Chinhan, another of three Han confederations in the south. It managed to stay out of the initial conflicts between Koguryo and Paekche. It remained in relative isolation, away from Chinese influence, and did not establish substantial contact with China until the sixth century CE. This proved to be a mixed blessing for Silla. With less influence from China, Silla had an opportunity to develop a political system of its own, a combination of both the Chinese bureaucratic model and the Korean aristocratic connection. Silla created seventeen grades, known as "bone ranks," to run its government headed by a king. These ranks were based on hereditary aristocracy instead of merit, which was emphasized in the Chinese system. Through the use of these ranks, the king of Silla could better incorporate the other chiefs in the Chinhan tradition into his aristocracy than Paekche could with Mahan chiefs. By the mid-sixth century CE, Silla had become an important ally with Paekche, and the two together defeated Koguryo and recovered Paekche's former capital near the Han River. Silla, however, soon turned against Paekche and took the lower Han River Valley, which gave Silla direct access to China. This proved to be very important for Silla in gaining Chinese support in its final struggle against both Paekche and Koguryo a century later.[108] By 562 CE, Silla had eliminated Kaya, which had been a foothold for Japan.[109]

Irritated by Silla's betrayal and control of the lower Han River Valley, Paekche tried to push Silla back to the south. In desperation, Silla asked China for help. China, which had failed in its repeated efforts to invade Korea from the north under the Sui dynasty and the early Tang dynasty, agreed to provide help to Silla. In 660, Silla and Tang joint forces defeated Paekch and eliminated it as a power.[110] By this time, Koguryo, which was initially the most formidable force among the three, had been greatly weakened by the repeated Chinese invasions from the north and its internal strife. In its weakened state, Koguryo could no longer hold against the invading forces of Silla and Tang, and surrendered in 668 CE.

With the help of Tang China, Silla finally eliminated its long-term competitors and for the first time in Korean history, put most of the Korean peninsula under the control of a single power. China, however, would not easily give up their opportunity to control Korea. This led to a six-year war between Silla and Tang China. Silla was able to rally the Korean forces from all of Korea, including forces from its former enemies, Paekche and Koguryo, and successfully drive the Chinese out of Korea by 676 CE. Relations with China were severed until the beginning of the next century when the Chinese Tang dynasty was eventually obligated to settle with accepting Silla as a tributary state.[111]

A new state, the state of Parhae (Bohai in Chinese, 698–926 CE), emerged in Southern Manchuria and northern Korea, an area that had formerly been controlled by Koguryo. Many people in Parhae were descendants of Koguryo people, but other minority groups also immigrated into the area from China. Its culture was a combination of both Chinese and Korean components.[112] As a result, there are still ongoing debates about whether the state of Parhae should be counted as part of Korean or Chinese history.

THE SILLA PERIOD

The formation of the United Silla (668–935 CE) was a significant event in Korean history. Under Silla, Korea became a unified state with the same language and customs; the Koreans, who had been divided by different economic and political interests, were able to build a single, homogenous political and cultural identity that continues today. As a tributary state to China, Silla regularly sent their students to China to bring back knowledge of Chinese political and cultural systems.[113] The Silla kings consolidated their political control through a centralized Tang-style administration, establishing a National Academy, which was devoted to Confucian teachings. Silla, however, did not adopt the civil examination system that had been implemented in Tang China, and the bureaucracy was still based on old-style, aristocratic "bone ranks" developed in the earlier Silla kingdom.[114] The country was divided into provinces and prefectures that were led by officials appointed by the central government. The Silla government attempted to implement land reform, which was intended to convert the estates owned by the aristocrats into lands assigned by the central government. This attempt at land reform, however, completely failed. Similar to the city of Nara in Japan, Silla's capital at Kyongju imitated the same checkerboard style of the Tang capital, Chang'an. The Silla army was organized into "oath banners"; three of them were Silla soldiers, whereas former soldiers of Koguryo and Paekche were put into separate banners.[115] Economically, Silla prospered through its trade with China. The artifacts that were excavated from the tombs of Silla's capital in Kyongju (also Gyeongju) included a golden crown, which illustrated the wealth of the Silla king and aristocrats.

Despite the heavy influence of the Chinese culture, the Silla period was known for its own gold, bronze, and granite artistic achievements, especially in the art forms that related to Buddhism. During the Silla era, Buddhism developed into the national religion with generous patronage from the kings who granted large amounts of land and generous funds to the monasteries. Similar to Ashikaga Japan, Buddhist temples became important centers of new architecture and art forms in Korea. Huge pagodas, as well as stone and bronze statues of Buddha, were among the most accomplished achievements of this era. For example, the three-story pagoda in the Pulguksa (also spelled Bulguksa) temple, which was built in 535 and enlarged in 735, remains as Korea's national treasure. The granite statue of Buddha at Sokkuram grotto (Stone Cave Hermitage) is also one of a kind, and UNESCO has declared Sokkuram as a site of world cultural heritage.[116] A great bronze bell, eleven feet high and several tons in weight, is another precious relic from Silla Korea.[117]

Similar to the case in Japan, up to the Silla period, Korea did not have its own written script, but instead used Chinese characters for its writings. Chinese characters, however, are monosyllabic in their pronunciation and thus, were not a good fit for Korean words, which are polysyllabic in nature. An important cultural development of the Silla period was the creation of a writing system for the Korean language, known as *idu*, which was developed by a Korean scholar around 694 and based on selected Chinese characters. It remained in use for several centuries until the *Hangul* alphabet was invented in the fifteenth century. With the help of *idu*, poetry, which was a dominant literary form during the Tang Dynasty in China, also became popular in Silla Korea.[118] The Koreans are especially proud of the *Chomsongdae* (star observation tower), which was built in 647 and is one of the world's oldest observatories. This milk-bottle shaped observatory has twelve pieces of base stone, which symbolized the twelve months of a year, and 365 stones altogether, representing 365 days in a year.

Toward the end of the eighth century, the United Silla became politically fragmented owing to the challenge of the old-style aristocrats whose tribal related traditions and values had never been destroyed. There was also a rising merchant group who greatly benefited from Korea's trade with China, and some of them, by this time had become actively involved in the political struggles. The Silla kings/queens started to lose control of the provinces, and the assassination of the Silla king in 780 marked the beginning of their decline. After 889, the country once again was split into competing kingdoms, and this gave the name "the Late Three Kingdoms" to the last part of the Silla era.[119] The remnants of the old three kingdoms reappeared to claim their independence. Kyon Hwon, who claimed to be the king of Later Paekche in 900, forced the Silla king to commit suicide in 927, but soon Kyon Hwon himself became disheartened by the power struggles of his own sons. In 935, he fled to Koryo (a short form for Koguryo), another kingdom that was established in 918 by a former merchant named Wang Kon. This led to the establishment of a new dynasty, the Koryo dynasty, which was named after Wang Kon's Koryo kingdom.

THE KORYO DYNASTY

In 935, Wang Kon became the ruler of the Korean peninsula after his kingdom had eliminated other competing powers. The Koryo dynasty (918–1392) under him and his heirs dominated the Korean peninsula for the next five centuries, providing the Koreans a more definitive identity. The word Koryo is the origin of the word "Korea," which is the modern name for both the peninsula and the countries on the peninsula.[120] Wang Kon, the founding emperor, who was given the Chinese-style title of Taejo, established his capital at Kaesong, a city located closer to the most productive areas of the country than the earlier capitals of Pyongyang or Kyongju, and rebuilt the city on the pattern of the Tang capital. Taejo and other Koryo kings actively followed the Chinese model in reshaping the political and economic structure of the country, and laid a solid foundation for the impressive achievements that Korea made during the Koryo dynasty.[121]

The Koryo dynasty, however, was not a simple replica of the Chinese system. Some Korean traditions survived, even within a Chinese style administration. For example, the civil service examinations that Korea adopted in 958 were supposedly open to a broader range of social groups, but commoners were largely excluded from the government, and the hereditary aristocracy completely controlled the court as they had before.[122] The kings usually appointed the sons of aristocrats to high-ranking positions without requiring them to take the exams.

Similar to the previous Silla period, Buddhist art dominated Koryo culture. Korean Buddhism continued to develop as its own unique version of Buddhism, which incorporated shamanistic and Taoist elements, and also placed a particular emphasis on new Buddhist schools developed in China, such as the Tiantai and the Chan sects. The Koryo period saw the peak of Buddhism in Korea. The Buddhist monasteries were big landholders, rich, and powerful; they were constantly involved in court politics and even engaged in the banking business. One of the most outstanding achievements of the Koryo era was a massive printing of the entire Buddhist Tripitaka, one of the three categories of Buddhist canon, in the eleventh century.[123] The ambitious project was encouraged by printing technology, developed in the late Tang era and arrived in Korea during the Koryo dynasty. Thousands of woodblocks were cut for this purpose over a period of more than seventy years, but many of them were destroyed in the Mongol invasion in 1232. Between 1236 and 1251, the Koryo king ordered another set to be made, hoping that such devotion would convince Buddha to protect the Koreans from Mongol rule. More than 81,000 woodblocks were cut, and these woodblocks, together with the remnants of the earlier set, were put in the Haeinsa monastery, which was built on Mount Kaya in South Korea. This unique collection of early printing materials, sometimes known as Haeinsa tablets, is still kept there today.[124] Another equally impressive achievement was the use of movable metal type for printing. Although China might have invented a similar technology earlier, the Koreans were the first to use metal movable type around 1230. Both inventions in China and Korea, it is said, preceded Gutenberg movable type (ca.1440) by more than 200 years.

Similar to the situation in China during the Song dynasty, Buddhism started to decline during late Koryo period. This, however, gave rise to more secularly-oriented cultural developments in other artistic forms, such as landscape painting and porcelain making. The pale green Koryo celadons, which were very different from the Song style, are among the most famous porcelain arts in the world.[125] The earliest remaining book on Korean history, *The History of the Three Kingdoms*, compiled by Kim Pusik in 1145, was another noticeable achievement of the Koryo dynasty.

THE MONGOL INVASION AND THE END OF THE KORYO DYNASTY

From the early stage of the Koryo dynasty, Korea had problems with its northern neighbors: the Khitan kingdom of Liao first, then the Jurchens, and eventually the Mongols. In 1010, the Liao invaded Koryo and sacked the capital, causing nearly a decade of war between the two. After the Jurchens defeated the Khitans, they also forced Koryo into a tributary state. The greatest threat, however, were the Mongols who overwhelmed Korea after they destroyed the Song dynasty in China. In 1231, the Mongols invaded Korea. Koryo put up a severe fight to defend their kingdom, but the Mongols, who had already subjugated China, central Asia, and Russia, proved to be too strong for Korea's resistance. The Koryo court was moved to an island off the west coast of Korea until 1259 when they formally surrendered.[126] The Mongols annexed the northern part of the peninsula and controlled the rest of the peninsula through garrisons.

The Mongol rule of Korea was a quite devastating experience for all Koreans, from the king to the peasants. The Mongols tried to legitimize their control over Korea through forced marriages between Mongolian "princesses" and the Koryo kings, and coerced Korean aristocrats to accept Mongol culture and values. Thousands of Koreans were forced into military service or slave labor. When the Mongols invaded Japan in 1273 and 1281, their emperor in China, Khubilai Khan, forced Koryo to participate, providing 900 ships for each occasion and collecting enormous amounts of supplies and labor from Korean peasants. Meanwhile, in order to push their culture through the Koreans, the Mongols destroyed the Silla pagoda at the Hwangnyongsa temple, an act that contributed to the Koryo court's decision to carve the second set of Buddhist Tripitaka and hide them in the Haeinsa Temple, in order to preserve the Korean Buddhist tradition.[127] As a result, even if the Koryo dynasty survived the Mongol invasion, it continued to decline and approached its end after the Mongol Empire fell apart in the middle of the fourteenth century.

In the 1340s, frequent Chinese rebellions broke out against Mongol rule. Under their rebel leader, Zhu Yuanzhang (see chapter 9), the Chinese drove the Mongols out of Beijing by 1368 and established a new dynasty, the Ming Dynasty (1368–1644), in China. In pursuing the Mongols, who were retreating to Manchuria, the Chinese rebel forces followed them and subsequently invaded Korea in 1361. After the Ming dynasty was formally established, the Koryo king had to choose between the Mongols and the Chinese. In 1388, the Koryo king sent General Yi Song-gye to fight against the Ming forces, but when General Yi encountered the Chinese forces, he started to realize the absurdity in fighting the Chinese on behalf of the Mongols. Instead of fighting against the Chinese, General Yi returned his army to the Koryo capital and took control of the court. In 1392, Yi Song-kye took the throne himself and, thus ended the Koryo dynasty, which had ruled Korea for over four hundred years.[128] The new dynasty established by Yi Song-gye was known as the Choson Dynasty, after the ancient Choson kingdom, but it was also sometimes called the Yi Dynasty, after the name of the imperial family.

For more information about the topics discussed in this chapter, please visit the website for this textbook. This website can be accessed from http://www.grtep.com/.

1 Fairbank et al., *Tradition*, 324.
2 Fairbank et al., *Tradition*, 325; and Conrad Schirokauer, *A Brief History of Japanese Civilization* (Philadelphia: Harcourt Brace College Publishers, 1993), 5.
3 World Development Indicators and Global Development Finance World databank, accessed on June 4, 2012, at http://databank.worldbank.org/ddp/home.do.
4 Fairbank et al., *Tradition*, 326.
5 Mikiso Hane, *Modern Japan: A Historical Survey* (Boulder, CO: Westview, 1992), 3.
6 "Japan," CIA World Factbook, accessed on June 4, 2012, at https://www.cia.gov/library/publications/the-world-factbook/geos/ja.html.
7 Fairbank et al., *Tradition*, 325–327.
8 For more on the Ainu, see William W. Fitzhugh and Chisato O. Dubreuil, eds. *Ainu: Spirit of a Northern People* (Seattle: University of Washington Press, 2000); Brett L. Walker, *The Conquest of Ainu Lands: Ecology and Culture in Japanese Expansion,1590–1800* (Berkeley: University of California Press, 2006); D.W. Johnson, *The Ainu of Northeast Asia* (Idzat International, 1999); and Mark Hudson, *Multicultural Japan: Palaeolithic to Postmodern* (New York: Cambridge University Press, 2001), 22–23.
9 Takehiro Sato et al, "Origins and Genetic Features of the Okhotsk People, Revealed by Ancient Mitochondrial DNA Analysis," *Journal of Human Genetics* 52 (7): 618–627.
10 Peter Duus, *Modern Japan*, 2nd ed. (Boston: Houghton Mifflin, 1997), 5.
11 Patricia Ebrey, Anne Walthall, and James Palais, *Pre-Modern East Asia: To 1800* (Boston: Houghton Mifflin, 2006), 138; and Fairbank et al., *Tradition*, 329.
12 James McClain, *Japan: A Modern History* (New York: W. W. Norton, 2002), 12; and Fairbank et al., *Tradition*, 329–330.
13 McClain, *Japan*, 12; and Schirokauer, *Japanese Civilization*, 13.
14 Schirokauer, *Japanese Civilization*, 9–10; and Edwin O. Reischauer and John K. Fairbank, *East Asia: the Great Tradition* (Boston: Houghton Mifflin, 1958), 456–457.
15 Hane, *Modern Japan*, 7–8.
16 Reischauer and Fairbank, *East Asia*, 459–461.
17 Schirokauer, *Japanese Civilization*, 10–11.
18 Reischauer and Fairbank, *East Asia*, 469–470.
19 Schirokauer, *Japanese Civilization*, 30.
20 Schirokauer, *Japanese Civilization*, 15; and Reischauer and Fairbank, *East Asia*, 471–472.
21 Reischauer and Fairbank, *East Asia*, 475–476.
22 Schirokauer, *Japanese Civilization*, 30–31.
23 Reischauer and Fairbank, *East Asia*, 478-479.
24 Reischauer and Fairbank, *East Asia*, 479–480.
25 Reischauer and Fairbank, *East Asia*, 464–465.
26 For more on *Manyashu* poems, see Schirokauer, *Japanese Civilization*, 34; and Reischauer and Fairbank, *East Asia*, 496–497.
27 Schirokauer, *Japanese Civilization*, 35–38.
28 Reischauer and Fairbank, *East Asia*, 489–491.
29 Schirokauer, *Japanese Civilization*, 41.
30 Reischauer and Fairbank, *East Asia*, 480.
31 Fairbank et al., *Tradition*, 351.
32 Fairbank et al., *Tradition*, 352–353.
33 Fairbank et al., *Tradition*, 351.
34 Reischauer and Fairbank, *East Asia*, 516–517.
35 Reischauer and Fairbank, *East Asia*, 514–515.
36 McClain, *Japan*, 14.
37 Reischauer and Fairbank, *East Asia*, 520–521; and Hane, *Modern Japan*, 8.
38 Ethan Segal, "The Shoen System" in *Japan Emerging: Premodern History to 1850*, ed. Karl Friday (Philadelphia: Westview, 2012), 167–177.
39 Fairbank et al., *Tradition*, 358–360.
40 For more on the warrior class, see Karl Friday, "The Dawn of the Samurai," in Friday, 178–188; and Reischauer and Fairbank, *East Asia*, 522–523.
41 Heike is the Sino-Japanese pronunciation of the Chinese character for Taira, literally means "house of Taira."
42 "Genji" was the Sino–Japanese pronunciation of the Chinese characters for Minamoto (gen) and family (ji).
43 Reischauer and Fairbank, *East Asia*, 521–522.
44 Fairbank et al., *Tradition*, 360–362.
45 vReischauer and Fairbank, *East Asia*, 527–528.
46 Fairbank et al., *Tradition*, 361.
47 Reischauer and Fairbank, *East Asia*, 528–529; and Andrew Edmund Goble, "The Kamakura Shogunate and the Beginnings of Warrior Power" in Friday, 189–191.
48 Fairbank et al., *Tradition*, 360–362.
49 Ebrey et al., *Pre-Modern East Asia*, 213–215.
50 Schirokauer, *Japanese Civilization*, 75–77.
51 Reischauer and Fairbank, *East Asia*, 531.
52 Ebrey et al., *Pre-Modern East Asia*, 215.
53 Walter Wallbank, *Civilization, Past and Present* (Boston: HarperCollins College Publishers, 1996), 195; and Ebrey et al., *Pre-Modern East Asia*, 208.
54 Ebrey et al., *Pre-Modern East Asia*, 214–215; and Fairbank et al., *Tradition*, 366.

55 Hane, *Modern Japan*, 10.
56 Murphey, *History*, 127; and John Whitney Hall and Kōzō Yamamura, *Cambridge History of Japan*, vol. 3, *Medieval Japan* (Cambridge: University of Cambridge Press, 1990), 138.
57 Reischauer and Fairbank, *East Asia*, 539; and Hall and Yamamura, *Cambridge History*, 146.
58 Ebrey et al., *Pre-Modern East Asia*, 222–223.
59 Hall and Yamamura, *Cambridge History*, 130.
60 Reischauer and Fairbank, *East Asia*, 552–553; and Hall and Yamamura, *Cambridge History*, 153.
61 Hall and Yamamura, *Cambridge History*, 178; and Fairbank et al., *Tradition*, 375–376.
62 Hall and Yamamura, *Cambridge History*, 183–185.
63 Ebrey et al., *Pre-Modern East Asia*, 253.
64 Hall and Yamamura, *Cambridge History*, 175.
65 Ebrey et al., *Pre-Modern East Asia*, 253–254.
66 Conrad Schirokauer, *Japanese Civilization*, 98–99.
67 Ebrey et al., *Pre-Modern East Asia*, 259.
68 Schirokauer, *Japanese Civilization*, 99–100; and Reischauer and Fairbank, *East Asia*, 558–559.
69 Ebrey et al., *Pre-Modern East Asia*, 258.
70 Murphey, *History*, 144
71 Schirokauer, *Japanese Civilization*, 99–100.
72 Ebrey et al., *Pre-Modern East Asia*, 259.
73 Schirokauer, *Japanese Civilization*, 103.
74 Schirokauer, *Japanese Civilization*, 108; and Reischauer and Fairbank, *East Asia*, 564–565.
75 Reischauer and Fairbank, *East Asia*, 560–561; and Schirokauer, *Japanese Civilization*,100.
76 Schirokauer, *Japanese Civilization*, 108.
77 Schirokauer, *Japanese Civilization*, 108; Ebrey et al., *Pre-Modern East Asia*, 259; and Reischauer and Fairbank, *East Asia*, 567–568.
78 Donna Schaper and Simon Dorrell, *The Art of Spiritual Rock Gardening* (West Linn, OR: Hidden Spring, 2001), 134.
79 Schirokauer, *Japanese Civilization*, 109.
80 Ebrey et al., *Pre-Modern East Asia*, 259.
81 Ebrey et al., *Pre-Modern East Asia*, 259; and Reischauer and Fairbank, *East Asia*, 565–566.
82 Murphey, *East Asia*, 222
83 Reischauer and Fairbank, *East Asia*, 569–570.
84 Reischauer and Fairbank, *East Asia*, 570–571.
85 Fairbank et al., *Tradition*, 379–381; and Reischauer and Fairbank, *East Asia*, 573–574.
86 Mikiso Hane, *Japan: A Historical Survey* (New York: Scribner, 1972), 113; and Fairbank et al., *Tradition*, 396.
87 Schirokauer, *Japanese Civilization*, 121; and Reischauer and Fairbank, *East Asia*, 583–585.
88 Murphey, *East Asia*, 224.
89 Murphey, *East Asia*, 224; and Schirokauer, *Japanese Civilization*, 121.
90 Hane, *Japan*, 115.
91 Richard L. Greaves, *Civilizations of the World: The Human Adventure* (New York: Harper Collins College Publishers, 1993), 328; and Reischauer and Fairbank, East Asia, 586–588.
92 Hane, *Japan*, 135–136; and Reischauer and Fairbank, *East Asia*, 589–590.
93 G.B. Sansom, *Japan: A Short Cultural History*, rev. ed. (New York: Appleton-Century-Crofts, 1962), 410, quoted from Murphey, *East Asia*, 224.
94 Hane, *Modern Japan*, 152.
95 Hane, *Modern Japan* 152–153.
96 Reischauer and Fairbank, *East Asia*, 591.
97 Reischauer and Fairbank, *East Asia*, 594–595.
98 Murphey, *East Asia*, 178.
99 Ebrey et al., *Pre-Modern East Asia*, 116–117.
100 Michael J. Seth, *A Concise History of Korea: From the Neolithic Period Through The Nineteenth Century* (Lanham MD: Rowman & Littlefield, 2006), 10–11.
101 Murphey, *East Asia*, 177; and Ebrey et al., *Pre-Modern East Asia*, 119.
102 Murphey, *East Asia*, 177.
103 Ebrey et al., *Pre-Modern East Asia*, 119–120; and Mark E. Manyin, Larry A. Niksch, and Edgar V. Connor, *Korea: Current Issues and Historical Background*, (Hauppauge, NY: Nova Science Publishers, 2003), 166; and Murphey, *East Asia*, 178.
104 Murphey, *East Asia*, 179.
105 Ebrey et al., *Pre-Modern East Asia*, 121–122.
106 Fairbank et al., *Tradition*, 282.
107 Ebrey et al., *Pre-Modern East Asia*, 123–124.
108 Murphey, *East Asia*, 180; and Ebrey et al., *Pre-Modern East Asia*, 124–125.
109 Reischauer and Fairbank, *East Asia*, 410.
110 Ebrey et al., *Pre-Modern East Asia*, 126–127; and Murphey, *East Asia*, 180–181.
111 Reischauer and Fairbank, *East Asia*, 409–410; and Ebrey et al., *Pre-Modern East Asia*, 127.
112 Reischauer and Fairbank, *East Asia*, 414.
113 Murphey, *East Asia*, 180–181, and Reischauer and Fairbank, *East Asia*, 411–412.
114 Fairbank et al., *Tradition*, 288.
115 Ebrey et al., *Pre-Modern East Asia*, 129.
116 Ebrey et al., *Pre-Modern East Asia*, 133–134; and Fairbank et al., *Tradition*, 288–290.

117 Fairbank et al., *Tradition*, 290.
118 Ebrey et al., *Pre-Modern East Asia*, 133; and Fairbank et al., *Tradition*, 291.
119 Ebrey et al., *Pre-Modern East Asia*, 176–177; Reischauer and Fairbank, *East Asia*, 414–415; and Fairbank et al., *Tradition*, 291.
120 Reischauer and Fairbank, *East Asia*, 416.
121 Fairbank et al., *Tradition*, 293–295.
122 Fairbank et al., *Tradition*, 293.
123 Murphey, *East Asia*, 183.
124 Fairbank et al., *Tradition*, 295; and Seth, Concise *History*, 88.
125 Fairbank et al., *Tradition*, 295.
126 Reischauer and Fairbank, *East Asia*, 423–424.
127 Fairbank et al., *Tradition*, 287–298; and Murphey, *East Asia*, 182–183.
128 Reischauer and Fairbank, *East Asia*, 425–426; and Fairbank et al., *Tradition*, 300–312.

Chapter 8: Early Kingdoms in Southeast Asia

Present-day Southeast Asia

Similar to the case of African history, the early history of Southeast Asia is full of ambiguity, at least until the tenth century. A study of the early history of Southeast Asia usually runs into at least two general problems. The first is the scarcity of reliable sources available to historians in attempting to reconstruct an accurate early history. Archaeological discoveries provide evidence of a hunting and gathering culture in the region about 10,000 years ago and of human activities, such as farming in northern Vietnam and sea faring explorations in Java as early as 8000 BCE.[1] By 3000 BCE, the cultivation of rice became common in Southeast Asia, as did the cultivation of yams, taro, and bananas. By the sixth century BCE, there emerged socially and technologically sophisticated communities with populations exceeding two million, and these communities left large bronze ceremonial drums throughout the region.[2] However, our knowledge about the people responsible for these activities is still limited.[3] Written sources from China and India only provide us with fragmented information about the early history of the area. Even the term "Southeast Asia" is a relatively modern invention. The early Chinese and Arab mariners and traders gave the area various names such as "Nan Yang" (southern oceans) or "land below the winds."[4] The European explorers first viewed the region as an extension of China or India. The French referred to their colony in Southeast Asia as "Indochina"; the British called their colony "Malayan India"; and the Dutch referred to theirs as "Netherland's India" or "Dutch East Indies." The term "Southeast Asia" was first used during World War II to distinguish Southeast Asia from East Asia.[5]

The second problem is that it is difficult to make any conclusive generalizations about the region. Southeast Asia is more diverse than South Asia or East Asia. In geographical terms, the countries in Southeast Asia generally fall into two categories: "mainland" countries and island countries. The former include Vietnam, Laos, Cambodia, Myanmar, and Thailand; the latter refers to the Philippines, Indonesia, Malaysia, Singapore, Brunei, and East Timor, the youngest Southeast Asian country.[6] These countries have different cultural and historical origins, multiple ethno-linguistic groups, and a variety of religious practices. All of the major religions in the world are practiced in Southeast Asian countries. While Buddhism is the dominant religion in the continental countries, such as Thailand, Myanmar, Laos, and Cambodia, Islam has a strong presence in most insular Southeast Asian countries including Indonesia, Malaysia, and Brunei. Christianity prevails in the Philippines and East Timor. Vietnam and Singapore, on the other hand, have strong Confucian traditions. Religious diversity even appears in a single country. Indonesia, for example, is a predominantly Muslim country and actually has the largest Muslim population of any country in the world. Significant pockets of Christianity, however, can be found throughout the country, and Bali retains its Hindu traditions.[7]

Ethnicity and language also vary greatly among Southeast Asian countries. Although linguists still do not agree with each other on the grouping of some major languages spoken in the region, there are roughly four major language families in Southeast Asia: the Austronesian group (Malayo-Polynesian), which includes Javanese, Malay, and Sudanese; the Austro-Asiatic group, which includes Mon, Khmer, and Vietnamese; the Sino-Tibetan group, which includes Burmese, Karen, Chin and Miao; and the Tai-Kadai group, which includes Thai, Lao, and Shan.[8] The earliest residents of Southeast Asia may have come from southern China or Eastern Tibet. These immigrants came to Southeast Asia in waves that stretched between two and five thousand years before the Christian era began.[9]

Scholars who study early Southeast Asia have not reached a consensus concerning the chronology of early immigration. The earliest migrations that historians know of may have been of those who spoke Austronesian languages, as they became dominant throughout present-day Malaysia, southern Vietnam, and Indonesia between 2500 and 500 BCE. They probably entered the region in staggered waves.[10] Some of them, such as the Malay, moved in from southern China as early as 2500 BCE, but others in this group, who were probably sea-faring people, moved from China, by way of Taiwan, to the islands of Southeast Asia, and then up to the mainland Southeast Asian region. Their descendents account for the large populations of people who speak an Austronesian language today in Indonesia, Malaysia and the Philippines.[11]

Another ethno-linguistic group, a group of Austro-Asiatic speakers, moved out of southern China and eastern Tibet into Southeast Asia at what may have been an even earlier time. When the Malays reached the region, the Mons may have already been farming in Cambodia and the Vietnamese, in southern Vietnam. The Mons and the Vietnamese may have been in the region as early as 3500 BCE and spread throughout Southeast Asia as far as northern Sumatra.[12] The spread of two other ethno-linguistic groups, the Tai-Kadai group and the Sino-Tibetan group, however, eventually pushed the

Austro-Asiatic group south. Chinese records dated 110 BCE indicate that Tai-Kadai speakers, who originally dwelt in southern China, moved into northern Vietnam and then spread southwestward.[13]

As in the case of some other regions, geography played an important part in leaving Southeast Asia politically fragmented. Mountains, jungles, forests, and swamps prevented easy penetration of neighboring states. Historically, no single power has ever controlled the entire region, or even a large part of the region, as the Ashoka Empire did in South Asia or the Han dynasty did in East Asia.[14] Most early kingdoms were relatively weak and unconsolidated, and as a result, they were often unable to endure the challenges of new immigrants. Probably due to its earlier political disunity, today Southeast Asia has greater ethnic and linguistic diversity than other Asian regions. Today's Indonesia, for example, boasts over 300 different languages and dialects, and there are over 100 different ethnic groups in Myanmar.[15] Even smaller countries, such as Laos and Cambodia, are equally diverse. Laos has forty-seven ethnic groups within its population of five million.[16]

EARLY KINGDOMS IN SOUTHEAST ASIA

FUNAN AND CHAMPA

Two cultures, Indian and Chinese, exerted a strong influence over early Southeast Asian kingdoms. The emergence of the early kingdoms was, in a sense, the direct result of these influences. As early as 200 BCE, many Indian merchants travelled across the Bay of Bengal to Southeast Asia. Along with their merchandise, they brought social and religious ideas. Some of the early chiefdoms in Southeast Asia embraced the new ideas and used the religious principles to redefine their kingship over their domains.[17] Meanwhile, developments of maritime trade and agriculture also provided favorable conditions for the emergence of local powers.[18] Due to the large-scale penetration of Indian and Chinese cultures that occurred after the Qin dynasty in China and Ashoka Maurya in India, several kingdoms emerged on the mainland of Southeast Asia after the first century CE.

Funan (ca. first to sixth centuries CE) was one of the earliest kingdoms known to historians. The Funanese were probably related to the Mon-Khmer people who spoke an Austro-Asiatic language. According to one legend, a Hindu Brahman, who followed his dream to arrive in Funan in the first century CE, founded the kingdom. After defeating a local queen, he married her and started the royal line of the Funan kingdom.[19] Funan, accordingly, was a Hindu kingdom that was heavily influenced by Indian culture, probably as a result of their close contacts with Indian traders. Under its greatest ruler, Fan shih-man (r. 205–225 CE), Funan subjugated other states in the area and extended its power into southern Vietnam, Cambodia, central Thailand, northern Malaya, and southern Myanmar.[20]

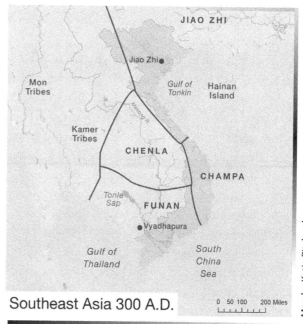

Southeast Asia 300 A.D.

Map by Katie Pitchard

Southeast Asia c. 300 CE

The Funan kingdom prospered through its active participation in the maritime trade that had developed between India and China. Situated in a strategic position overseeing the major sea routes and equipped with a great fleet, Funan became a powerful maritime force and played an important role in international maritime trade. Excavations at Oc Eo, one of the kingdom's major ports, revealed evidence of goods from India and China, and even golden coins from Rome were discovered among the artifacts.[21] Funan maintained a relatively cordial relationship with China and remained a tributary state of China from 357 CE to the end of the kingdom in the sixth century. Most of what is known about Funan comes from the records of two Chinese envoys who visited the kingdom in the middle of the third century CE.[22]

The Funan kingdom declined in the sixth century probably as a direct result of the decline of maritime trade around the region. New seafaring technology made it possible for ships to sail away from coasts, and thus bypass Oc Eo. The Cham, who took advantage of the reduced status of Funan, defeated them and established themselves north of Funan. According to Chinese records, a warrior from Chenla (or Zhenla), who might have been related to the king of Funan, finally eliminated the state, and Chenla replaced Funan as the dominate power of the region. To some scholars, Chenla is an important link that may be able to connect Funan with the Khmers, who established their powerful Khmer Empire in the ninth century CE in what is today's Cambodia.[23]

The Champa kingdom (192–1700 CE) was one of the longest, if not the longest, lasting civilizations in Southeast Asia. It was founded in 192 CE by a Han official from China, who established his own kingdom, known as Linyi, in the present city of Hue, taking advantage of the breakup of the Han dynasty of China.[24] Linyi was the first Champa state.[25] Champa later became a confederation of four different states. Unlike their neighbors in northern Vietnam, Champa was a Hindu kingdom. As early as the fourth century, Champa was influenced by Indian culture when it expanded southward into the areas that had been controlled by Funan. Their contact with Indian culture in what had been Funan gradually changed Champa into a Hindu kingdom, and its kings assumed the Indian-style of kingship, using *varman* as part of their names.[26] The term *varman* originated from the Hindu religion and was originally associated with warrior or ruling elites in Vedic-Hindu society. It was later adopted in early Southeast Asian kingdoms, such as the Champ kingdoms and the Khmer empire, as the official title of their kings.[27]

For more than a thousand years, the Cham withstood invasions from China, Vietnam, the Khmers, and later, the Mongols. After the Vietnamese Kingdom of Dai Viet was established in the tenth century CE, they forced the Cham to relinquish the northern part of their territory. Then, during the twelfth and thirteenth centuries CE, Champa had major problems with aggressive Khmer kings and fought hard to maintain their independence. Afterward, they faced an even more formidable competitor, the Vietnamese, whose many wars of aggression greatly weakened the Champa kingdom. In 1471, the Vietnamese delivered a major blow to Champa, killing more than 60,000 Cham.[28] A remnant of Champa lingered on, but was eventually absorbed into Vietnam in 1720. The last Cham king fled to Cambodia. Today, about 40,000 Cham live in southern Vietnam and about 85,000 live in Cambodia.[29]

Although Vietnamese culture was heavily influenced by China, the Cham in the south had a different cultural heritage, which was more influenced by Hindu culture. Champa left a significant cultural legacy in southern Vietnam. As a result, there is a noticeable contrast between the Sinicized culture in the north of Vietnam and Indinized culture in the south of Vietnam. The present city of Hue, the early Champa capital, is one of the most beautiful cities in Vietnam, adorned by elaborate palaces constructed in Cham style and tombs of early Champa kings. Hindu-based social and religious practices are still the backbone of the Cham society, including such practices as the caste system and the worshiping of the Hindu gods Shiva, Brahma, and Vishnu.[30]

PYU AND PAGAN

Similar to the situation of Funan and Champa, there is no agreement among scholars about the chronology of migration to today's Myanmar. The Mons from southwest China and the Karens from east Tibet were probably among the earliest ethnic groups who moved to the area.[31] Settling down in central Myanmar first and later moving southward to lower Myanmar, the Mons were among the first people in Southeast Asia to gain knowledge of Indian culture, which was brought over by Indian merchants who travelled along the east coast of Bengal to the lower Burma area. As early as the third century BCE, Emperor Ashoka sent two Buddhist monks to Myanmar to spread the Buddhist faith. Along with knowledge of Buddhism, the Mons also spoke the Indian languages of Sanskrit and Pali, and even modified their own script to conform to these languages.[32]

The Pyu, who were remotely related to the Burmans and spoke a Tibeto-Burman language, established the first historically significant city-kingdoms in Myanmar. The Pyu probably originated from southeast China, following the same paths as the Mons into Myanmar around the first century CE, and establishing their city-kingdoms at Binnaka, Beikthano, Halin, Shri Kshetra (southeast of modern day Prome), and Mongamo.[33] The Pyu built the earliest urban sites in Southeast Asia. From the excavations at Sri Kshetra, scholars have concluded that the Pyu's culture flourished in the area between the first and ninth centuries CE. Chinese records, *The Old and the New Tang Histories*, identify eighteen Pyu city-kingdoms, describing the Pyu governments as humane and the Pyu lifestyle as elegant and graceful.[34] The Pyu seemed to have a luxurious lifestyle, including "golden knives and utensils and art objects of gold, green glass, jade, and crystal."[35] Men wore gold and silver ornaments on their hats, and women wore silk scarves.

The Pyu are described as peace-loving people. According to Chinese records, the crime rate in Pyu society was negligible, and prisons were non-existent. It is believed that this passivity strongly influenced Burmese society until the nineteenth century.[36] The Pyu probably first adhered to Hinduism. The name of Beikthano, for example, means "city of Vishnu."[37] By the seventh century CE, however, Theravada Buddhism seemed to have become the dominant faith. The Pyu monarchs built numerous Buddhist monuments, including Buddhist stupas, tall bell domes with pointed tops, which were originally designed to contain the relics of Buddhist saints. The Pyu style became the principle architectural theme of Buddhist architecture in Myanmar.[38] Several of the most exquisite pagodas in today's Myanmar, such as the Shwezigon Pagoda (built in the eleventh century CE) at Pagan and the Shwedagon Pagoda in Yangon (also known as Rangoon) resemble the early Pyu style. The mild nature of the Pyu, however, may have eventually cost them their independence when the Mons defeated them in the eighth century CE, causing them to flee northward. The new Pyu kingdom became a vassal to the powerful kingdom of Nanchao between the eighth and tenth centuries CE in southern China.[39]

The people who were eventually responsible for the demise of the Pyu kingdom were the Burmans, who came from east Tibet and moved into Myanmar in the second century CE. After 500 CE, the Burmans gradually penetrated central Myanmar, where the Pyu people had settled, and took the Pyu's capital in 832 CE. By 849 CE, they had established their capital in Pagan. Not much is known about the early history of the Burmans before the eleventh century when their greatest king, Anawratha or Anniruddha (r. 1044–1077 CE), came to power. King Anawratha, who is credited as the founder of the Pagan kingdom, the first united state of Myanmar, greatly extended the Burmans' control of upper Myranmar.[40]

The Pagan era (1044–1287 CE) was also an important era in terms of spreading the Buddhist faith in Myanmar. Similar to Emperor Ashoka, King Anawratha became a zealous advocate for Buddhism after he was converted to Buddhism in 1056 CE. He defeated the Mons who had established their kingdoms in two separate regions, Pegu and Thaton, between 600 and 1000 CE. At the time, the Mons were probably one of the most cultured peoples in Southeast Asia. The Mons shared many similarities with the Pyu, against whom they had had earlier wars. Similar to the Pyu, the Mon kingdoms were Indianized kingdoms; however, the Mon kingdoms may even have exceeded the level of Indianization of the Pyu. The Mon kings had adopted the Hindu idea of divine kingship and their devotion to Theravada Buddhism was undeniable. The Mons were also described as peace-loving people, despite their wars against their neighbors.

In 1057, Burman King Anawratha agreed to help the Mons resist an invasion from the Khmers, but he did so only with the intention of securing precious Buddhist scriptures that were kept in Thaton. After the Mon king refused to surrender the scripts to him, Anawratha sacked Thaton, returning to Pagan with thirty sets of Tripitaka and 30,000 prisoners, including the king of Thaton and many Mon artists.[41] The conquest of the Mon states had far-reaching significance to the history of Myanmar. Some of the Mon monks who served at Anawratha's court introduced Theravada Buddhism to the king and his kingdom, and many Mons served at Anawratha's court. As a result, the Mon culture dominated both the Burmese court, as well as the city of Pagan. The Burmans were gradually assimilated into the Mon culture. Anawratha even modified Burmese script according to the Mon script. These events had enduring consequences on the further development of Burmese culture. Through the Mon culture, the Burmans were introduced to the Indian concepts of kingship, law, and literature, which helped consolidate Pagan as a well-structured state. Initially, the assimilation of the Burmans into Mon culture may have helped mitigate the wrath of the Mons, but the Mons never forgave the Burmese for destroying their hometowns. They continued to refuse to reconcile politically with the Burmans, and this resulted in centuries of warfare between the two.[42]

After his conquest of the Mon kingdoms, King Anawratha also subjugated the Shakingdom in the North and the Arakan kingdom in the West. By the time of Anawrath's accidental death in 1077 CE, he had laid a solid foundation for the Burmese domination of Myanmar, which has lasted to present day. The period under his reign is considered the golden age of Buddhist art and architecture, which was first sustained by Mon artistic value, but was continuously supported by the Burmese court for the next 200 years. Thousands of Buddhist pagodas and shrines flourished throughout the Pagan kingdom, including the famous Shwezigon pagoda in Pagan, which was built by order of King Anawratha to enshrine a sacred relic of the Buddha that he had obtained from the Mons. Representing a Mon artistic theme in Buddhist architecture, the Shwezigon pagoda is a huge terraced plinth about 100 meters tall, square below and circular above, with a bell-shaped stupa at the top, which symbolizes a sacred mountain in Buddhist culture. Painted with gold and decorated with thousands of diamonds and other precious stones, this golden mass carries an air of mightiness and stability.[43] For centuries, its beauty has inspired many to copy its design throughout Myanmar. Pagan, at its zenith, became one of the greatest learning centers of Buddhism. The financial burden of building and maintaining the Buddhist monasteries and building more Buddhist pagodas, however, exhausted the kingdom of its money and labor. The state started to decline in the thirteenth century CE, and in 1287 CE, the Mongols under Khubilai Khan sacked the city and thus ended the Pagan kingdom.

THE KHMER EMPIRE

The highlight of the early Southeast Asian States was the power and achievement of the Khmer Empire (802–1431), which existed between the ninth and fifteenth centuries CE. The Khmers were related to the Mons, but it is not clear whether they belonged to the same ethnic group as the Funanese.[44] Their first state in Southeast Asia was Chenla, which was a vassal state to the Funan Empire, but in the middle of the seventh century CE, they overthrew Funan and became a dominant power in the Mekong Delta.[45] Afterward, they began expanding into lower Myanmar, central Thailand, and southern Vietnam. According to Chinese records, the Khmers were divided, and in 706 CE, their kingdom was separated into Upper Chenla, which was probably in today's southern Laos, and Lower

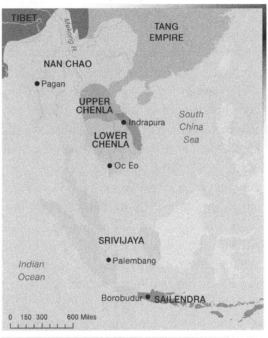

Southeast Asia, c. 800 CE

or Water Chenla, which was located in the Mekong Delta.[46] Other than this, not much is known about the early history of the Khmers.[47] It seems that the divided Khmers became vulnerable to new threats, and in 790 CE, Lower Chenla was invaded by a rising sea power, the Sailentras of Java, who took advantage of the Khmers' inability to replace Funan as a seafaring power. The king of Lower Chenla was killed, and his family was taken to Java as hostages.[48] When a prince, later known as Jayavarman II, returned to Chenla after having spent some time in Java as a hostage, he rallied all of the Khmers, both in Upper and Lower Chenla, and successfully resisted new invasions from the Sailendras.[49] In 802 CE, he crowned himself as the king, and thus began a new era for the Khmers, known as the Angkor Empire. Jayavarman II's long reign, from 802 to 850 CE, laid a solid foundation for Angkor's dominance over the next six centuries.

During the Chenla era and even during their vassalage to the Funan kingdom, the Khmers had already been exposed to Indian culture and accepted many of the values of that culture. The title for the Khmer kings, for example, was evidence of Hindu influence. Jayavarman II further consolidated his power by accepting the Indian notion of "god-king" (*devaraja*) and invited an Indian Brahman to design an elaborate ceremony to establish him as a manifestation of the god Shiva, one of the supreme deities in Hinduism.[50] By reinforcing the notion of the god-king, he successfully legitimized his kingship as divine and hence claimed for himself absolute sovereignty over all of the Khmers. His employment of the concept of divine kingship was probably one of the most important factors accounting for the power and durability of the Angkor Empire. From then on, the power of Angkor was centered on the king, who was an ultimate defender of the faith and had absolute control over his bureaucracy and society.

Using a connection to god Shiva in order to justify the Khmer king's rule, however, did not mean that the Khmers were devoted exclusively to Hinduism. The early Khmers learned about Hinduism from their Funan connections, but subsequently Buddhism, both in the forms of Mahayana and Theravada, was introduced to the Khmer kings. For their convenience, the Khmer kings mixed ideas and concepts from both religions. Actually, this was not an unusual practice among the early Indianized states in early Southeast Asia. New faiths were first introduced to the state ruler, who practically chose the concepts or deities that would support his control over the state and the society. These rulers were not necessarily devoted to the theological dogma of one particular religion. As a result, in the minds of the religious devotees in the Khmer Empire and other kingdoms, there was probably no clear distinction between Hinduism and Buddhism. Their loyalty could go to god Shiva, god Vishnu and Buddha all at the same time.[51]

Other strategies that contributed to Khmer success include Jayavarman II's clever choice of the location of his capital. While his major competitors were in the south and east, he moved further west from the Mekong Delta to the area north of Tonle Sap Lake in western Cambodia. This gave the Khmers a safe buffer to consolidate their kingdom on the fertile agricultural land of Cambodia and opened the door for the Khmers to expand further northward and westward.[52] The later expansion, however, put the Khmers into conflicts with other formidable forces like the Anman in northern Vietnam, the Cham in central Vietnam, and the Thai in Siam.[53]

The subsequent Khmer kings exalted Jayavarman II as the true founder of the Khmer empire, and closely followed Jayavarman II's design to expand the kingdom and build new Khmer capitals. It was not, however, until the fourth king, Yasovarman I (r. 889–900 CE) that the Khmers built their capital at Angkor. Yasovarman I built an elaborate capital after the previous capital was burned during the ensuing power struggle upon the death of his father. The entire design of the new capital city reflected a Hindu understanding of the universe. The city was surrounded by a wall and a moat, which symbolized Hindu thinking of the universe as being delimited by rock and ocean. At the exact center of the city stood Phnom Bakheng Hill, an artificial mound that represented the sacred Mount Meru in the Himalayas. According to Hindu tradition, Mount Meru was the heavenly residence of Hindu gods.[54] A temple was built on the top of the hill. The temple, with its galleries facing all four directions, was considered the center of the universe. Yasovarman I declared that he was "Ruler of the Universe." All of the subsequent Khmer kings inherited this title and employed this Hindu concept of universe to design their own capitals and temple complexes.[55]

Another significant achievement of Yasovarman I was the construction of one of the largest reservoirs in the Angkor Empire. It had the capacity to store enough water to irrigate as many as 20,000 acres of farmland. According to Helen Ibbitson Jessup, this project was "a staggering example of the hydraulic ambitions of the Khmer, since its construction entailed altering the course of the Siem Reap River."[56] Agriculture was the greatest resource of wealth for Angkor. Some scholars calculated that during the Angkor era, engineers developed a sophisticated irrigation system, which included reservoirs, storage tanks, canals, and dams. It covered 12.6 million acres of farmland that were able to yield three or four harvests a year.[57] The greatest wealth of the Khmer kings was essentially the agricultural capacity of their kingdom, which could sustain a large population and source of labor.[58]

The Khmer kings closely followed the footsteps of their predecessors and further enhanced Angkor's power and glory through their territorial expansion. By the death of Yasovarman I, the Khmer empire may have already achieved hegemony over a large area, which included parts of today's Myanmar, Thailand, Cambodia, and Vietnam. Suryavarman I (1002–1050 CE) was the first king to turn that hegemony into an empire. He expanded the Khmer kingdom into the Chao Phraya River Valley, and added into his territory the fertile land that stretched into the Malay Peninsula.[59] This greatly increased the king's revenue and helped fund the large-scale construction of religious temples and monasteries. Suryavarman II (1113–1150 CE), the most ambitious Khmer king in terms of territorial expansion, expanded this territory in all directions. He invaded Champa in central and southern Vietnam and controlled the area for nearly two decades until the Cham regained control of their capital in 1150 CE. Amidst his war against Champa, he also sent an unsuccessful expedition against Dai Viet in northern Vietnam in 1132 CE.[60] His conquering of several city-states extended his power to as far north as present day Laos; as far south as today's southern Thailand in the upper Malay Peninsula, and as far west as the border of the Pagan kingdom. In 1177 CE, however, Suryavarman II suffered a severe setback when the Cham, who learned to use cavalry and naval forces instead of traditional fighting techniques, sacked and destroyed the Khmer capital that had been built by Yasovarman I. The Khmers, however, soon recovered from this disaster. Unified under their great king Jayavarman VII (1181–1219 CE), who liberated the state from the Cham, the Khmers retaliated against the Cham and sacked the Champa capital in 1190 CE.[61] King Jayavarman VII's reign marked the apogee of the Khmer civilization,

Southeast Asia, c. 900 CE

and his empire dominated a large part of Southeast Asia until the middle of the fifteenth century. Zhou Daguan, a Chinese traveler who visited Angkor in 1296, was impressed by the wealth of the Khmer king and the layout of the city, describing the city of Angkor as the richest in Southeast Asia.[62]

The most important legacy of the Khmer Empire, however, was extensive monument building during the Angkor era. Many Angkor kings were great builders. King Suryavarman II, for example, is best remembered for his ambitious construction of Angkor Wat (*wat* means temple), one of the most important temple complexes in the world. Angkor Wat was built between 1112 and 1152 CE as a Vishnu temple celebrating Suryavarman II as the incarnation of the god Vishnu. It is an immense rectangle, measuring about 1,300 by 1,500 meters (about 4,265 by 4922 ft), surrounded by

a thick brick wall and a moat, which is almost 200m (656 ft) wide.[63] The entire structure was built according to the same Hindu principles discussed earlier. The central structure was five towers linked by galleries, which signified Mount Meru and the other four nearby sacred hills, the heavenly residence of Hindu gods. The open ground space between the towers and the surrounding walls was filled with galleries and libraries, which were lavishly decorated with thousands of fine bas-reliefs depicting Hindu legends and Khmer history. Some of them depicted episodes of the *Ramayana* and *Mahabarata*, two great Hindu epics,

Angkor Wat

Angkor Thom

and others portrayed their king, Suryavarman II inspecting his troops. "Suryavaman II was probably Cambodia's most assiduous empire builder," claimed Jessup, "but had he achieved nothing else, the construction of Angkor Wat would ensure his place in the pantheon of contributors to civilization."[64] Since it is a splendid example of Khmer architecture, Angkor Wat is a major tourist attraction in Cambodia and one of the greatest wonders of the world today.

The greatest builder of the Khmer kings, however, was Jayavarman VII, who constructed a new capital after the Cham had destroyed the old capital. The new capital, known as Angkor Thom, was situated on the right bank of the Siem Reap River and partially overlapped with the old capital. Again, the city was surrounded by thick stone walls and a moat, and was entered through one of the five monumental gates, guarded by statues of colossal heads of generals and courtiers.[65] At the center of the city is the Bayon Temple, which is famous for its fifty towers, each bearing four massive stone faces, each face pointing to one of the four cardinal directions. Unlike his predecessors who devoted themselves mostly to Hinduism, Jayavarman VII was a Mahayana Buddhist. As a result, the Bayon Temple is a Buddhist temple and was the official state temple at the time, in contrast to Angkor Wat, which is a temple of Vishnu. The faces on the towers conveyed the Buddhist message of looking in all directions for souls to save. Because of the lack of reliable archival sources, however, the debate concerning the identity of these identical gigantic and mysterious faces is still ongoing.[66] Some believe that they are the faces of the Bodhisattva of Mercy, but others point out the striking resemblance of these faces to a sculpture of Jayavarman VII's own face, which had the same gentle smile known as the Khmer smile.[67] In addition to these towers, Bayon also contains galleries decorated with extraordinary bas-reliefs, which tell the history and everyday life of the Angkor Empire. In the words of a Japanese team that is involved in preserving the temple, Bayon is "'the most striking expression of the baroque style' of Khmer architecture, as contrasted with the classical style of Angkor Wat."[68]

DECLINE OF THE KHMER EMPIRE

Jayavarman VII was the last great king of the Angkor Empire. His reign marked the zenith of power and prosperity for the Angkor Empire, but also the beginning of its decline. One foremost reason for the decline was Jayavarman VII's large-scale construction projects, which eventually took a toll on his kingdom's finances. In addition to Angkor Thom, the Bayon temple, and other monuments, Jayavarman VII also built the roads that linked his capital with the provinces. During his time, according to D. R. SarDesai, the king built 102 hospitals, 101 rest houses for pilgrims, and over 20,000 shrines. The state also supported all of these hospitals and shrines, and nearly 300,000 priests and monks were on the state payrolls. All of this proved to be too much of a burden on the villagers, artisans, and even his officials who had to organize and supervise thousands of laborers for the king's continuous projects.[69]

The weakened economic structure, in turn, could no longer sustain the military supremacy of the kingdom. Angkor was subject to threats from the Cham in the east and especially from the Thai in the west.[70] The Thai, whose hometown in Nanchao was overrun by the Mongols in the thirteenth century, aggressively expanded south and became an emerging power in Southeast Asia. When Jayavarman VII died in 1219 CE, the Thai took the opportunity to declare their independence from Khmer rule and established their kingdom at Sukhotai.

In 1431 CE, the Thai captured and sacked Angkor Thom after a seven-month siege. The subsequent Thai invasions permanently destroyed the vital irrigation system of the region and forced the Khmers to abandon Angkor to move further south to Phnom Penh, despite briefly recovering their capital.[71] The mighty Angkor Empire, which had dominated a large part of Southeast Asia for more than five centuries, gradually sunk into oblivion. Angkor Wat, the ruins of Angkor Thom, and the remains of other monumental buildings built by the Khmer kings vanished in the jungle. Although Angkor Wat was not totally abandoned and was preserved better than Angkor Thom and the other remains, they did not get much attention outside of Cambodia until the nineteenth century.[72] The rich Khmer cultural heritage, represented by its extraordinary achievements in architecture and arts, however, survived long after the kingdom disappeared. The Thai, for example, absorbed much of the Khmer legacy, which became obvious in later developments of Thai architecture, their concepts of administration, and even the Thai written language.[73]

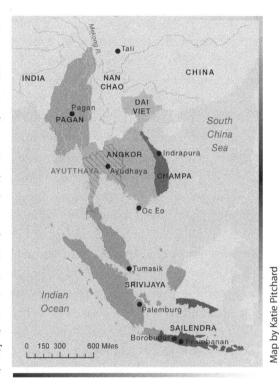

Map by Katie Pitchard

Southeast Asia in the Thirteenth Century

EARLY KINGDOMS IN VIETNAM

Although destruction of the Angkor Empire had little to do with the state of Vietnam, the decline of Angkor encouraged the Vietnamese to expand further south after the fifteenth century. The Vietnamese had long been an active player in Southeast Asia. The Vietnamese probably originated in South China and established their legendary kingdoms in the Red River Valley thousands of years before the Christian era. The first historically known kingdoms were Van Lang (also known as Hong Bang dynasty, (2879 ?–258 BCE) and Au Lac (also known as the Trieu dynasty, 257–207 BCE). They were connected to the Dong Son culture, which,

Artist unknown.

Dong Son drum

according to archaeological evidence, lasted from about 1000 BCE to the first century CE.[74] The Dong Son culture was characterized by the early cultivation of rice and domestication of animals, and the production of huge bronze ceremonial drums, known as Dong Son drums, which have been discovered throughout Southeast Asia.[75] Archeological evidence from northern Vietnam also indicated that the Vietnamese were among the earliest peoples to cultivate rice.

Au Lac, the last of the pre-historical Vietnamese states, was short-lived and was conquered by a Chinese general, Trieu Da (Zhao Tuo in Chinese), who took advantage of the chaos following the collapse of the Chinese Qin dynasty and carved out his own kingdom in 207 BCE in southern China and Northern Vietnam. This was the first Chinese-Vietnamese kingdom, known as Nam Viet (or Nan Yue in Chinese, and also known as the Trieu dynasty).[76] For a longtime, the Vietnamese accepted Nam Viet as the first Vietnamese state, but seemed to have recently changed that notion.[77] In 111 BCE, Chinese armies under the Han dynasty conquered Nam Viet and incorporated it into the Han Empire under the new name of Jiaozhi. During this first Chinese domination, Chinese administrators set up Chinese-style political institutions, and Confucianism became the official ideology. The Chinese language was also introduced and adopted as the official language. Chinese art, architecture, and music also flooded in and exercised a powerful impact on the local culture.[78]

The Chinese rule, however, was quite oppressive to the Vietnamese. The early history of Vietnam was, in effect, dominated by the theme of the Vietnamese resistance against the Chinese, who frequently penetrated into, and often exerted direct control over, northern Vietnam. In 39 CE, a noble woman, Trung Trac, the wife of a local Lac lord who had been executed by the Chinese, led a rebellion against the Chinese. Trung Trac and her sister declared themselves queens and set up their administration at the former capital of the Au Lac kingdom.[79] Although the revolt led by the Trung Sisters lasted only three years, the Trung sisters are honored in Vietnamese history as heroines who dared to engage in a struggle against Chinese rule.

Chinese control of northern Vietnam continued for the next few centuries. In 539 CE, another attempt at independence temporarily interrupted the Chinese reign. Taking advantage of disunity in China, Ly Bi, the magistrate of Jiaozhi, claimed himself as emperor and established the Early Ly dynasty in 544 CE. Freedom from Chinese rule did not last long. The Chinese, under the Sui dynasty, soon returned, and the Tang dynasty continued Chinese rule of Vietnam and renamed the area Annam, a name that continued to be used by outsiders as a reference to northern Vietnam until the colonial era.[80] It was not until the prolonged chaos of the late Tang era in the tenth century that the wishes of the Vietnamese to become independent were finally fulfilled. The collapse of the Tang dynasty provided a great opportunity for the Vietnamese to gain their freedom. In 939 CE, a Vietnamese general, Ngo Quyen, successfully defeated the Chinese and drove them out of northern Vietnam. Ngo Quyen established a new Vietnamese kingdom, Dai Viet, and his Ngo dynasty (939–967 CE). Although short lived because of domestic problems and its conflict with Champa, Dai Viet paved the way for an independent Vietnam for centuries to come.

The inconsistent Chinese reign over Vietnam for over a millennium left a long-term impact on the formation of Vietnamese culture. Although it is difficult to evaluate the depth of Chinese influence because of the love-hate relationship between the two states, there is little doubt that Chinese culture left a strong impact on the development of Vietnamese culture. The most important aspect of Chinese influence is in the area of ideology, which is defined in terms of "three teachings," namely, Confucianism, Buddhism and Daoism.[81] The Chinese style of administration, overseen by an emperor and carried out by a mandarin bureaucracy, continued into later Vietnamese dynasties. Similar to the situation when the French culture dominated the early English court, the Chinese culture and language were well accepted by the Vietnamese elites for a long time.[82] Besides, the Chinese introduced many important technical and cultural innovations to northern Vietnam. Many Vietnamese family names were derived from the Chinese, and even the Vietnamese language, which is believed to be related to Cambodian rather than Chinese, is heavily influenced by Chinese in terms of vocabulary and grammar.[83] In comparison to other Southeastern Asian countries, Vietnam remains to be the only country where its early culture was Sinicized instead of Indianized,[84] although this approach of describing early Southeast Asia as either Indianized or Sinicized is challenged by some experts of Southeast Asian history.[85] Because of the peculiar nature of early Vietnamese history, some scholars believe that Vietnam belongs to the Confucian world of East Asia, and hence, include a study of Vietnam in their studies of the history of East Asia.[86]

For more information about the topics discussed in this chapter, please visit the website for this textbook. This website can be accessed from http://www.grtep.com/.

1 Craig Lockard, *Southeast Asia in World History* (Oxford: Oxford University Press, 2009), 7–8.
2 J. M. Barwise and N. J. White, *A Traveler's History of Southeast Asia* (New York: Interlink Books, 2002), 20–30; and Lockard, *Southeast Asia*, 10–18.
3 Lockard, *Southeast Asia*, 10–13.
4 D. R. SarDesai, *Southeast Asia: Past and Present* (Boulder, CO: Westview Press, 2003), 1; Duiker and. Spielvogel, *World History*, 6; and Barwise and White, *Traveler's History*, 10.
5 Barwise and White, *Traveler's History*, 9–10; and Milton Osborne, *Southeast Asia: An Introductory History* (Crows Nest, Australia: Allen & Unwin, 2010), 6.
6 SarDesai, *Southeast Asia*, 6.
7 Barwise and White, *Traveler's History*, 4.
8 Raymond Scupin, "Mainland Southeast Asia," in *Peoples and Cultures of Asia*, ed. Raymond Scupin (Upper Saddle River, NJ: Person Prentice Hall, 2006), 337–338; and M.C. Ricklefs, Bruce Lockhart , Albert Lau, Portia Reyes, and Maitrii Aung-Thwin, *A New History of Southeast Asia* (New York: Palgrave MacMillian, 2010), 1–2.
9 SarDesai, *Southeast Asia*, 10; Lockard, *Southeast Asia*, 13; and Barwise and White, *Traveler's History*, 25–26.
10 Duiker and Spielvogel, *World History*, 433.
11 Lockard, *Southeast Asia*, 13–15.
12 Duiker and Spielvogel, *World History*, 433; and SarDesai, *Southeast Asia*, 12.
13 Lockard, *Southeast Asia*, 13; and Barwise and White, *Traveler's History*, 25–26.
14 SarDesai, *Southeast Asia*, 6.
15 Peter Church, ed. *A Short History of Southeast Asia*, 5th ed. (Singapore: John Wiley & Sons, 2009), 108.
16 Barwise & White, *Traveler's History*, 1; and Ronald Lurkens-Bull, "Island," in Scupin ed., *Peoples*, 388.
17 Lurkens-Bull, "Island", 340–341.
18 SarDesai, *Southeast Asia*, 21–22.
19 SarDesai, *Southeast Asia*, 22; and Duiker and Spielvogel, *World History*, 435–436.
20 SarDesai, *Southeast Asia*, 22–23.
21 SarDesai, *Southeast Asia*, 22–23; and Helen Ibbitson Jessup, "Southeast Asia: the Khmer 802–1566," in *The Great Empires of Asia*, ed. Jim Masselos (Berkeley: University of California Press, 2010), 75.
22 SarDesai, *Southeast Asia*, 22–23; and Thomas R. Leinbach and Richard Ulack, *Southeast Asia: Diversity and Development* (Upper Saddle River, NJ: Prentice Hall, 2000), 49.
23 Jessup, "Southeast Asia," 75–76.
24 SarDesai, *Southeast Asia*, 23–24; and Encyclopaedia Britannica, Inc, *The New Encyclopaedia Britannica*, 15th ed., Vol. 3 (London: Encyclopaedia Britannica, 1998), 71.
25 Ricklefs et al., *New History*, 27.
26 SarDesai, *Southeast Asia*, 24.
27 For more on this, see Benjamin Walker. *The Hindu World: An Encyclopedic Survey of Hinduism* (New York: Frederick Praeger, 1968).
28 Barwise and White, *Traveler's History*, 50–52.
29 SarDesai, *Southeast Asia*, 24.
30 Leinbach and Ulack, *Southeast Asia*, 49–50.
31 SarDesai, *Southeast Asia*, 11.
32 SarDesai, *Southeast Asia*, 30–31.
33 Ricklefs et al., *New History*, 25–26.
34 Encyclopaedia Britannica Inc. *Encyclopaedia Britannica*, 2003, vol. 27, 760; and D.G.E. Hall, *Burma* (Hesperides Press, 2008), 8–10.
35 *Encyclopedia Britannica*, 2003, vol. 27, 760.
36 SarDesai, *Southeast Asia*, 31.
37 Ricklefs et al., *New History*, 26.
38 Encyclopaedia Britannica, *The New Encyclopaedia Britannica*, Vol. 9, 56.

39 SarDesai, *Southeast Asia*, 31.
40 SarDesai, *Southeast Asia*, 32.
41 SarDesai, *Southeast Asia*, 32.
42 SarDesai, *Southeast Asia*, 33.
43 Encyclopaedia Britannica, *The New Encyclopaedia Britannica*, Vol. 9, 56; and Ran'kun' Takkasuil, *Glimpses of Glorious Pagan* (Yangon: Universities Press, 1996), 7.
44 Murphey, *History*, 127; SarDesai, *Southeast Asia*, 24; and Jessup, "Southeast Asia," 75.
45 SarDesai, *Southeast Asia*, 24.
46 Church, *Short History*, 13; Ricklefs et al., *New History*, 29; and Leinbach and Ulack, *Southeast Asia*, 53.
47 For more on the Khmers before the eighth century, see Jessup, "Southeast Asia," 76–79.
48 SarDesai, *Southeast Asia*, 24.
49 SarDesai, *Southeast Asia*, 26.
50 Jessup, "Southeast Asia", 79–80.
51 SarDesai, *Southeast Asia*, 27.
52 SarDesai, *Southeast Asia*, 26.
53 Stanley Sandler, *Ground Warfare: an International Encyclopedia*, Vol. 1 (ABC-Clio, 2002), 460–61.
54 Murphey, *History*, 127; and Jessup, "Southeast Asia", 86.
55 Murphey, *History*, 127; and SarDesai, *Southeast Asia*, 27.
56 Jessup, "Southeast Asia," 86.
57 Church, *Short History*, 14; and SarDesai, *Southeast Asia*, 28–29.
58 Osborne, *Southeast Asia*, 27.
59 Jessup, "Southeast Asia," 93.
60 Sandler, *Ground Warfare*, 460–61; and Jessup, "Southeast Asia," 96–97.
61 Sandler, *Ground Warfare*, 461; and Jessup, "Southeast Asia," 100.
62 Osborne, *Southeast Asia*, 29; and Jessup, "Southeast Asia," 102.
63 Jessup, "Southeast Asia," 97.
64 Jessup, "Southeast Asia," 98.
65 Murphey, *History*, 127–128.
66 Jessup, "Southeast Asia," 101; and Leinbach and Ulack, *Southeast Asia*, 54.
67 Maurice Glaize, *The Monuments of the Angkor Group*. Translated into English from the French, revised 1993. An online version is available at <http://falcon.arts.cornell.edu/am847/pdf/angkor-guide%5B1%5D.pdf>, accessed on April 2, 2012; and Janet Arrowood, *Cambodia Travel Adventures* (Madison SD: Hunter Publishing, 2011), 47–48.
68 JSA, *The Bayon Symposium*, accessed on April 2, 2012, http://www.unesco.org/culture/Bayon/interface/en/temple.html.
69 SarDesai, *Southeast Asia*, 29; and Ricklefs et al., *New History*, 43.
70 Leinbach and Ulack, *Southeast Asia*, 54–55.
71 Sandler, *Ground Warfare*, 461; and SarDesai, *Southeast Asia*, 29.
72 Ricklefs et al., *New History*, 44–45.
73 Osborne, *Southeast Asia*, 30.
74 Ricklefs et al., *New History*, 32–33.
75 SarDesai, *Southeast Asia*, 33–34; and Leinbach and Ulack, *Southeast Asia* , 41.
76 SarDesai, *Southeast Asia*, 34.
77 Ricklefs et al, *New History*, 33.
78 Duiker and Spielvogel, *World History*, 433–435; and Ricklefs et al., *New History*, 33.
79 Duiker and Spielvogel, *World History*, 434.
80 Church, *Short History*, 183; and Duiker and Spielvogel, *World History*, 434.
81 Ricklefs et al., *New History*, 34.
82 Church, *Short History*, 184.
83 Ricklefs et al., *New History*, 34.
84 SarDesai, *Southeast Asia*, 34–35.
85 See, for example, Ricklefs et al., *New History*, 18–23.
86 See for example, Chapter 10, "Vietnam: A Variant of the Chinese Pattern," in Fairbank et al, *Tradition*, 256–276; and Chapter 9, "Premodern Vietnam and Korea, in Murphey, *East Asia*, 168–189.

Chapter 9 Imperial China

Between the thirteenth and nineteenth centuries, China found itself in its high imperial stage. Of the dynasties that reigned during this era, the Yuan (1271–1368), the Ming (1368–1644), and the Qing (1644–1911), two of them, the Yuan and the Qing, were of foreign origin. Nevertheless, Chinese political and cultural systems continued to develop based on the autocratic model developed during the Song dynasty, despite the non-Chinese background of the Yuan and the Qing. This durability of Chinese political order "lay partly in its capacity to let non-Chinese, when they were strong enough, rule over it without changing its fundamental features."[1]

FORMATION OF THE MONGOL EMPIRE

In the thirteenth century, the political threat of the Jin kingdom in northern China to the Southern Song dynasty became minor in comparison to an even bigger threat from the rising Mongols, who soon established their dominance not only in China and Korea, but also in Russia, Persia, and all of central Asia. At the height of their power, the Mongols controlled over 14 million square miles on

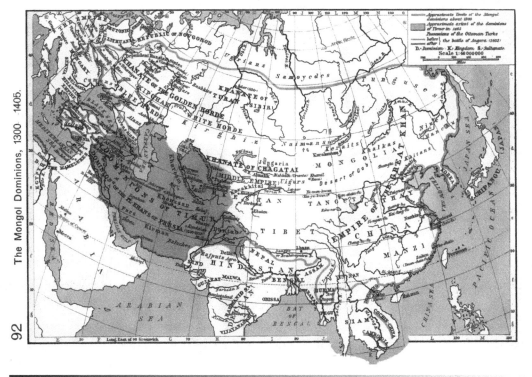

The Mongol Empire

Courtesy of the University of Texas Libraries, The University of Texas at Austin.

Eurasia, "an area roughly the size of the African continent."[2] The Mongol success started with their legendary leader, Temujin, or "man of iron" (1167–1227), who is more widely known by his title of Chinggis Khan, (more commonly spelled as Genghis Khan).[3] In the thirteenth century, he led his sons, and later grandsons, to create the largest contiguous empire that the world had ever known, leaving a permanent legacy on its historical development.

Temujin was born to a minor Mongolian chief and endured hardships during his childhood after enemies killed his father and forced his family into exile.[4] Temujin's personal strengths, such as courage, patience, and ambition, coupled with his strategies of cleverness and aggression, helped him survive and reemerge even stronger. After he defeated Toghril, a Khan of the dominant tribe of central Mongolia in 1204, Temujin unified the tribes of Mongolia into Khamag Mongol Ulus (the All Mongol State) in 1206 and then assumed the title of Chinggis Khan, meaning "Fierce or Resolute Ruler."[5]

image © qian, 2012. Used under license from Shutterstock, Inc.

Chinggis Khan

The unification of the Mongolian Steppes was the first step for Chinggis Khan in building his Mongolian empire. His troops soon began to raid and loot the neighboring areas, including the Xi Xia and Jin dynasties in northern China. Although Chinggis Khan may not have had a grand plan to conquer the world, his initial military successes and his yearning for a continuous victory inspired him to lead the Mongols, who were less than a million in numbers, to expand from northern China all the way to Russia and into Poland and Prussia. "Man's highest joy is in victory," Chinggis Khan reportedly claimed.[6]

In less than a century, the Mongols had subdued most of the population from the Pacific to the Danube.[7] Although scholars still debate about the reasons for the successful Mongol expansion, two critical reasons were the Mongols' military mobility and their strategy of terror, especially at the initial stage of the expansion. Their horses could travel more than 100 miles a day, so they often caught their enemies by surprise.[8] After their conquest, the Mongols, who did not respect city dwellers because of their own nomadic tradition, would burn down houses and conduct large-scale slaughters of local populations, leaving the cities in ruins. People would flee the area as soon as they heard that the Mongols were coming. During the years of 1212 and 1213, Chinggis Khan was said to have left more than ninety Chinese cities and towns in rubble. The Chinese population was reduced by 30 percent during the Mongol's rule; initial Mongol campaigns may have caused the deaths of forty million people.[9]

Chinggis Khan died in 1227. After assuming the title of the Grand Khan, Ogodei, Chinggis Khan's second son, adopted the idea that Heaven had chosen the Mongols to rule the world, in order to justify his own authority as well as the Mongols' continuing conquests. While Ogodei's troops were finishing the conquest of the Jin dynasty in northern China, other Mongol princes and generals led their troops into Iran, Iraq, Russia, Poland, and Hungary.[10] Although Poland and Hungary were spared from occupation, owing to Ogodei's death in 1241, the Mongols firmly controlled most areas in Eurasia by the 1280s. The central power of the Grand Khan, however, soon declined due to succession problems after the death of Ogodei. As a result, Chinggis Khan's sons and grandsons divided the Mongol Empire into four khanates: the Grand Khanate in China and Mongolia; the Golden Horde in Russia; the Il Khanate in Persia, Iraq, Turkey, and part of Afghanistan; and the Chagadai Khanate in Central Asia.[11] These Mongol Khanates went their own ways, pursuing different patterns of development based on the local physical, cultural, and religious characteristics. The Mongols' rule of the Il-Khanate was the first to end in 1333, and this was followed by their fall from power in China in 1368. Remnants of the Golden Horde, however, lingered in Russia at least until 1502. According to Timothy May, the last Chinggisid ruler in Khiva, Russia was not removed from his throne until 1920 by the Bolsheviks.[12]

Despite their initial brutality during the process of subjugation, the Mongols were eventually able to maintain peace in their occupied areas for a century and established an era of *Pax Mongolica* or *Pax Tatarica* (Mongol Peace), a term that some scholars coined to compare it to *Pax Romana* (Roman Peace). The term is used to describe the stabilizing effects on the social, cultural, and economic life of the inhabitants of the vast Eurasian territory that was under the Mongols' control in the thirteenth and fourteenth centuries.[13] It was the first time that a single power controlled most of Eurasia, thus facilitating inter-regional travel and trade. The Silk Road, both the inland and maritime routes, once again became important for linking different regions. Many influential world travelers, such as Marco Polo and Ibn Battuta (1304–1368) traveled unmolested from the Mediterranean to China and Southeast Asia by way of the Silk Road and other travel routes.

Marco Polo, who traveled from Venice all the way to China, was one of the first Europeans to travel extensively in China, where he stayed for over fifteen years, and brought back to Europe fresh knowledge about this relatively unknown country. Excerpts of his *Description of the World*, which he dictated to a writer when they were in prison together, were translated into Italian, Latin, French, and other languages, although the original did not survive.[14] Many Europeans at the time could hardly believe Polo's story that "black stones" (coal) could be used to make fire or that paper could be used as money.[15] It is said when Marco Polo's friends urged him to recant for the sake of his soul and admit that his accounts about China were nothing but his imagination, his reply was that "I have not told half of everything I saw."[16]

Meanwhile, the Mongols were able to adjust their rules according to geographical, cultural and religious variations. Despite their ill reputation as "barbarians" in the eyes of the natives, the Mongols exercised the rule of law in the administration of their empire. Chinggis Khan created a law code, known as *the Great Yasa*, which was promulgated in 1206. The *Yasa*, which was a collection

1324. Artist unknown.

Marco Polo traveling

of imperial decrees based on steppe nomadic tradition, laid out the basic rules of administration, as well as moral behavior based on nomadic customs.[17] The initial importance of Chinggis Khan's *Yasa* was to turn unruly nomadic tribes into more orderly organizations, which in turn, encouraged a more durable tradition of obeying the law. Their respect for law and order may help to explain the Mongols' pragmatic political style. In exchange for political stability, the Mongols were tolerant of all the religions in their ruling domains, so long as they did not in conflict with their *Yasa*. They treated all the religious sects, Nestorian or other Christian denominations, Islam, Buddhism, Shamanism, Confucianism, and Daoism, with respect, and generally exempted clergy of all faiths from taxes on the condition that they would pray for the Mongol rulers. Mongol rulers and their queens were known for their generous donations for the building of not only Christian churches, but also Muslim mosques and Buddhist temples.[18] It is said that the religious tolerance of the Mongols resulted in a faster spread of Islam and Buddhism within the Mongols' domains, since these were the majority religions in these areas. However, the number of Christians declined during Mongol rule. This decline of Christian control of the region may have facilitated the rise of Muslin empires in the areas of the Mediterranean, Central Asia, and India after the fourteenth century.[19] The impact of the Mongol Empire, thus, continued long after the Mongol Khanates were gone.

THE YUAN DYNASTY IN CHINA

Although Chinggis Khan died during his battle against the Xi Xia dynasty in northern China, his son and successor Ogodei soon uprooted the Xi Xia in 1227. In 1234, Ogodei overthrew the Jin dynasty of the Jurchens. He then attempted to conquer the rest of China, but, upon the advice of his major advisors, he soon gave up the idea in order to focus on consolidating his kingdom.[20] The Mongols did not return to eliminate the Southern Song until the second half of the thirteenth century.

The fourth Grand Khan, Mongke (r. 1250–1259), undertook two campaigns simultaneously against Persia and China. While Persia was conquered in 1256, southern China managed to stand against the Mongol invasion. Meanwhile, disagreement over who would become the Grand Khan after

Mongke's death in 1259 diverted the Mongols' attention from further expansion. The competition between Mongke's three brothers, Khubilai (1215–1294) who controlled northern China, Hulegu (1217–1265) who had conquered Persia, and Arik Boke (1219–1266) who was elected as the Grand Khan in the absence of Khubilai and Hulegu, caused civil unrest. The subsequent civil war resulted in the disunity of the early Mongolian empire. Since each brother ruled a separate Mongolian khanate, the four khanates went their own ways.[21]

In 1264, Khubilai consolidated his position as Grand Khan, although his authority as the Grand Khan may never have been truly recognized throughout the entire Mongolian Empire. Instead of continuing his fight with other Mongol rulers, he began focusing on China. In 1271, following Chinese tradition, he renamed his empire, which included China and Mongolian central Asia, the Yuan Dynasty (1271–1368) and made Dadu (today's Beijing) his capital. From Dadu, he resumed the Mongols' efforts to eliminate the Southern Song. In 1276, the imperial family of the Southern Song surrendered to Khubilai, and the Mongols finally took Hangzhou, the capital of the Southern Song dynasty, and put all of China under their control.[22] The last Song emperor drowned in a sea battle in 1279, and thus ended the Song dynasty.

Khubilai Khan established the first non-Chinese dynasty in Chinese history and in accordance with Chinese tradition, he was known posthumously as Yuan Shizu, the ancestral emperor of the Yuan Dynasty. Khubilai's success in China, however, did not satisfy him. After stabilizing China's situation, he soon turned his attention to China's neighboring countries. Korea had already been brought into tributary vassalage to the Mongols as early as 1260, but Japan refused to yield to the Mongols' power. Khubilai sent envoys to Japan to demand that Japan become a vassalage state of the Mongolian Empire, but Kamakura Shogunate of Japan rejected this demand and even executed Khubilai's messengers. In 1274, Khubilai sent his mighty fleet on a punitive expedition against Japan. His troops landed at Hakata Bay and sent the Japanese samurai on the run. Unfortunately for Khubilai, a typhoon came and destroyed his fleet overnight. A few years later, in 1281, Khubilai assembled an even larger fleet to pursue his dream of conquering Japan. Once again, however, bad weather, as well as some fatal design flaws in his ships, shattered his fleet. After these two setbacks, Khubilai finally dropped his plan of invading Japan. The threat of a possible return of the Mongols, however, contributed to the eventual fall of the Kamakura shogunate.

Khubilai proceeded further south, sending envoys to Vietnam, Annam, and even Java to solicit their surrender.[23] However, Khubilai's subsequent four land expeditions against Vietnam and five penetrations into Burma all failed to subjugate these nations. He eventually managed to make Vietnam accept his suzerainty and pushed forward to other areas in Southeast Asia.[24] The Mongols destroyed the city of Bagan, the capital of the Pagan Kingdom in Burma, and between 1278 and 1294 forced the Khmer kingdom to accept Khubilai as their overlord. The Thai kingdoms of Sukhotai and Chiangmai also accepted the status of vassalage to Khubilai. His punitive expedition to Java in 1293, however, failed to produce any positive results. Nevertheless, the Mongols exerted a strong influence on the political landscape of Southeast Asia—new states emerged from the ruins of the old kingdoms that the Mongols had devastated.[25]

CHINA UNDER THE MONGOL RULE

The Mongols' rule in China lasted less than a century. The initial construction of the Mongol empire in China was devastating to the Chinese. It is said that under the Mongol rule, the Chinese population dropped from 108 million in 1220 to 75 million in 1229.[26] From the beginning, the Mongols encountered severe problems as a minority surrounded by a large population with a strong cultural tradition. Facing native hostility, the Mongols initally filled many administrative positions with foreigners from central Asia and even from Europe, whom they could trust more than the Chinese. Marco Polo, for example, may have served at Khubilai's court for many years.[27] In effect, the Mongols facilitated the spread of Islam in China through their employment of Iranian officials. Khubilai Khan even established an Islamic Academy, which undertook the translating of Arabic texts into Chinese.

After the Mongols gradually learned that they could not rule such a vast and diverse area without adapting to the local political tradition and culture, they started to include the Chinese in governmental administration, especially at the local level.[28] Even at the central government level, the Yuan continued the Chinese political structure established in the Tang-Sung era with a division of responsibilities among three major government branches: civil administrative, military, and censorial. Recognizing the important connection between religion and politics, Khubilai tolerated the practice of Confucianism in China and even exempted Confucian scholars from taxation. However, he terminated the civil service examinations, fearing that his court would be flooded with Confucian scholars. Even after the examination system was partially restored after 1315, the Confucian scholars were not necessarily selected as top candidates.[29]

At least at the beginning, Khubilai's economic policies were effective and flexible. He maintained the Southern Song dynasty's policy of landholding and kept intact the Song dynasty's basic economic structure. The Mongols encouraged economic and commercial development for their own benefit. For example, the Grand Canal, which had become inoperative because of the territorial retreats of the Southern Song, was rebuilt and extended to Beijing for the purpose of transporting grains from the South to the capital.[30] Trade was facilitated through merchants of other Mongol khanates in Central Asia and the Mediterranean. In order to meet the requirements of large-scale commercial transactions, Khubilai created a nationwide financial system based on a paper currency that had been in use during the Song dynasty, a system of which greatly impressed Marco Polo.[31] Khubilai also built China into a sea power, increasing its influence on South and Southeast Asia. As stated previously, his fleets had visited Ceylon and Southern India, and attacked Java without success.[32] Despite the initial destruction that the Mongols brought to China, the Chinese economy survived and fared relatively well under the Yuan dynasty.

Despite a century of rule, the Mongols' impact on Chinese culture was limited. The Mongols struggled to avoid being assimilated into the Chinese tradition even though the daily contact with the Chinese was unavoidable. Some of them were drawn into certain Chinese living and cultural styles, such as painting, but most Mongols preferred not to mingle with the Chinese culture. With a lack of official patronage, traditional Chinese culture based on Confucianism did not flourish under the Mongols, but it did not suffer a devastating blow either. The Chinese continued to develop their culture on the basis of the achievements of the Tang-Song era without much interference. The historical tradition of composing the official histories of the previous dynasties went forward under the sponsorship of the Mongol administration. The drama and the novel emerged during the Yuan era as influential new literary genres.[33] The Chinese dramas produced during the Yuan dynasty were semi-operatic combinations of singing, dancing, delicate gestures, humorous dialogue, and brilliant costuming. They gained great popularity during the Yuan era. The development of these new literary genres represented both "the vitality of Chinese culture" and "the frustration of the scholar class" under the Mongols.[34]

The early prosperity of the Yuan was largely credited to the capable founder of the dynasty, Khubilai Khan. After his death in 1294, few of the remaining Yuan emperors were capable of executing strong leadership. By the mid-fourteenth century, Mongol rule completely lost its vitality when its emperors had neither enough ambition nor enough capability to maintain the Mongol dominance over China. Seven rulers ascended the throne in quick secession, and after a civil war started in 1328, the Yuan dynasty rapidly approached its end. Taking advantage of the weakness of the Mongol court, the Chinese rose to rebel against them. One commoner, Zhu Yuanzhang (1328–1398), gained prominence among all of the rebel leaders. After he led his troops to conquer Beijing in 1368, Zhu announced the establishment of a new Chinese dynasty, the Ming.[35]

EMPEROR HONGWU AND THE ESTABLISHMENT OF THE MING DYNASTY

The Ming dynasty (1368–1644) was one of the strongest and most important dynasties in Chinese history. It not only returned control of China to the Han Chinese, but also spread China's influence to areas as far away as Sri Lanka and the east coast of Africa. The Ming dynasty constructed such an orderly government, as well as a stabilized social and economic structure, that the Ming system persisted even under another alien dynasty, the Qing dynasty.[36]

The Ming, more than any of the other early dynasties, owed its style and governance to its founder, Zhu Yuanzhang, known as the Hongwu emperor, or posthumously as Ming Taizu. Zhu originally chose Hongwu as the name of his "year period," which usually specified the first year of a new emperor, but he continuously used it for the rest of his reign. As a result, Zhu transformed Hongwu into his reigning title, a fashion that was continued by the other emperors of the Ming and Qing dynasties.[37]

1905. Louis le Grand.

The Ming Empire

Zhu was the first commoner to become emperor since Liu Pang, the founder of the Han dynasty. He was an orphan who grew up as a Buddhist monk. He joined the anti-Mongol rebellion of the Red Turbans, who were related to a Buddhist sect, the White Lotus, and eventually became a successful general.[38] His troops captured Nanjing in 1356, but Zhu did not declare himself emperor until after he seized Beijing, the Yuan capital, in 1368. His expedition forces pursued the fleeing Mongols into Mongolia in 1372, and by 1379, Zhu's new empire had been accepted not only by the Chinese, but also by some of the Chinese neighbors, such as Korea and Tibet.[39]

After Zhu's establishment of the Ming dynasty, his personal style, more than anything else, was responsible for the national policies of the Ming dynasty. Hucker describes Zhu's personal style as "somewhat populist mediocrity."[40] In comparison to the glamorous aristocratic culture of the Han and the Tang, or the cultural magnificence of the Song, the Ming culture was in general mediocre and less colorful. Coming from a poor peasant family with an understanding of the plight of the poor, the Hongwu emperor catered many of his policies toward the poor in China. He confiscated large amounts of land from rich landlords and rented them to the poor peasants. His government levied extremely high taxes on commercial transactions and forced many rich merchant families to relocate from the Hangzhou-Suzhou area to his new capital of Nanjing. Emperor Hongwu's policies, however, did not deprive the region of its continuing prosperity.[41] The rich could continuously create and enjoy material and cultural wealth in the thriving cities of the Hangzhou-Suzhou region. Hongwu also fostered education in the countryside, establishing elementary schools for villagers. During the Ming dynasty, the villages were largely autonomous and enjoyed a certain kind of self-government.

Meanwhile, Hongwu greatly centralized his administration and deliberately reduced the power of the privileged groups. He curbed the power of the court eunuchs and fragmented the power of the military generals to make sure that he alone would have direct control of the military.[42] Although he restored the system of the civil service examination, the scholar-officials never enjoyed the same level of power as they had in the Song dynasty. Hongwu, thus, enjoyed a level of autocracy that few past Chinese emperors had ever had. This was especially true after he abolished the position of grand chancellor. The grand chancellor had been in charge of the central administration of the government ever since the Tang dynasty. Hongwu eliminated the position because of his great disappointment with his grand chancellor, Hu Weiyong, who had been a close friend, but had been involved in a conspiracy to usurp the emperor's power. Hongwu ordered Hu's execution in 1380 and took over direct responsibility of all the departments and ministries, although he did establish a grand secretariat to aid him in managing the court. As a result, the Hongwu emperor alone had absolute power, and all of the officials only functioned as his personal servants. His style of governance continued to influence not only the reign of other Ming emperors, but also some modern Chinese leaders such as Mao Zedong.[43]

One outstanding legacy of the Hongwu emperor was his creation of *Da Ming Lu* (The Great Ming Code), which started as early as 1367 even before Zhu formally established the Ming dynasty. The original version contained an impressive 430 articles, but seven years later, the second edition added even more articles, totaling 606 articles in thirty volumes. When it was finally promulgated in 1397, a year before Zhu's death, the code was reorganized again with its total number of the articles being reduced to 460.[44] The code represented a comprehensive plan of rebuilding the Chinese empire, dealing with every aspect of Ming China, including a justification of the emperor's power, the structure of the political institution, social customs, and a code for moral behavior.[45] *The Great Ming Code* is one of the most valuable collections of documents for studying the Ming society, as well as the legal history of China.

The last stage of Emperor Hongwu's reign was one of the darkest eras in Ming history. Toward the end of his thirty-year rule, the emperor became increasingly paranoid, especially after the death of his wife, Empress Ma, who had been a source of great comfort for him.[46] Hongwu was so distraught over her death that he refused to have a new empress. Isolating himself from others, Hongwu's paranoia drove him into believing that many at his court conspired against him. He imaged that they laughed at his humble origins behind his back and mocked his ugliness due to the large pits on his face from a childhood case of the measles. His distrust of his high-ranking officials seemed to be confirmed by the failed conspiracy of his grand chancellor Hu Weiyong in 1380. Not only did Emperor Hongwu order the execution of Hu Weiyong, he also put to death everyone in Hu Weiyong's family together with thousands of others who were remotely connected. Emperor Hongwu's ruthless purges had eliminated tens of thousands of officials along with their entire families, and only his death in 1398 put an end to it.[47] It is said that many court courtiers would bid farewell to their family in the morning before they attended the court, because they were not sure whether they would return home safely in the evening. The victims directly related to the emperor's purges totaled nearly 40,000 over the years.[48]

After the Hongwu emperor's death, a brief civil war over the succession broke out. The emperor had passed the throne to his grandson, Zhu Yunwen, whose father, the crown prince, had died earlier. This aroused jealousy from Emperor Hongwu's other sons, especially from Zhu Di, the fourth and most capable son. Zhu Di, the Prince of Yan at the time, decided to compete for power against his nephew. In the subsequent civil war, Zhu Di defeated his nephew and claimed himself as the Yongle emperor in 1402, becoming the third emperor of the Ming Dynasty. Despite his infamous ways of gaining power, which haunted him for the rest of his reign, the Yongle emperor proved to be the most successful of the remaining Ming emperors.[49] Yongle started with stabilizing the national economy. He made extensive plans to restore agricultural work in rural areas and promote production around the country. He rebuilt the grand canal to ensure a better connection between the prosperous south and Beijing in the north, the capital of his princedom that his father had bestowed to him. Emperor Yongle eventually moved the Ming capital from Nanjing to Beijing in 1421, and Beijing remained as the imperial capital until the fall of the Qing dynasty.

Militarily, the Yongle emperor was successful in eliminating the remaining Mongol threat and secured the northern borders for the Ming. The Mongols, however, never ceased to be the major threat to the Ming. In order to eliminate the Mongol threat, he led at least five campaigns into the steppe of Mongolia, but few of them produced significant results.[50] The pressure of guarding the northern border was one of the foremost reasons behind the emperor's decision to transfer the capital to Beijing. Emperor Yongle also turned his attention further south, sending troops to the Vietnamese Tran kingdom upon the request of the Tran king, who had lost his throne to a usurper. After Ming troops occupied northern Vietnam, which was known as Annam at the time, the Yongle emperor decided to annex Annam as a Ming province. This proved to be a mistake. Many Annamese resisted the Chinese occupation and engaged in guerrilla warfare against the Ming troops. They eventually regained their independence from the Ming under the leadership of their hero, Lê Lợi, who later established the Lê Dynasty, the longest-ruling dynasty of Vietnam from 1428 to 1788, with only a brief interruption.[51]

ZHENG HE AND HIS SEA VOYAGES

The most ambitious project of the Yongle emperor was his commissions of sea expeditions conducted under the command of Admiral Zheng He (1371–1433), his trusted advisor. Between 1403–1427, Admiral Zheng He led China's dragon fleets to the coasts of Southeast Asia, South Asia, the Middle East, and Africa. Zheng He had an unusual background. In addition to being an admiral, a diplomat, and an explorer, Zheng He was a eunuch and a Muslim. His family may have come to China from Persia, and both his great grandfather and grandfather served under the Mongol Yuan dynasty. During the Chinese rebellion against Mongol rule in the late Yuan period, the Chinese troops killed his father and captured seven-year-old Zheng He. They made him a eunuch as punishment and sent him to prince Zhu Di as a servant. Zheng He later aided Zhu Di in his war of succession against his nephew, and his loyalty earned him trust from Zhu Di, who became the Yongle emperor. In 1403, the Yongle emperor ordered Zheng He to conduct a sea voyage, the first of seven sea voyages in the next twenty-four years. The purposes of the voyages were not clear, but they might have included enticing the countries in Southeast Asia into China's tributary system; gaining firmer court control of the oversea trade between China and other countries; and hunting down Emperor Yongle's major competitor, his nephew Jianwen.[52]

Zheng He's first voyage of 1405–1407 was one of the most impressive. He set out from south China with an estimated 317 vessels, including sixty-two treasure ships. These treasure ships were 370 to 440 feet in length, 150 to 180 feet in width, and each had four decks.[53] One scholar estimates that "these treasure ships must have displayed about 3,000 tons apiece" and with "four to nine masts up to 90 feet high, a dozen water-tight compartments, and stern-post rudders." Each treasure ship could carry as many as 500 men.[54] According to Rhoads Murphey, these treasure ships were larger than any previously built ships in the world, but "were reported nonetheless to be faster sailors than the Portuguese caravels or Spanish galleons of a century or two later, especially with a favorable wind."[55] On his first voyage, Zheng He commanded a force of 27,870 men, accompanied by medical personnel, astrologers, and military officers.[56] Following the traditional trade routes, Zheng He visited the seaports of Southeast Asia, the east and west coasts of India, Ceylon, the Persian Gulf and the Straits of Hormuz, the Red Sea, and the east coast of Africa. Some ships may have gone even further around the Cape of Good Hope.[57] His fleets brought tributary envoys from nearly thirty countries to China, together with gifts including such exotic animals as giraffes, zebras, and ostriches, and then took these envoys back to their home countries.

At the time, these large-scale sea expeditions of Zheng He were unprecedented in the world. The voyages, however, were quite different from the European sea explorations conducted nearly half a century later, such as those of Vasco da Gama or Christopher Columbus. Diplomacy, rather than commerce or conquest, was the basic motivation of the Chinese dragon fleets. As a result, Zheng He conducted most of his voyages peacefully with only occasional violence.[58] They worked well as showcases of China's might and pride, but economically China benefitted little from these expensive sea expeditions. As the threat to China's northern border increased, the Yongle emperor temporarily suspended the sea voyages after Zheng He embarked on his sixth voyage in 1421–1422. After the Yongle emperor died in 1424, the succeeding Hongxi emperor (r. 1424–1425), issued an imperial decree to make that suspension permanent during his reign. The next emperor, the Xuande emperor (r. 1426–1435), ordered Zheng He to embark on his last sea voyage in 1430 in order to send some foreign envoys back to their countries in the Persian Gulf.[59] Zheng He and his fleet sailed out in 1433, but Zheng He died on his way back to China. The era of Chinese sea voyages ended with the death of this great Chinese admiral.

The later Ming rulers turned away from the sea, following Confucian doctrine that strongly favored an inward looking policy. While the Europeans started to conduct their overseas expansions zealously into other continents in the second half of the fifteenth century, the Ming emperors officially banned seafaring enterprises. Several factors may have caused the demise of China's seafaring business, including the financial burden of continuing the expensive sea voyages, the increasing threat from the Mongols at China's northern border, and strong opposition from Confucian scholar-officials.[60] As a result, after the Emperor Xuande, none of the Ming emperors was interested in sea voyages. Instead, they returned to the policy of *Hai jin* (sea ban), first proposed by the Emperor Hongwu in 1371, which banned maritime activities.[61] Although that policy was implemented inconsistently in the following years, the damage had been done. Not only were the treasure ships destroyed and sea maps burned, the Chinese were also discouraged from doing business overseas. By the late sixteenth century, the Ming's naval capability had deteriorated so much that it could not deter pirates from Japan and other countries who frequently looted the towns and village along China's seacoasts. The Ming spirit of expedition had changed into "a xenophobic isolationism," which turned China completely away from the sea.[62]

GOVERNANCE AND ABSOLUTISM OF THE MING

Many scholars characterize the politics of the Ming as a conservative "Ming absolutism."[63] The political structure established by the Hongwu emperor was initially headed by a grand chancellor, who was in charge of routine national business; a bureau of military affairs; and the censorate, who oversaw the officials' work. Hongwu later abolished the position after his execution of his last chancellor in 1380 and tended to state affairs himself.[64] This was probably the most important step toward Ming absolutism. In the previous dynasties, it was the grand chancellor or the chief minister, not the emperor, who was in charge of imperial administration. The administration under the grand chancellor was more or less independent from the emperor and thus allowed bureaucratic stability. Driven by his ambition of achieving absolute power, Hongwu decapitated the civil bureaucracy and fragmented the military commission. He formulated elaborate rituals in order to create an atmosphere where he was seen as a divine ruler, and he punished those who criticized him with humiliating retribution, such as beating their bare buttocks in public. Few could survive after this torture. Thus, the Emperor Hongwu became the most powerful and feared despot in Chinese imperial history. The Tang emperors sat down with their grand chancellors to discuss national affairs, and the Song emperors allowed their courtiers to stand in front of them to voice their opinions, but Ming officials were required to kneel down and kowtow in the presence of their emperors.[65] It is believed that the Emperor Hongwu's ambition of concentrating all of the power into his hands actually precipitated the political decline of the Ming; he permanently damaged a functional administrative body that could have been an insurance against incompetent emperors.

A high concentration of power in the hands of the emperor also meant an extraordinary burden for the Ming emperor, who had to handle enormous administrative duties in person. Other than a few capable early emperors such as Hongwu or Yongle, few of the remaining Ming emperors cared to emulate their ancestors. This led to another important aspect of Ming politics—the control of the court by the eunuchs. Tired of taking on enormous administrative responsibilities, the later Ming emperors tended to rely on the eunuchs in administrative and military affairs.[66] Some emperors, such as the Emperor Chenghua (r. 1465–1487) preferred to isolate himself from the court because of a speech impediment, but other emperors did so only to pursue their personal interests. The Jiajing emperor (r. 1522–1566) withdrew himself from court duties for a lengthy period in order to follow his passion for Daoist rituals.[67] Similarly, the Wanli emperor (r. 1573–1620) chose to abandon his administrative bureaucracy, refusing to meet with his officials, to read memorials, or to make reappointments for vacant positions for years.[68] The capricious behaviors of the Ming emperors gave the eunuchs opportunity to rise to dominance. At the beginning of the Ming dynasty, the Hongwu emperor, who was well aware of the problematic eunuchs, made a strict rule to prevent the eunuchs from interfering with government affairs. He managed to keep the number of court eunuchs down to a few hundred. That number, however, increased to about 10,000 by the end of the fifteenth century and nearly 100,000 toward the end of the dynasty.[69]

MING ECONOMY AND OVERSEAS TRADE

Despite political problems during the late Ming, the Ming dynasty was one of the most prosperous Chinese dynasties and one of the richest in the world. The Ming dynasty experienced one of the greatest economic expansions in Chinese history. It is said that "Ming China—not London or Seville—was the economic centre of the world in 1600; its global importance was analogous to Britain in 1850 or to the United States today."[70] Benefiting from the systems and technology developed during the early Tang and Song dynasties and its expanding overseas trade, the Chinese economy at the time of the Ming "was sophisticated and productive beyond comparison with any other region."[71]

Overseeing the large area traditionally known as "China proper," which refers to the area traditionally controlled by the Chinese, excluding Tibet, Mongolia, central Asia, and Manchuria, the Ming prospered from the tax of the cultivated land, which amounted to over 500 million *mu* (a *mu* is about one seventh of an acre) by the end of the dynasty. An agricultural revolution, which had begun under the Song, continued to increase the production of wet-rice agriculture during the Ming dynasty, especially under the patronage of the emperor Hongwu. An earlier introduction of what is called "Champa rice" from Southeast Asia greatly boosted rice production. Although Champa rice was less nutritious than traditional Chinese rice, it was more drought-resistant and required less time to mature, reducing the rice-growing season by half, from 120 days to sixty days, and eventually even to thirty days by the late Ming and the early Qing dynasties.[72] Meanwhile, under the Ming dynasty, China continued to adopt new crops from other areas, such as sweet potatoes, corn, and peanuts, and this resulted in boosting cultivation of the dry-fields in China.[73] All this, together with the technology of crop rotation, continued to sustain lucrative agricultural production, which in turn led to a booming of the Chinese population. During the 270 years of Ming rule, the Chinese population more than doubled, from about sixty-five million in 1368 to between 150 million and 200 million in 1644.[74]

The population boom created an increasingly larger demand for commercial goods. As a result, a form of urbanization and a related commercial revolution were well underway. The level of urbanization under the Ming, however, was maintained on a relatively small scale. Instead of forming large cities, as occurred during the Tang and Song dynasties, the Ming saw a flourish of medium-sized cities. These cities usually served as commercial centers that benefited the surrounding countryside. It is said that by 1800, there was virtually no village in China that did not have an easy access to these market towns.[75]

This does not mean that the big cities stop growing. Large industrial centers continued to merge throughout the Ming dynasty. Following the Tang-Song tradition, the Ming government maintained control of large-scale construction, military manufacturing, and other large projects. It monopolized certain commodities such as salt and closely supervised domestic, as well as international trade. The colossal government projects often employed tens of thousands of craftsmen and laborers. Meanwhile, the private sector, which had gradually broken free from state control, progressed to meet the increasingly large demand for manufactured products. Merchants dealing with the same products started to cluster together by profession and location. They formed associations similar to the guilds of early modern Europe and tended to have their shops clustered along the same streets in the same city.[76] Northern China gradually recovered from the political and economic depression that had troubled the area since the Southern Song, and the Ming saw the booming of commercial centers across the country.

As a result, the domestic industry steadily grew to meet the increasingly larger domestic market, especially in terms of cotton, silk, paper, and porcelain. Cotton grown in southern China supported the new textile industry around the traditional centers of silk production in Suzhou and Hangzhou. Paper and printed material manufacturing resulted from the success of commercial books. One district in Jiangxi alone had thirty paper mills, each employing 1,000 to 2,000 workers.[77] The printing industry, which had developed steadily since the Tang dynasty, played an important role in preserving knowledge and spreading new technology to Chinese society. While Tang China produced both the "oldest datable printed materials" (770), and the "oldest extant printed book" (868), Song China manufactured, between 972 and 983, one of the most monumental printing jobs in world history—the publication of the entire *Tripitaka* (the Buddhist canon) in 1,521 volumes, totaling about 130,000 pages.[78] The Ming greatly benefited from this tradition, and its printing industry laid the foundation for many great achievements of Ming culture and literature.

The Ming dynasty also saw a remarkable expansion of overseas trade. While importing large quantities of raw materials from South and Southeast Asia, Ming China was the world's largest exporter of manufactured goods.[79] Silk continued to be the major export, but porcelain had also become an important part of China's trade with the outside world. Having benefited from the previously developed technology of producing ceramics, the Ming dynasty produced large amounts of porcelain, not only for daily usage, but also as a form of decorative art. As discussed earlier, the technology of hard-glazed porcelain had developed during the Tang-Song era. Song porcelain, produced near the Song capital of Kaifeng, was famous for its thin eggshell style in blue-gray or pure white colors. During the Ming era, more colorful and elaborate decorative wares were developed in the south, especially in Jingdezhen in Jiangxi, one of the major concentrations of porcelain production.[80] At its peak, Jingdezhen could produce over a million pieces a year. In addition to filling out special orders for the imperial court, its products were exported to Japan, Southeast Asia, the Middle East, and Europe; many of the products even carried specially designed Christian or Islamic motifs. Jingdezhen's blue and white porcelain was especially popular in Europe after the late sixteenth century, and the best examples of this porcelain can be found in great museums around the world.[81] The Ming's porcelain style influenced the later development of the porcelain of the Qing dynasty and the modern era.

© Heritage Images/Corbis

Porcelain bowl made during The Ming Dynasty

THE DECLINE OF MING EMPIRE

As powerful and prosperous as the Ming Empire had been, it fell into the same dynastic cycle as the previous Chinese dynasties. Scholars of Chinese history often use the dynastic cycle to explain the rise and fall of the Chinese dynasties. They begin with a strong start owing to the work of able and hardworking founding emperors, but eventually experience tragic declines at the hands of their less motivated and less capable successors. The Ming dynasty followed the same pattern.

The political decline of the dynasty started with irresponsible emperors. As discussed earlier, the political structure created by the Hongwu emperor, in which there was a heavy concentration of power in the hands of the emperor, was actually responsible for the decline of the dynasty. Except for the first few, the Ming emperors were known for their capricious and bizarre behaviors, such as allowing the eunuchs and others to take control of the court and even the military. There was no effective mechanism other than an absolute emperor himself to check the power of corrupt high officials. If the emperor was weak, which was the case with many Ming emperors, his powerful subordinates abused power at their wills. One of the most notorious cases of powerful eunuchs was Wei Zhongxian under the Tianqi emperor (r. 1621–1627). Young and incapable of leadership, the Tianqi emperor made Wei Zhongxian a "kind of associate emperor," an unprecedented arrangement in the Ming history.[82] With the endorsement of the emperor, Wei ruthlessly purged his political opponents, putting hundreds of them to death. The emperor gave Wei so much power that all later imperial edits were co-signed by the emperor and the "depot minister," Wei's official title as head of the Eastern Depot, a eunuch-run police and investigation agency.[83] As a result, Wei Zhongxian had become "the most notorious palace eunuch of all Chinese history."[84]

Other than the incompetent emperors, however, the decline of the durable Ming empire, which had lasted more than 270 years, was also the work of more formidable internal and external sources. One problem was that the Ming court had to deal continuously with a financial deficit. As discussed earlier, one major factor that pushed the Hongxi emperor to abolish Zheng He's sea voyages was the financial burden that resulted from these voyages. Corruption and the decline of the military forces were other problems for the late Ming dynasty. The weakness in its military made the late Ming dynasty especially vulnerable. Military leaders seldom played a crucial role in the court politics of the Ming other than in the era of great sea expeditions. The weakening of the military leadership became obvious by the middle of the fifteenth century. The Tumu incident in 1449, during which the Zhengtong emperor (r. 1435–1449; 1457–1464) allowed himself to be captured by the Mongols when he led a punitive campaign against the Mongols, marked a turning point. After a eunuch-led palace coup restored Zhengtong to the position of emperor, he ordered the execution of General Yu Qian, who had taken leadership to save the dynasty after the Tumu incident.[85] The Zhengtong emperor resumed his reign and changed the Ming's military strategy from the offensive expansion of the Hongwu-Yongle era to defensive maneuvers of repairing and extending the Great Wall, adding towers and using bricks and stones to strengthen the structure.[86] For the rest of the Ming era, none of the military generals obtained the same level of power as civilian prime ministers such as Zhang Juzheng, who was the prime minister at the beginning of the reign of the Emperor Wanli, or eunuch officials, such as Wang Zhen under the Zhengtong emperor or Wei Zhongxian under the Tianqi emperor.

The military weakness of the Ming, however, was not a salient problem in the absence of substantial external threat. The dynasty managed to continue for over 270 years, but its luck started to wear out when the Manchus, descendents of the Jurchens of the earlier Jin kingdom in northern China, emerged to form a powerful threat. After their innovative leader, Nurhachi (1559–1626), announced the establishment of a latter Jin dynasty in 1616, the Manchus began to loot the Ming cities along the northeastern borders. This threat also coincided with widespread domestic disturbance. A large-scale peasant rebellion broke out and eventually brought down the Ming dynasty.

The peasants, who had always been at the bottom of the society, had been subjected to abuse at the hands of local landed gentry and corrupted officials at various levels. Their rebellions were most common cause of the fall of a Chinese dynasty. Because of the political and economic decline of the late Ming dynasty, the peasant revolts increased dramatically toward the end of the dynasty.[87] In 1628, a famine led to widespread banditry, and Li Zicheng (1606–1645), who was a messenger in a post office in the Shaanxi province, became the leader of a peasant revolt. By 1643, Li controlled large areas, including Henan and Shaanxi. Li called himself the "Dashing King," and designated Xi'an as his western capital.

He then turned his forces north and captured the Ming capital of Beijing in April 1644. Feeble and weak, the Chongzhen emperor (r. 1627–1644), the fourteenth and last emperor of the Ming, was incapable of rallying enough defense for his palace, and in desperation, the emperor hang himself over a tree in the royal garden. Li, however, could not hold Beijing for long. The combined forces of Wu Sangui, a Ming general, and Dorgon, the Manchu leader, drove Li's forces out of Beijing in June. It is said that Li was soon killed in his foraging to the north.

THE RISE OF THE MANCHUS

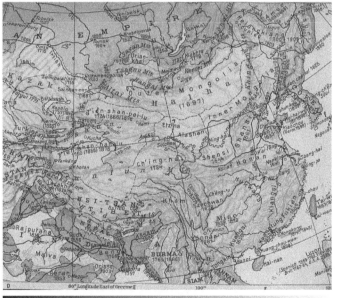

1905. Louis le Grand.

The Qing Empire

The Qing dynasty that replaced the Ming dynasty is the second alien dynasty that ruled China and the most powerful dynasty in Chinese history. At its peak, the Qing dynasty had the largest population and controlled the largest territory that China had ever seen, doubling the size of the territory that had been controlled by the Ming. This dynasty was one of the longest-lasting dynasties, spanning from 1644, making it a contemporary of American colonies, to 1911. The Ming and the Qing dynasties together provided China with unprecedented peace, stability, and prosperity. The Ming's conservatism and the Qing's eagerness to maintain the Chinese traditions, on the other hand, may have resulted in China's stagnancy, especially in terms of the development of science and technology. This conservatism formed a sharp contrast to the spirit of innovation and exploration that existed in European countries at this time. The prosperity and stability that China enjoyed under the Ming and the Qing dynasties may have accounted for China's falling behind Europe in the eighteenth and nineteenth centuries.[88]

Similar to the legendary story of the rise of the Mongol empire, the success of the Manchus started with their mighty leader, Nurhachi (1559–1626) and his sons. The Manchus were related to the Jurchens, who had previously established their Jin kingdom in northern China between 1122–1234. For centuries, they existed in separate tribes in Manchuria, hunting, doing some agricultural work, and trading with the Chinese in the Liaodong peninsula and southern Manchuria. By the beginning of the seventeenth century, their population was about three million. In order to appease these tribes, the Ming emperors established a number of commanderies in the area, headed by hereditary chieftains. After the first Jurchen commandery was established in Liaodong in 1404, the chieftains conducted regular tributary envoys to Beijing.[89] Nurhachi was born to a minor tribal leader, but when he was young, both his father and grandfather were killed in a fight that involved the Chinese. Similar to the case of Chinggis Khan, Nurhachi gradually eliminated his rivals and unified four main Jurchen tribes by 1586.[90] Trying to avoid conflict with the Chinese at this stage, he led a tributary envoy to Beijing in 1590, and in 1595, the Ming Wanli emperor gave him the title "Dragon-Tiger General," the finest ever given a tribal chief.[91] He continued to send tributes to Beijing until 1609.

Meanwhile, Nurhachi focused on organizing his tribes into an orderly state, following the Chinese model as closely as he could. Staying close to the Chinese borders and having accepted the Ming emperor as an overlord, the Manchu tribes had a long history of interacting with the Chinese. Nurhachi was keen on making his tribes more state-based, in accordance with the Chinese model. One important effort toward this goal was the development of a writing system for their language, which had only been used for oral communication up to this time. In 1599, he hired scholars to create a Manchu script based on a modified Mongolian alphabet. After its final creation in 1632, the new written language became an important tool for the Nurhachi to use to learn the regulations of the Chinese government. He had some important Chinese works translated into the Manchu language so that he and his sons could systematically study the Chinese way of managing a state, focusing on the role of the ruler and his bureaucracy.[92]

Another important endeavor of Nurhachi was his creation of the Eight-Banner system, which successfully turned all of his tribes into administrative-military unities. Starting in 1599, he reorganized his tribes into companies, each with 300 warriors, and fifty of such companies formed one of the four bigger units known as "banners" because of the distinctive flag that each unit carried. These flags were one of four colors: yellow, white, blue, or red.[93] All of the warriors, together with their families and slaves, were registered with one of these banners, and were organized and taxed through these banner units. These banners became multifunctional units; in addition to serving as military organizations during the war, they also operated as administrative units for tax assessments in peacetime.

Nurhachi appointed officials to the banner units and hired clerks to keep records for them, but reserved the leadership positions for his sons. As his forces grew, he added four more banners, using the same four colors but including a border of red, except for the red banner, which was bordered with blue. The creation of this Eight-Banner system proved to be the most effective way for Nurhachi to transform the Manchu tribes into a Manchu state.[94]

After all of these preparations, Nurhachi was ready to challenge the Chinese. In 1616, he founded a Later Jin dynasty, as if it was a continuation of the Jurchen's Jin dynasty of 1122–1234, and assumed the title of the Tianming (the Heaven-designed) emperor. Two years later, he issued a document that listed his seven grievances against the Ming, including the murder of his father and grandfather, and used these grievances as his justification to start a war against the Ming.[95] He took the Chinese city of Fushun in 1618 and then, Liaoyang and Mukden (today's Shenyang) in 1621. In 1625, he moved his capital to Mukden and started to build an elaborate palace for his dynasty, where the next two Manchu emperors would be enthroned. One year later, however, Nurhachi was wounded when he attempted to take another Chinese city, Ningyuan, and died a few days later.[96]

Nurhachi's death, however, did not halt the Manchu advance into China. Huang Taiji (1592–1643), who was Nurhachi's eighth son, and often mistakenly called Abahai, continued what his father started. He even broke through the Great Wall and looted the Chinese cities. In 1635, Huang Taiji officially changed the name of his people from Jurchen to Manchu and the next year renamed his dynasty the Qing Dynasty.

The Qing dynasty was run by a central civil administration consisting of six boards, the same style that the Chinese had used since the Tang dynasty. With an ambition to conquer China, but understanding that the Manchus would always be a minority among millions of Chinese, Huang Taiji employed Chinese as his administrative officials and military generals, a decision that proved to be crucial for later Manchu success in China. It is said that it was these Chinese generals who accomplished the final conquest of south China. Without their aid, the Manchus might not have been able to conquer and control all of China and might have been restricted to controlling northern China only, as their Jurchen ancestors had done.[97] By 1643, Huang Taiji had a force totaling about 170,000 troops under his command, including 278 Manchu, 120 Mongol, and 165 Chinese companies.[98] His unexpected death that year, however, deprived Huang Taiji of an opportunity to realize his ambition of conquering China. Nevertheless, he laid a solid foundation for the Manchus' success in taking control of China the next year.

BUILDING OF THE MANCHU EMPIRE

The opportunity for the Manchus to conquer all of China finally presented itself when the rebel Li Zicheng attacked Beijing. The Chongzhen emperor summoned his generals to come to his rescue. One of them, General Wu Sangui, (1612–1678), responded by marching his troops to Beijing. Before he was able to approach Beijing, the city fell into the hands of the rebels, and the last emperor committed suicide. The rebels pursued him when General Wu retreated back to his base at Shanhaiguan, where the Great Wall meets the sea. Instead of surrendering to Li's rebel troops, Wu decided to ask the Manchus for help. He invited Dorgon, Huang Taiji's brother, to come to the other side of the Great Wall through the Shanghaiguan Pass, and together they fought against rebel troops and eventually drove Li Zicheng out of Beijing. Li was killed during his retreat back to central China. Regardless of what General Wu's original intention may have been when he had invited them in, once the Manchus controlled Beijing, they had no intention to return to Mukden. Instead, the Manchu emperor moved his capital from Mukden to Beijing. Thus, the Manchus' seizure of the Chinese throne was made much easier by their being allowed through the gate of the Great Wall.[99]

The Ming, on the other hand, could only put up a limited resistance against the Qing invasion because of ineffective leadership. The Ming remnant forces retreated to Nanjing, where Prince Fu assumed the throne as the Hongguang emperor, but this temporary court lasted for less than a year. The Manchus soon conquered Nanjing and executed the Hongguang emperor. There were other efforts to hold onto a Ming court, but all met a similar fate. The last Ming remnants moved further south, but were eventually eliminated by the Chinese generals serving under the Manchu, such as Wu Sangui, who pursued the last Ming prince, a grandson of Wanli emperor, all the way to Burma and strangled him to death in 1662.[100] Wu later built his own power in Yunnan, and together with two other Chinese generals who had joined the Manchus in their Mukden days, they controlled most of southern China. In 1674, these three Chinese generals, known collectively as the "three feudatories," rebelled together against the Qing, but the Manchu troops under the Emperor Kangxi (r. 1661–1722) eventually subjugated their rebellion in 1681.[101]

It took much more effort for the Qing to gain control of more remote areas. The island of Taiwan or Formosa (beautiful island in Portuguese), for example, caused the Manchus much trouble before the Qing could finally annex it for the empire. By the time that the Manchus started their conquest of the Ming, Taiwan was under the colonial rule of the Dutch, who colonized the entire island after they expelled the Spaniards from northern Taiwan in 1642.

In 1661, a Ming loyalist, Zheng Chenggong (1624–62), known in the West as Koxinga from the title *guoxingye* (Lord of the Imperial Surname) that the last Ming prince gave to him, arrived at Taiwan after his anti-Qing fleet was devastated by the Qing troops. Zheng Chenggong was born to a powerful Chinese pirate-trader and his Japanese wife, and the family resisted the Manchu conquest from their hometown in Fujian. His father was instrumental in putting another Ming prince on the throne in 1645 after the fall of Beijing, but could not help maintain this court in Fuzhou. After Zheng Chenggong became the head of the Zheng family, he kept the family's pledge of allegiance to the last Ming prince and controlled the Fujian coast in the 1650s.[102] In 1659, however, he suffered a severe loss of 500 ships when he tried to recover Nanjing from the Manchus, and after that, he turned his attention to Taiwan. Zheng placed a siege on the island for nine months, before he eventually drove the Dutch out of the island in 1661.[103] He also wanted to conquer the Spanish Philippines, but his death in 1662 interrupted his plan.

Today, Zheng is still considered a national hero, especially in Taiwan.[104] Zheng Jing, his eldest son, succeeded him as the King of Taiwan and continued the battle against the Qing along the south and southeast coasts of the mainland. He even temporarily took control of some coastal cities. The Qing could not eliminate Zheng Jing's threat along the Fujian coast until he died in 1681, and two years later, a Manchu fleet led by Shi Lang, one of the former subordinates of Koxinga, managed to take control of Taiwan for the Qing. In 1684, the Emperor Kangxi officially announced the annexation of Taiwan into the Qing Empire.[105]

Similarly, the Manchus also incorporated other areas into Chinese territory, areas that the Chinese seldom controlled in the past, such as parts of the Inner Asia controlled by the Mongols and Tibet. The Tibetans had a long history of independent kingdoms. The date of the first Tibetan king can be traced back to as early as 126 BCE, when the early Han dynasty of China exited. From the seventh to the eleventh century, an influential Tibetan kingdom, ruled by a series of capable kings, had firm control of the area. King Songtsan Gampo (ca. 605–649 CE) was famous for causing important cultural changes to Tibet through his political marriages. Songtsan Gampo had several wives, including a Nepalese princess and a Chinese princess, Wencheng, both of whom were responsible for introducing Buddhism to Tibet. He was also credited with the creation of a script for the Tibetan language, which was based on an Indic script. At the height of its power, the Tibetan Kingdom extended its influence to as far as Bengal and Mongolia.

During the Ming era, Tibet maintained a tributary relation with the Ming court. It also went through dramatic religious reforms, which gave rise to a dominant Buddhist "Yellow Sect," which was distinct from the traditional Buddhist "Red Sect." Their leader, later known as the Dalai Lama, also became the temporal ruler of Tibet.[106] When the Manchus established the Qing dynasty in China, Tibet was under the rule of their fifth Dalai Lama. While recognizing the suzerainty of the Qing, the Dalai Lama managed to conduct foreign policy independently of the Qing and served as a mediator between the Qing and the Mongol tribes. It was only after his death in 1582 that the Qing started to deal with the Mongols directly. The Kangxi emperor destroyed a Mongol state in 1693 and renamed the area as Qinghai, a name the area still bears today. In 1720, the Qing had its first direct intervention in Tibet, and several years later, a civil war in Tibet ended with the second Qing intervention. In 1751, the Kangxi emperor finally brought Tibet into the Qing Empire, ruling it through a council of four ministers.[107]

QING ADMINISTRATIONS AND CULTURAL ACHIEVEMENTS

The Manchus did not consolidate their empire until their fourth emperor, the Kangxi emperor, who was the second emperor who reigned from Beijing. From the reign of Kangxi to that of his grandson, the Qianlong emperor (r.1736–1795), the Qing dynasty was at its zenith. It oversaw the largest territory that China had ever had under its control, covering five million square miles, much larger than today's People's Republic of China, which has only 3.7 million square miles.[108] Chinese culture also reached a peak of development. Under Qing emperors, the Chinese cultural achievements exceeded the levels of success in any other Chinese dynasties. Scholars still debate how the Manchus, who were only about 2 percent of the total population, could build such a successful administration over China for nearly three centuries, whereas the Mongols lost their control of China in less than a century.

In contrast to the Mongols, from the very beginning, the Manchus tried to adopt the Chinese style of ruling their empire. As mentioned earlier, Nurhachi had replicated the Chinese style of administration during their formation period at Mukden. After conquering Beijing, the Manchu rulers claimed that they had come to Beijing to eliminate the anti-Ming rebels, and they would restore the peace and order in China. The Qing emperors later portrayed themselves as the "Son of Heaven," who had obtained the Mandate of Heaven, a concept that the Chinese had used to legitimize the forming of a new dynasty. They buried the last Ming emperor with honor and hired Confucian scholars to compile an official history of the Ming dynasty.[109] The Chinese were basically left alone so long as they submitted to the new regime. The early Qing emperors even reduced the tax rates, which had overburdened the peasants during the late Ming period. Throughout their reign, the Manchus seldom introduced any significant social or agrarian changes. One of the few social norms that they imposed upon the Chinese was to force all of the Chinese men to have Manchu haircuts—shaving their hair in front and wearing a long braid in the back.[110]

In order to govern the country more effectively, the Manchus purposely recruited Chinese elites into their administrations, allowing them to hold positions at the highest levels. Some scholars describe the Qing administration as a "Manchu-Chinese dynarchy," a joint administration managed both by the Manchu and the Chinese. This nature of the Manchu regime was obvious even during its formative years at Mukden. Many Chinese from Liaodong aided the Manchu conquest of China, and some later assumed important positions in the Qing administration. One such example was Hong Chengchou (1593–1665), who had been a Ming governor-general of five provinces in the South, but was later transferred to the North to fight the rebel Li Zicheng. After Hong surrendered to the Manchus, he was made a Grand Secretary and played a principal administrative role. At the early Manchu court, three of the six grand secretaries were Chinese, and all of the six ministries had two presidents, one Manchu and one Chinese.[111] In order to find capable administrators, the Qing adopted the civil service examinations, which produced over 25,000 degree-holders after each county level examination, 1,400 at the provincial level and over two hundred after a palace examination.[112] These graduates provided administrators for the Qing administration not only at the central level, but also at the provincial and local levels. At the county level, the Chinese carried out almost all administrative duties. Of course, the Manchu officials were better trusted than their counterparts were, and the Chinese officials seldom had complete control.

In this way, the Manchus could enjoy their privileges without being burdened with the enormous administrative duty of running their vast empire. Throughout their reign, the Manchus carefully preserved their privileges through a series of methods, including special stipends and land to all their bannermen, exempting them from local Chinese jurisdiction, and maintaining their homeland in Manchuria exclusively for the Manchus. In addition, the Manchus forbade mixed marriages and applied policies of segregation in Beijing and other big cities.[113] The Manchu emperors always enjoyed absolute power in the same manner that the Ming emperors did, and they also maintained tight control of the military through the Banner forces, which grew from 169,000 in 1644 to 350,000 strong by the eighteenth century. The Chinese troops were mostly relegated to the "Army of the Green Standard," which were separate from the Manchu Banners.[114]

The joint Manchu-Chinese administration created language problems at the beginning. The early Qing court was conducted in the Manchu language, and translators were hired to facilitate communications between Manchu and Chinese officials. As many Manchu officials and their emperors mastered the Chinese language, the need for bilingual procedures disappeared. By 1670, interpreter positions had been reduced or abolished, and Manchu language examinations attracted less and less candidates. As the court language gradually shifted from Manchu to Chinese, Manchu was used mostly in translating Chinese documents into Manchu or for ceremonial purposes.[115]

In addition to a stable and effective administration, the vision and hard work of the early Qing emperors accounted for much of the continuing success of the Qing. The Kangxi emperor, for example, was one of the most capable rulers of the Qing, if not of all the emperors in Chinese history. He ascended to the throne in 1661, at the age of seven, and reigned until his death in 1722. As a result, he holds the record for the longest reigning of any Chinese emperor. He was a vigorous military leader. At the age of twenty-seven, he successfully suppressed the revolt of Three Feudatories, the biggest crisis that the Qing encountered. He later led his troops into Mongolia and brought Taiwan under Qing control. In 1689, he signed the Treaty of Nerchinsk with Russia, which was the first treaty that China signed with a Western power; this treaty defined the borders between the two countries.[116]

Kangxi was also a diligent administrator, whose court usually started at 5 am.[117] In order to know the land and culture under Qing control, he conducted six great tours of southern China and went as far as to the lower Yangtze River areas. After gaining knowledge of these areas, he paid special attention to the flooding of the Huai and Yellow rivers. In order to curb corruptions among the administrators, he issued an edict in 1670, which was later known as the Sacred Edict (Sheng yu), which laid out the moral standards for the officials. As a result, one scholar described his reign, together with the reigns of his son, the Yongzheng emperor (r. 1723–36), and his grandson, the Qianlong emperor (r. 1736–1795), as "the reign of moral order."[118] The Yongzhen emperor later revised and enlarged Kangxi's Sacred Edict, and had it publicly read aloud throughout the country.

Kangxi also took great interest in China's immense wealth of cultural heritage. He was a great patron of Chinese culture, comparable to the most successful Chinese emperors in China's imperial history. He was fluent in the Chinese language, an accomplished poet, and a calligrapher. His works still rank among the finest examples of excellent calligraphy. *Kangxi zidian* (The Kangxi Dictionary), a dictionary that bears his name, is still one of the best dictionaries in the Chinese language. It gives the meaning and usage of over 42,000 Chinese characters.[119] He sponsored fifty-seven official publications, including an anthology of the Tang poets in 1703, *Quan Tang shi* (A Complete Collection of Tang Poems) that collected 48,900 poems from 2,200 different poets in the Tang era.[120] The most ambitious project was to compile a massive encyclopedia, *Gujin tushu jicheng* (Synthesis of Books and Illustrations of Ancient and Modern Times), which ended with 10,000 rolls, 800,000 pages, and 100 million Chinese characters.[121]

Other Qing emperors emulated the Kangxi emperor's endeavor to preserve Chinese culture. The Qinglong emperor admired his grandfather so much that he voluntarily retired after 59 years of his reign in order to preserve his grandfather's record, although he continued control of the court as the regent. Qianlong eventually incorporated Chinese Turkestan and renamed it *Xinjiang* (New Territory), and brought Tibet under Qing control. Qianlong's military campaigns carried the Qing troops into Vietnam, Burma, and even Nepal, and forced the local rulers to enter the Qing's tributary system.[122] Under the reign of Qianlong, the Qing was undoubtedly the most powerful and prosperous empire in the world.

The Emperor Qianlong also engaged in several large-scale cultural projects, including compiling a great imperial manuscript, *Siku quanshu* (The Complete Library of the Four Treasures). *The Four Treasures* referred to the four different branches of Chinese literature: classics, history, philosophy, and anthologies of literature. The court hired 360 scholars to search for the books and manuscripts, and 15,000 copyists to copy the rare works from *Yongle da dian* (The Yongle Encyclopedia), an early Chinese encyclopedia of the Ming dynasty, and other sources. When the project was completed, *The Four Treasures* contained nearly 36,000 volumes and 79,582 chapters, in comparison to 11,905 chapters of *the Yongle Encyclopedia*.[123] According to R. Kent Guy, this is "final affirmation of the unity of knowledge and power in Chinese history."[124] It is by far the largest collection of books in Chinese history and the most ambitious literary project in the history of the world. On top of all of this was the encouragement of the development of literature in all forms. The Qing era produced several monumental works of Chinese literature, such as *Jing ping mei* (Golden Lotus), China's first realistic novel by a single author, and Cao Xueqin's *Honglou meng* (The Dream of the Red Chamber), one of the four great literary classics of China.

The reign of the Qianlong emperor, however, also marked the beginning of a decline of Qing power. After nearly two centuries of a successful rule, the Qing dynasty started to experience the same problems that had brought down the other Chinese dynasties, such as over spending, corruption, and the officials' abuse of power. It followed the same dynastic cycle: a strong start with a few motivated founders, followed by a decline. In addition to the traditional problems that early Chinese dynasties faced during their declines, the Qing also encountered new challenges, such as the foreign intrusion from emerging Western powers. The eventual destruction of the Qing and the consequences of that destruction will be discussed in Chapter 12.

For more information about the topics discussed in this chapter, please visit the website for this textbook. This website can be accessed from http://www.grtep.com/.

1 John King Fairbank, Edwin Reischauer, and Albert M. Craig, *East Asia, Tradition and Transformation, revised ed.* (Princeton: Houghton Mifflin, 1989), 152.
2 Timothy May, "Central Asia: The Mongols, 1206–1405," in *The Great Empires of Asia*, ed. by Jim Masselos, (Berkeley: University of *California Press*, 2010), 34.
3 May, "Mongols", 24.
4 Thomas Walter Wallbank, Alastair M. Taylor, Nels M. Bailkey, and George F. Jewsbury, *Civilization Past and Present, 8th ed.* (New York: Harpercollins College Division, 1995), 224; and Fairbank et al., *Tradition*, 163.
5 May, "Mongols", 23–24; and Fairbank et al., *Tradition*, 163.
6 Fairbank et al., *Tradition*, 164.
7 Hucker, *Imperial*, 283.
8 Fairbank et al., *Tradition*, 163–164.
9 William Bonner and Addison Wiggin, *Empire of Debt: The Rise of an Epic Financial Crisis* (New York: John Wiley and Sons, 2006), 43–44; and Hucker, *Imperial*, 285.
10 May, "Mongols", 27–28.
11 Wright, *History*, 84; and Fairbank et al., *Tradition*, 166.
12 May, "Mongols", 40.
13 Hucker, *Imperial*, 285.
14 Fairbank et al., *Tradition*, 171.
15 Hucker, *Imperial*, 286; and Fairbank et al., *Tradition*, 171–174.
16 Thomas J. Craughwell, *The Rise and Fall of the Second Largest Empire in History: How Genghis Khan's Mongols Almost Conquered the world.* (Beverly, MA: Fair Winds Press, 2010), 243.
17 Fairbank et al., *Tradition*, 163; and May, "Mongols," 38–39
18 May, "Mongols," 44; and Fairbank et al., *Tradition*, 169.
19 May, "Mongols," 44.
20 Wright, *History*, 83.
21 May, "Mongols," 40–43.
22 Wright, *History*, 85.
23 Hucker, *Imperial*, 285; and May, "Mongols," 30–31.
24 Fairbank et al., *Tradition*, 167; and Conrad Schirokauer and Miranda Brown, *A History of Chinese Civilization, 2nd ed.* (Belmont, CA: Thomson & Wadsworth, 2006), 174–175.
25 Fairbank et al., *Tradition*, 167.
26 Schirokauer and Brown, *Civilization*, 177.
27 May, "Mongols," 36; Hucker, *Imperial*, 286; and Fairbank et al., *Tradition*, 168.
28 Fairbank et al., *Tradition*, 162; and Schirokauer and Brown, *Civilization*, 174–175.
29 Fairbank et al., *Tradition*, 168–169; and Schirokauer and Brown, *Civilization*, 175.
30 Hucker, *Imperial*, 286; Schirokauer and Brown, *Civilization*, 176; and Fairbank et al., *Tradition*, 170.
31 Fairbank et al., *Tradition*, 171.
32 May, "Mongols," 42; and Fairbank et al., *Tradition*, 167.
33 Fairbank et al., *Tradition*, 175–176; and Gernet, *Civilization*, 382–383.
34 Fairbank et al., *Tradition*, 176; and Schirokauer and Brown, *Civilization*, 181–184.
35 Hucker, *Imperial*, 287; and Fairbank et al., *Tradition*, 170.
36 Fairbank et al., *Tradition*, 177.
37 Fairbank et al., *Tradition*, 180.
38 Hucker, *Imperial*, 288–289; J.A.G. Roberts, "China: The Ming 1368–1644" in Masselos, 49; and Fairbank et al., *Tradition*, 179–180.
39 Roberts, "Ming," 49; and Schirokauer and Brown, *Civilization*, 191.
40 Hucker, *Imperial*, 288. Also see John King Fairbank, *China, A New History*, (Cambridge: the Belknap Press of Harvard University Press, 1992), 128–129.
41 Hucker, *Imperial*, 287; and Schirokauer and Brown, *Civilization*, 191–193.
42 Hucker, *Imperial*, 289.
43 For more details, see Anita M. Andrew and John A. Rapp, *Autocracy and China's Rebel Founding Emperors: Comparing Chairman Mao and Ming Taizu* (Lanham, MD: Rowan & Littlefield Publishers, 2000).
44 "*Da Ming lu*" (The Great Ming Code), accessed on January 2, 2012, at http://baike.baidu.com/view/46444.htm.
45 Jiang Yonglin, *The Mandate of Heaven and the Great Ming Code* (Seattle: University of Washington Press, 2011), 3–5; and Edward Farmer, *Zhu Yuanzhang and Early Ming Legislation: The Reordering of Chinese Society Following the Era of Mongol Rule* (New York: E.J. Brill), 10.
46 Roberts, "Ming," 52.
47 Roberts, "Ming," 50; and Schirokauer and Brown, *Civilization*, 193.
48 Fairbanks, *Tradition*, 129–130.
49 Roberts, "Ming," 52; and Schirokauer and Brown, *Civilization*, 193.
50 John Dardess, *Ming China, 1368–1644: A concise History of a Resilient Empire* (New York: Rowman & Littlefield Publishers, 2012), 14–55.
51 Darness, *Ming*, 4–5.
52 Edward L. Dreyer, *Zheng He: China and the Oceans in Early Ming Dynasty, 1405–1433* (New York: Pearson-Longman, 2006), 27–35.
53 Murphey, *History*, 200–201; Fairbank, *Tradition*, 137–138; and Roberts, "Ming," 54.
54 Fairbank, *Tradition*, 137.
55 Murphey, *History*, 201.
56 Roberts, "Ming," 54.

57 Murphey, *History*, 200; and Schirokauer and Brown, *Civilization*, 194.

58 Dreyer, *Zheng*, 28–30; Murphey, *History*, 202; and Fairbank et al., *Tradition*, 138.

59 Roberts, "Ming," 55; and Dreyer, *Zheng*, 32.

60 Fairbank et al., *Tradition*, 138–39; and Schirokauer and Brown, *Civilization*, 193–194.

61 For more on this, see Richard Von Glahn, *Fountain of Fortune: Money and Monetary Policy in China, 1000–1700* (Berkeley: University of California Press, 1996).

62 Hucker, *Imperial*, 291. For more on Zheng He's voyages, see Louise Levathes, *When China Ruled the Seas: The Treasure Fleet of the Dragon Throne, 1405–1433* (Oxford: Oxford University Press, 1997).

63 Roberts, "Ming," 58.

64 Roberts, "Ming," 50; and Hucker, *Imperial*, 289.

65 Hucker, *Imperial*, 304.

66 Fairbank et al., *Tradition*, 130.

67 Dardess, *Ming*, 50–52; and Roberts, "Ming," 70.

68 Fairbank et al., *Tradition*, 141; and Dardess, *Ming*, 54–55.

69 Albert Chan, *The Glory and Fall of the Ming Dynasty* (Norman: University of Oklahoma Press, 1982), 18, 32; Roberts, "Ming," 59; and Dardess, *Ming*, 64–65.

70 Francesca Bray, *Technology and Society in Ming China (1368–1644)* (Washington DC: American Historical Association, 2000), 4, quoted from Roberts, "Ming," 61, note. 16.

71 Hucker, *Imperial*, 356.

72 Hucker, *Imperial*, 342–343.

73 Hucker, *Imperial*, 344–345; and Schirokauer and Brown, *Civilization*, 200–202.

74 Roberts "Ming," 59; and Hucker, *Imperial*, 292.

75 Hucker, *Imperial*, 333–334.

76 Hucker, *Imperial*, 349; and Schirokauer and Brown, *Civilization*, 201.

77 Hucker, *Imperial*, 333–334; and Bray, *Technology*, 7–17.

78 Hucker, *Imperial*, 336–337.

79 Roberts, "Ming," 60.

80 Hucker, *Imperial*, 410–411; and Schirokauer and Brown, *Civilization*, 197.

81 Hucker, *Imperial*, 412–413; and Roberts, "Ming," 60–61.

82 Dardess, *Ming*, 56–57; and Roberts, "Ming", 71.

83 Dardess, *Ming*, 57.

84 Hucker, *Imperial*, 293.

85 Roberts "Ming," 57; and Schirokauer and Brown, *Civilization*, 195.

86 Arthur Waldron, *The Great Wall of China: From History to Myth* (Cambridge: Cambridge University Press, 1992), 55–164.

87 James W. Tong, *Disorder under Heaven: Collective Violence in the Ming Dynasty* (Stanford: Stanford University Press, 1991), 192–203.

88 Fairbank et al., *Tradition*, 211; Hucker, *Imperial*, 294–295; and Schirokauer and Brown, *Civilization*, 235.

89 Fairbank et al., *Tradition*, 211–212.

90 Roberts, "Ming," 71; and Fairbank et al., *Tradition*, 213–214.

91 Edwin O. Reischauer and John King Fairbank, *East Asia: the Great Tradition* (Boston: Houghton Mifflin, 1960), 351.

92 Fairbank et al., *Tradition*, 214; and Schirokauer and Brown, *Civilization*, 236.

93 Roberts, *Concise*, 139; and Gernet, *Civilization*, 466.

94 Fairbank et al., *Tradition*, 214.

95 Fairbank et al., *Tradition*, 214–215; and Roberts, *Concise*, 139.

96 Fairbanks et al., *Tradition*, 215; and Gernet, *Civilization*, 466.

97 Hucker, *Imperial*, 295; and Gernet, *Civilization*, 446–467.

98 Fairbank et al., *Tradition*, 214.

99 Fairbank et al., *Tradition*, 216; Gernet, *Civilization*, 466–467; and Hucker, *Imperial*, 294–295.

100 Fairbank et al., *Tradition*, 216–217; and Gernet, *Civilization*, 469–470.

101 Fairbank et al., *Tradition*, 216; and Gernet, *Civilization*, 471–473.

102 Fairbank et al., *Tradition*, 216–217.

103 Gernet, *Civilization*, 470.

104 Hucker, *Imperial*, 296.

105 Gernet, *Civilization*, 470.

106 Fairbank et al., *Tradition*, 220.

107 Fairbank et al., *Tradition*, 221–222; and Gernet, *Civilization*, 481.

108 Gernet, *Civilization*, 482.

109 Gernet, *Civilization*, 476; and Schirokauer and Brown, *Civilization*, 237.

110 Gernet, *Civilization*, 468.

111 Fairbank et al., *Tradition*, 225–226.

112 Fairbank et al., *Tradition*, 228.

113 Fairbank et al., *Tradition*, 222–223; and Gernet, *Civilization*, 467.

114 Fairbank et al., *Tradition*, 222–223.

115 Gernet, *Civilization*, 295; and Fairbank et al., *Tradition*, 227

116 Hucker, *Imperial*, 299.

117 Schirokauer and Brown, *Civilization*, 242.

118 Gernet, *Civilization*, 474–475.

119 Gernet, *Civilization*, 511; and Schirokauer and Brown, *Civilization*, 242.

120 Gernet, *Civilization*, 511.
121 Gernet, *Civilization*, 511.
122 Schirokauer and Brown, 244; and Gernet, *Civilization*, 481–482.
123 Gernet, *Civilization*, 511-512; Schirokauer and Brown, *Civilization*, 244; and Fairbank et al, *Tradition*, 234.
124 R. Kent Guy, *The Emperor's Four Treasures: Scholars and the Rise of the State in the Late Ch'ien-lung Era* (Cambridge: Harvard University Press, 1987), 37, quoted from Schirokauer and Brown, *Civilization*, 385.

Chapter 10: Southeast Asia and the Periods of Colonial Rule

INTRODUCTION

For centuries, Southeast Asia existed with well-established empires and kingdoms even prior to European nations founding colonies within the mainland and maritime countries of Southeast Asia, countries where development arose with major trading ports. Along with trade came cultural and religious influences that contributed to the assimilation of indigenous and feudal polity and peoples of a different culture. The religious influence would provide new insights into new traditions, but also lead to conflict as development took precedence over the traditions that identified the people of Southeast Asia. Before the West colonized Southeast Asia, Asian cultural colonialism from India and China had already affected the region. This effect influenced the art, language, literature, and religious traditions in Southeast Asia and subsequently diversified each country as they assimilated and adopted those traditions of other countries. Three hundred years before the European traders arrived, Southeast Asia had its share of conquests and invasions. Prior to 1400, the Mongols attempted to traverse the region, trampling on Burma, Thailand, Cambodia, Laos, Vietnam, Malay, and Indonesia. While China's intrusion into the region conflicted with pre-existing empires and kingdoms, a bridge of understanding in the form of intellectual and educational development was established. The historical accounts by travelers, missionaries, monks, and the imperial records of Chinese, Indian, and European scribes uncovered the cultural, political, and economic influence that came about before and after 1400 in Southeast Asia.

Western connections contributed to the identification of Asian and Southeast Asian countries on the map and led to the establishment of European settlements within the regions of Greater India, Little China, and the Indo-Pacific. By the twentieth century, these regions had become even more clearly demarcated due to their international relations, world war conflicts, and the Cold War ideology that drew partitions but later encouraged independence.

BURMESE DYNASTIES AND EARLY ENGLISH ENCOUNTER

Having shared a border with the subcontinent of India, Burma thrived on her own, especially with the establishment of one of her most vibrant periods of history, the Pagan Dynasty. During this time, Burma experienced cultural assimilation through Buddhism and the ethnic migration of non-Burmese peoples called Mons, who originated from Burma's southern regions. In 1287, a Mongol invasion took hold of the Mons, which led to the collapse of the Pagan Dynasty.

Burma's colonial beginnings date back to the fifteenth century during the Toungoo Dynasty (1531–1732), one of Thailand's peaceful periods. During this time period, 1486 to 1752, Western trade expanded into the country while Burma attempted to unify its rule over its multi-ethnic society. This era ended without leaving a lasting cultural legacy, but the Toungoo dynasty eventually expanded during its conquest of the Shan states' and Laos.

Courtesy of Library of Congress.

Young Burmese Buddhist Monk circa 1880s

In the early sixteenth century a new Burmese dynasty began that showed growing dominance over maritime trade, a dominance that increased revenue and fueled conquest and political authority along the coast. Traded commodities included natural resources, but as the capital experienced political upheaval, the improvement of Portuguese-supplied guns took precedence. By the early nineteenth century, the Konbaung dynasty (1752–1885), a result of Thailand's Ayudhya Kingdom, encountered constant wars instigated by Burmese kings between Burma and regions of Thailand. Notwithstanding, one of her last dynasties ended as it had begun; there were bitter remnants of past invasions of the Mons and regions of the Pagan Dynasty, which the Mons believed hindered their independence. As a result, the Mons struck the Burmese capital, Ava, only to be deterred by the Burmese who proclaimed Alaungpaya as the Burmese leader of the country. He and his armies launched further confrontations against the Mons, which led to a migration across the southeast boundaries of Burma to Ayudhya.

Despite the invasions that took place throughout the late Toungoo and early Konbaung dynasties, trade flourished and proved beneficial, especially for the British. They launched aggressive moves into the upper and lower most regions of Burma that led to three major skirmishes: the first Anglo-Burmese war of 1824–1826, followed by the second Anglo-Burmese War in 1852 and the third Anglo-Burmese war in 1885. These events proved Britain's interest in expanding into Burma.

THAILAND AND INFLUENTIAL BORDERS

Pocketed between Burma and the countries of Indochina, Burma's neighbor and constant rival, Thailand, bypassed colonial control by any European nation due to its political and diplomatic associations and the strength of the country's monarchical rule. Much like Burma and

Vietnam, Thailand possessed a vibrant historical past as told by archaeological remnants that reveal a Chinese-influenced civilization existing for at least 4,500 years. The migration and re-migration of peoples that crossed its borders and the border of China's Yunnan Province consisted of two major ethnic groups: the Mons, who occupied central and northern Thailand, and northern Burma; and the Khmers along the Mekong River. The Chinese and Indian peoples influenced the culture of the Thais; perhaps the best examples of this are Theravada Buddhism, which became the state religion, and Hinduism, a religion brought by missionaries and traders from Sri Lanka and India that influenced art and literature within Thai culture.

The country became culturally and politically rich by the time the great Khmer Angkor Kingdom existed and stayed so up until its decline in the thirteenth century when a new state situated north of Bangkok called Sukhothai gained prominence in 1238. The Sukhothai represented a long legacy of diplomatic relations with China and India. China and India continued the cultural exchange during the Khmer Angkor Kingdom. Thailand modeled its kingdoms after India, especially by its emphasis on Brahmanical thought and during the state ruled by Ramkhamhaeng, "Rama the Great," from 1277 to 1317.

After the fall of the Sukhothai, the Kingdom of Ayudhya (1351–1767) relied on support from China, India, and Europe to increase the wealth of their kingdom. During the sixteenth century, European nations, such as Portugal, established a string of formal treaties between themselves and the King of Ayudhya; these treaties were designed to sustain the monarchy and increase the wealth within the country in 1561. Thailand also made treaties with England, Japan, Persia, Spain, and India. However, two dominant forces involved in Southeast Asia, the Vereenigde Oostandische Compagnie or Dutch East India Company (VOC) and English East India Company (EEIC), established an economic and political activity that foretold Thailand's future.[1] This allowed factories to be built near the ports and diplomatic missions that helped the country maintain its monarchical rule and keep Western nations' involvement in trade and politics at bay so as not to dominate Thailand. However, the Dutch attempted to bypass the Thais by demanding extraterritorial rights which would exempt them from Thai laws as long as they operated within the country in order to trade freely.

Dutch and the English trade grew and proved beneficial. However, activities outside of trade proved detrimental and interfered with Thai traditions. For example, religious proselytization by French missionaries conflicted with Thai Buddhist communities and their beliefs. This interference bred resentment between the two groups and resulted in the downfall of the French and other religious groups that attempted to convert Thai Buddhist followers. These efforts eventually led to the closing of Thailand from the West for 150 years.

Thailand's troubles did not end at that point; the country had to contend with an invasion by Burma and her interest in expanding her boundaries. The Burmese invasion took place at Ayudhya in 1767 when forces captured, destroyed, and pillaged the city; but after the siege, the Chinese invaded Burma, which led to a Burmese defeat. This gave Thailand the opportunity to regroup and establish a new leader, Thai military commander Phraya Taksin. This leader and his armies resisted the Burmese invasions, thus enabling the reunification of provinces and the annexation of the state of Chiang Mai. Life prospered in Thailand with a new capital at Thon Buri, situated south of the former capital of Ayudhya, and with Taksin assuming the throne; unfortunately, Taksin's self-righteousness did not fare well with the ministers of the kingdom so he was later deposed and executed. King Rama I, seized power to help defeat the Burmese and expand Thai territory. The outcome of this was the establishment of the Chakkri Dynasty (1782–present), which controlled Cambodia, Laos, and parts of the Malay States.

A series of changes took place, which expanded trade activity for the country: a major port was established at Bangkok, religious laws were revised, and reforms centered on Buddhist scriptures occurred. These changes bred a Thai society heavily influenced by Indian culture, a society where scholars produced historical and literary works that contained a new edition of the Indian epic the *Ramayana* in Thai.

Well into 1795, and with the help of Vietnam, the Thais helped to protect the Cambodian territories from the British threat along the Battambang and Siem Reap regions. However, this would not have been possible without the Burney Treaty, which allowed trade concessions between Thailand and Great Britain. In 1833, Thailand and the US also negotiated a similar treaty. British and French territorial and trade endeavors did not end with the implementation of treaties or with the death of Rama III. British and French colonists took hold of tributary provinces.

Mongkut, the brother of Rama III and a monk, succeeded the throne in 1824. He used his monastic experience in Buddhism as well as his toleration of Western culture to help reform the monastic community. These reforms involved Catholic and Protestant missionaries, education in foreign studies that leaned on the Western languages of English and Latin, and the study of science and mathematics. By 1855, treaties between Thailand and Great Britain abolished old trade monopolies. The Treaty of Friendship and Commerce (Bowring Treaty) allowed extraterritorial rights and a consulate at Bangkok. Without these essential treaties, Thailand would not have established an international relationship with Western nations that provided the rights of free trade and limited import and export fees. As a result, trade increased, thus economically transforming the country by integrating it into the global economy.

VIETNAM AND CHINA'S IMPERIAL INFLUENCE

Vietnam experienced major upheavals throughout its history and along its geographic borders of the Red River and the Ma River, upheavals that involved Chinese rule and Western colonialism. Chinese feudalism helped to assimilate the people of Vietnam in the form of Sinicization or Chinese colonization that began during the Qin dynasty. The Qin dynasty established a Chinese settlement that stretched from the north of Vietnam to the south of Vietnam. An independent kingdom called Nam Viet became a part of a Sino-Vietnamese state. China ruled Vietnam for most of the years between 200 BCE to 938 CE. Chinese rule in Vietnam operated under a Chinese cultural model that incorporated Chinese characters and Confucian philosophy and played an essential role in structuring the government. Chinese feudalism dominated the tenth century and the basic foundations of Confucius' teachings structured the government and society.[2]

Chinese aristocrats, scholars, officers, and wealthy Chinese migrated to the Tonkin delta and the Au Lac Kingdom dating to the ninth century CE and helped to structure Vietnamese society under a Chinese model which influenced political and social development. Government officials married into the Vietnamese aristocracy, a major force for the educated class of Sino-Vietnamese, or people of mixed Chinese and Vietnamese ethnic backgrounds. Emigrants built schools and temples and ordered the construction of major networks of canals, dikes, roadways, and bridges to facilitate the movement of people and resources and the production of rice. The government, modeled after the Han, divided the prefectures into seven Chinese divisions. The Chinese government granted land to the soldiers from the Han and took up farming in Vietnamese villages, which led to 700 years of discontent. Due to rebellions, the lack of equal distribution of land allotments, and an increase in taxes, the kingdom suffered; poor government and natural disasters also contributed to peasant sufferings.

China's rule of Vietnam came to an end by 950 CE as a result of anarchy and civil war. China would not rule Vietnam again until it invaded Vietnam in 1414. Invasion, however, did not prevent Vietnam from maintaining a succession of independent dynasties.

In 965 Dinh Bo Linh, a peasant, proclaimed himself king of Northern Vietnam and ruled the country until 980. Between 980–1009 Le Dai Hanh ruled the short-lived early Le dynasty only to be overthrown by Ly Thai To, who founded the Ly Dynasty, in 1009. The Ly experienced its demise when it fell to the Tran Dynasty in 1225.[3] With the endless invasions of rivaling dynasties, Vietnam continued to live in the shadow of the country's Champa kingdom.

Fighting between the Tran dynasty and the Mongols affected the southern coastal boundaries where the former Champa kingdom had existed. In a region comprised of seafaring people of Malayo-Polynesian descent, an endless degree of invasion and migration often allowed the infusion a culture and language with Indic

Courtesy of Library of Congress.

A Mandarin in Saigon, Vietnam, circa 1923

script, Brahmanist religion, and neo-Confucianist thought, and the Khmer tradition. The people of Vietnam's southernmost region along the Mekong Delta and the Funan kingdom became a part of the culture and language within Vietnamese society.[4] Despite the cultural assimilation, invasions launched by the Mongols affected political development and pre-existing tensions in the North with the Champa. However, the Mongols could not withstand the Ly kingdom's strength with strategist and tactician Ly Thuong Kiet, a military official of royal blood, at the helm.[5] The Ly dynasty fell to rebels that overthrew their rule and established the Tran Dynasty in 1226. The Trans also inherited the endless threats by the Mongols, but the Vietnamese eventually successfully deterred Kublai Khan and his armies by thrusting Mongolian supremacy into the south.[6] As a result, Vietnam increased in size with the annexation of Cham territory and further weakened the Champa state.

The brief Ho dynasty reigned from 1400–1407, followed by the Ming (1414–1427), and the Le dynasty (1428–1788), which was the longest dynasty in Vietnam's history. After the fall of the Le dynasty, the Nguyen dynasty (1802–1945) continued the succession of Vietnam's dynastic cycle with Gia Long as one of its most important rulers who also maintained the Chinese model structured under Confucius principles and Chinese culture.

MARITIME SOUTHEAST ASIA COUNTRIES

Indonesia, Malaysia, and the Philippines interacted with countries neighboring their islands through cultural, religious, and trade connections. Major European countries became associated with these archipelagos through maritime trade. India's culture and religion played an essential role in influencing the people of Indonesia and Malaysia. Traditions were spread through language and goods and

Courtesy of Library of Congress.

Philippine Indigenous Peoples of the island of Luzon aiming their arrows, circa 1890s

services, such as bronze, stone, copper, Sanskrit, old Malay, old Javanese and old Balinese. China and India contributed to the development of the history of the major trading ports of Sumatra and Java.

Imperial annals have recorded the historic events of Malaysia and Vietnam and their shared kingdoms, rulers, and embassies. Specifically, trade proved beneficial to the countries of Southeast Asia. Accounts recorded by Marco Polo and the Mongols about Indian traders showed an abundance of imports, agriculturally productive regions, and the presence of monsoon winds.

Sumatra, Java, and the Straits of Malacca are all central points that provided access for maritime activity and connections, and by the sixteenth century, were an alternate trade route through the Sunda Strait. Competition of trade between Indonesian kingdoms, one of which being Srivijaya, the greatest maritime kingdom from the seventh to thirteenth centuries, created a successful pathway between major trading ports that served beneficial for sailing ships navigating monsoon winds.

Political activist Jose Rizal called the Philippines the "Pearl of the Orient," a term used to refer to this area as the gateway to the East with its 7,000 islands, including the two largest archipelagos, Luzon in the North and Mindanao in the South. Within these archipelagos, the peoples of the islands did not operate in kingdoms or empires as their neighboring Southeast Asian mainland and archipelagos did prior to Spanish colonization. The islands were comprised of indigenous peoples, tribal communities that spoke different languages and dialects and believed in animistic spirits called the *Bathala*, and *anitos*. These beliefs were especially strong in the central and northern islands where Christianity became the predominant religion for the country. Before that took place, between the thirteenth and fourteenth centuries, Islamic conversion existed within the archipelagos of Malaya, South Vietnam, and Indonesia and Southern Philippines. Arab Muslims controlled trade in these areas, especially during the fifteenth century and in Mindanao, the southernmost island of the Philippines, converted inhabitants on the island to the Muslim religion. Muslim origins began with the ruler Sulu who converted to Islam. He held court in Mindanao where Islam influence grew to the North, to the islands of Luzon and Manila where he ruled as an Islamic ruler.

The Majapahit kingdom, one of the last Hindu kingdoms of Southeast Asia, was involved in this religious conversion to Islam, which served to be beneficial as it expanded trade and religious influence within the island; trade connections, furthermore allowed Indian trade from major Indian ports, Gujarat to flow to Southeast Asia, especially during the Mughal dynasty that contributed to the extension of the Islamic dynasties and religious conversion took place by 1208 in Delhi and spread to the southeast islands of Indonesia and Malaysia.

Initial contact, as a result of the peaceful religious schism in the Middle East, showed a demand for Asian goods. Gujarat served as a portal for commerce. It was in Gujarat where the trading of sugar and spices, textiles, and luxury goods, and Islamic conversion took hold. This new cultural association generated competition between Hinduism and Islam or the Hindu-Buddhist tradition, but Islamic influence within the region did little to disrupt Hindu practices especially within marriage or the polity, economy, and culture. Religion provided a bridge toward alliance, whether political, economic, or social. Islamic customs and rituals became a shared way of life that culturally and militarily affected society, marriage, and the conversion of armies. For example, Malacca was comprised of Javanese mercenaries and Javanese slaves of merchants, and its administration structurally operated under Islamic law, headed by the Sultan who infused Islam with Hindu-Buddhist courts. Arab and Persian traders helped to establish an empire and political center with the Chief Minister or *bendahara*, Tun Perak (1456–1498), in charge of the hereditary office, within Southern Malaya.

SOUTHEAST ASIA AND COLONIALISM

During the sixteenth and eighteenth century, when the Enlightenment advanced science and technology and expanded philosophical reflections, Asia experienced an influx of productivity infused with political and cultural influences. The mercantilist economy gave rise to the industrialist/capitalist society. Southeast Asian countries impacted by colonialism continued to generate financial investment, but also experienced exploitation of their material and human resources. In turn, economic activities led to the establishment of direct political control over colonies, administered through elaborate colonial bureaucracies.

As a result of pre-industrial development and scientific discovery, European cultural attitudes changed to those of aggression and dominance resulting in racist overtones, which led to territorial control of national states in Asia. Elevated power status equated with the possession of overseas colonies and policymakers used economic arguments to explain the necessity for expansion. Imperialism was supported by all classes, including workers, and even trade union leaders, and socialists who were enthusiastic about colonial expansion. Colonial settlements, however, did not happen overnight.

INDONESIA AND PORTUGUESE AND DUTCH SETTLEMENTS

The establishment of the East India Company brought much economic growth to the countries of Southeast Asia and at the forefront of this hub of trade activity was Indonesia and neighboring Malaysia. Portuguese trade and religious proselytization dominated the archipelagos along with the trading ports established in Goa, Melaka, Malaysia, Ambon, Timor, and Macau, China. The golden age of Portuguese trade spanned from the sixteenth to the seventeenth centuries, especially within the region of Java and its northern coastline, until a foothold of Dutch trade dominated the archipelagos. By the 1600s and onward, the Dutch developed competitive trade monopolies and rivalries with the establishment of colonial posts in Jakarta, renamed Batavia (capital of the Dutch East Indies).

During the seventeenth and eighteenth centuries, the Dutch East Indies Company controlled a large part of the trade in the region and Dutch trade dominated the region. However, by the eighteenth century, competition existed between the Dutch and British, especially after the Napoleonic Wars when the British showed a tremendous interest in expanding into the islands. Thereafter, with fears of imminent British control, the Dutch government reacquired control and expanded to Sumatra and Eastern Indonesia.

By 1911, the Dutch government ruled Bali, which became a centralized state with Batavia as the capital. With established economic and political ties with the Dutch, Indonesia provided an abundance of resources and had an efficient system of cultivation. The cultivation system gave the Dutch an advantage in terms of building an economy based on the cash crops of sugar, indigo, coffee, and tea, which were sold to European markets. By the twentieth century, Sumatra provided essential tobacco and rubber resources, but despite these valuable resources, Indonesia and its neighbors, especially China, experienced overpopulation and poverty within the rural population. To compensate for the poor living conditions and to keep up with production, Chinese immigrants became an integral labor force as production continued to grow. The country became a wealth of resources as urbanization continued to propel Dutch development. Consequently, a Western style of education was introduced, an education system that focused on the elite classes and the production of skilled labor.

SETTLEMENTS IN MALAYA

The Malay Peninsula has a history as old as Vietnam and China. Archaeological evidence shows the earliest inhabitants dating back to 10,000 years ago and Neolithic culture existing between 2500–1500 BCE.[7] The peninsula experienced a series of early migrations and developments during the fourteenth century that influenced the people of the peninsula with the culture and tradition of China and India. By 1400, an influx of trade further increased this influence as explorers and traders made their way along the Straits of Malacca. Beyond trade, claims to the land surrounding Melaka and southern Sumatra also took hold of the region due to the decline of the Srivijaya Kingdom, and rulers fled to new locations. Prince Parameswara of Palembang claimed Melaka, brought wealth to his kingdom, and made the peninsula a center of trade. The Straits of Malacca served as a corridor for trade and also allowed a pattern of migration of diverse populations which settled within the region. The geographic terrain benefited the

Courtesy of Library of Congress.

Wealthy Malays in Singapore, circa 1923

people and the country, which established economic and political relations and provided an important navigational outlet that allowed thousands to pass through the archipelago to acquire natural resources such as rubber, spices, and tin. With the immense amount of resources, kingdoms gained a wealth of riches and control of the Malay Peninsula, northern region of Borneo, eastern Sumatra, and the Straits of Malacca.[8] The fleets of ships that carried goods and services also brought Christian and Islamic influences to Melaka. Muslims in Melaka began to identify themselves as "Malay" in the fifteenth century and communities designated their language and culture of the "Malay world."[9]

By 1511, European exploration and navigational interests focused on the Straits of Malacca and the Spice Islands. The Portuguese played an influential role in the region by trade activities and their territorial claim of the Malay states. Explorer Afonso de Albuquerque and his forces ended Malay's golden age and began a period of Portuguese colonial claims that rivaled with the Netherlands. The Dutch captured Malay in 1641 and ruled it for over 150 years, dominating the spice trade that prompted the migration of the Minangkabau peoples from Sumatra by the late 1800s. This skirmish opened the door to countless invasions by the Bugis of Celebes and sultans controlling of the regions of Selangor and Jahon.[10] European settlements competed with the endless invasions of Malay states, but Portuguese and Dutch settlements, during the period of their slow downturn in the eighteenth century, faced a bigger challenge with the arrival of the British. By 1786, the roots of modern Malaysia had become evident on the island of Penang.[11] In 1819, British agent Sir Thomas Stamford Raffles established a trading post on Singapore Island and Penang Island, smaller geographic regions of the Malay Peninsula. The British established colonial rule in areas of northern Borneo and the Malay Peninsula. In 1824, the British acquired Melaka from the Dutch in exchange for a port in Western Sumatra. This territorial acquisition sealed British colonial rule in Melaka and encouraged the necessary resources to operate their colonial system of political and economic influence in the region. The Malay Peninsula provided efficient farming, British mining, rubber tree plantations, tin mines manned by Chinese labor, and plantations run by Indian labor.[12]

Rubber Trees in Singapore, circa 1890s

Courtesy of Library of Congress.

Malay states gained economic and political advantages under British control, but disadvantages also affected the people of the islands. Measures were put in place that divided the communities comprised of the Malays, Chinese, and Indians from the British. This type of division was not unusual under British rule for it had already existed in well-established settlements and prevented integration between ethnic groups and the British.[13]

By 1941, independence from colonial rule would come to light as Japanese forces seized the islands, but complete independence would not come until 1957.

PHILIPPINES AND SPANISH COLONIAL RULE

In 1493, Pope Alexander VI established a line of demarcation which ran from north to south through the middle of the Atlantic Ocean. Spain was given rights over land west of this line.[14] While Portugal's voyages dominated trade with the Indies by way of the Indian Ocean, Spain headed towards the West and East Indies to trade and spread Christianity during the late fifteenth century, and found its way to the Philippine archipelago. With the arrival of Dutch and Muslim trading ships, which came from as far away as Ceylon and the Indian Ocean, traveled through the Straits of Malacca and Sumatra and Java, and brought fine tea and silk and later spices of the East Indies, Christian and Muslim cultural exchanges were also taking place. The Moros, a term the Spanish used to refer to Islamic followers, dominated the southern realms of the islands with the Sulu and Muslims populating the region of Mindanao and competing for territory as well as religious influence upon the people of the Philippines.[15]

By 1500, trade between China, Arabia, and the Middle East had expanded, and thus connected markets with Southeast Asia and provided an advanced form of technological navigation of the seas. This allowed explorers to navigate through alternate sea routes.[16] The Philippines did not possess the spices that Arab and Western traders had already found within the bastion of the Spice Islands to the south of the Philippine archipelagos, Moluccas, Malaya, Indonesia, and New Guinea. However, merchants and traders saw the southern regions of the islands as a major trading port and link to other trading networks that competed with China, Singapore, and the Dutch.

FERDINAND MAGELLAN AND THE INDIES

The sixteenth century saw navigational advances and explorers utilized new methods to find efficient routes of travel. Expeditions were driven by monarchical endeavors. Declared by Queen Elizabeth I of England and King John I of Portugal and his son Prince Henry, these endeavors led them along with other European nations, such as Spain, to the exotic islands of Southeast Asia. Ferdinand Magellan, a Portuguese navigator from Spain, arrived in the Philippines in March 1521 after sailing an alternate route from Spain to the East Indies through the Americas and the Pacific Ocean. There he planted a Christian cross, and made alliances as well as enemies. Chief Lapu Lapu of Mactan Island killed Magellan and became a Filipino national hero for challenging the colonial invasion of the islands. Spain's attempts to acquire the islands did not end with Magellan's demise. King Philip II of Spain reigned from 1556–1598 and conquered the islands in 1571. In 1580, Philip officially proclaimed the Philippines, named in his honor, to be a Spanish colony that mirrored the empire in the Americas ruled by the viceroyalty of Nueva España (New Spain) in Mexico. King Philip sent Spanish galleons to the Pacific and Asia. These galleons carried and transported crops, silk, and porcelain goods acquired from China and sent to Manila from 1565–1815.

Courtesy of Library of Congress

Dock workers in Hong Kong, circa 1890s

Courtesy of the University of Texas Libraries, The University of Texas Austin.

The Philippines

SPANISH SETTLEMENT

The Spanish established their first settlement in 1565 in the city of Cebu. Six years later the central and northern regions of the islands became the center of Christianity and expansion when Miguel Lopez de Legazpi (1502–1572), a Basque Spanish Conquistador, established Manila as the capital of the Spanish East Indies. Legazpi was made *adelantado* ("Governor-General") of the city, opening trade doors within the country and allowing the import and export of major cash crops such as sugar, tobacco, coffee, and abaca. Production of these products increased between 1825 and 1875 as Chinese immigrants began to establish and own the production of these commodities.

Trade played a major role in the Philippines but not without the control by the Spanish government that came in the form of the Council of the Indies in Spain, a royal order based on religious edicts known as "Laws of the Indies."[17] As a part of this order, Roman Catholic friars served as administrators, while Jesuits, Franciscans, Dominicans, and Augustinians became the core Church officials. In order to attract new converts, animistic believers could still practice their beliefs but had to pay tribute to the Church as protection from non-believers. This form of religious assimilation took place while Spanish priests and friars educated the Filipino people about Christianity, and in turn, Filipinos taught the language of Tagalog to the priests. The friars and the priests not only provided salvation, but also were charged with managing the land estates owned by the Church under the provisions made with the *encomiendas*, or royal grants.[18] These grants were ordered by the Spanish to maintain colonial rule. To properly maintain the lands, villagers had *gobernadorcillos* (little governors) who supervised the village that fostered relations between the Church and peoples through financial arrangements made by the *encomenderos* that took tribute and labor from families, and in return, gave protection to these families from non-Christians if they converted to Christianity.[19] The Spanish granted stability to the Filipino people. The British invaded the islands in 1762 during the Seven Years' War (1756–1763) in order to prevent French threat to Chinese trade in Manila. The Spanish empire began to decline and roots of anti-Spanish dissent began to rise.

VIETNAM AND FRENCH SETTLEMENT

During the fourteenth and fifteenth centuries and before the French colonization of Vietnam, the region experienced a series of wars with the Cham Kingdom of Central Vietnam. The Vietnamese forces captured the Champa capital at Da Nang. This led to conflicts that were indicative of the Vietnamese resistance to Chinese imperial rule within the country. Despite this resistance, China continued to expand into Vietnam, especially during the Ming dynasty, as the Chinese occupied the region by way of a politicized version of Confucianism, forced labor, and exploitation.[20]

In 1428, rebel leader Le Loi defeated the Chinese and established the Le Dynasty; in the South, along the Mekong Delta, the Le colonized the former Khmer Empire and in 1516, the French and Europeans arrived. Into the seventeenth and eighteenth century, feudalism weakened and peasant revolts occurred. The Vietnamese defeated the Khmer and subsequently, French missionaries arrived and traded along the Mekong Delta. The event opened the door for French colonization. By 1615, Jesuit missionaries established missions, and beginning in 1627, Alexandre de Rhodes, a member of the missionary effort, spent over four decades establishing missionaries within Vietnam. Rhodes' contributions to Vietnamese culture included Christian conversion and Latin, which was an essential part of learning and communication in the Church. The Vietnamese people's religious beliefs leaned towards the ancient Chinese model of the "Mandate of Heaven," supernatural and moral forces centered on Confucianism and Daoism, and a tenet where the emperor signified the "son of heaven," an intermediary between the earth and supernatural.[21]

BRITISH IN BURMA

British influence spread to Burma during the Konbaung dynasty, established in 1752 under King Alaungpaya, and allowed an increase of Western trade to occur in the country. This increase in trade affected neighboring Southeast Asian countries such as Thailand and smaller states. Greater economic and territorial interests began to take hold of the region, and Alaungpaya focused on protecting the country's initial borders. These borders were affected by warfare and conquest, which involved the Mons, Arakanese, and Siamese. The Burmese fought with the Siamese, taking the capital of Ayudhya in 1767. They endured devastating invasions by the Chinese, and constant battles with the Siamese. While Siam's advances waged on, by the late nineteenth century, Burma also contended with the imminent fear of the British Empire that sought to advance from India to extend its economic and political influence within the country.

ENGLISH EAST INDIA COMPANY AND BURMA'S BORDERS

The British expanded their India policy into Burma. Since Burma was adjacent to India, the first priority was to maintain security of the border. Burma failed to respond in a trustful way. Its rulers, the Konbaung dynasty, with their capital at Ava, showed a Southeast Asian lack of interest in protecting its borders. Thereafter, expansionist campaigns in Arakan penetrated into Assam and brought conflict with the English East India Company. Burma failed to achieve an alliance with the French to forestall three successive British military campaigns. The British entered Burma in 1824 and expanded their holdings through three wars. With the first war, the British were in dispute over the geographic borders, trade, and diplomatic relations, resulting in an invasion lasting from 1824–25.

The First Anglo-Burmese War resulted in the loss of the peripheral Burmese provinces of Arakan and Tenasserim to the British. Between 1824 and 1826, British control of Assam and Arakan was confirmed and a British resident was installed at the court of Mandalay; the British captured the Burmese cities of Rangoon (Yangon), in 1824, and Ava, in 1826. Temporary peace occurred with the Treaty of Yandabo where the British granted the Arakan and Tenasserim regions, a part of the Kingdom of Manipur, to the Burmese while the British ruled from Calcutta.

The Second war in 1852 was to punish the king's arrogance. This war ensued because of the imprisonment of two British ship captains who were charged with murder and forced to pay a large ransom to secure their release. With the British annexation of lower Burma, including the port of Rangoon, British control of the Lower Burma kingdom was secured. The core area of Upper Burma was arid and nonviable territory where famine ensued, and the opening of new land in the delta of Lower Burma attracted thousands of refugees and immigrants to British territory. British armies captured the cities of Yangon and Prome and gave way to the annexation of lower Burma to the British crown and the British gaining full control of all trade and shipping on the Irrawaddy River.

While British rule looked imminent, the monarchy remained in place after the death of Pagan Min. A new king, Mindon Min, became one of the great kings of Burma.[22] He moved the capital to Mandalay and instituted new reforms such as the improvement of the administrative structure of the state, introduction of an income tax, building of new roads, initiating a telegraph system, and building modern factories using European machinery with European managers. He signed a commercial treaty with Britain.

After a brief respite from invasion, a third war followed in 1885, partly to deter the French from expanding from Indochina, and building a railway between Haiphong in Vietnam and Mandalay. Still under British rule, and after the death of King Mindon, Thibaw maneuvered onto the throne by Mindon's wives and her daughter, Supayalat. Thibaw massacred all contenders to the throne and their supporters.[23] With the conquest of the capital at Mandalay, the British abolished the Konbaung, ending the monarchy, and the land became known as "Further India", an extension of British colonial India.

BRITISH MODERNIZE BURMA

The British divided and occupied Burma's upper and lower regions. They allowed the tribes of the Shan, Karen, Kachin, Chin, and Naga, to retain their tradition of leadership (though rebellions erupted). The British built a large bureaucracy to assist in ruling India. Indian civil servants who ruled in Burma created great resentment and racial antagonism among the native people because few Burmese, lacking administrative experience that would prepare them for independence, were able to become part of the ruling class or allowed to serve in the army. During the 1920s, the Burmese, like the Indians, took part in the independence movement, a move towards self-government with the drive to organize strikes and school boycotts. These activities spread across the country and involved religious and political infractions between Buddhist establishment and the British government that created tensions between the people, who were devout Buddhists. The Burmese demanded more autonomy and these activities continued well into the 1930s and during World War II.

Despite political and social upheavals, the economy flourished and rice exports increased with the opening of the Suez Canal. By 1930, cultivated land in southern Burma, the Irrawaddy Delta area, increased ten times and rice exports increased five times.[24] Indian Chettiars (money lenders) were sent by the British to encourage Burmese farmers to settle new land and undertake the work of draining, and growing crops. These moneylenders made cheap loans more readily available to the Burmese farmers.[25]

With the outbreak of WWII, the Burmese continued to seek independence from British rule and joined forces with the Japanese to drive the British out of Burma. However, the Burmese switched alliances by mid-1945 and aided the US and British forces. After the war, the Burmese sought complete political and economic independence from Britain and a constitution was completed in 1947 and eventually granted in January 1948.

FRENCH IN VIETNAM AND THE END OF THE DYNASTY

By 1771, steps to end feudal lordship began to take root with a peasant uprising of landowners, Chinese bureaucrats, and the hereditary monarchy known as the Tay Son Movement (1773–1802). This event involved the capture of the Binh Dinh Province in southern Vietnam by three brothers, Nguyen Hue, Nguyen Nhac, and Nguyen Lu, and the defeat of the Nguyen family of the south. The Nguyens then fought the Trinh family of the north. They fought in the name of the Le Dynasty but then turned against the Le emperors and took the country for themselves. Nguyen Hue took the throne under the name Quang Trung and established the Tay Son Dynasty.

The establishment of this dynasty reunited the country, abolished the old tax system and replaced it with a Vietnamese model rather than a Chinese one, and gave women given more rights, and improved village education. The reign was short lived and after Quang Trung's death, the throne was

French Indochina

given to his ten-year-old son who eventually disabled the dynasty. As the French assisted Vietnam with administrative and education reforms, they overthrew regional feudal lordships, which opened the door for Nguyen Anh of the defeated Nguyen family to take over the ruling power in the south and establish the Nguyen Dynasty. Established in 1802, and the first to rule where current day Vietnam exists, this was the last royal dynasty in the country's history that contained a succession of rulers. Vietnam continued to deal with peasant unrest while the French quickly settled within the country participating in trade and religious activities. The reign of Tu Duc (1848–1883), the last emperor of independent Vietnam, led to the dynasty's downfall and allowed the French to invade and occupy the country.

FRENCH INVASION BEGINS IN 1858

French presence during the Tay Son Movement showed that Western influence was evident in Vietnam and contributed to the weakness of the Nguyen government by 1859. The French invasion of the south and Saigon was a response to brutal acts that pre-dated the 1830s. These brutal acts involved the persecution of Christians, French missionaries, and Vietnamese who converted to Catholicism. The capital of Hue generated much strength for the French conquest of Vietnam that proceeded with events of 1862 and the establishment of Cochin China. Cochin China consisted of a French colony within Southern Vietnam, Annam in Central Vietnam, and Tonkin in the North. By 1884, it had culminated into a colonial settlement with a colonial government that controlled the entire Vietnamese territory and proclaimed itself as a colonial sphere in Southeast Asia.

French Cochin China expanded with the annexation of Cambodia and Laos, and the defeat of Chinese forces that had been sent to protect their tributary state. Northern Vietnam experienced small industrial growth in the area around Hanoi and the northern port of Haiphong, a densely populated region organized by the Chinese model. Although these areas remained the least commercially developed, Southern Vietnam compensated for that deficiency and became a major exporter of rice and rubber. These products were grown in the Mekong delta and exported through the capital and chief port of Saigon.

Northern Vietnam remained influenced by China's influence, but by the late 1880s, the French administration tried to impose their culture on these territories and collectively called the region Indochina. Europeans controlled and exploited the labor in Vietnam and the cultural influence of French literature, language, and history affected the Vietnamese people. Many Vietnamese Catholics entrusted their spiritual well being to the French. This bears resemblance to Spain's monastic sovereignty in the Philippines. However, with Tuc Duc's presence as eminent ruler during the "Pacification Period" (1859–1897) this influence was not readily accepted. This struggle lasted for thirty years costing the lives of many Vietnamese, but strengthening French authority. After the "Pacification Period," Governor-General Paul Doumer focused his energy on "modernizing" Vietnam with a network of communications and the construction of railroads, bridges, and highways. In addition to moving the capital to Hanoi, Doumer also introduced forced labor, heavy taxes, and a centralized government. These "improvements" were designed to maximize profits in the area, and did not benefit the peasant community. The elite prevailed with Vietnamese collaboration.[26]

By the twentieth century, the doors opened for nationalism and de-colonization as Vietnamese confidence grew during 1907 and 1908 in the form of nationalist fervor. The printing press gave way to accessible forms of literature and communication that expanded Vietnamese public opinion and their ability to poetically and politically express themselves. As a response to French colonization, the cultural and intellectual development of the Free School Movement emphasized Vietnamese identity rather than French or Chinese.

In Vietnam, the Chinese Revolution of 1911 was an inspiration to many and led to the founding of the Vietnamese Nationalist party; a party based on the ideas of Sun Yat-sen, who had a strong influence on Ho Chi Minh. Ho Chi Minh, the most famous Vietnamese student-intellectual, traveled to France, Russia, and other areas of Europe, creating his own brand of Communism. In Hong Kong, he organized the Vietminh, an Indochinese Communist party (Viet Nam Doc Lap Dong Minh). The party attacked the French colonial government in 1929 and was completely destroyed by the early 1930s, leaving the field to the Indochinese Communist party. Nationalism emerged in the 1930s. The events that corresponded with Chinese nationalism filtered into Vietnam and slowly forced a French departure by the 1950s, despite France's unwillingness to leave. The siege in 1954 at Dien Bien Phu signified the end of the French Colonial period but divided the country. Western intervention by the United States opened another chapter to another phase of war in Vietnam.

SPANISH RULE IN DECLINE

By the nineteenth century, anti-Spanish sentiment spread and individuals that supported Nationalism took part in protests. Dr. Jose Rizal, a brilliant doctor, would become the most famous Filipino nationalist hero of the nineteenth century and who is known as the father of Philippine nationalism. Born in 1861, Rizal was the son of a sugar-planter of Filipino ancestry on his father's side and Chinese ancestry on his mother's side. He was educated at the Dominican University of Santo Tomas but later traveled to Madrid to study medicine and visited Paris and Heidelberg.[27] While overseas, Rizal wrote novels that reflected upon his travels in Europe and Asia. The first work, was entitled *Noli Me Tangere* (Touch me Not); the title comes from the words that Jesus uttered to Mary Magdalene at the Resurrection. The sequel, *El Filibusterismo* (The Subversive), was thought to have intimations of hatred towards submission to Spain and the Mother country, and as a result, was banned.[28]

Rizal was exiled to Europe and sent to Dapitan on Mindanao in 1892. In 1896, the Spanish executed Rizal. His death made him a martyr, spurning nationalism and anti-imperialist sentiment. Anti-imperialists and democrats looked at the relationship between the Philippines and United States as a corrupt alliance and one that contradicted American ideals and prevented the development of Filipino society. Disjointed party lines rooted in nationalism attracted an elite and educated class, known as the Ilustrados who were caught between Spanish rulers and Filipino peasantry with whom they could not identify.

SPANISH-AMERICAN WAR IN THE PHILIPPINES

Parallel to what had occurred in Cuba and a response against Spanish rule, the conflict began in 1895. A revolutionary society, known as the Katipunan, with Masonic and traditional overtones formed was founded by Andres Bonifacio, a patrician leader, son of a tailor and a Mason. The political execution of the revolutionary movement was conducted by town mayor Emilio Aguinaldo. At the end of the year, he reached a truce, mediated by Pedro Paterno, with the Spanish authorities. Aguinaldo and others went into exile in Hong Kong. The Spaniards hoped the revolution would subside. For the revolutionaries, it was a time for regrouping and for spreading unrest outside the Tagalog provinces.

The revolutionaries now placed their hopes on the United States. The United States did indeed intervene, fending off the Germans as well as the Japanese. By defeating Spain, the United States

Map of the Philippines which
indicated the location of certain
resources

helped the Philippines to end 400 years of Spanish rule in the country. This was a symbolic event that showed the first stirrings of anti-colonial rule to take place in the Philippines. After three centuries of Spanish rule that spread a common language and religion among the national elite, an emerging middle class of educated people, Ilustrados, acted against the government that they considered to be foreign rulers within their country.

RESULTS OF THE SPANISH-AMERICAN WAR

Open warfare ensued. It was neither a success nor a failure, yet in April 1898, the Spanish-American War began at the Battle of Manila Bay (May 1, 1898) with US Naval Admiral Dewey sending a fleet of ships that included the USS Olympia. Defeat appeared imminent for the Spanish fleet. With this incident, US involvement and Philippine participation in the Spanish-American War resulted in independence declared on June 12, 1898. Provisions outlined with the Peace Treaty at Paris (ratified February 6, 1899) specifically declared the US purchase of the Philippines from Spain for 20 million dollars. However, the islands' problems did not end with Philippine independence from Spain by the United States. Philippine revolutionaries against Spain further fueled their political cause for complete Philippine independence after the United States intervened to revitalize the country. General Emilio Aguinaldo responded with opposition to US intervention in the form of warfare. The Philippine and American War broke out on February 2, 1899 between Aguinaldo's army and US infantrymen. By 1902, most of the fighting was quelled except for in the South. US economic expansionists sought Chinese markets and navies sought the islands for its harbors and fuel resources.

AFTERMATH OF THE PHILIPPINE AND AMERICAN WAR AND US ANNEXATION

The Philippine and American War consumed the country. After Aguinaldo was captured in March 1901 and surrender took place in April 1902, Aguinaldo was relentless to pursue any form of non-foreign rule in the Philippines by establishing the Republic of the Philippines. His attempts to maintain the Republic became a challenge after the United States defeated Spain. The United States government under President William McKinley affirmed annexation and the goal to pursue a Philippine self-government. Despite the promise to establish stability, Aguinaldo and members of the Philippine Republic lacked confidence that Philippine autonomy would come about.

This concern caused tension. The Republic, set up in June 1898, had to prove to foreign powers that it could govern. It needed the elite, and it needed the support from the peasants. The problem was that the Republic demanded labor and services similar to the Old Spanish regime; the other major concern involved the elite's fear that the peasants and their reaction to this plan would cause another revolution. However, the difference between the Spanish and the United States was that the United States operated as a transitional government for the Filipinos, despite their depreciation of Filipino achievements. Jacob Gould Schurman established a policy known as Benevolent Assimilation that provided the hope that the Filipinos needed to revitalize the country and to reshape Filipino society but under a policy that the United States instituted.[29] The islands became governed by the United States, and officials implemented reform programs that included education, literacy, and modern health care.[30] Among the early allies of the Americans was a group of upper class Manilenos, led by T.H. Pardo de

The Philippine Rebellion

Courtesy of Library of Congress.

Tavera. They formed a Federal party in 1900 aimed at making the Philippines a state of the Union, first patronized by Governor-General William H. Taft. The party offered the Americans an advantage for their support with the resistance: mobilize the Filipinos for their friendly rapport and support for the American cause, and in return, they offered statehood, a tutelage, and protection without colonial inequality or second-class citizenship. Despite these efforts, the Filipinos rejected statehood.[31] Instead, plans already in progress to grant national sovereignty to the Philippines were under way by the 1920s and 1930s with several government acts implemented throughout the decades, Jones Act (1916) went through revisions until a definite act that declared Philippine independence for the people and the country was in place, the Tydings-McDuffie Act (1934).

For more information about the topics discussed in this chapter, please visit the website for this textbook. This website can be accessed from http://www.grtep.com/.

1 D.R SarDesai, *Southeast Asia: Past and Present*, 6th ed. (Pennsylvania: Westview Press, 2010), 62.
2 Alexander Woodside, "Territorial Order and Collective-Identity Tensions in Confucian Asia: China, Vietnam, Korea, *Daedalus* 127, no. 3 Early Modernities (Summer 1998), 205.
3 Windows on Asia, Michigan State University: Vietnam. http://asia.isp.msu.edu/wbwoa/southeast_asia/vietnam/history.htm#bullet4, accessed on May 4, 2011.
4 Milton Osborne, *Southeast an Introductory History* (Australia: Allen and Unwin, 1979 reprinted 2010), 7.
5 Windows on Asia, Michigan State University: Vietnam.
6 Windows on Asia, Michigan State University: Vietnam.
7 History of Malaysia, http://www.kiat.net/malaysia/history.html accessed on June 9, 2012.
8 Osborne, 85.
9 Craig Lockard, *Southeast Asia in World History* (New York: Oxford University Press, 2009), 69.
10 History of Malaysia, http://www.kiat.net/malaysia/history.html accessed on May 4, 2011.
11 Osborne, 86.
12 Lockard, 100.
13 Lockard, 99.
14 "Treaty of Tordesillas." Britannica: Academic Edition. http://www.britannica.com/EBchecked/topic/599856/Treaty-of-Tordesillas accessed August 23, 2012.
15 Lockard, 80.
16 Lockard, 63.
17 "Spaniards as Colonial Masters." Philippine History. http://www.philippine-history.org/spanish-colonial-masters.htm accessed June 10, 2012.
18 SarDesai, 67.
19 Ibid.

20 Alexander Woodside, "History, Structure, and Revolution in Vietnam," *International Political Science Review* 10 no. 2 (April 1989), 146.

21 Woodside, "History, Structure, and Revolution in Vietnam," 146.

22 Windows of Asia, Michigan State University: Burma, http://asia.isp.msu.edu/wbwoa/southeast_asia/burma/history.htm, accessed March 2, 2011.

23 Windows of Asia, Michigan State University: Burma.

24 Windows of Asia, Michigan State University: Burma.

25 Windows of Asia, Michigan State University: Burma.

26 Windows on Asia, Michigan State University: Vietnam.

27 H.W. Brands, *Bound to Empire: The United States and the Philippines*, (New York: Oxford University Press, 1992), 40.

28 Ibid.

29 Lockard, 117.

30 Ibid.

31 Brands, 86.

Chapter *11* Mughal Empire and Colonialism in South Asia

After Timur sacked Delhi in 1398, the Delhi Sultanate could never restore its earlier glory. Although the Sultanate regained some strength during the last Lodi dynasty, it soon faced a more formidable challenge from the Mughals, who would build one of the greatest empires in Indian history. Between the sixteenth and the eighteenth centuries, the Mughals unified almost all of the Indian subcontinent, making their empire one of the largest in Indian history. During their three-century rule, the Indian subcontinent experienced a depth of long-term peace and prosperity that it never had before. At its height, the Mughal Empire was one of the three Muslim empires, comparable with that of the Ottomans and Safavids in the Middle East.[1]

The Mughal era began with the territorial expansion by Mughal rulers, Babur, Jahangir, Akbar, and Shan Jahan, who extended the boundaries of their empire to match those of the Mauyan Empire, which had existed nearly 2000 years prior. The resilience of their empire depended more on their political reforms than their military triumphs. Unlike the previous Delhi dynasties, the Mughal rulers followed the territorial conquests with successful political consolidation. The flexibility and openness of the administrative institutions created by the Mughal emperor Akbar evolved over the years into a multi-ethnic and multi-cultural system that had won not only the cooperation of Hindu Rajputs (son of a king, generally used to refer to Hindu warrior classes in north India) and other elites, but also the loyalty of their diverse subjects. As a result, the Mughals eventually turned their empire into a new kind of cosmopolitan Indian empire, despite the fact that they initially moved into India as foreign invaders.

None of the earlier invaders of the northern India, such as the Greeks, the nomadic groups from the Central Asia, or other Muslim groups, enjoyed the fame and success as the Mughals did for more than three centuries. Through their tolerant attitudes and inclusive policies toward non-Muslims, they managed to blend many local societies together under their rule instead of alienating them.[2] The Mughal era, in the words of Barbara and Thomas Metcalf, "was one of far-reaching political, economic, and social reconfigurations."[3] This produced an Indian state that is a fusion of both traditional Indian and Muslim cultures.

After two centuries of rule, however, the empire started to lose its vitality. Following the death of their last capable emperor, Aurangzeb, in the early eighteenth century, the empire began to fall apart. The British started to move into this power vacuum and gradually seized control of trade routes and the right to govern increasingly larger areas of India.[4] After the mid eighteenth century, the British gradually reduced the Mughals into a regional power confined in Delhi. In 1858, the British finally deposed the last Mughal emperor and exiled him to Burma.[5] The decline of the Mughal Empire, however, is still open to debate. Although the British East Indian Company takes the blame for the fall of the Mughals, some scholars "see the seeds of decay less in the challenge from abroad than in internal weakness—in the very nature of the dynasty itself, which was always more a heterogeneous collection of semiautonomous political forces than a centralized empire in the style of neighboring China."[6]

BABUR AND THE NEW DYNASTY

Babur (1483–1530), a prince of Kabul, was the founder of the Mughal Empire. He had an unusual pedigree: on his father's side, he was a descendent of Timur, who had established an early dynasty over a vast region of Persia and Central Asia and sacked Delhi in 1398; on his mother's side, he was descended from the legendary Mongol ruler Chinggis Khan.[7] Consequently, Babur and his family were known as "Mughals," a Perso-Arabic term for Mongols.[8] At the age of twelve, he inherited a fragment of Timur's empire, which is present-day Uzbekistan. Facing increasingly severe challenges from other emerging powers, such as the Uzbeks, Babur and his warriors moved southeast and seized Kabul in 1504.[9] Stationed in Kabul, the young Babur, who had lost hope in recovering his home-town, began to direct his ambition to a new area and had "never ceased to think of the conquest of Hindustan."[10]

The opportunity finally came twenty years later. After a few adventures into northern India resulted in small victories, Babur entered India again in 1524 for the fourth time upon receiving an invitation from the ruler of Lahore in Punjab, Daulat Khan Lodi, a brother of the sultan of Delhi, Ibrahim Lodi (r. 1517–26). Dualat Khan asked Babur to support him in his conspiracy against the sultan. Babur was more than happy to accept the invitation and took this opportunity to further his plan to conquer India. He not only defeated Ibrahim Lodi's troops, but also weakened the power of Daulat Khan Lodi, and thus paved the way for his future control of Punjab.[11] Two years later, he eliminated Daulat Khan on his way to Delhi and defeated Ibrahim Lodi in a decisive battle at Panipat, about 70 miles from Delhi.

It is said that Babur's victories were partially due to his advanced weapons, including light field artillery, a new technology that the Turks had brought to Asia from the West, and his effective use of cavalry, which he had learned from the Uzbeks.[12] His artillery had a decisive advantage over the war elephants of his opponents. In the Battle of Panipat, he crushed Ibrhim's forces, even though Ibrahim had ten times as many troops as he did.[13] This victory increased Babur's confidence, and he soon controlled Delhi, a city of great meaning to him, and ended the rule of Delhi Sultanate. Although the Lodis had moved their capital away from Delhi to Agra, the city of Delhi was symbolic to Babur; not only because he wanted to replicate Timur's victory over the city more than a century before, but also because Delhi had become a religious and cultural center of northern India.[14] In the following year, he won another great victory over the overwhelming forces of the Rajput Confederacy. By the time of his death in 1530 at the age of 47, Babur had added most of northern India to his newly claimed Mughal Dynasty.[15]

At the beginning, Bubar's new dynasty seemed to suffer in the same ways as the short-lived dynasties of the Delhi Sultanate. Despite his great military achievements, Babur ruled only four years and died prematurely in 1530 without being able to consolidate his conquests in India. He may have died after a compassionate prayer to exchange his life for the life of his dying son, but Humayun (1508–1556), the son on whom Babur had placed so much hope, failed to meet Babur's expectations.[16] Humayun, in the words of an English historian, was "intelligent but lazy"[17] and prob-ably more interested in "astrology, illustrated books, and in building innovative palaces" than power.[18] Lacking both the personality and determination of his father, Humayun gradually lost control of

Afghan generals who were powerful enough to compete with him for the throne. The crisis finally came in 1540 when his advisor, Sher Shah (r. 1540–1545), temporarily put an end to the Mughal kingdom and forced Humayun to flee westward to Persia.

Sher Shah ruled only for several years before his accidental death in 1545. However, he made a permanent mark on the history of South Asia through his far-reaching administrative initiatives and his ambitious construction projects. He introduced the notion of measuring land for tax purposes, the standardization of a silver-based monetary system, and a law system for the fair execution of justice for all subjects. Emperor Akbar, Humayun's successor, later adopted and refined many of Sher Shah's measures for his own administrative system.[19]

Sher Shah also undertook ambitious construction projects, including the extension of a major road in north India to connect East Bengal to West Punjab, passing through Agra, Delhi, and Lahore. The road, known later as the Great Trunk Road, is one of the oldest and longest roads in South Asia.[20] The structure and the grand size of the tombs that he built for his grandfather, father and himself became an inspiration for later Mughal emperors to build their own.[21]

However, his rule, together with that of his son and grandson, proved to be only a short-term deterrence from the restoration of the Mughal Dynasty. With the help of the Safavid Dynasty in Persia, Humayun retook Delhi and recovered his throne 1555. Eight months later, however, he reportedly fell from the terrace of his library after smoking a pipeful of opium and died from the resulting injuries, leaving the empire to his thirteen-year-old son, Akbar (1542–1605).[22]

AKBAR AND HIS ACHIEVEMENTS

Akbar was the greatest Mughal ruler and one of the greatest rulers in Indian history. Neither Babur nor Humayun could secure the borders of the dynasty.[23] It was Akbar who built the dynasty into an empire. During his half-century rule, he gradually extended Mughal control over the entirety of north India and continuously pushed the Mughal frontier southward. By the end of his reign, his empire had extended from Kabul in the west to Bengal in the east and from Kashmir in the north to the Godavari River in the south.[24] He established a successful administration over the vast empire and exercised policies of tolerance toward different religions. As a result, he won the cooperation of local elites and respect from his diverse subjects. His governance laid the foundation for a great Mughal empire that had a lasting impact over the subcontinent.

Akbar was born in 1542 when his father, Humayun, was still in exile in Persia. At first, it was difficult for the young Akbar to manage the Mughal Dynasty. Taking advantage of his young age, some Afghan generals rebelled against him and even temporarily took Delhi away from him. Fortunately, he had help from his tutor, Bairam Khan, who was also a trusted friend of his father, Humayun. Bairam Khan became Akbar's regent and protector, and helped him to suppress all of the rebellions within the coming years. Akbar claimed full control of the court himself in 1560 after he became increasingly uncomfortable with Bairam's power over the Mughal administration and his brutality over their enemies.[25]

As his primary concern at the time was to secure the empire that the Mughals had only recently recovered, Akbar continued Bairam's policies of expansion. He pushed the Mughal frontiers beyond their previous heartland, and by 1581, he had exercised a firm control over Gujarat, Rajasthan, the Deccan, and the Bengal.[26] During his entire reign, Akbar never abandoned the policy of military conquest, which, by his own account, was vital for the survival of his empire. "A monarch," he remarked, "should be ever intent on conquest, otherwise his neighbors rise in arms against him. The army should be exercised in warfare, lest from want of training they become self-indulgent."[27]

Akbar, however, was better known for his achievements in administrative reforms, religious tolerance, and cultural patronage.[28] As early as the 1570s, after he securely put northern India under his control, he began focusing on building a solid administration over his vast empire. Viewing himself as "an Indian ruler, not a foreign despot," he recognized the pluralistic character of Indian society.[29] Similar to the great Indian rulers before him, his political and religious policies were lenient toward different ethnic and religious groups. Akbar's administrative elites were comprised not only of different groups of Muslims from central Asia and Persia (who were Shiites instead of Sunni Muslims), but also Rajputs, Brahmans and other Hindus. He appointed Hindu officials and Rajputs, many of whom were former leaders who had rebelled against him, to the important positions. The characteristics of his administration, and the Mughal administration in general, have led to debates among scholars concerning the nature of Mughal rule. Some scholars characterize Akbar's rule as "Indo-Muslim" rule, instead of pure Muslim rule, but others ponder on the true meaning of the over 300 year rule of the Mughal dynasty.[30] The latter argue that while the Mughal monarchs were Muslims who "justified their existence in Islamic terms," non-Muslim elites were essential to the administrations of the Mughal regime, and the Mughal emperors did not execute "programs of mass, much less forced, conversion."[31] Furthermore, they believe that the notion that "the Hindus and Muslims came to see themselves as distinct religious communities, even two nations" is only a modern phenomenon, and hence may not have its historical roots in India's past, during which there were numerous examples of diverse ruling elites such as those at the Mughal courts.[32]

In order to win support and loyalty from non-Muslim elites, Akbar employed various means, including the establishment of matrimonial alliances with the proud Rajputs. Two of his wives were Hindu princesses and one Christian. Unlike the previous practices that had usually included humiliation of the in-laws, Akbar treated the family members of his wives with equal respect and made them court nobles.[33] The interaction between these Hindu nobles and Muslim nobles enhanced the understanding between the two cultures. Furthermore, some of Akbar's children were born with a mixture of Mughal and Rajput blood. One of his Hindu wives, for example, gave birth to his son, Jahangir (r. 1605–1628), who later became his heir.[34]

Because of the diverse ruling elites at his court, "the unifying ideology of the regime," observed by Barbara D. Metcalf and Thomas R. Metcalf, "was that of loyalty, expressed through Persianate cultural forms, not a tribal affiliation (like that of the Ottomans), nor an Islamic or an Islamic sectarian identity (like that of the Safavids)."[35] These policies of Akbar were so successful that many Rajputs became his strongest allies and constantly assisted him in his struggle against his other rivals, especially in Akbar's conquest of Gujarat in 1572.[36] The conquest of Gujarat gave the Mughals access to the sea and an initial contact with the Portuguese who had established themselves at Diu.[37]

The evolution of Akbar's social policy also reflected his understanding of the subcontinent as a diverse society. To bring his subjects together, he began his social reforms by changing some of the harsh Muslim-based policies against infidels and replacing them with policies that would provide better social justice to all of his subjects.[38] He even applied Hindu law to settle disputes in the area settled by Hindus.[39] Among his most beloved policies was the outlawing of forcible conversion to Islam and the special tax on Hindus as infidels, the tax that had been collected by previous Muslim rulers for years.[40] Further, around 1580, Akbar's administration granted equal rights to the non-Muslim population through a policy known loosely as "universal toleration." This policy became a cornerstone of his governance.[41] His relatively benign social policies won him loyalty from his subjects, especially among non-Muslims populations.

Akbar's open-mindedness was best demonstrated in his view of religion. Born an orthodox Muslim, he was extremely open to other religious beliefs and showed interest in philosophy and religion of all kinds. Not only did he tolerate Hindu practices throughout his empire, but he also expressed interest in the Christian view of the Jesuit missionaries and the view of Jain monks. After he completed most of his conquests, his curiosity in philosophical thinking grew even stronger. He held a series of religious debates at his new court at Fatehpur Sikri, during which Muslim scholars would debate with Hindu Brahmins, Sikhs, Jains, Jews, and Portuguese priests.[42] He instructed his scholars to translate into Persian the books that were important to other religions, including the Christian gospels and Hindu epics of *Ramayana* and *Mahabharata*.[43] While he granted lands and money to build Muslim mosques, he also sponsored the building of Hindu temples in north India and Christian churches in Goa. He also granted land to the newly born Sikh faith in Amristar, Punjab where the Sikhs erected their famous Golden Temple.[44]

Akbar's interests in different religions and philosophies ultimately led to his creation of a new faith of his own. Out of his sincere belief that there should be "a universal faith in an all-powerful creation," Akbar promulgated Din-i-Illah (the divine faith), which in his belief would "merge the best of the Indian traditions" with that of Islam.[45] Akbar's new faith was generally interpreted as a new religion, which has led some scholars to question whether Akbar eventually abandoned Islam as his faith. Others, however, argue that what Akbar created was merely a "new discipleship order intended to bind the highest ranking nobles in complete loyalty to the emperor."[46] Akbar may have only wanted to secure loyalty from all of his officials and subjects through this new faith. In either case, Akbar's new faith was a noticeable departure from orthodox Islam, which upset many Muslim elites. Some of them merely showed open hostility against this new faith, while others revolted against his regime. As a result, his "divine faith" vanished quickly after he died.[47]

Akbar is a fascinating figure who has inspired many studies. Because of his tough childhood, he remained illiterate, but he demonstrated higher intellectual capacity and versatility than his well-educated father and grandfather.[48] He had over 24,000 manuscripts in his library and sometimes had his courtiers read them to him several hours a day. He had remarkable talents in many areas, such as sports (polo), painting, and music, and even left behind a few inventions, including a lighted polo ball that enabled him to play in the evening and a gun that could fire multiple rounds.[49]

Despite all of the fame and wealth that he had enjoyed, however, Akbar's life was not a perfect one. One of his more personal problems was the lack of an heir; twenty six years of age is usually quite late for producing heirs in the Indian tradition. In desperation, he went to a Sufi saint, Shaikh Salim Chishti, who predicted that Akbar would actually have several children in his life. True to his words, Akbar's first surviving son, Jahangir, was born the next year. As a gesture of gratitude, Akbar built a new mosque next to the saint's humble cottage near Agra and later a new capital nearby. It was the first planned city of the Mughal era and one of the oldest examples of the splendid Mughal style of architecture.[50] Akbar was so emotionally attached to the place that he decorated this magnificent capital at Fatehpur Sikri with the best architecture, in a style that was a distinctive fusion of Indian and Persian styles.

Akbar showed amazing originality in the architectural choices of his new capital. The city had beautiful ensembles of highly individualized buildings using a unifying material of warm red sandstone. Among the most impressive were the grand gate, the Buland Darwaza, the great mosque, which was dedicated to Salim Chishti, and Salim's white marble tomb. Akbar's own spectacular palace was behind a pool of water and decorated with exquisite carvings, wall paintings, and pillars covered with precious stones.[51] Fatephur Sikri became a model for later Mughal architects. It took fifteen years to build Fatehpur Sikri, but it served as Akbar's capital only from 1571 to 1585. Because of the water supply problem, Akbar had to abandon the city after fourteen years, shifting his capital to Lahore and then back to Agra in 1599.

Akbar was miserable when he did not have an heir, but his life was more miserable after he had one. The last few years of his life was marred by his son's disloyalty. His ambitious heir, Jahangir, engaged in rebellions against him and eventually may have poisoned him to death.[52] Actually, the Mughal monarchs were always troubled by succession problems in their later years. From the time of Akbar, every Mughal emperor faced the rebellion of his own sons. This problem originated through a Timurid tradition that did not recognize the right of the eldest son as heir to the throne. This always resulted in a heated competition among the emperor's capable sons, a competition that wasted many resources and much energy, and had probably done more damage to the empire than any other outside forces.[53]

JAHANGIR AND SHAN JAHAN

Jahangir was a capable ruler who quickly overcame the animosity toward him after he ascended the throne. In order to rule Akbar's vast empire, an empire that contained an estimated 110 million people, Jahangir continued his father's political and religious policies for most of his rule.[54] He strengthened Mughal control of north and central India, and his administration ran smoothly, much like the one that his father had established.[55] He was especially famous for his strong sense of justice. He set up a golden "chain of justice" outside of his palace of Agra. Anyone could ask his personal hearing for justice by pulling the chain of one of the sixty bells.

Jahangir, together with his wives and courtiers, indulged themselves in a more luxurious life style than his father had had. He and his favorite wife from Persia, Nur Jahan (the Light of the World), adorned Agra with new palaces, gardens, and tombs, and took delight in silks, perfumes, wine, troupes of dancing girls, and month long parties.[56] The city of Agra grew into a size that was twice that of Isfahan, the capital of the Safavid Empire in Persia, and with a population of half a million. Because of his Persian wife's influence, the city became a favorite place of Persian poets, musicians, artists and architects. Gradually the Persian influence merged with traditional Indian fashion to produce a luxurious life style that had a widespread influence over the Mughals and other elites. Observers at the time could not help but notice that there were "no sharp distinctions in either dress or appearance between the Great Mughal emperors and princes and their leading nobles or other contemporary Hindu chiefs."[57]

Further, as a great patron of arts, especially of painting, Jahangir sponsored many court painters, whose portrait paintings of Jahangir and his family introduced a new style of realistic portraiture into Mughal arts. Relying on Jahangir's perception of himself as "a light-filled ruler," his royal painters often depicted Jahangir as a divine figure at the center of the universe.[58] Jahangir's artistic influence, together with those of his son, Shah Jahan, inspired some to name their reigns the "golden age of the Mughal culture."[59]

Jahangir's rule, however, was troubled with many problems, as his father's reign before him. With the exceptions of invasions and rebellions, many problems were a result of his family. Jahangir seemed to be easy-going by nature and "only wanted a bottle of wine and a piece of meat to make merry," according to his memoirs.[60] Soon after his marriage to Nur Jahan, his strong-minded Persian wife became a source of trouble at court. As the favorite of Jahangir's wives, she took advantage of Jahangir's weaknesses to manipulate him and hence became a power in her own right. She appointed her father and brothers to the highest positions, and arranged for her daughter from her first marriage to marry Jahangir's youngest son. This last move caused a split between her and prince Khurram, also known as Shah Jahan, who viewed the empress' move as a deliberate undermining of his position as the heir apparent, even though Nur Jahan had arranged for her niece, Mumtaz Mahal, to marry Shah Jahan.[61] Additionally, her extravagant life style nearly bankrupted the country.

Similar to the case of his father, Jahangir's bigger issues came from his heir, his third son Shan Jahan. In order to eliminate competition for the throne, Shah Jahan murdered Jahangir's eldest son and then competed vehemently against the empress for control of the court. In 1622, he openly defied his father's (or Nur Jahan's) order to lead a military expedition to regain the territory of Kandahar from a resurgent Iranian ruler, for fear that

1616. Artist unknown.

Jahangir giving a robe of honor to a courtier while being watched by Sir Thomas Roe, the English Ambassador

Nur Jahan would maneuver against him in his absence. The problems between him and the empress eventually provoked a three-year revolt against his father and stepmother. Although his father and brother eventually suppressed his revolt, Shah Jahan eventually secured the Mughal throne after Jahangir's death in 1627.[62]

Shah Jahan (Emperor of the World, r. 1627–1658) was one of the most accomplished rulers of the Mughal Empire.[63] He was a more militarily vigorous ruler than either his father or grandfather, and probably more ruthless than either as well.[64] After his inauguration, he immediately put most of his rivals to death and forced Nur Jahan to retire, although he allowed some of her relatives to remain at court.[65] During his three-decade reign, he expanded Mughal control through Deccan to south India; both Shah Jahan's father and grandfather had dreamed of this expansion, but neither could obtain the area. His ambition to follow his Timurid ancestry in conquering Balkh in northern Afghanistan, however, was less successful.[66]

Shah Jahan's domestic policies were not dramatically different from those of Akbar and his father. Shah Jahan, however, was not as supportive of his grandfather's cornerstone policies of tolerance. Instead, he was in favor of a more traditional interpretation of Islam and geared his policies toward that direction. As a result, his most significant change of Akbar's policies was in religion. He appeared in public as a devout Muslim, and his adherence to fasting in the month of Ramadan even amazed his close friends. He curtailed the constructions of new Hindu temples and limited the privileges of non-Muslims.[67] Some of these changes may have been a result of his father Jahangir's lavish lifestyle, his own massive construction projects, as well as his expensive military campaigns. In order to have better control over his court, Shah Jahan also changed the ethnic composition of his administration, giving in to the pressure of promoting more Persia-Muslim nobles, a practice that probably had begun with the domination of Nur Jahan's family at his father's court.[68]

With the domination of the Persian-Muslim elites came more influence from Persian culture. As a result, Shah Jahan's reign saw a maturation of the Mughal culture, an "Indianized Muslim culture," according to some scholars.[69] Actually, as in the case of their predecessors, Jahangir's and Shah Jahan's cultural policies were equally as important as their political ones.[70] Mughal Persian-influenced art and architecture reached its peak at this time. As mentioned earlier, Jahangir often used the arts to enhance his own political image as a semi-divine ruler. Probably drawing their inspiration from medieval European church paintings, the Mughal painters often drew a halo over Jahangir's head. Although Shah Jahan was less interested in the idea of the Christian-affiliated halo, he did reinforce the link between political power and spiritual influence through many of his portraits.

The important cultural legacy left by the Mughal emperors was their architectural achievements in Delhi, Agra and other places, including gardens, palaces, and tombs.[71] The Mughal emperors enjoyed gardens from the time of Babur, who often saw his garden as an important manifestation of his rule. Babur tells us, through his own memoir, that his gardens epitomized his own desire to turn "an unruly India into a site of order and control."[72] Later, gardens became an important part of imperial mausoleums built for each Mughal monarch and their family.[73] The most famous of these is the Taj Mahal in Agra, a tomb Shah Jahan built for his beloved wife Mumtaz Mahal, who died at the age of 39 when she gave birth to their fourteenth child.[74] Despite Shah Jahan's propensity for a lavish lifestyle as well as his possession of hundreds of concubines, his devotion to his beautiful wife Mumtaz Mahal was legendary. "Empire has no sweetness, life has no relish for me now," moaned Shah Jahan after he heard of the death of Mumtaz Mahal.[75]

Soon afterwards, Shah Jahan ordered the construction of the Taj Mahal, the most lavish tomb in India's history. Designed by two Persian architects, but following traditional Indian style, the Taj Mahal is often considered the greatest single masterpiece of Indian culture, one of the most beautiful structures in the world, and a symbol of permanent love. The milky white marble dome on top of the marble structure was adorned with semi-precious stones outside and inside, a monument that has awed visitors from all over the world for centuries. This famous monument was built and erected at the expense of many Indian people. It took 20,000 workmen nearly twenty years to complete this construction.[76] India actually suffered one of the worst famines in its history, from 1630 to 1632, when Shah Jahan began constructing the Taj Mahal at a staggering expense.[77]

The famine, however, did not stop Shah Jahan from taking on projects that were even more ambitious. Instead of helping devastated peasants, Shah Jahan increased their taxes in order to sustain the financial needs not only for the Taj Mahal, but also for his other extravagant constructions. In 1638, the massive construction of a new capital in Delhi began, even before his workmen finished the Taj Mahal. Shah Jahan's decision to move his capital from Agra to Delhi may have been prompted by his troubled memory of Mumtaz Maha, or by his passion for building his own capital.[78] Using the traditional material of red sandstone, which gave the name "the Red Fort" to the complex, Shah Jahan designed his new capital on a grander scale than his grandfather Akbar's capital. When the new capital was erected in 1648, it occupied an area of nearly five million square feet in Delhi. This city within the city is sometimes known by its Mughal name, *Shah Jahanabad* (Shah Jahan's city).[79] Inside its thick walls were palaces, royal halls, mosques, military barracks, a treasury, a mint, as well as thousands of houses for the princes and princesses, royal relatives, courtiers, servants, and slaves.[80] An inscription on the wall of *Diwan-I Khas* (the Hall of Private Audience) best symbolizes the beauty of the Red Fort, "If there be Paradise on earth, it is Here, It is Here, It is Here!"[81] Sitting on his famous Peacock Throne, which was made of pure gold and decorated with the largest precious stones that the world had ever seen, Shah Jahan, in the words of Wolpert, was "a king mightier than England's monarch, richer than China's and as strong as Persia's."[82]

AURANGZEB AND MUGHAL DECLINE

Shah Jahan's power and wealth further destroyed the lives of the Indian people. The lavish construction projects as well as his wasteful military expenses forced Shah Jahan to raise tax rates to double what it had been under his grandfather Akbar. In addition to his financial problems, Shah Jahan also had to deal with the century-old Mughal problem of succession. When Shah Jahan fell seriously ill in 1657, it triggered palace intrigue among his four capable sons, all of whom immediately claimed to be the next Mughal emperor. Eventually, Aurangzeb eliminated all of the other powerful contenders and ascended to the throne in 1658. It might have been unfortunate for the Mughals that Shah Jahan's favorite son, Dara, who was "a philosopher and mystic like his great-grandfather Akbar," lost in this power competition, despite support from his father.[83] Otherwise, the Mughals might have seen another enlightened ruler.[84]

Aurangzeb, or Alamgir (World Conqueror, r. 1658–1707) by his reign name, was the most controversial ruler in Mughal history.[85]Although killing family members was a general practice when Mughal royal princes competed for the throne, cold-blooded Aurangzeb did more than necessary to his father and brothers. In order to obtain this long desired throne, he poisoned or assassinated a dozen of his brothers and half brothers, and put countless others to death. After he defeated Dara, he cut off his brother's head and sent it to his father, who spent the last eight years of his life in Aurangzeb's prison in Agra.[86] It is said that after he heard that the old man could still get some comfort from staring at the Taj Mahal through the window of his cell in Agra, Aurangzeb gave an order to have the old man's eyes put out.[87]

What Aurangzeb did to his courtiers and subjects was even more controversial. During his long reign from 1658 to 1707, he completely abandoned Akbar's model that assured his subjects' loyalty through benevolence and tolerance, and preferred instead to rule by terror and coercion. He reinforced orthodox interpretations of the Koran and reversed the long-supported Mughal policy of cultural pluralism. Accordingly, he banned Hindu festivals and practices throughout his domain and even ordered the demolition of Hindu and Sikh temples. He cruelly tortured the ninth Sikh guru to death and thus made himself a permanent enemy to the Sikhs.[88] In order to deal with his financial problems, he reinstalled the hated *jizya*, the special tax for non-Muslims, and doubled the taxes on Hindu merchants.[89] Meanwhile, his court became more austere when he prohibited the use of gold in men's garments and wine consumption according to *sharia* law. In addition to banning music and other entertainment at his court, Aurangzeb also put a death knell to other art forms, such as painting, at least in his domain.[90]

His unpopular policies soon backfired. A few years into his reign, he encountered a number of popular revolts. This, however, only pushed Aurangzeb to employ more forceful measures against his disobedient subjects. His military decisions assured his successful suppression of rebellions and enabled him to extend his power further into central and south India. Different from his predecessors who usually focused on north and west India,[91] Aurangzeb focused on the territory of Deccan and beyond. He spent the second half of his reign engaging in expensive but eventually unsuccessful

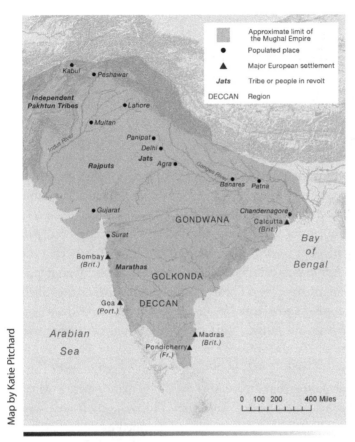

The Mughal Empire

Map by Katie Pitchard

wars against the lords in Deccan.[92] His goals included incorporating the semi-independent sultanates in Deccan into his Mughal Empire, preventing them from helping his worst opponent, the Marathas, and eventually eliminating this dangerous enemy.[93] In order to achieve these goals he even moved his capital from Delhi to Deccan in 1681 and stayed there until his death in 1707.[94]

Although he temporarily brought the Mughal Empire to new heights, many argue that his passion to conquer Deccan accounted for the rapid decline of the Mughals. Financial burdens and human losses were staggering during his campaigns at Deccan. Aurangzeb would annually lose about 100,000 men and over 300,000 transport animals, both of which he needed to reacquire from the peasants. In addition, a famine occurred in 1702–1703, which cost nearly two million lives.[95] As a result, the Mughal emperor permanently lost the support of a majority of its people.

Scholars still debate to what extent Aurangzeb's unpopular reign was responsible for the rapid decline of the Mughal Empire. It is true that his orthodoxy of Islam brought about widespread resistance, especially among the Rajputs, the Sikhs, and other non-Muslim populations. His archenemy, the Marathas, for example, rallied massive support against Aurangzeb in the name of the restoration of Hindu rule. Still, many argue that he was a capable ruler, and the problems of his reign may have been exaggerated.[96] Many of his policies may have been more politically and economically oriented than religiously driven. His immediate return to Muslim orthodoxy, for example, may have been the justification for the violent oustings of his father and brothers. He claimed afterwards that his opposition to his family was out of a defense for Islam, not over a personal grudge. As mentioned before, he may have justified his decision to reinstall *jizya* because of a hard-pressed need to raise enough revenue to sustain his military activities. He may also have used his departure from this father's and grandfather's luxurious lifestyle as a way to insert his own absolute authority over his courtiers and other elites, from whom he required more fear than admiration. While he destroyed Hindu temples and humiliated Sikh gurus, he also violently eliminated Muslim sultanates who chose to defy his orders.[97] Some scholars also point out the fact that the number of Hindu courtiers serving at Aurangzeb's court actually increased in the last decades of his reign after he appointed many courtiers of Hindu origin from Deccan.[98] Above all, Aurangzeb may not have been the heartless tyrant that he is usually portrayed as being. He died in 1707 as a miserable old man. "I came alone and I go as a stranger. I do not know who I am, nor what I have been doing," confessed Aurangzeb to his son before he died. "I have sinned terribly and I do not know what punishment awaits me."[99]

In any case, the effective rule of the Mughals ended with the death of Aurangzeb. None of its later rulers could save the empire from the irreversible problems of widespread rebellions, incompetent rulers, greedy factionalism, and new invasions from the northwest.[100] During the reign of the next several Mughal rulers, local rebellions became epidemic. The Rajputs, the Sikhs and above all the Marathas emerged as parallel powers to the Mughals, too strong for the late Mughal rulers to eliminate.

The Sikhs' relations with the Mughals experienced ups and downs since the founding of the Sikh faith by its first guru, Nanak, in the early sixteenth century. Many of its early followers were the hard-working peasants in Punjab.[101] The Sikhs initially benefited from Akbar's open policies toward other religions. Their third guru received patronage from Akbar, and the fourth one served at Akbar's court and obtained a royal grant for the land where Sikhs later built their sacred capital Amristar. However, the fifth guru, Arjun, was in trouble with Jahangir who charged him with treason and tortured him to death, because Arjun supposedly provided aid to Jahangir's rebellious son, Khusrau. This incident motivated his son, the next guru, to modify their basic pacifist faith in non-violence. He organized, instead, a new military order to defend their faith and their lands.[102] By1650 the number of Sikhs greatly increased, and military actions became part of their identities. The seventh guru, Har Rai, supported Shah Jahan's son, Prince Dara, against his brother Aurangzeb and therefore drew hatred from the latter. Aurangzeb eventually retaliated against the ninth guru, Tegh Bahadur, and tortured him to death in 1675. Tegh Bahadur's son, the tenth and the last guru, vowed to avenge his father's death and turned his communities into formidable military forces. The Sikhs saw themselves as a separate state and never stopped fighting against the Mughals. When the rule of the Mughals eventually weakened, the Sikhs established their new kingdom in Punjab and controlled the area until the early nineteenth century when the British finally annexed their home in Punjab.[103]

The most dangerous enemy to the Mughals, however, were the Marathas, whose leader Shivaji Bhonsle (1627–80) launched long-term guerrilla warfare against the Mughals during the reign of Aurangzeb and in 1674 created a new Hindu state in Maharashtra in West India.[104] Aurangzeb spent his last years operating in Decca against Shivaji, pursuing him for nearly twenty years and eventually capturing him. The Marathas, however, always found a way to bounce back.[105] Aurangzeb professed to his dismay, "My armies have been employed against him [Shivaji] for nineteen years, and nevertheless his state has always been increasing."[106] Although the true nature of Shivaji's relationship with Aurangzeb is still under debate, the Hindus, especially the Marathas, have to this day viewed Shivaji as their hero against the Mughals' rule.[107] Shivaji himself did not live long enough to witness the death of Aurangzeb, but his successors eventually built a Maratha kingdom after the decline of Mughal rule. At its peak in the 1760s, the Maratha Confederacy, as it was called, had become the greatest power in India, exerting its power from the area near Delhi to central and south India. It seemed for a while that the Maratha Empire would grow into a great Hindu empire and might have a chance to defend India from foreign encroachments, but unfortunately, the kingdom was only short-lived and collapsed after the new invaders from Iran defeated them.[108]

These new Invaders were troops led by Nadir Shah (r. 1736–1747), the Shah of Iran, who invaded Mughal India in 1738–1739. He also sacked Delhi and looted the city, carrying away with him the city's greatest treasures, including the Peacock Throne.[109] As a result, the Mughal empire faded behind the shadow of its earlier glories and was never able to recover. Although scholars still debate the reasons for the collapse of the Mughal Empire, obviously a combination of different factors was at work.[110] It was at this time that the British began to insert their control of India; their control lasted for nearly two centuries and undoubtedly brought about the biggest political change that the subcontinent had ever experienced in its 3,000 years of existence.

ARRIVALS OF THE PORTUGUESE

As mentioned before, the sea explorations of the European countries, which had been facilitated by new technologies, connected all of the continents for the first time in history. The zeal of some European monarchs to spread Christianity and the greed of the merchants to pursue the highly profitable overseas spice trade motivated the European captains to explore far away from their homeland. The Portuguese were the first Europeans to arrive on the Indian subcontinent. When Vasco da Gama sailed around the Cape of Good Hope and arrived at Calicut on the Indian Malabar coast in 1498, neither he nor the local ruler fully understood that this was the beginning of centuries of European presence on and control of the Indian subcontinent.[111]

At the time, Calicut was a thriving port, where Arab and Chinese merchants had frequented for years. Somewhat overwhelmed by the prosperity and large population of the area, da Gama was uncertain of his power, even though over twenty cannons were mounted on his flagship alone. He asked his crew to exercise caution and not to bargain with the local merchants. Da Gama and his men were probably tricked by the seasoned local merchants into overpaying for products, but they still earned a record profit of 3,000 percent from selling the cargo that they had purchased in India. The amount of money they pocketed was about sixty times more than the total cost of da Gama's two-year voyage.[112] When the news of da Gama's success spread, more ships were immediately assembled to sail to India under the command of Pedro Alvarez Cabral. After he arrived in India, Cabral sought a long-term arrangement with the local ruler and secured a treaty from him; this treaty allowed the Portuguese to buy a warehouse so that they could continue to buy spices off-season and store them for the next shipment. Leaving behind fifty-four merchants to continue trading with the locals, Cabral returned to Portugal with his ships loaded with pepper and other spices.

The initial contact between the Portuguese and the Indians, however, was not smooth. On his way back home, Cabral raided a Muslim ship, and in retaliation, the Muslims executed all of the Portuguese merchants who were left behind. Vasco da Gama returned in 1502 with a large, vengeful fleet. Not only did he blast the port into ruins, but he also captured approximately 800 Muslims, cutting off their hands, ears and noses, and sent them to their lord for "his highness's 'curry'."[113] Using their powerful gunships and brutality against the locals, the Portuguese seized control of the Indian Ocean and monopolized the Indian maritime trade until the mid-sixteenth century. Portugal benefited economically from its spice trade with India and other Asian countries.[114] The import of spices from India rose from a quarter of a million pounds in 1501 to 2.3 million pounds in 1505.[115]

Along with the merchants came Portuguese missionaries. As mentioned before, Jesuit priests participated in the religious debates at Akbar's court. Saint Francis Xavier (1506–1552), one of the most important Jesuit missionaries in Asia, visited Goa in 1548, but he soon left India for Japan as he realized that there was little opportunity to convert local Hindus and Muslims. Although the Jesuits failed in their mission to convert the Mughals, they managed to exert considerable influence over the Mughal rulers.

Other than the earlier bloodshed between the Portuguese and the Muslims in the area, the Portuguese had a relatively decent relationship with the Mughals, which at the time were an emerging power in northern India. The Portuguese had fortified a few places along the Malabar Coast, such as in Goa, Daman, and Diu, under the directorship of Don Affonso de Albuquerque, viceroy of Portugal in the East from 1509 to 1515.[116] The function of these fortresses was to protect their trade monopoly in the Indian Ocean, rather than to aid further territorial expansion. As a result, the Portuguese focus on maritime trade did not conflict with the territorial ambition of the early Mughal emperors. For the Mughals, who were only interested in building a powerful land empire, the Portuguese, as a sea power stationed at a few cities along the Malabar coast, were merely a mild irritant.[117] Even after his conquest of Gujarat in 1574, which put him in direct contact with the Portuguese in Diu, Akbar made peace with them in exchange for Portuguese protection of his family's pilgrimages to Mecca.[118]

As a result, the challenge to Portuguese domination of the maritime trade in India came from elsewhere. The lucrative profit of the spice trade induced jealousy from other Europeans, such as the Dutch, the British, and the French, who soon followed suit and came to India and other parts of Asia. This caused a heated competition among the European powers in Asia. While the Dutch mainly focused on the islands of Ceylon and of those in today's Indonesia, they allied with the British to break the Portuguese monopoly over the trade, only to fight later against the British for control of India.

THE ADVENT OF THE BRITISH

While the Portuguese reaped enormous benefits from the spice trade in Asia, the British became increasingly frustrated with their inability to participate in this productive venture. The controlling Portuguese blocked the Britain's first few attempts to reach Asia, but after Queen Elizabeth I granted a royal charter to the English East India Company in 1600, the Company eventually broke Portugal's monopoly of the Indian trade through their persistent and systematic efforts.[119]

The Company first reached Southeast Asia through the sea routes that were different from the ones used previously by the Portuguese. Their first several voyages to the area were successful, having brought back an average profit of 170 percent per trip. This convinced the Company's board members that going to Asia was a worthwhile investment. The Company's first successful trip to India was under the command of Captain William Hawkins who anchored his ships in 1607 at Sarut, a principle port on the Malabar Coast.[120] Hawkins served as an envoy from the British Monarch, carrying a letter from King James I to the Mughal Emperor Jahangir requesting a treaty of trade.[121] His mission, however, was much less satisfactory than he had expected. Not only was Captain Hawkins ignored and humiliated by the Mughal officials, but his mission was also sabotaged by the Jesuits at the Mughal court, who had established a better relationship with the Mughal Emperor. Additionally, Hawkins was also robbed of his gold by Portuguese pirates.[122] It was not until British Captain Thomas Best defeated the Portuguese fleet at the Battle of Swally near Surat in 1612 that the Mughal court started to pay attention to the British. When King James I sent another ambassador, Sir Thomas Roe, to visit Jahangir in 1616, the emperor received him in a much more cordial manner, hoping that he could make use of Britain's superior naval power the same way he had used Portugal's.[123] Still, it took three more years before Sir Roe could obtain royal permission to open a "factory" (warehouse) at Surat. After the Company built its first warehouse in 1619, Surat became the first headquarters of the English East India Company and remained the center of the Company's activities until the Company shifted its focus in 1687 to Bombay, an area consisting of several offshore islands on the west coast of India. In 1534, the Portuguese obtained Bombay through a treaty with a local Sultan, and then gave it to Charles II in 1661 as part of the dowry of his wife, Portuguese Princess Catherine of Braganza. A few years later, Charles II turned Bombay over to the English East India Company in 1668 for an annual rent of 10 pounds.[124]

THE ENGLISH EAST INDIA COMPANY

Following their establishment at Surat, the English East India Company was on a fast track to set up their residence in other Indian seaports. By 1700, the Company had established several important fortified bases at Surat, Bombay, Madras, and Calcutta. From there, it gradually extended its control over almost all of the Indian subcontinent over the next century and half.[125] The Company began as a trading company that had a royal endorsement to monopolize British trade with Asia. The Company had a rough start, but its power was greatly increased by King Charles II (r. 1649–1685), who became a powerful patronage to the Company. King Charles II granted the Company not only economic privilege over the trade, but also the right to maintain its own military forces, to exercise full jurisdiction over the English subjects in India, and above all, to "make war or peace with 'non-Christian powers' in India."[126] As a result, by luck or by design, the Company gradually transformed into a *de facto* government of India until it lost all of its privileges in 1858.

In order to stay in India, however, the Company initially had to fight with other European powers even after they obtained permission from the Mughal emperors. Until the middle of the eighteenth century, the British probably fought more battles against other European powers in India than against the declining Mughal power or other local rulers. Lack of sufficient support from their home government, the Portuguese largely abandoned their trade interest in India by the middle of the seventeenth century, leaving behind them a legacy of "Portuguese India" which lingered on until 1961.

Subsequently, the Company had to deal with the more aggressive Dutch, who had allied with them in their struggle against the Portuguese, but soon turned against the Company once their common threat was gone.[127] Fortunately for the English East India Company, the Dutch East India Company (VOC), which was chartered in 1602, two years after the English East India Company was established, was preoccupied with the island of Ceylon, the Spice Islands (or the Maluku Islands) and the area later known as the Dutch East Indies. Although they were instrumental in clearing the Indian Ocean of the Portuguese fleets and temporarily controlled Calicut and other areas, by 1721 the Dutch had abandoned their competition with the British and the French over the Malabar Coast, and instead, focused their efforts on control of Southeast Asia. Their departure yielded the entire Malabar Coast to the English East India Company.

Neither the Portuguese nor the Dutch mounted a formidable resistance against the British. The challenge from the French, however, proved to be a different case. France, who did not establish their East India Company until 1664, was the last European country to join in the Indian trade. Their aggressive policies and commercial success in India, however, soon put the British on the defense. Within a decade of its establishment, the French East India Company under the directorship of Francois Martin, French Viceroy in India, established its headquarters at Pondicherry, south of Madras on the Coromandal coast of southeast India.[128] By the time the Dutch retreated from the Indian Ocean, the French fleet had already reached Indian ports for a swift takeover of these seaports. The following decades witnessed the peak of French trade with India; the French East India Company reaped an annual average of 25 percent profit. In contrast, the profits of the English East India Company were down to merely 10 percent, even though British imports from India at the time were over one million pounds per year.[129] This problem, as well as the animosity between their home countries in Europe, soon put the British and the French at war in India. Consequently, the first half of the eighteenth century saw severe competition between the British and the French over the control of India's southeast and east coasts.

The architect behind the success of the French East India Company was its president, Joseph Francois Dupleix (1697–1764). A son of the French Company's director-general, Dupleix lived in India for nearly twenty years and hence probably understood Indian politics better than any other European leader in India. He was a master at playing one Indian ruler against another and rallied strong local support for the French in the process. When the War of Austrian Succession (1740–1748) broke out in Europe, which ignited conflicts between Britain and France that would continue over the next half century, it soon bred a conflict between the French and the British in India.[130]

Dupleix initially gained an upper hand over his opponents. In 1746, he even captured the British Fort St. George at Madras and drove the British out of the area. Among his prisoners was Robert Clive (1725–1774), a clerk of the English East India Company who later played a crucial role in the Company's expansion in India.[131] Dupleix's next victory was over a local ruler, which gave him more confidence in his military capability. In order to defend his newly gained Madras, his 230 French men, plus a support of 700 trained *sepoys* (a word that refers to European trained Indian soldiers), defeated an Indian army of ten thousand cavalry. This victory rendered Dupleix the position of *de facto* ruler of the Carnatic, a word used to refer to a region that is located in Southern India between the Eastern Ghats and the Coromandel Coast.[132]

According to Wolpert, with his political foresight and military talent, Dupleix might have become the *de facto* ruler of all of India, securing control of India for France the same way that Robert Clive later did for England, had he had more support from home. Unfortunately for him, with their preoccupation in Europe, neither his King nor his Queen could care less about what happened in India.[133] The Treaty of Aix-la-Chapelle (1748) returned his hard-earned Madras to the British, strengthening the British position in the area. His main British opponent was now Robert Clive, who had learned from Dupleix how to maneuver among the local forces. With the help of the local *nawab* (a title for a Mughal provincial governor), he successfully curbed Dupleix's ambition of further territorial expansion. The French government, which was anxious to make peace with the British, recalled Dupleix back to Paris in 1754, charging him with wasteful spending of the government's investments in India.[134]

Dupleix's return to Paris greatly weakened the French position in India and gave the English East India Company an opportunity in the Carnatic. Taking advantage of this and the continuous decline of the Mughal control of the subcontinent, the Company advanced its power beyond their early settlements under their now Lieutenant Colonel Clive, who had earned a great reputation because of his bravery. In 1751, he led two hundred Englishmen and three hundred *sepoys* to capture the palace of the *nawab* at Arcot, a strategically located town with over one million inhabitants. Clive was so successful with his military strategy, as well as his manipulation of the local rulers, that he soon replaced Dupleix as "*nawab* maker" of the Carnatic.[135]

The Seven Year War (1756–1763) over Charles VI's empire triggered another round of Anglo-French competition in India, but by this time, the French in India were too weak to be of any substantial threat to the British. Instead, the biggest threats to the British were ambitious *newabs* who had gained independence from the Mughals. The most severe challenge to the British military forces came from the local authority of Bengal. Ever since the British had settled in Surat, they had always actively sought to have more bases on India's east coast where they would have better access to higher-quality cotton as well as to rich resources like saltpeter, a key ingredient of gunpowder. In 1639, the Company gained permission from the Mughal emperor to build a warehouse at a place later known as Fort George, or Madras, and in 1690, the Company gained permission to build Fort William, known later as Calcutta. The settlement in Calcutta gave them access to the finest-quality gunpowder in the Bengal area, which is said to have helped the British in their victories against Louis XIV and Napoleon of France.[136] In the eighteenth century, the Company had focused their business more on the east coast of India than that on the west.

After the death of Aurangzeb, the increasing chaos in India compelled the Company to organize its own military forces to protect its properties. As the disorder prevailed, more and more Indian merchants, who had become easy prey to robberies, started to seek protection from the British. As the size of the British settlements grew, their military capacity, reinforced by their fleet, became stronger and stronger. Still the local Indian forces easily outnumbered them, making the British vulnerable to the threat of some ambitious independent rulers. In 1756, a young ambitious *nawab* of Bengal, who had become jealous of the increasing power of the British, decided to teach them a lesson with the excuse that the British had expanded Fort William without his permission.[137] He ordered a large force of 50,000 to push toward Fort William. The British governor of Calcutta, who had only 1,000 troops under his command, decided to abandon the fort, leaving behind some soldiers, women and children. The English prisoners were thrown into a tiny lockup, called the "black hole," where they spent a hot summer night. When the door was opened the next morning, only twenty-one out of sixty-four remained alive; others had died of suffocation. This was known as the "Black Hole of Calcutta," which later became a textbook example of the "barbarism" of the Indians in British history.[138] To retaliate against this brutality, Clive organized a military operation and retook the fort in 1757. He won a decisive victory over the huge army of the Bengal *nawab* at the battle of Plassey, and replaced the *nawab* with one of his royal relatives. Clive soon became a *de facto* ruler of Bengal.[139]

FROM TRADING COMPANY TO GOVERNMENT

The great victory at the Battle of Plassey and the Company's subsequent control of Bengal marked a significant change in the Company's role in India. From the Battle of Plassey in 1757 to the *Sepoy* Rebellion of 1857, the Company experienced a transition from a trading company to a *de facto* government of the Indian subcontinent.[140] Clive was appointed the first governor of Bengal in 1758. By this time, the Company had already played an important role in global markets with an annual import of over two million pounds from India to Europe.[141] As secure and profitable as this trade had been, the Company's control of Bengal opened a new source of revenue to the Company as well as to its employees. In 1765, the Mughal emperor granted the Company the right to collect revenue from Bengal and other provinces on behalf of the emperor in exchange for an annual tribute from the Company.[142] The Company's initial intention was to secure some extra revenue for the Company's army, but the opening of the wealthy and heavily populated Bengal area to the Company as a large revenue base gradually changed the company's focus in India. In the eyes of some company employees, this also offered an opportunity to grab a personal fortune; an opportunity that was too good to pass up.[143] For example, after the Battle of Plassey, Robert Clive himself immediately gained a reward of £234,000 for his assistance to the new *nawab* of Bengal; this was in addition to "an annual salary of £30,000 in rent from the Twenty-four *Parganas* (regions) of Bengal, some 880 square miles south of Calcutta," which later became his private domain.[144] According to Wolpert, Clive became one of the wealthiest English subjects overnight and used to bring bags of Indian jewels and gold with him when he returned to London.[145]

Clive's immediate affluence prompted widespread corruption among Company's employees, who now found an easier way than managing trade to reap a fortune—collecting tax revenue from the Indians and keeping some for themselves. Similar to the previous rulers of India, the Company benefitted from land revenue and gradually shifted its focus from international trade to the generation of revenue internally in India, and this policy reorientation coincided with the continuous decline of Mughal control of India. More and more local lords and Indian merchants sought protection from the Company's army, and in return, they bestowed the Company more land and privileges. Since Clive still recognized the sovereignty of the *nawab* of Bengal in name, the Company administration soon found itself in a unique position of power, from which they could guarantee benefits to the company without any of the normal responsibilities or obligations that a government would have to the people under its jurisdiction. It was the worst type of government: "those with responsibility possessed no power, and those with power felt no responsibility."[146]

The Company's plunder of Bengal became so rapacious that it soon reduced the rich area of Bengal to a land of desolation. In 1769–1770, a series of massive famines may have taken the lives of about one-third of the population under the Company's administration.[147] The corruption and scandals of the East India Company began to draw attention from the British Parliament. In 1767, the Parliament called Clive back to London and charged him with felony of corruption. Although Clive was eventually acquitted, the Parliament passed a bill, known as the "Regulating Act of 1773" or "Lord

North's India Bill," which established the position of Governor-General of India, who would be in charge of all of the British controlled areas in India, including Surat, Bombay, and Calcutta. The bill also established a Council of Four appointed by the Crown in order to have better supervision of the East India Company's operation in India.[148]

The British government's intervention, however, may not have been solely based on its concern for humanitarian issues. The Parliament may have been more alarmed by the financial problems of the East India Company. After the Company took control of Bengal, the Company's financial situation declined. The Company had appealed to the government for a loan of one million pounds to cover its "deficit" in Bengal.[149] As a result, the first measures that Warren Hastings (1773–1785), the first Governor-General of India, took were to strengthen the company's finance.[150]

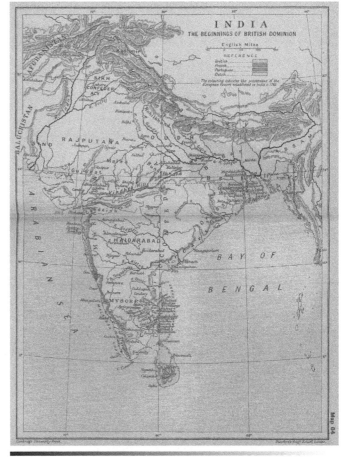

Courtesy of the University of Texas Libraries. The University of Texas at Austin.

Areas in India under European control, c. 1783

He centralized the revenue collection system to make sure that the agencies would have less opportunity to cut out a share during the process. While Clive had already recognized the possibility of British control of all of India by the time of his victory in Bengal, he did not follow that direction and still acknowledged the rule of the local *nawab* as well as that of the Mughal court.[151] Hastings, however, quickly changed this pattern and stripped the *nawab* of Bengal of his remaining power. He also withdrew the Company's annual tribute to the Mughal emperor and thus saved over half a million pounds annually.[152] With the power that the Parliament granted the governor-general to make peace or war, Hastings and subsequent governors vigorously pursued policies that would allow them to acquire more territory in India, though they each may have had different reasons for doing so.

For Hastings, it may have been the financial need of the company. His territorial ambition often put him into conflict with the local rulers, especially with the rising power of Maratha. Hastings' constant military actions, plus the Company's responsibility to fulfill its financial obligations to the British government, further bankrupted the Company. Out of desperation, the Company monopolized the collection and sale of salt in India as well as the production and sale of opium to China, the details of which will be discussed later.[153] Although Hastings was very much concerned with providing civil rule to India through his new legal system, he found that he often had to "squeeze" more resources out of those in his protectorate, which led to his impeachment by the parliament and forced him later into retirement.[154]

The next few governor-generals, such as Lord Charles Cornwallis (1786–1801), Lord Richard Wellesley (1798–1805), and Lord Francis Rawdon-Hastings (1812–1823) continued what Clive and Hastings had started and accelerated the process of establishing British rule over all of India. Meanwhile, the Parliament passed more acts to set up the guidance of Indian affairs and gradually took matters out of the hands of the Company and into its own. The second East India Company Act or Pitt's India Act in 1784 set up a new London-based Board of Control under the Crown, which would oversee major British policies concerning India. The result was that the East India Company's political functions were now separated from its commercial activities.[155] The members of the Control Board in London could make decisions about vital Indian policies without consulting anyone in the Company. Although these acts made it possible for the British government to supervise Indian affairs, the "dual control" of the Parliament and the Company created some problems for the governor-generals in India.[156] The Parliament may have felt obligated to respond to Indian complaints on a humanitarian basis, but left it unclear as to what would happen if "the interests of British commerce and imperialism clashed with the interests of the indigenous population."[157]

The biggest problem for the Company was that the government was neither responsible for financing the Company's operation and its army, nor did they have any intention of reducing the Company's obligation to pay its annual dues to the government. From time to time, the Company had to rely on measures that were more coercive than usual to increase its revenue. A few early Indian governor-generals fell victim to this dilemma. Hastings, for example, cried out during his impeachment, "I sent forth its armies with an effectual but economical hand, through unknown and hostile regions, to the support of your other possessions... I gave you all, and you have rewarded me with confiscation, disgrace, and a life of impeachment."[158]

The next act, the Act of 1786, may have been a response to the dilemma of dual control. It strengthened the power of the governor-general over his council and over the Company's military forces, allowing the same person to hold simultaneously both the position of governor-general and that of commander-in-chief. With these new powers endorsed upon him, Lord Cornwallis carried out impressive reforms in India. As part of his efforts to curb corruption among the Company employees, he devised an extensive structural reform that turned the Company employees into salaried government civil servants.[159] Furthermore, he regulated the Company's administrative system with a Code of Forty-Eight Regulations, which "laid the foundations for British rule throughout India, setting standards of the services, courts, and revenue collection that remained remarkably unaltered over the time."[160]

In order to consolidate the area under Company control, Cornwallis formulated a socio-economical system known as *zamindar* landlordism. A *zamindar* was an Indian aristocrat who ruled over enormous tracts of land and lived on the tax collected from the peasants of the land. These *zamindars* traditionally served more as tax collection agencies than as landlords. More often than not, they would avoid paying promised taxes, using as an excuse the peasants' absconding from the land.[161] Cornwallis may not have originated the idea of tying the responsibilities of the *zamindars* with their estates, but he forcefully executed this policy—the Company would protect the private properties of the *zamindars* if they paid a specified amount of annual revenue to the Company.[162] Otherwise, the Company would auction off their estates.[163] The system was intended to stabilize the *zamindars'* relations with the Indian peasants much like the British landlords with their tenants.

Although Pitt's India Act of 1784 disclaimed the desire for territorial acquisition in India, none of the governor-generals could ignore the challenge of the local rulers and thus resist the temptation to gain control of more lands.[164] Under the more aggressive policies of Lord Wellesley and Marquis of Hastings, the Company extended control over almost all of the Indian subcontinent. They vigorously pursued their dream of a global British Empire, probably inspired by the new imperialistic ideology and the competition among the Western Powers to build empires. By the time that Marquis Hastings left India, the Company government had become the master of the Indian subcontinent.[165]

The Company's more aggressive actions in India may also have been the result of the increasing difficulty of reaping enough profits through its trade with Europe. While Napoleon's expansion to Egypt and other areas had somewhat blocked the Company's exportation of Indian products to Europe, the Industrial Revolution in England, especially in the textile industry, also diminished the demand for Indian textiles.[166] As a result, the export of textiles from Bengal dropped by more than one-third within a decade, from £1.4 million in 1800 to only £0.9 million in 1809. In addition, the British government abolished the trading monopoly of the East India Company in 1813, which forced the Company to look elsewhere for revenue.[167] While the Company tried to pursue the trade as well as the market in China more vigorously, the governor-generals also embarked on aggressive actions towards territorial acquisition.

It is still difficult to this day to determine an overall evaluation of the Company rule in India. The regulated Company rule brought positive results to the subcontinent, such as banning the practice of *sati*, a practice of forcing a surviving widow to throw herself into the fire that was burning her husband's body, and limiting the activities of banditry that had plagued India for centuries. Some governor-generals also encouraged education in India, which produced new generations of Indian elites who would later lead nationalist movements in India.[168] Their political and cultural policies over India, however, had become increasingly arrogant under a premise that the British were better-qualified rulers of the subcontinent than the Indians themselves.[169] Moreover, the economic system of *zamindar* landlordism did not turn out to be an effective system. Peasants at the bottom fell victim to increasing exploitation by landowners and their agencies. All of this led to a widespread revolt in 1857, which ended Company rule of India.

THE REVOLT IN 1857

A sepoy mutiny against the British officers triggered a widespread revolt in northern India in 1857. Although the sepoys were never treated equally in the Company army, they initially took some pride in their roles before the eighteenth century. Hastings, for example, took special measures that were more sympathetic toward traditional Indian culture, such as not employing sepoys overseas and allowing the celebration of Hindu festivals in the barracks.[170] The Company army steadily grew to 100,000 strong in 1789, and then to 155,000 in the early nineteenth century.[171] Lord Cornwallis' regulation of the Company officers' payments, however, led to changes in the Company army. After 1790, no sepoy was allowed to rise through the ranks to be a commissioned officer.[172] With the arrival of the young and well-educated British officers who had been attracted only by the good salary, and who had little interest in Indian culture, a gulf widened between these English officers and their sepoy soldiers.

Adding to the dismay of the sepoys was the Company's aggressive policy to gain greater control of the land that had originally belonged to the Company's Indian allies. After the Company lost its trade monopoly over India in 1813 and then over China in 1833, the Company had to make further adjustments to meet its financial needs.[173] It penetrated deeper into the interior of India in order to make more revenue settlements in landlocked provinces and focused more on building enterprises in India, such as a railroad network.[174] Consequently, the Company needed to control the pockets of lands that were still in the hands of its rival and to annex the lands that belonged to its former Indian allies.[175] In 1849, the Company finally gained control of the vast and rich area of Punjab after its two bloody wars against the Sikhs.[176]

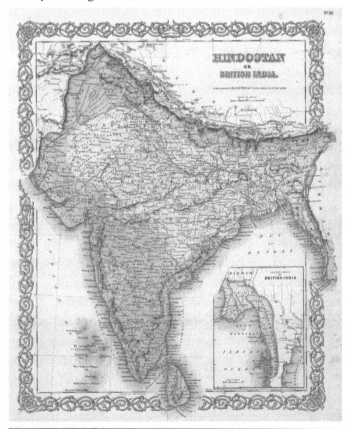

Joseph Hutchins Colton

1855 Map of British India

Furthermore, Lord Dalhousie (1847–1856), the Company's governor-general, decided to ignore all of the treaties that the Company had previously signed with India's princely states and forced the Indian princes to surrender their lands to the Company under the pretext of a "Doctrine of Lapse," according to which, the Company would take control of their states, if Indian princes died without an heir.[177] The Company subsequently embarked on taking the small states in India one way or another. In 1849, the Company took a few princely states in central India and the Bengal area. By 1850 they had taken those in Punjab; in 1852, the Rajputs in Udaipur of northwest India; in 1854 the huge state of Nagpur in central India that had over four million Marathas; and most importantly in 1856, Oudh, one of the richest regions in the Gangetic plain's heartland.[178]

This last occupation, according to Wolpert, was the "worst blunder" of Lord Dalhousie, although Dalhousie may have believed at the time that it was a reasonable decision.[179] Many sepoys, especially those who were originally from Punjab, Oudh, and Bengal, were heart-broken and disillusioned when they witnessed their homelands become the prey of the East India Company. Unlike the composition of the soldiers in many other countries, many sepoy soldiers came from higher classes of Indian society, such as Brahmins and Rajputs if they were Hindus. They had many family and caste connections with their home areas and hence, were more sensitive to the situations that would affect the well-being of their families.[180]

The causes of the mutiny were deeper than military discontent. In addition to the reasons discussed above, the Company's last governor-general, Lord Charles John Canning (1837–1859), who was less sensitive to the Indian traditions, implemented several unpopular measures, including the General Service Enlistment Act, which required Indian soldiers to be in service anywhere, including Burma, the Company's newly annexed territory. To Hindu soldiers, especially Brahmins, these requirements violated their Hindu principle which prohibited the crossing over "dark waters" (the sea) to Burma.[181] They would be rejected by their families, friends and even their caste if they did so.[182] The last straw that added to the accumulated dissatisfaction of the sepoys was the introduction of a new muzzle-loaded Enfield rifle. The new rifles required the soldiers to bite off the tip of the cartridge before they could load the gunpowder into the muskets. These cartridges, however, were greased with animal fat. Most Indian sepoys, Hindus and Muslim alike, were bound by their religious obligations not to touch animal fat, and hence, they felt greatly violated by this requirement. To many, this only confirmed an earlier widespread suspicion among the sepoys that the Company had reversed its policies in the eighteenth century, including the former policy of not supporting missionary activities in the English settlements and intentionally tried to convert the sepoys to Christianity.[183] Most of their British officers, however, only ignored the complaints of the sepoys, and even severely punished those who refused to comply with the new requirement.[184]

The revolt started at Meerut, a city located about thirty-six miles northeast of Delhi on Saturday, May 9, 1857. The rebellious sepoys soon took control of Delhi, the seat of the last Mughal Emperor, and were joined by the sepoys of other regiments and rulers in other cities of northern India.[185] Later developments proved that the uprising was not simply a mutiny. It reflected a general discontent among the Indians who were not simply "perpetually docile subjects."[186] For a while, it greatly terrified the British in India, who quickly lost control over the Gangetic heartland as well as of portions of the Punjab and Deccan. After several months, however, the revolt gradually lost its momentum, owing to the problem of a lack of a cohesive leadership, which led to a lack of the necessary cooperation of different sepoy regiments as well as different states.[187] The last Mughal Emperor also failed to explore the situation to restore the Mughals' power, even after the sepoys initially went to him for help. On the other hand, the British, angered by the violence ignited by the rebellious sepoys against British citizens in Delhi and Lucknow, organized effective counterattacks and eventually regained control of Delhi and other areas. Still, it took eighteen months for the British to extinguish the rebellion completely at a cost to England of £36 million, a full year's worth of Indian revenue.[188] Some of the battles were "the fiercest, bloodiest war(s) ever fought on Indian soil."[189] The British officers retaliated against the revolting soldiers with brutality—blowing away the captured mutineers "from cannons to which they had been surely strapped."[190] The revenge even extended to Indian women and children.[191]

Vasily Vereshchagin

A reproduction of *Blowing from Guns in British India*, a painting by Vasily Vereshchagin

The Revolt of 1857 itself was short-lived. Nonetheless, it brought lasting changes to India, in spite of an ongoing debate about its long-term significance—whether it was the "First Indian War of Independence" to the radical Indian nationalists or the "mutiny" preferred by the British.[192] Not only did the revolt result in Britain's formal termination of the Mughal Empire, whose last emperor was exiled to Burma and died there a couple of years later, but it also brought a demise to the Company rule of India.[193] The news of this large-scale Indian rebellion against the East India Company greatly upset the Parliament and challenged some fundamental beliefs in the progress of the Victorian English.[194] On August 2, 1858, the British Parliament passed the Government of India Act, which terminated all of the rights that the East India Company had in India and transferred them to the Crown.[195] The great days of the East India Company were over, and so was the Company itself and its history of two and a half centuries.[196]

For more information about the topics discussed in this chapter, please visit the website for this textbook. This website can be accessed from http://www.grtep.com/.

1   Catherine B. Asher and Cynthia Talbot, *India before Europe* (Cambridge: Cambridge University Press, 2006), 152.
2   Asher and Talbot, *Before Europe*, 115.
3   Metcalf and Metcalf, *India*, 25; and Asher and Talbot, *Before Europe*, 131.
4   Duiker and Spielvogel, *World History*, 629.
5   Asher and Talbot, *Before Europe*, 119.
6   Duiker and Spielvogel, *World History*, 629.
7   *Memoirs of Aebir-ed-Din Muhammed Babur*, 2 vols. trans. J. Leyden and W. Erskine, rev. L. King (London: Oxford University Press, 1921), quoted from Wolpert, *New History*, 122, note 4; and Duiker and Spielvogel, *World History*, 630.
8   Asher and Talbot, *Before Europe*, 116; and Murphey, *History*, 176.
9   Duiker and Spielvogel, *World History*, 630; and Kulke and Rothermund, *History*, 139.
10   Wolpert, *New History*, 122.
11   "Mughal Dynasty-Babar," accessed September 5, 2011, at http://www.indiabuzzing.com/2011/06/14/mughal-dynasty-babar-2.
12   Kulke and Rothermund, *History*, 139.
13   Murphey, *History*, 176–177; Duiker and Spielvogel, *World History*, 630–631; and Asher and Talbot, *Before Europe*, 116.

14 Asher and Talbot, *Before Europe*, 116–118.
15 Wolpert, *New History*, 122; and Murphey, *History*, 176–177.
16 Barbara D. Metcalf and Thomas R. Metcalf, *A Concise History of Modern India*, 2nd ed. (Cambridge: Cambridge University Press, 2006), 15; and Kulke and Rothermund, *History*, 142.
17 Duiker and Spielvogel, *World History*, 631.
18 Asher and Talbot, *Before Europe*, 119.
19 Asher and Talbot, *Before Europe*, 120–121.
20 Metcalf and Metcalf, *India*, 15; and Asher and Talbot, *Before Europe*, 121.
21 Asher and Talbot, *Before Europe*, 121–122.
22 Duiker and Spielvogel, *World History*, 631.
23 Metcalf and Metcalf, *India*, 15.
24 Metcalf and Metcalf, *India*, 15; and Duiker and Spielvogel, *World History*, 631.
25 Murphey, *History*, 177; and Asher and Talbot, *Before Europe*, 124–126.
26 Muphey, *History*, 179–180; and Asher and Talbot, *Before Europe*, 124–126.
27 Duiker and Spielvogel, *World History*, 631.
28 Craig et al, *Heritage*, 646; and Asher and Talbot, *Before Europe*, 126–144.
29 Murphey, *History*, 178.
30 Duiker and Spielvogel, *World History*, 632.
31 Metcalf and Metcalf, *India*, 27.
32 Metcalf and Metcalf, *India*, 27–28.
33 Murphey, *History*, 178–179.
34 Metcalf and Metcalf, *India*, 17.
35 Metcalf and Metcalf, *India*, 17, and 20.
36 Satish Chandra, *History of Medieval India* (New Delhi: Orient Longman, 2007), 231–232.
37 Vincent A. Smith, *The Oxford History of India* (Oxford: Oxford University Press, 2002), 342–343.
38 Irfan Habib, *Akbar and His India* (New Delhi: Oxford University Press, 1997), 84–85; and Sanjay Subrahmanyam, *Mughals and Franks* (Oxford: Oxford University Press, 2005), 55.
39 Duiker and Spielvogel, *World History*, 632.
40 Murphey, *History*, 180; and Asher and Talbot, *Before Europe*, 128.
41 Asher and Talbot, *Before Europe*, 129.
42 Murphey, *History*, 180–181; and Asher and Talbot, *Before Europe*, 129.
43 Metcalf and Metcalf, *India*, 18; and Murphey, *History*, 180–181.
44 Nurul Hasan, *Religion, State and Society in Medieval India* (New Delhi: Oxford University Press, 2007), 85; and Asher and Talbot, *Before Europe*, 129.
45 Murphey, *History*, 180.
46 Asher and Talbot, *Before Europe*, 130; Duiker and Spielvogel, *World History*, 632; and Metcalf and Metcalf, *India*, 17–18.
47 Duiker and Spielvogel, *World History*, 632.
48 Kulke and Rothermund, *History*, 142; Duiker and Spielvogel, *World History*, 631; and Murphey, *History*, 180.
49 Murphey, *History*, 180.
50 Asher and Talbot, *Before Europe*, 129; and Kulke and Rothermund, *History*, 147.
51 Kulke and Rothermund, *History*, 147.
52 Wolpert, New *History*, 134.
53 Murphey, *Asia*, 182; Asher and Talbot, *Before Europe*, 153; and Kulke and Rothermund, *History*, 148.
54 Metcalf and Metcalf, *India*, 18; and Asher and Talbot, *Before Europe*, 152.
55 Murphey, *History*, 182.
56 Wolpert, *New History*, 149–150; and Murphey, *History*, 182.
57 Wolpert, *New History*, 150.
58 Asher and Talbot, *Before Europe*, 155.
59 Craig et al., *Heritage*, 646.
60 Duiker and Spielvogel, *World History*, 633.
61 Duiker and Spielvogel, *World History*, 633; Asher and Talbot, *Before Europe*, 154, 204; and Wolpert, *New History*, 148.
62 Asher and Talbot, *Before Europe*, 153; Murphey, *History*, 182, and Wolpert, *New History*, 152.
63 Murphey, *History*, 182; and Wolpert, *New History*, 153.
64 Duiker and Spielvogel, *World History*, 633; and Asher and Talbot, *Before Europe*, 154.
65 Murphey, *History*, 182; Asher and Talbot, *Before Europe*, 154; and Wolpert, *New History*, 152.
66 Asher and Talbot, *Before Europe*, 155.
67 Asher and Talbot, *Before Europe*, 226–227.
68 Asher and Talbot, *Before Europe*, 155–156.
69 Wolpert, *New History*, 150.
70 Asher and Talbot, *Before Europe*, 187.
71 Metcalf and Metcalf, *India*, 18.
72 Asher and Talbot, *Before Europe*, 118.
73 Asher and Talbot, *Before Europe*, 194.
74 Murphey, *History*, 182.
75 Murphey, *History*, 182; and Wolpert, *New History*, 154.
76 Murphey, *History*, 182; and Wolpert, *New History*, 149.
77 Murphey, *History*, 187.

78 Wolpert, *New History*, 155.
79 Murphey, *History* 182.
80 Wolpert, *New History*, 155; and Asher and Talbot, *Before Europe*, 197–201.
81 Wolpert, *New History*, 156.
82 Wolpert, *New History*, 155.
83 Murphey, *History*, 183.
84 Murphey, *History*, 188.
85 Wolpert, *New History*, 158.
86 Murphey, *History*, 183; and Wolpert, *New History*, 158–159.
87 Murphey, *History*, 183.
88 Murphey, *History*, 184; and Wolpert, *New History*, 158–159.
89 Murphey, *History*, 183.
90 Asher and Talbot, *Before Europe*, 227.
91 Murphey, *History*, 183–184.
92 Murphey, *History*, 184.
93 Asher and Talbot, *Before Europe*, 233; and Murphey, *History*, 184–85.
94 Asher and Talbot, *Before Europe*, 233.
95 Murphey, *History*, 187.
96 Asher and Talbot, *Before Europe*, 227–231; and Metcalf and Metcalf, *India*, 21–25.
97 Asher and Talbot, *Before Europe*, 227–236.
98 Kurzke and Rothermund, *History*, 150; and Metcalf and Metcalf, *India*, 23.
99 Waldemar Hansen, *The Peacock Throne* (New York: Holt, Rinehart and Winston, 1972), 485, quoted from Wolpert, *New History*, 168, note 4.
100 Wolpert, *New History*, 174.
101 Wolpert, *New History*, 161.
102 Wolpert, *New History*, 162; and Metcalf and Metcalf, *India*, 32–33.
103 Wolpert, *New History*, 162; and Murphey, *History*, 185.
104 Murphey, *History*, 185–86; and Wolpert, *New History*, 163–164.
105 Asher and Talbot, *Before Europe*, 231–236.
106 Murphey, *History*, 186.
107 Wolpert, *New History*, 163–66; Murphey, *History*, 185; Metcalf and Metcalf, *India*, 25; and Asher and Talbot, *Before Europe*, 238.
108 Murphey, *History*, 186; and Asher and Talbot, *Before Europe*, 241–242.
109 Metcalf and Metcalf, *India*, 33.
110 Duiker and Spielvogel, *World History*, 635–636.
111 Wolpert, *New History*, 135.
112 Wolpert, *New History*, 136.
113 Wolpert, *New History*, 136.
114 Kulke and Rothermund, *History*, 156–158.
115 Wolpert, *New History*, 138.
116 Wolpert, *New History*, 137.
117 Kulke and Rothermund, *History*, 155–158.
118 Kulke and Rothermund, *History*, 158; and Murphey, *History*, 271.
119 Wolpert, *New History*, 139–142.
120 Wolpert, *New History*, 142.
121 Wolpert, *New History*, 142; and Murphey, *History*, 272.
122 Wolpert, *New History*, 142–143; and Murphey, *History*, 272.
123 Wolpert, *New History*, 143; and Murphey, *History*, 272.
124 Wolpert, *New History*, 144; Metcalf and Metcalf, *India*, 48; and Murphey, *History*, 273.
125 Metcalf and Metcalf, *India*, 47–48.
126 Wolpert, *New History*, 147.
127 Wolpert, *New History*, 143–144.
128 Wolpert, *New History*, 175.
129 Wolpert, *New History*, 176.
130 Metcalf and Metcalf, *India*, 49.
131 Wolpert, *New History*, 176; and Metcalf and Metcalf, *India*, 49–50.
132 Wolpert, *New History*, 176.
133 Wolpert, *New History*, 176–177.
134 Wolpert, *New History*, 178; Murphey, *History*, 275; and Kulke and Rothermund, *History*, 168.
135 Wolpert, *New History*, 178; and Kulke and Rothermund, *History*, 167–168.
136 Murphey, *History*, 273.
137 Metcalf and Metcalf, *India*, 51–52.
138 Danis Judd, *The Lion and the Tiger: The Rise and Fall of the British Raj, 1600–1947* (Oxford: Oxford University Press, 2004), 39-40; Wolpert, *New History*, 180; and Murphey, *History*, 275.
139 Murphey, *History*, 275; and Wolpert, *New History*, 179–181.
140 Judd, *Lion*, 30.
141 Metcalf and Metcalf, *India*, 45.
142 Metcalf and Metcalf, *India*, 53.

143 Metcalf and Metcalf, *India*, 54.
144 Wolpert, *New History*, 181.
145 Wolpert, *New History*, 181; and Metcalf and Metcalf, *India*, 54.
146 Wolpert, *New History*, 187.
147 Duiker and Spielvogel, *World History*, 639.
148 Wolpert, *New History*, 190; and Judd, *Lion*, 32–35.
149 Wolpert, *New History*, 190.
150 Metcalf and Metcalf, *India*, 56.
151 Wolpert, *New History*, 185–186.
152 Wolpert, *New History*, 189.
153 Wolpert, *New History*, 199.
154 Metcalf and Metcalf, *India*, 56–60; Wolpert, *New History*, 193–94; and Kulke and Rothermund, *History*, 179–180.
155 Wolpert, *New History*, 194.
156 Judd, *Lion*, 35–36.
157 Judd, *Lion*, 36.
158 Sir G.W. Forrest, *Selections from the State Papers of Hastings*, vol. 1, 290, quoted from Wolpert, *New History*, 193, footnote 3.
159 Kulke and Rothermund, *History*, 183.
160 Wolpert, *New History*, 198–199.
161 Kulke and Rothermund, *History*, 182.
162 Murphey, *History*, 284; and Wolpert, *New History*, 191–197.
163 Kulke and Rothermund, *History*, 182.
164 Wolpert, *New History*, 195.
165 Metcalf and Metcalf, *India*, 68.
166 Metcalf and Metcalf, *India*, 76.
167 Kulke and Rothermund, *History*, 183.
168 Wolpert, *New History*, 210–214; and Metcalf and Metcalf, *India*, Chapter 3, "The East India Company Raj, 1772–1850," 56–91.
169 Murphey, *History*, 284–285.
170 Metcalf and Metcalf, *India*, 61.
171 Metcalf and Metcalf, *India*, 61.
172 Wolpert, *New History*, 197.
173 Metcalf and Metcalf, *India*, 76.
174 Kulke and Rothermund, *History*, 185.
175 Wolpert, *New History*, 224–225.
176 Wolpert, *New History*, 214–223; and Judd, *Lion*, 75–76.
177 Kulke and Rothermund, *History*, 191; Judd, *Lion*, 76–77; and Metcalf and Metcalf, *India*, 95–96.
178 Wolpert, *New History*, 225–230; and Judd, *Lion*, 47.
179 Wolpert, *New History*, 230; and Judd, *Lion*, 68.
180 Judd, *Lion*, 76.
181 Wolpert, *New History*, 230–231; and Judd, *Lion*, 73.
182 Judd, *Lion*, 76.
183 Metcalf and Metcalf, *India*, 47–48; and Kulke and Rothermund, *History*, 189.
184 Wolpert, *New History*, 231; and Judd, *Lion*, 71–73.
185 Judd, *Lion*, 71, and 77–78.
186 Judd, *Lion*, 70.
187 Kulke and Rothermund, *History*, 188; Judd, *Lion*, 77–82; and Metcalf and Metcalf, *India*, 101–102.
188 Judd, *Lion*, 77; and Wolpert, *New History*, 237.
189 Wolpert, *New History*, 236; and Metcalf and Metcalf, *India*, 103.
190 Wolpert, *New History*, 235; and Judd, *Lion*, 82.
191 Judd, *Lion*, 82–84.
192 Judd, *Lion*, 84–86; and Metcalf and Metcalf, *India*, 98.
193 Judd, *Lion*, 84–87; and Metcalf and Metcalf, *India*, 103–104.
194 Judd, *Lion*, 85.
195 Wolpert, *New History*, 237.
196 Judd, *Lion*, 87; and Metcalf and Metcalf, *India*, 103–104.

Chapter 12: Colonial Impact on East Asia: Decline of China

The nineteenth century saw a dramatic political change in East Asia. Although none of the East Asian countries fell completely into the hands of any particular Western power, colonialism had a strong impact on the historical development of East Asia in the nineteenth and early twentieth centuries. While China was in a continuous decline after the Opium War, until the fall of the Qing dynasty in 1911, Japan was able to avoid going down the same path and redeemed itself through the Meiji Restoration in 1868. Korea, on the other hand, eventually fell as a colony to Japan in 1910 after its long struggle for independence against its two powerful neighbors.

CHINA'S FOREIGN POLICIES DURING THE QING DYNASTY

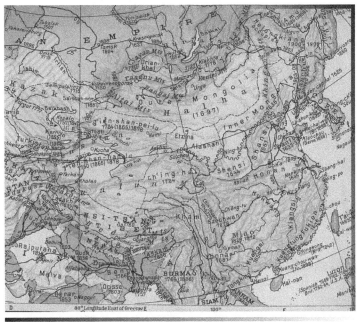

1905. Louis le Grand

The Qing Dynasty

As discussed before, the Qing dynasty was the last and strongest dynasty in Chinese history. Under the Qianlong emperor, the Qing dynasty reached its apex in terms of political and territorial consolidation, and economic development. The Qing Empire controlled a vast area, which was much larger than today's China. Until 1850, the Chinese economy was probably larger than all of the Western countries combined. Some studies of the known world economy and trade in the eighteenth and nineteenth centuries show that the total world GNP (gross national product) was 155 billion dollars (measured in 1960 US dollars) in 1750. 120 billion or 77 percent was produced in Asia, whereas only 35 billion or 23 percent was produced in the West. In 1800, the world's GNP was 183 billion dollars, of which 137 billion or 75 percent was produced in Asia. In 1860, 165 billion or still 60 percent of the world GNP of 280 billion dollars was produced in Asia.[1] Meanwhile, an estimate of GNP per capita also shows that in 1800, China's GNP per capita was $228, whereas in England and France, it ranged from $150 to $200, even though China's population in 1800 was 315 million, whereas that of all of Europe was 173 million.[2]

After the seventeenth century, the world became increasingly connected to each other because of international trade and technological improvements. China, however, had limited foreign relations, except for its relations with its tributary states, up to the late Qing dynasty. The theory and practice of the tributary system reflected China's worldview: a belief that China was the center of the known civilized world, and all of the countries that desired to have a relation with China should accept the status of a tributary state.[3] Chinese rulers clung to this view in their relations with neighboring countries, since China had been the most powerful state in East and Southeast Asia for centuries. The Ming dynasty built the tributary system into a cornerstone of China's foreign policy. The Ming court developed a hierarchical system that put China at the center of leadership, and made many other Asian countries, such as Korea, Ryukyu, Annam (Vietnam), Burma, and Thailand, into tribute states. Admiral Zheng He's sea expeditions extended China's tributary system to include some of the Middle Eastern and African countries. The Chinese courts decided on the frequency and the routes of tributary missions, based on the importance of a nation in China's foreign relations. China would finance the tributary missions, but the tribute states had to go through complicated rituals to present their gifts to the Chinese court.[4]

The Qing state inherited this system of tributary states from the Ming dynasty and did not establish a Ministry of Foreign Affairs to handle China's relations with other countries until the middle of the nineteenth century. Until that time, the Qing court handled their relations with foreign countries in three separate offices. While Lifan yuan (Office of Border Affairs) handled the relations with the peoples on China's northern and northwestern borders, such as the Mongols and the Russians, the Office of Imperial Household supervised the activities of European missionaries. The officials in the Ministry of Rituals handled relations with the tribute states, most of which were Asian countries.[5] Although the Qing dynasty, in terms of their management of foreign relations, seemed to be more flexible than the Ming Dynasty had been, the Qing court shared with the Ming dynasty the central value that China was a middle kingdom, whereas all other nations were peripheral.

This China-centered worldview was shattered after the Western powers approached China in the late sixteenth century. Taking advantage of newly developed seafaring technology, European explorers reached the Indian coast and Southeast Asia; they eventually arrived on Chinese waters at the turn of the Ming-Qing dynasties. Initially, their appearance did not pose much of a challenge to the Chinese emperor, who managed to employ the centuries-old notion of the tributary system to deal with the new comers. With their sense of superiority, the Western powers eventually clashed with China's ethnocentric worldview, and their advanced Western technology and military power soon proved to be too formidable for the Chinese rulers. As one Asian country after another fell as victims of Western colonization, the Qing dynasty also experienced a rapid decline caused by the colonial powers.

The arrival of Europeans in China followed a common pattern of Western colonization in Asia: merchants and missionaries first, and then military forces. Jesuit missionaries were the first to come to China to carry out missionary work. Francis Xavier (1506–1552), a great Jesuit pioneer, was the first Jesuit who attempted to reach China. After his successful pioneer work in Japan, he was on his way to China when he got sick and died on an island near today's Hong Kong in 1552.[6] Another great Jesuit missionary, Matteo Ricci (1552–1610), entered China via Macau in 1582. He studied the Chinese culture and language intensively, and even adopted a Chinese name, Lima Dou, in order to communicate better with the Chinese. After gradually working his way northward, he arrived in Beijing in 1598 and developed a good relationship with the Ming Wanli Emperor, owing to his knowledge as a mathematician and a cartographer. With the permission of the emperor, Ricci established a church in Beijing, which became the oldest Catholic Church in the city.

The work of Ricci paved the way for other Jesuit missionaries to obtain positions at the Ming and later, Qing courts for the next century and a half.[7] Several of them, such as Jesuit astronomers Johann Adam Schall von Bell and Ferdinand Verbiest, became trusted advisers to the Ming and Qing emperors. Jesuit influence peaked during the reign of the Kangxi Emperor, who studied Western sciences in his youth under Jesuit tutors. The emperor appointed Adam Schall to the position of court astronomer and later gave him the title, "Master of Universal Mysteries."[8]

image © William Ju, 2012. Used under license from Shutterstock, Inc.

The Bronze Celestial Sphere of the Beijing Observatory

Verbiest became Emperor Kangxi's Head of the Mathematical Board and Director of the Observatory, and was asked to supervise several projects, including the casting of cannons for the imperial army and building an imperial observatory. Verbiest designed several instruments for this observatory, which was later known as the Beijing Observatory.[9]

Other Catholic missionary orders, such as the Franciscans and the Dominicans, arrived in China in the 1630s. They started to compete with the Jesuits and criticized Jesuit practices in China, including their accommodation of China's centuries-old rituals, such as ancestral worship. This led to a so-called "Rite Controversy" among the Catholic missionary orders, which lasted for over 100 years until 1742 when the Pope ruled against the Jesuits and discredited Chinese Christians' performances of their traditional rites and ceremonies based on Confucianism. The Pope's decision greatly upset the Kangxi Emperor, who began detaching himself from Rome, and the Jesuits lost their favored status.[10]

A bigger setback for Catholic missionaries in China, however, was yet to come. After the death of Kangxi, a brief succession struggle broke out among Kangxi's capable sons. Eventually, Kangxi's fourth son ascended to the throne and became the Yongzheng Emperor. Angry with the Catholic missionaries who had supported his Christian brother, the Yongzheng Emperor issued an order to limit missionary activities in China. Although he did not totally ban missionary activities, his orders began to confine Christian missionary activities to Canton.[11] After the throne passed to the Qianlong Emperor, the emperor issued an imperial edict in 1757 to initiate a "Closed Door Policy," which reinforced Yongzheng's earlier policy and limited trade activities to Canton. This caused a continuous decline of Christianity in China for over a century. Nevertheless, Catholic missionaries were of central importance to Western entry into China.

CANTON TRADE SYSTEM

With the missionaries came European merchants, who followed the newly discovered sea routes to arrive in Macau in the early sixteenth century. The Europeans, however, initially entered into trade with China through the tributary system, which was the centerpiece of Chinese world order. During the Ming dynasty, the centuries-old tributary system had developed into a "tribute-trade system."[12] As mentioned earlier, the first emperor of the Ming, Zhu Yuanzhang, issued an order of *Haijin* (sea ban) shortly after he gained power, probably with the intention of monopolizing the maritime trade that had developed during the Song dynasty. All of the foreign countries who wanted to trade with China could only do so through the tributary system. They were asked to accept the status of a tributary state, and their envoys would go through established rituals, including kowtowing to the Chinese emperor and exchanging valuable gifts at the Chinese court. Only then would they be granted certain trade privileges and be allowed to trade in China. Usually, trade with China was more important to the tributary states than to the Chinese emperors, who often viewed international trade as a privilege that they could grant or withdraw as they wished.[13] Studies by Takeshi Hamashita convincingly argued that the Chinese tributary system was by nature a tribute-trade system, which was supported by a trade network that covered East Asia, part of Central Asia, and most of Southeast Asia.[14] This tribute-trade system "governed the entirety of the late Chinese empire's international relations along with that of the entire East Asia region."[15]

When Portuguese merchants came to conduct trade in China, it was natural for them to enter China, as well as the countries on China's periphery, through this well-established trade network. The Ming court registered Portugal into the tribute-trade system and granted Portuguese traders the right to anchor at Macau in 1535.[16] In 1553, the Portuguese obtained temporary permission from the local authority to have storage receptacles on shore, and in 1557 the Portuguese were granted permission to establish a permanent settlement, contingent on their paying an annual rent of 500 taels (one tael equals approximately 38 grams) of silver to the local authorities.[17] In order to maintain their trade privileges, the Portuguese paid a few tributary visits to the Ming and the Qing courts.[18] After the Dutch conquered Taiwan in the 1620s, they followed the Portuguese pattern and sent tribute missions to China, hoping they would gain similar trade concessions. They failed, however, to get what they expected to gain, and their interest in trading directly with China declined, especially after the Qing dynasty gained control of Taiwan in 1684.[19]

The Qing conquerors initially maintained the same tribute-trade policy that had existed under the Ming dynasty, but the system was failing. It had become too expensive to prevent smuggling and piracy on the Chinese coasts because the volume of private business greatly increased as the trade with the European merchants became much more profitable. In 1683, after the Manchu gained control of Taiwan, the Emperor Kangxi lifted the sea ban, and this led to a gradual separation of maritime trade from the tributary system.[20] The court no longer required the Western powers to accept the status of a tribute state before they could conduct trade in China.[21] As a result, the British, who started to appear in Chinese waters beginning in 1635, managed to stay outside of the tributary system. British merchants were also allowed to trade in seaports, such as Canton, Zhoushan, and Xiamen with private Chinese merchants, who could now conduct foreign trade legally and openly. In order to manipulate the price, these merchants in Canton organized into *Cohong* (a corruption of *Yang-hang*, combined merchant companies, a kind of trade guild) in 1720. Canton gradually replaced Macau as the center of the foreign trade.

Lifting the sea ban and separating maritime trade from the tributary system, however, did not mean that the Qing court would relax its control over trade. After the Qing court limited missionary activities to the city of Canton, it also set up a single-seaport system, which was known as the Canton Trade System. Between 1757 and 1760, the Emperor Qianlong issued a series of edicts, which restricted international trade to the city of Canton; granted the *hong* merchants, who were members of *Cohong*, the exclusive rights to trade with foreign merchants; and limited the trading season to a few months, from October to March. When the trading season ended, all of the foreign merchants had to leave and were only allowed to return for the next season.[22] At the beginning, the European merchants, who wanted to continue to trade with China, had no other choice but to accept this system. They, however, became increasingly frustrated by the fact that all of them had to deal exclusively with the *hong* merchants, who usually belonged to one of only ten to thirteen companies. These *hong* merchants not only monopolized maritime trade in Canton, but were also manipulative and corrupt. What was making the situation worse was that when problems arose, the European merchants could not lodge complaints with the Chinese government, but could only lodge their complaints to the *hong* merchants themselves, who were designated by the Qing court as the sole group to deal with the European merchants because of their knowledge of Western languages.[23] Moreover, matters concerning legal jurisdiction became more problematic because of the differences between Chinese and Western legal practices. The Chinese would hold an entire ship crew liable if one of its sailors fought with a Chinese. The foreign defendants were subjected to Chinese law, and quite often, harsh punishments over minor crimes terrified the Europeans.[24]

Despite all of these problems, the volume of European-Chinese trade continued to increase. The British East India Company, who was granted a monopoly of British trade with the Far East, took the lead in trade with China because of a flourishing triangular trade between China, India, and Britain. After 1751, half to two thirds of the European ships sent to China were from England. For example, ten out of nineteen ships visiting China in 1751 were from England; sixty-two out of eighty-one in 1787; and thirty-nine out of fifty-seven in 1792.[25] Tea became the Chinese product that was most sought after by the British, because drinking tea became a national habit in England during the first quarter of the nineteenth century. The demand for tea surged, and the amount of Chinese tea imported into Britain rose from 2.6 million pounds in 1762 to 13.3 million in 1800. Thereafter, the British East India Company bought an average of 23 million pounds of Chinese tea at the cost of 3.6 million English pound per year.[26] Tea sometimes accounted for about 90 percent of the British imports from China. Meanwhile, exports to China were flat and even declined, especially when China's demand for Indian cotton dramatically declined after China started to grow cotton in its own southern region.

The result was a serious imbalance in British-Chinese trade. Lacking products that could balance trade with China, Britain had to pay for the tea and other Chinese products in silver. According to Immanuel Hsu, 90 percent, sometimes 98 percent, of the cargo of the British East India Company's ships from London to China was gold and silver.[27] In the 1760s, the surplus silver flowing into China exceeded three million taels. That number grew to 7.5 million in the 1770s, and 16 million by the 1780s. These bullion settlements of commercial transactions that China had with European countries, plus an unknown amount of silver that China received from Asian countries, made China "the ultimate sink of the world's silver," in the words of Andre Frank.[28]

In order to improve the trade balance with China, in 1793, Earl George Mccartney was chosen as the British envoy to China, under the pretext of commemorating the Emperor Qianlong's 80th birthday. The mission had eighty-four members, including scientists, artists, and military officers, and they also brought expensive birthday gifts for the emperor. The purpose of the mission was to negotiate better trade conditions for British merchants. More specifically, Britian wanted their merchants to be allowed to have a residential settlement at an island near Canton and to purchase warehouses for their goods.[29] In addition, the British government also wanted to have a permanent British embassy in Beijing and to negotiate a commercial treaty in order to expand the volume of trade with China, Japan, and neighboring countries.[30]

The Qianlong Emperor was very much flattered by the first English "tributary" mission. He issued a few edicts, asking the Chinese officials to receive Lord Macartney in an appropriate manner and allocating a daily allowance of 5,000 taels of silver to cover the mission's stay in Beijing. Despite all of the courtesy and special treatment, the Macartney mission failed, and Lord Macartney left China without getting any promises from the Qianlong Emperor.[31] The primary reason for the failure was that China was not ready to give up on its tributary system, and the Qianlong Emperor's letter to British King George III clearly illustrated this. In this letter, the emperor, who followed the idea that China was the center of known civilization, treated Britain the same way as China treated tributary states. He condescendingly rejected all of the British requests, telling the king that a British embassy in Beijing would be "indeed a useless undertaking," since "he is not like the Europeans, who come to Peking as Chinese employees, live there and never return home again, nor can he be allowed to go and come and maintain any correspondence." (See the Emperor Qianlong's letter, available at primary source section for this chapter). As for trade, "we possess all things, I set no value on objects strange or ingenious, and have no use for your country's manufactures."[32] Lord Macartney's refusal to kowtow to the Emperor Qianlong may also have contributed to the failure of his mission.

Meanwhile, trade in Canton continued to develop largely due to private trade. The "country trade," which was conducted by the Indian merchants under the British East India Company, had risen from one million taels to 3.7 million by early 1880s.[33] Trade directly controlled by the East India Company, known as the "company trade" also rose. Between 1781 and 1790, the British paid 16.4 million taels of silver to China; between 1800 and 1890, that amount increased to 26 million taels.[34] By the early nineteenth century, about 150,000,000 pesos worth of bullion had entered the Middle Kingdom, averaging between two to three million pesos (57,500–82,250 kilograms) per year.[35] It is said that over half of the silver production of the world ended up in China.[36] The Chinese, however, had not yet developed much interest in Western exports such as furs, clocks, and other mechanical curiosities. The increasing trade deficit alarmed the British government, as well as the British East India Company. The company had to find a way to solve this financial problem, and eventually, the British East India Company found a promising commodity that would solve its financial predicament. The illegal opium trade with China organized by the British East India Company skyrocketed during the first few decades of the nineteenth century. The efforts of the Qing court to prohibit the opium trade in China eventually led to a showdown between Great Britain and China.

THE OPIUM WARS

Many Chinese scholars refer to the First Opium War (1839–1842) as a turning point in modern Chinese history. The Qing dynasty was at its zenith in the late eighteenth and early nineteenth centuries, but after the First Opium War, they faced increasingly severe problems of foreign encroachments and domestic turmoil, which led to the social, political, and economic decline of the Qing dynasty. According to some scholars, the Opium War ushered in an era of "a hundred years of humiliation" for China in the hands of Western power.[37]

There are still debates concerning the causes of the Opium War. Some see it as an inevitable clash between two different ideological systems: China's ethnocentric worldview, which was embodied in the system of the tributary state, and the view of free trade and the free market held by Western colonial powers.[38] Others, however, maintain that self-centered economic interests were actually the origins of the war. Still others, especially those scholars in China, view the war as nothing but sheer evidence of Western imperialist exploitations of China.

The Arabs had introduced opium to China as early as the eighth century; its chief use at this time was medicinal. In the seventeenth century, it became popular for people to mix it with tobacco for smoking. The Emperor Yongzheng banned the smoking of opium in 1729, and the Emperor Qianlong banned the importation and cultivation of opium in 1796.[39] However, the Qing could not effectively enforce this policy. The problem worsened after the British East India Company started to foster opium production in India and then hired "country merchants" to ship the opium to Chinese coastal cities, from which the opium was distributed by the Chinese merchants.[40] The volume of opium that was smuggled in from India increased, from 200 chests in 1729 to 4,570 in 1800, and 23,570 in 1832. Each chest contained about 140 pounds of opium. As a result, an estimated fifteen tons of opium were smuggled into China in 1730 and in 1773, seventy-five tons.[41] The number continued to rise; over 30,000 chests were shipped to China in 1835 and 40,000 in 1838.[42] This supply, plus the opium smuggled in from other sources and the homegrown variety, could support at least two million addicts in China.

The opium trade reflected social problems in China. In order to sustain a profitable opium trade in China, several factors had to be present: a strong motivation to invest and organize the trade, a large quantity of available land, a substantial amount of cheap labor, an affluent but stagnant society in which people wanted to indulge in temporary ecstasy, and a government that was ineffective in solving social problems. In the first half of the nineteenth century, this "perfect storm" of factors brought China into "[a] particularly agonizing cycle of its modern history."[43] As mentioned earlier, the British East India Company controlled large areas in India and had access to large amounts of cheap labor. China, under the late Qing, suffered the same problems that had brought the early Chinese dynasties into a rapid downturn. According to Hsu, there was a wide range of opium addicts in China at the time, from court officials to the coolies at the bottom of the society; about 10 to 20 percent of the Chinese officials smoked opium.[44]

What really alarmed the Qing rulers, however, were the financial consequences of the opium trade. In 1825, it was the first time since the beginning of the dynasty that China suffered a net loss of silver. With about 4,500 chests of opium illegally entering China each year during the 1830s, the East India Company made ten million rupees in 1832, twenty million in 1837, and thirty million in 1838. With the lucrative profit of the opium trade, the company began to balance its trade. In 1836, for example, the British sold eighteen million pounds worth of opium to China, but imported seventeen million pounds worth of tea and other commodities from China.[45] When China's trade balance shifted from positive to negative, and the loss of bullion was generally related to the opium trade, the Qing court decided to adopt a more forceful scheme in solving the opium problem. The Emperor Daoguang (r. 1820–1850) appointed Lin Zexu (1785–1850) as the imperial commissioner to handle the opium problem.

After Commissioner Lin arrived at Canton in 1839, his campaign against the Chinese opium dealers was very successful. His investigations, however, also drew his attention to the foreign traders who smuggled opium from India and stored the cargo in their "factories" (warehouses) in Canton; they then sold it to Chinese opium traders, who would then distribute the opium inland throughout the country through an extensive trade network. In order to reason with the British government, Commissioner Lin wrote two letters to Queen Victoria in 1839, making a plea to her to prohibit her citizens from involving themselves in the opium trade. (See the primary source section of Chapter 12.)[46] Neither the British Government nor the British East India Company responded to Lin's requests. Commissioner Lin then felt obligated to employ coercive methods against the foreign traders. He ordered the siege of the thirteen factories and the compound where about 350 foreign traders lived. Among the people who were confined to their residences was the Queen's representative, Captain Charles Elliot, who was appointed by the British government as Chief Superintendent of Trade in 1836.[47] Commissioner Lin gave the foreign traders, most of them British, an ultimatum: surrender the opium stocked in these factories by May 18 or suffer the consequences. After Elliot delivered 21,306 chests of opium to Lin, the commissioner publicly destroyed the confiscated opium at Bogue (*Humen* in Chinese) as an example of his determination to stop the opium trade in China.[48]

Although it may not have been Commissioner Lin's intention to use force, much less to provoke armed conflicts, the British government took Lin's confiscation of British merchants' opium as an insult to the Crown and dispatched forces from India to aid the British citizens in Canton. Fighting broke out between the British and the Chinese naval forces in late 1839, but the war was not officially announced until January 1840, when the Indian government, on behalf of the British crown, declared war against China. The initial armed conflicts, however, were not substantial, and the result was Qing government's decision to stop "forever" the trade with the British.[49]

The war escalated in June 1840, when a British expeditionary force under Admiral George Elliot arrived. With a fleet of sixteen warships and several other ships, the British blockaded Canton. The fleet sailed northward, blockading Ningbo and occupying Zhoushan, an island outside of Shanghai. When the British fleet approached Tianjin, a city that was situated at the mouth of the Beihe River leading to Beijing, the Emperor Daoguang became alarmed. He asked Qishan, a grand secretary and the governor-general of the capital province of Zhili, to meet with Admiral Elliot to determine what the British wanted.[50] Qishan successfully persuaded the British fleet to return to Canton, where the British and the Chinese negotiated for two months.

In January 1841, Qishan and the British reached an agreement, by which China would pay six million taels of silver in indemnity, cede up Hong Kong to Britain, and reopen the Canton trade to foreign traders, and so on. When this agreement reached the Emperor Daoguang, the emperor was so angry that he immediately dismissed Qishan and even ordered his execution, a sentence that was later changed to banishment.[51] The British government was equally enraged, blaming Elliot for getting "far short of those which you were instructed to obtain," claimed Lord Palmerston, British Foreign Secretary at the time.[52] Lord Palmerston also dismissed Captain Charles Elliot, who had negotiated the agreement on behalf of the British government, replacing him with Sir Henry Pottinger. "Her Majesty's Government cannot allow that, in a transaction between Great Britain and China, the unreasonable practice of the Chinese should supersede the reasonable practice of the rest of mankind."[53]

When Pottinger arrived in China with the new instructions in August 1841, the situation had deteriorated in Canton. Captain Elliot had captured the Bogue forts, destroyed the Chinese defense, and was occupying part of Canton. A truce was negotiated after the Chinese agreed to pay six million taels. After Captain Elliot left for Britain, Pottinger and his fleet proceeded north in order to carry out the order to deal directly with the Chinese emperor, capturing Xiamen, Ningbo and Zhoushan again along the way. After receiving reinforcements from India, he captured Shanghai in June 1842, and a couple of seaports in Zhejiang the next month, thus blocking the traffic to the Grand Canal and the lower Yangtze River. When his fleet approached Nanjing, the first capital of the Ming dynasty, and took a position to capture the city, the Qing emperor sued for peace.[54]

The Treaty of Nanjing was signed on August 29, 1942. As part of the treaty, China agreed to pay 21 million taels of silver, instead of the previously agreed 6 million taels, for the cost of war and the loss of the British merchants' opium. China would end the Canton Trade System and open five seaports for foreign trade, including Canton, Xiamen, Ningbo, Fuzhou, and Shanghai; cede Hong Kong to Great Britain; and have a fixed tariff of 3 percent for British imports and exports, and so on. The Treaty of Nanjing did not give China anything in return, and thus, it became the first of a series of "unequal treaties" that the Western power forced upon China and later upon Japan and other Asian countries.[55] Both the Emperor Daoguang and Queen Victoria subsequently ratified the treaty and thus, ended the First Opium War.

AFTERMATH OF THE WAR

Although the war did not result in a substantial loss of human lives or the destruction of Chinese cities, it inflicted a far more damaging blow to China's ethnocentric worldview. The superiority of British fighting power proved that China had fallen behind the Western powers in terms of science and technology, especially that of military technology. China had lost the ability to defend itself and was forced into a new legal structure, that of an "unequal treaty" system, when dealing with the Western powers.

Other countries immediately followed suit and forced similar treaties upon China. In October 1843, Britain and the Qing court signed a supplementary treaty, the Treaty of Bogue, which gave the right of extraterritoriality to British citizens in port cities and added a "most-favored-nation" clause. The United States signed its first treaty with China in July 1844, the Treaty of Wangxia, and France signed the Treaty of Whampoa on October 24, 1844, both of which requested the freedom of Christian missionaries in China.

These treaties greatly shattered China's centuries-old tributary system. The new treaty system, especially the fixed tariff, the extraterritoriality, and the most favored nation status, according to Hsu, were especially damaging to China's sovereignty, even though the Qing court may not have fully realized the consequences at the time.[56] When the Qing court struggled to understand the situation and was reluctant to accept diplomatic relations on Western terms, more severe conflicts ensued. In 1858, an incident occurred on board the *Arrow*, a Chinese ship that was registered with Britain in Hong Kong. This incident led to the *Arrow* War, or the Second Opium War (1856–1860) between China and the allied forces of Britain and France. The *Arrow* was anchored off the coast of Canton in October 1856 when Chinese officials and soldiers boarded the ship under the

A drawing of the aftermath of a battle which occurred during the Second Opium War. The bridge is known as Eight Mile Bridge

pretext of searching for a pirate, whom they believed to be hiding on the ship. In the chaos, the British flag was hauled down and stepped upon. This and subsequent anti-western episodes, convinced the British and the French governments that it was necessary to send joint expedition forces to China to protect their citizens.[57] After the Anglo-French forces took Canton in December 1857 and set up a puppet regime, they proceeded north in March 1858, and took Tanggu forts and Tianjin, a city that was about one hundred miles southwest of Beijing. Shocked by these developments, the court sent representatives to negotiate with the Western powers, four in number now after Russia and America joined the British and the French.

The subsequent negotiations resulted in the Treaty of Tianjin (1858) between China and Great Britain, France, Russia, and America. The treaty focused on four areas: Western diplomatic residence in Beijing, opening more trade cities along the Yangtze River, travel freedom for Western merchants, and indemnity. The Qing court conceded in all areas. The Chinese emperor, however, was most reluctant to grant the permission of the permanent residency of foreign diplomats in Beijing, which would facilitate the demise of the Chinese tributary system, the cornerstone of Chinese foreign relations. When the diplomats from Britain and France arrived in China the next year, they found that the Chinese officials tried to defer them to Shanghai. Despite the warning of the Chinese officials, the British proceeded to Beijing, but suffered a heavy loss from the attack of newly strengthened Dagu forts. In retaliation, the Anglo-French forces attacked Beijing in August 1860, sending the Emperor Xianfeng on the run. As a punishment, the British command, Lord Elgin gave an order to sack and then set fire to the Summer Palace, which for the previous 139 years had been the place of administration, vacation, and residence for five Qing emperors between the Chinese New Year and the end of the summer.[58] It was, at the time, one of the most beautiful imperial gardens in the world, occupying 150,000 square meters, with more than 160 scenic attractions including imitations of scenic mountains, rivers, and gardens in China. The buildings and the gardens were a combination of Chinese and Western styles with unique artistic and architectural values. It is said that it took over a week for the fire in the palace to be extinguished.

On October 24, the Convention of Beijing was signed. The British gained the right to establish permanent residence in Beijing and received eight million taels of silver in indemnity, and the concession of the Kowloon Peninsula near Hong Kong. France got eight million taels in indemnity as well as the right for the Catholic churches to own property. Tienjin was opened to foreign trade. With the series of treaties, from the Treaty of Nanjing in 1842 to the Convention of Beijing in 1860, the Western powers forced upon China a treaty system, from which China could not free itself until the 1940s.[59]

DOMESTIC REBELLIONS

Despite all of the problems with the Western powers, scholars of modern Chinese history still debate about what eventually brought down the Qing dynasty. Was it the work of the Western powers, or was it the domestic turmoil that eventually brought demise to the Manchu rule? Judging from the extent of the social and political problems that the Qing state suffered toward its end, some argue that even without the encroachment of the Western powers, the traditional dynastic cycle would have eventually taken its toll on the Qing dynasty.[60]

In the dynastic history of China, the forces that eventually overthrow a dynasty are usually peasant rebellions. While the Qing government was greatly troubled by the unequal treaties imposed by the foreign powers, it also faced increasingly stronger social upheavals during the nineteenth century. The Chinese population rose from 143 million in 1741 to 430 million in 1850, which is an increase of 200 percent, but the cultivated land only increased from 549 million mou (one mou equals one sixth of an acre) to 737 million in 1833, which was only a 35 percent gain.[61] The shrinking of the land to person ratio, in conjunction with other problems, such as corrupt officials who were only interested in personal gain, pushed the peasantry to a breaking point. The White Lotus Rebellion (1796–1804) was the first large-scale rebellion against the Manchu. It started as a tax protest led by the White Lotus Society, a secret religious society, and quickly spread across what is today the Sichuan and Hubei provinces. It was eight years before the Qing court managed to suppress it in 1804. The White Lotus Rebellion, however, was only the beginning of large-scales Chinese peasant revolts.

The most detrimental rebellion to the Qing court was what is known as the Taiping (Heavenly Peace) Rebellion (1850–1864), which began in the Jintain county of today's Guangxi province. The leader, Hong Xiuquan (1814–1864), was an extremely interesting figure in modern Chinese history. He was born into a family of Hakka (guest settlers), who originated in central China, but migrated to Guangxi and Guangdong during the Southern Song dynasty. They had their own dialects and habits, and this made them a kind of social "out-group." Hong Xiuquan, an independent thinker, took the civil service exam four times at the local level, but failed each time. He fell seriously ill after his third exam with a fever that lasted for over a month. He told others later that he was actually taken to heaven, where he was told that he was the younger son of God and a younger brother of Jesus Christ![62]

Hong and his associates studied Christian tracts, and later initiated a rebellion under their new faith in late 1850. With nearly 20,000 believers answering his call, on January 11, 1851, his 38th birthday, Hong proclaimed himself as the Heavenly King (Tian wang) of the "Heavenly Kingdom of Great Peace" (Taiping tianguo). As many poor peasants joined them, the Taiping troops became 500,000 strong in two years. They broke into Hunan, took control of three cities of Wuhan in Hubei, and sailed along the Yangtze River to approach Nanjing. In March 1853, the Taiping forces seized Nanjing, where Hong established his capital. The Heavenly King then issued several scripts to introduce new policies, including a land reform policy, and new regulations for military, financial, judicial, and educational institutions. He also banned many old practices, such as opium smoking, foot-binding, prostitution, the sale of slaves, and gambling. Hong also issued an order giving women equal rights with men.[63] Because of the radical nature of his policies, some scholars refer to the Taiping Rebellion as the Taiping Revolution.[64]

The Taiping Kingdom controlled Nanjing until 1864. An internal power struggle in 1856 greatly weakened the Taiping leadership. In subsequent years, the Taiping lost three of its five original leaders, including its prime minister who had been largely responsible for Taiping's military and administrative success. This greatly deprived the Taiping of its early effective and visionary leadership.[65] What was even more problematic to Hong, however, was the fact that he failed to attract more support to his rebellion. The Western powers, which were initially excited about this rebellion in the name of Jesus Christ, were soon disappointed after they learned more details of Hong's new faith. Moreover, the Taiping further alienated themselves from the major Western powers with their policy of prohibiting the opium trade and their condescending treatment of the British representative who came to Nanjing to gain more information about the Taiping. All of the Western powers in China remained neutral during the Taiping Rebellion, and some of them even fought against the Taiping when the Taiping troops tried to capture Shanghai.[66]

The Taiping also failed to attract more support from local Chinese. As most of the Taiping leaders were Hakka, who spoke a different language and had different customs from most Chinese, many Han Chinese perceived them with suspicion. Their policies against some of the Han Chinese customs, such as foot-binding and polygamy, did not help them to win support from the local elites.

The poor local Chinese were infuriated when the Taiping came to the villages to destroy their temples and idols, and further forbade them from performing ancestor worshiping.[67]

In addition, Hong's devotion to his interpretation of Christian faith prevented him from taking advantage of the established social structure, which often gave rise to rebellions driven by secret societies, such as the earlier White Lotus Rebellion.[68] Some other peasant rebellions occurred around the same time. The Nian Rebellion (1853–1868), for example, broke out in 1853 in northern China, which includes today's Shangdong, Henan, Gansu, and Anhui provinces. The Nian forces were an association of secret societies, known as Nian (literally band). Inspired by the Taiping Rebellion, the Nian leaders imitated the Taiping organization.[69] However, Hong, who had become more focused on his new faith than military and political objectives, did not seek a vigorous collaboration with the Nian forces. After the Taiping Rebellion was suppressed in 1864 by a joint force of Qing troops and foreign troops, the remaining Taiping forces joined the Nian forces; this only postponed the eventual failure of the Taiping forces and the Nian forces, which would occur four years later.

The Taiping Rebellion was the most damaging rebellion in China in the nineteenth century. It lasted fifteen years and affected two thirds of the provinces. Nearly 600 cities in central and south China changed hands between the Taiping and the Qing forces, and these battles may have claimed about 500,000 lives. The Taiping and other rebellions, including two Muslim rebellions, one in Yunnan between 1855 and 1873, and the other in Shaanxi and Gansu between 1862 and 1873, greatly affected Manchu rule in China. The Qing court's inability to suppress the rebellions exposed the weaknesses of the Qing military forces, which were corrupt and ineffective. This gave rise to capable Chinese elites who organized local militias to protect their properties. This practice eventually led to the emergence of personal armies under the command of talented Chinese generals who later played important roles in politics at the Qing court. Zeng Guofan's (1811–1872) Xiang Army, Li Hongzhang's (1823–1901) Huai Army, and Zuo Zongtang's (1812–1885) Chu Army were all instrumental in the eventual victories over the Taiping, Nian and Muslim rebellions.[70]

POLITICAL REFORMS IN LATE QING

Foreign encroachment and domestic turmoil greatly weakened Manchu control of China. The Qing dynasty, however, did not immediately collapse. Owing to a series of political reforms implemented by the Qing court, the dynasty managed to continue for another half of a century. The first of such reforms was loosely known as the "Tongzhi Restoration" during the reign of the Emperor Tongzhi (1862–1874); the name is quite ironic as the emperor did not play a leadership role during the reform.[71] To a certain extent, the Tongzhi Restoration of the 1860s and 1870s was comparable to the Meiji Restoration in Japan, but lacked the rigor and revolutionary nature of the latter. In the 1860s, the court appointed Zeng Guofan and others to important provincial positions; these key individuals played important roles in suppressing the Taiping Rebellion. The new leadership, headed by Prince Gong (1832–98) at the court and supported by Zeng Guofan, Zuo Zongtang, and Li Hongzhang in the provinces, brought a temporary revival of the Qing dynasty.

Prince Gong was the sixth son of the Emperor Daoguang and brother of the Emperor Xianfeng (1851–1861). He was the major negotiator with the Western powers at the end of the Second Opium War in 1860 and was in charge of Beijing when the Emperor Xianfeng fled the city. When the Emperor Xianfeng died the next year, a joint *coup d'état* of Prince Gong and Empress Dowager Cixi, a shrewd and calculative empress who dominated the Qing court for the next 47 years from 1861–1908, rendered the Qing court into their hands. Highly intelligent and quick thinking, Prince Gong initiated foreign policy reforms and then advocated a movement, known as the "Self-Strengthening Movement," to modernize the Chinese military forces. Prince Gong created new government offices to handle foreign affairs and foreign trade, including the *Zongli Yamen* (Office of Foreign Affairs) in March 1861; the Superintendent of Foreign Trade in Tianjin, which was parallel to an existing position in Shanghai; and the *Tongwen Guan* (College of Foreign Languages) in Beijing in 1862.[72] The Western powers welcomed these efforts at modernizing China's diplomacy, and as a result, they were at peace with China for nearly two decades.

Meanwhile, Prince Gong became the chief promoter of the Self-Strengthening Movement, which lasted from 1861 to 1895. The theme of the movement came from an idea set forth by Feng Guifen (1809–1874), which emphasized a doctrine of "Chinese learning as the fundamental structure and Western learning for practical use."[73] Most of the successful projects of the Self-Strengthening Movement were initiated and carried out at the provincial level; these successful projects were in large part due to the vision and hard work of Zeng Guofan and Li Hongzhang. Zeng Guofan was probably "the most respected and the greatest scholar-official of nineteenth century China."[74] He was a pioneer in experimenting with ways to modernize China on the one hand, but maintain certain Chinese traditions on the other. He was a devoted Confucianist, believing that China's main problem was a "spiritual collapse" from the true faith of Confucianism. Zeng advocated the return of China to a Confucian order. Zeng, however, was not a simple-minded conservative. As governor-general of Liangjiang, (Jiangxi, Anhui, and Jiangsu), he sponsored programs to modernize the Chinese military by adopting Western military technology. He helped to establish the Jiangnan Arsenal in Shanghai, which opened in 1865. It was the first major achievement in the Self-Strengthening Movement.[75]

After Zeng died in 1872, Li Hongzhang, his major follower, became the central figure of the movement. Even though he remained mostly a provincial leader, the governor-general of Zhili, he functioned as a national leader when coordinating the Self-Strengthening Movement. He implemented several successful projects toward the modernization of the Chinese military: the Fuzhou Dockyard was built in 1866; the Nanjing Arsenal was opened in 1867; a naval military academy was established at Tianjin in 1880; another military academy was established in 1885; and the *Peiyang* (Northern Sea) fleet was established in 1888. On the recommendation of Zeng and Li, China dispatched thirty teenage students to Hartford, Connecticut in 1872, and more followed over the years. By 1881, 120 boys had been sent to the United States with the intention of eventually studying in an American military academy. The mission, however, failed when the United States government refused to enroll these Chinese students at a military academy. Later, some of these Chinese students were sent to Germany, France, and Great Britain.[76]

In addition to military improvements, Li Hongzhang sponsored many modern enterprises. The China Merchants' Steam Navigation Company was inaugurated in 1872; the Bureau for Kaiping Coal Mines was created at Tianjin; the Shanghai Cotton Cloth Mill was opened in 1877; the first telegraph line between Dagu and Tianjin was built in 1879; and two years later, the Imperial Telegraph Administration was created. In 1881, a six-mile-long railway was built in Tianjin; and in 1882, Li ordered the construction of a harbor and a shipyard at Port Arthur (today's Lushun). More than 90 percent of the projects launched during the Self-Strengthening Movement were under the guidance of Li Hongzhang. For this reason, Li Hongzhang is known as the father of China's early modernization.[77]

The conservative officials of the Qing court, however, strongly opposed the Self-Strengthening Movement, which was sometimes also known as a movement of "foreign matters" (*yangwu yundong*), since most of the inspiration for the projects came from the West. Empress Dowager Cixi took advantage of this controversy for her own benefit. Jealous of Prince Gong's increasing popularity, she used conservative forces to balance Prince Gong's power and eventually pushed Prince Gong to resign in 1884. The Qing court was thus deprived of capable leadership and was easily manipulated by the Empress Dowager Cixi, who is often blamed for the problems of the last stage of the Qing dynasty. It seems that the ultimate goal for this ambitious lady was to secure her own power over the court. She was not happy with her son, the Emperor Tongzhi, because the emperor often expressed his resentment of his mother's manipulative control over him. It is said that when her son became seriously ill, the Empress Dowager did nothing to help him. Instead, she focused on demanding that the court find a boy emperor of her son's generation so that she could continue to be the "Empress Dowager-Mother" instead of the "Empress Dowager-Grandmother," who would lose the position of regent to the mother of the future emperor. This move was a violation of the established rules of the Qing dynasty, and some courtiers even committed suicide in protest against her, following the Chinese tradition of "death remonstration."[78] Nothing, however, could stop her from maintaining her power. After the death of the Emperor Tongzhi at the age of nineteen in 1875, her four-year-old nephew became the Emperor Guangxu (1875–1908).

This development at court only further damaged the Self-Strengthening Movement, which had already suffered from limited vision and weak central leadership. Most later projects merely satisfied local interests, and strong regional sentiments eventually led to the failure of the movement. In 1884, the Beiyang (north ocean) fleet and the Nanyang (south ocean) fleet refused to rescue the Fujian fleet when it was under attack by the French, who wanted to annex Annam (north Vietnam). In 1894–1895, during the First Sino-Japanese War, the Beiyang fleet fought alone against the Japanese, which led to a total annihilation of the fleet by the Japanese Imperial Navy.[79] The limitations of the Self-Strengthening Movement became too obvious to be ignored.

A HUNDRED-DAY REFORM

The fact that China lost to the Japanese in the First Sino-Japanese War in 1895 served as another wakeup call to the Qing leadership. Even the Emperor and the Empress Dowager could no longer deny that China needed reforms that were more profound than what had been carried out superficially under the pretentiousness of "Western learning for practical use," if the dynasty wanted to survive in the modern world. The question was what kind of institutional reforms would the court or the Empress Dowager Cixi allow?

When the young Emperor Guangxu was finally allowed to assume "personal rule" in 1889, he was initially attracted to the ideas of a moderate institutional reform proposed by a Confucian conservative, Weng Tonghe (1830–1904), who advocated for limited administrative reorganization. The emperor, however, was soon won over by the more radical ideas of Kang Youwei (1858–1927), a remarkably open-minded intellectual who embraced some Western ideas and strongly advocated the idea that China should follow the models of Peter the Great of Russia and the Meiji Emperor of Japan in reorganizing its administrative structure to meet the challenges of the modern world. "Without the reform, the sovereign might not even have the chance of becoming a commoner in the future," exclaimed Kang in one of his memorials to the Guangxu Emperor.[80] The emperor was very much impressed by Kang's audacity and was even more impressed by his novel ideas. In spite of the opposition of the conservatives at court, the emperor appointed Kang as secretary of Office of Foreign Affairs.

With the encouragement of Kang and Liang Qichao (1873–1929), a talented student of Kang, the Emperor Guangxu issued the first of his reform edicts on June 11, 1898, asking his court officials and commoners alike to learn Western knowledge.[81] In the next 103 days, until September 20, the emperor issued as many as fifteen edicts to implement reforms in three major areas: education, political administration, and industry. In terms of education, the old writing style, known as "eight-legged" essay writing, required by the civil service examination, would be abolished, and new subjects, such as political economy would be added to the exam; a new imperial university with a medical school would be established in Beijing; other schools, from elementary schools to colleges, would be established in each province; and the court would publish an official newspaper.[82] As for the political administration, some "unnecessary" offices would be abolished, including the Banqueting Court, the Court of State Ceremonies, the Imperial Stud, and the Court of Sacrificial Worship. Meanwhile, the court would appoint progressives to supervise the preparation of a budget and to improve legal codes. As for industry, the emperor ordered railroad construction, industrial and commercial developments, and encouraged invention.[83]

The radical reforms pushed by the emperor and his advisors, Kang Youwei and Liang Qichao, scared many senior officials at court, as well as at the local level. Many of them boycotted the reforms, hoping that the Empress Dowager, who had stayed in the Summer Palace since her retirement in 1889 without losing her power over court politics, would interfere with the emperor's reforms. This was exactly what happened. The Empress Dowager was alarmed by the young emperor's radical programs and assumed that his reform programs were a scheme to deprive her of her power. On September 21, the Empress Dowager Cixi suddenly sent troops to raid the imperial palace and put the Emperor Guangxu under house arrest. She subsequently issued an order to arrest those who helped the emperor stage the reforms. With the help of foreign powers, Kang Youwei and Liang Qichao managed to escape and eventually went to Japan, but six other reformers, including Kang's brother, were arrested and executed. In the following months, most of the reforms were reversed, except for the newly established university and other schools.[84] The Hundred-Day Reform, which might have given the Qing dynasty an opportunity to revitalize itself, thus failed under the suppression of the Empress Dowager Cixi. She might have tolerated some conservative reforms, but her highest priority was preserving her power despite what would benefit the nation. The Qing dynasty collapsed only three years after her death in 1908.

THE BOXER REBELLION

The failure of the Hundred-Day Reform had far-reaching consequences. It resulted in restoring power to the hands of conservative Manchu officials instead of moderate or radical Chinese officials. At the turn of the twentieth century, widespread anti-foreign sentiment had become prevalent in the Qing court; this resurgence of the conservatism of the Qing court soon put the country into conflict with the Western powers .

The treaty system established after the 1860s opened the Chinese markets to foreign countries, and large amounts of foreign commodities flowed into China. Because of the fixed 3 percent tariff, many foreign goods, such as cotton cloth from Britain, were sold for only one-third of the price of the domestic product, putting many local textile manufacturers out of business. In 1899, China's trade deficit amounted to 69 million taels, and the government was 12 million taels in debt.[85] In order to increase government revenue, the Qing court levied heavy taxes against its subjects, and this added more hardship to the townspeople who had already been impoverished by the decline of domestic commerce and rising unemployment.

Life in the countryside was even worse because the peasants were subjected to central, provincial, and local taxes. In addition, natural disasters worsened toward the end of the century. The Yellow River, which had changed its course from Heman to Shandong in 1852, flooded more frequently than before. In 1898, it flooded hundreds of villages in Shandong affecting millions of people. The Yangtze River also flooded Sichuan, Jiangxi, and Anhui in the same year. Two years later in 1900, a severe draught occurred in Northern China. Superstitious central, local, and societal leaders started to blame foreigners for all of the misfortune, claiming that *feng-sui* (a Chinese system of geomancy) was negatively affected because foreigners damaged the "dragon vein" (*long mai*) by constructing railroads across the land and let out "precious breath" (*bao qi*) by digging mines in the mountains.[86]

These circumstances provoked the Boxer Rebellion in northern China. The name Boxers referred to the members of a Chinese secret society, *Yihe quan* ("Righteous and Harmonious Fists"), which was related to the secret societies that had led the earlier White Lotus Rebellions. First appearing in the Qing records as early as 1808, the Boxers were described as local bandits harassing villagers and townsmen, and were eventually banned by the Qing dynasty.[87] In the last decade of the nineteenth century, however, the Boxers turned from anti-Manchu to anti-foreign; some of them even created a slogan, "Support the Qing and destroy the foreigners" (*fuqing mieyang*).[88] The officials of the Qing dynasty, especially the governor-general of Shandong, who wanted to use the Boxers to get rid of some of the foreign missionaries and merchants, quickly encouraged this mentality. Some conservative high officials at court also welcomed the opportunity and encouraged the Empress Dowager Cixi to endorse the Boxer movement so that the Qing court could use it as a means of limiting foreign influence in China. The Empress Dowager Cixi gladly complied with these suggestions. On January 12, 1900, she stated in a decree that "People drilling themselves for self defense and for protection of their villages should not be considered bandits."[89] In May, the Empress Dowager Cixi secretly summoned the Boxers to Beijing and asked the court officials and Qing military troops to practice the Boxers' arts and rituals, which, according to the Boxers, would make them immune to bullets.

With the encouragement of the Qing court, the Boxers attacked boldly against foreign residents, burning down churches, shops, and schools owned by foreigners and massacring foreigners as well as Chinese Christians in Tianjin and other northern cities. This greatly worried the foreign legations in Beijing because rumors spread that the Qing Court may have decided to kill all of the foreigners in the capital.[90] In desperation, they asked their governments for help. An international force of 2,100 soldiers was dispatched from Tianjin, but the Boxers blocked the troops halfway between Tianjin and Beijing. Meanwhile, the Boxers were out of control. In early June, they burned the British legation and killed the chancellor of the Japanese legation in Beijing.

Instead of putting constraints on the Boxers, the Empress Dowager Cixi wanted to utilize the Boxer forces to fight against the foreign powers. A few Qing court officials incorporated the Boxers into their own forces and encouraged them to kill more foreigners. In late June, the court formally ordered provincial officials to organize their Boxers and join the court to expel the foreigners from China.[91] However, many governor-generals in South and Southeast China, including Li Hongzhang at Canton, Zhang Zhidong at Wuhan, and Yuan Shikai (1859–1916), the new governor-general in Shandong, rejected this order. Some of them secretly reached agreements with foreign communities, promising them protection if they came under the threat of the Boxers. In mid-July, thirteen provincial officials in the Southeast submitted a memorandum urging the court to suppress the Boxers, but this did not prevent some hotheaded Qing officials from pressing the Empress Dowager Cixi to continue her hostile policies against the foreign powers.[92]

In August, an international relief expedition, consisting of troops from seven countries, Japan, Russia, Great Britain, the United States, France, Austria, and Italy, arrived in Beijing; German troops would arrive later. The allied forces stormed Beijing, which relieved the foreign legations. The Empress Dowager Cixi, the Emperor Guangxu, and a small cohort escaped from the city and all the way to Xi'an. The allied forces occupied Beijing for over a year until September 1901; during the occupation, the allied forces looted the city, including the palaces, turning the occupation of Beijing into an "orgy of looting."[93]

In desperation, the exiled Empress Dowager Cixi asked Li Hongzhang to go to Beijing to negotiate with the foreign powers. After much hesitation, Li eventually agreed to go to make peace settlements with the allied forces. By this time, the foreign powers were arguing with each other over how to divide the spoils of the war. It was not until December 1900 that the allies finally reached an agreement, focusing on two areas: punishment of the guilty and indemnity. The Boxer Protocol, signed on September 7, 1901, required China to pay war reparations of 450 million taels

A cartoon depicting the demands upon China for indemnity after the Boxer Rebellion

to the countries that had participated in the expedition. As the entire annual revenue of the Qing dynasty was around 250 million at the time, the payment would be completed in thirty-nine years until 1940. Adding 4 percent interest each year, China's total payment amounted to almost one billion taels by December 31, 1940, when the debt was cancelled, an equivalent value, by some calculations, of sixty-one billion dollars in 2010.[94]

The Qing dynasty quickly declined after the Boxer Rebellion. The foreign encroachments had dismantled the Qing Empire. Russia controlled Manchuria and Ili (Yili) in today's Xinjiang; France had taken control of China's formal tribute state Annam after the war of 1884–1885, and from there they extended their sphere of influence into Yunnan; Japan engineered the ending of Korea's tributary relations with China in 1895 and later formally annexed Korea as a Japanese colony in 1910. Japan also forced China to cede Taiwan, the Liaodong Peninsula, and the Pescadores after the first Sino-Japanese war of 1894–1895. While the British established their sphere of influence in the Yangtze River Valley, the Germans took Qingdao, a port city in Shandong. Concessions were given to foreigners in big cities such as Shanghai, where the foreign powers exercised their rights of extraterritoriality. The United States did not claim any territorial control of China. In 1900, following an initiative from Great Britain, the US Secretary of State, John Hay, under President Woodrow Wilson, issued notes to other powers who had interest in China, urging them to have an "OpenDoor Policy." According to this Open Door policy, all of the countries could trade with China, but no one should single handedly colonize China.[95] All of the interested countries agreed, in principle, that China should uphold its territorial and administrative integrity, although in reality, China under the Qing dynasty had assumed a semi-colonial status in the eyes of the world powers.

1911 REVOLUTION: THE FALL OF THE QING DYNASTY

The Qing government's mishandling of the Boxer Rebellion was seen as proof that the Qing rulers had lost the Mandate of Heaven. Social disturbances increased after China's defeat in the First Sino-Japanese War, and now, revolutionary movements aimed at overthrowing the Qing dynasty were well underway. Chinese intellectuals were at the forefront of the revolutionary movements. Many of them had gone to study in Japan after the First Sino-Japanese War and returned to China after the Boxer Rebellion. Unlike Zeng Guofan, Li Hongzhang, and others, who had wanted to make changes within the system of the Qing dynasty, the students who returned from Japan believed that Manchu rule was the source for all of the evils that China had suffered recently, and they started to call for a revolution to overthrow the Qing dynasty. Zou Rong (1885–1905) and Zhou Shuren (1881–1936, more popularly known by his pen name, Lu Xun) were among these young radicals.

After Zou Rong returned from Japan, he lived in the British Concession in Shanghai where he had more freedom to publish anti-Manchu ideas because the British had extraterritorial rights there. His book, *The Revolutionary Army*, called for his fellow Han Chinese to reject the rule of the Manchu, who had turned the Han Chinese into their slaves. Zou condemned such men as Zeng Guofan, who, claimed Zou, was far from a hero, because he only helped the Manchu kill his own people.[96] Furious about Zou's anti-Manchu statements, Qing officials put pressure on the British to yield Zou to the Manchu authorities, but their request was refused. Eventually Zou was put on trial in the Shanghai Mixed Court, where he was found guilty of distributing anti-Manchu writings and received a two-year sentence. Unfortunately, Zou got sick and died in prison in 1905 at the age of 19.[97]

Another young man, Zhou Shuren, also used writing to inspire social reforms in China. He later became one of the most famous writers in Chinese literature, using his pen name Lu Xun. While Lu Xun was studying medicine in Japan, he was shocked to learn about an event where several Japanese soldiers accused a Chinese man of being a traitor and beheaded him in front of a large group of apathetic Chinese. After that, he decided to give up studying medicine to become a writer, a career that would enable him to "wake up" more Chinese and save more lives than a medical doctor.[98] His novel, *The Story of Mr. Q* and his satire, *The Diary of a Madman*, exposed social problems of China in the late Qing period.

Some of the Chinese students in Japan were young women who bravely broke away from the role of the traditional Chinese woman and were later involved in the revolutionary movement. Qiu Jin was the most famous among them. She was from Zhejiang province, married young, and had two children. In 1904, she suddenly abandoned her home and left to study in Japan, where she was drawn to the revolutionary movement. After she returned home in 1906, she engaged in revolutionary movements against the Qing dynasty and even attempted an uprising against the Manchu in her hometown. The local authorities arrested her and executed her after a short trial. Her courageous resistance against tradition and the Manchu has made her an inspiration to generations of Chinese women.[99]

The central figure of the revolutionary movement was Sun Yat-sen (1866–1925, also known as Sun Yixian, or Sun Zhongshan), who was later known as the "father of the Chinese Revolution." Sun was born into a peasant family in Guangdong. At the age of thirteen, he moved to Hawaii to join his brother. After he graduated from high school in 1883, he left Hawaii for Hong Kong, where he was Christianized. In Hong Kong, Sun began to develop ideas of overthrowing the Qing dynasty, but the early part of his career as a revolutionary was not easy. After nearly twenty years of trial and error including two failed uprisings against the dynasty in 1895 and 1900 respectively, and being kidnapped and kept in the Qing legation in London in 1896, Sun eventually emerged as a famous and mature revolutionary leader.[100] He and his *Tongmeng Hui* (Chinese Revolutionary Alliance), established in 1905, became the most formidable force against the Qing dynasty.

Meanwhile, the Empress Dowager Cixi, who was deeply ashamed of the Boxer fiasco, initiated her own political reforms. In 1901, she accepted responsibility for the Boxer calamity and proclaimed her intention of implementing institutional reform.[101] The proposed reform included abolishing some old offices and replacing them with new ones, and other military, educational, and social reforms—all of which were actually similar to what the Guangxu Emperor had suggested in his Hundred-day Reform in 1898. A constitutional movement was also underway after 1905, and some court officials even proposed a "constitutional monarchy," which would entail the establishment of a national assembly and drafting a constitution.[102] Few of those in charge of the reforms, however, dared even to mention the expression "Western methods" in front of the Empress Dowager Cixi; this undoubtedly would offend her, since she obviously still loathed anything Western, due to the deep humiliation that she had suffered at the hands of the Western powers. As a result, these reforms largely remained only on paper until her death in 1908. The Emperor Guangxu, who reportedly had good health until then, also mysteriously died the day before her death.[103]

The throne went to her three-year old grandnephew, Pu Yi, who was the last emperor of the Qing dynasty. His father and the regent, Prince Chun, was a Manchu conservative, whose priority was to restore the power of the court to the Manchu. By this time, however, the constitutional movement had widely been accepted by the provinces, whose leaders constantly appealed to the Qing court for an immediate convening of a national assembly. Prince Chun, however, stubbornly rejected these appeals. Seeing no hope of getting any compromises from the Qing court, many provincial leaders became sympathetic to the idea of a revolution.

The issue that led to the widespread revolt that finally brought down the Qing dynasty was the nationalization of the railroads that had been built after the First Sino-Japanese War. Many of these railroads were built with mixed funds: foreign loans secured by the court and local investments. In early 1911, the Qing court approved a proposal to nationalize the main railroads that connected Sichuan, Hubei, Hunan and Guangdong. The court offered 100 percent compensation to Hubei and Hunan, and 60 percent to Guangdong, but only gave Sichuan enough funds to cover the railroad capital and the actual construction cost, with the excuse that Sichuan officials had embezzled government funds before.[104] This unfair treatment enraged the people of Sichuan, who quickly organized the "Railroad Protection Club." When a mass rally was staged in Chengdu, the provincial capital of Sichuan, fighting broke out between the demonstrators and government troops. In order to control the situation in Sichuan, the court transferred some troops from Hupei to Sichuan. This gave the revolutionaries in Hupei an opportunity to stage a revolution in Wuhan.

Between 1906 and 1911, the revolutionaries under *Tongmeng Hui* had already made eight attempts at gaining control of the local governments: six in Guangdong, one in Guangxi, and one in Yunnan. Together with the earlier two led by Sun Yet-sen, these ten unsuccessful attempts at revolution all took place in the south. Now, the revolutionaries turned their eyes to Hubei of central China, hoping that a disturbance in central China would have a stronger impact on Beijing in the north.[105] The weakening of the Qing troops in Hubei provided the revolutionaries with a good opportunity to execute their plan, since they had already won support from some local troops known as the New Army.

On the morning of October 10, an engineer unit of the New Army seized control of a government munitions depot in Wuchang and attacked the office of the governor-general, who managed to flee upon the arrival of the rebels. By noon that day, the revolutionaries controlled the city of Wuchang and made Li Yuanhong, a brigade leader, the military governor of Hubei. The revolutionaries soon took control of two other cities, Hanko and Hanyang, and by October 12, the tri-cities of Wuhan had been in their hands. These events triggered the 1911 Revolution, also known as the *Xinhai* Revolution (*Xinhai* was the name of the year of 1911 according to the Chinese lunar calendar). The success of the revolution in Wuhan soon encouraged other provinces to stage their own revolutions. Within the next two and a half months, fifteen provinces and municipalities declared independence, including Hunan, Yunnan, Shanghai, Zhejiang, Fujian, Sichuan, and Guangdong. Although the Qing army under Yuan Shikai recaptured Wuhan in November, their victory was quickly counterbalanced by their loss of Shanghai, where the revolutionaries established their revolutionary government, headed by Huang Xing (1874–1916), a co-founder of the *Tongmeng Hui*, and Li Yuanhong.[106] The revolutionary government, however, postponed its election, waiting for the return of Sun Yet-sen, who had travelled to the United States and then to Europe, trying to rally support for the revolution.

Upon his return in late December, Sun was elected by a nearly unanimous vote, sixteen out of seventeen, to be the provisional president of the Republic of China. Li Yuanhong became the provisional vice-president, and Huang Xing, the minister of war. January 1, 1912 was designated as the first day of the Chinese Republic, and Nanjing would be the capital.[107] The question for the new republic now was how to overthrow the Qing dynasty.

Back in Beijing, Prince Chun had resigned, leaving national matters to Yuan Shikai, a calculating opportunist and the most powerful military general of the late Qing period. After he was appointed as Prime Minister at the Qing court, Yuan, on the one hand, tried to impress the Manchu leaders with his recapture of Wuhan from the revolutionaries, but on the other hand, secretly approached Sun's revolutionary government to negotiate about how to guarantee his own benefit through the revolution. Reluctantly, but persuaded by his colleagues who believed that Yuan was the only person that could prevent China from being divided, Sun promised Yuan the position of the President of the Republic of China if Yuan could persuade the emperor to abdicate. And indeed that was what Yuan did. He convinced the Empress Dowager that it was better for the emperor to abdicate voluntarily in exchange for a better outcome than losing everything. After the Empress Dowager agreed on the voluntary abdication of the emperor, Sun's government agreed to treat the emperor with courtesy, subsidize him with four million taels a year and allow him to live in the Summer Palace. On February 12, an imperial rescript, countersigned by Yuan Shikai as premier, documented the formal abdication of the Emperor Xuantong, the last Qing emperor, and thus, ended 268 years of Manchu rule in China.[108] In October 1913, Yuan was formally inaugurated as President of the Chinese Republic, a year and a half after he had assumed the position of provisional president in Beijing in March 1912.[109]

The 1911 Revolution successfully overthrew the Qing dynasty and established the first republic in Chinese history. It brought an end to the Chinese dynastic system, which had lasted for over three thousand years. The revolution, however, was an incomplete one. The power went to Yuan Shikai, who would soon betray the revolution and seek to be an emperor

1911. Artist unknown.

A picture taken during the beginning of the first republic of China. There are two flags of the Wuchang Uprising in the background

himself. The swiftness of the revolution, from the Wuchang uprising in October to the establishment of the republic in January the next year, did not allow enough time for extensive social and political reforms before Yuan stole the power from the revolutionaries. It would take a couple of more decades before a real republic would function in China under the Goumingdang (GMD), or the Nationalist Party.

For more information about the topics discussed in this chapter, please visit the website for this textbook. This website can be accessed from http://www.grtep.com/.

1 Andre Gunder Frank, *Reorient: Global Economy in the Asian Age* (Berkeley: University of California Press, 1998), 171–172.
2 Frank, *Reorient*, 170 and 173.
3 Immanuel Hsu, *The Rise of Modern China*, 4th ed. (Oxford: Oxford University Press, 1990), 130.
4 Hsu, *Modern China*, 131–134.
5 Jonathan Spence, *In Search for Modern China*, (New York: W.W. Norton & Company, 1991), 117–120.
6 Hsu, *Modern China*, 97.
7 Hsu, *Modern China*, 97–99; and Fairbank et al, *Tradition*, 224–225.
8 Hsu, *Modern* China, 100.
9 William T. Rowe, *China's Last Empire: The Great Qing* (Harvard: the Belknap Press of Harvard University Press, 2009), 139–140.
10 Hsu, *Modern China*, 100–103.
11 Spence, Search, 90.
12 Rowe, *Last Empire*, 133–135.
13 Hsu, *Modern China*, 142.
14 Takeshi Hamashita, *Trade and Finance in Late Imperial China: Maritime Customs and Open Port Market Zones* (Singapore: National University of Singapore Press, 2010), 155–157; and Frank, *Reorient*, 111–116.
15 Rowe, *Last Empire*, 135.
16 Hsu, *Modern China*, 133.
17 James Graham, "China's Growing Sea Trade with Europe 1517–1800," available at <http://www.historyorb.com/asia/china_trade.shtml>, accessed on April 17, 2012; and Bongyin Fung, *Aomen gai lun* (*Macau: A General Introduction*) (Hong Kong: Joint Publishing , 1999), 5–7. For more on this, also see Zhidong Hao, *Macau History and Society* (Hong Kong: Hong Kong University Press, 2011).
18 Spence, *Search*, 120.
19 Graham, "Sea Trade".
20 Rowe, *Last Empire*, 136–137; and Hsu, *Modern China*, 133–134.
21 Spence, *Search*, 120–122; and Graham, "Sea Trade".
22 Hsu, *Modern China*, 142; Rowe, *Last Empire*, 141–142; and Spence, *Search*, 121.
23 Spence, *Search*, 121; and Hsu, *Modern China*, 142–148.
24 Hsu, *Modern China*, 152–154; and Fairbank et al, *Tradition*, 254–257.
25 Hsu, *Modern China*, 148–149.
26 Spence, *Search*, 122; and Hsu, *Modern China*, 149–150.
27 Hsu, *Modern China*, 168.
28 Frank, *Reorient*, 115.
29 Hsu, *Modern China*, 155–156.
30 Hsu, *Modern China*, 156.
31 Hsu, *Modern China*, 157–161.
32 Hsu, *Modern China*, 161; and also Qianlong's letter in primary source section.
33 Hsu, *Modern China*, 166.
34 Hsu, *Modern China*, 166.
35 Frederic E. Wakeman, Jr., *Telling Chinese History: A Selection of Essays*, selected and ed. Lea H. Wakema, (Berkeley: University of California Press, 2009), 28; William S. Atwell, "International Bullion Flows and the Chinese Economy Circa 1530–1650," *Past and Present* 95 (May 1982): 74; and John E. Wills, Jr. "Maritime China from Wang Chih to Shih Lang: Themes in Peripheral History," in *From Ming to Ch'ing Conquest, Region and Continuity in Seventeenth-Century China*, ed. Jonathan D. Spence and John E. Wills Jr. (New Haven: Yale University Press, 1979), 213.
36 Frank, *Reorient*, 147–148.
37 Hsu, *Modern China*, 192.
38 Fairbank et al, *Tradition*, 454.
39 Hsu, *Modern China*, 168–169.
40 John K. Fairbank, *China: A New History*, Revised & enlarged ed. (Harvard: Belknap Press,1998), 198–199.
41 Hsu, *Modern China*, 169; and Lapo Salucci, "Depths of Debt: Debt, Trade and Choices," a paper presented at Midwest Political Science Association (MPSA), Chicago, April 12–15, 2007, 8, accessed on May 15, 2012, at http://sobek.colorado.edu/~salucci/assets/MPSA07_Salucci.pdf.
42 Spence, *Search*, 151.
43 Spence, *Search*, 129.
44 Hsu, *Modern China*, 172.

45 Hsu, *Modern China*, 173.
46 Hsu, *Modern China*, 179–182.
47 Hsu, *Modern China*, 177–180.
48 Spence, *Search*, 154; and Hsu, *Modern China*, 182.
49 Hsu, *Modern China*, 184.
50 Hsu, *Modern China*, 187.
51 Hsu, *Modern China*, 186–187.
52 Spence, *Search*, 158.
53 Daniel Nadler, *China to Order: Focusing on the Xixth Century and Surveying Polychrome Export Porcelain Produced during the Qing Dynasty (1644–1908)* (Paris: Vilo International, 2001), 91.
54 Hsu, *Modern China*, 188–191.
55 Hsu, *Modern China*, 190.
56 Hsu, *Modern China*, 191.
57 Hsu, *Modern China*, 205–206.
58 Hsu, *Modern China*, 205–215.
59 Hsu, *Modern China*, 209–219.
60 Spence, *Search*, 167.
61 Hsu, *Modern China*, 222.
62 Hsu, *Modern China*, 226–227; and Fairbank, *New History*, 207.
63 Hsu, *Modern China*, 232–233.
64 Hsu, *Modern China*, 226.
65 Spence, *Search*, 172–174; and Hsu, *Modern China*, 242–243, 250.
66 Hsu, *Modern China*, 236–238, 246–247; and Spence, *Search*, 178.
67 Spence, *Search*, 177.
68 Fairbank, *New History*, 207; and Hsu, *Modern China*, 444.
69 Spence, *Search*, 183–186; and Hsu, *Modern China*, 253–255.
70 Hsu, *Modern China*, 238–248.
71 Hsu, *Modern China*, 261–262.
72 Spence, *Search*, 197–202; and Hsu, *Modern China*, 268–272.
73 Fairbank et al, *Tradition*, 560–561; and Hsu, *Modern China*, 276–277.
74 Hsu, *Modern China*, 248.
75 Spence, *Search*, 193–197; and Hsu, *Modern China*, 278–279.
76 Spence, *Search*, 218–219; and Hsu, *Modern China*, 282–284.
77 Hsu, *Modern China*, 284–288.
78 Hsu, *Modern China*, 309.
79 Hsu, *Modern China*, 288–289.
80 Hsu, *Modern China*, 370.
81 Hsu, *Modern China*, 371–372; and Spence, *Search*, 228–229.
82 Spence, *Search*, 228–229.
83 Hsu, *Modern China*, 375–376.
84 Spence, *Search*, 229.
85 Hsu, *Modern China*, 389–391.
86 Hsu, *Modern China*, 390.
87 Hsu, *Modern China*, 391.
88 Joseph Esherick, *The Origins of the Boxer Uprising* (Berkeley California: University of California Press, 1988), 143–144.
89 Hsu, *Modern China*, 393.
90 Hsu, *Modern China*, 393.
91 Hsu, *Modern China*, 394–395.
92 Spence, *Search*, 231–232; and Hsu, *Modern China*, 396.
93 James L. Hevia, "Looting and Its Discontents: Moral Discourse and the Plunder of Beijing, 1900–1901," in *The Boxers, China, and the World*, eds. Robert Bickers and R. G. Tiedemann (Lanham, MD: Rowman & Littlefield, 2007), 94.
94 Spence, *Search*, 233; and Hsu, *Modern China*, 405.
95 Hsu, *Modern China*, 349–350.
96 Spence, *Search*, 236.
97 Spence, *Search*, 237.
98 Spence, *Search*, 240.
99 Spence, *Search*, 239–240.
100 Spence, *Search*, 266–267; and Hsu, *Modern China*, 454–466.
101 Hsu, *Modern China*, 408.
102 Hsu, *Modern China*, 409–416.
103 Hsu, *Modern China*, 416.
104 Hsu, *Modern China*, 467; and Spence, *Search*, 247–251.
105 Spence, *Search*, 457–458; and Hsu, *Modern China*, 456.
106 Spence, *Search*, 468–470.
107 Spence, *Search*, 258–262; and Hsu, *Modern China*, 470.
108 Hsu, *Modern China*, 472–474.
109 Spence, *Search*, 263; and Hsu, *Modern China*, 478.

Chapter 13   Japan in the Era of Transformation

Map of Present-Day Japan

In late Qing dynasty, China continued to decline under the pressure of domestic rebellions and foreign encroachments. The irony is that the Chinese court still did not understand the extent of the problems that China was facing and still clung to the idea that the Chinese were superior to "barbarians," a word that the Chinese used to refer to other "uncivilized" people. Empress Dowager Cixi, who dominated the Qing court in its last half century, was only concerned about clinging to her own power. She had a new summer palace built for her at the cost of thirty million taels of silver, using the money that was supposed to go to the Beiyang fleet. Instead of building new warships for the Navy, she accepted a new marble boat for her luxurious Summer Palace. Japan, under Tokugawa control, well understood the problem of Western military superiority, and its leaders decided to follow the road of the Western powers in modernizing their country. This led Japan to embark on a different road that eventually allowed Japan to emerge as a world power.

TOKUGAWA: THE GREAT PEACE

When China started to have problems with the Western powers, Japan was under one of its strongest and most powerful military governments, the Tokugawa Bakufu. This government was established by Tokuguwa Ieyasu in 1600, after he eliminated the forces of his opponents who were loyal to Toyotomy Hideyori, the son of his predecessor, Toyotomy Hideyoshi, at the Battle of Sekigahara in 1600. Until the time of the Meiji Restoration in 1868, the Tokugawa Bakufu provided over 250 years of peace to Japan, largely owing to the policies created by the first of a few very capable shoguns.

In order to legitimize his rule, Ieyasu obtained the title of Shogun from the Japanese emperor in 1603, but retired after only two years from this position in 1605. Tokugawa probably wanted to secure a peaceful succession for his son, especially in light of the previous failure of the Toyotomy family after Hideyoshi died. Despite his retirement, Ieyasu, continued to control the bakufu until he died in 1616. Together with the second shogun, Tokugawa Hidetada (r. 1605–1623), and the third shogun, Tokugawa Iemitsu (r. 1623–1650), Ieyasu laid the political, social, and economic foundation for the long-lasting Tokugawa bakufu.

At the beginning, the most acute problem for the bakufu was how to control the *daimyo*, who had gained a strong socio-political status over the past few centuries. The bakufu tried to solve this problem by establishing Tokugawa hegemony over the rest of the *daimyo*. The Tokugawa family controlled a large domain, which yielded about a quarter of the agricultural production of the whole country. The family controlled large cities, such as Edo, Kyoto, Osaka, and Nagasaki, and owned the most important mines. The bakufu often ordered other *daimyo* to share the expenses of national projects, including the building of Edo castle.[1] This established the Tokugawa shogun as a super lord over other *daimyo*.

Ieyasu and other shoguns invented and consolidated the *baku-han* system to regulate the relationship between the shogunal government and local *daimyo*. *Han* referred to the domains of *daimyo* who were supposed to be semi-independent, at least in theory. *Daimyo* maintained the right to collect taxes, to have their own retainers, and to retain the ownership of their domain. Their obligations to the shogun included sharing the cost of national projects, such as road building, and supplying soldiers when needed. In reality, the bakufu had developed several mechanisms to control the *daimyo*. During the Tokugawa era, the shogunal government controlled the number of *daimyo*, which was usually between 245 and 295, with an average of 265.[2] The shogun had the right to reward someone with the title of *daimyo*, or deprive the title from a family; to endorse or reject a marriage application, which was required from the *daimyo* if they wanted to have a marriage bond; and to forbid the building of more than one castle in their *han*.

Ieyasu created a hierarchical system, which divided the *daimyo* into different categories. The highest group, consisting of approximately twenty-three Tokugawa families, was known as *shimpan* (related) *daimyo*. They were given the richest and most strategically located places as their domains, as well as hereditary positions as high officials. The three most important *shimpan daimyo* were Ieyasu's three sons, whose families would provide heirs to the shogun in case the main family line extinguished. The next group was known as *fudai* (house) *daimyo*, which was the title given to those *daimyo* who had followed Ieyasu before his victory at the Battle of Sekigahara in 1600. They were also generously awarded rich domains in good locations. Their domains, however, were relatively small because they were in more densely populated areas. The third group, *tozama* (outer) *daimyo*, consisted of those who claimed allegiance to the Tokugawa only after the battle of 1600. They were given domains in remote areas and were under closer watch by the shogunal government.[3]

Keeping hostages had often been a tactic used during the *Sengoku* era before Tokugawa Ieyasu gained power. Toyotomi Hideyoshi, for example, required other *daimyo* to send their family members to Osaka. It was under the Tokugawa, however, that a more elaborate system, known as *sankin kotai* (alternative residence), was developed. In 1633, it became mandatory for all of the *daimyo* to live in Edo every other year, and even when they returned to their own *han*, they had to leave their families in Edo. The system was designed for the shogun to keep a close eye on the *daimyo* and thus, to reduce the possibility of a conspiracy. It was expensive for the *daimyo* to maintain one or more extra residences in Edo, and added to this burden was the expenses of their travel to and from Edo. Many *daimyo* felt obligated to turn the pilgrimage into a parade and competed with each other for scale and grace. This further weakened the *daimyo* financially.

In order to maintain social stability, the Tokugawa shogun continued Hideyoshi's social policies. Hideyoshi had forbidden peasants and commoners from possessing swords with his famous "sword hunt" in 1588. Tokugawa shoguns not ouly continued this policy of keeping swords out of the hands of commoners, but also followed Hideyoshi's policy to freeze social mobility. The Tokugawa divided Japanese society into four categories: samurai, peasants, artisans, and merchants, each following different rules. The line between the samurai and the commoners was strictly preserved.[4]

The last measure, but by no means the least, was the Tokugawa's *sakoku* (close country) policy, which was aggressively enforced after 1633. As discussed earlier, Hideyoshi banned Christian missionaries in Japan in 1597. Similarly, Tokugawa Ieyasu also viewed Christianity as a subversive force, and in 1612, the second shogun, Hidetada, banned all missionary activity in Japan. The prosecution of foreign missionaries and Japanese Christians reached its peak between 1637–1638 when Christian peasants in Shimabara staged an uprising against oppressive taxation. The Shimabara Revolt, which was soon suppressed, marked an official end to Christianity in Japan during the Tokugawa era. Afterwards, all of the Christians in Japan were forced to register at Buddhist temples, and Christianity was not openly practiced until after the Tokugawa bakufu was overthrown in 1867.[5]

Similar to China's Canton Trade System, in 1616, the Tokugawa limited trade to two ports, Nagasaki and Hirado, both on the Island of Kyushu. As the Tokugawa imposed more regulations and constraints on foreign traders, the British left Japan in 1623. The Spanish were expelled from Japan in 1624, and so were the Portuguese in 1639. Only the Dutch were allowed to trade on the small island of Deshima in Nagasaki harbor. Two other countries also remained to trade with Japan: Korea through the *daimyo* of Tsushima and China through the kingdom of Ryukyu, the island chain south of Kyushu. The king of Ryukyu continued to conduct frequent tributary missions to China in the seventeenth and eighteenth centuries. Moreover, in 1635, all Japanese were banned from leaving the country, and those who had already lived outside of Japan were forbidden from returning.[6]

The *sakoku* policy, together with the other policies discussed above, resulted in a deep isolation of Japan during the Tokugawa era. Relatively free from outside influence, Japan was able to consolidate its social and political system based on its own tradition, which, in turn, provided more than two and half centuries of much needed peace for Japan. The Japanese economy developed considerably under this peaceful and stable environment. The Tokugawa era saw an early urbanization in Japan. Edo grew into a city of more than one million people. Other cities, such as Osaka and the capitals of large *han*, contained populations between 100,000 and 400,000.[7] Many castle towns, which emerged around the castles of *han* leaders and the residences of the samurai, also mushroomed throughout Japan. The *sanki kotai* system greatly contributed to the emergence of a national market, owing to the improvement of roads that connected every *han* to the Tokugawa headquarters at Edo. Businesses, such as restaurants, inns, and sake-drinking houses, boomed at emerging market towns along the major roads.

COMMODORE PERRY AND THE OPENING OF JAPAN

The peace enjoyed by Japan due to its isolation was greatly disturbed in the middle of the nineteenth century, and this time, it was the work of Americans. As part of the competition among the Western powers to build their colonial empires, Russia, Britain, and the United States all started exploring Japanese shores. Russia was the first to approach Japanese waters. As early as 1771, a Russian explorer sailed into a harbor in Shikoku, pretending to be a Dutchman. In the following years, more Russian merchant ships arrived in Japan, asking for a commercial treaty with Japan, but the local Japanese authorities turned all of the Russian ships away. In the early nineteenth century, the British also became interested in returning to Japan; they sent a vessel to Uraga near Edo, asking Japan to enter into a commercial treaty, but Japanese officials turned them away.[8] Because of the increasing activity of foreign ships in Japanese waters, the shogun issued an order in 1825, which gave the Japanese permission to fire upon foreign ships, "with no second thought."[9] Americans, however, were eager and determined to "open" Japan, since China had already been opened. As American whaling had extended into the Pacific, Japanese seaports would be ideal locations for American ships to obtain their supplies. The Japanese, however, promptly drove away a few early American ships. Eventually, the US government assigned Commodore Matthew C. Perry to go to Japan to negotiate a treaty with the Japanese emperor. On July 8, 1853, Commodore Perry commanded his fleet, consisting of four warships, to anchor at Uraga at the mouth of the Edo Bay, despite protests from smaller Japanese vessels. By this time, Japan had already heard the news of China's defeat in the recent Opium War. The sheer power of the US Navy shown by Perry's fleet left the Bakufu little choice but to allow Commodore Perry to land. Perry delivered a letter from US President Fillmore, which asked the Japanese government's permission to allow American ships to use Japanese ports for making repairs or getting supplies. He left afterwards, but promised to return in a year for a reply from the emperor, even though he had no idea that in Edo, he had only dealt with the shogun, not the emperor.[10]

Perry's appearance at Edo Bay presented the worst political crisis that the Tokugawa bakufu had ever experienced since the beginning of its power. It became obvious to the shogunal government that Japan in general had been left behind in terms of military technology. In light of the fact that China, its powerful neighbor and friend, had easily been defeated by the British Navy, the Japanese Navy, similarly, may not have been able to defeat the American Navy. The government split in terms of how to deal with the situation. Some insisted on the policy of *joyi* (repelling the barbarians,), but others suggested a more cautious handling of the issue. In desperation, the shogun invited opinions from all of the *daimyo*. This proved to be a big mistake, as the door opened for many *daimyo*, especially the *tozema daimyo*, who had been kept outside of government decisions. Many believed that the arrival of Commodore Perry ushered in an era of *bakumatsu* (end of bakufu).[11]

The Delivery of President Fillmore's Letter

Commodore Perry returned early the next year because he had learned about the increasing activity of the Russians along the Japanese coasts. Perry did not want to lose the opportunity to negotiate the first treaty with Japan. To press the Japanese government into accepting US requests, Perry brought even more warships this time, eight of the world's most lethal warships.[12] Overwhelmed by this show of force, the shogunal government signed the Treaty of Kanagawa on March 31, 1854. Japan would open two seaports, Shimoda at Izu Peninsula and Hakodate in Hokkaido for US ships; allow an American consulate to be established at Shimoda; and also give the Unites States the status of most-favored nation, even though the issue of trade remained unsettled.[13] In 1858, the trade issue was eventually solved by a separate treaty negotiated by the US Consul General to Japan, Townsend Harris. The commerce treaty required Japan to open four more cities for trading; open Edo and Osaka for foreign residence; and establish fixed tariffs and extraterritorial privileges for the Americans. Other Western powers, such as Russia, Britain, France, and the Netherlands, soon obtained similar treaties from Japan. Through these treaties, the Western powers were eventually able to open Japan.

THE MEIJI RESTORATION

All of these unequal treaties put Japan in an "unequal treaty system," similar to the one which China was forced to accept. Japan, however, embarked on a road that was quite different from the one that China was taking. At this critical junction, Japan's dual political structures, where power had been separated from the emperor, proved to be a disguised blessing. The Meiji Restoration in 1868 was one of the most important political events in modern Japanese history. Not only did it end the Tokugawa bakufu that had ruled Japan for over 250 years, but it also opened the door for Japan to modernize itself. A few decades later, Japan emerged as a modern world power, the only one in Asia, while other Asian countries fell into the hands of colonial powers.

The Meiji Restoration occurred as the result of two simultaneously emerging forces: the imperial court and the leading *tozama han*, such as Satsuma and Choshu, who actively participated in national politics. As mentioned earlier, the bakufu made the mistake of seeking advice from all of the *daimyo*, including those of *tozama han*, on the issue of whether Japan should sign a treaty with the United States.[14] Once the door opened, there was no way to stop those *tozama han* from participating in national politics. The bakufu made another mistake when they decided to sign the treaty with Commodore Perry in 1854, despite the opposition of the *daimyo* who preferred a *joi* policy. The bakufu's assumption that there would be no problems in getting the emperor to endorse the treaty turned out to be dead wrong. Some of the emperor's advisors, who took it as a perfect opportunity to insert imperial authority, successfully persuaded the emperor to withhold his sanction, though he did not reject the treaty outright. This brought public humiliation to the Tokugawa.[15] When the Tokugawa bakufu sought the emperor's approval of the commercial treaty in 1858, the emperor again gave an ambiguous reply. The emperor eventually endorsed both of the treaties, but these episodes clearly demonstrated that the emperor's power over national policies could no longer be ignored.

The idea of restoring to the emperor the power of making national policies was further supported by some of the *tozama han*, such as Choshu at the western tip of Honshu, Satsuma in southern Kyushu, and Tosa in southern Shikoku, all of which had previously been blocked by the Tokugawa from participating in national politics. Once they were allowed on the national stage, these *han* proved to be extremely dangerous to the Tokugawa. Although they were located at peripheral areas, Satsuma and Choshu were among the largest and richest *han*, ranking the second and the ninth, respectively, in income among all the *han*. Satsuma and Choshu also had a higher ratio of samurai to commoners than the national average. Satsuma had about 27,000 samurai, at a ratio of one to three, instead of the national average of one to seventeen, whereas Choshu had about 11,000 samurai at a ratio of one to ten.[16] Like many other *tozama han*, whose ancestors had been loyal retainers of Toyotomi Hideyoshi, there were strong anti-bakufu sentiments in both *han*. It is said that the samurai of Satsuma slept with their feet pointing in the direction of Edo in order to show their contempt for the Tokugawa.[17] Also, their remote geographical locations were actually an advantage because the bakufu had less control over these areas than many other areas whose locations were strategically important. Satsuma, for example, greatly benefited from trade with China through the Ryukyu kingdom, which was ruled by the Satsuma lord. Their relative wealth allowed them to purchase new weapons from the West.

All of this made Satsuma and Choshu especially dangerous to the Tokugawa. Fortunately for the bakufu, Satusma did not get along with Choshu until the mid-1860s due to their jealousy against each other, and their disagreements over Japan's foreign policy. Choshu's leadership was increasingly influenced by radical samurai, known as *shishi* (men of high purposes), who had anti-bakufu and anti-foreign mentalities. Their leading spokesman was Yoshida Shoin (1830–1859), a scholar who studied "Dutch Learning," a term used to describe Japan's knowledge of the West through the Dutch, Neo-Confucianism, and military strategy, although he was a loyal adherent to Japan's own Shintoism. He believed that the old bakufu system was completely incapable of solving national crises after Perry's arrival, and his thinking strongly influenced his students, including the architects of the Meiji Restoration and future national leaders such as Kido Koin (also known as Kido Takayoshi, 1833–1877), Ito Hirobumi (1841–1909), and Yamagata Aritomo (1838–1922), all of whom came from Choshu. Shoin also endorsed the idea of *sonno* (honor the emperor), which, together with that of *joi* (expel the barbarians), became popular slogans at the time.[18]

The rise of Choshu and Satsuma coincided with the emergence of the imperial court at the center of national politics. The moderate Choshu leaders were the first to propose an idea of *kobu gattai* (union of court and shogun) and tried to serve as a mediator between the bakufu in Edo and the imperial court in Kyoto, but they were soon by-passed by the representatives from Satsuma, who approached the shogunal government with more specific ideas. The idea of *kobu gattai* was soon adopted by the *fudai daimyo*, Ii Naosuke (1815–1860), who became the leader of the Council of Senior Advisors to the shogun. Ii tried to restore the power back to the Tokuguwa by ordering the arrest and execution of those who disagreed with his policy. His victims included Yoshida Shoin. In retaliation to the death of their master, some now masterless samurai assassinated Ii in 1860, and thus deprived the Tokugawa bakufu of their last strong leader.

Meanwhile, radical *shishi* strongly influenced the *han* politics of Choshu, although the lord of Satsuma managed to keep his *han* leadership free from the influence of radical samurai. Choshu's representative at court persuaded the emperor to give a deadline to the shogun to adopt the *joi* policy. When that failed, Choshu alone opened fire against foreign ships, which led to the destruction of Choshu forts by American and French warships. After several failed anti-Western incidents, the *shishi* in Choshu dropped their anti-Western orientation. Ito Hirobumi and others went to England to study Western technology, and Choshu leaders were determined to strengthen their military with Western warships and weapons.

In 1864, the Tokugawa organized a punitive expedition force of 150,000 strong against Choshu, and this led to a brief civil war within Choshu. The conservatives returned to power in Choshu and negotiated a compromise with the bakufu, but the radical samurai under the leadership of Kido refused to cooperate with the *han* government and eventually took control of the Choshu capital. In order to bring the rebellious Choshu samurai under control, the shogun ordered the second expedition against Chusho in August 1866. The shogunal forces, however, were weaker than they had been during the first expedition against Choshu. Satsuma, whose representatives in Kyoto had already entered into a secret agreement with the representatives of Choshu in March of that year, refused to participate in the second expedition.[19] Failing to rally enough support, the expedition forces were unable to subjugate Choshu's resistance and were eventually compelled to sue for peace.

The second punitive expedition against Choshu was a fiasco for the bakufu. When a single *han* could defeat the shogunal forces, it would only be a matter of time before Tokugawa control ended. A few simultaneous events in 1867 led to a great change in Japan's leadership structure. Keiki, a reform-minded politician, assumed the position of shogun in January 1867. Realizing that the bakufu was losing its power over the *daimyo*, Keiki accepted a proposal, known later as "Tosa Memorial" from the *daimyo* of Tosa, another *tozama han*, to return his political power to the emperor in exchange of heading the new government. Meanwhile, the leadership in Kyoto changed when the Emperor Komei died in early 1867 and passed the throne to his fourteen-year-old son, Mutsuhito, known later as the Meiji (enlightened rule) Emperor. Having learned the content of the "Tosa Memorial," Satsuma and Choshu representatives acted promptly against the Tokugawa. With the help of a court noble, Iwakura Tomomi (1825–1883), they obtained an "imperial rescript," which called for the destruction of the Tokugawa Bakufu.[20]

In January 1868, an imperial restoration occurred when the Emperor Meiji entered Edo, where the Tokugawa headquarters were located, and renamed it Tokyo, "the east capital." Keiki retreated from Edo to Osaka to avoid conflict. Some shogunal forces put up a fight, but were soon subjugated by the forces of Satsuma and Choshu. By May 1869, all of the shogunal forces surrendered, and Japan was under the control of the revolutionaries.[21]

CREATION OF A NEW GOVERNMENT

The Meiji Restoration in 1868 was a revolutionary event in modern Japanese history. The restoration had far more overreaching consequences than simply restoring political power back into the hands of the emperor. What happened after the restoration was, in a sense, a socio-political revolution that totally changed Japan from an isolationist society dominated by native values to a modern state influenced by Western thinking and practices.

This amazing transition was largely the work of a group of young, audacious, and visionary Meiji leaders. The Emperor Meiji was still too young to provide effective rule, even though the entire revolution was carried out in his name. Other than a few court nobles, such as Prince Iwakura, most of the new leaders had been relatively low-ranking samurai in Satsuma and Choshu, two leading *tozama han* of the Tokugawa era. The new leaders were young and ambitious. Prince Iwakura, the oldest, was forty-three in 1868, and Ito, the youngest, was only twenty-seven.[22] Their relatively humble origins had deprived them of any chance to have real power in the *baku-han* system, and thus made it easy for them to detach themselves from the Tokugawa bakufu. It was their loyalty to the emperor that had justified their move against the bakufu. As a result, they were extremely loyal to the emperor, without whom they would not have any legitimate power.

1868–1870. Artist Unknown

The young Meiji Emperor and others

The transition started with the destruction of the Tokugawa's *baku-han* system, and this was achieved in a relatively short period. In March 1869, the two most powerful Meiji leaders, Kido Koin and Okubo Toshimichi (1830–1878), successfully persuaded their *daimyo* in Choshu and Satsuma, respectively, to return their domains to the emperor. Many *daimyo* followed suit, and those who did not were ordered to do so in July.[23] By August 1871, the *baku-han* system was completely abolished. The new government divided all of Japan into three metropolitan areas (*fu*) and seventy-two prefectures (*ken*), and appointed governors for these areas. Many of these governors, however, were former *daimyo*.

With these swift political changes came widespread social changes. As early as April 1867, the new leaders asked the emperor to issue a five-article "Charter Oath." One of the articles promised equal rights to all of the Japanese. "The common people, no less than the civil and military officials, shall each be allowed to pursue his own calling so that there may be no discontent."[24] Accordingly, the new government removed class distinctions in 1869; allowed commoners to have a family name in 1870; and promised all Japanese full legal equality in 1871. As a result, the samurai lost all of their social and economic privileges, and, after 1876, were even forbidden to carry their swords, the symbol of their privilege during the Tokugawa era. In 1876, after the *baku-han* system was abolished, the government promised to pay stipends in the form of government bonds to the samurai, but their stipends were reduced to roughly half of what had already been reduced by their previous *han* leaders. Many samurai soon sank into poverty, and the samurai as a class gradually extinguished.

The destruction of the bakufu and the *baku-han* system was accomplished with relative ease, but the construction of a new system to replace the Tokugawa system proved to be far more difficult. There were no precedents in Japanese history for the new leaders to follow, and none of them had extensive administrative experience. It took more than two decades of trial and error before a new system was finalized with the promulgation of the Meiji Constitution in 1890.

By the time of the Meiji Restoration, the Meiji leaders had grown out of their crude *joi* mentality, and the Japanese in general had accepted the fact that Japan needed to learn from the West if it wanted to avoid the fate that many other Asian countries were forced to accept. The Meiji government set a new goal for the country, *fukoku kyohei* (a rich country and strong army). A new centralized armed force was established, consisting mostly of samurai and soldiers from Choshu and Satsuma. In January 1873, a universal conscription law, prepared by Yamagata Aritomo, was issued, requiring that all men above the age of twenty-five serve at least three years of active military duty. This law, according to Fairbank and others, was the most revolutionary step towards modernizing Japan. Under the Tokugawa, commoners were banned from participating in military activities. In the era of *Bakumatsu*, Choshu broke this law and drafted peasants into its army, and this resulted in Choshu's defeat of the shogunal army in 1866. Now the entire military system was centralized and expanded, laying a solid foundation for Japan to modernize its military forces.[25]

The two most difficult issues for the Meiji government were its foreign policy and the structure of the new government. The focus of the foreign policy of the new government was to eliminate the unequal treaty system by revising the treaties signed earlier with the Western powers. As early as 1871, Prince Iwakura led a government delegation, including Kido, Okubo, and Ito, to the United States and Europe in an effort to seek treaty revisions, while also studying Western systems. The first purpose of this two-year mission failed, but the group was able to gain first-hand knowledge of the West.

A crisis over Japan's foreign policy toward Korea broke out in 1873, before the Iwakura mission returned to Japan. In light of the discontent of the samurai, who were being deprived of their social and economic privileges, some Meiji leaders believed that a foreign war would help to boost the samurai's pride. At the time, Korea was an easy target, since it had rejected Japan's request to improve the relations between the two countries.[26] Saigo Takamori (1828–1877), who was probably the most conservative among the Meiji leaders and was sympathetic for the samurai, planned to create an "incident" on Korean Waters as an excuse for Japan to invade Korea. Some new leaders supported Saigo, while others opposed the plan. When the word about Saigo's plan reached Iwakura, who was still in Europe, he immediately sent Kido and Okuba back to Japan in the middle of 1873 to block Saigo's plan. However, Prince Sanjo Sanetomi (1837–1891), who was in charge of the government, decided to send Saigo to Korea anyway to solicit an "apology" from the Korean government for "insulting the Japanese government."[27] Upon his return to Japan, Iwakura managed to persuade Saigo to reverse his decision and cancel his trip to Korea.

Furious over Iwakura's decision, Saigo resigned from the government and returned to his home of Kagoshima (in former Satsuma *han*). Many samurai followed him back to Satsuma, and by this time, there was widespread discontent among the samurai, who were well educated and had an elitist mentality. Believing that they were left out of the new government, some of them returned to their traditional way of expressing discontent—forcing the issue with swords and guns. Samurai riots broke out in many areas, including the former Choshu and Satsuma *han*. Samurai rebellion reached its peak when Satsuma decided to secede from the new government. About 15,000 soldiers, led by Saigo, marched toward Tokyo with the intention of overthrowing the government and restoring samurai privileges. Many samurai joined the rebellion, making Saigo's forces 42,000 strong.[28] It was the largest samurai rebellion since the Meiji Restoration, but the last one as well. The rebellion was doomed to fail, when Saigo's forces met with a large government army of 60,000 soldiers. Saigo committed *seppuku* and was subsequently condemned as a traitor by the Meiji government. The Meiji Emperor, however, later posthumously pardoned him in 1889. Saigo remains a legendary hero in Japan, and many Japanese still admire him today.

The Satsuma Rebellion is considered the last stand of the samurai, and it brought mixed consequences. Some forms of protest against the government continued, including attacking high officials. In 1878, a sympathizer of Saigo assassinated Okobu who was also from Satsuma but did not join Saigo. Others, however, started to seek nonviolent ways of breaking the dominance of the Satsuma and Choshu clan, also known as a Sat-Cho clique, in the government. These efforts led to the rise of the "people's rights movement" and eventually to the rise of political parties. One leader of this movement was Itagaki Taisuke (1837–1919), a samurai of Tosa and a councilor of state, but resigned from the government in 1873 because of his harsh stand against Korea. Another leader was Okuma Shigenobu (1838–1922), a samurai from Saga and a major competitor of Ito; Okuma was forced out of the central government in 1881. Both of them started to organize political parties through the popular rights movements and advocate a parliamentary system in order to break up the dominance of the Sat-Cho clique of the government.[29]

THE MEIJI CONSTITUTION

The Satsuma Rebellion and the party movements highlighted a central political issue of the early Meiji government: what kind of government should Japan have? From the very beginning, the Meiji leaders understood the need for a representative government, but Japan's tradition of a government run by a few powerful figures remained strong. Between 1868 and 1870, there were attempts to create a deliberative assembly, but none of them was successful.[30] In the early 1880s, Ito and other members of the Sat-Cho clique started to focus on designing a permanent form of government; this happened after they gained control of the government by expelling other politicians, such as Okuma, from the central leadership.

In March 1882, Ito led the Meiji Constitutional Commission to Europe to study the constitutions of European countries. Ito firmly believed that Japan's constitution should not be a simple duplication of any of the Western models. Instead, it should reflect both Western values and Japanese practices. The actual work of drafting a constitution started in 1886, and after two and half years of study and preparation, Ito and his colleagues finished drafting the constitution, which was largely based on the Prussian constitution.[31] One of the major reasons that the conservative German model was especially attractive to Ito was that the Prussian constitution positioned the monarch above the legislature. Ito's loyalty to the Japanese emperor explained why the constitution was eventually presented to the nation as "a gift from the emperor" on February 11, 1890, the official anniversary of the supposed founding of Japan in 660 BCE.[32]

The Meiji Constitution was a combination of Western values and structures, and Japanese practices. Following the German system, Japan would establish a bicameral parliamentary body called the Diet. The members of the upper house, the House of Peers, most of whom were higher-ranking nobles, were to be appointed by the emperor. The members of the lower house, the House of Representatives, would be elected, but only by a small pool of voters. In 1890, some 450,000 Japanese, which was only 5 percent of the adult male population and 1 percent of the entire population, could meet the requirement of paying fifteen yen or more in taxes[33] The House of Representatives would have power over the budget, but its power would be limited. If it failed to pass a new budget, the cabinet would have the option to renew the previous year's budget. Its legislative power would also be limited, because both the emperor and the House of Peers would have veto power. Besides, the Diet would have no power over government officials, who would report directly to the emperor. The Prime Minister and members of the cabinet would be appointed by the emperor, and the cabinet would be directly responsible to the emperor, not the Diet. This "transcendent" nature of the cabinet allowed the *genro* (senior politician), most of whom were from the Sat-Cho clique, to control Japanese politics through the cabinet positions and the office of the prime minister in the name of the emperor.[34] For the next half century, these *genro* served alternately as the prime minister, a variety of other ministers, or as members of the Privy Council, which, according to the Constitution, were to serve as appointed advisors to the emperor.

The Constitution was designed by Ito to "strengthen the authority of the ruler and make it weightier," and, therefore, it recognized the sovereignty of the emperor.[35] The emperor had broad executive authority, including the power to declare war, make peace, and institute treaties. His administrative power, as mentioned above, included the right to appoint officials, including the members of the cabinet and upper-level positions of the Diet. The emperor would hold the right to institute or dissolve the two houses of the Diet. The emperor also had supreme authority over the legislative body, including the power to veto legislation passed by the Diet. The emperor was the supreme commander of the armed forces, which bypassed the Diet and answered directly to the emperor.[36] This proved to be problematic later in the 1920s and 1930s when Japanese military forces went out of control.

As a result, the Meiji Constitution represented many conflicting ideas of Ito and his colleagues. They wanted to see the Constitution shore up the emperor's power, as clearly stated by Ito, on one hand, but to "limit the authority of the ruler and protect the subject's rights," in Ito's own words, on the other.[37] Despite all of these problems, the Meiji Constitution was a remarkably progressive document, considering Japan's feudal background and its zero experience as a democratic system. More importantly, the Meiji Constitution established Japan as a "modern nation" in the eyes of the Western powers. This was soon reflected in Japan's improved relations with the Western powers and would greatly change the orientation of Japan's foreign policy.

MEIJI IMPERIALISM

Two major goals of Japan's foreign policy after 1890 were to gain an equal status with the Western powers through revisions of unequal treaties and to achieve national security. The two were tightly related to each other. Yamamoto, under the influence of his teacher, Yoshida Shoin, strongly advocated the idea that Japan's defense should "lay far beyond the line of sovereignty."[38] He viewed Korea as the biggest threat to Japan's security; this idea was represented in the famous saying—Korea is a dagger pointed at the heart of Japan. This line of thinking brought further tension to already strained relations between Japan, Korea, and China as well, since Korea was still a tribute state to China. Although Saigo's plan of invading Korea was blocked by moderate factions in the government in 1873, Japan secured the treaty of Kanghwa from Korea in 1876, forcing Korea to open three seaports to Japanese trade and grant Japan extraterritorial rights. This was the first unequal treaty that Korea signed with a foreign power, a treaty that was similar to the unequal treaties that the Western powers had imposed on Japan two decades ago. Japanese traders quickly took advantage of this treaty and expanded their exports to and imports from Korea. By the 1870s, about 90 percent of Japan's imports were from Korea.[39]

Meanwhile, Korea, under the Choson Dynasty, suffered from domestic strife. In the 1880s, it was under the control of a powerful regent Yi Ha-ung (1812–1898), often known by his title Tae-wongon (lord of the grand court). The regent was a conservative exclusionist at first, fighting for keeping Korea away from foreign control and rejecting Japan's early request to revise existing relations between the two nations.[40] He was, however, impressed by Japan's achievements after the Meiji Restoration, so he intended to initiate some reforms according to the Japanese model, but a power struggle interrupted his efforts.

After his son, King Kojong (r. 1864–1907) began his rule in 1873, Queen Min and her family became increasingly powerful. Taewongon, who was jealous of the queen's increasing power, was determined to limit the queen's power. The subsequent conflict between the queen's supporters and her detractors led to an insurrection against the queen in 1882. The movement against the queen also had animosity toward Japanese merchants, whose speculations, according to many Koreans, caused a rice shortage in Korea. Several Japanese officers at the Japanese legation lost their lives. Taewongon, who had been out of power since 1873, seized the opportunity to return to leadership. On the request of Queen Min, however, China sent troops under Yuan Shikai to Korea and soon suppressed the uprising and took Taewongon into custody.[41] Japan's war faction under Yamagata also tried to intervene, but by the time they arrived in Korea, the Chinese had already subdued the riot. Japan had to be satisfied with soliciting indemnities from the Korean government. Japan started to strengthen its Imperial Navy with the anticipation of future showdowns with the Chinese over the Korean Peninsula.

In 1884, two Korean reformers, Kim Ok-kyun and Pak Yong-hyo, both of whom were heavily influenced by Fukuzawa Yukichi (1835–1901), an influential scholar of the Meiji era, staged a coup d'état against Queen Min. With secret support from the Japanese legation, they assassinated conservative ministers and threatened the safety of the king and the queen. Chinese forces, which had been present in Korea since 1882, quickly crushed the rebellion, and Japanese ministers fled with the reformers.[42] The Japanese government dispatched their foreign minister, Inoue Kaoru, and two battalions of troops to Seoul, demanding an apology as well as indemnities from the Korean government, since the Korean troops attacked Japanese legation during the suppression of Kim-Pak coup. Public opinion in Japan called for a war with Korea and China. Probably realizing that Japan was not ready for war yet, Ito preferred a more responsible stand. He went to Tianjin to negotiate a peace agreement with China and reached an agreement with Li Hongzhang. The resulting Li-Ito Convention promised the withdrawal of both Chinese and Japanese troops from Korea, and a notification to the other party in future, if either country sent troops to Korea.[43]

The agreement kept both Chinese and Japanese military forces out of Korea for a decade, but in 1904, domestic problems in Korea again caused clashes between Chinese and Japanese troops, and this led to the First Sino-Japanese War (1894–1895). In 1894, another revolt, led by the Tong Hak

Society, who were similar to the Boxers in China in that they were a religiously based secret society with a strong anti-foreign, especially anti-Japanese, mentality, broke out in Southern Korea. The Korean government asked China for help again. Upon receiving the information about the Chinese move from the Japanese legation in Seoul, Japan immediately dispatched troops to Korea even before they received notification from China. The Japanese troops seized the Korean palace, put Taewongon in power, and through him, asked the Chinese troops to withdraw.[44] On July 25, the Chinese navy and Japanese navy engaged in a battle off the Korean coast, and Japanese battleships overwhelmed the Chinese vessels. Several days later, on August 1, Japan declared war against China. The Japanese army moved into Pyongyang in northern Korea and proceeded into Manchuria, China. After the Japanese navy defeated the Chinese Beiyang fleet and gained control of the Yellow Sea in September, Japan's Second Army Corps was shipped across the sea to the Liaodong Peninsula.[45] As the Japanese troops formed a threat to Beijing toward the end of 1894, China was willing to negotiate a settlement.

1894. Oomoto

Picture taken during the First Sino-Japanese War

In March 1895, Li Hongzhang arrived in Shimonoseki to negotiate a treaty with Japan. The treaty which was agreed upon is known as the Treaty of Shimonoseki. According to this treaty, China would recognize Korea's "independence"; cede the Liaodong Peninsula, Formosa (Taiwan), and the Pescadores (Penghu Islands) to Japan; pay an indemnity of 200 million taels; open an additional four seaports to Japanese trade; and allow Japanese ships to navigate the Yangtze river, and so on.[46] Japan's victory over China in the First Sino-Japanese War undoubtedly placed Japan with the Western powers as a modern world power. In 1900, Japan joined other Western powers in the International Relief Expedition to China, and Japan actually provided about half of the total number of the expedition forces.[47]

Japan's progress impressed the Western powers, who would reconsider their relations with Japan. In 1894, Great Britain was the first to accept Japan's plea for revising the early unequal treaties and relinquished their extraterritorial privileges in 1899. Other Western powers followed the British example, and Japan regained complete control of its tariffs in 1911.[48] Japan became the first Asian country to sign treaties with Western powers as an equal partner. Through the Anglo-Japanese Alliance in 1902, both countries agreed to recognize each other's special interests in East Asia: Britain's in China and Japan's in Korea. They also agreed that each would remain neutral if the other nation was under attack by a third power. With this promise from Britain, Japan would be able to maneuver against another dangerous competitor in East Asia, Russia, whose interest in both Manchuria and Korea would be a great threat to Japan's goal of obtaining security beyond its borders.[49]

Russia showed its calculative animosity toward Japan at the end of the First Sino-Japanese War. After Japan and China concluded the Treaty of Shimonoseki, Russia, in alliance with two other Western powers, Germany and France, intervened on "China's behalf," forcing Japan to return the Liaodong Peninsula to China. Japan could, according to these three powers, ask China instead to pay more money as indemnity. Japan was very reluctant, but had no other choice but to comply. Obviously, Japan was not strong enough to confront three Western powers simultaneously. The Triple Intervention greatly hurt Japan's national pride.[50] Added to this humiliation was the very next year, Russia's obtaining of a ninety-nine year lease over the same Liaodong Peninsula from China through a secret treaty, the Li–Lobanov Treaty. The agreement also gave Russia the right to build railroads in Manchuria, which would connect the Russian Trans-Siberian Railway to Vladivostok. In return, Russia agreed to defend China against future Japanese attacks.[51]

Meanwhile, Russian influence on Korea was on the rise. In 1895, the Japanese minister to Korea had Queen Min assassinated. The king fled to the Russia legation in Seoul to avoid possible Japanese plots against him. The fact that Russia became the protector of the king made Japan more suspicious of Russia's intentions in Korea, even though Russia had agreed not to "hinder the development of commercial and industrial relations between Japan and Korea," when Russia signed a couple of agreements with Japan. To many Japanese leaders, a war with Russia had become inevitable.

On August 9, 1904, Japan launched a surprise attack on a Russian fleet at Port Arthur on the Liaodong Peninsula and declared war two days later. This was very similar to the situation of Japan's surprise attack on an American fleet at Pearl Harbor nearly four decades later. Caught by surprise, the Russian fleet was quickly crippled. Japan scored a few victories at first, because it had the advantage of having the war close to Japan. Without any interference from China, it was easy for Japan to transport its troops to China. In 1904, it had about 189,000 in active service and 850,000 in total trained manpower.[52]

The Japanese Navy had also been greatly strengthened after the Meiji Restoration and after the First Sino-Japanese War; it was equipped with modern British-built ships. Russia, on the other hand, was caught by surprise because they did not expect a Japanese attack, even though they may have noticed Japan's early maneuver toward Port Arthur. Russia only had about 135,000 troops east of Lake Baikal when the war started, and the Trans-Siberian Railroad had not been completed. Russia could only transport, at the most, about 7,000 soldiers a month to the Liaodong Peninsula.[53]

The land war, however, proved to be difficult for the Japanese army. Russia after all was a strong Western power with enormous firepower. Japan suffered 56,000 casualties at the Battle of Port Arthur and about 70,000 at the Battle of Mukden, when nearly 600,000 Russian and Japanese soldiers fought hard against each other. Both sides were exhausted after their combined casualties reached 150,000 at the Battle of Mukden.[54] In effect, as early as January 1905, President Theodore Roosevelt of the United States took the initiative to invite both Russia and Japan to the United States to have a peace negotiation. Japanese officials seemed to be willing to accept the offer, but Russia was not ready to settle yet, because they were expecting reinforcement from the Baltic Fleet, which was on its way to the Liaodong Peninsula. After its eighteen thousand mile trek, the Baltic Fleet arrived at the Tsushima Strait between Japan and Korea in May 1905. However, it only sailed into an ambush by the Japanese navy under Admiral Togo, who had been waiting for the Russians there. Within twenty-four hours, the Japanese fleet scored a total victory against the Baltic Fleet, destroying twenty Russian ships and damaging another eleven.[55] Completely exhausted by the late summer of 1905, both countries were willing to accept the early offer of President Roosevelt. The Treaty of Portsmouth was signed in September 1905. Russia agreed to transfer its lease of the Liaodong Peninsula and the southern section of the Chinese Eastern Railroad to Japan. Russia would also cede the southern half of Sakhalin Island to Japan and recognize Japan's "paramount political, military, and economic interests" in Korea.[56] Japan, however, could not obtain any indemnities for war loss because the Tsar of Russia simply refused to pay any money to Japan. This very much overshadowed Japan's victory over Russia. Japan was frustrated since their national debt jumped during the war from 600 million to 2.4 billion yen. Japan, however, had no leverage in forcing Russia to budge. President Roosevelt later received the Nobel Prize for Peace for his successful mediation to end the Russo-Japanese War.[57]

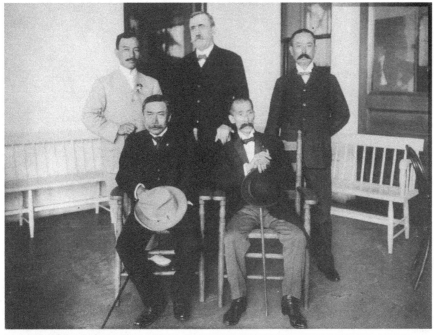

Courtesy of Library of Congress

Japanese delegation to Portsmouth w/Willard Denison

In a subsequent secret agreement with the United States, Japan gained consent from the United States for its control of Korea and in return, Japan promised not to interfere with the United States' affairs in the Philippines. This further deprived Korea of the possibility of soliciting international support. Two months after the Russo-Japanese War was over, Korea was forced to accept being a Japanese protectorate, and Ito Hirobumi became the first Resident General of Korea. The Koreans, however, never stopped their resistance against Japan. Between July 1907 and July 1908, for example, some 11,962 Korean rioters were killed. In October 1909, a Korean patriot assassinated Ito at the Harbin railroad station in China. Japan reacted with a formal annexation of Korea as a colony in August 1910.[58]

The Emperor Meiji died in 1912 and thus, closed the Meiji era, an era that marked Japan's successful transformation into a modern country. Japan's victories in the First Sino-Japanese War and the Russo-Japanese War had firmly established Japan as a world power. It had fully realized its Meiji dream of building Japan into a "rich country" with a "strong military." The Japanese Empire now included the Japanese home territory, the Ryukyu Islands, Taiwan, the Pescadores, Korea in the south, and the Kuril Islands and southern part of the Sakhalin Island in the north. However, the Meiji Imperialism, as a result of Japan's pursuit of an empire and a status as a great world power, led the country onto a bumpy road toward an uncertain future.

For more information about the topics discussed in this chapter, please visit the website for this textbook. This website can be accessed from http://www.grtep.com/.

1 Fairbank et al., *Tradition*, 399–400.
2 Fairbank et al., *Tradition*, 400.
3 Fairbank et al., *Tradition*, 400–401.
4 Fairbank et al., *Tradition*, 406–407.
5 Fairbank et al., *Tradition*, 408.
6 Fairbank et al., *Tradition*, 409.
7 Fairbank et al., *Tradition*, 414.
8 Hane, *Modern Japan*, 65–66.
9 Fairbank et al., *Tradition*, 485.
10 Fairbank et al., *Tradition*, 486–487; and Hane, *Modern Japan*, 67.
11 Fairbank et al., *Tradition*, 487; and Hane, *Modern Japan*, 69–71.
12 McClain, *Japan*, 138.
13 Fairbank et al., *Tradition*, 488.
14 Louis G. Perez, *The History of Japan* (Westport, CT: Greenwood Press, 1998), 86.
15 Andrew Gordon, *A Modern History of Japan*, 2nd ed., (Oxford: Oxford University Press, 2009), 58.
16 Fairbank et al., *Tradition*, 494.
17 Perez, *Japan*, 87.
18 Fairbank et al., *Tradition*, 494.
19 Fairbank et al., *Tradition*, 499–500.
20 Hane, *Modern Japan*, 80.
21 Fairbank et al., *Tradition*, 500–501.
22 Fairbank et al., *Tradition*, 502.
23 Fairbank et al., *Tradition*, 505–506.
24 Fairbank et al., *Tradition*, 503.
25 Fairbank et al., *Tradition*, 506–507.
26 Fairbank et al., *Tradition*, 510.
27 Hane, *Modern Japan*, 122.
28 Hane, *Modern Japan*, 115; and Schirokauer, *Japanese Civilization*, 464.
29 Fairbank et al., *Tradition*, 536–540.
30 Fairbank et al., *Tradition*, 535.
31 Fairbank et al., *Tradition*, 540–543.
32 Hane, *Modern Japan*, 129; and Fairbank et al., *Tradition*, 544.
33 Fairbank et al., *Tradition*, 543–544.
34 Gordon, *Modern History*, 91–92.
35 Hane, *Modern Japan*, 139.
36 McClain, *Japan*, 204.
37 Hane, *Modern Japan*, 129.
38 Fairbank et al., *Tradition*, 552.
39 Hane, *Modern Japan*, 171.
40 Hsu, *Modern China*, 334.
41 Hane, *Modern Japan*, 158; and Hsu, *Modern China*, 335–336.
42 Hane, *Modern Japan*, 158–159; and Hsu, *Modern China*, 337–338.
43 Hane, *Modern Japan*, 158–159.
44 Gordon, *Modern History*, 114–116; and Hsu, *Modern China*, 338–339.
45 Hane, *Modern Japan*, 160; and Hsu, *Modern China*, 340–341.
46 Hane, *Modern Japan*, 161.
47 Fairbank et al., *Tradition*, 555–556.
48 Fairbank et al., *Tradition*, 554.
49 Hane, *Modern Japan*, 173.
50 McClain, *Japan*, 301–302.
51 Hane, *Modern Japan*, 178.
52 Hane, *Modern Japan*, 174–175.
53 Hane, *Modern Japan*, 175.

54 McClain, *Japan*, 304; and Hane, *Modern Japan*, 176.
55 McClain, *Japan*, 305–306; and Hane, *Modern Japan*, 176.
56 Fairbank et al., *Tradition*, 556.
57 Hane, *Modern Japan*, 178–179.
58 McClain, *Japan*, 310–312.

Chapter 14 East Asia in the Era of War and Revolution

The success of the 1911 Revolution ushered in a new era in Chinese history, a republican era (1911–1916). The first Republic of China was established on January 1, 1912, but was soon overshadowed by Yuan Shikai's dictatorship and betrayal. Yuan eventually terminated the Chinese Republic when he restored a short-lived imperial system in China in 1916. The subsequent chaos plunged China into an era of disintegration dominated by warlords, who controlled separate areas of China and competed with each other for more power, wealth, and territory.

YUAN SHIKAI AND THE PROBLEM OF THE REPUBLIC

From the very beginning, Yuan Shikai did not intend to follow his pledge to protect the republic and prevent a restoration of the monarchy. His first step in pursuing his monarchical dream was to grasp as much power as possible, making the premier and the cabinet nothing but his puppets. Positions of important ministers, such as that of Foreign Affairs, Internal Affairs, War, and Navy, were filled with his subordinates; whereas, Huang Xing, the Minister of War under Sun, was only reappointed governor of Nanjing. Yuan later refused to subsidize Huang's soldiers in Nanjing, effectively forcing him to dissolve them.[1] Yuan then turned against the Nationalist Party, which was established in 1912. Under the leadership of Song Jiaoren, the Nationalist Party achieved a sweeping victory in the first parliamentary elections in December 1912, taking 269 seats out of a total of 596 in the Lower House.[2] After failing to win Song's support through bribery, Yuan had Song assassinated in March 1913 and dissolved the Nationalist Party in November. The "Second Revolution" occurred when Yunnan and six other provinces declared independence in July and August 1913. Yuan, however, was able to suppress these rebellions without much trouble.[3] Sun Yat-sen escaped to Japan after the "Second Revolution" failed.

In order to gain foreign support, Yuan secretly negotiated an agreement, known as the Twenty One Demands, with Japan, agreeing to yield many specific privileges to Japan. In return, Japan started to express interest in supporting a "constitutional monarchy" in China. On December 13, 1915, Yuan announced that he would rule as an emperor, and his new reign, Hongxian (the Glorious Constitution), would start on January 1, 1916. What Yuan Shikai did not expect was the tenacity of the opposition to his restoration of the monarchy in China. Even his closest followers refused to accept the new appointments at his new court. Less than two weeks after his announcement, Yunnan announced independence on December 25, followed by Guizhou on December 27. On March 22, 1916, Yuan was forced to give up his new reign, and a few months later, he died of uremia.[4]

PERIOD OF WARLORDISM

China began to fall apart immediately after Yuan's death in 1916. Li Yuanhong, who was Yuan's vice president, took over the presidency, but many immediately challenged his legitimacy, arguing that Yuan was only acting as the president, but was not the true president since he had not gained the position in accordance to the Constitution of 1914. As a compromise, Li appointed Duan Qirui, Yuan's former assistant, as premier.[5] Duan became the most powerful figure in the government, but was not powerful enough to control all of the warlords. After the death of Yuan, the Beijing government, which was sometimes known as the Beiyang government because most of the "presidents" were former generals of Yuan Shikai's Beiyang Army, could hardly function as a national government.

The warlords during this period (1916–1927) were from a variety of backgrounds and controlled their domains differently. Many of them, like Duan Qirui and Cao Kun, had risen through the ranks of Yuan's Beiyang army; others had held the government position of provincial governor-general, such as Yan Xishan in Shanxi; and still others were simply self-made, such as Zhang Zuolin in Manchuria.[6] In terms of ideology, some of them were loyal Confucian scholars, such as Wu Peifu, but others, such as Feng Yuxiang, were attracted to Christianity and other Western ideas. Their political views also varied greatly; some of them recognized the legitimacy of the Beijing government, but others preferred Sun's government in Guangdong. Some of them ruled their area virtuously and were relatively benign to the local people, whereas others, such as Zhang Zongchang, one of the most brutal and ruthless warlords, simply exercised brutality and heavily exploited the local people. These warlords often had connections to different foreign powers in order to solicit financial aid from foreign governments.

The 1920s saw a civil war among the warlords. The most powerful warlords formed cliques in order to compete for control of the central government. Dun Qirui, who initially dominated the Beijing government, headed the Anhui Clique, named after Dun's hometown; Feng Guozhang, another former attaché of Yuan Shikai, who felt jealous of Dun's power, formed the Zhili Clique; and Zhang Zuolin in Manchuria led the Fengtian Clique. The competition and wars among these cliques resulted in frequent changes in the Beijing government. There were also forces independent of the above cliques, such as those of Yan Xishan in Shanxi, Li Zongren in Guangxi, and above all, Sun Yat-sen in Guangdong, where he established a military government.[7]

INTELLECTUAL MOVEMENT AND THE RISE OF THE POLITICAL PARTY

The period between 1917 and 1923 also saw a rigorous intellectual movement in China, led by the returning students from the West. These returning students brought back to China a wide range of Western ideas, from John Dewey's pragmatism to Karl Marx's Communism. They called for a critical re-evaluation of Chinese heritage and aroused Chinese nationalism. The resulting New Culture Movement and the May Fourth Movement in 1919 dramatically changed the views of many Chinese, who adopted radical ideas such as democracy and nationalism.

Among the most prominent returning students were Chen Duxiu (1879–1942) and Cai Yuanpei (1976–1940) from France, and Hu Shi (1891–1962) from the United States. Cai Yuanpei studied in Germany between 1907 and 1911, before he returned to China to join the 1911 Revolution. He left

China again, this time to study in France, after Yuan Shikai took the presidency. In 1916, he returned from France to become chancellor of Beijing University. During his tenure, he turned the university into a cradle of revolutionary intellectual movements. Chen Duxiu stayed in France between 1907 and 1910, and returned to China for the 1911 Revolution. After the failure of the Second Revolution, he fled to Japan, but returned to China in 1915 to protest Yuan Shikai's acceptance of Japan's Twenty-one Demands. Hu Shi won a government scholarship to study in the United States in 1909 and returned to China in 1916 with a BA from Cornell University and a PhD from Columbia University. The Chancellor Cai of Beijing University hired both Chen and Hu after they returned to China. Chen became the Dean of the School of Letters, and Hu became a professor of literature.

Under the leadership of the Chancellor Cai, professors at Beijing University became the impetus behind the New Cultural Movement, which spread quickly across the country. Chen and others assumed a strong anti-Confucian stand. Through new journals, such as *the New Youth*, a monthly periodical that Chen founded in 1915 in Shanghai, Chen called on Chinese youth to break away from China's old traditions. "I would rather see the ruin of our traditional 'national quintessence' than have our race of the present and future extinguished because of its unfitness for survival," claimed Chen.[8] Hu Shi, an energetic advocate of scientific thinking and pragmatism, also believed that Confucianism had become "out of touch with the realities of the modern world."[9] His greatest contribution to the New Culture Movement, however, was his initiation of a dramatic change to the Chinese language: replacing the Chinese classical writing style with the vernacular style of writing or *baihua*, in Chinese. He successfully invented a simple and plain style of writing, which immediately became popular and greatly helped the radical Chinese intellectuals influence more people with their novel ideas.[10] It is in this social and intellectual environment that the students at Beijing University took the lead in a massive national outburst, the May Fourth Movement, in 1919.

The movement was triggered by the signing of the Treaty of Versailles that ended World War I. China did not directly participate in the war, but after 1916 the Chinese government under Duan Qirui sent many Chinese laborers to France. By late 1917, 54,000, and by late 1918, 96,000 Chinese laborers had been in France and Great Britain, building barracks and hospitals, digging trenches, and handling logistical needs. In addition to the casualties caused by German bombs, many of them fell ill because of poor working conditions and "strange food."[11] With these men's sacrifices, the Chinese expected to get something in return after the war. The Western powers, however, ignored China's request to get back the Shandong Peninsula from Germany and instead, allowed Japan to control that area in China. When the news reached China, about three to five thousands students of Beijing University and thirteen other universities gathered at Tiananmen Square before they marched to the foreign legation to protest Japan's takeover of the Shandong Peninsula. They later broke into the house of the Chinese Minister of Communications and burned it down. In subsequent conflicts with the police, one student was wounded and later died in the hospital, and ten were arrested. Inspired by the students, other Chinese also joined in the protest. The widespread discontent eventually forced the Chinese government delegates in France to change their stand and refuse to sign the Treaty of Versailles.[12] This massive protest, known later as the May Fourth Movement of 1919, was the first outburst of Chinese nationalism. Many Chinese students, especially those at Beijing University, used the May Fourth Movement as an expression of discontent over Western imperialism, as well as with the Chinese government.

The most important political movement in China in the 1920s was the rise of political parties. After Russia's Bolshevik Revolution in 1917, the idea of Communism attracted some intellectuals, including Chen Duxiu, who was arrested during the May Fourth Movement because of his fervent support of the students; he was forced to resign from Beijing University after his release. Chen Duxiu went to Shanghai where he became interested in Marxist theory and had *The Communist Manifesto* translated into Chinese and published in 1920.[13] He organized the Marxist Study Society in May 1920, which was a forerunner of the Chinese Communist Party. Li Dazhao, who was a librarian at Beijing University, organized the Society for the Study of Socialism; among his followers was the young and ambitious Mao Zedong. With the encouragement of agents from the Third Communist International, or Comintern for short, Chen in the South and Li in the north became important leaders of the Communist movement.[14]

On July 1, 1921, the First Congress of the Chinese Communist Party (the CCP) was secretly held in Shanghai with twelve delegates representing fifty-seven party members. It was first held in the French Concession of Shanghai, but moved to the countryside after they became suspicious of being followed. Chen Duxiu and Li Dazhao were honored as the co-founders of the party, and Chen Duxiu was elected party secretary-general, even though neither Chen nor Li attended the meeting. Some Chinese students in Japan and in France also formed Communist groups. The French group was particularly important to the Chinese Communist movement, and several important future CCP Leaders, including Zhou Enlai, Deng Yingchao (Zhou's wife), Li Fuchun, and Deng Xiaoping were among this group.[15]

Meanwhile, Sun Yat-sen in Canton also sought ways to reorganize his party and to carry out his goal of achieving national unity through the military. Sun was disappointed with his party, the Chinese Revolutionary Party (1914–1918), a forerunner of the Nationalist Party, which was weak and had become factionalized. He spent several years reorganizing his party, emphasizing discipline and personal loyalty in his party. After he returned in 1916 from Japan, which he had fled to after the failure of the Second Revolution, he founded a military government in Canton in 1917. Sun, however, withdrew from the government the next year. In 1920, he found protection from a Guangdong warlord, Chen Jiongming, and became president of the "Chinese People's Government." Chen, however, drove Sun out of Canton in 1922, because he did not agree with Sun's plan of national unification.[16] Sun left Canton for Shanghai where he focused on reorganizing the Goumindang (GMD, or Kou-min-tang, KMT, the Nationalist Party) and made it more appealing to various social groups for support.

Equally annoying to Sun was his lack of financial support from foreign powers. Japan supported the Anhui Clique held by Dun Qirui, and Britain favored the Zhili Clique under Wu Peifu. In his frustration, Sun turned his attention to the Soviet Union after the Bolshevik Revolution in 1917. Sun was impressed by the success of the revolution led by the Soviet Communist Party, which was well organized and disciplined. He was equally impressed by Lenin's anti-imperialist stand. Lenin openly announced that his government would renounce Russia's privileges in China obtained under the Tsarist governments. Meanwhile, the recently established Chinese Communist Party also took a strong anti-imperialist stand.

Sun, however, firmly believed in a nationalist revolution instead of a communist revolution. His ideas for a nationalist revolution were represented by his "Three People's Principles," which were nationalism, democracy, and people's livelihood. When a Comintern agent approached him and indicated that the Comintern would like to negotiate with him, Sun insisted that his different perception of China's future needed to be specified in the formal agreement. On January 26, 1923, Sun signed the Sun-Joffe Agreement with Adolf Joffe, who had been sent to China by the Comintern to work with Sun. The agreement made it clear that China would not carry out a communist revolution at present, and that the Soviet Union would reconfirm its renunciation of the Tsarist privileges in China and support Sun in achieving national unification.[17] At the same time, the Comintern instructed the members of the CCP to join the GMD individually in order to support Sun's national revolution. This established the first alliance between the GMD and the CCP, known as the First United Front.

The first National Congress of the GMD was held in January 1924, during which Sun announced his three policies of "Allied with the Soviet Union; Allied with the CCP; and Support the Workers and Peasants." With Soviet support and his newly strengthened military forces under the control of his best assistant, Chiang Kai-shek, Sun was ready to carry out a northern expedition to achieve national unification, but his illness prevented him from achieving that goal. Sun died in Shanghai in March 1925.[18]

UNIFICATION OF CHINA UNDER THE NANJING GOVERNMENT

Sun's death greatly overshadowed the future of the First United Front, the alliance between the GMD and the CCP. The right wing in the GMD, who, from the very beginning, did not want to cooperate with the Communists, became more resolute. The GMD's future leader, Jiang Jieshi (Chiang Kai-shek), was also deeply suspicious about the Communists' intentions. Even though Sun did not name Jiang as his successor, Jiang Jieshi, as the commandant of the Whampoa Military Academy, soon emerged as the *de facto* leader of the GMD. Jiang's army, led by Whampoa cadets and supplied with Russian rifles, machine guns, and artillery, soon became the backbone of the GMD military.[19] Under his leadership, the National Revolutionary Army declared the Northern Expedition against the major warlords in July 1926 and pressed northward from Canton. After taking control of Changsha, the capital of Human province, Jiang's troops captured Wuhan on October 10, and in mid-December, they captured Fuzhou, the capital of Fujian province. By the end of the year, the GMD controlled seven provinces: Guangdong, their home base; Hunan, Hubei, Jiangxi, and Fujian by force; and Guangxi and Guizhou through negotiation.[20] In January 1927, the GMD decided to move its government from Canton to Wuhan, and Wang Jingwei (1883–1944), who was sympathetic to the Communist movement and was advised by one of Joseph Stalin's agents, controlled the Wuhan government.

Early the next year, the GMD government in Wuhan directed Jiang to move north to attack Beijing, but Jiang ignored the directives and pressed toward Shanghai instead.[21] By mid-March, his troops had entered Shanghai with the help of the Shanghai General Labor Union, which had organized a general strike in Shanghai under the guidance of the CCP. Jiang, however, had no intention of working with the CCP to support the workers. Shanghai was the financial center of China, where many foreign concessions were located, and many rich entrepreneurs and bankers lived. In order to protect their citizens, a large number of foreign troops and warships were also present in Shanghai. Even before Jiang's march to Shanghai, the Shanghai Chamber of Commerce visited Jiang in Nanchang in late December to offer him financial support. Jiang accepted the offer and entered into a few secret agreements with the banks and commercial circle in Shanghai.[22] On April 10, soon after he controlled Shanghai and Nanjing, Jiang organized a "purge committee" (*qingdang*). In the early morning of April 12, 1927, an anti-union organization in Shanghai, which acknowledged the authority of the foreign powers over the foreign concessions and later supported Jiang's National

Revolutionary Army, raided the headquarters of all the large unions in Shanghai. When Shanghai workers, townspeople, and students staged a protest rally the next day, Jiang's troops fired upon them with machine guns, killing about one hundred people. More purges of union leaders and CCP members followed in the next few weeks.[23]

The Wuhan government dismissed Jiang as commander-in-chief of the National Revolutionary Army on April 17, but Jiang was unshaken. He announced the establishment of his own government in Nanjing the next day. Eventually, in July, Wang Jingwei and his Wuhan government also decided on a total removal of CCP members from the GMD, and this finalized the split between the two parties.[24] Some units under CCP control staged an uprising in Nanchang on August 1, 1927 and then retreated to the mountainous areas in Jiangxi. After both the Nanjing and Wuhan governments purged CCP members, the two governments reconciled, and the Wuhan government was dissolved in February 1928. Jiang resumed his northern expedition, and in June, with the help of warlords Feng Yuxiang and Yan Xishan, he defeated the Manchu warlord, Zhang Zuolin, who controlled the Beijing government at the time, and took control of Beijing.[25] By the end of 1928, Jiang had unified most of China under the GMD government in Nanjing. The GMD government, however, could hardly enjoy any peace before Japan exerted its control over Manchuria.

RISE OF MILITARISM IN JAPAN

By the late Meiji Era, Japan had already embarked on the road to empire building. Japan had already defeated China and Russia, taking control of Korea and Taiwan, and forced Russia to transfer to Japan the railroads that the Russians had built in southern Manchuria. As a result of the Great Depression in the late 1920s, Japan was compelled to rethink their foreign policy. With its rich resources and fertile land, Manchuria drew attention from many Japanese political and military leaders. Driven by a concern for economic security, many Japanese leaders favored a radical expansionist policy, and this, in turn, paved the road for the rise of militarism in Japan.

Some scholars, however, prefer to call the Taisho era (1912–1926) that followed that of Meiji the era of Taisho democracy. They believe that the Taisho era was probably the only period before World War II that the political parties in Japan had some opportunity to prevail in Japanese politics. The Japanese political system, set up by the Meiji Constitution, was "constitutional," but not really "parliamentary."[26] Several groups of elites played important roles in Japan's decision-making process, and some of them, according to the constitution, were independent from the Diet. For example, the chiefs of staff of the army and navy, who reported to the emperor directly, had their "right of autonomous command" and had leverage over the Diet by withdrawing their ministers or refusing to submit new candidates.[27]

Other "extra-legal" bodies included the elites that were close to the emperor, who often controlled the selection of the prime ministers and foreign policies from behind the curtain. Before Yamagata died in 1922, a group of *genro* appointed by the emperor manipulated Japanese politics. The members of the Privy Council, who were also appointed by the emperor, would advise the emperor on the appointment of the prime minister and foreign policy. Yet another elite group was made up of the leading financiers and industrialists, whose businesses were known as *zaibatsu* (financial clique). Most of these business giants rose to prominence after the Meiji Restoration and greatly expanded their businesses during Japan's economic boom between 1890 and 1920. Unlike Western corporations of the time, Japanese *zaibatsu* would often be involved in many different sectors, from mining, to transportation, to marketing, to manufacturing, and to financing. For example, Mitsui, one of the largest *zaibatsu* before 1945, consisted of one holding company and 70 direct corporate affiliates, which in turn, had 265 affiliate companies. The largest Mitsui subsidiary, Mitsui Trading, alone had 126 affiliates.[28]

These elites groups did not just compete with each other. They also cooperated and compromised with each other depending on the situation. Up until 1905, the *genro* mediated among the elites. After 1905, the party movement was on the rise under the leadership of Saionji Kinmochi (1849–1940) and his close protégé, Hara Kei (or Hara Takashi, 1856–1921). After both Ito and Yamagata died, Saionji became one of the most important politicians in Japan. After the Meiji Restoration, he spent several years in France extensively studying European systems. In 1900, Ito formed his own party, known as the *Rikken Seiyukai* (Friends of Constitutional Government) or just the *Seiyukai*. Saionji was among the first people to join the *Seiyukai*. Saionji, due to his European experiences, favored a parliamentary government, believing that, instead of having a cabinet appointed by the emperor, the majority party should have the right to form a party cabinet. In 1900, Saionji replaced Ito as president of the Privy Council and in 1903, Saionji replaced Ito as president of the *Seiyukai*. However, the *Seiyukai* was not successful in gaining power until it was in the hands of Hara Kei, a brilliant party politician in Japan's early party politics. Hara belonged to a different generation than the Meiji leaders. He worked as a newspaper reporter and an officer in the Foreign Services before he became the leader of the *Seiyukai*. Sharing Saionji's view that Japan should be led by a party government, instead of by the oligarchs, Hara worked extremely hard to build his party's power.[29] He formed a coalition with other elite groups and also worked with local elites, especially those in the countryside, who would rally the votes for his party at the local level. From 1905 to 1913, the *Seiyukai* became the only political party that influenced cabinet politics.

The *Seiyukai*'s power peaked in 1918 when Hara was appointed prime minister. The position gave Hara opportunities to push forward his goal of a more democratic government, even though he did not want to change the basic government structure defined by the Meiji Constitution. He increased the autonomy of local governments, which were relatively easy to bring under *Seiyukai* control, and established small electoral districts. He also reduced the minimum amount of taxes a Japanese man had to pay in order to qualify for voting rights from ten to three yen, so that more people in the rural areas could vote.[30] The trend toward making Japan more democratic continued even after Hara's tragic death at the hands of an ultranationalist in 1921. His death temporarily delayed the process of establishing party cabinets, because three non-party prime ministers ran the government between 1922 and 1924. With the blessing of Saionji, the only *genro* left after the death of Yamagata and others, a rule seemed to have been set, before the rise of the militarism, that the party who won a majority in the lower house would automatically take power.[31]

The party government returned in 1924, when Kato Komei (or Kato Takaaki, 1860–1926), who was the president of the *Kenseikai* (renamed the *Minseito* in 1927), a political party established in 1916, was appointed as Prime Minister. Kato's appointment ushered in an eight-year period during which the president of one of the two major parties held the post of prime minister. Although he was conservative in nature and despite his close ties with other elites, Kato introduced impressive measures to regulate the party government during his tenure. The highlight of his achievements was the passage of a universal male suffrage bill in 1925, which increased the electorate from 3 to 12 million.[32] Other accomplishments of the Kato cabinet included new laws that were favorable to workers, including the National Health Insurance Law and the Labor Disputes Mediation Law. Kato also pushed reform concerning the House of the Peers. Although he could not change the constitution to limit the power of the House of Peers, he managed to reduce the number of the positions held by nobility. The military budget was cut from 42 percent of the budget in 1922 to 29 percent in 1925.[33]

After Kato died of pneumonia in 1926, the party government continued until 1931, when the last party prime minister was assassinated. The party government, however, was in trouble long before that. After the power and prestige of the major political parties greatly increased, due to the efforts of such party leaders as Hara and Kato, many top elites, including many in the military, were drawn to a political party. General Tanaka Giichi, a close protégé of Yamagata, for example, became the president of the *Seiyukai* in 1925, and the prime minister in 1927 after he brought the *Seiyukai* back to power. Tanaka's cabinet, however, marked the beginning of the military's increase in power in Japan. Tanaka aggressively worked to combat "dangerous thought," and he would issue an emergency ordinance to enforce his policy if it was blocked by the Diet.[34] His policy toward China was aggressive, and his support to the efforts of the Japanese Kwantung Army in Manchuria to strengthen Japan's position in Manchuria aroused an anti-Japanese mentality in China. In 1928, officers of the Kwantung Army assassinated the Manchurian warlord, Zhang Zuolin, when he was on his way back to Manchuria after being ousted from the Beijing government by the GMD. When the Japanese government became aware of what happened, Tanaka tried to cover up for the Kwantung Army and even lied to the Emperor Hirohito, who ascended to the throne after his father died in 1926. When the truth eventually came out, the emperor was angry and called Tanaka a liar. Tanaka soon resigned from office.[35]

A bigger problem that contributed to the demise of the party government was that Japan's economy was stagnant between 1920 and 1930, after decades of rapid growth. Japan's economy had greatly depended on the Western markets, but after World War I, these markets shrank dramatically. Japan's exports decreased, and this soon resulted in a negative trade balance for Japan. The domestic economy did not fare any better. The price of rice in Japan dropped rapidly after 1913, because of the cheap rice that Japan imported from Korea and Taiwan; this led to a steady drop in the real income of Japanese farmers.[36] By 1929, nearly 40 percent of farming households had to look for extra income, such as raising silk worms to produce raw silk.[37] Government expenditures, which had increased six fold between 1890 and 1913, also dropped because of a decrease in the military budget. In 1926, the domestic economic recession in Japan led to a bank crisis, during which several weaker banks were wiped out.[38]

When the New York stock market collapsed in 1929, Japan's economic depression became even worse. Japan's exports dropped 50 percent from 1929 to 1931. The real income of Japanese workers dropped from an index of 100 in 1926 to 81 in 1930, and to 69 in 1931; and unemployment skyrocketed to three million. The rural areas suffered even more than the urban areas: within a year, from September 1930 to September 1931, the price of raw silk fell 65 percent; and between 1926 and 1931, rural cash income fell from an index of 100 to 33.[39] The gloomy picture of Japan's economy led to severe criticism of the party government. Many started to believe that building a self-sufficient empire through overseas expansion might provide a viable solution to Japan's economic problems. More aggressive foreign policy, in turn, precipitated the rise of militarism in Japan in the 1930s.

As mentioned earlier, military elites were allowed by the Meiji Constitution to act independently, and they were not shy in doing so. During the early "Taisho Political Crisis" in 1912–1913, the resignation of the army minister brought down Saionji's cabinet, and later, the Navy's refusal to provide a navy minister prevented the formation of a functional cabinet for a lengthy period.[40] Under the party cabinets of the 1920s, the power and prestige of the military declined, but in the early 1930s, many Japanese elites leaned toward the military for a solution to Japan's problems. Actually, even the party elites, who may have had different approaches in terms of how to govern Japan, were equally aggressive in terms of foreign policy. In 1915, Kato, who was then the foreign minister, delivered the Twenty-one Demands to China without consulting Yamamoto, who was concerned about stirring up anti-Japanese activities in China.[41] The reasons behind the rise of militarism in the 1930s were quite complicated, although the Japanese military was largely responsible for the misstep of Japan's pre-war foreign policy.

MANCHURIAN INCIDENT AND MANZHOUGUO

Manchuria in northeast China is known for its vast fertile land and rich mineral resources. Japan's expansionists had long harbored desires for the area ever since the First Sino-Japanese War and especially after the Russo-Japanese War. After taking the railroads in southern Manchuria from Russia and the annexing Korea, Manchuria, to many Japanese, especially the officers of Japan's Kwantung Army, seemed to be a logical next step for Japan's foreign expansion.[42] In 1906, after the Russo-Japanese war, the Kwantung Army was created to guard Japan's railroad zone in southern Manchuria, and later, the Kwantung Leased Territory, including Port Arthur and the city of Dalian.[43] Relatively free from home control, the Kwantung Army took the issue in China into their own hands, and by the late 1920s, they were ready to push their plan forward if the Japanese government was not prepared to take action.

In June 1928, some officers in the Kwantung Army assassinated the Manchurian warlord Zhang Zuolin under the assumption that his son, Zhang Xueliang, would be easier to manipulate into collaboration with Japan. Zhang Xueliang, who is often referred to by his nickname, the Young Marshal, was furious about his father's assassination and claimed allegiance, instead, to Jiang Jieshi's Nanjing government.[44] With little hope of persuading the Young Marshal to change to their side, the officers in the Kwantung Army planned to stage another "event" that could be used as an excuse for the army to take actions in Manchuria.

Back in Japan, the Japanese government headed by General Tanaka was sympathetic toward the Kwantung Army officers and even tried to cover up their plot. After the economic depression deepened, many men in a position of authority in the army started to share the Kwantung army's vision of Manchuria. The *zaibatsu* also thought of Manchuria as a logical "extension" of Japan, since as much as 75 percent of the foreign investments in the area were from Japan.[45] These economic overlords, therefore, also favored an expansionist policy. When the Kwantung Army sent an officer to Tokyo to ask for permission to take action in Manchuria, the request won substantial support. However, the emperor, who was concerned about the army's imprudent behavior, asked the Kwantung Army to exercise caution and sent a general to Manchuria to deliver his message. Secretly tipped off by army sympathizers in Tokyo, Kwantung Army officers took the general directly from the airport to a geisha house for a lavish dinner and entertainment before he could deliver the emperor's message.[46]

Around 10 p.m. that day, September 18, 1931, a bomb exploded at a stretch of railroad outside of the city of Mukden, where the Kwantung Army had moved their headquarters after 1928. The damage from the explosion was limited, but a Chinese garrison stationed nearby exchanged fire with the Japanese. Several hours after the incident, the Kwantung Army took control of the entire city.[47] When news of the event reached Tokyo, the civilian cabinet urged the Kwantung Army to exercise restraint and refused the Army Minister's request to send reinforcements to the Kwantung Army. The cabinet's decision, however, had little effect on the Kwantung Army in Manchuria. Japan's army commander in Korea sent his troops to Manchuria on his own authority. Over the next several days, Japanese troops captured one major city after another in Manchuria.

The Mukden Incident could not have happened at a worse time for Jiang's nationalist government. After coming to power, the regime faced the enormous problems of consolidating the power of the GMD and reviving the national economy. In the summer of 1931, Yangtze River floods devastated several provinces and left fourteen million people homeless.[48] Politically and militarily, the GMD regime had not achieved complete national unity. In some areas, the "new warlords" still acted semi-independently, despite their allegiance to the Nationalist government. Also, Communist troops had retreated into the mountainous areas of the Jiangxi province and named their bases there the Jiangxi Soviets. Working closely with the poor peasants in the area, the Communists strengthened their power and military forces within a few years. Jiang Jieshi, who was determined to eliminate the Communist troops, launched five encirclement campaigns against the Jiangxi Soviets between 1930 and 1934.[49] As a result, when the Mukden Incident occurred in 1931, the bulk of Jiang Jieshi's forces were in southern China combating the Communist troops in the Jianggang Mountains in Jiangxi. Jiang gave an order of non-resistance to Zhang Xueliang, the Young Marshal in Manchuria, asking him to retreat his troops south of the Great Wall without engaging the Japanese troops.[50] Instead of fighting directly against the Japanese, Jiang appealed to the League of Nations for help.

An international sanction, however, was slow to come. Most European countries were still struggling to recover from the devastation of World War I, and could not be concerned with what Japan did in the Far East. Both Britain and the United States were actually rather sympathetic to the Japanese government and willingly accepted the notion that the Kwantung Army acted on its own without the permission of the Japanese government. China was largely left alone to handle the situation by itself.[51]

Without effective international sanctions or organized Chinese resistance, Japan gained control of Manchuria in five months. Japan's invasion of Manchuria aroused deep resentment from the Chinese, who organized non-military acts of resistance against Japan, such as boycotting Japanese goods and attacking Japanese shops in Shanghai and other cities. In retaliation, Japanese marines landed in Shanghai in late January and exchanged fire with GMD troops. The Japanese government subsequently ordered the bombing of Shanghai, followed by a full-scale attack on Shanghai, where they met with severe resistance from GMD troops. In May, China and Japan negotiated an armistice, and Japan agreed to withdraw from Shanghai.[52]

In order to legitimize Japan's control of Manchuria, Japan invited Puyi, the last emperor of the Qing dynasty, to come to Manchuria as the head of an independent Manzhoukuo (or Manchukuo, Manchu State), which was officially established on March 9, 1932. China once again appealed to the League of Nations. This time, the League of Nations reacted by sending a commission led by Lord Lytton, a former Viceroy of India, to China to investigate the situation. The report of the Lytton Commission refuted Japan's claim that their troops only acted in order to support a Manchu independence movement. Infuriated with the report, Japan withdrew from the League; this was the first mistake that Japan made, which alienated the United States and other Western allies.[53] Other than a verbal condemnation of Japan's aggression in Manchuria, however, the League of Nations could do nothing about Japan, and this resulted in Japan's further moves into China. Japan further advanced into the Rehe of Hebei province afterwards, and by April, Japan had completed the conquest of the four northeastern provinces of China, and successfully created a buffer zone that separated Manchuria from the rest of China. On March 1, 1934, Puyi was enthroned with the reign title of *Kangde*, which means "prosperity and virtue."

THE XI'AN INCIDENT AND THE SECOND UNITED FRONT

While Japanese troops consolidated their control of Manchuria, Jiang's GMD troops were still busy fighting against the Communists in Jiangxi. His first four encirclement campaigns, which were between 1930 and 1933, failed to drive the Communist troops out of their bases. In the fall of 1934, Jiang started his fifth campaign with 700,000 of his best troops trained by German military advisors. He followed his German advisors' strategy of being "strategically offensive but tactically defensive" and approached the Communist bases slowly but firmly, using the blockhouses that had been built along the roads as their resting points.[54] This strategy worked and soon forced the Communist troops to retreat.

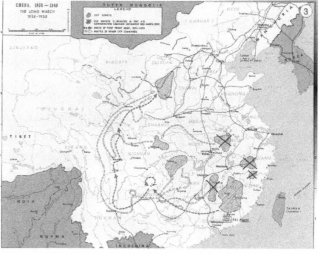

The Jiangxi Soviets and The Long March

History Department of the U. S. Military Academy West Point

In order to avoid being totally annihilated, the Communist leaders decided to evacuate their bases and embark on what would later be known as the Long March toward northern China. About 85,000 Communist soldiers of the First, the Second, and the Fourth Red Armies; 15,000 government and party officials; and thirty-five women, who were wives of high officials, started to leave the Jiangxi Soviets on October 15, 1934. The troops had to choose difficult routes, climbing up the snow-covered mountains of the Tibetan highlands and trekking across grassy swamps in order to avoid a fatal confrontation with GMD troops, who closely pursued them. They lost nearly one tenth of their troops when the Red Army was engaged in a bloody battle with the pursuing GMD troops at the bank of the Xiang River. At another battle, where control of the Luding bridge of the Dadu River was at stake, the Red Army narrowly escaped the fate of annihilation at the hands of local warlords. After a year of enduring struggle, in October 1935, Mao's central Red Army arrived at Yan'an in the Shaanxi province, where other Red Armies joined them. By now, only about 8,000 troops of the original 100,000 had survived this Long March of 25,000 *li* (one *li* equals half of a kilometer).

In early December 1936, Jiang Jieshi flew to Xi'an to arrange a final campaign of annihilation of the greatly weakened Red Army stationed at Yan'an, a county not very far from Xi'an. He had no idea that a mutiny was waiting for him in Xi'an, led by the Young Marshal Zhang Xueliang, whose troops had retreated from Manchuria after the Mukden Incident in 1931 and had stationed themselves in Xi'an. After his troops retreated from Manchuria, Zhang had followed Jiang to fight against the Communists, but became increasingly disappointed with Jiang Jieshi's policies of "non-resistance" against the Japanese and "unification before resistance." He was impressed by the student movements in Beijing, Shanghai, and other cities, which called for the government to change its policy of non-resistance against the Japanese. He also had second thoughts about fighting against the Communists, who had stated their willingness to ally with the GMD in order to fight against the Japanese.[55] Jiang, however, stubbornly rejected all of these ideas and was determined to finish off the

Communists once and for all before he dealt with the Japanese invasion. Meanwhile, the Japanese continued to push into other provinces in northern China. Agitated by all of these developments, Zhang and other generals decided to force Jiang to change his mind.

In the early hours of December 12, Zhang's troops stormed Jiang's residence, killed most of his bodyguards and eventually captured Jiang. That morning, Zhang issued a telegram, announcing to the whole country his eight demands of Jiang, which included reorganizing the Nanjing government to include all parties for future national policies, terminating civil strife, and releasing all political prisoners, and so on.[56] The Xi'an Incident shocked the nation, and the Nanjing government immediately split upon it received the news. Jiang's wife and friends tried to rescue him, while his opponents tried to further aggravate the situation at the risk of Jiang's life. The Communists at Yan'an were excited, but also confused. Some saw it as an opportunity to get rid of Jiang, but Mao and others were persuaded by Stalin to mediate with Zhang on Jiang's behalf. Under the influence of Stalin, the Communists changed their policy from "against Jiang and against Japan" to "ally with Jiang against Japan."[57]

Zhou Enlai, a leader of the CCP arrived in Xi'an on December 16 and had a private conversation with Zhang, during which he suggested a united-front government under Jiang. The Young Marshal agreed to release Jiang after Jiang verbally agreed to consider Zhang's demands.[58] Zhang voluntarily accompanied Jiang back to Nanjing on Christmas day, but was arrested and court-marshaled upon his arrival in Nanjing. Zhang was sentenced to ten years in prison after a brief trial. The sentence, however, was soon changed to house arrest, under which condition Zhang stayed for the next forty years until Jiang died in 1976. Although Jiang denied having signed any agreement with Zhang, he did change his policy afterwards. The anti-communist campaigns were cancelled, and Jiang expressed his willingness to allow the Communist troops to participate in future fighting against the Japanese. The Second United Front between the GMD and the CCP was formed, although Jiang was still hesitant to commit fully to it.[59]

UNDECLARED WAR AND THE NANJING MASSACRE

The Xi'an Incident affected the historical course of China in more than one way. After the Xi'an Incident, anti-Japanese sentiments rose in China, and this made the situation in northern China more difficult for the Japanese. After taking control of Manchuria, Japan continued their encroachments into northern China in order to create a buffer zone for Manchuria. Japan also sought to reach certain diplomatic solutions with the Chinese government, but the GMD government refused to contact the Japanese government, following Jiang's policy of "nonresistance, noncompromise and nondirect negotiation."[60]

Meanwhile, Japanese militarists and ultranationalists, many of whom were mid-ranked military officers, were determined to exert their influence on Japan's national politics and foreign policy. These radicals and "self-appointed national savors of the country" resorted to extreme means to achieve their goals, including assassinating high officials in Japan.[61] On May 15, 1932, a group of junior naval officers assassinated Prime Minister Inukai Tsuyoshi, who had wanted a peaceful solution to the issue of Manchuria with China, and attacked the Tokyo police station, the headquarters of the *Seiyukai* party, and the buildings of the Mitsubishi Bank. They called on the people to rise for a "Showa Restoration" in the name of the Emperor Showa (1926–1989) and to eliminate those who did not support their ideas of expansion. All of the participants in the attempted coup were arrested, but received only light sentences. The death of Inukai marked the end of the party cabinets, which would not return until after World War II.[62]

On August 12, 1935, an army lieutenant colonel assassinated Major-General Nagata Tetsuzan, head of the Military Affairs Bureau, because he blamed General Nagata for dissolving ultranationalist factions in the army. In February 1936, an ultranationalist organization in the army staged another coup against the government. Fourteen hundred soldiers from three regiments occupied the buildings of the Diet and the War Ministry, and raided the residence of the prime minister; unfortunately, they killed his brother-in-law by mistake. Others who were killed included a former prime minister, Admiral Saito; the minister of finance, Takahashi; and the inspector-general of military education, General Watanabe.[63] Martial law was declared, but the army did not do anything to put down the mutiny until the emperor expressed his discontent by referring to the mutineers as rebels. Only after that, did the army leadership call in forces to subdue the rebellion. Although all of these coup attempts eventually failed, the result was that moderate politicians gave way to more radical thinking statesmen, who preferred to have a more aggressive foreign policy toward China.

These developments both in China and in Japan did not help ease Japan's problems in Manchuria and northern China. Up to this time, to Japanese army leaders, the Soviet Union was their topmost concern for a future war. The primary goal of the Japanese army was to secure their control of Manchuria by creating a buffer zone in northern China. Then they would have a freer hand to deal with Soviet threat without worrying about being attacked from the north and the south at the same time. Japan tried a few times to sponsor a movement that would call for independence from China for five provinces in northern China: Hebei, Chahar, Suiyuan, Shanxi, and Shandong. Japan wanted to turn this area into a second Manchuria, but the plan could not be carried through.[64] On the contrary, calls for resistance against Japan increased in the area after the Xi'an Incident. On July 7, 1937, a few unplanned events led to an armed clash between Japanese and Chinese troops at the Marco Polo Bridge in the suburb of Beijing. On that day, some Japanese troops held a field exercise near the bridge and claimed that one soldier was missing. Using this as a pretext, the Japanese troops demanded to enter the nearby town of Wanping to search for the missing soldier. After the demand was rejected, the Japanese soldiers and local Chinese troops exchanged fire. Within a few hours, the Japanese troops occupied the town. Although few people realized it at the time, the Marco Polo Bridge Incident started the Second Sino-Japanese War, also known as the China Incident, since the war between China and Japan was never formally declared.[65]

Feelings about the incident were tense in both Japan and China. Prince Konoe Fumimaro, the Japanese prime minister, demanded an apology from the Chinese government for these "illegal anti-Japanese actions."[66] Jiang Jieshi emotionally announced that because they were pushed into a corner, China had no choice but to throw their "last ounce of energy into a struggle for national survival."[67] Soon afterwards, Japan sent reinforcements from Manchuria and the homeland to northern China; Jiang ordered four divisions to move into Beijing area. The CCP issued a manifesto claiming that the CCP would abolish the policy of resistance against the GMD government, reorganize its military forces under the control of the Military Commission of the GMD, and fight the Japanese at the front.[68] A full-fledged Japanese invasion seemed to have cemented the Second United Front, the alliance between the GMD and the CCP.

Despite their resolute and strong rhetoric, however, the Chinese troops proved to be no match for the better-equipped and better-trained Japanese. When the Japanese were ready to take Beijing, the Chinese government ordered an evacuation of the city on July 28, 1937, in order to spare the historical city from the destruction of warfare. Two days later, the Japanese also took Tianjin. On

August 13, the Japanese opened a second front in Shanghai in an attempt to take control of China's financial center. Jiang used his best German-trained troops to defend Shanghai, and they successfully stopped the Japanese advance for three months. Japanese troops gained control of Shanghai only after they tactically outflanked the defenders. The Japanese then advanced to Nanjing, which had been the capital of the Nationalist government. They did not encounter a lot of resistance in Nanjing, because Jiang had moved the capital to Chongqing, a city in the mountainous areas of the Sichuan province, before the Japanese approached the city.

Japanese navy enters Nanjing

The fall of Nanjing was followed by the notorious "Rape of Nanjing," during which hundreds of thousands of Chinese were indiscriminately massacred, and thousands of women were raped. The exact number of Chinese casualties is still in dispute. While China insists that about 300,000 Chinese lost their lives during the massacre, some Japanese claim that the entire event was nothing but Chinese fabrication and exaggeration. Even today, China and Japan have not yet reached reconciliation concerning the issue of the Nanjing Massacre, and it remains to be the thorniest issue between the two countries.

When the war first expanded from Manchuria to northern China, the Japanese government again accepted the *fait accompli* initiated by the field-level army officers in China. After sending reinforcements to China and opening the second front in Shanghai, it became virtually impossible for the Japanese government to stop what it had started and halt the further invasion of China. Encouraged by its early military success in Manchuria and northern China, the Japanese government expected a quick victory, which would force Jiang's government to yield to Japan's will within three months of the beginning of the war in July.[69] Even after the fall of Nanjing, however, Jiang refused to surrender. He established his headquarters in Wuhan where he could organize an effective resistance, after the Nationalist government had moved to Chongqing. This drew the Japanese further into central and southern China. Canton fell to the Japanese on October 21, 1938, and Wuhan finally fell in December 1938. The fall of Wuhan ended the first phase of the Sino-Japanese War, which took sixteen months.[70]

JAPAN'S ROAD TO PEARL HARBOR

The war in China proved to be a technical success, but a strategic blunder for Japan. It was impossible for Japan to conquer all of China, one of the largest and most populous countries in the world. Jiang's government understood this fact well and adopted the strategy of "trading space with time," waiting for the opportunity to recover its losses, even though international sanctions and support were limited and slow to come about, due to the rise of Fascism in Europe. The CCP troops, which had been reorganized into two Nationalist armies, the Eighth Route Army, and the New Fourth Army, were basically engaged in guerrilla warfare in the areas occupied by Japan.

In order to get out of this conundrum and find a peaceful solution, Japan changed its focus after it took Wuhan. Japan tried to establish a puppet government in China, following the same model of the "Manchu state." Unable to solicit cooperation from Jiang Jieshi, Japan found a collaborator, Wang Jingwei, who had been competing with Jiang for the leadership of the GMD ever since the death of Sun Yat-sun. In March 1940, Wang set up a government in Nanjing under Japan's tutelage. Most Chinese did not accepted Wang's government, even though Wang claimed that his intention was to bring peace to China and protect the Chinese in the areas occupied by Japan.[71]

These unfortunate events in China, however, do not explain why Japan attacked Pearl Harbor in 1941, which initiated the Pacific War with the United States and the Allied Forces. Japan's atrocities in China, including the Nanjing Massacre, aroused worldwide sympathy for China, but Japan's war in China alone did not precipitate an even larger war in the Pacific. Even in the middle of the Second Sino-Japanese War, one priority of the Kwantung Army was to strengthen its position against the Soviet Union. Actually, ever since the Russo-Japanese War, Japan's foreign policy had seldom deviated from Japan's preparation for a future war with Russia. As early as 1918, Japan eagerly participated in an Allied intervention in Russia, after the Bolshevik Revolution in 1917, and sent its troops to Siberia. Once the government was committed to sending troops, the Japanese army took advantage of its "autonomy of command" and sent in 74,000 troops, which was several times more troops than the 12,000 that the Japanese government had originally agreed upon. After the troops of other countries had withdrawn by June 1920, the Japanese extended their occupation to northern Sakhalin and did not withdraw from Siberia until October 1922 or from Sakhalin until 1925.[72]

Meanwhile, the Soviet Union apparently did not give up strengthening its position in the Far East. By 1935, Russia had 240,000 troops in its Far Eastern Provinces, whereas Japan had 160,000 in Manchuria. In 1935, the Soviet government announced that Germany and Japan were the enemies of the Soviet Union; and in March 1936, the Soviet Union concluded a mutual defense pact with Outer Mongolia.[73] All of this, in the eyes of the Kwantung Army, was evidence of Russia's hostility toward Japan. In order to balance against the Soviet Union's moves, Japan concluded an Anti Comintern Pact with Germany on November 25, 1936, in hopes that Hitler would back up Japan if there was a war between Japan and the Soviet Union.

In July 1938, a border dispute broke out between Japanese and Soviet troops at the Zhanggufeng-Lake Khasan area where the borders of Siberia, Manchuria, and Korea meet. A number of Kwantung army officers who believed that the Soviet threat was bigger than the Chinese threat decided to use the border dispute as an excuse to engage the Soviet Union in a war. On July 29, the commanding general in the area took the initiative and ordered Japanese troops to attack the Soviet troops.[74] However, the Russian troops, equipped with airpower, heavy artillery, and tanks, forced the Japanese troops to withdraw. Unwilling to accept defeat, the Kwantung Army engaged Soviet forces in another "border incident," this time at Nomonhan at the border of Manchuria and Outer Mongolia, in May 1939. After the Kwantung Army received the go-ahead from the Minister of War, it soon turned the border conflict into a major war against Soviet troops in June. In August, the Soviet troops under General Georgy Zhukov (1896–1974) launched a counterattack supported by air power and soon won a decisive victory against the Japanese troops. The Kwantung Army asked for reinforcements from Japan, but the Army leadership stood firm this time in refusing to allow the Kwantung Army to further aggravate the situation.

Toward the end of 1939, the dream of those Japanese who were pro-Germany and advocated "going north" to wage a major war against Russia was shattered by Hitler's surprising decision to enter into a Treaty of Non-Aggression with the Soviet Union on August 23, 1939. The treaty eliminated the threat from the east so Germany would be able carry out its aggression against other European countries. When Japan received the news, many felt that they had been fooled by Hitler, especially in light of the Kwantung Army being engaged in a border war at Nomonhan with the Soviet Union. When the Japanese prime minister resigned, he claimed that "Japan's foreign policy is in a state of having been practically betrayed."[75]

Hitler's successful invasions of European countries one after another, Poland in September 1939; Denmark and Norway in April 1940; and France, Belgium, the Netherlands, and Luxembourg in May 1940, greatly impressed the Japanese government. The Japanese government saw an opportunity to expand its empire in Asia, since Nazi Germany had devastated most of the colonial powers in Asia. The possibility of expanding the Japanese empire southward led to a reorientation of Japanese foreign policy, especially concerning its policy toward the Soviet Union. In September 1940, Japan signed the Tripartite Pact with Germany and Italy to formalize the Axis Powers. Afterward, it proceeded to improve its relations with the Soviet Union and sought to form a military alliance with Germany and Soviet Union together. Germany, who had already planned an attack on Russia, refused Japan's suggestion without revealing its reasons. As a result, Japan alone signed a neutrality pact with the Soviet Union in April 1941.[76]

A couple of months later, Hitler launched a blitzkrieg attack against Russia on June 22, 1941 without notifying Japan in advance. Japan was shocked by this move and once again felt betrayed by Hitler. Hitler then doubled the humiliation by asking Japan to attack the Soviet Union from the east side. This led to a serious debate between those who favored going north to have a war with Russia and those who wanted to go south to establish Japan's own empire. Japan eventually decided that if Hitler were successful in subjugating Russia, as he had been in other European countries, Japan would join Germany in attacking Russia. Germany's advance, however, was stopped short in Moscow in September.[77] On July 2, 1941, at a conference at which the emperor attended, the cabinet and the supreme commander decided on a new policy that affirmed Japan's intention to establish a new order in Asia, "A Greater East Asia Co-prosperity Sphere" led by Japan; to end the war against China; and to advance to the south to build a self-sufficient empire.[78] Japan, thus, decided to ignore Hitler's request and honor its neutrality pact with the Soviet Union.

While the Second Sino-Japanese War was largely the fault of the Japanese Army, Japan's Imperial Navy was crucial in getting Japan to move south, which eventually led to the conflict with the United States. Actually, Japanese and Western interests started to diverge as early as the years following World War I. While the Western powers were exhausted from World War I and were longing to seek long-term peace through disarmament, Japan was more interested in further expanding its empire in Asia. The Japanese Navy had long been unhappy about the West's push for disarmament, reflected by treaties reached at the Washington Naval Conference between November 1921 and February 1922. The Washington Naval Limitation Treaty, or the "Five Power Pact," signed by Japan, Britain, the United States, France, and Italy in February 1922, specified what would be the ratio of capital ships, battleships and battle-cruisers, between the five countries as 5-5-3-1.75-1.75. Britain and the United States were allowed to have the greatest amount of capital ships in terms of tonnage, and they were the two "5s" in the 5-5-3-1.75-1.75 ratio, under the excuse that both had two-ocean fleets. Japan, on the other hand, was given a "3" because it could only claim a one-ocean fleet. In other words, the tonnage of Japan's capital ships was only allowed to be 60 percent the size of the tonnage of Britain or the United States' capital ships. The other two countries, France and Italy, accepted the ratio of 1.75 each on their capital ships after they obtained better terms on cruisers and submarines.

The Japanese Naval authorities were not happy with this decision and wanted to be at least 70 percent the size of the US Navy in terms battleships, so a 5:3 ratio or 60 percent was not acceptable. However, lacking any leverage, Japan had to accept the ratio insisted upon by the Western powers.[79] In early 1930 when the five signatories of the Washington Naval Limitation Treaty met in London to discuss a similar treaty, Japan succeeded in securing a ratio of 10:10:7 (US: Britain: Japan, respectively) in destroyers, but had to accept a 10:10:6 ratio in heavy cruisers. The treaty was never fully accepted in Japan, because the militarists and right-wing radicals in the Navy severely criticized the party cabinets for accepting the treaty and put those who supported the London treaty on their list of those of being considered for assassination.[80] On January 15, 1937, these radicals in the Navy eventually forced the Japanese government to withdraw from the international disarmament system, which was established by the Second London Conference and was in effect between 1935 and 1941. Free from the treaty, Japan secretly expanded its navy, and by 1940, its navy had been greatly strengthened.[81]

After Japan signed the Tripartite Pact with Germany and Italy in September 1940, Japan's relations with Britain and United States further deteriorated. When Japan moved into French Indochina in July 1941, taking advantage of France's fall to the Germans, the United States imposed a total embargo on all exports to Japan. The United States had warned Japan earlier that it would consider Japan's moving into French Indo-China as a first step toward getting control of Singapore and the Philippines, and the United States would not stay idle if this happened. Great Britain soon followed suit and imposed embargos on Japan, as well. This put Japan into a difficult economic situation. Japan had relied heavily on the United States and Britain for resources since the 1920s. Two thirds of Japan's trade was with, and the most strategically important materials that Japan needed came from, these two countries. By the late 1930s, Japan had received 74 percent of its imported scrap iron, 60 percent of its imported machine tools, 93 percent of its imported copper, and 90 percent of its imported oil from the United States.[82] With a daily consumption of twelve thousand tons of oil, it was estimated that the Japanese navy's oil reserves would last less than two years, if Japan did not get more oil from abroad.[83]

The navy now strongly favored immediate action and advocated a plan to get Japan into the oil-rich Dutch East Indies (today's Indonesia), even if it meant a full-scale war with Britain and the United States. The plan would risk war with Britain and the United States because Japan would need to pass Singapore and the Philippines in order to get into the Dutch East Indies. Konoe, Japan's prime minister at the time, preferred to seek diplomatic solutions first. The subsequent negotiations with the United States, however, did not go anywhere because both sides refused to compromise on certain issues, especially on issues concerning China. Cordell Hull, the US Secretary of State, proposed that negotiations be based on moral principles, such as respecting the territorial integrity and sovereignty of every nation, and adherence to the principle of noninterference in the internal affairs of other nations.[84] Hull insisted that Japan make some concessions on vital issues, such as withdrawing from the Tripartite Pact and getting its troops out of northern China, but Japan was not willing to compromise on either issue. As a result, United States-Japan negotiations would go nowhere.[85]

While Japanese diplomats were in Washington DC negotiating for more oil, the Imperial Navy was preparing for war with the United States. The Naval authorities and other ultranationalists felt that war with the United States had become inevitable, because they believed that Japan had only two choices: either move into the oil rich Dutch East Indies and establish a self-sufficient empire, or withdraw from China and lose face. The Navy General Staff warned that if no action was taken by October 1941, it would be too late to take any action, and Japan would lose all that it had achieved so far. This either-or logic gained momentum at a meeting of Japanese leaders on September 3, 1941.

The Navy Chief of Staff argued that Japan was like "a patient who was critically ill, an operation, though extremely dangerous, might save his life."[86] It was then decided that if Japan could not reach an agreement on oil with the United States by October, Japan would go to war with the United States.

Prime Minister Konoe was thus under pressure to secure some sort of agreement with the United States if he wanted to avoid a major war. The plan was to obtain promises from the United States that they would 1) not interfere in the war in China; 2) not establish any more bases in Southeast Asia; and 3) restore trade, especially the oil trade, with Japan. In return, Japan would agree 1) to withdraw from Indochina as soon as a peace settlement was achieved with China; 2) to guarantee the neutrality of the Philippines; 3) to honor the neutrality pact with the Soviet Union; and 4) to automatically revoke Japan's obligation to the Tripartite Pact should America enter the war in Europe.[87] These terms, however, were unacceptable to Hull, who insisted on the terms that he had proposed earlier. Unable to achieve anything through negotiation, Konoe, the last civilian prime minister before World War II, resigned on October 16, 1941.

When General Tojo Hideki succeeded Konoe as prime minister, the emperor asked him to reevaluate the situation. After weighing all of the alternatives, Tojo chose the middle ground. He decided to continue diplomatic negotiations, while, at the same time, prepare for war. The new deadline was December 1. In addition to what Japan had proposed before, it offered further concessions: agreeing to withdraw troops from China in two years with the exception of critical areas, such as northern China, Inner Mongolia, and Hainan Island, and refraining from any further advances into Southeast Asia (except for Indochina).[88] The military authorities in Japan strongly objected to these terms. The Army worried about having to give up their conquest in China, and the Navy was concerned with the shipbuilding program launched by President Roosevelt in 1940, which would soon strengthen the US position in the Pacific.[89] Tojo, however, managed to keep them in line.

Again, the negotiations went nowhere. The United States actually took an even harsher stand than they had in the last round of discussions, probably because of their growing power in the Pacific. On November 26, Japanese envoys received a note from Hull in which he suggested Japan withdraw all troops from China and Indochina; avoid invoking the Tripartite Pact; and allow the United States to mediate between Japan and China. The United States, in return, would resume economic relations with Japan and supply Japan with oil and rice.[90] When the Japanese authorities in Tokyo received the note, they interpreted it as an ultimatum. The plan to go to war was finally decided upon at an imperial meeting, and Admiral Yamamoto Isoroku, commander of the combined Japanese fleet, was ordered to sail his fleet from Etorofu Isand of the Kuril Islands toward Hawaii. His fleet included six aircraft carriers, two battleships, three cruisers, nine destroyers, and numerous submarines. The Japanese envoys in Washington DC were ordered to deliver the message of Japan's declaration of war against the United States at 1 pm on Sunday, December 7, but were not given the details of the plan. Due to a technical problem in deciphering the message, Japanese diplomats did not arrive at the office of the Secretary of State until 2:20 pm, an hour *after* Japan's attack on Pearl Harbor![91]

Japan's surprise attack against the US Pacific Fleet at Pearl Harbor was a total victory for Japan. It started with an air strike. Three hundred and fifty Japanese aircraft left their carriers, which were from 250 miles away from Pearl Harbor. They approached from north of Oahu and dropped their first bomb at 7:55 am. Japanese torpedoes quickly ripped into US battleships, which were lined up in "battleship rolls." The Battleship Oklahoma was hit by five torpedoes, the West Virginia by seven, and the California by two. The USS Arizona exploded instantly and lost 1,103 men, out of a crew of 1,400, including its captain, Franklin von Valkenburgh, and Rear Admiral Isaac Cassin Kidd. By the end of the air raid at 10:00 am, the United States had lost seven battleships, three destroyers, and several other ships; nearly 200 aircraft, which was about half of the total number of aircraft at Pearl Harbor and other bases in Hawaii; and about 4,000 Americans. Japan, on the other hand, lost 29 planes and 64 men.[92]

This brilliant tactical victory, however, only led Japan on a dangerous path against one of the greatest industrial powers of the time. Ironically, even Admiral Yamamoto Isoroku, the genius behind this victory, was uncertain about an ultimate victory over the United States. He had argued that the Japanese Navy, with its limited

The Attack on Pearl Harbor. The ship in the middle of the picture is the USS California

resources, would not be able to sustain its dominance in the Pacific for long. He had cautioned the government about the diminishing chances of a Japanese victory, "if the war dragged on for two or three years." A war with the Unites States, however, would "necessarily be a protracted one," according to calculations made by him and Navy staff.[93] His apprehension about the industrial power of the United States was not unwarranted. After the disaster of Pearl Harbor, public opinion in the United States was immediately unified. Only America's policy of "Europe first" withheld the United States from launching an immediate counterattack in the Pacific.

US INVOLVEMENT IN CHINA

Before the Pacific War broke out in December 1941, China largely fought alone against Japan. Some support came from the Soviet Union, but it was totally stopped after Hitler attacked the Soviet Union. In 1939, America's financial support to China amounted to 150 million dollars at a very low interest rate of 3 percent, but that support dwindled after Hitler's war against Europe started. In 1940, France closed the railroad service from Vietnam to Kunming, China in order to avoid provoking Japan, and Britain closed the Burma Road, which was built by Chinese laborers in 1937 to connect Lashio, Burma to Kunming. The British had been transporting materials to China through the Burma Road, but with its closing, China was completely isolated from the outside world by the mid-1940s. In early 1941, President Roosevelt made the Lend Lease program[94] available to China, but the amount available to China was only 21 million dollars, 1.7 percent of the total to all countries.[95]

Japan's surprise attack on Pearl Harbor on December 17, 1941 started the Pacific War with the United States. On the next day, President Roosevelt declared war against Japan. China now became an important member of the Allied Powers. Actually, President Roosevelt insisted that China become one of the Big Four, despite opposition from Britain and the Soviet Union, the other two members of the Big Four. The Allied Powers established a China-Burma-India Theater of war appointing Jiang Jieshi as the Supreme Commander of the China Theater, whereas the Burma-India Theater was under the command of the British. General Joseph Stilwell was appointed as Jiang's chief of staff and the commander of the China-Burma-India Theater responsible for all Lend-Lease supplies to China.

From 1942 to 1946, China received 500 million dollars worth of loans from the United States and 1.54 billion through the Lend-Lease program.[96]

China welcomed this much-needed support. Jiang Jieshi, however, soon had some problems with General Stilwell over issues of war strategy and control of Lend-Lease supplies. The first issue was about Stilwell's strategy to defend the Burma Road, which was the only passage for China to connect with the outside world, after Japan controlled all of coastal China.

After the Burma Road reopened, US Lend-Lease supplies were shipped to Rangoon, Burma, and from there they were transported to Lashio and then, through the Burma Road, to Chongqing. As a result, it became the major target of the Japanese Army. In early 1942, Japanese troops invaded Burma and captured Rangoon on March 8, 1942. By late April, they captured the city of Lashio and thus cut off China's lifeline through the Burma Road.

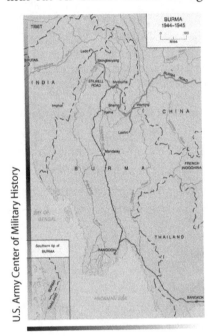

U.S. Army Center of Military History

The Burma and Ledo Road

Courtesy of Library of Congress

Chinese Laborers working to reopen the Burma Road in southwest China, 1944

Stilwell's prime goal was to reopen the Burma Road so that the Lend-Lease supplies to China could get through. Due to Japan's control of northern Burma, all of the supplies by now had to be transported by air with the help of General Claire Chennault and his "flying tigers," originally the "American Volunteer Group" to China in 1937 and later part of 14th US Air Force after 1941. The "Flying Tigers" flew from the airfields in Assam, India over "the hump," and the eastern end of the Himalaya Mountains to Chongqing. With limited capacity, however, the goods transported through air were far from enough for Jiang's poorly equipped troops. Jiang was initially willing to cooperate with Stilwell's plan and committed two of his best-equipped armies for the Burma expedition. Due to problems of communication and poor cooperation between the Chinese and the British troops, which were mixtures of British, Burmese, and Indian units, the Allied powers quickly collapsed, and the remnant of Jiang's troops dispersed into India and northern parts of Burma. Jiang was furious over this loss and started to question Stilwell's ability as a military commander. Jiang later repeatedly refused Stilwell's proposal to send Chinese troops to Burma, even believing that such an action would be for no other reason than to help restore British colonial control of Burma.[97] The relationship between the two started to sour.

Jiang's stubbornness frustrated Stilwell, who from the very beginning had little respect for Jiang.[98] Stilwell was even more disappointed after he learned that Jiang actually used his best troops, as many as 400,000, not for combating the Japanese, but for blocking the Communist bases in the Yan'an area in order to prevent them from getting basic supplies for living, such as salt, medicine, and other daily necessities, in addition to putting a stop to their subsidies.[99] When Stilwell suggested using these Nationalist troops for his planned operations against the Japanese, Jiang again rejected the idea. Instead, Jiang accepted an alternative strategy proposed by General Chennault, which emphasized the merit of air power. Chennault argued that the principal strategy against Japan should be building airbases in southwest China for the US Air Force to use to transport Lend-Lease supplies, and in the future, the bases could be used for bombing Japan's home islands. Stilwell, on the other hand, believed in training the Chinese troops for conventional military battles.[100] Jiang sided with Chennault, making Stilwell more frustrated. Stilwell was also frustrated by Jiang's repeated requests to control the Lend-Lease supplies without committing more of his troops to confronting the Japanese.

For a while, Chennault's vision of an air war seemed to bring positive results. On June 15, 1944, America's new powerful B-29 bombers took off from these new airbases in southwest China and dropped 221 tons of bombs on Kyushu Island, one of the four main home islands of Japan. These bombers also carried out missions against military targets in Thailand, Manchuria, Sumatra, and Taiwan. In retaliation, Japan launched Operation Ichigo (number one) in the summer of 1944, and by November captured Changsha (Hunan Province), Guilin (Guangxi Province), Liuzhou (Guangxi Province), and Guiyang (Guizhou Province), and even threatened Chongqing itself. The Chinese Nationalist troops were easily defeated, and all of the airbases, as Stilwell warned would happen, were lost. After this fiasco, the Joint Chiefs of Staff suggested that President Roosevelt consider Stilwell's suggestion of using the Chinese Communist troops and urge Jiang Jieshi to relinquish his command of the Chinese troops to Stilwell.[101]

This was the last straw to an already strained relationship between Stilwell and Jiang. Deeply hurt by these requests, Jiang instead asked the President not to put the Communist troops under Stilwell's command and to give Jiang complete control of the distribution of Lend-Lease supplies.[102] Jiang also asked the President to recall Stilwell. The last thing that Jiang wanted was to give the Communist troops access to Lend-Lease supplies. Already anticipating and preparing for the future showdown with the CCP in China, Jiang's priority was to preserve his troops and equipment for that anticipated conflict.

In September 1944, the President sent General Patrick Hurley to China as his personal emissary to find a way to mediate between Jiang and Stilwell. Sympathetic to Jiang, Hurley assured the president later in his report that there was no other issue between the President and Jiang but Stilwell. "My opinion is that," continued Hurley, "if you sustain Stilwell in this controversy, you will lose Chiang Kai-shek [Jiang Jieshi] and possibly you will lose China with him."[103] China was a crucial partner in the Pacific War and was tying up more than half of all the Japanese troops available at the time. This was especially significant after the British forces in Asia had collapsed as Japan advanced into Southeast Asia. Among Japan's fifty army divisions, thirty-four were in China and Manchuria, whereas only ten were in Southeast Asia and the Pacific.[104] Under this circumstance, the President could not risk losing China to Japan. On October 1944, President Roosevelt recalled General Stilwell even though the Joint Chiefs of Staffs fully supported Stilwell in this controversy.

On the issue of the Communist troops, however, Hurley's opinion differed from that of Jiang. As early as the first half of 1943, John P. Davis, a political adviser to Stilwell, recommended three times to Stilwell, as well to the State Department, to dispatch American observers to the Communist bases.

He argued that the CCP was probably the most "cohesive, disciplined, and aggressive anti-Japanese force in North China." Worried about Jiang's reaction, the president let the matter drop at the time.[105] In June, a Foreign Service officer, John S. Service, initiated another effort to contact the CCP, and this time the president concurred after he secured consent from Jiang. On July 22, 1944 eighteen American officers under the command of Colonel Davit D. Barrett arrived at Yan'an, the Communist capital, and opened the Dixie Mission (July 1944–March 1947) there. During their stay in Yan'an, these officers noticed the nationalism and pragmatism of the Communist leaders and were impressed by better discipline and higher morals among their troops. In their culminating report, they called the Communist controlled areas a "different country," and Yan'an, "the most modern place in China."[106] Later, both John Service and John Davis were convinced that Jiang would not be able to wipe out the Communists. "The Communists are in China to stay," claimed Davis, "and China's destiny is not Chiang [Jiang]'s but theirs."[107]

Based on these assessments, Hurley, who became the ambassador to China in November 1944, worked to reconcile the two parties. Hurley visited Yan'an himself in November. He was also impressed by what he observed there, and after a two-day conference in Yan'an, Hurley reported in his letter to the Secretary of State, "there is little difference, if any, between the avowed principles of the National Government of Kuomingtang [Guomindang] and the avowed principles of the Chinese Communist Party."[108] This observation by Hurley, together with the earlier reports of Stilwell's staff and the staff of the US Embassy in China, formed the basis of US post-war China policy.

THE ATOMIC BOMBS AND JAPANESE SURRENDER

Back in the Pacific, Japan scored one victory after another after their victory at Pearl Harbor in December 1941. Another disaster for the United States occurred the very next day after the attack on Pearl Harbor. Having learned of Japan's attack at Pearl Harbor, General Douglas MacArthur, the commander of US troops in the Philippines, ordered his planes to take off immediately in order to avoid a fiasco similar to Pearl Harbor. However, when these planes landed for refueling around lunchtime, they were caught on the ground by Japanese bombers.[109] Two British ships in the area, the battleship Prince of Wales and the battle cruiser, the Repulse, were sunk off the coast of Malaysia the following day.

After these victories, Japanese troops advanced into Southeast Asia. In January 1942, Japan battled British Malaya, capturing it on January 31 after Japan drove the defending armies of British, Indian, Australian, and Malayan forces to Singapore. On February 15, 1942, Japanese troops penetrated the Malayan jungle, which was thought to be "impenetrable," and overwhelmed the remaining forces of the Allied Powers in the region. About 80,000 British, Indian, and Australian troops became prisoners of war. Japan then embarked on taking the Dutch East Indies; Bali, Timor, and Sumatra fell in February 1942. On March 1, Japanese forces landed on the island of Java from where they further advanced into northern New Guinea.

In the Philippines, the US forces and the Filipinos resisted until early May. General MacArthur had left for Australia by personal order of Roosevelt in March, leaving behind 80,000 soldiers who were later ordered to surrender on May 6, 1942. American POWs in the Philippines were soon forced into the Bataan Death March to the interior of the island; nearly 10,000 prisoners died during the trip. From Malaya, Japanese forces pushed toward northern Burma, and by the end of May, they reached Lido, Burma and closed the Burma Road to China. By the summer of 1942, Japan had created a vast empire stretching four thousand miles from Sakhalin in the north and close to Australia in the south; six thousand miles from Burma in the west to the Gilbert Islands in the east.[110]

Japan embarked on creating a "Greater East Asia Co-Prosperity Sphere" to pursue its goal of economic autonomy.

The Allied counterattack in the Pacific was delayed, largely owing to the joint decision to defeat Germany in Europe first. The Battle of the Coral Sea northeast of Australia in May 1942 was the first significant sea battle against Japan after Pear Harbor. It was the first major carrier battle in history during which the opposing fleets fought without seeing each other; the entire battle was fought by aircraft. Neither side could claim a victory in the battle. Strategically speaking, Japan suffered its first major setback in the Pacific with its advance toward Australia being halted.

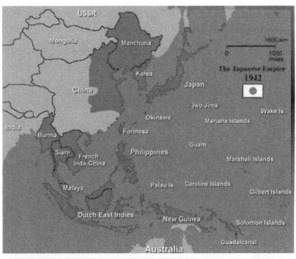

The Japenese Empire, 1942

1942. United States Army

A turning point came a month later at the Battle of Midway. In June, a large Japanese fleet approached Midway Island at the westernmost part of the Hawaiian chain, hoping to finish off the US Pacific Fleet once and for all. Having broken Japan's naval codes, American aircraft from US carriers nearby ambushed the approaching Japanese fleet and sank four Japanese aircraft carries. This was a great victory for the Allied Powers. During the war, Japan was never able to replace these precious aircraft carriers or the experienced pilots that they had lost at the battle. It was exactly six months after Pearl Harbor, echoing Yamamoto's comments that his success at Pearl Harbor would only be able to give Japan six months to one year to win. After that, he was not sure what would happen. After losing its striking force in the Battle of Midway, Japan was on the defensive thereafter.

In the middle of 1943, the United States and Britain designed a strategic plan, known as "island hopping" offensives. Two great amphibious island-hopping offensives struck the Pacific toward the home islands of Japan. One was led by General MacArthur in the Southwest Pacific Theatre through the Solomon Islands to New Guinea, and then to Luzon (the Philippines); the other, led by Admiral Nimitz, pushed through the Central Pacific Theatre from the Gilbert Islands to the Marshall Islands, and then took a jump to the Mariana Islands and Iwo Jima.[111] In April 1945, the two offensives joined at Okinawa. In June 1945, the Philippines were recaptured; MacArthur kept his pledge of returning. Allied control of Saipan, a Mariana island, brought Japan within the range of powerful US B-29 bombers.

The Allied forces captured some of these islands relatively easily as they were able to bypass some heavily fortified islands. Other battles, however, were far bloodier than was originally expected. The battle of Iwo Jima and the battle of Okinawa were such examples. Iwo Jima is a volcanic island in the Bonin Islands in the Pacific Ocean. It is only eight square miles in area and is located halfway between Saipan and the Japanese home islands. Control of the island would eliminate the possible danger of Japanese planes taking off from the island to intercept US bombers and would provide an ideal place for US disabled bombers on their way back to Saipan from Japan.[112] What the Allied forces did not know was that the Japanese commander on Iwo Jima, General Tadamichi Kuribayashi, who had anticipated an attack since March 1944, had greatly strengthened the defense of the island by covering it with underground passages and fortified caves formed by Mount Suribachi. Kuribayashi ordered his men to kill ten Americans before they themselves died at battle or through suicide.

When the US Marines finally landed on February 14, 1945, they engaged in a bitter battle. The US Marines suffered more casualties at Iwo Jima than they had in any earlier battles. By the time Japanese resistance ended, only 212 out of 22,000 Japanese defenders were left to surrender. The Marines suffered over 25,000 casualties, with nearly 7,000 killed.[113] The picture of four Marines putting the American flag on Mount Suribachi became one of the most memorable pictures of World War II.

The last stronghold of the Japanese defense was in Okinawa in the Ryukyu Islands. The battle of Okinawa occurred between April 2 and June 22, 1945 and was the most difficult battle in the Pacific theater, during which about 110,000 Japanese soldiers and 100,000 Okinawans, almost a fourth of Okinawa's population of 450,000, perished. US casualties amounted to nearly 45,000, including 12,500 killed in land or naval combat.[114] Japan lost nearly 8000 planes and fifteen warships, including the Yamamoto, the largest warship in the world at the time. Japan used 1,900 *kamikaze* attacks, the suicidal plane attack that Japan had used since October 1944. Thirty US ships were sunk, 368 damaged, and 763 aircraft were lost due to these *kamikaze* attacks. Control of Okinawa opened the door for the Allied forces to take the main Japanese islands.

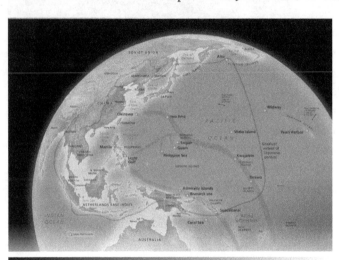

Major battles fought in the Pacific Theatre

The savageness of the battle of Okinawa, however, weighed heavily on the Allied commanders as they considered their next move. It would definitely cost more lives, maybe as many as a million according to some estimations, if the Allied forces invaded the main home islands of Japan, which contained a population of 71,000,000 in 1945. However, some scholars argue that the number of possible casualties may have been exaggerated.[115]

On July 26, 1945 the United States, Great Britain, and China issued the Potsdam Declaration, which called for Japan to surrender unconditionally or "face prompt and utter destruction."[116] Japan, however, refused to surrender. The United States government started to consider using the atomic bombs, which had recently been developed. Weighing the choice of either using atomic bombs or a possible protracted and ferocious war that might cost millions of lives, President Harry Truman decided to use the new weapon against Japan. At 8:15 am on August 6, the bomber Enola Gay dropped the first atomic bomb on the city of Hiroshima. The bomb released a force equivalent to 20,000 tons of TNT. An intensive white flash created a temperature of 7000 degrees Fahrenheit, turning the city into a "living inferno." Everything

Hiroshima after the bomb

within a mile-and-a-quarter radius of the explosion was burnt, and everyone within this radius was killed instantly.[117] The bomb left 140,000 dead, tens of thousands injured or exposed to radiation, and over 80 percent of the buildings in Hiroshima in ruins. For the Japanese survivors, this was the most horrible thing that they had ever experienced. They, however, "bored their suffering with stoic dignity."[118] "The hurt ones were quiet;" observed Father Kleinsorge, a Catholic priest in Hiroshima at the time, "No one wept, much less screamed in pain; no one complained...."[119]

Despite the catastrophe at Hiroshima, Japan's military, which still had 5.5 million enlisted men, was reluctant to surrender.[120] On August 8, the Soviet Union declared war against Japan, after refusing to renew the neutrality pact with them. The next day, the second atomic bomb was dropped on Nagasaki, a city that manufactured many goods for the military. More than 70,000 Japanese died, and another 60,000 were injured. The Japanese government finally agreed to accept the terms set forth by the Potsdam Declaration, with one exception: the Japanese emperor should be allowed to remain as sovereign of Japan. The United States rejected this proposal and stated that after he surrendered, the status of the emperor would be "subject to the Supreme Commander of the Allied Powers."[121] At the subsequent meetings of the cabinet and the Supreme Council, the military leaders still strongly opposed the idea of surrender, and as a result, no decision could be made. Finally, Prime Minister Suzuki presented the issue to the emperor. At the imperial conference on August 14, the Emperor Hirohito finally spoke, saying that "he could no longer allow his people to suffer death and destruction," and asking the military officials "to endure the unendurable" to end the war.[122] On the early morning of August 15, the emperor announced Japan's surrender on the radio. It was the first time that the Japanese ever heard their emperor's voice. Numerous generals and admirals committed *seppuku*, the ritual suicide, and more than 500 military personnel followed suit. On September 2, General Umezu, representing Japan, signed the surrender with General MacArthur, representing the Allied powers, on board the Missouri in Tokyo Bay. Japan's war in Asia, which started with Japan's invasion of Manchuria in 1931, finally ended after having caused an incalculable loss of human lives and property across Asia.

ALLIED OCCUPATION OF JAPAN

When General MacArthur and Allied troops arrived in Japan at the end of August 1945, Japan was in poor condition. The war had caused a tremendous loss of Japanese lives and almost all of the major cities had been laid to waste by bombings, except for Kyoto because of its historical and cultural value. Conventional Allied bombing of Japan's home islands since October 1944 actually caused more damage than the two atomic bombs did. The firebomb raids in Tokyo in March 1945 alone killed about 100,000 people, and the total number of victims of the Allied air raids was over 500,000.[123] The military casualties were even worse. According to Mikiso Hane, the Japanese Army suffered nearly five million casualties, including 1,140,000 dead, 300,000 wounded, and 4,470,000 sick (of whom 40,000 died later); the casualties of the Japanese Navy included 415,000 dead and 1,400 missing.[124]

The surrender shattered Japanese pride and sense of direction. Many Japanese expected a cruel and harsh occupation, similar to the Japanese occupation of Korea, China, and other Asian countries. The Allied Occupation, however, was carried out in a peaceful manor with little or no violence involved. The Occupation, in theory, was carried out by a four-power Allied Council for Japan in Tokyo and supervised by a thirteen-nation Far Eastern Commission in Washington. In actuality, General MacArthur, who had been appointed Supreme Commander for the Allied Powers (SCAP) (the whole

Occupation administration under him was also known as SCAP), and his American staff handled most policies of the Occupation.[125] Unlike Germany, which was governed directly by foreign troops, Japan maintained its own government during the Occupation. The General Liaison Office under the SCAP handled communication between the general headquarters of the SCAP and the relevant offices in the Japanese government. After the initial reforms were accomplished in 1948, the Liaison Office was abolished, and the SCAP gradually turned over the reins to the Japanese government.[126]

The first responsibility of the SCAP was to decide on the fate of the Japanese emperor. General MacArthur had conversations with the Emperor Hirohito and was impressed by the emperor's gentleness. He decided that the emperor should be exempted from criminal prosecution and maintain his monarchical position. "I believe that if the emperor were indicted and perhaps hanged as a war criminal, military government would have to be instituted throughout all of Japan, and guerilla warfare would probably break out," reasoned MacArthur.[127] However, he encouraged the emperor to renounce his divinity and to come out of his palace more often to mingle with people. On New Year's Day, 1946, the Emperor Hirohito officially announced to his subjects that he was not divine, and this shocked many Japanese.

The next step was to dismantle Japan's military machine and put war criminals on trial. The Japanese empire was dismantled, and about six million servicemen returned to Japan by the end of 1947. The Japanese military was demobilized; ultranationalist organizations were dissolved; military industries were dismantled; and the police were decentralized.[128] Then the SCAP proceeded to remove the old leadership, with the exception of the emperor. The International Military Tribunal for the Far East, also known as the Tokyo War Crimes Trials, opened in May 1946. Twenty-five top leaders were tried as Class A war criminals who committed crimes against peace by waging war. All were found guilty. Seven of them, including General Tojo, received death sentences, sixteen life sentences, one twenty years, and one seven years. Two died during the year and a half long trial, and one went insane. The death sentences were carried out in December 1948. The surviving defendants who were in prison ended up being released in April 1958. Twenty high-ranking military officers were charged as Class B criminals, being charged with command responsibility for the troops who committed war crimes, but they were all acquitted.[129] A total of 5,700 of lesser officers and soldiers were tried as Class B and Class C criminals for committing war atrocities. Of this number, 984 initially were condemned to death; 475 received life sentences; and 1,018 were acquitted.[130] The whole procedure was completed by the fall of 1949.

Over the next a few years, the Allied Occupation focused on political, economic, and social reforms. In addition to dismantling the Japanese war machine, the political reforms also included dismantling Shintoism as a national ideology and severing the ties between the government and the Shinto shrines; making the executive branch of government responsible to the people through their representatives; and putting liberal minded people into government offices to ensure a democratic style of leadership.

In terms of economic reforms, the most important step was to eliminate *zaibatsu*, which by the end of the war probably dominated about 75 percent of the national economy. The SCAP took steps against the major *zaibatsu* giants, freezing their family assets and breaking the conglomerates into smaller companies. The Mitsui and Mitsubishi *zaibatsu*, for example, were broken into 240 separate firms. Anti-monopoly laws were issued in order to prevent the reestablishment of these giants. In December 1947, SCAP planned to dissolve another 1,200 companies, but the plan was later dropped.[131] Along with eliminating the *zaibatsu*, efforts were also made to improve working conditions by giving workers the right to organize, bargain, and strike. Workers' unions mushroomed; by mid-1948, 6.7 million workers had joined 33,900 unions.[132]

Another very important economic achievement was land reform. In 1945, about seventy percent of Japanese farmers had to rent land. Under the direction of SCAP, the Japanese government passed the Farm Land Reform Laws in October 1946. Landowners were allowed to keep two and half acres to be farmed by their families, and up to five acres for renting. The government would purchase the rest of the land from them and then sell it to farmers who did not have any land. These farmers would receive low interest mortgages to allow them to purchase the land.[133] By 1947, the percentage of land worked by hired hands was down from 46 percent to 10 percent.[134]

Social reforms significantly changed the status of women. After the reforms, women had the same rights as their husbands: they were allowed to divorce their husbands, to own property independently, and had the right to vote. Education reforms were implemented to get rid of militaristic and ultra-nationalistic materials from the schools and to purge the teachers who held these ideas. Textbooks were revised, eliminating the influence of Shintoism and adding information about the problems of the old Japanese systems. New universities were established to meet the needs of higher learning.[135]

The most significant achievement of the reforms was the new constitution of 1947, which was drafted by the staff of SCAP and later presented to the Japanese government for adoption. It was put into effect in May 1947. The new constitution reduced the power of the emperor. It made it clear that the sovereign power resides with the people, and the emperor derives his position from the will of the people. Both houses of the Diet would now be elected, and party government, which struggled in the 1920s and was eliminated in the middle 1930s, eventually returned with full constitutional support. An important part of the 1947 constitution is Article IX, the "No War" clause, which states that the Japanese people will forever renounce war as a sovereign right of the nation and will not maintain regular military forces anymore. Instead, self-defense forces will be responsible for maintaining national security.[136] Article IX has been at the center of the debate over the constitution ever since its adoption.

By the end of 1947, the Occupation had achieved its primary goals. The Occupation, however, continued for another five years because the Soviet Union delayed the signing of a peace treaty with Japan. On September 8, 1951, in San Francisco, Japan was finally able to sign a peace treaty, known as the San Francisco Peace Treaty, with the United States and forty-seven other countries. The Soviet Union, Poland and Czechoslovakia attended the San Francisco conference, but did not sign the treaty, and China was not even invited because the change to their government in 1949.[137] By signing the treaty, Japan gained its independence, but lost all of the territory outside Japan that it had gained since the Meiji Restoration. On the same day, Japan signed a bilateral treaty with the United States, the US-Japan Security Treaty. According to this treaty, America agreed to provide protection for Japan in case of war. In exchange, Japan would allow American troops to be stationed at a few military bases in Japan. Six years after the horrible Pacific War, Japan became an ally of the United States once again. This dramatic change was due to some unexpected developments in East Asia, which will be covered in Chapter 16.

THE CIVIL WAR AND THE
PEOPLE'S REPUBLIC OF CHINA

After Japan surrendered on August 16, 1945, China was also in a devastating situation. According to the Chinese nationalist government's calculation, the Chinese troops suffered more than 5.6 million casualties since the China war started, and civilian loss was over 1.1 million. Property damage exceeded 29.42 billion of prewar Chinese yuan.[138] China, however, did not have much time to enjoy the peace before a civil war broke out between the GMD and the CCP. As soon as Japan surrendered, the GMD and the CCP started to compete, as each tried to acquire quickly as much of the land that had been controlled by Japan as they could. They also tried to gather Japanese military equipment. The military equipment was of particular importance to the CCP, since they were poorly equipped as a result of being cut off from American aid. Washington ordered American troops in China to help Jiang get into crucial cities, but try to avoid direct involvement in the GMD-CCP conflict. The US Tenth Air Force airlifted over 110,000 of Jiang's troops to key cities. Japanese troops were also told not to surrender to the Communists, and in some cases, they continued to fight with the Communists until the Nationalist troops arrived.[139]

The United States hoped that it would be able to mediate between the two parties in order to prevent a civil war in China. In August, Ambassador Hurley flew to Yan'an and personally escorted Mao Zedong from Yan'an to Chongqing for a negotiation with Jiang Jieshi concerning the future of China. In the subsequent Chongqing negotiations, Jiang and Mao agreed on some points, such as having a democratic government to guarantee freedom for the people and all parties. Jiang also agreed to establish a Political Consultative Conference where all political parties could participate. The two sides, however, had problems in reaching an agreement on military issues. They agreed on the general principle of having a unified army, but were reluctant to give in to the other party's demands. With the mediation of the United States, Jiang and Mao jointly issued a final communiqué on October 10, 1945, but it had little effect on what was happening on the battlefields. After Mao returned to Yan'an, he increased the number of troops in his army in preparation for a civil war.[140] Seeing no hope in fulfilling his mission of mediation, Ambassador Hurley resigned in November 1945. In his letter to the president, however, he accused American foreign-service officers in China of undermining his efforts out of their sympathy for the Communist troops.[141]

President Truman then sent General George Marshall as his envoy to China in December 1945. The Marshall Mission introduced a shift in US-China policy from unconditional support of the Nationalist government to conditional support. Marshall made it clear to Jiang that continuing US support (up to 600 million dollars) would be contingent on the achievement of a truce and national unity.[142] He also delivered the three primary goals of the mission to both parties: 1) a cease-fire; 2) the establishment of a conference to discuss a coalition government; 3) the integration of all military forces into a national army.[143]

Because of the high reputation that Marshall enjoyed, both Jiang and Mao were willing, at least on the surface, to follow Marshall's guidance. As a result, Marshall quickly scored satisfactory achievements. In January 1946, the Political Consultative Conference convened, and a cease-fire was accomplished. Marshall even successfully persuaded the GMD and the CCP to agree upon the integration of their troops into a national army. They agreed that, within a year, the GMD forces were to be reduced to ninety divisions and the CCP forces to eighteen divisions; and then in six months after that both would have further reduction, the GMD forces to fifty divisions and the CCP to ten divisions. Satisfied with the results, Marshall returned to Washington in March to arrange a loan of 500 million dollars for China.[144] Soon after Marshall left, however, military strife broke out in Manchuria. The Communist troops under the command of Lin Biao, one of their best generals, took control of Changchun in Manchuria in mid-April, but lost it to the Nationalist troops in May. When Marshall returned to China, he managed to arrange another fifteen-day truce on June 6, but the war resumed in July. Jiang, who was now very confident that he would be victorious over the Communists, was reluctant to follow Marshall's directives. On December 1, 1946, he even told Marshall, "the enemy forces could be wiped out in eight to ten months."[145] Under these circumstances, Marshall could do nothing but admit failure, and in early January 1947, President Truman recalled Marshall from China.

Jiang's confidence in a quick victory over the Communist troops was based on his successful military campaigns between July and September 1946, during which the Nationalist troops won practically every battle. The Communists were in retreat, and their territorial holdings shrank by 165 towns and 174,000 square kilometers of territory.[146] In March 1947, Jiang's troops managed to drive the Communists out of their headquarters in Yan'an, which seemed to replicate the situation of capturing the Communist bases in Jiangxi that forced the Communist troops into the Long March in October 1934. Things, however, were different this time. The Communists employed a "strategic retreat," which would allow them to avoid a head-on collision with the superior Nationalist troops and would scatter their troops among the rural areas. This strategy seemed to work for them, and they soon rebounded back with stronger forces. When the civil war started, the Communists had barely one million poorly equipped troops under their command; whereas, the Nationalists had about five million troops. By mid-1947, the number of CCP troops had reached 1.95 million. They also had much better equipments, since the Soviet Union provided them with the equipments that came from the Kwantung Army. The Communists also captured American equipment from the defeated nationalist troops. The number of Nationalist troops, however, had shrunken to 3.37 million.[147]

Mid-1947 saw a turning point in the Chinese civil war. The Communist troops started to launch offensives against the Nationalist troops. By June 1948, each side had about an equal number of well-armed troops: the Nationalists had 980,000 well-armed troops, whereas the Communists had 970,000 well-armed troops. The Nationalists, however, had three times as many poorly armed troops as the Communists had. The artillery pieces also became equal in number.[148] It became clear that the Nationalist troops could no longer hold their momentum against the Communists. In September 1948, the Communist troops under Lin Biao scored a decisive victory in Manchuria. Between mid-September and early November, Lin Biao led over 700,000 Communist troops against 1.3 million Nationalist troops in Manchuria. During this campaign, which was later known as the Liao-Shen (Liaoning-Shenyang) campaign, Lin's troops scored impressive victories against the Nationalist troops. Within fifty-two days of the Liao-Shen Campaign, Jiang lost four army groups, eleven armies, and thirty-three divisions, which totaled about 472,000 of his best trained and best equipped troops. Lin Biao's troops captured equipment from the Nationalists, including nearly 13,000 cannons, over 180 tanks, 22 planes, over 2,500 armored vehicles and trucks, and nearly 420,000 guns. Manchuria was in the hands of the Communists.

This was only the beginning of Jiang's fiasco. The second decisive showdown between the GMD and the CCP occurred between November 1948 and January 1949 in central China. About 800,000 Nationalist troops fought against about 600,000 Communist troops in what is known as the Huai-Hai (the Huai River and the Hai River) Campaign. Jiang lost over 555,000 of his troops, many of whom simply surrendered to the Communists without fighting due to low morale. Meanwhile, another impressive campaign, known as the Ping-Jin (Beiping, an old name of Beijing, and Tianjin) Campaign, was occurring in northern China between November 1948 and January 1949 after Lin Biao's troops advanced to northern China from Manchuria. The GMD's losses in the Ping-Jin Campaign were just as catastrophic as their losses in Huai-Hai campaign. Overwhelmed by the Communists, the commander of the Nationalist troops in Beiping surrendered without a fight after the CCP took Tianjin. Jiang lost another half a million Nationalist troops in this battle.[149]

From September 1948 to January 1949, the GMD lost 1.5 million troops. It became virtually impossible for the Nationalist government to recover from these staggering losses. In January 1949, Jiang was forced to resign and was replaced by Li Zongren, who started to seek negotiations with the Communists. With a total victory in sight, Mao refused to compromise. On April 21, his troops crossed the Yangtze River and took control of Nanjing and Shanghai. The Nationalist government retreated to Taiwan. On October 1, 1949, Mao announced the establishment of the People's Republic of China on top of the Tiananmen in Beijing, and this opened a new era in Chinese history.

For more information about the topics discussed in this chapter, please visit the website for this textbook. This website can be accessed from http://www.grtep.com/.

1 Hsu, *Modern China*, 475–476.
2 Hsu, *Modern China*, 477.
3 Hsu, *Modern China*, 477–478.
4 Hsu, *Modern China*, 481–482.
5 Hsu, *Modern China*, 482–483.
6 Spence, *Search*, 283–284.
7 Hsu, *Modern China*, 484–486.
8 Cezong Zhou, *The May Fourth Movement: Intellectual Revolution in Modern China* (Stanford: Stanford University Press, 1967), 46; and Hsu, *Modern China*, 498.
9 Hsu, *Modern China*, 499.
10 Hsu, *Modern China*, 500–501.
11 Spence, *Search*, 286–287.
12 Spence, *Search*, 300; and Hsu, *Modern China*, 501–505.
13 Hsu, *Modern China*, 516; and Spence, *Search*, 309.
14 Hsu, *Modern China*, 516–517.
15 Hsu, *Modern China*, 517; and Spence, *Search*, 310.
16 Spence, *Search*, 324–315; and Hsu, *Modern China*, 518.
17 Hsu, *Modern China*, 520–521.
18 Spence, *Search*, 327; and Hsu, *Modern China*, 525.
19 Spence, *Search*, 322.
20 Spence, *Search*, 331.
21 Hsu, *Modern China*, 527.
22 Spence, *Search*, 333–334.
23 Hsu, *Modern China*, 528–529; and Spence, *Search*, 336.
24 Hsu, *Modern China*, 528–531.
25 Hsü, *Modern China*, 530–531.
26 Fairbank et al., *Tradition*, 682.
27 Fairbank et al., *Tradition*, 682.
28 Fairbank et al., *Tradition*, 656.
29 Fairbank et al., *Tradition*, 684–685.
30 Fairbank et al., *Tradition*, 691–692.
31 Peter Duus, *Modern Japan*, 2nd ed. (Boston: Houghton Mifflin, 1998), 178–179.
32 Fairbank et al, *Tradition*, 698; and Gordon, *Modern History*, 163.
33 Fairbank et al., *Tradition*, 698–700.
34 Hane, *Modern Japan*, 236–237.
35 Fairbank et al., *Tradition*, 700.
36 Schirokauer, *Japanese Civilization*, 237.
37 Duus, *Modern Japan*, 195.
38 Fairbank et al., *Tradition*, 703.
39 Fairbank et al., *Tradition*, 703–704.
40 Fairbank et al., *Tradition*, 687–690.

41 Gordon, *Modern History*, 174.
42 Hsu, *Modern China*, 545.
43 Hsu, *Modern China*, 546.
44 Spence, *Search*, 368–369.
45 Hsu, *Modern China*, 547.
46 Hsu, *Modern China*, 548.
47 Spence, *Search*, 369; and Hsu, *Modern China*, 348.
48 Spence, *Search*, 383.
49 Hsu, *Modern China*, 557–558.
50 Spence, *Search*, 370.
51 Hsu, *Modern China*, 549.
52 Spence, *Search*, 371–372.
53 Hsu, *Modern China*, 551; and Spence, *Search*, 372.
54 Spence, *Search*, 395; and Hsu, *Modern China*, 557–558.
55 Spence, *Search*, 404–405.
56 Hsu, *Modern China*, 564; and Spence, *Search*, 407–408.
57 Hsu, *Modern China*, 565.
58 Spence, *Search*, 409.
59 Hsu, *Modern China*, 565.
60 Hsu, *Modern China*, 550.
61 Hsu, *Modern China*, 579.
62 Hsu, *Modern China*, 580; Fairbank et al., *Tradition*, 709–710; and Hane, *Modern Japan*, 243, 252–253.
63 Hsu, *Modern China*, 581.
64 Fairbank et al., *Tradition*, 714.
65 Hsu, *Modern China*, 582–583; Spence, *Search*, 419–421; and Fairbank et al., *Tradition*, 713–715.
66 Spence, *Search*, 421.
67 Hsu, *Modern China*, 583.
68 Hsu, *Modern China*, 588.
69 Hsu, *Modern China*, 583.
70 Hsu, *Modern China*, 584.
71 Hsu, *Modern China*, 585–586.
72 Janet Hunter, *Concise Dictionary of Modern Japanese History* (Berkeley: University of California Press, 1984), 205; and Fairbank, et al., *Tradition*, 683.
73 Fairbank et al., *Tradition*, 731.
74 Hane, *Modern Japan*, 497.
75 Fairbank et al., *Tradition*, 716.
76 Hane, *Modern Japan*, 292; and Fairbank et al., *Tradition*, 717.
77 Fairbank et al., *Tradition*, 719.
78 Hane, *Modern Japan*, 295; and Fairbank et al., *Tradition*, 719.
79 Fairbank et al., *Tradition*, 694.
80 Hane, *Modern Japan*, 252–253.
81 Fairbank et al., *Tradition*, 715.
82 McClain, *Japan*, 471–472.
83 Hane, *Modern Japan*, 279.
84 Hane, *Modern Japan*, 295.
85 Hane, *Modern Japan*, 297–298.
86 Fairbank, et al., *Tradition*, 719–720.
87 Hane, *Modern Japan*, 299–301.
88 Hane, *Modern Japan*, 302–303.
89 Fairbank et al., *Tradition*, 721.
90 Hane, *Modern Japan*, 304.
91 Hane, *Modern Japan*, 305.
92 Fairbank et al., *Tradition*, 808.
93 Hane, *Modern Japan*, 305.
94 "Lend Lease" was approved by the US Congress in 1941. Supplies were available through "Lend Lease" to the countries of the Allied Powers, and these supplies were free if they were used in the common cause against the enemy of the Allied Powers.
95 Hsu, *Modern China*, 600.
96 Hsu, *Modern China*, 601.
97 Jay Taylor, *The Generalissimo:Chiang Kai-shek and the Struggle for Modern China* (Harvard: Belknap Press of Harvard University Press, 2009), 208–209.
98 Spence, *Search*, 446.
99 Spence, *Search*, 443; and Hsu, *Modern China*, 603.
100 Britannica Educational Publishing, *The History of China*, ed. Kenneth Pletcher (London: The Rosen Publishing Group, 2010), 288–289; and Spence, *Search*, 452–453.
102 Hsu, *Modern China*, 604.
103 Hsu, *Modern China*, 605.
104 Spence, *Search*, 445.

105　Hsu, *Modern China*, 597.

106　Hsu, *Modern China*, 598.

107　John S. Service, *The American Papers: Some Problems in the History of US-China Relations*, (Berkeley, University of California Press, 1971), 162. Quoted from Hsu, *Modern China*, 598, note 39.

108　Hsu, *Modern China*, 607.

109　Fairbank et al., *Tradition*, 809.

110　Fairbank et al., *Tradition*, 810.

111　Fairbank et al., *Tradition*, 814; and Hane, *Modern Japan*, 320–321.

112　Hane, *Modern Japan*, 329.

113　Hane, *Modern Japan*, 329.

114　Hane, *Modern Japan*, 330–331.

115　McClain, *Japan*, 513.

116　Hane, *Modern Japan*, 335.

117　McClain, *Japan*, 513.

118　Hane, *Modern Japan*, 336.

119　John Hersey, *Hiroshima* (New York: Knopf, 1946), 60; quoted from Hane, *Modern Japan*, 336, note 15.

120　McClain, *Japan*, 510.

121　Hane, *Modern Japan*, 337.

122　Hane, *Modern Japan*, 338.

123　McClain, *Japan*, 514.

124　Hane, *Modern Japan*, 339.

125　Fairbank et al., *Tradition*, 818.

126　Fairbank et al., *Tradition*, 818.

127　Hane, *Modern Japan*, 569.

128　Fairbank et al., *Tradition*, 820; and John Dower, *Embracing Defeat: Japan in the Wake of World War II* (New York: W. W. Norton & Company, 1999), 73–78.

129　Hane, *Modern Japan*, 346.

130　Dower, *Embracing Defeat*, 443–447.

131　Fairbank et al., *Tradition*, 822.

132　McClain, *Japan*, 546.

133　McClain, *Japan*, 547.

134　Fairbank et al., *Tradition*, 822.

135　Hane, *Modern Japan*, 348–350.

136　For details of the Article IX, see Toshio Nishi, *Unconditional Democracy: Education and Politics in Occupied Japan*, 1945–1952 (Stanford: Hoover Press, 2004), 126–129.

137　McClain, *Japan*, 557.

138　Hane, *Modern Japan*, 339.

139　Spence, *Search*, 459–460.

140　Hsu, *Modern China*, 623.

141　Spence, *Search*, 462.

142　*United States Relations with China: with Specific Reference to the Period*, 1944–1949 (Washington D.C., 1949), 133, 605–607; quoted from Hsu, *Modern China*, 624, note 15.

143　Hsu, *Modern China*, 625.

144　Hsu, *Modern China*, 625–626.

145　*United States Relations with China*, 212, quoted from Hsu, *Modern China*, 629, note 21.

146　Hsu, *Modern China*, 630.

147　Fairbank et al., *Tradition*, 938.

148　Spence, *Search*, 483.

149　Hsu, *Modern China*, 632.

Chapter *15* Nationalism to Independence

The years prior to the end of World War II in Asia were years of political struggle within Southeast Asia. After 1945, Asia had no choice but to confront its colonial past and the long road to achieve independence. Political movements played an essential role in the road to independence for Southeast Asian countries. These movements attracted a massive following and were often led by prominent people that spoke of freedom and peace. The political sentiments of these movements spread beyond Asia, resonated within the Western hemisphere, and influenced generations during the twentieth century.

ROOTS OF NATIONALISM IN SOUTH AND SOUTHEAST ASIA

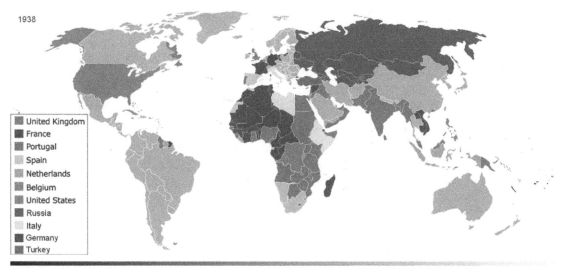

1938

United Kingdom
France
Portugal
Spain
Netherlands
Belgium
United States
Russia
Italy
Germany
Turkey

Colonial Control in 1938

A strong nationalist sentiment in Asia is not new. Early opposition and reaction to colonial and imperial policies originated from political infighting and insurgencies that eventually culminated in major nationalistic movements in Southeast Asia.[1] Several factors contributed to the quest for independence in Asia's colonial states. Political and social movements affected both the impoverished and under-represented within a colonial society, and its government of elite and aristocratic members.[2] After the decline of Spanish rule of the islands, the Philippines led a movement of nationalistic and political action. Filipino nationalism actually began before the Spanish departed in the late 1890s. In the Philippines, an organized group of educated individuals known as the *ilustrados*, which included future Filipino nationalist hero Jose Rizal, fought against oppression. The Philippines and other regions in Southeast Asia, such as Indonesia, Java, Burma, Cambodia, Laos, and Malaya thereafter, launched independence movements.[3] The Philippines began its independence movement in 1895. It was followed by India, Vietnam, and Burma. These countries were experiencing modernization but at the same time attempting to preserve the customs and traditions that they embraced with much loyalty.

Japan intervened in Southeast Asia with a policy known as the Greater East Asia Co-Prosperity Sphere. This policy involved the occupation of French Indo-China by the Japanese, during which they utilized the people and the resources of this region.[4] The Philippines and Indonesia were also occupied by Japan and were a part of this policy. The Japanese presented themselves as liberators to the oppressed colonial states of Southeast Asia. However, relations deteriorated when World War II erupted in Asia and the people of the affected countries were exploited. It became commonplace for them to be forced into labor and prisoner of war camps. The term "occupier" replaced the term "liberator". The aftermath of Japan's policies in Southeast Asia resulted in misconstrued alliances.

The main intent of the nationalist movements was to achieve independence for most of the Asian countries affected by colonial rule; the temporary interruption of war did not deter these movements. The affected countries forged ahead in constructing and assembling a political structure and policies that allowed for self-government. Until this was possible, newly independent countries and people stood under an umbrella of limited support from the previous colonial governments.

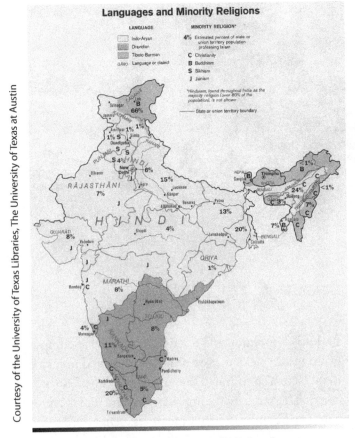

Courtesy of the University of Texas Libraries, The University of Texas at Austin

India's "Languages and Minority Religions"

INDIA AND THE ROAD TOWARD INDEPENDENCE

By 1939, when World War II occurred, Gandhian influence had taken hold in India and it had become apparent that the British would eventually need to make some concessions toward Indian independence. In the Asian theatre of the war, all eyes were on the Japanese. Colonial governments scrambled and organized to deter the Japanese imperial forces, and priorities of political activism shifted to the war effort. However, the desire for national independence did not go away, especially in India and the Philippines. The Philippines already had a time stamp for independence to be proclaimed by 1945. The Government of India Act of

1935 was to provide increased autonomy for India.[5] The Act was a stepping-stone toward Indian and Pakistani independence. It even served as a model to the Indian constitution of 1950.[6] In order to understand why the Government of India Act was put in place, one needs to understand the role of the Indian National Congress. The Indian National Congress was established in 1885. Initially, its main goal was to have its members play an active role in the law-making process. Its members included Hindus, Muslims, and Sikhs. Members of the Indian National Congress typically came from educated, intellectually elite classes within the caste system. Many members of the Indian National Congress were key individuals in the process which led to India's independence. The Government of India Act and the Indian National Congress' role in its creation established the goal for the active participation of Indians in the law-making process in India's British ruled government. English official Allan Octavian Hume (1829–1912) recognized the abilities of each member of the Indian National Congress. He also understood the need for Indian representation within a predominantly British government.

By 1909, two separate agendas for Indian independence were already on the horizon. December 6, 1906 marked the birth of the Indian Muslim League in Dacca (a city which would later become the capital of Bangladesh). The Indian Muslim League issued a memorandum that showed loyalty to the Crown, but also a desire for self-government. The memorandum also acknowledged the need for different religious groups, as well as the feudal class and zamindars (large landlords), to have representation in government.[7] The Muslim league began to focus on gaining representation in institutions of political importance.[8] The Act of 1909 made separate representation for Muslims a reality, but not without political allowances that pitted Muslims against Hindus and that undermined the Indian nationalist movement.

© Bettmann/CORBIS

Gandhi and members of a nationalist party, 1922

Despite future plans for partition, the events associated with the Muslim League did not hinder the goals outlined by the Indian National Congress. Members of the Congress soon realized it would take petitions, prayers, and protests, to reach their goals. A young lawyer, Gujarat-born Mahatma Gandhi (1869–1948), who had already incited action in Johannesburg, South Africa by holding demonstrations against discriminatory practices against non-English or non-European citizens, became a leader in the Indian nationalist movement. Roots of change spread and Gandhi gained a large following by the 1920s. The protests that occurred in South Africa found their way back to India.

After World War I, US President Woodrow Wilson's sympathy for national self-determination, his Fourteen Points, and the Versailles Peace Conference had a profound impact on the nationalist movement for Asians abroad and activists such as Gandhi and Ho Chi Minh. The independence movement transcended more so to *satyagraha*, which emphasized non-violent civil disobedience. It also involved religious overtones and prayer. Gandhi continued the movement well into World War II. The British government began to attempt to grant concessions toward independence for India. One example of such an attempt was the Cripps Mission of 1942 that showed signs of sympathy from the British. Sir Stafford Cripps (1889–1942), a Labor Leader and cohort to Jawaharlal Nehru, was one of several Labor Party members who sympathized with the Indian nationalist movement and urged dialogue with Indian leaders; he understood the complex dynamic between the Indian National Congress and the Indian Muslim League. In order to reconcile the differences between the Indian National Congress and the Indian Muslim League, Viceroy Lord Linlithgow, who did not fair well with Gandhi, sent the Cripps Mission.[9] However, the Cripps Mission was not helpful to the plan for a free country because it offered "dominion status after the war, allowed any province to opt out of that dominion", which conceded to the Muslims' demands. Furthermore, it did not help to reconcile relations between Gandhi and Linlithgow.[10] Despite this attempt at reconciliation, many demonstrations occurred during the war. None of these demonstrations was as monumental as the Quit India Movement of 1942–1943.

QUIT INDIA MOVEMENT AND AFTERMATH

On August 9, 1942 the Quit India Movement began. It was the last major effort to convince the British government to fulfill Gandhi's demands. A committee of the Indian National Congress gathered at the historic Gowalia Tank to pass a resolution demanding the withdrawal of British power from India. This resolution was known as the "Quit India" resolution, an outcry to immediately end British rule in India.[11] Gandhi was successful in drawing attention to the anti-colonial movement in India, but not without 90,000 Indian National Congress members and additional supporters. It has been estimated that millions of people throughout the country, cities, towns, and villages took part in the demonstration, and many were jailed for the violence that ensued.[12] Although deemed as a failure, though not in comparison to the Cripps Mission, this massive movement did not go unnoticed by British officials. In 1945, Japan withdrew from Southeast Asia, and the British were authorized to occupy Southeast Asia south of the fourteenth parallel. Under the supervision of Lord Louis Mountbatten (1900–1979) of the Southeast Asia Command, the British returned to their former colonies of Burma, Malaya, and Singapore.[13] The war had taken a heavy toll upon the war torn regions and colonies. Rebellions among British Indian armed forces undermined morale.[14] 40,000 British Indian troops in Singapore defected and joined the newly created Indian National Army.[15] The English government granted the Muslim League and their leader, Muhammad Ali Jinnah (1876–1948), their demands for an independent Muslim state.

After the collapse of the Mughal empire, power had been consolidated into the hands of the British Raj. The British Crown ruled India, but allowed the establishment of princely states as a political and economic peace keeping act. Former Mughals were made princes of these independent states, but the British government supervised them. When the power of the East India Company diminished after the Great Uprising of 1857, the British "fervently protected the feudal rights and privileges of the princely order, leaving the tens of millions under them away from the democratic winds sweeping the subcontinent."[16] An alliance was established between the British and Indian Muslims, an alliance that benefited both modernization, and the preservation of culture and tradition in the country.

In 1946, Jinnah and English officials agreed on concessions that would allow for the creation of a separate Muslim state of Pakistan where the heritage and identity of Muslims could be preserved. Muslims could live and thrive and practice their faith freely. With the independence of India in August 1947, the

Jinnah and Nehru Meeting, 1946

© Bettmann/CORBIS

Muslim state of Pakistan was also established. Pakistan was originally established in two geographically separate areas. One of these areas, known as West Pakistan, was located in a historic region of the subcontinent, the area where the former Indus Valley Civilization had existed. It was adjacent to West Punjab, Sindh, and Baluchistan. The second area, known as East Pakistan, was located in what had been referred to as Bengal. This was a monumental event that led to a religion-inspired migration from north to south or south to north. India remained mostly Hindu. The migration into and out of India was accomodated by the British-Muslim alliance. This event did not occur without some violence between Muslims and non-Muslims. Jawaharlal Nehru became president of India and defined this moment in a 1947 speech when he spoke of his vision of India's future. Despite the declaration of two new governments and the proclamation of independence handed down by the British, the political division of what had been British India turned into a long-standing struggle drawn along political and religious lines. The peoples of India would have to choose into which state to migrate.

To add to these already tense matters, in 1948 a Hindu radical assassinated Mahatma Gandhi. The Constitution of India was drafted in 1946, adopted in 1949 and enforced in 1950. The document was influenced by India's Western allies: the United States, the United Kingdom, Ireland, Canada, and South Africa. The Indian Parliament was established with a lower and upper house of elected officials. The prime minister is the head of the government but the president, an office with limited power, is the head of state.

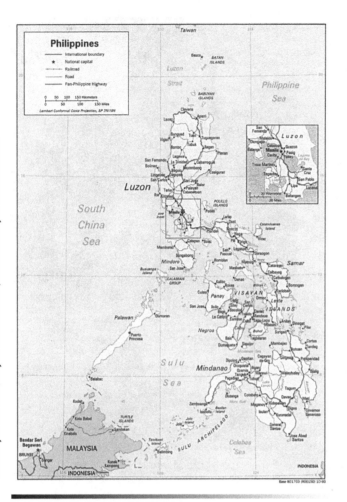

The Philippines

PHILIPPINES

After the end of Spanish rule, the Philippines went into the hands of the United States. The difference between the United States' control of the Philippines and the way countries such as Great Britain, France, and even Spain controlled their colonial possessions was that when the United States intervened in the Philippines, they made an effort to politically and socially rebuild the country so that it could become an independent and sovereign nation. Unlike Vietnam, the Philippines had never been unified under a common government prior to colonial rule.[17] In 1935, the Philippines established a commonwealth free from Spanish or US control. The Commonwealth of the Philippines was confident of its ability to maintain a self-governing state.

Mass groups of people in the Philippines organized to address economic equity, social justice, and public participation in the government. These people were seeking guarantees of political, economic, and social freedom.[18] The concept of individual rights, as expressed in Western philosophies and ideologies, became the cornerstone of the nationalistic independence movements. Filipino leaders and organizers believed in individual rights, and Jose Rizal (1861–1896) was one such leader. Rizal's views were expressed in his first novel, *Noli Me Tangere*. This novel introduced readers to the earlier years of Spanish rule and Rizal's personal experiences and dreams for the country. His second novel, *El Filibusterismo*, came out thirteen years later. *El Filibusterismo* was a cry for freedom from an oppressive government. Rizal and his supporters sought to create a shared sense of identity that the country and people had not experienced under Spanish rule. The political and social patterns that had existed within neighboring Asian countries did not go unnoticed. The political bantering that took place in other Asian countries affected Rizal. Like India and Southeast Asian countries, after World War I, the continued resistance to colonialism in the Philippines was focused on social, economic, and political factors.[19] Rizal would not see the fruits of his political influence come to fruition. However, revolutionaries who supported his cause would help lead the movement for Philippine independence. Members of the *ilustrados* formed politically driven organizations, such as the *Katipunan*, and moved forward after Rizal's demise. Emilio Aguinaldo (1869–1964) spearheaded the movement to end Spanish rule and organized a military approach to the independence movement. His efforts contributed to the establishment of a provisional government of the Republic of the Philippines well before the end of the Spanish American War and the US intervention of 1898.

Courtesy of Library of Congress

Then U.S. Secretary of War William H. Taft and U.S. Governor-General of the
Philippines Lloyd Wright leaving a landing place at Manila

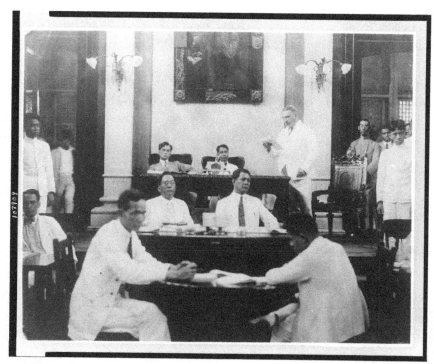

Courtesy of Library of Congress

Philippine Islands, General Leonard Wood reading his message before the
members of the Philippine legislature ca. 1900–1923

A political blunder that took root between the American Consul to Singapore and Admiral George Dewey who was responsible for defeating the Spanish fleet at Manila Bay prevented Aguinaldo from being at the forefront of the new Philippines. The blunder involved unofficial oral assurances between Dewey and Aguinaldo that led Aguinaldo to presume that the granting of complete independence to the Philippines was a done deal. However, that was not the case because the agreement was never officially signed nor was it ever shared with anyone in Washington. It was merely an ill promise that Aguinaldo misunderstood and responded to in the form of a revolt known as the Philippine American War.[20]

The United States took possession of the Philippines following the Spanish-American War. The Philippine Commonwealth had established a Philippine Congress to maintain independence. A series of reforms were implemented during the period when the United States helped to revitalize the Philippines. In July 1901, then "Judge (later president) William H. Taft replaced military rule that had been under the wings of General Leonard Wood from 1906 to 1910 with civilian governors and a year later," Taft declared a state of peace and general amnesty.[21] The Taft Commission acted as the legislative and executive body of the government, but allowed elections of Filipino representatives at the municipal and provincial levels.[22] In 1902, the Organic Act provided the separation of church and state, and lands owned previously by friars were sold to the public.[23] As the Philippines realigned its social structure, the Jones Act of 1916, which was signed by President Woodrow Wilson on August 29, 1916, promised that full political autonomy would eventually be granted to the Philippines; "this set the pattern for the government of the Philippines that obtained until the creation of the commonwealth in 1936."[24] The Jones Act did not, however, give a time frame for when independence was to be achieved. The Philipine Congress was established in 1936 after the Tydings-McDuffie Act was enacted. Unlike the Jones Act, The Tydings-McDuffie Act did give a timeframe for independence. It stated that independence was to be achieved within ten years. In 1935, US President Roosevelt approved a constitution that established the elections of the first Philippine President, Manuel Quezon (1878–1944), and the first Philipine Vice President, Sergio Osmeña. Both men spearheaded the Philippine independence movement from the beginning. The transition to self-government occurred rather swiftly between periods of war. For the most part, the Philippines modeled its government after the American model.[25] The Commonwealth of the Philippines developed their own politicians during the 1930s, which showed that the future looked promising for the Philippines. The Philippines eventually achieved independence on July 4, 1946. The aftermath of World War II and societal division in the form of ethnic, economic, and regional gaps and lines was the challenge that the people of the Philippines had to confront in the proceeding decades of the 1950s and 1960s.[26]

VIETNAM

In Vietnam, a dominant colonial presence and government intervention ceased any form of demonstration and political activism, so nationalistic fervor occurred later in Vietnam than it had in the Philippines or India. A call for political action in Vietnam did not come overnight, but was a gradual process. By the time the British had established settlements in India and Burma, France was already beginning to establish territorial claims in northern Vietnam, Laos, and Cambodia. By 1886, after Burma had fallen to Britain, Vietnam, along with Laos and Cambodia, had become French Indo-China. France controlled Vietnam in the late nineteenth and early twentieth centuries. Colonial events and imperial endeavors inflicted pain and wounds within countries such as Vietnam.

Group of children with baskets, posed under palm tree, Saigon, South Vietnam

Fortunately such treatment did not affect the Vietnamese culture and heritage that fostered nationalism and the preservation of Vietnamese identity. However, due to an increase in socio-economic inequity that had similarly occurred in India and Burma while under British rule, a political movement formed in Vietnam.

The Russian Revolution had a great affect on Ho Chi Minh (1890–1969), a Vietnamese nationalist who recognized the injustices placed upon the peoples of his country. Ho Chi Minh's concerns were similar to those of Gandhi but were much more politically generated, rather than religiously or philosophically centered. The revolutions in Beijing and Russia spoke to the Vietnamese nationalism that later transcended towards Marxist and Communist thought. Ho Chi Minh focused on the impoverished people in Vietnamese society. Under the umbrella of French colonial rule, there existed a socio-economic inequity between north and south. In the south, there was greater French influence, while in the north, Ho had an advantage to lead a revolution and reform against colonial

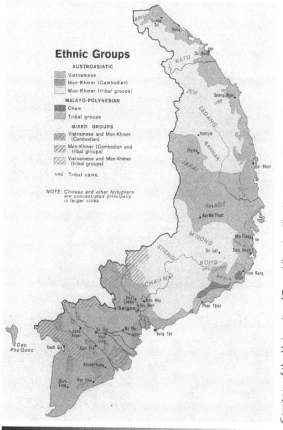

"Ethnic Groups" of Vietnam

exploitation and repression that affected the peasant population. The Great Depression of 1930 intensified demonstrations led by groups of peasants that sympathized with Indonchinese Communists (ICP) and their reaction to crop failures and strikes in factories.[27]

Resistance to the French colonial government drove the Vietnamese nationalist movement. A generation of educated and intellectual Vietnamese individuals reacted to the oppressive and exploitative actions of the colonial government. Their actions led to reactions from the French government. Ho Chi Minh and hundreds of other individuals who fought against the oppression were punished, exiled, or fled the country to safer havens where they could exercise their right to free speech and their right to protest. This made the movement even greater upon their return.

After having formed the French Communist party in France during the 1930s, Ho Chi Minh returned to Vietnam to transform the nationalist sentiment in Vietnam into a communist sentiment with the Indochinese Communist Party. Support for Ho's leadership grew and in 1941 when World War II broke out, Ho formed the Viet Minh, after Ho's relations with the Soviet Union fell apart; the Viet Minh included "nationlists in a Marxist-led united front that worked toward revolution and independence."[28] During World War II, Ho's Viet Minh worked against the Japanese occupation and the French Vichy Regime. The nationalist movement never lost momentum and became allied with Ho and the Vietnamese Communists. This alliance was based on a shared anti-colonial sentiment.

Following Japan's surrender in August 1945, Ho Chi Minh declared independence and established the Democratic Republic of Vietnam.[29] The Declaration of Independence that Ho Chi Minh wrote looked very similar to the American Declaration of Independence in rhetoric and principles. This document provided the foundation for the political changes and struggle which occured in Vietnam when the French continued to occupy the country after the Japanese had surrendered. In 1946, a war between France and Ho Chi Minh's Vietnamese forces began. This war was known as the French Indo-China War or the the First Indo-China War. Vietnamese General Vo Nguyen Giap and his troops often engaged in guerilla warfare against the French. Giap and his troops defeated the French at the Battle of Dien Bien Phu, which is considered to be France's last stand in Indo-China. After this defeat, the French called for peace.[30]

At The Geneva Peace Conference in 1954, France agreed to grant independence to Vietnam. This conference occured during the early part of the Cold War and some of the agreements made there paralleled agreements made at the end of the Korean War. Similar to the situation in Korea, Vietnam was divided with a partition at the 17th parallel. This separation was meant to be temporary. The Cold War, however, was already in progress and the fear of Communism and its possible spread led to US involvement in Vietnam. In 1954, the Second Indochina War (also known as the Vietnam War) began due, at least in part, to the desire of the United States to prevent the spread of Communism to the Southeast Asian states of Laos and Cambodia.

COLONIES AND SETTLEMENTS IN DECLINE POST-1945

INDONESIA

Indonesia was a different story in terms of their nationalistic endeavors. From the late nineteenth to the early twentieth century, the country was under a Dutch policy which provided a cultural boundary between the people of Indonesia and the Dutch colonial government. This policy initially prevented the kind of uprisings and protests that occurred in neighboring Asian countries from

Indonesia

occurring in Indonesia. But like Indonesia's neighbor Vietnam, nationalism in Indonesia was strong by the 1930s and into World War II. The Indonesian Communist Party (PKI) was founded in the 1920s with the support of Muslims in Java, but was later banned by the Dutch. However, Indonesians did not halt their activism; leaders such as Sukarno (1901–1970) organized a much more political entity, the Indonesian Nationalist Party (PNI), and worked towards ending the constricting policies imposed upon the people of Indonesia. Sukarno attracted a mass following because of his use of Javanese religion and cultural symbols.[31] Sukarno had been born into an aristocratic Javanese family. Sukarno's familial background, however, did not hinder his political and social influence upon the people of Indonesia.[32] Much like his counterparts, Ho Chi Minh and Rizal, Sukarno was influenced by Western ideas and philosophy. He had been educated within the Dutch educational system in Java and his political views involved Javanese, Islamic, and Marxist sentiments that represented a form of Indonesian nationalism. Sukarno was well spoken and admired as the most popular nationalist in Indonesian history. He was banned from protesting and was exiled. He did not return to Indonesia until the end of Dutch rule.

Sukarno's departure led to infighting within the country. The Japanese occupation had a tremendous affect on Indonesia. Indonesia's pre-war political associations ceased to exist, although religious groups remained.[33] Indonesia became a republic in 1945.[34] Indonesia's independence was declared by two of Indonesia's major political figures: Sukarno and Mohammad Hatta. However, Indonesia remained the center of attention for the Netherlands that still considered itself the sovereign power of the islands due to the economic wealth that it gained from them. This is where the Marshall Plan served as a springboard for economic relief and a door for independence for Indonesia; this economic plan allowed the Dutch to concentrate on industrializing the Netherlands and focus less on Indonesia. Due to reduced international support for Dutch control of Indonesia and domestic economic troubles, the Netherlands recognized Indonesia's independence in 1949. However, Indonesian independence resulted in mistrust between the Netherlands and Indonesia. Despite this mistrust, Indonesia became the sixtieth member of the United Nations.

Indonesia established a parliamentary form of government; a constitution was adopted and elections were held. Sukarno emphasized "unity and diversity" as his goals for the country.[35] This slogan stressed equal representation and participation of Indonesians in the parliament. The parliament was divided into political parties, which allowed Indonesians the power to write and implement laws. Islam is an essential part of Indonesian society. Sukarno recognized and defended the Islamic traditions of the country, and went so far as to preserve a secular state based on monotheism, humanitarianism, national unity, and representative democracy as declared in the Constitution. Despite this major Constitutional provision, Muslim groups preferred a Muslim state or a preamble provision that adhered to Islamic law.[36]

Courtesy of Library of Congress

Dr. Sukarno, president of Indonesia, during his trip to Washington, D.C.

BURMA

Burma was considered part of British India and the people of the country struggled as the British imposed their traditions over Burmese customs. Buddhist monks and Burmese intellectuals at Rangoon University led one of the first nationalist movements during the 1920s. Policies implemented in India were generally implemented in Burma as well, where a fragmented political and social structure equated to an unbalanced society for the people of the country. Indian civil servants and local Burmese workers were barred from holding government positions beyond clerkships. During the late 1920s and 1930s, there were protests and strikes led by students, teachers, and intellectuals such as Rangoon University student union vice president Ba Maw who was a strict proponent for women's rights and reform.[37] In 1929, the Great Depression affected Burma and its rice industry. This contributed to the economic and political turmoil against the British government.[38]

In 1935, Aung San (1915–1947), a young law student of the Rangoon University Student Union, became the leader of the nationalist movement in Burma and spearheaded political action towards independence. Already by 1935, several political parties had formed out of Rangoon University such as the Thakins ("lords"), which became a political force that allied with Aung San. The Government of Burma Act of 1935, similar to the policy in India, granted greater autonomy to Burma. This represented a major step for Aung San and his supporters, who were now less restrained by the British, but this did not cease protests and demonstrations as they continued well into 1936 when Thakin Nu, the Student Union president, and Aung San were expelled for protesting.[39] When Burma became formally separated from British India by 1937, a constitution was written, and legislative elections were held.

In 1941, Japan occupied Burma. British colonialists and the colonial government fled the country. The Japanese military declared an "Independent Burma."[40] Aung San, at first, was supportive of the Japanese as they sympathized with Burma's sentiments to be free from western rule and also enticed local politicians to become, at least in theory, a part of the administrative structure.[41] He solicited the support of thirty comrades who briefly dispensed to Japan for military training. Meticulous changes took place while Japan offered an empty promise in granting Burma their freedom.

Japan used the declaration of independence of Burma merely as a propaganda tool to gain support from the people of Burma, so that it could strengthen its military and acquire natural resources from the region. Japan's grand plan was to combine asian countries such as Burma into "Greater East Asia." Burma possessed an abundance of rich mineral resources and agricultural products, but when the British departed, they destroyed the modern infrastructure, buildings, communication, and transportation lines. The Japanese utilized Burmese citizens, Indian citizens, and Allied prisoners of war as workers to rebuild the Burmese infrastructure. The infamous railway system between Burma

Courtesy of Library of Congress

Chinese laborers working to reopen the Burma Road in southwest China, 1944 and Thailand is a testament to their arduous labor and to the deaths of thousands of workers. The occupation of Burma by Japanese forces took its toll alongside unfilled promises, which prompted Aung San to change sides. Burma began assisting the British in their fight against the Japanese.

Aung San was instrumental in moving Burma toward independence. However, Burma's independence did not come until 1948, after Aung San and members of his cabinet had been assassinated. U Nu (1907–1995) became the first prime minister of an independent Burma and a major political figure in the country during the 1950s.[42] The year 1948 may have ushered in Burma's independence, but this was the early part of the Cold War. The Cold War brought with it the threat of communism. Burma also suffered from ethnic conflicts over unequal representation in the government, civil wars, empty promises in granting independence to states of the Shans and the Karens, and a debilitating economy. Burma was led down a road of political struggle and turmoil. U Nu stepped down in 1958, but was later reinstated in 1960. Political finagling by General Ne Win led to a coup and military regime.

After 1945 and even before the end of World War II, Burma experienced a confused state of alliances between allies and enemies that the country and its neighbor Thailand experienced as a result of a series of treaties that were in place before the war. These pre-war treaties temporarily granted immunity from invasion and territorial annexation by Great Britain and other Western nations. However, when World War II broke out, things changed. When the Japanese invaded Burma and Thailand, both countries suffered political turmoil and a division of loyalties between the British and the Japanese. Burma, under the leadership of General Aung San, sided with the Japanese in order to deter British presence in the country. However, by 1945, things changed and Burma allied with the United States and Great Britain with the fall of the Japanese occupation of Rangoon. In the process, Burma sought economic and political independence from Britain. Burma's request was granted in 1947 with the Burmese constitution and Burmese independence officially established in 1948.[43] Aung San was assassinated before the constitution took effect. Much like in Indonesia, a parliamentary style of government was established. Burma's central government, however, was weak. This weakness led to political and social upheaval, which led to suffering.

MALAYA

British colonies existed in Hong Kong and Canton, and further south, in Malaya and Singapore. Like Malaya's neighbors, Burma and India, Malaya also experienced a surge of nationalism. The approaches that the colonial government in Malaya took to prevent the spread of nationalism were similar to the approaches used in India when the British colonized the country and people. Malayans became mindful of their past, and their historical traditions as they unearthed archaeological artifacts, and temples. The colonizers were greatly interested in Malay culture and tradition. However, beneath the surface, a nationalist front generated as a result of events taking place in nearby countries such as China and Vietnam that resonated into Malaya. A significant nationalist movement in Malaya, however, would not occur until much later, after 1945.

Malaya and Singapore experienced and participated in nationalistic movements much later than their neighbors, Burma and Vietnam. The strong alliance between the British authorities and Malay officials despite deep ethnic divisions, the economic deterioration of Southeast Asian markets, and the rich tin and rubber industry which was beneficial to the region along the Straits of Molucca and in the Malaya peninsula were all factors which helped delay a significant Malayan independence movement.[44] Early nationalist movements in Malaya originated in China during the 1930s as the

Communist party gained momentum and support from poor residents.[45] The political ideas of the Chinese Communist Party influenced the Malays and in 1930, the Malayan Communist Party (MCP) was formed.[46] Exploitation, however, did not become a major concern in Malaya because British laws protected Malays and Chinese immigrant workers. This swayed people away from protesting and rebelling against the government. However, by the time mass demonstrations started to take place in China and Vietnam during the early twentieth century, it was obvious that the influence of political gatherings and protests would dominate even the most productive regions of Malaya. Chinese immigrants who were influenced by Communism, began to view productive labor and wealth distribution differently. Chinese Communists and Nationalists organized resistance to British rule. Influenced by the political movements generated by the outbreak of war, invasion by Japan, and weak Western colonialism, nationalistic forces began to emerge. Japanese forces had utilized propaganda to draw Malays to their cause to establish an Asian empire, an "Asia for Asians." This propaganda tactic was intended to further Japan's interests in rubber, oil, and timber from Indonesia, Sarawak, Brunei, and Malaya.[47] The Japanese occupied Malaya. At the end of the war in 1945, restructuring took place. Much like the rest of Southeast Asia, the attempt to become one unified independent state happened very gradually.

In 1946, the United Malaya National Organization (UMNO) was formed to promote nationalism and negotiate with the British for the guarantee of Malay rights.[48] In 1948, the kingdoms on the Malayan Peninsula, plus Melaka and the island of Penang, united to form the Federation of Malaya, an independent territory under British protection. A Communist party also formed in Malaya and a guerilla uprising known as the Emergency, ensued against the British in June 1948.

Malaya experienced a period of revolutionary transitions and struggles against Communism. The British intervened in these struggles.[49] Britain also remained economically involved in Malaya, even after its independence. The British rubber industry had a large influence in the country until 1955. A "new imperialism" created by the British rubber industry delayed complete political independence for Malaya. This "new imperialism" caused friction between British elites and the Malayan government.[50] Malaya eventually joined Sarawak and Sabah, regions in Borneo, and formed Malaysia.[51] By 1957, Malaysia achieved independence and Singapore followed in 1965.[52]

NATIONALISM TO INDEPENDENCE

Nationalism served as the foundation for the independence movements in Southeast Asia. However, despite nationalism's importance as a major factor in Southeast Asia's independence movements, by the 1960s, the revolution was over. Replaced by authoritarianism, revolutionary goals were ignored or forgotten. A major war against communism broke out in Vietnam.[53] The Philippines encountered several economic and political upheavals that affected the country and the democratic ideals that the government and people wanted to maintain throughout the twentieth century. Countries such as the Philippines met political and social challenges that are still an issue today. The partition of India led to civil wars between East Pakistan and West Pakistan, which led to their becoming two separate countries in 1971: Pakistan and Bangladesh. Further South, Ceylon was renamed Sri Lanka. The peoples of South and Southeast Asia embraced and utilized the influences of the west that developed during the periods of colonial rule. These influences affected political and social revitalization, infrastructures, education, institutions, and industry. These countries eventually transitioned into economic and cultural modernization.

For more information about the topics discussed in this chapter, please visit the website for this textbook. This website can be accessed from http://www.grtep.com/.

1 SarDesai, *Southeast Asia*, 134.
2 SarDesai, *Southeast Asia*, 134.
3 Lockard, *Southeast Asia*, 112.
4 A. J. Grajdanzev, "Japan's Co-Prosperity Sphere," *Pacific Affairs* 16, no. 3 (Sept. 1943): 5
5 D.R. SarDesai, *India the Definitive History*, 294.
6 SarDesai, *India*, 294.
7 SarDesai, *India*, 282.
8 SarDesai, *India*, 282.
9 SarDesai, *India*, 303.
10 SarDesai, *India*, 304.
11 SarDesai, *India*, 304.
12 SarDesai, *India*, 305.
13 SarDesai, *India*, 305.
14 SarDesai, *India*, 306.
15 SarDesai, *India*, 306.
16 SarDesai, *India*, 292.
17 SarDesai, *Southeast Asia*, 133.
18 SarDesai, *Southeast Asia*, 134.
19 Osborne, *Southeast Asia*, 133.
20 H.W. Brands, *Bound to Empire: The United States and the Philippines*. (New York: Oxford University Press, 1992, 45.
21 SarDesai, *Southeast Asia*, 145.
22 SarDesai, *Southeast Asia*, 145.
23 SarDesai, *Southeast Asia*, 145.
24 Brands, 116.
25 Brands, 162.
26 Lockard, *Southeast Asia*, 163.
27 SarDesai, *Southeast Asia*, 173.
28 Lockard, *Southeast Asia*, 141.
29 Global Edge, Michigan State University: Vietnam History, accessed on May 8, 2012, www.globaledge.msu.edu/countries/vietnam/history.
30 Battlefield Vietnam: A Brief History, accessed on May 8, 2012, www.pbs.org/battlefieldvietnam/history.
31 Lockard, *Southeast Asia*, 138.
32 Osborne, *Southeast Asia*, 142.
33 László Sluimers, "The Japanese Military and Indonesian Independence," *Journal of Southeast Asian Studies* 27, no. 1 (March 1996), 28.
34 Colonialism and Nationalism in Southeast Asia, accessed on May 8, 2012, www.seasite.edu/crossroads/wilson/colonialism.htm.
35 Lockard, Southeast Asia, 162
36 Global Edge: Indonesia: History, accessed on May 8, 2012, www.globaledge.msu.edu/countries/indonesia/history
37 Lockard, *Southeast Asia*, 142.
38 SarDesai, *Southeast Asia*, 162.
39 Lockard, *Southeast Asia*, 142.
40 Donald Seekins, "Burma's Japanese Interlude, 1941–1945: Did Japan Liberate Burma?" Japan Policy Research Institute, JPRI Working Paper no. 87 (August 2002), accessed on May 9, 2012, www.jpri.org/publications/workingpapers/wp87.html.
41 Osborne, *Southeast Asia*, 165.
42 Osborne, *Southeast Asia*, 205.
43 History of Burma, accessed May 2012, http://www.cfob.org/historyOfBurma.shtml
44 Lockard, 144.
45 Lockard, 144.
46 Lockard, 144.
47 Lockard, 144.
48 Lockard, 167.
49 Kiat.net, History of Malaysia, accessed on May 9, 2012, http://www.kiat.net/malaysia/history.html.
50 Nicholas White, "The Frustration of Development: British Business and the Late Colonial State in Malaya, 1945–1957," *Journal of Southeast Asian Studies* 28, no. 1 (March 1997), 104.
51 Robert Shaplen, "Southeast Asia: Before and After," *Foreign Affairs* 53, no. 3 (April 1975), 536.
52 Lockard, 168.
53 Shaplen, "Southeast Asia," 539.

Chapter *16* Cold War and Globalization in Asia

The post World War II era saw three major developments in Asia. The first major development was the independence movements, which occurred under the influence of nationalism, as was discussed in chapter 15. While some Asian countries regained their independence from colonial powers, such as Vietnam, Burma, and Cambodia, several newly independent countries emerged in Asia after Japan's surrender in 1945, such as Indonesia, the Philippines, Malaysia, and Singapore. The second major development was the emergence of the Cold War in Asia, which exerted tremendous influence over regional politics. Between the 1950s and the 1970s, East Asia became a major battlefield in the Cold War between the Communist countries and the US led anti-Communist coalition. The last focus of this chapter is the economic development in Asia after 1950. The rebound of Japan's economy in the post-war era was considered an "economic miracle." This was followed by the success of the countries collectively known as the "Four Asian Tigers." Considering the success of the Four Asian Tigers and the recent economic success of other Asian countries such as China, India, Thailand, and Indonesia, it is likely that Asian countries will continue to have a strong influence in the world in the twenty-first century.

Present-day Asia

COLD WAR EMERGING IN ASIA

The success of Mao Zedong's Communist revolution in China changed the political terrain of East Asia. The United States viewed the Communist success with great caution in light of the increasing concern about Communist expansion led by the Soviet Union, which had successfully built a Communist bloc in Eastern Europe. China became the first major Communist country in Asia. Will other Asian countries follow suit? This became a major concern for the US. After Mao Zedong announced the establishment of the People's Republic of China (PRC), the Soviet Union and several Eastern European countries, such as Romania, Bulgaria, Yugoslavia, Hungary, and Czechoslovakia immediately recognized Mao's China. In January of the next year, Great Britain, Norway, Denmark, Israel, Finland, and Sweden also recognized the PRC as legitimate. The United States, however, adopted a "wait and see" strategy. Despite the Truman administration's earlier commitment to the Nationalist government in China, they hesitated to get involved in the anticipated China-Taiwan conflict as the president was very disappointed with Jiang Jieshi's government. In a statement issued on January 5, 1950, President Truman announced that "the United States has no predatory designs on Formosa [Taiwan], or on any other Chinese territory," and he believed that "the resources on Formosa are adequate to enable them [the Nationalists] to obtain the items which they might consider necessary for the defense of the island."[1]

Six months later, what happened on the Korean Peninsula changed the president's view, as well as US foreign policy, toward China and East Asia in general. Similar to the division of Germany into East Germany and West Germany after World War II, the Korean Peninsula was divided into South Korea and North Korea along the 38th parallel. South Korea was occupied by the United States, and North Korea was occupied by the Soviet Union. The arbitrary division of Korea at the 38th parallel was a result of President Truman's fear of the Soviet occupation of the entire Korean peninsula, after Soviet troops entered Manchuria. Despite the separate occupational zones, both the United States and the Soviet Union were still committed to the original design for Korea. As early as the Yalta Conference in February 1945, Franklin Roosevelt, Winston Churchill, and Joseph Stalin all agreed that Korea would be under an international trusteeship, which would supervise a general election of a unified Korean government. By mid-1948, however, no agreement concerning the details of such a unified government had been reached. The United States simply went ahead and had a general election in South Korea in May 1948. Crediting Korea with little strategic value in America's postwar security design, the United States withdrew the last of its occupation troops from Korea in June 1949, leaving the Korean issue to the United Nations.[2] The Soviet Union, likewise, evacuated most of its troops from North Korea, leaving only some military advisors, after North Korea established its own government in August 1948.

THE KOREAN WAR

Because of the emerging Cold War, Korea was divided and ruled by two separate governments: the Republic of Korea (ROK), headed by Syngman Rhee, an American educated conservative in South Korea, and the Democratic People's Republic of Korea (DPRK), headed by a Communist, Kim Il Sung. Both leaders were headstrong nationalists, and neither of them would settle for a permanent separation of Korea, since the arbitrary separation of Korea at the 38th parallel had neither historical nor cultural value for the nationalistic Koreans.

On June 25, 1950, the Korean War (1950–1953) broke out near the 38th parallel when North Korean troops crossed the border and attacked the South Korean troops. The North Korean military had several advantages over the South Korean military. They had a large group of veterans who had participated in the wars in China, and they were armed with Soviet equipment. The South Korean defense quickly collapsed. Within three days, the North Koreans captured Seoul, the capital city of South Korea and then marched southward.

After the United States learned about the war, its first reaction was that the war was part of a Soviet-led Communist conspiracy in Asia, and that Communist expansion had to be stopped. The United States immediately presented the case to the Security Council of the United Nations (UN), which swiftly passed a resolution the same day, condemning the North Korean invasion of South Korea. Ironically, the Soviet Union, who had veto power at the Security Council, boycotted the Security Council meetings because the seat held by Taiwan was not given to the PRC. Two days later, President Truman ordered the US Air Force and Navy to help the South Koreans. US air support, however, could not stop the North Korean troops. By September, the North Korean troops had almost reached the southern tip of the peninsula. On September 15, General MacArthur was appointed Supreme Commander of the UN army, which included 83,000 Americans. The UN troops landed at Inchon, cutting off the retreating routes of the North Koreans, and soon pushed the North Koreans back to north of the 38th parallel.

Douglas MacArthur in Korea, 1951

Courtesy of Library of Congress

MacArthur's next move, an attempt to reunify Korea, is still very much under debate. Some scholars believe that it was an "uncontroversial" decision by the United States, whereas others believe that MacArthur had become carried away by his initial victories over the North Koreans.[3] Whatever the reason behind this decision, the UN troops crossed the 38th parallel and continued their advance all the way up to the Yalu River, the border between Korea and China. When the UN troops first approached the 38th parallel, Zhou Enlai, China's new premier, sent out warnings through Indian government that China would not tolerate America's advance into North Korea, but the American government brushed them off as a bluff.[4]

On October 14, Chinese "volunteers" started to move into North Korea, largely undetected by US intelligence. MacArthur's troops continued to push forward after they captured Pyongyang on October 20, and on November 21, an American unit reached the Yalu River. By this time, General MacArthur had certainly "exceeded his instructions in using American troops so close to the Chinese border," even if his move across the 38th parallel may not have been his own decision.[5] US bombers started to bomb the North Korean area near the Yalu River, and some of the bombs landed on the Chinese side of the river.

As many as 300,000 Chinese troops moved into North Korea. When MacArthur started his last counter-offensive to complete the UN occupation of North Korea, the Chinese troops, under the command of Marshall Peng Dehuai, joined the remaining North Korean troops to engage in fighting against the UN forces. Totally caught by surprise and outnumbered, the UN troops soon retreated to south of the 38ᵗʰ parallel, where both sides continued to engage in bitter fighting. In retaliation, MacArthur suggested to President Truman that he bring the war to China and ask Taiwan to attack China from the south. Disagreeing with these imprudent measures, the president ordered the Seventh Fleet to enter the Taiwan Strait to prevent a war between China and Taiwan from occurring.[6] The Korean War dragged on for two more painful years. By the time an armistice was signed in July 1953, which ended the military conflict, the number of US casualties had reached over 160,000, including 54,000 deaths. South Korea suffered about 400,000 casualties, whereas North Korea lost about 600,000 people. The Chinese government never publicized the number of casualties that incurred in the Korean War, but the number of its casualties was estimated to be between 700,000 to 900,000.[7]

The Korean War had become the impetus behind the Cold War in Asia and had significant political and economic consequences. In retrospect, it was not a "Communist conspiracy." It started as a move toward national reunification. Stalin was not committed to supporting North Korea, even though he might have encouraged Kim Il Sung's aggressive actions against South Korea. Mao Zedong might have actually disagreed with Kim's plan and as a result, was not informed of the details of Kim's.[8] He only ordered his troops to go into North Korea when he perceived the Americans' move toward the Yalu River as a threat to China's security. When the war ended, most Korean cities were reduced to rubble, and Korea remained divided.

The Korean War greatly damaged US-China relations. China's fighting against the United States in Korea convinced the US government that China was a firm ally of the Soviet Union, and therefore on the opposing side of the Cold War. This perception eliminated the possibility of the United States recognizing Mao's China, and the war interrupted normal diplomatic relations between the two nations for the next two decades. In the United States, the Korean War shocked conservative politicians who brought up the question of "Who lost China?" In the early 1950s, Joseph McCarthy, a senator from Wisconsin, claimed that there were "Communists" in the State Department who deliberately aided the Chinese Communists. The subsequent purge eliminated most of the experts on China in the State Department and the foreign services. This may have resulted in a lack of understanding of China's strategy during the Korean War and later during America's War in Vietnam. The United States may have misunderstood the nature of the relationship between China and the Soviet Union.[9] Only in light of the open arguments between China and the Soviet Union in the 1960s, and the border wars between the two in 1969, was Dr. Henry Kissinger, a foreign affairs advisor to President Nixon, eventually convinced that it might be worthwhile to explore the possibility of engaging China as an ally against the Soviet Union.

Nationalist Taiwan and newly independent Japan benefited from the situation following the Korean War. Nationalist China, once again, was put under the protection of the United States. It was considered the legitimate government of China in the eyes of most countries and represented China in the Security Council of the United Nations until 1971. Japan became a strategic partner with the United States and remained one of the most trusted allies of the United States in its Cold War against the Soviet Union. US foreign aid, as well as contracts for war supplies and repairs due to the Korean War, poured into Japan and greatly helped its post-war economic recovery. One of the most important legacies of the Korean War, however, was America's increasing involvement in Asia, especially in Vietnam.[10]

THE WARS IN VIETNAM

After the Korean War, the center of the Cold War in Asia changed to Vietnam. Between 1946 and 1975, two wars occurred in Vietnam. The first of these wars, the First Indochina War, was basically an anti-colonial war against the French that lasted from 1946 to 1954. The second war, the Vietnam War, occurred from 1959 and 1975. The United States' reason for getting involved in this war was similar to its reason for getting involved in the Korean War; namely, the United States wanted to keep "Communist North Vietnam" from taking over "democratic South Vietnam."

The First Indochina War, which was discussed in the last chapter, started as a war against the return of French colonial rule over Vietnam after Japan's surrender in 1945. Unlike the division of Korea, the division of Vietnam was more of a legacy of French colonial government than of allied occupations after World War II. Vietnam was under French colonial rule before Japan started its move toward Southeast Asia. In 1940, Japan obtained an agreement from the collaborative Vichy government in France that allowed Japan to move into Vietnam. After Japan's attack at Pearl Harbor, Japan ruled Vietnam through the French colonial government and only ousted that government in March 1945, for fear that the French colonial government would shift their support to the Free French under de Gaulle.[11]

After Japan's surrender in August 1945, Ho Chi Minh, a leader of the Indochinese Communist Party of Vietnam, led his forces into the power vacuum and took control of Hanoi. In early September, Ho established the Republic of Vietnam. His government, however, was weak and had problems gaining support from well-to-do and well-educated Vietnamese. In order to gain broader support, Ho was willing to compromise and he even dissolved the Communist Party in November 1945.[12] Instead, Ho strengthened the Viet Minh (League for the Independence of Vietnam), a military organization established in 1941 for the purpose of national unification. After the Allied forces arrived in mid-September, the Chinese forces under the Nationalist government occupied the area north of the 17th parallel, and the British occupied the area south of it. Sympathizing with France's desire to restore its sense of national glory by holding on to its colonial empire, the British, before they left in January 1946, allowed the French to retake Saigon and other major cities in South Vietnam. The Nationalist Chinese, on the other hand, allowed Ho's Viet Minh to continue their control in the North, and this prevented the French from returning to North Vietnam. The Chinese Nationalist government, however, pushed the Viet Minh to negotiate with the French. The Viet Minh and the French soon reached an agreement, by which the French would recognize Viet Minh's Democratic Republic of Vietnam in exchange for Viet Minh's promise to "become a part of the Indochinese Federation and the French Union."[13] The terms of the agreement were too vague to prevent belligerence from resurfacing. In December 1946, motivated by a strong desire to unify Vietnam, Ho's government declared war against the French colonial government, and that war lasted until 1954.

In 1948, in order to balance Ho's state in North Vietnam, the French established another government in Saigon headed by Bao Dai, the last emperor of the Nguyen Dynasty (1802–1945). The Americans initially were not keen on the idea of France's reinstating its colonial rule over Vietnam. Around the time of the Korean War, however, the United States changed its position and began to see North Vietnam's war against the French as another example of "Communist expansion." This view was reinforced in February 1950, when Ho asked both Stalin and Mao for support. The next year, Ho reinstituted a Communist Party in Vietnam, the Vietnam Worker's Party (also known as the *Lao Dong* Party), using the Soviet Communist Party as a model. America then joined Great Britain's efforts in supporting Bao Dai's regime in the South; whereas, the Soviet Union and China, now under Communist rule, aided Ho's regime in the North. As a result, Vietnam's struggle against French colonial rule became a part of the emerging Cold War in Asia.[14]

In April 1954, the army of the Viet Minh, under General Vo Nguyen Giap (br. 1912), scored a decisive victory against the French at Dien Bian Phu and forced the French to surrender in May. As the war in Vietnam became increasingly unpopular at home, the French Government decided to quit. At an international conference at Geneva, Switzerland in 1954, both sides agreed on a temporary partition of Vietnam at the 17th parallel near the city of Hue. This resulted in there being two governments in Vietnam: the Democratic Republic of Vietnam (DRV), headed by the Viet Minh and the State of Vietnam, headed by Emperor Bao Dai. A general election for a united government of Vietnam, according to the Geneva Accords, would be held in 1956, and the French would leave the country.[15]

Ngo Dinh Diem, premier of Emperor Bao Dai, soon became a real power player in South Vietnam. With the support of the United States, he announced that the government in South Vietnam disagreed with the terms of the Geneva Accords of 1954 from the very beginning, and accordingly, would not participate in the scheduled general election in 1956. He argued that his government could not trust the Communist government to have a fair election in the North. Instead, a referendum concerning the future of South Vietnam was held in October 1955. It was supervised by Diem's brother. Diem claimed that he got 98% of the votes, 600,000 votes in total, even though the total number of registered voters was only about 450,000.[16] A few days later, Diem declared himself to be the President of the Republic of Vietnam, which replaced the State of Vietnam, and ousted Emperor Bao Dai.

The DRV in the North was not happy with the developments in the South, but its government had its own problem: consolidating its control of North Vietnam. The rigid land reform imposed by the Communist party alienated many Vietnamese in the North, and the situation became so bad that the Viet Mihn quickly lost popular support. In the following years, the government had to focus on repairing the damage done by its radical policies, and its attention was temporarily diverted from the issue of reunification.[17] The leadership of the DRV actually split into two groups. One group promoted the idea of "North first," which meant that the economy in the North should be strengthened before making an attempt at re-unification. The other group preferred a more aggressive policy, arguing that their main priority should be achieving national unity, even at the risk of a war with the United States.[18] By mid-1959, the group preferring a more aggressive policy gained an upper hand, and a decision was made to establish the National Liberation Front (NLF), widely known as the Viet Cong, in order to support the anti-government movements in the south, which had already gained momentum in the countryside of South Vietnam as a result of Diem's abusive policies toward the peasants. This indicated a major shift of DRV policy toward becoming involved in the resistance movement in the South, as one member of the Foreign Ministry explained, "We had given up a strategy of purely political struggle, which could not succeed due to Ngo Dinh Diem's brutal tactics against our people."[19] In May 1959, the Lao Dong Party, the Communist party in Vietnam, publicly identified "the United States as the main obstacle to the realization of the hopes of the Vietnamese people, and as an enemy of peace."[20]

America's war in Vietnam, usually dated from 1959 to 1973, did not have a clearly defined beginning. It was the result of a series of events beginning in 1959 and a gradual escalation of America's involvement. In August 1959, North Vietnam established the Ho Chi Mihn Trail, through which many former Viet Minh members who had left South Vietnam for the North after the Geneva Accords in 1954 were sent back to the South to strengthen the anti-government movement there. In 1960, the NLF was formally established, and by 1962, its forces had grown to an estimated 300,000 members.[21] The violence in South Vietnam extended to Americans in the area as well. In 1961, President Kennedy decided to send 600 American military advisors to South Vietnam in order to save Diem's government from falling into the hands of the Communists.[22] Under the influence of the Cold War, the JFK administration firmly believed that NLF's guerrilla warfare in South Vietnam was directly controlled by the North, which in turn, was controlled by the Chinese and Soviet Communists. Therefore, it was considered important to prevent a Communist victory in Vietnam. Robert McNamara, the US Defense Secretary, later commented: "We believed that if the South Vietnamese domino fell, then all of Southeast Asia—Thailand, Indonesia, Malaya, the Philippines, even Japan—could be at risk."[23] Due to its commitment to Cold War ideology, the United States became increasingly involved in the Vietnam War. In November 1961, President Kennedy dramatically increased US aid to Diem's government, even though that government was proven to be corrupt.[24] At the end of 1962, the number of US military advisors in Vietnam was about 12,000.[25]

In November 1963, Diem was assassinated at the hands of his own officers who were under the influence of the United States. Afterwards, the situation in the South became more chaotic.[26] Like Diem's government, the subsequent military governments in the South were corrupt and lack of popular support. This helped to strengthen the Communist-led resistance movement.[27] The United States became deeply involved in the Vietnam War without being able to win a decisive victory over the NLF. The basic problem was that America failed to understand the depth of the peasants' wrath toward Diem and other South Vietnamese government officials, and the depth of their ardor for reunification. The US government at the time still clung to the idea that the resistance in the South was only manufactured by the North. This misunderstanding led to the escalation of the war in 1965, when President Lyndon Johnson ordered a systematic bombing of North Vietnam and put US ground troops into combat in South Vietnam, where "the rice paddies and jungles" constituted an "impossible terrain in

which to engage our forces," warned George Ball, the Under Secretary for Economic and Agricultural Affairs under President Kennedy.[28] This decision may have been, in a sense, a response to the early infiltration of North Vietnamese troops into the South. After the escalation, however, the DRV poured even more troops into the South. This opened a new stage of the war, "Americanization," which changed the nature of the war from a war primarily characterized by resistance against the South Vietnamese government to a major war between the United States and the

United States Department of Defense

Picture from the Vietnam War

combined troops of the NLF and the DRV.[29] By early 1968, there were more than 500,000 US troops in South Vietnam, fighting an impossible war to defend an indefensible regime in the South.

As the Vietnam War continued, it started to lose public support back in the United States. The open split between Mao's China and the Soviet Union over ideological issues in the early 1960s strongly undermined the early theory of "Communist conspiracy." As war losses dramatically increased on both sides, the anti-war movement reached a new level in the United States by the late 1960s. The public demanded answers to the question, "Why are we there?" In 1968, peace negotiations between the United States and North Vietnam started in Paris. After President Nixon got into office, he started the process of "Vietnamization" of the war in June 1969, in order to reduce the number of US troops in Vietnam. By 1973, when the Paris Peace Accords were signed, over 58,000 Americans and over 500,000 Vietnamese soldiers had died in the war.[30] Vietnam suffered overall more than six million casualties. According to Rhoads Murphey, the United States may have dropped more bombs in the Vietnam War, maybe twice as much in terms of tonnage, than it did in World War II.[31] Two years after the Paris Peace Accords, the South Vietnamese government collapsed. The DRV sent administrators to Saigon on April 30, 1975, only hours after the last units of American troops left the city.[32] In 1976, the United Socialist Republic of Vietnam was established with its capital in Hanoi, and Saigon was renamed as Ho Chi Minh City.[33]

The Vietnam War, in a sense, was an indirect result of the McCarthyism of the early 1950s, during which many Chinese and Asian specialists were purged as Communist sympathizers. Few advisors of military and foreign policy to the JFK and Johnson administrations probably understood what was happening in Vietnam or in the Communist bloc in general at the time.[34] Henry Kissinger and President Nixon's surprise visits to Mao's China, in 1971 and 1972 respectively, in the middle of the Vietnam War, were a major breakthrough of the Cold War. With the endorsement of the United States, the People's Republic of China took a seat at the United Nation and the UN Security Council in 1971 and has since established diplomatic relations with the United States, Japan, and many other countries.

MAO'S CHINA

When the Communists won the civil war in China in 1949, the Chinese people, in general, welcomed the new regime. After having experienced nearly four decades of war and chaos since the end of the Qing dynasty, China was badly in need of peace and stability. A new regime seemed to promise that to the Chinese people. The acceptance of the new government was made easier in light of a horrible economic crisis that pushed the national economy to the verge of collapse. Inflation skyrocketed between 1947 and 1949. If the wholesale price index measured 100 in May 1947, it rose in June to 112, in July to 130, in September to 179, in October to 282, and in December to 389, which was a 544 percent increase from that in May. In 1948, that index continued to rise to 780 in February, in May to 2100, in June to 7650, and in July to 11,100![35] The rapid rate of inflation was catastrophic to life in China, especially in major cities. In Shanghai, for example, a bag of rice (about 171 pounds) cost twelve yuan in 1937, but 6.7 million yuan in early June 1948, and 67 million yuan in August 1948. A forty-nine-pound bag of flour cost forty-two yuan in 1937, but 1.95 million yuan in June 1948, and 21.8 million yuan in August 1948.[36] In the second half of 1948, Jiang resorted to drastic methods for curbing inflation and issued a new bank note, the "gold yuan," to replace the old "fabi." This, however, did not work. The Shanghai wholesale price index continued to rise. If the index in August 1948 is considered to be 100, it rose to 1,921 by the end of the year, and to 40,825 in February 1949.[37]

This economic disaster completely destroyed the credentials of Jiang's GMD government. As Dean Acheson noted, "The decay which our observers had detected in Chungking [Chongqing] early in the war had fatally sapped the power of resistance [to the Japanese] of the Kuomintang. Its leaders had proved incapable of meeting the crisis confronting them, its troops had lost the will to fight, and its Government had lost popular support."[38]

Mao's new government, however, was not democratic, even though a Political Consultant Conference was immediately established with representatives from all the political parties, including the GMD, represented by the GMD members who chose to stay on the Mainland after 1949. The Organic Law of 1949 described the PRC as a "Democratic Dictatorship" led by a single party, the Communist Party, on the basis of a four-class alliance: workers, peasants, petty bourgeoisie, and national capitalists. The four-class alliance, which represented over 95 percent of the Chinese, gave the government a "democratic" portrayal; whereas, the unyielding dictatorship would be used against "counterrevolutionaries" and "enemies of the people."[39] The Organic Law remained in force for five years, and was replaced by a Constitution of 1955. Under the new constitution, the highest state organ was the National People's Congress, which convened every four years. The government would be headed by the State Chairman, and other major central offices including a State Council, headed by the Premier, a Supreme People's Court, and a Supreme People's Procuratorate. Under the central government, there were provinces, municipalities, and autonomous regions. Similar to the organizational structure of Jiang's GMD government, the real power resided with the Communist Party, whose Central Committee and Politburo were in charge of national policy.[40]

The initial priority of the new government was to stabilize the national economy. In May 1949, the People's Bank of China issued new banknotes, *reminbi* (people's currency) and banned the circulation of foreign currencies. In order to reduce the amount of paper currency in circulation and curb inflation, the government introduced a "wage-point" system to pay the salaries of government employees.[41] A wage-point was based on the prices of five basic items: rice, oil, coal (for cooking), flour, and cotton cloth; the value of these points would rise or fall according to the prices of these commodities.[42] In 1950, the government managed to control inflation and balance its budget. It was a great achievement in light of the fact that under Jiang's government in the previous year the budget deficit was 75 percent.

The government then moved to economic reconstruction by introducing land reform in the countryside in the mid-1950s. The government divided the rural population into five different categories: the landlords, the rich peasants, the middle peasants (who worked their own lands without renting them out), the poor peasants, and the hired hands. The government confiscated most of the land owned by families in the first two categories and redistributed it to those in the last two categories. By December 1952, the agrarian revolution had been completed, and nearly 700 million *mu* had been distributed to 300 million poor peasants.[43]

The CCP, however, did not allow land to be in the hands of private owners for long. The government soon made the peasants to give up private ownership of their land and organized them into farming collectives. By the end of 1956, 96 percent of peasant households were enrolled into 760,000 to 800,000 cooperative organizations. In 1958, these farming organizations were combined into a socialist agrarian organization, the People's Commune.[44]

The government policies aimed at the urban populations were initially more lenient than their policies for those in the countryside. The People's Government was anxious to gain the support of the urban population and was concerned about restoring the national economy, which had plunged to between 56 and 75 percent of its prewar peak. The CCP government initially allowed most city officials to stay at their posts and factory owners to manage their own factories.[45] It seemed that most of the CCP's initial policies worked. In 1952, grain output amounted to 308.8 billion *jin* (one *jin* is half kilogram), an increase of 42.8 percent from 1949; and the gross output of industry reached 34.33 billion yuan the same year, a 144.9 percent increase from 1949. According to Immanuel Hsu, by 1952, "not only had the prewar peaks been matched, but those of 1949 were surpassed by 77.5 percent."[46]

Encouraged by this early success, the CCP became more confident and started to push forward more and bigger projects. Following the Soviet model of a planned economy, the CCP started to prepare for the First Five-Year Plan in 1953. Due to a lack of expertise in handling the preparation, however, the plan was not launched until February 1955. As a result, the First Five Year Plan was only a three-year plan. Even though the plan was shortened, the results were quite encouraging. The targets of the First Five-Year Plan were exceeded by an average of 19 percent. In many categories, such as in the production sector (i.e. machinery, chemicals, steel ingots, electric power, internal combustion engines, generators, electric motors, machine tools, trucks, bicycles, and transformers), the output exceeded the target by 20 to 134 percent.[47] The first decades of the PRC were largely a success.

The success of the First Five-Year Plan was followed by the more ambitious Second Five-Year Plan (1958–1962), which called for an overall increase in output of 75 percent in national industry and agriculture, as well as a 50 percent increase in national income.[48] In order to fulfill this overly ambitious plan, the government soon started a national movement known as the "Great Leap Forward." It called for about a 20 percent increase in major industrial categories, such as steel production, electricity, and coal production. With little professional advice, the Central Committee of the CCP arbitrarily raised the steel production target twice within three months from an already inflated goal of 6.2 million tons in February 1958, to 8.85 million tons in May, and to 10.7 million tons in August of the same year. The production of steel in 1957 was only 5.35 million tons, and steel production from January 1958 up to August 1958 was only four million tons. To fulfill the projected 10.7 million tons meant that the daily production had to be 60,000 tons. What was the rationale for such an extremely bold move?

Mao Zedong was a true believer in the power of mass movements, which had brought him success in wartime. Now, Mao and his comrades were counting on a mass movement to promote the production of steel. Leaders at various levels were mobilized to organize a mass movement to boost the production of steel. By the end of 1958, over 600,000 small "backyard" blast furnaces were operating across the country. The number of people mobilized to work the mines and furnaces jumped from 240,000 in August to 50,000,000 by September and eventually reached 90,000,000. Iron and steel production spread everywhere, to fields, to schools, to the streets, to the courtyard of the Ministry of Foreign Affairs, and even to State Vice-Chairman Madame Song Qingling's backyard.[49] By the end of the year, the Party announced that the goal of producing 10.7 million tons of steel had been met, but more than a quarter of the produced steel and iron was useless. Consequently, the Great Leap Forward movement proved to be a total economic failure. The movement resulted in an enormous waste of resources and damaged the agricultural sector. Over thirty-eight million peasants had to stop farming to produce steel in August and September, and this left many crops unharvested due to insufficient hands in the fields. This, plus the natural disasters that hit the country over three consecutive years, resulted in a great famine between 1960 and 1962, during which an estimated ten to thirty million Chinese died of starvation. The official statistics are still unavailable.[50]

In the late 1950s, Mao faced criticism from both the Chinese people and his own comrades. Mao took the criticism personally, and viewed it as a challenge to his power. The CCP tightened their control over Chinese society through political movements. For example, the first phase of a movement known as the Anti-Rightist Campaign was held between 1957 and 1959, which produced 500,000 to 750,000 victims, most of whom were intellectuals.[51] The loss of support and expertise from

intellectuals was one of the reasons for the economic disasters during the Great Leap Forward movement. The second phase of the Anti-Rightist Campaign was connected to the power struggle within
the CCP. General Peng Dehuai, Minister of Defense, and several other top leaders were ousted because
they voiced their opinion that Mao Zedong was responsible for the economic failure of the Great
Leap Forward. Mao resigned from the State Chairmanship in 1959 and was succeeded by Liu Shaoqi.

The PRC in the 1950s and 1960s suffered from relative international isolation as a result of the
Cold War. After the Korean War, the United States decided not to recognize Mao's government as a
legitimate regime, and as a result, the GMD government in Taiwan held China's seat in the United
Nations. Many countries followed the US foreign policy of isolating China. By 1969, only forty-
eight countries around the world recognized the PRC, whereas seventy-one countries recognized the
Republic of China in Taiwan. International isolation reduced China's chances of securing international support during difficult periods, such as the great famine in the early 1960s.

In the second half of the 1950s, China's relations with the Soviet Union also went sour after Nikita
Khrushchev (1894–1971) became the First Secretary of the Communist Party of the Soviet Union
in 1953, when Stalin died. Mao became especially alarmed in 1956 when Khrushchev delivered a
"secret speech," which denounced Stalin, at the Twentieth Party Congress of the Soviet Union. Even
though Mao himself had had problems with Stalin, especially over Stalin's policy toward China,
the disrespect that Khrushchev showed to Stalin shocked Mao in a profound way both politically
and psychologically. Politically, Mao believed that Khrushchev damaged not only the reputation of
Stalin, but also the reputation of the entire Communist world. Also, in the eyes of Mao, Khrushchev's
foreign policy toward the United States discredited him as the leader of the Communist world, and
this would provide Mao with an opportunity of claiming himself a leader.[52] All of this motivated him

to lead the CCP into an open split with the Soviet
Union in the early 1960s. In retaliation, Khrushchev
withdrew all of the Soviet experts in China, experts
that were in China to help with new industrial projects that were part of China's first two Five-Year Plans.
During the Khrushchev era, China's relations with the
Soviet Union went from lukewarm to cold, and eventually, to hostile. The CCP openly accused the Soviet
Communist Party of being a "revisionist" party, which
meant that it was no longer a real Communist party.

Khrushchev's "de-Stalinization" movement also
had a profound psychological impact on the aging
Mao, who became increasingly convinced that the
Soviet Union was his real enemy internationally.
Domestically, he viewed his own comrades within
the CCP as potentially dangerous to him. Mao was
determined to start another revolution to eliminate
"China's Khrushchev" from his party before it was
too late. Otherwise, both his party and his country
would "change their color," which meant that China
would become a capitalist country and the Communist Party, a "revisionist party." In August 1966, Mao,
at the age of seventy-three, started his last revolution,

A poster from the Cultural Revolution

the Chinese Cultural Revolution (1966–1976), which eventually turned the entire country upside down. Mao designated his wife, Jiang Qing, as the leader of this revolution and used teenage students as his "Red Guards" to attack other CCP leaders under the excuse that they had chosen to go along the capitalist road as "Capitalist roaders." The initial victims of this "Cultural Revolution" included Liu Shaoqi, the State Chairman, who was soon labeled as "China's Khrushchev," and Deng Xiaoping, the General Secretary of the CCP Secretariat. By the end of 1966, the Red Guards had brought total chaos to major cities. They beat many teachers who had "bad-class" origins to death and harassed whoever they perceived as targets of the revolution. Hundreds of thousands of CCP cadres were ousted as followers of the "Liu-Deng Capitalist Headquarters," and no one was safe from the terrorism of the Red Guards.

Mao obviously underestimated the grievances of the people, and once his revolution started, it went out of control. After the workers and peasants joined the revolution, the entire country slipped into a *de facto* civil war for power, since the government had collapsed at all levels. Eventually, Mao had to bring in the military, which was the only government institution left intact, to restore national order. The Cultural Revolution turned out to be an even bigger disaster than the Great Leap Forward. It negatively touched the lives of nearly all Chinese people, and even Mao himself eventually became a victim of his own delusions, which compelled him to find and destroy his imagined enemy for the sake of his revolutionary legacy. His Cultural Revolution, however, did nothing but destroy that legacy. As soon as he died in September 1976, the CCP ended the Cultural Revolution in October. Jiang Qing, his wife, and her Cultural Revolution colleagues were arrested a month after Mao's death. The country suffered tremendous damage from the Cultural Revolution, during which nearly 100,000,000 people were mistreated in one way or another.

ECONOMIC DEVELOPMENTS IN JAPAN

A 1984 public opinion poll in Japan named Yoshida Shigeru (1878–1967) as "the greatest Japanese figure of the twentieth century."[53] Yoshida was Japan's Prime Minister from May 1946 to May 1947 and from February 1949 to December 1954. Under Yoshida's leadership, Japan started to rebuild its industry and focus on economic recovery. His major policies, known as the "Yoshida Doctrine," which emphasized economic development and a reliance on the United States for military protection, laid the foundation for Japan's post-war national policies. When the Cold War emerged in Asia with the outbreak of the Korean War in June 1950, Japan came under increasing pressure from the United States to rearm itself. Yoshida, however, successfully defended Japan's decision not to be drawn into the Cold War by citing Article IX of Japan's 1947 Constitution, which maintains that Japan will never maintain regular armed forces. Yoshida argued that Japan's small defensive forces did not give Japan the ability to be involved in the war effectively. As a result, he was able to keep Japan out of the military conflicts of the Korean War, although Japan did provide aid to US troops at the Incheon Landings.[54] After Japan established its Self-Defense Forces, the government managed to keep its military budget at less than 1 percent of Japan's Gross Domestic Product (GDP); this became the norm in Japan throughout the Cold War era.[55]

The Korean War provided Japan a much needed opportunity for economic recovery. Japan's manufacturing sector boomed when four billion dollars worth of American military procurement orders poured in. By the time Yoshida's last term ended in December 1954, Japan had recovered economically from the devastation of World War II, and by 1955, Japan's productivity had risen to match that of the prewar era.[56]

From the 1950s to the 1970s, the Japanese economy developed at a miraculous speed, with an average growth rate of 11 percent each year. In 1973, Japan's economy became the third largest in the world, behind that of the United States and the Soviet Union, both of which were much larger continental countries. Many scholars believe that Japan created an economic miracle. While some scholars believe that Japan's economic boom was a combination of a favorable international environment and Japan's national policy of economic development, others point out several special characteristics in Japan that help account for this "economic miracle."

The high productivity of Japanese industry largely depended on Japanese workers, who are known for their diligence, discipline, and skill. By the 1960s, Japan had created a workforce that was probably the best in the world, and the work ethic of the Japanese greatly contributed to the economic development of the country.[57] Other factors included a low military budget and the relatively low cost of buying or licensing new technology, instead of developing it in Japan. One lesson learned from Japan's experience is that it is generally cheaper to buy than to develop new technology. This, however, does not mean that Japan did not invest in the development of technology. By 1988, Japan's investments in research and technology had reached 3 percent of its GDP, which was higher than Germany, Britain or France, and about the same as the United States.[58] Also, during these years, the Japanese saved on average four to five times more than Americans did. Between 1970 and 1972, Japanese households saved about 26 percent of their disposable income, whereas the average household savings in Western European countries was between 15 and 17 percent.[59] Japanese banks encouraged people to save more, and in 1970, one advertiser popularized the saying, "Happiness is a bank account of 1 million yuan (about $3,000)."[60]

The Japanese government also played a crucial role in this economic boom. Japan is a democratic country, but the government's involvement in planning Japan's economy was much more than any other democratic countries. Some scholars argue that Japan's economy actually developed under "Japan Inc.," a term that describes the close cooperation between private businesses and the Japanese government, which would provide guidance and support, but others question such a characterization.[61] Much of the Japanese government's involvement with the economy was done through the Financial Ministry and the Ministry of International Trade and Industry (MITI). These agencies collaborated with each other through the Economic Planning Agency to decide on the direction of Japan's economic development. The Bank of Japan, for example, would generously back commercial bank investments in the areas that the MITI perceived as vital for Japan's economic development. Many Japanese companies, if they followed the government's guidance, could borrow as much as two-thirds of their capital requirements from the bank; whereas American companies usually could not borrow more than one-third of their capital requirements.[62] The MITI, however, was not always successful in knowing which sector to promote. Japan's automobile industry, for example, developed against the MITI's instructions.[63] In order to protect infant industries in Japan, the Japanese government often employed means such as "walls of tariffs, quotas, currency controls, foreign investment controls, and bureaucratic red tape."[64] In 1985, Japan's economy became the second largest economy in the world, after that of the United States, and continued to hold that position for twenty-six years until 2011 when its economy was surpassed by that of China.

FOUR ASIAN TIGERS

The economic development of Asian Countries in the post-war era was not balanced. Some countries followed Japan's model and became economically successful, but others only had marginal development, and still others even experienced a decline in their economic development. After the 1970s, Japan's economic model was successfully adopted by four areas in Asia: South Korea, Taiwan, Singapore, and Hong Kong. These four areas are collectively known as the "Four Asian Tigers" or sometimes as the "Four Little Dragons in Asia."[65]

South Korea was devastated by the Korean War, which ended in 1953. Due to paranoia caused by the horrible experiences of the Korean War, Syngman Rhee's government placed a high priority on building up the military. Rhee did not hesitate to crack down on his critics, adopting a political style that was more dictatorial than democratic.[66] Rhee was forced to resign in 1960 and was replaced by General Park Chung-hee, who seized power through a military coup. Park later attempted to legitimize his position as President of South Korea through an "election" and ruled the country until 1979, when he was assassinated by a member of the secret military police, which he had set up to terrorize people. Another military general, Chun Doo-hwan, gained power. It was not until 1987 that the South Koreans had a chance to vote directly for their president. Roh Tae-woo became the first South Korean President who won the position by popular election instead of by military coup. After his election, South Korea gradually moved toward a democracy.[67]

South Korea's economy did not fully recover from the war until 1960. Both Park and Chun's governments encouraged economic development. In a more democratic environment under President Roh, the economy in South Korea grew in strength. The government gradually built strong relations with the business circle, following Japan's model of success. Giant Korean conglomerates emerged in the 1970s. These conglomerates are known as *chaebol*, which is the Korean pronunciation of the same Chinese character that is pronounced as *zaibutsu* in Japanese. Examples of *chaebol* include Hyundai, Samsung, and SK Group. Like many other Korean companies, they started in light industries, and then moved to heavy industries and high tech products, such as construction, chemical and energy industries, shipbuilding, steel, automobiles, and electronics. These *chaebol* enjoyed close ties with the government and took advantage of various governmental subsidies. For example, the president of the SK Group, Chey Tae-won, the eldest son of the founder, the late Chey Johnphyun, is married to the daughter of former President Roh Tae-woo. The close ties between the government and the *chaebol* resulted in widespread corruption in South Korea.[68] In the 1980s, the ten largest *chaebol* dominated the South Korean economy, and accounted for nearly 70 percent of the GNP and the same percentage of South Korea's exports.[69] On the Fortune Global 500 in 2011, Samsung ranked number 22, Hyundai, number 55, and SK Group, number 88. Led by these *chaebol*, the South Korean economy took off rapidly after the late 1970s and became an integral part of the global economy. Its exports rose from 33 million dollars in 1960 to 47 billion dollars in 1987.[70] Several Korean companies have become household names in the United States and other countries.

Japanese investments in South Korea may also have helped to boost South Korea's economy in the 1980s. In 1988, Japan's total cumulative

image © Andrew Park, 2012. Used under license from Shutterstock, Inc.

Buildings in Seoul, South Korea

direct investment in South Korea reached 3.3 billion dollars, which amounted to about 10 percent of Japan's total overseas investments in Asia. As an important export and import partner to Japan, Korea similarly drew from existing technologies, taking advantage of technological support provided by its close neighbor Japan. This was particularly true in the development of South Korea's automobile industry. In 1985, only 8 percent of the automobiles made in South Korea were sold in overseas markets, but five years later, in 1988, that number increased to 70 percent. In the 1980s, the Hyundai Motor Company received 50 percent of its capital equipment from Japan, and 15 percent of its shares was directly owned by the Japanese Mitsubishi Corporation. Following Japan's example, South Korea's direct investment overseas rapidly grew in the 1980s, from 633 million dollars in 1986 to 1.2 billion dollars in 1988, an almost 100 percent increase in just two years.[71] Like its neighbor, Japan, the South Korean economy had remarkable growth, at an average rate of 9.5 percent, in the 1980s and 1990s, and its GNP rose from 2.7 billion in 1953 to about 120 billion in 1988, and to 1.1 trillion in 2011.[72] As a result, since the 1990s, South Korea, which is similar in land area to Iceland and Portugal, and ranks number 109 in land area among all the countries in the world, has consistently ranked within the 15 largest economies in the world.[73]

Taiwan became a Japanese colony in 1895, after the First Sino-Japanese War. The Cairo Declaration of 1943 restored Taiwan and the Pescadores to the Republic of China under the Nationalist government. In August 1945, Jiang Jieshi's government took control of Taiwan and established its rule by suppressing the local residents. In a massacre that occurred on February 28, 1947, thousands of Taiwanese were slaughtered, giving way to bitter memories not easily forgotten by local Taiwanese. In late 1949, upon failing in the Chinese Civil War, Jiang's GMD government led over two million Nationalists in retreat from mainland China to Taiwan and established the capital of the Republic of China in Taipei (Taibei).[74]

The initial rule of the GMD in Taiwan was conducted under the assumption that the GMD government in Taiwan was the legitimate ruler of China, and the government would eventually return to the mainland after their temporary stay in Taiwan. The government maintained a structure similar to the one it had before it evacuated from the mainland. It maintained a National Assembly in Taipei with legislators, who had been elected in 1948 to represent all the provinces of China. It was planned that these representatives would hold these positions until the GMD government returned to mainland China. When a representative passed away, the government initially would appoint another legislator to replace the deceased, but after 1969, the vacancies were filled through election.[75] The president, in theory, was supposed to be chosen by an election and was supposed to be limited to two consecutive terms of six years each. After Jiang Jieshi was elected in 1954, however, he held that position until 1975 when he died.[76]

In 1978, Jiang Jingguo, Jiang Jieshi's son, became the President of the Chinese Republic. During his tenure, Taiwanese politics started to depart from the earlier focus of returning to the mainland. Although Jiang Jingguo started his political career in an authoritarian style, he understood the importance of gaining the support of the local Taiwanese better than his father did and was keener on improving the GDP's relations with the Taiwanese. He opened the door for more Taiwanese to become members of the government. His own vice president, Lee Denghui, was a local Taiwanese man. Under Jiang Jingguo, politics in Taiwan became much more flexible and tolerant. In 1986, he allowed the candidates from other parties to run in the election, even if these parties were still deemed illegal at the time, and in 1987, he lifted the martial law that had been implemented since 1949. When he died in 1988, he held high esteem from the local Taiwanese.[77]

When the nationalist government retreated to Taiwan, the economy in Taiwan was predominantly agricultural. The GMD government resorted to harsh methods toward the local Taiwanese in order to sustain the newly added population of over two million who had retreated from the mainland. Since most of the land was owned by the Taiwanese, in 1949 the government limited the amount of rent that could be charged for use of land to 37.5 percent of the value of the main crop harvest and also secured tenure for tenants. In 1953, it put a ceiling of about 7.4 acres on landholding and redistributed the excess land to landless families.[78]

Taiwan had little industry left by the end of World War II. As many experienced workers and engineers came to Taiwan in 1949, Taiwan's industry started to become much stronger. By 1952, Taiwan's industry had recovered to the pre-war level, and by 1960, it was twice the size that it was in 1952.[79] The structure of the Taiwanese economy also changed. In the 1950s, two-thirds of the economy was owned by the state, but in the 1960s, the state's share was reduced to only one-third of the economy. This shift was largely due to the government's 1953 four-year plan where ownership of dozens of government-confiscated industries was transferred to private enterprises. A more democratic political structure after the 1980s further improved the Taiwanese economy. In 1988, Taiwan's GNP reached 95 billion dollars, and its GNP per capita was $4,820, more than ten times higher than the GNP per capita of mainland China.[80]

Taiwan's success in attracting a considerable amount of direct foreign investment was one of the reasons for its early, rapid economic recovery and growth. After the Korean War, Taiwan became an important partner in the United States' containment policy in Asia. In 1954, the United States signed a mutual defense treaty with Taiwan, thereby assuring Taiwan's protection by the United States. In the 1950s and 1960s, America poured large amounts of aid money into Taiwan. Even after the aid from the US slowed down in the 1970s, due to US-mainland China rapprochement, America continued to give Taiwan between 4.8 billion and 5 billion dollars in aid by 1990.[81] In the 1960s, the Vietnam War further boosted the Taiwanese economy, just as the Korean War had boosted the Japanese economy. Many of Taiwan's companies engaged in capital-intensive industries, such as steel and petro-chemicals. After the 1960s, when Taiwan's economy shifted to a focus on exports, America opened its markets to Taiwan and took nearly half of Taiwan's exports.[82] In 1989, America's trade deficit to Taiwan amounted to 12 billion dollars.

Japan followed the United States and established diplomatic relations with Taiwan in 1952. Encouraged by the government's favorable investment laws, Japan's investment in Taiwan continued to grow, especially after the 1980s when Japan's domestic labor became too expensive to keep the retail price of Japanese products low. In the 1980s, Taiwan's export of calculating machines, colored TV sets, and radios increased from 5.5 percent of the total volume of Japan's imported of those goods at the beginning of the decade to 9.1 percent by the end of the 1980s, largely because of the high demand for these products in Japan.[83] Taiwan was also heavily dependent on Japan for imports. In 1989, about a third of Taiwan's imports came from Japan. Similar to the situation in South Korea, Japan played an important role in the prosperity of Taiwan's economy.

Taiwan's relationship with mainland China will continue to be a tough issue in the realms of Asian collective security and US foreign policy. In addition to losing its diplomatic relations with many countries after the United States formally recognized the PRC in 1978, Taiwan also lost its membership in the United Nations and the World Bank, and its seat on the UN Security Council. This, however, did not stop Taiwan from being an active player in the international community. After withdrawing their diplomatic relations with Taiwan, many countries established "trade offices" in Taiwan, which house administrators who serve as unofficial consulates to Taiwan. In 2011,

Taiwan's GDP was 466 billion dollars, making the Taiwanese economy the twenty-sixth largest national economy in the world, ahead of such places as Thailand, Denmark, Greece, Singapore, and Hong Kong. It has become too important an economic player to be ignored.

After the PRC reentered the international community in the late 1970s, Taiwan became one of mainland China's most important economic partners. In 1995, Taiwanese investment in China amounted to 31.62 billion dollars, second only to the amount of investment from Hong Kong. Although Taiwan did not change its policy of no direct trade with China until 2008, the value of Taiwan's indirect trade with China rose from 5.17 billion dollars in 1990 to about 21 billion dollars in 1995.[84] In 2010, two years after the opening of direct trade between Taiwan and the PRC, the value of the trade between the two reached about 110 billion dollars. China had become Taiwan's largest export market.

The trade between the two will probably continue to grow, especially after Taiwan and the PRC signed the Economic Cooperation Framework Agreement (ECFA) in June 2010. According to the terms of the agreement, the PRC will have tariff concessions on over 539 of Taiwan's products, and Taiwan will do the same for 267 mainland products. The PRC will also open their market to Taiwan in about a dozen service sectors, such as banking, securities, insurance, hospitals, and accounting, whereas Taiwan would likewise open their market to China in several areas, including banking and visual arts.[85] It seems that despite their political differences, including the tough issue concerning Taiwan's independence, the economic relations between the two will continue to develop. Different from the investment pattern of the United States or Japan, which are largely based on big international corporations, the trade between China and Taiwan is largely sustained by a large number of small to medium-sized businesses in Taiwan. A common cultural heritage and linguistic environment make people from both sides of the Taiwan Strait feel comfortable doing business with each other. It is hoped, at least from the viewpoint of the PRC, that continued economic cooperation between Taiwan and China will gradually reduce hostility between the two. A rational and responsible PRC government should not be too eager to bomb its "Bank of Taiwan."

SINGAPORE AND HONG KONG

The two other "Asian Tigers" are Hong Kong and Singapore, both of which were former colonies of Great Britain. China ceded Hong Kong Island to Britain after the Opium War in 1842. After Britain obtained Kowloon in 1860, Britain made another agreement in 1898 with the Qing court, whereby Britain would lease another area, known as New Territories, from the Qing court for ninety-nine years. These three areas, totaling about 403 square miles, were the British Hong Kong colony. In 1997, when Hong Kong was returned to China, it had a population of about 6.5 million.[86] Singapore, which is located at the tip of the Malay Peninsula, is only about half the size of Hong Kong. Similar to the history of Hong Kong, Singapore was originally established as a British colony in 1819 and was occupied by the Japanese in World War II. It became independent in 1959, and in 1963, it joined the Federation of Malaysia. The federation, however, did not work. Singapore's population is about 74 percent Chinese, and many Malaysian leaders feared that an increase in the Chinese population in the federation would jeopardize the privileges that the Malays enjoyed in Malaysia. Two years after they had joined, Singapore was voted out of the federation, and it became the independent Republic of Singapore in August 1965.[87]

Hong Kong and Singapore have several things in common and have had similar patterns of development. Both are small in size with few natural resources; both enjoyed relative political stability under British rule; both are in a favorable location for transshipment and have developed excellent port facilities; and both have a hard-working and skilled work force.[88] In the 1950s and 1960s, when China was closed to much of the world and isolated from free-market economies, Hong Kong took the opportunity to develop itself into a trading *entrepot* that connected China to the outside world. While Hong Kong depended on China for its food, water, and other daily necessities, China, in exchange, obtained information, technology, and capital from Hong Kong.[89] Before China opened itself in the late 1970s, Hong Kong was its major source for foreign capital; in fact, half of its foreign exchange came from Hong Kong.[90] Between 1987 and 1989, 25 percent of Hong Kong's exports went to China, while 18 percent went to Japan. The value of Hong Kong's exports to China increased from 21.9 billion dollars in 1989 to 35.98 billion dollars in 1995.[91] In 2001, Hong Kong's investment in China reached 174.2 billion dollars, accounting for 48.45 percent of all foreign investment in China.[92]

Hong Kong was not content to remain just a transshipment center. Taking advantage of its cheap but skilled laborers, as well as its deep harbor, Hong Kong soon developed itself into a manufacturing center for textiles in the 1960s, and later, for electronics in the 1970s and 1980s. These economic developments were largely driven by exporting conducted by private entrepreneurs. In the 1990s, Hong Kong developed into one of the world's leading financial centers with the Hong Kong Stock Exchange, the world's seventh largest stock market. In 2009, it raised 22 percent of worldwide initial public offering capital and thus, was the easiest place to raise capital.[93] Hong Kong's GDP in 1997 was 180 times the size of its GDP in 1961, and its GDP per capita in 1997 was eighty-seven times the size of its GDP per capita in 1961.[94] In 2010, Hong Kong's GDP per capita was $46,502, about the same as the United States.[95]

During these years of economic development, the Hong Kong government seldom interfered with economic activities, and there were few industrial policies or regulations governing exports and imports. Some argue that Hong Kong's economic model was "Big Market, Small Government," and as a result, Hong Kong's economic development is one of the most successful stories of "laissez-faire capitalism."[96]

The government of Singapore, on the other hand, exerted considerable control over the economic development of the country. Lee Kuan Yew, Singapore's first prime minister, directly governed the country for over three decades and continued to exert a strong influence afterward. During his administration, Lee was a strong autocratic leader and did not have much tolerance for different opinions. One of his most controversial policies was his advocacy of caning, an old Chinese tradition to punish students with beating them with a cane if they did not study hard. His highhanded supervision of national policies often drew criticism. Lee's authoritarian rule, however, did not hinder the development of Singapore's economy. On the contrary, Singapore's economy took off under his guidance. In the mid 1960s, Singapore had few resources other than its hard working people. Despite its strategic location, fabulous harbor, and shipping facilities, disputes with its neighbors often limited its role as a trans-shipper. Lee's government decided to rely on foreign capital for its industrial development. Capital from foreign corporations poured in, and low-paid, but highly skilled, Singapore workers produced watches, cameras, and electronic gadgets for foreign companies. By the 1980s, about 70 percent of Singapore's industries were foreign owned.[97] Soon, it became a major regional shipping and financial center owing to its secure and stable environment sustained by Lee's authoritarian rule. In 1985, Singapore's GDP reached 16.2 billion dollars, and its GDP per capita amounted to $6,230. Although its 2010 ranking as the forty-second largest economy in the world may not be as impressive as the top economies, its GDP per capita was $57,932 in 2010, the third highest in the world, ahead of the United States and Hong Kong.[98]

EAST ASIAN SUCCESS AND CONFUCIAN VALUES

The above success stories of rapid economic development in East Asia have attracted scholars far and wide. In a study finished in 1993, the World Bank characterized the remarkable records of high and sustained economic growth in East Asia as the "East Asian Miracle." It maintains that the economies in East Asia, including Japan, the four Asian Tigers, and China, had faster economic growth from the 1960s to the 1990s than any other region in the world. The report identified a few common economic factors that helped sustain economic growth in the region, such as "private domestic investment" and "rapidly growing human capital."[99] However, certain common historical and cultural heritages that are shared among these East Asian economies may provide further understanding of the East Asian miracle.

It is probably not merely a coincidence that all of the areas, Japan, South Korea, Taiwan, Hong Kong and Singapore, either have adopted Confucian ideology or have been heavily influenced by Confucian values. Some scholars argue that some core Confucian values, such as hard work, frugality, sacrificing individual interests for the sake of one's family and country, and the emphases on family, education, and collaboration greatly contributed to some generally held characteristics identified by the World Bank report mentioned earlier."[100] Japan's economy, for example, benefited greatly from the frugality of the Japanese. Some argue that Japan's high growth rate was supported by capital made by savings. As mentioned earlier, the average household saving in Japan was much higher than the Western countries, such as the United States, Germany, France, and Italy. These savings became a powerful engine in Japan's economic development, and the reinvestment rate was also considerably higher in Japan than in European countries.[101]

East Asian economies are often praised for another commonality: the "high productivity of their work force." This has much to do with the Confucian emphasis on education. Usually the second largest investment for East Asian families, next to their house, is their children's education. East Asian governments understand the importance of education. South Korea, for example, invests heavily in the nation's education program. The South Korean government announced in June 2011 that it will replace all of the printed textbooks with electronic versions by 2014 and will invest two billion dollars in the next two years to provide all elementary school students, and to all high school students by 2015, with free electronic tablets with Internet capability. This will give Korean students an even greater educational advantage. In 2011, South Korean students ranked second in reading comprehension on the Programme for International Student Assessment Test. Their Chinese peers from Shanghai ranked first, and American students ranked seventeenth.[102] Better education will result in a higher quality work force, which in turn, will further increase economic productivity.

RISE OF THE CHINESE ECONOMY

Confucian values by themselves cannot account for economic development in East Asia. Social and political environments are more important factors in economic development. North Korea, which has the same cultural heritage as South Korea, had the worst record of economic performance in East Asia and is far behind other East Asian countries due to its rigid political dictatorship. Another such example is Mao's China. During the years of Mao's socialist revolution, the Chinese economy did not fare well. The great famine in the early 1960s cost millions of Chinese lives, and the Cultural Revolution greatly interrupted the social order in China. According to data from the World Bank, the

GDP growth rate in China in 1961 was -27 percent, and in 1962, -6.11 percent. The GDP growth rate became positive in 1963, at 10.34 percent, but plunged into negative numbers after the Cultural Revolution started; it was -5.7 percent in 1967, and -4.1 percent in 1968. In 1976, the year that Mao died, the growth rate plunged again to -1.6 percent.[103] Two important events in the 1970s changed the political environment in China. The first was President Nixon's visit to China in 1972, and the second was Deng Xiaoping's return to power in 1978.

As discussed earlier, after the Korean War broke out, the United States decided not to recognize the PRC and severed all contacts with China until 1971 when Henry Kissinger, the US Secretary of State under President Nixon, secretly visited Beijing. It was the first time since 1950 that a high-ranking US official met with Mao and Zhou Enlai, Premier of the PRC. When President Nixon announced Kissinger's visit to China in July 1971, it shocked the American public and the world. Despite receiving criticism for his decision, President Nixon visited China and met Mao in February 1972. Nixon's delegation negotiated with Zhou Enlai in Shanghai for a joint communiqué, the Shanghai Communiqué of 1972, where both sides promised to improve commercial and cultural contacts and eventually normalize diplomatic relations.[104] In May 1973, liaison offices were opened in Beijing and Washington DC. Some unexpected events, however, slowed down the process of normalization. The Watergate scandal, which started in June 1972, eventually forced President Nixon to resign in 1974. The American public, whose memories of the Korean and Vietnam wars were still fresh, was not ready to accept the PRC, especially at the cost of severing relations with Taiwan. China, on the other hand, was engaged in a power struggle after Mao's health deteriorated; he eventually died in 1976. The normalization of diplomatic relations between the two countries did not finalize until January 1979 when President Jimmy Carter recognized the People's Republic of China as the legitimate government of China.

Although the normalization of diplomatic relations between China and the United States was a slow process, China immediately benefited from its improved relations with the United States. In October 1971, China was admitted to the United Nations after the United States changed its position on the issue of China's membership. In 1972, Japan normalized its relations with China and many other countries switched their diplomatic relationships from the Republic of China in Taiwan to the People's Republic of China in mainland. The number of countries that recognized the PRC jumped to 171, while only twenty-three countries maintained diplomatic relations with Taiwan's government. None of the Asian countries had a diplomatic relationship with Taiwan anymore, and the Vatican is the only country in Europe that still has a formal relationship with Taiwan. In 1980, the People's Republic of China took Taiwan's place at the International Monetary Fund and the World Bank, and in 2001, 142 members of the World Trade Organization (WTO) voted unanimously in favor of China's application to join the WTO. All of this opened the door for China to have access to international funds and markets.[105]

Another significant event in China in the 1970s was Deng Xiaoping's return to power in 1978. Deng had been one of the most important CCP leaders since the 1920s, but was purged by Mao twice during the Cultural Revolution, due to his having views on China's future that were different from Mao's. After the economic disasters of the early 1960s, Deng, together with Liu Shaoqi, the state chairman after Mao resigned from that position, and Zhou Enlai, the premier, worked diligently together to restore the national economy. China's economic growth rate increased from -6.11 percent in 1962, to 10.34 percent in 1963, 15.84 percent in 1964, and 16.36 percent in 1965. When Mao started the Cultural Revolution in 1966, the Chinese economy was, in effect, at its highest point since 1949. Mao, however, felt being left out and was determined to redeem himself through another revolution, that is, the Cultural Revolution. As soon as the Cultural Revolution began, Mao ousted Liu Shaoqi and Deng Xiaoping, labeling them as "Capitalist roaders." Liu died of exposure in 1969, but Deng survived.

The Lin Biao Incident in 1971 gave Deng an opportunity to return to power. The Lin Biao Incident refers to the sudden death of Lin Biao, the only remaining Vice Chairman of the CCP after Mao started the Cultural Revolution, and Mao's designated successor, in a mysterious plane crash. The official explanation from the Chinese government was that Lin and a group of generals had conspired against Mao, and after his "conspiracies" were exposed, Lin and his family boarded a Trident jet and escaped the country. The plane crashed outside China in the Mongolian Republic. Despite these heavily worded charges, the Chinese government never released convincing evidence to support their story. As a result, the Lin Biao Incident still remains an unsolved mystery.[106] Mao's extensive purge after the Lin Biao Incident greatly damaged the military leadership. The victims of the purge included the Chief of Staff of the People's Liberation Army (PLA), four associate Chief of Staff, the Commander in Chief of the PLA Air Force, the Political Commissar of the PLA Navy, and the Director of the PLA Logistic Department. The purge of the military was so thorough that the position of PLA chief of staff remained vacant until 1975 when Mao invited Deng Xiaoping to take the position. Upon the recommendation of Zhou Enlai, Deng also became the First Vice-Premier the same year. Under the leadership of Zhou and Deng, the GDP growth rate rose from 2.3 percent in 1974 to 8.7 percent in 1975. In early 1976, Mao, who would die in a few months, dismissed Deng from office again, worrying that Deng would reverse the changes made by his Cultural Revolution after his death.

After Mao died in September 1976, Deng returned to power and became the CCP Vice-Chairman in July 1977. As one of the few survivors among the senior veterans of the earlier Communist revolution, Deng controlled the CCP and the government until his death in 1997. Deng's reforms transformed China into a modern society, and the high speed at which Chinese economy grew in the 1980s and 1990s even exceeded Japan's miraculous growth in the 1960s and 1970s. When China's economic reforms started in 1978, China's GDP was 148 billion dollars, far behind Japan's 982 billion dollars. Three decades later, in 2008, China's GDP reached 4.52 trillion dollars, whereas Japan's GDP was 4.87 trillion dollars. [107] In 2010, China surpassed Japan, becoming the second largest economy in the world, only behind the United States. (see the chart blow)

ECONOMIC DEVELOPMENT IN EAST ASIA, 1970–2011 IN GDP (NOMINAL)				
	China	Japan	South Korea	Hong Kong
1970	91.5 billion	206 billion	8.9 billion	3.8 billion
1978	148.1 billion	982 billion	51.1 billion	18.2 billion
1985	306 billion	1.36 trillion	51.1 billion	35.3 billion
1995	728 billion	4.64 trillion	517.1 billion	144.2 billion
2005	2.25 trillion	4.55 trillion	844 billion	177.7 billion
2010	5.92 trillion	5.45 trillion	1.01 trillion	224.4 billion
2011	7.2 trillion	5.8 trillion	1.1 trillion	243.3 billion

Source: Data from World Bank[108]

In a sense, the rise of the Chinese economy followed a path similar to the one taken by other East Asian economies, such as Japan and the Four Asian Tigers. In light of the earlier discussion on East Asian Confucian values, the rise of the Chinese economy is probably not a mere coincidence. China, the home of Confucianism, inherited a strong Confucian tradition which dominated its dynastic history for thousands of years.. The Confucian ethics of hard work, education, and group collaboration stood untouched during Mao's socialist revolution, even though Mao's regime no longer honored Confucianism as a national ideology. China's rapid economic development is, in effect, the result of both Deng's policies in the reform era, and the work ethic and entrepreneurial skills of China's people.[109] Once the government loosened political control and changed its economic policies in order to give better material incentives to the people, over a billion Chinese people channeled their energy and creativity into economic development. The result is astonishing. Within a few decades of its economic development, China had created a middle class consisting of nearly three hundred million people.[110] Scholars and the media began to popularize the saying that "China shakes the world," instead of referring to China as another "economic miracle."

The magnitude of the Chinese economy has had a profound impact on the world economy. Since 2003, China has been exporting about 1.2 trillion dollars worth of goods and services annually, while only importing about one trillion dollars in goods and services annually, thus creating an annual trade imbalance of about 200 billion dollars with the rest of the world. In 2010, China emerged as the second largest trading economy in the world, with total annual trade (imports plus exports) equaling 2.97 billion dollars.[111] Foreign direct investment (FDI) poured into the country in large quantities. In 2010, China attracted 185 billion dollars of FDI, the second largest recipient of FDI, only behind the United States, who received 236 billion dollars of FDI the same year.[112] By 2009, over 400 "Fortune 500" companies had opened their offices in China.[113]

China's rapid economic development has increased its demand for energy and raw materials, driving up the prices of these products. In 2010, China became the world's largest energy consumer, being responsible for more than 20 percent of global energy consumption and consuming an amount of energy equivalent to 2.3 billion tons of oil. The United States was the second largest, with 2.2 billion tons of oil equivalent, accounting for 19 percent of the world's consumption. China accounts for nearly half of the worlds' coal consumption, followed by the United States. China's oil consumption in 2010, however, was nine billion barrels, while the United States consumed nineteen billion barrels.[114]

Similar to other historical cases of economic success, rapid economic growth came with a high price. The foremost problems caused by China's economic success include environmental issues and the centuries old problem of disparity between the rich and the poor. Due to the rapid increase of energy consumption and the lack of effective regulation over decentralized economic activities, air pollution became the number one problem in China. Smog in Beijing, Shanghai, and other major cities has affected the health of millions of Chinese people. Linfen, Yangquan, and Datong in the Shanxi province, the "capital of coal" in China, have become the "most polluted places that you will find on earth."[115] China's Environmental Protection Ministry reported in November 2010 that a third of China's 113 surveyed cities failed to meet air standards established by the ministry.[116] Water pollution is also a significant health issue that China faces today. A World Bank report in 2006 labeled nearly one-third of the water in all of the monitored river sections as having "very restricted functionality." In 2009 none of the lakes met Grade I standards for water quality, and 34.6 percent of the lakes in China did not meet even Grade V standards.[117] Providing effective regulations to protect the environment before it is too late has become the biggest challenge for the Chinese government. An even more severe challenge for the Chinese government will be whether the government can maintain social and political stability, which will be crucial for China's continuing economic progress as it works to transform itself into a more democratic regime. Cases of human rights violations in China are still regularly reported by Human Rights organizations.

Since the end of the Cold War, China has continued to rise as a world power. China's ability to reconcile the irreconcilable is worth studying: an authoritarian regime, which is supposedly an obstacle to economic development on the one hand, and a prosperous capitalist market economy on the other. China is now "the single largest market for Internet and telecommunications use in the entire world" and "the largest foreign holder of US treasury bonds."[118] It is predicted that the Chinese economy could exceed the size of the United States' economy as early as 2020, and it is also estimated that at its current rate of growth, the world's grain markets will not be able to meet China's needs by 2030.[119] In today's environment of globalization, either continued prosperity or an economic disaster in China would inevitably have a strong impact on the world.

Other Asian countries will also have an important impact on the world. India, one of the oldest civilizations in the world, will likely not be far behind China in its economic development. With its recent economic boom and a GDP growth rate of 8.8 percent in 2010, it is predicted to be the third largest world economy in 2025. In addition to the continuing development in Japan and the other East Asian economies discussed earlier, the Philippines (7.6 percent GDP growth rate in 2010), Thailand (7.8 percent in 2010), and Malaysia (7.16 percent in 2010) have now entered the list of what is known as the "Newly Industrialized Countries" (NICs) and joined other Asian economies to make a greater contribution to the world economy.[120]

What does this mean to the rest of the world? While some suggest that the twenty-first century is an Asian century, others predict that the twenty-first century is a "Pacific Century," with "North America (including Mexico) on the eastern side of the Pacific and East Asia on the other side," comprising a region where economic development will continue to surpass the growth of other regions.[121] In either case, Asia, which is home to more than half of today's world population, will continue to play an increasingly important role in the world economy and politics. For this reason alone, we need a better understanding of Asia's past and present.

For more information about the topics discussed in this chapter, please visit the website for this textbook. This website can be accessed from http://www.grtep.com/.

For more information about the topics discussed in this chapter, please visit the website for this textbook. This website can be accessed from http://www.grtep.com/.

1 John Spanier, *The Truman-MacArthur Controversy and the Korean War* (New York: The Belkap Press of Oxford University Press, 1965), 55.
2 Roger C. Thompson, *The Pacific Basin since 1945*, 2nd ed. (New York: Longman/Pearson Education, 2001), 15–17.
3 Thompson, *Pacific Basin*, 43; and Dennis D. Wainstock, *Truman, MacArthur, and the Korean War* (Westport, CN: Praeger, 1999). For more on this, see Stanley Weintraub, *MacArthur's War: Korea and the Undoing of an American Hero* (Free Press, 2008).
4 Thompson, *Pacific Basin*, 44.
5 Thompson, *Pacific Basin*, 45.
6 Thompson, *Pacific Basin*, 45; and Fairbank et al., *Tradition*, 916.
7 Spence, *Search*, 505; and Fairbank et al., *Tradition*, 915.
8 Thompson, *Pacific Basin*, 42–43.
9 Thompson, *Pacific Basin*, 47.
10 Vera Simone, *The Asian Pacific: Political and Economic Development in a Global Context*, 2nd ed. (New York: Longman, 2001), 319.
11 Fairbank et al., *Tradition*, 885.
12 Fairbank et al., *Tradition*, 887.
13 Fairbank et al., *Tradition*, 887.
14 Fairbank, et al., *Tradition*, 889.
15 Fairbank, et al., *Tradition*, 890.
16 Edwin E. Moïse, "The Aftermath of Geneva, 1954–1961" in "The Vietnam Wars," Section 5, accessed May 31, 2010, at http://www.clemson.edu/caah/history/FacultyPages/EdMoise/viet5.html
17 Moïse, Section 5.
18 Cheng Guan Ang, *The Vietnam War from the Other Side* (New York: Routledge Curzon, 2002), 16, 21.
19 Thompson, *Pacific Basin*, 63.
20 "Origins of the Insurgency in South Vietnam, 1954–1960" in *The Pentagon Papers*. The Senator Gravel Ed. Vol.1, Chapter 5 (Boston: Beacon Press, 1971), 242–314, accessed May 30, 2012, at http://www.mtholyoke.edu/acad/intrel/pentagon/pent11.htm.
21 *The Pentagon Papers*, 242–314.
22 Fairbank et al., *Tradition*, 890.
23 Thompson, *Pacific Basin*, 75.
24 Thompson, *Pacific Basin*, 74–76; and David L. Anderson, *Trapped by Success: The Eisenhower Administration and Vietnam, 1953–1961* (New York: Columbia University Press, 1991), 196–197.
25 Stanley Karnow, *Vietnam: A History*, rev. ed. (New York: Penguin, 1997), 694; and Thompson, *Pacific Basin*, 75.
26 Thompson, *Pacific Basin*, 78.
27 Thompson, *Pacific Basin*, 63.
28 Thompson, *Pacific Basin*, 75, 123.
29 Fairbank et al., *Tradition*, 892.
30 Ricklefs et al., *New History*, 354.
31 Murphey, *East Asia*, 442.
32 Church, *Short History*, 195.
33 Murphey, *East Asia*, 442.
34 Thompson, *Pacific Basin*, 76–77; and Fairbank et al., *Tradition*, 893.
35 Spence, *Search*, 476.
36 Spence, *Search*, 477.
37 Spence, *Search*, 448–449.
38 Dean Acheson, "United States Position on China, August 1949" in Internet Modern History Sourcebook, ed. by Paul Halsall, accessed June 1, 2012, at http://www.fordham.edu/halsall/mod/1949-acheson-china.html.
39 Hsu, *Modern China*, 646–647; and Fairbank et al., *Tradition*, 940–941.
40 Fairbank et al., *Tradition*, 941.
41 Spence, *Search*, 943.
42 Hsu, *Modern China*, 652.
43 Hsu, *Modern China*, 652–653.
44 Fairbank et al., *Tradition*, 951; and Hsu, *Modern China*, 653.
45 Spence, *Search*, 492.
46 Hsu, *Modern China*, 654.
47 Spence, *Search*, 516.
48 Hsu, *Modern China*, 654.
49 Jin Qiu, *The Culture of Power: The Lin Biao Incident of the Cultural Revolution* (Stanford: Stanford University Press, 1999), 24–25.
50 Jin, *Culture*, 25.
51 Fairbank et al., *Tradition*, 954.
52 Spence, *Search*, 364–365.
53 Fairbank et al, *Tradition*, 823.
54 Thompson, *Pacific Basin*, 55–56.
55 Fairbank et al., *Tradition*, 825–826.

60 Fairbank et al., *Tradition*, 829.
61 Murphey, *East Asia*, 420.
62 Suzuki, "Japanese Model," 308–309
63 Fairbank et al., *Tradition*, 831–832.
64 Fairbank, et al., *Tradition*, 831.
65 Thompson, *Pacific Basin*, 198–202; and Murphey, *East Asia*, 452.
66 Murphey, *East Asia*, 436.
67 Murphey, *East Asia*, 436–437.
68 Gerardo R. Ungson, Yim-Yu Wong, *Global Strategic Management* (New York: M.E.Sharpe 2008), 462.
69 Murphey, *East Asia*, 437.
70 Fairbank et al., *Tradition*, 921.
71 Thompson, *Pacific Basin*, 188–189.
72 Fairbank et al., *Tradition*, 921–922; and "List of countries by GDP (nominal)," accessed June 1, 2012, at http://en.wikipedia.org/wiki/List_of_countries_by_GDP_(nominal)
73 "Historical list of ten largest countries by GDP," accessed June 1, 2012, at http://en.wikipedia.org/wiki/Historical_list_of_ten_largest_countries_by_GDP.
74 Milton W. Meyer, *Asia: A Concise History* (Lanham, MD: Rowman and Littlefield, 1997), 478–479.
75 Fairbank et al., *Tradition*, 902–903.
76 Meyer, *Asia*, 479.
77 Fairbank et al., *Tradition*, 902–903.
78 Meyer, *Asia*, 481.
79 Meyer, *Asia*, 481.
80 Fairbank et al., *Tradition*, 905.
81 Meyer, *Asia*, 479–480.
81 Fairbank et al., *Tradition*, 905.
83 Thompson, *Pacific Basin*, 199.
84 Stephen M. Goldsten, "Terms of Engagement: Taiwan's Mainland Policy" in *Engaging China*, eds. Alastair I. Johnston and Robert S. Ross (New York: Routledge, 1999), 70–72; Mei-ling T. Wang, *The Dust that Never Settled: The Taiwan Independence Campaign and US-China Relations* (Lanham, NY: University Press of America, 1999), 314–321; and Suisheng Zhao, "Economic Interdependence and Political Divergence: A Background Analysis of the Taiwan Strait Crisis" in *Across the Taiwan Strait: Mainland China, Taiwan, and the 1995–1996 Crisis* ed. Suisheng Zhao (New York: Routledge, 1999), 24–25.
85 "ECFA signing scheduled for June 29" Taiwan News Online, 2010-06-25, Etaiwannews.com, accessed June 2, 2012 at http://www.etaiwannews.com/etn/news_content.php?id=1299089&lang=eng_news&cate_img=83.jpg&cate_rss=news_Politics_TAIWAN; and "China Pulls Taiwan Closer With Historic Trade Deal," *Business Week* 2010-06-29, accessed June 2, 2012, at http://www.businessweek.com/news/2010-06-29/china-pulls-taiwan-closer-with-historic-trade-deal-update1-.html.
86 Fairbank et al., *Tradition*, 925.
87 Murphey, *East Asia*, 449.
88 Fairbank et al., *Tradition*, 925–926.
89 Thompson, *Pacific Basin*, 201; Organization for Economic Co-operation And Development, *The Newly Industrializing Countries: Challenges and Opportunities for OECD Industries* (Paris, 1988), 47–52.
90 Fairbank et al., *Tradition*, 926.
91 Thompson, *Pacific Basin*, 201, 289.
92 Yin Zhili, "Hong Kong Investment in China's Mainland Come to Over US$170 Bn," *The People's Daily*, May 24, 2001, accessed June 3, 2012, at http://english.people.com.cn/english/200105/24/eng20010524_70925.html.
93 "Hong Kong: A Symphony of Lights," Thomas White International, Thomaswhite.com, 2009-10-16, accessed June 3, 2012, at http://www.thomaswhite.com/explore-the-world/hong-kong.aspx.
94 Rikkie Yeung, *Moving Millions: The Commercial Success and Political Controversies of Hong Kong's Railways* (Hong Kong: Hong Kong University Press, 2008), 16.
95 "List of countries by GDP (PPP) per capita," accessed June 3, 2012, at http://en.wikipedia.org/wiki/List_of_countries_by_GDP_(PPP)_per_capita.
96 Donald Tsang, "Big Market, Small Government" (Press release), Hong Kong Government, September 18, 2006, accessed June 3, 2012, at http://www.ceo.gov.hk/eng/press/oped.htm; and "End of an Experiment," *The Economist*, July 15, 2010, accessed June 3, 2012, at http://www.economist.com/node/16591088.
97 Fairbank, et al., *Tradition*, 27.
98 "List of countries by GDP (PPP) per capita."
99 World Bank, *The East Asian Miracle: Economic Growth and Public Policy* (Oxford: Oxford University Press, 1993), 5.
100 Fairbank et al., *Tradition*, 876–877.
101 Suzuki, "Japanese Model", 305.
102 Andres Oppenheimer, "South Korea Investing in Education," *The Miami Herald*, July 14, 2011, accessed June 3, 2012, at http://www2.ljworld.com/news/2011/jul/14/south-korea-investing-education.
103 "Gross Domestic Product Growth Rate, China," accessed June 4, 2012, at http://www.google.com/publicdata/explore?ds=d5bncppjof8f9_&met_y=ny_gdp_mktp_kd_zg&idim=country:CHN&dl=en&hl=en&q=china+gdp+growth.
104 Fairbank et al., *Tradition*, 972.
105 "China Officially Joins WTO" CNN World," November 10, 2001, accessed June 4, 2012, at http://articles.cnn.com/2001-11-10/world/china.WTO_1_wto-meeting-wto-director-general-mike-moore-world-trade-organization?_s=PM:asiapcf.
106 For more on the Lin Biao Incident, see Jin Qiu, *Culture*.

107   Data from World Bank, accessed June 4, 2012, at http://www.google.com/publicdata/explore?ds=d5bncppjof8f9_&met_y=ny_gdp_mktp_cd&idim=country:CHN&dl=en&hl=en&q=gdp+china; and http://www.google.com/publicdata/explore?ds=d5bncppjof8f9_&met_y=ny_gdp_mktp_cd&idim=country:JPN&dl=en&hl=en&q=japan+gdp.

108   Data from World Bank, accessed June 4, 2012, at http://www.google.com/publicdata/explore?ds=d5bncppjof8f9_&met_y=ny_gdp_mktp_cd&idim=country:CHN&dl=en&hl=en&q=gdp+china.

109   Linda Benson, *China Since 1949*, 2nd ed. (New York: Pearson, 2011), 106.

110   For more on this, see Helen H. Wang, *The Chinese Dream: The Rise of the World's Largest Middle Class and What It Means to You* (CreateSpace, 2010).

111   Doug Guthrie, *China and Globalization: The Social, Economic and Political Transformation of Chinese Society* 3rd ed. (New York: Routledge, 2012), 95–98.

112   Greyhill Advisors, "FDI by Country," accessed June 4, 2012, at http://greyhill.com/fdi-by-country/.

113   Benson, *China*, 106.

114   Guthrie, *Globalization*, 159–163.

115   Guthrie, *Globalization*, 158.

116   "Air Pollution in China", Facts and Details, accessed June 4, 2012, at http://factsanddetails.com/china.php?itemid=392&catid=10&subcatid=66.

117   Guthrie, *Globalization*, 168.

118   Guthrie, *Globalization*, 6.

119   For more on this, see Lester Brown, *Who Will Feed China* (New York: W.W. Norton, 1995).

120   Paweł Bożyk, "Newly Industrialized Countries," in *Globalization and the Transformation of Foreign Economic Policy* (London: Ashgate Publishing, 2006), 164; and David Waugh, Geography: *An Integrated Approach*, 4th ed. (Cheltenham, UK: Nelson Thornes, 2009), 552–586.

121   Murphey, *East Asia*, 451–452.